perspectives

Intercultural Communications

Academic Editor
Gaye Perry
University of Houston

coursewise publishing inc.

Bellevue • Boulder • Dubuque • Madison • St. Paul

Our mission at **coursewise** is to help students make connections—linking theory to practice and the classroom to the outside world. Learners are motivated to synthesize ideas when course materials are placed in a context they recognize. By providing gateways to contemporary and enduring issues, **coursewise** publications will expand students' awareness of and context for the course subject.

For more information on **coursewise,** visit us at our web site: http://www.coursewise.com

To order an examination copy: Houghton Mifflin Sixth Floor Media 800-565-6247 (voice); 800-565-6236 (fax)

coursewise publishing editorial staff

Thomas Doran, ceo/publisher: Environmental Science/Geography/Journalism/Marketing/Speech
Edgar Laube, publisher: Political Science/Psychology/Sociology
Linda Meehan Avenarius, publisher: **courselinks**™
Sue Pulvermacher-Alt, publisher: Education/Health/Gender Studies
Victoria Putman, publisher: Anthropology/Philosophy/Religion
Tom Romaniak, publisher: Business/Criminal Justice/Economics
Kathleen Schmitt, publishing assistant

coursewise publishing production staff

Lori A. Blosch, permissions coordinator
Mary Monner, production coordinator
Victoria Putman, production manager

Note: Readings in this book appear exactly as they were published. Thus, inconsistencies in style and usage among the different readings are likely.

Cover photo: Copyright © 1997 T. Teshigawara/Panoramic Images, Chicago, IL. All Rights Reserved.

Interior design and cover design by Jeff Storm

Copyright © 1999 by **coursewise publishing,** Inc. All Rights Reserved.

Library of Congress Catalog Card Number: 98-96802

ISBN 0-395-97223-X

No part of this publication may be reproduced, stored in a retrieval system, or transmitted, in any form or by any means, electronic, mechanical, photocopying, recording, or otherwise, without the prior written permission of the publisher.

Printed in the United States of America by **coursewise publishing,** Inc.
1559 Randolph Avenue, St. Paul, MN 55105

10 9 8 7 6 5 4 3 2 1

from the
Publisher

Tom Doran
coursewise publishing

My Uncle Kenny, a Minnesotan, argues against the teaching of foreign languages in the local high schools and colleges. He questions the time, attention, and tax dollars spent on a tool that the typical Minnesotan will have few opportunities to use.

Arguing with Kenny about the value of learning about other cultures—including their language—is a waste of time. I know because I tried. I pointed out that my kids attend an inner-city school, where English is the second language for many of the Hmong children. And that my kids are learning about the Hmong culture—including pieces of their language—through commonplace child's play. And that experience is making my kids a bit smarter about what the world is and how it works.

"They should allow only English while on school property" was Kenny's response, reducing a discussion about cultures into his issue with "foreign" language. Kenny probably has more company sharing this outlook than I want to consider. Forget ideals for a minute. The pragmatist in me shivers at this kind of thinking. The world is blending, and cultures are overlapping and creating new subcultures. This trend is obvious even up here in Minnesota—a state known for its abundance of Scandinavian heritage.

You know that all demographic and economic trends indicate that intercultural encounters will become increasingly more common. It only makes sense to sharpen our skill-set to be as effective with and prepared for intercultural communications as we are trained to be for inner-cultural communications. So hat's off to you for taking this course and welcome to our *Perspectives* and **courselinks**™ publications!

There are three reasons why we think you'll like this work. The first is Gaye Perry, the Academic Editor. Gaye gave this project a great deal of thought and consideration before agreeing to take it on. It was important to Gaye that this reader was done right. She had/has very specific ideas about the topics to be covered, the makeup of the Editorial Board, and how the web site was to work. For more on this, be sure to check out the interesting note from Gaye on page iv.

The second reason you'll like this publication is the highly pragmatic, yet balanced approach found in the material herein. Gaye and the members of her Editorial Board provide you with a savvy collection that's organized in a practical fashion. There's a hands-on emphasis featuring readings you can use immediately as you set off to work or to other studies—even in the articles that help you understand the theory of intercultural communications!

The third reason is the **courselinks** site for Intercultural Communications, which Gaye also edits. Note I use the present tense. The site is a dynamic publication that features, among other things, updates and new readings that Gaye and the members of her Editorial Board have assembled.

My thanks to Gaye and her Editorial Board members for their savvy work. I know you'll find it enriching.

Good luck with your intercultural studies. Let us know how we did. Write to me at: tomd@coursewise.com   Know that I'll use any endorsements sent my way in my next round with Uncle Kenny.

from the
Academic Editor

Gaye Perry
University of Houston

As a child I lived in Tucson, Arizona, which is close to the United States and The Republic of Mexico border. I attended University Heights Elementary School there while my mother completed law school at the University of Arizona. Because of my school's close proximity to the university, as well as Tucson's international trade status, my classmates came from the diverse student parent population which made up my school district.

Hearing multiple languages, experiencing different ways of living, and viewing the world made an indelible impression on me. That was my life, and I had little with which to compare it. In retrospect, I was blessed by this experience, as we were a tiny version of the world toward which we are evolving today.

On the school sandlot, we played hard and argued vociferously over who was out and who wasn't. We knew who had great athletic abilities and who had academic skills of higher caliber than others, who was our best friend and who could not be trusted. We based our judgments on skills and experiences with classmates; thus, in our protected corner of the world, culture and ethnicity were nonissues. We accepted variety in patterns of behavior, religions, languages, communication styles, and general ways of living, and we adapted accordingly.

In my elementary school, another factor also came into play. It was our good fortune that we came from families who understood we would be in a global world. They wanted us to develop the skills to communicate comfortably and effectively within multicultural groups.

My grandmother, Thelma Sapp Malone, in particular, wanted this for me. Having spent much of her younger years in Silsbee, a small town in East Texas, she was determined not to pass on some of the negative attitudes toward other races and cultures she had been raised with as a child. Thus, she greeted my friends at school programs with a graciousness that I now appreciate as an adult. She supported my activities with friends and broke the cycle which continues to imprison others.

Having gone full circle, I live in Houston, Texas, an international city, where both professionally and personally my world is multinational. An average day finds me in contact with ten to fifteen different populations. This is the norm in my small piece of geography.

Our Houston circle expands globally, as international trade is a major part of our economy. Employees may never travel out of Houston, but by the nature of their jobs they are in daily contact with customers or company offices located in all regions of the world via fax, telephone, e-mail, and video conferencing, as well as in person. Houstonians regularly work in multinational teams or with individuals from diverse cultures.

My early positive cross-cultural experiences left me with a fascination for the wide variety of living patterns which societies create. As I increase my knowledge of others' cultures, I also increase my insight into my own culture. For many people, their culture is as familiar as the roads they take

---

Dr. Gaye Perry is an assistant professor in the College of Technology at the University of Houston. Her doctorate is in communication arts and sciences from the University of Southern California. She teaches technical communication as well as training and development courses in classroom settings and on television. Her research interests include international training, distance learning, organizational development, intercultural and health communication, and virtual groups. Her consulting work includes managing multinational teams, intercultural communication, organizational communication audits, customer service, and conflict resolution.

each day and they are only aware of the nature of their well-traveled road when faced with the experience of a cultural detour.

As sophisticated satellites increase the opportunity and speed with which we can exchange thoughts and data internationally, there is a concern that our ability to interface interculturally has not grown as rapidly. We have the ability with "high tech" to interface instantly, but as yet we are not equally as sophisticated in human relations to create "high touch." We have seen the carnage which results from unresolved intercultural conflict and the inability to move toward closure in negotiations ranging from border issues to global environmental policies, all of which affect people individually and society as a whole.

The **courselinks** site for *Perspectives: Intercultural Communications* offers the reader the opportunity to focus on issues ranging from exploring one particular people to negotiating among multiple groups. Sites of professional groups which include a global emphasis on research or application of cross-cultural skills are also linked. The **courselinks** site includes guest columnists from a variety of world locations and organizations, who provide an additional insight into this expanding field.

As an avid "Star Trek" fan, I am drawn to many aspects of the series, but two have had the greatest philosophical impact on my personal and professional approach to life, one of which is the following directive: "These are the voyages of the starship *Enterprise*. Our ongoing mission: to seek out new life and new civilizations, to boldly go where no one has gone before." As we seek new methods to create cross-cultural relationships, we are indeed going to new worlds. The second aspect of "Star Trek" is the acceptance of new and different patterns of culture and the address of the ethical question of "doing no harm" when interfacing with one or multiple "civilizations" while still keeping one's own culture intact.

The starship *Enterprise* is only a Hollywood set, inhabited by actors pretending to resolve these galactic problems. The scenes which appear on "global village" television are only science fiction. We, however, are in the real world, with critical intercultural issues with which to wrestle, and without Star Fleet to come to the rescue. But, as we continue to expand our research and practices regarding intercultural communication, I believe, we, too, will develop the skills to create the world we now see only in electronic images on the screen.

Editorial Board

We wish to thank the following instructors for their assistance. Their many suggestions not only contributed to the construction of this volume, but also to the ongoing development of our Intercultural Communications web site.

Dorothy Lawrence Franzone

Associate Professor of Communication
Texas Southern University

Dorothy Franzone received an undergraduate degree in English and education, master's degrees from the University of Michigan in speech correction and in interpersonal and intercultural communication, and a Ph.D. in African American studies from Temple University. In addition, she studied at Stanford University's Summer Institutes and the University of Houston in the area of psychology. She is currently a member of the communications faculty at Texas Southern University, where she has conducted annual Intercultural Communication Conferences for the past two decades. These annual spring conferences have drawn the attention of national and international conferees and participants. She has presented professional papers at SCA, ICA, and SIETAR, which have earned her friendships and intercultural connections in the Netherlands, Toronto, Mexico City, Hong Kong, Malasia, Belize, Honduras, and the Virgin Islands. In these sites, she has researched aspects of the culture, presented papers, chaired sessions or workshops, and critiqued presentations.

Robert L. Kimmons

Managing Partner
Kimmons-Asaro Group Limited

Robert L. Kimmons is managing partner of the Kimmons-Asaro Group Limited, Inc., a Houston-based corporation founded in 1986 that is committed to the advancement of the project management profession and to the training and development of project managers and teams worldwide. He has fifty-one years of firsthand engineering, construction and project management experience on five continents. His workshops have been conducted throughout the United States and in Latin America, the Caribbean, Europe, Asia, and the Middle East.

Kimmons is editor of *Project Management: A Reference for Professionals* (1989) and author of *Project Management Basics: A Step-By-Step Approach* (1990), both published by Marcel Dekker, Inc., New York City. He has written over thirty technical and management papers for professional and industry publications. He recently authored "Controlling the Costs of Safety" from *The Engineers Cost Handbook* by R. E. Westney, MDI, New York (1997).

Larry Livingston

President
International Training Resources

Larry Livingston is the president of International Training Resources. His training career has spanned two continents, and he has worked for a variety of Fortune 500 companies.

Livingston has provided just-in-time international training to corporations and not-for-profit organizations doing business internationally. His training programs prepare employees for international assignments, build global work teams, and prepare managers to manage a multinational workforce. His international training expertise has been valuable to the International Space Station Training Working Group, where he worked with the International Space Station Partners.

Livingston is a certified instructional design trainer who has led results-oriented, customer-specific training workshops. Also, he is certified as a Ropes Course Facilitator. He is known for his professionalism and his flexibility to apply training examples to the student's specific training situation.

He has a bachelor of science degree from Illinois State University in sociology and anthropology and a master of science degree in sociology from Illinois State University.

Patty Lynam
Vice President of Human Resources Systems and Global Initiatives Kvaerner Process

Patty Lynam has a BA in human resources management from Wheeling Jesuit University and an MA in multicultural studies from the University of Houston–Clear Lake. She has over eighteen years of directly related experience in human resource management, functioning in a variety of roles. Her newly assigned role is that of global project manager for the implementation of a human resource information system. Her assignments with Kvaerner Process have provided many opportunities to travel to company offices around the world and to work on a multinational team.

Tulsi Saral
Professor of Clinical Psychology University of Houston–Clear Lake

Dr. Tulsi Saral is a professor of clinical psychology at the University of Houston–Clear Lake and teaches courses in culture and psychotherapy, group psychotherapy, transpersonal therapy, and sex therapy. At UH–Clear Lake, he served as program director of human sciences and founded a master's degree program in multicultural studies. Before that, he served as a research assistant professor at the University of Illinois' Institute of Communication Research and as university professor at Governors State University. At Governors State University, he also served as program coordinator of communication science, assistant dean, and later, as acting dean, of the College of Human Learning and Development.

Dr. Saral is the past chair of the Intercultural Communication Division of the International Communication Association and past secretary of the Society of Intercultural Education, Training and Research. He is also the past president of the American Association for the Study of Mental Imagery. Dr. Saral is the founding Editor of the *Journal of Communication Therapy* and founding associate editor of the *International Journal of Intercultural Relations*. He has published numerous articles and book chapters on the various aspects of intercultural communication, transpersonal communication, mental imagery, and psychotherapy.

WiseGuide Introduction

Question Authority

Critical Thinking and Bumper Stickers

The bumper sticker said: Question Authority. This is a simple directive that goes straight to the heart of critical thinking. The issue is not whether the authority is right or wrong; it's the questioning process that's important. Questioning helps you develop awareness and a clearer sense of what you think. That's critical thinking.

Critical thinking is a new label for an old approach to learning—that of challenging all ideas, hypotheses, and assumptions. In the physical and life sciences, systematic questioning and testing methods (known as the scientific method) help verify information, and objectivity is the benchmark on which all knowledge is pursued. In the social sciences, however, where the goal is to study people and their behavior, things get fuzzy. It's one thing for the chemistry experiment to work out as predicted, or for the petri dish to yield a certain result. It's quite another matter, however, in the social sciences, where the subject is ourselves. Objectivity is harder to achieve.

Although you'll hear critical thinking defined in many different ways, it really boils down to analyzing the ideas and messages that you receive. What are you being asked to think or believe? Does it make sense, objectively? Using the same facts and considerations, could you reasonably come up with a different conclusion? And, why does this matter in the first place? As the bumper sticker urged, question authority. Authority can be a textbook, a politician, a boss, a big sister, or an ad on television. Whatever the message, learning to question it appropriately is a habit that will serve you well for a lifetime. And in the meantime, thinking critically will certainly help you be course wise.

Getting Connected

This reader is a tool for connected learning. This means that the readings and other learning aids explained here will help you to link classroom theory to real-world issues. They will help you to think critically and to make long-lasting learning connections. Feedback from both instructors and students has helped us to develop some suggestions on how you can wisely use this connected learning tool.

WiseGuide Pedagogy

A wise reader is better able to be a critical reader. Therefore, we want to help you get wise about the articles in this reader. Each section of *Perspectives* has three tools to help you: the WiseGuide Intro, the WiseGuide Wrap-Up, and the Putting It in *Perspectives* review form.

WiseGuide Intro

WiseGuide Intro

In the WiseGuide Intro, the Academic Editor introduces the section, gives you an overview of the topics covered, and explains why particular articles were selected and what's important about them.

Also in the WiseGuide Intro, you'll find several key points or learning objectives that highlight the most important things to remember from this section. These will help you to focus your study of section topics.

At the end of the WiseGuide Intro, you'll find questions designed to stimulate critical thinking. Wise students will keep these questions in mind as they read an article (we repeat the questions at the start of the articles as a reminder). When you finish each article, check your understanding. Can you answer the questions? If not, go back and reread the article. The Academic Editor has written sample responses for many of the questions, and you'll find these online at the **courselinks**™ site for this course. More about **courselinks** in a minute. . . .

WiseGuide Wrap-Up

Be course wise and develop a thorough understanding of the topics covered in this course. The WiseGuide Wrap-Up at the end of each section will help you do just that with concluding comments or summary points that repeat what's most important to understand from the section you just read.

In addition, we try to get you wired up by providing a list of select Internet resources—what we call R.E.A.L. web sites because they're **R**elevant, **E**xciting, **A**pproved, and **L**inked. The information at these web sites will enhance your understanding of a topic. (Remember to use your Passport and start at http://www.courselinks.com so that if any of these sites have changed, you'll have the latest link.)

Putting It in *Perspectives* Review Form

At the end of the book is the Putting It in *Perspectives* review form. Your instructor may ask you to complete this form as an assignment or for extra credit. If nothing else, consider doing it on your own to help you critically think about the reading.

Prompts at the end of each article encourage you to complete this review form. Feel free to copy the form and use it as needed.

The courselinks™ Site

The **courselinks**™ Passport is your ticket to a wonderful world of integrated web resources designed to help you with your course work. These resources are found at the **courselinks** site for your course area. This is where the readings in this book and the key topics of your course are linked to an exciting array of online learning tools. Here you will find carefully selected readings, web links, quizzes, worksheets, and more, tailored to your course and approved as connected learning tools. The ever-changing, always interesting **courselinks** site features a number of carefully integrated resources designed to help you be course wise. These include:

- **R.E.A.L. Sites** At the core of a **courselinks** site is the list of R.E.A.L. sites. This is a select group of web sites for studying, not surfing. Like the readings in this book, these sites have been selected, reviewed, and approved by the Academic Editor and the Editorial Board. The R.E.A.L. sites are arranged by topic and are annotated with short descriptions and key words to make them easier for you to use for reference or research. With R.E.A.L. sites, you're studying approved resources within seconds—and not wasting precious time surfing unproven sites.

- **Editor's Choice** Here you'll find updates on news related to your course, with links to the actual online sources. This is also where we'll tell you about changes to the site and about online events.

- **Course Overview** This is a general description of the typical course in this area of study. While your instructor will provide specific course objectives, this overview helps you place the course in a generic context and offers you an additional reference point.

- **www.orksheet** Focus your trip to a R.E.A.L. site with the www.orksheet. Each of the 10 to 15 questions will prompt you to take in the best that site has to offer. Use this tool for self-study, or if required, email it to your instructor.

- **Course Quiz** The questions on this self-scoring quiz are related to articles in the reader, information at R.E.A.L. sites, and other course topics, and will help you pinpoint areas you need to study. Only you will know your score—it's an easy, risk-free way to keep pace!

- **Topic Key** The Topic Key is a listing of the main topics in your course, and it correlates with the Topic Key that appears in this reader. This handy reference tool also links directly to those R.E.A.L. sites that are especially appropriate to each topic, bringing you integrated online resources within seconds!

- **Web Savvy Student Site** If you're new to the Internet or want to brush up, stop by the Web Savvy Student site. This unique supplement is a complete **courselinks** site unto itself. Here, you'll find basic information on using the Internet, creating a web page, communicating on the web, and more. Quizzes and Web Savvy Worksheets test your web knowledge, and the R.E.A.L. sites listed here will further enhance your understanding of the web.

- **Student Lounge** Drop by the Student Lounge to chat with other students taking the same course or to learn more about careers in your major. You'll find links to resources for scholarships, financial aid, internships, professional associations, and jobs. Take a look around the Student Lounge and give us your feedback. We're open to remodeling the Lounge per your suggestions.

Building Better Perspectives!

Please tell us what you think of this *Perspectives* volume so we can improve the next one. Here's how you can help:

1. Visit our **coursewise** site at: http://www.coursewise.com

2. Click on *Perspectives*. Then select the Building Better *Perspectives* Form for your book.

3. Forms and instructions for submission are available online.

Tell us what you think—did the readings and online materials help you make some learning connections? Were some materials more helpful than others? Thanks in advance for helping us build better *Perspectives*.

Student Internships

If you enjoy evaluating these articles or would like to help us evaluate the **courselinks** site for this course, check out the **coursewise** Student Internship Program. For more information, visit:

http://www.coursewise.com/intern.html

Contents

section 1

Intercultural Communications

WiseGuide Intro   1

1. **The International Space Station: Multi-Culture on the High Frontier,** Larry Livingston. International Training Resources, Houston, Texas, 1998.
Livingston discusses the intercultural communication issues that the crew members of the international space station will face. He suggests that a third "space station" culture will be established as the international crew struggles to increase harmony and reduce conflict in the extreme environment.   **3**

2. **Intercultural Communication Competencies: Using Behavioral Objectives for the Introductory Course,** Dorothy Lawrence Franzone. Texas Southern University, 1998.
There are different criteria for measuring intercultural competence. Dr. Franzone summarizes this research on the dimensions of intercultural communication components and criteria for assessment, and provides insight into three different approaches to teaching intercultural communication.   **8**

3. **How Many Things Do You Like to Do at Once? An Introduction to Monochronic and Polychronic Time,** Allen C. Bluedorn, Carol Felker Kaufman, and Paul M. Lane. *The Executive: An Academy of Management Publication,* November 1992.
Bluedorn, Kaufman and Lane compare monochronic and polychronic cultural differences in temporal perspective. They also identify why patterns of time may create conflict among people and offer you an opportunity to identify your individual orientation to time.   **11**

4. **Cross-Cultural Communication for Managers,** Mary Munter. *Business Horizons,* May–June 1993.
Munter synthesizes multiple insights into developing cross-cultural communication management skills. She also explores cultural value systems and their impact on the communication process.   **18**

5. **Learning the Arabs' Silent Language,** Edward T. Hall interviewed by Kenneth Friedman. *Psychology Today,* August 1979.
The Friedman interview of Edward T. Hall provides insight into the man who some say founded the field of intercultural communication research. Hall shares not only his insights into the Arab culture but also into the complexity of cross-cultural communication situations.   **27**

6. **Computer Chip Project Brings Rivals Together, But the Cultures Clash,** E. S. Browning. *The Wall Street Journal,* May 3, 1994.
Browning explores the intercultural communication problems that developed in a computer business project supported by Toshiba Corporation of Japan, Siemens AG of Germany, and IBM-USA.   **33**

7. **It's a Small World After All,** Judith Stone. *Discover,* February 1992.
Stone provides insight into some of the troublesome myths and stereotypes regarding "other cultures" that create cross-cultural communication difficulties on space missions. She also explores "Star Trek" as a model of sensitivity to cultural differences in the exploration of space.   **36**

WiseGuide Wrap-Up   38

At **coursewise**, we're publishing connected learning tools. That means that the book you are holding is only a part of this publication. You'll also want to harness the integrated resources that **coursewise** has developed at the fun and highly useful **courselinks** web site for *Perspectives: Intercultural Communications*. If you purchased this book new, use the Passport that was shrink-wrapped to this volume to obtain site access. If you purchased a used copy of this book, then you need to buy a stand-alone Passport. If your bookstore doesn't stock Passports to **courselinks** sites, visit http://www.courselinks.com for ordering information.

section 2

Global Business

WiseGuide Intro **39**

8 **Cultural Constraints in Management Theories,** Geert Hofstede. *The Executive: An Academy of Management Publication,* February 1993.
Hofstede, one of the leading intercultural communication researchers, presents his model in which he categorizes worldwide differences in national cultures. He recommends the internationalization of management theories and provides suggestions for change. **41**

9 **Building Effective Teams in a Multicultural Environment,** Robert Kimmons. Kimmons-Asaro Group Ltd., Inc., Houston, Texas, 1998.
Kimmons addresses the concerns that project managers face when their workforce is multicultural. He offers strategies for building effective teams that create a customized road map of how the work will get done. **49**

10 **Using Cultural Skills for Cooperative Advantage in Japan,**
Richard H. Reeves-Ellington. *Human Organization,* Vol. 52, No. 2, 1993.
Reeves-Ellington discusses how Pharmco, a multinational pharmaceutical company, utilized an anthropologically trained manager to develop tools and a learning process for managers who previously had not worked in a global marketplace. Reeves-Ellington's discussion of the cultural logic of relationships and its application to Japan may be applied to other societies. **51**

11 **When Groups Consist of Multiple Nationalities: Towards a New Understanding of the Implications,** Donald C. Hambrick, Sue Canney Davison, Scott A. Snell, and Charles C. Snow. *Organization Studies,* February 19, 1998.
The authors provide an overview of success stories in the use of multinational groups, as well as the frustrations that occur in this type of team. The article explores the effects of multinational diversity on group functioning and performance. **64**

12 **Women Expats—Shattering the Myths,** Charlene Marmer Solomon. *Workforce,* May 1998.
Solomon examines some outdated beliefs about the acceptance of women managers for international assignments and offers suggestions for recruiting women for these positions. She also outlines the importance of international experience for all professionals. **77**

13 **Managing Globally Competent People,** Nancy J. Adler and Susan Bartholomew. *The Executive: An Academy of Management Publication,* August 1992.
According to Adler and Bartholomew, a global human resource department, by necessity, must be transnational in structure and operation. They advocate a paradigm shift in how such departments develop and manage globally competent people. A matrix of transnational skills is offered, along with a comparison of transnationally competent managers versus traditional international managers. **81**

14 **Cultural Awareness: An Essential Element of Doing Business Abroad,**
Gary Bonvillian and William A. Nowlin. *Business Horizons,* November–December 1994.
What is cultural awareness? Bonvillian and Nowlin elaborate and indicate why they consider cultural awareness so important in operating internationally. Cultural awareness also has application for firms whose employees communicate globally, even though they may not travel geographically. **90**

15 **The Making of a French Manager,** Jean-Louis Barsoux and Peter Lawrence. *Harvard Business Review,* July–August 1991.
Barsoux and Lawrence provide insight into the French approach to management. In France, management is viewed not as a task but as a "state of mind," a concept that worldwide managers need to understand. This reading also provides perspective on the different training that French managers receive, what is expected in behavior, and the role of the manager in relation to the firm. **96**

WiseGuide Wrap-Up **102**

section 3: Negotiating Across Cultures

WiseGuide Intro   103

16 **Expand the Pie Before You Divvy It Up,** Doug Stewart. *Smithsonian,* November 1997.
William Ury and Roger Fisher co-authored the best-selling book *Getting to Yes: Negotiating Agreement Without Giving In.* In this negotiating situation, William Ury is faced with a difficult task: to apply some of the negotiating strategies from the book to an impasse between the Russians and Chechens. Stewart's interview with Ury provides insight into the highs and lows of this type of cross-cultural negotiation.   104

17 **Conflict Resolution for Contrasting Cultures,** Clifford C. Clarke and G. Douglas Lipp. *Training & Development,* February 1998.
Initiating conflict is easy; it is conflict resolution that is more time consuming and difficult. Clarke and Lipp offer seven steps to assist people of contrasting cultures in working together. The goal of this process is for managers and other employees from different cultures to better understand how culture affects their expectations, reactions, and views of themselves and each other, including possible negative perceptions.   109

18 **Negotiating with "Romans"—Part 1,** Stephen E. Weiss. *Sloan Management Review Reprint Series,* Winter 1994.
In Part 1, Weiss combines a number of negotiating strategies in a cross-cultural negotiating framework. He also offers eight culturally responsive negotiating strategies for various countries.   121

19 **Negotiating with "Romans"—Part 2,** Stephen E. Weiss. *Sloan Management Review Reprint Series,* Spring 1994.
In Part 2, Weiss expounds on the cultural responsive negotiating model. However, he adds in other variables, such as knowledge of own cultural script, relationships, and circumstances, that may apply to negotiating across cultures.   130

WiseGuide Wrap-Up   142

section 4: Global Human Resources and Training

WiseGuide Intro   143

20 **Global Business Issues,** Patty Lynam. Vice President of Human Resources Systems and Global Initiatives, Kvaerner Process, London, England, 1998.
Lynam provides an overview of the communication issues that global companies must address to be effective. As part of a global human resource team currently setting up a worldwide human resource information system, Lynam draws from recent experience. She also discusses how all employees need to be aware of the limitations of language when English is used as the common language of trade.   145

21 **Colgate's Global HR Unites Under One Strategy,** Dawn Anfuso. *Personnel Journal,* October 1995.
The Colgate-Palmolive firm sells its products around the world. The firm's global success comes from a sensitivity to the culture of both internal and external customers. Its human resource department not only modeled the change to global human resources, but was a leader in moving the rest of the company in the same international direction.   147

22 **A Guide for Global Training,** Sylvia Odenwald. *Training & Development,* July 1993.
Odenwald summarizes some of the traits necessary for global effectiveness. She reviews course issues, culture-specific issues, and multicultural integration. She presents examples of effective global training programs, as well as general suggestions for trainers.   151

23 **Developing Global Managers,** Stephen Gates. In *The Changing Global Role of the Human Resource Function: A Research Report,* The Conference Board, 1994.
The results of a survey of 158 human resource managers in North American, European, and Asian companies are offered in a series of articles. The survey results indicated some priorities on the part of global human resource managers. The human resource managers saw a shift toward developing global executives, managing the return of expatriates effectively, promoting a company vision and values globally, and building a global human resource network. Gates outlines the concern of developing global managers.   156

24 **When Sexual Harassment Is a Foreign Affair,** Wendy Hardman and Jacqueline Heidelberg. *Personnel Journal,* April 1996.
Sexual harassment can be complex in a global business situation. Laws, customs, gender roles, and values may differ from society to society. Hardman and Heidelberg offer prevention strategies for human resource departments operating internationally. **162**

WiseGuide Wrap-Up **167**

section 5

Intercultural Communication Research

WiseGuide Intro **168**

25 **Concepts of "Culture": Implications for Intercultural Communication Research,** Dreama G. Moon. *Communication Quarterly,* Winter 1996.
Moon provides both a historical examination of intercultural communication research and suggestions for future research. She also examines the issues of economic, gender, and researcher bias in her effort to provide some direction for a paradigm shift. **169**

26 **The Study of Cross-Cultural Competence: Traditions and Contemporary Issues,** Brent D. Ruben. *International Journal of Intercultural Relations,* Vol. 13, 1989.
Ruben provides a good overview of different definitions of intercultural communication competence. In addition, he raises many questions that remain unanswered, such as, "How is cross-cultural competency measured?" **179**

27 **Traits, Attitudes, and Skills That Are Related to Intercultural Effectiveness and Their Implications for Cross-Cultural Training: A Review of the Literature,** Terence P. Hannigan. *International Journal of Intercultural Relations,* Vol. 14, 1990.
Hannigan looks at such terms as *adjustment, adaptation, acculturation, assimilation,* and *effectiveness,* which are frequently used in intercultural communication research literature. He provides a summary of research regarding each term and how each is applied to intercultural communication research. **185**

28 **Trainer Competencies: The Missing Conceptual Link in Orientation,** R. Michael Paige. *International Journal of Intercultural Relations,* Vol. 10, 1986.
Paige examines various contexts for intercultural communication training. Ethical issues in training, ranging from marketing to training environment, are also addressed. He provides a list of training competencies in the cognitive domain. This reading does not answer all the questions raised but provides good discussion questions. **196**

WiseGuide Wrap-Up **207**

section 6

Intercultural Ethics and Discussion Issues

WiseGuide Intro **208**

29 **Intercultural Ethics,** Tulsi B. Saral. University of Houston–Clear Lake, 1998.
As the rules of behavior vary greatly from culture to culture, so do the ethical values of different societies. Dr. Saral addresses the variables that influence ethics within a culture and recognizes that there are individual standards of ethical behavior. He also examines the dissonance in cross-cultural relationships from the need to adjust to the situation and other cultures and the need to keep one's own culture intact. **210**

30 **Crossing the Line,** J. Stark. *People, Places and Society,* College of Social and Behavioral Sciences, University of Arizona, Spring 1998.
Dr. Ed Williams, professor of political science at the University of Arizona, discusses the border issues that occur on any shared boundary. The maquiladora industry along the U.S. and Mexico border has many of the same problems associated with production-sharing in other parts of the world. Dr. Williams provides a quick overview of these issues. **214**

31 **Imagining La Frontera: SEDL's Border Colloquy,** Southwest Educational Development Laboratory. University of Texas–Austin, 1995.
A series of regional meetings was held in 1994–1995 along the Mexican and U.S. border for information-sharing purposes and planning for the future. This excerpt from the "Imagining La Frontera" report provides an understanding of the concerns on both sides of the border as the NAFTA agreement continues to be implemented. **215**

32 **Helping Mixed-Race People Declare Their Heritage,** David L. Wheeler. *The Chronicle of Higher Education,* September 7, 1994.
In this interview, Terry Wilson, professor of ethnic studies, University of California–Berkley, describes his experiences as a mixed-race person. Dr. Wilson also provides examples of the concerns of mixed-race people. **220**

33 **Cattle, Education, and the Masai Identity,** Francis Slakey. *The Chronicle of Higher Education,* December 5, 1997.
This reading examines the ethical considerations that Dr. Slakey addressed as he decided whether or not to provide educational scholarships to two young Masai. A narrative of the dissonance Dr. Slakey experienced raises ethical questions of a cultural nature. **222**

34 **The Sounds of Global Change: Different Beats, New Ideas,** David Rothenberg. *The Chronicle of Higher Education,* June 5, 1998.
Music is often seen as the international language. Does this mean that music follows an international cultural pattern? These and other questions about the introduction of international artists to the global marketplace are explored in this reading. **224**

35 **Virtual Teams,** Beverly Geber. *Training,* April 1995.
How can we be "high-tech" and still create a "high-touch" network? This is the conundrum facing members of virtual teams who interact over space and time. **227**

WiseGuide Wrap-Up **231**

Index **232**

Topic Key

This Topic Key is an important tool for learning. It will help you integrate this reader into your course studies. Listed below, in alphabetical order, are important topics covered in this volume. Below each topic, you'll find the reading numbers and titles, and also the R.E.A.L. web site addresses, relating to that topic. Note that the Topic Key might not include every topic your instructor chooses to emphasize. If you don't find the topic you're looking for in the Topic Key, check the index or the online topic key at the **courselinks**™ site.

Border Issues
30 Crossing the Line
31 Imagining La Frontera: SEDL's Border Colloquy

Conflict Resolution
17 Conflict Resolution for Contrasting Cultures

Decision Making
7 It's a Small World After All
9 Building Effective Teams in a Multicultural Environment

Ethics
24 When Sexual Harassment Is a Foreign Affair
29 Intercultural Ethics
33 Cattle, Education, and the Masai Identity
Institute for Global Ethics
http://www.globalethics.org/about/default.html

European Union
Welcome to Europa
http://europa.eu.int/index-en.htm

Human Resources
12 Women Expats—Shattering the Myths
13 Managing Globally Competent People
21 Colgate's Global HR Unites under One Strategy
23 Developing Global Managers
24 When Sexual Harassment Is a Foreign Affair
Society for Human Resource Management (SHRM)
http://www.shrm.org/

Intercultural Communication Competencies
1 The International Space Station: Multi-Culture on the High Frontier
2 Intercultural Communication Competencies: Using Behavioral Objectives for the Introductory Course
3 How Many Things Do You Like to Do at Once? An Introduction to Monochronic and Polychronic Time
4 Cross-Cultural Communication for Managers
14 Cultural Awareness: An Essential Element of Doing Business Abroad
16 Expand the Pie Before You Divvy It Up
26 The Study of Cross-Cultural Competence: Traditions and Contemporary Issues
29 Intercultural Ethics
Cross-Cultural Resource Library
http://darkwing.uoregon.edu/~oieehome/oiee/resourcelibrary.html
Student and Educational Development
http://www.dist.maricopa.edu/eddev/

Intercultural Communication Research
8 Cultural Constraints of Management Theories
10 Using Cultural Skills for Cooperative Advantage in Japan
25 Concepts of "Culture": Implications for Intercultural Communication Research
26 The Study of Cross-Cultural Competence: Traditions and Contemporary Issues

27 Traits, Attitudes, and Skills That Are Related to Intercultural Effectiveness and Their Implications for Cross-Cultural Training: A Review of the Literature
28 Trainer Competencies: The Missing Conceptual Link in Organizations
National Communication Association (NCA)
http://www.natcom.org/

International Internships
Idealist
http://www.idealist.org/

International Travel
Bureau of Consular Affairs
http://travel.state.gov/

International Music
34 The Sounds of Global Change: Different Beats, New Ideas

Language Differences
1 The International Space Station: Multi-Culture on the High Frontier
4 Cross-Cultural Communication for Managers
6 Computer Chip Project Brings Rivals Together but the Cultures Clash
14 Cultural Awareness: An Essential Element of Doing Business Abroad
20 Global Business Issues
31 Imagining La Frontera: SEDL's Border Colloquy

Latin America
American Network Information Center
http://lanic.utexas.edu/

xvii

Management

- 3 How Many Things Do You Like to Do at Once? An Introduction to Monochronic and Polychronic Time
- 4 Cross-Cultural Communication for Managers
- 6 Computer Chip Project Brings Rivals Together but the Cultures Clash
- 8 Cultural Constraints in Management Theories
- 9 Building Effective Teams in a Multicultural Environment
- 12 Women Expats—Shattering the Myths
- 13 Managing Globally Competent People
- 15 The Making of a French Manager
- 23 Developing Global Managers

Multicultural/Multinational Teams

- 4 Cross-Cultural Communication for Managers
- 6 Computer Chip Project Brings Rivals Together but the Cultures Clash
- 9 Building Effective Teams in a Multicultural Environment
- 11 When Groups Consist of Multiple Nationalities: Towards a New Understanding of the Implications
- 22 A Guide for Global Training
- 24 When Sexual Harassment Is a Foreign Affair
- 35 Virtual Teams

Negotiation

- 16 Expand the Pie Before You Divvy It Up
- 18 Negotiating with "Romans"—Part 1
- 19 Negotiating with "Romans"—Part 2

Adil Hajam: MIT Chlorine Negotiation Simulation on the Global Environment
http://www.mit.edu/people/anajam/cl-game.html

Harvard Law School: The Program on Negotiation at Harvard Law School
http://www.pon.harvard.edu/

Nonverbal Communication

- 1 The International Space Station: Multi-Culture on the High Frontier
- 3 How Many Things Do You Like to Do at Once? An Introduction to Monochronic and Polychronic Time
- 5 Learning the Arabs' Silent Language
- 14 Cultural Awareness: An Essential Element of Doing Business Abroad

Russian and East European Countries

The Reese Web at the University of Pittsburgh
http://www.pitt.edu/~cjp/rees.html

Self-Concept

- 32 Helping Mixed-Race People Declare Their Heritage
- 33 Cattle, Education, and the Masai Identity

Social Skills

- 5 Learning the Arabs' Silent Language
- 6 Computer Chip Project Brings Rivals Together but the Cultures Clash
- 10 Using Cultural Skills for Cooperative Advantage in Japan
- 14 Cultural Awareness: An Essential Element of Doing Business Abroad
- 15 The Making of a French Manager

Total Quality Management

- 10 Using Cultural Skills for Cooperative Advantage in Japan

Training

- 22 A Guide for Global Training
- 27 Traits, Attitudes, and Skills That Are Related to Intercultural Effectiveness and Their Implications for Cross-Cultural Training: A Review of the Literature
- 28 Trainer Competencies: The Missing Conceptual Link in Organizations

American Society for Training and Development (ASTD)
http://www.astd.org/

Society for Human Resource Management (SHRM)
http://www.shrm.org/

Virtual Teams

- 35 Virtual Teams

section 1

Intercultural Communications

Learning Objectives

- Increase awareness of the importance of intercultural communications.
- Understand the relationship between culture and communication.
- Expand knowledge of the intercultural communications field.
- Develop better understanding of own cultural patterns.
- Increase intercultural communications skills.

WiseGuide Intro

Canadian communication theorist Marshall McLuhan envisioned a "global village" being technologically possible in the future. The interconnected world we inhabit far exceeds McLuhan's vision. As we "talk" via technology or "face-to-face" cross-culturally, we rely on the patterns learned from the society within which we were raised. When we interface with someone who has a "talking" pattern different than our own, we do not always know what to say or understand what was said. Edward Hall, an anthropologist whom many feel was the originator of the intercultural communication field, saw this relationship between culture and communication as "culture is communication and communication is culture."

One of the best ways to understand our own culture is to meet people with other backgrounds, recognizing that the process will be filled with false steps and moments of insight. We frequently do not understand our own patterns until we bump against others. Culture has multiple levels, which impact on us in a variety of ways. As we examine different nationalities and their organization of thoughts, topics of conversation, length and type of silence, eye gaze patterns, perceptions of what is humorous and what is not, gender expectations, power, use of time and authority, and patterns of "talk," we see that these cultural expectations are transmitted via channels of communication.

In communicating cross-culturally, we must recognize that errors will occur, but we must seek to minimize them. We may understand one aspect of a culture, but other aspects and contexts may cause confusion or missed communication. Various cultures place different responsibility for communication on the sender and receiver of messages. The signals for receipt of messages and sending messages vary. There is great variety in both the verbal and nonverbal aspects of the communication process.

An example of this occurred in a communication class at Texas Southern University, where I have had the good fortune to work with students from Kenya, Nigeria, Cameroon, South Africa, and Ethiopia. In my health communication class, when talking with students from the African continent, they did not maintain eye contact. Recognizing that different cultures have different gaze patterns, I did not take offense. After a period of time, I discussed cultural variations in nonverbal communication, gaze being an example. These African students then recognized they shared the indirect gaze norm when talking to an older person or, to one with higher status. It was a delightful revelation for me when they shared that professors are held in high esteem, hence the respectful downward gaze. In addition, they held people older than themselves in high regard, as being wiser. This insight led to class discussions of differences in eye contact patterns. Students were then able to decode the gaze patterns of their patients with new acceptance of cultural variety. Others decided to make adjustments in their gaze patterns as they worked with different patients.

These adaptable health professionals used their knowledge of nonverbal patterns to create better cross-cultural relationships with patients.

This section provides an overview of different cross-cultural situations. We have selected a wide variety of global contexts ranging from space, to organizations, to face-to-face situations. Articles focus either on a single culture or on multinational teams. In addition, these readings present a variety of approaches to increasing one's awareness of, knowledge of, and skills regarding effective intercultural communication.

Questions

Reading 1. Space—the final frontier . . . How will a multinational astronaut crew adapt to different languages and cultures, as they work to carry out their mission, to construct and work in the International Space Station?

Reading 2. What are intercultural communication competencies? Is it possible to learn them in a classroom or training setting? How can we assess intercultural interaction?

Reading 3. Attitudes, values, and beliefs about time can differ among cultures. Are there differences you have observed? Differences may include doing one or multiple things at a time; take the test to discover your pattern. How might differences impact relations? Would this interfere with getting work completed?

Reading 4. Culture consists of the values, attitudes, and behaviors of a particular group; might differences in work-related values have communication implications? In working with various cultures, what communication objectives might be reasonable within time constraints? What would be the most effective communication style?

Reading 5. In the 1950s, Edward Hall was director of the Point IV Training Program at the Foreign Service Institute, where he and others trained diplomats in intercultural communication. He and George Trager wrote the first manual for cross-cultural training. In this article, he offers insights into the Arab cultures. Are his comments accurate today? What changes in the Arab cultures do you believe have occurred, or what has remained the same? Does culture change or remain constant?

Reading 6. IBM USA, Siemens AG of Germany, and Toshiba Corporation of Japan brought a multinational team together to develop a computer chip; what got in the way? What might be done differently if they were to attempt it today?

Reading 7. Putting different cultures into tight quarters may create difficulties. Stone's article presents some funny and not so funny cross-cultural situations which have occurred in space. How should the international space effort resolve some of the issues of communication style, gender expectations, and privacy issues? Have there been any cross-cultural problems during recent joint space efforts on the Russian Space Station *Mir*? What might be future issues on the International Space Station?

Space—the final frontier... How will a multinational astronaut crew adapt to different languages and cultures, as they work to carry out their mission, to construct and work in the International Space Station?

The International Space Station

Multi-culture on the high frontier

Larry Livingston

Globalization is resulting in major projects being undertaken by multinational corporations. Whether it a single firm with world outlets or joint ventures, companies are using multinational managers and crews to do these projects.

When multinational employees are used on construction and operating projects, culture is an important underlying factor. On such a project, the combinations of languages, values, beliefs and attitudes and cultures is vast and its influence on the project is significant.

The International Space Station (ISS), nicknamed *the Station*, is a large-scale construction and operating project that will soon begin. The culture of the participants will affect the project, and the effects of zero-gravity, spacesuits and impaired communication will complicate this further.

The Station is a global joint venture between the United States, Canada, eleven countries of the European Space Agency, Japan and Russia. After over a decade of planning, the in-orbit construction of the station is planned to begin toward late 1998. Operating the Station will occur as soon as the Habitat (life support) Module becomes functional. The Station will include a main United States Habitat and Laboratory Module, a European and a Japanese Module. In addition, there will be substantial hardware contributions by Russia. Each international space agency will have its national/multinational goals.

The construction and occupation of the station will demonstrate the use of low gravity to pursue medical and technological research. In addition, the station will serve as a laboratory to demonstrate a new frontier of multiculturalism.

This article will explore:

- The influence of zero gravity on cultural rules
- Interaction between multicultural crew in zero-gravity
- Strategies to increase harmony and reduce conflict in an isolated, confined, extreme (ICE) environment
- Establishing a third culture

Space Construction

The construction of the Station can be compared to large multinational joint-venture projects on earth. To achieve a projects' goals, international organizations agree on who is responsible for what aspect of the project. A multinational task force is assembled with managers and employees from many different cultures.

On an earthbound multinational construction project, the workers interact with each other, communicate on the task to be achieved, make decisions and implement solutions. Adding the ingredient of culture to the physical aspects of space results in cultural dynamics different from what is experienced on earth.

On earth, gravity is always with us. We are used from birth to interacting and communicating in its presence. In the hostile vacuum and annoying zero-gravity environment of space, some rules change. In the space environment, construction workers must wear life support suits. Maneuvering is also difficult. The space construction workers wear portable Man Maneuvering Unit (MMU) backpacks—without it, they would float away and be lost.

The Station's construction requires crews to use the MMU to maneuver themselves into the payload bay of the Space Shuttle and take out predetermined building pieces. The number of crew assigned to assemble at any given time is determined by the task. Large task, such as attaching the Habitat or Laboratory Module may require five or six at one time. Simpler tasks, such as assembling the Station's solar panels or electronics, may take fewer.

"The International Space Station: Multi-Culture on the High Frontier," Larry Livingston. Reprinted by permission of the author.

The crew will have rehearsed and practiced pre-assembling the Station components on earth. Management will first take place at earth sites, then from the Space Shuttle until the Habitation Modules are ready for occupancy, then transition to that module.

Communicating During Construction of the Project

Although the MMU gives some mobility, the space environment limits personnel in the use of conventional methods of interacting and communicating. The communication technology used while in space suits is built-in radio transceivers which allow the crew to communicate with each other and to keep in touch with support personnel in the Space Shuttle, Habitat Module and ground-based personnel around the world.

Because of the environment of space and the technologies needed to deal with it, both verbal and nonverbal communication change.

Verbal Communication in a Vacuum

The space environment and the equipment necessary to work in it effects communication in general, and in particular affects communication among an international crew.

The official language spoken on the International Space Station project is English, with the exception of the Russian involvement. Preplanning has worked out the language between the Russians and the International Astronaut Corp. The language of choice will be Russenglish, agreed upon vocabulary that will be used by the international partners in space. For, example during the earlier joint U.S. Apollo and Soviet Soyuz program Russenglish was used as the main language. During a French visit to the Mir Space Station, a combination of French and Russian were used by the international partners to communicate (NASA, 1993). The use of a common language ensures that all participants are able to communicate or receive instructions equally well without the use of interpreters.

Unfortunately, the use of a common language on multinational projects has limitations, such as mispronunciations or heavy accents that cause misunderstandings and hence miscommunications. Bluth (1981) reported on the effects of language in multinational Russian crews. She indicated that "foreign accent deform Russian expressions, leading to misunderstanding" (Campbell, 1985). In addition the lack of gravity complicates this further by altering the function of the larynx, changing voice tone and timbre.

Multinationals working together during an Extra Vehicular Activity (i.e., spacewalk) may misunderstand each other as a result of using English as a second language. If Russians are conducting a joint assembly exercise, lack of familiarity of common Russenglish synonyms, acronyms, abbreviations may cause misunderstandings. This could cause serious problems in an emergency.

At a multinational project worksite on earth it is easy enough for multinational workers to misunderstand verbal messages by misunderstanding both the words being used and changes in a speaker's tone of voice. To overcome ambiguities, the communicator has the choice to use non-verbal communication such as facial and body gestures, as well as touch to overcome the cultural barriers that the spoken word has presented. In space, the multinational crew have more limited options available to them to clarify miscommunications.

Nonverbal Communication During Construction

Unlike the process used to clarify communication on earth, conventional facial expressions or other nonverbal communications can not easily be used to verify the intent of the message being sent. The space-suit helmets make facial gestures difficult to perform as well as see, and heavy space suits hobble body language and gestures.

Not only are the means to convey non-verbal communications thwarted, but the pre-existing mix of cultures in the crew means that what gestures can be seen might be misinterpreted because many gestures do not keep a consistent meaning across cultures. The traditional tip-of-thumb-to-tip-of-finger "OK" sign, for example, is not easily understood across cultures, and may mean something totally different than what the sender had in mind. In space even this simple sign is not easily made, and such failings can further distort the message being communicated.

Even the use of touching may be limited to pats on the back to show approval, acknowledgement, or to get a person's attention. Communication will thus be limited to the verbal communication, intonation of the voice and limited non-verbal communication.

The activities that are associated with construction involve management/supervisors to continually meet with the workforce on each aspect of the construction, take measurements, and perform quality control. In an international setting this routine takes more time, since translations may need to be made between languages of the manager and language of the workers.

The crew must be able to query the speaker and other sources that are on-line monitoring the communication, to receive feedback clarifications of communication if necessary.

Culture on the Space Station

As the Station construction becomes habitable, changes of selected international crewmembers will be assigned to staff the Station on a rotating basis during the twenty-five years of its planned operating life.

Living and working in space will be an international activity and cultures will be carried into space. The Space Station will be constructed for a "shirtsleeves" environment. Space suites will not obstruct interactions and communication in day-to-day operations once the Station is completed and staffed.

Although, space has no geopolitical borders, spacefarers are no different from their earth-bound relatives. The numbers of countries that have had citizens in space are numerous. Between the Russian and the United States space programs, a number of guest astronauts and Cosmonauts from many countries have gone into space, such as Canada, Czechoslovakia, East and West Germany, France, Japan, Italy, Mexico, the Netherlands, Saudi Arabia and Switzerland (Harris, 1992).

According to Bluth (1982) culture, "ideas, values, beliefs, assumptions, and ways of thinking are an ongoing background factor in crew activity, performance and expectations that are part of the varied demands of a space mission."

Social scientists have conducted research on the effect of Isolated Confined Extreme (ICE) environments on humans. Only recently they have turned their attention studying international groups and ICE. They have recognized that culture plays a major role in determining the success of international members in reaching their goals.

Four cultural variables have been studied extensively by social scientists

Group dynamics

Intercultural relations

Communication

Non-verbal communication

Group Dynamics

Group interaction will be essential to ensure that the Space Station is operational. The Station will require "numerous individuals working in close-net, efficient teams" (Santy, 1983). Each member will be required to be highly specialized. A crew member's degree of specialization will be one of several criteria taken into account to be selected for the Space Station. Since specialization is important, the make-up of the crew who rotates into the Station for stays of from 30 days to six months could be composed of any international mixture.

Two important aspects of group dynamics will evolve. The first is formal groups, made-up of the chain-of-command within the Station and professional or job task groups. The second is informal groups—small groups of 2 to 3 people, or a coalition who have common interest. Groupings in space will form along similar lines as they do on earth (Leonov, Lomov, and, Lebedev, 1976).

Past Space flights have seen groupings form along national or language similarities (Bluth, 1986, Oberg, 1981, Tajfel, 1982). These groupings could result in intergroup competition or conflict.

As a result of crew rotation, new members coming on board the Station will continually shape group composites and hence the constantly unfolding changes in group dynamics.

The U.S. Space Shuttle program has involved individuals from a variety of cultures, for example Franklin Chang Diaz, who immigrated to the United States from Costa Rica and Sidney Gutierrez, a Mexican-American from New Mexico (Peña, 1989). Other groups assigned to a Space Shuttle crew have included Black females and males, and a Chinese American, etc.

Although this article has been limited to the discussion of the multicultural crew, the crew's composition will be both males and females. The United States and the Russian space programs have had women in space. The U.S. space program has included women from different ethnic backgrounds, including a female Japanese Astronaut.

Periodically, members will leave the crew and new members will be added. Members from one's own country will be added or subtracted, as the task required is completed and they are no longer needed. Group dynamics and the interchange between members will be a matter of constant flux.

Once the Space Station becomes operational and other space goals are identified, the presence of married couples in space could become standard practice. This will add a new dimension to group dynamics (Santy, 1983, Bluth, 1986, O'Leary, 1987).

Intercultural Relations

International flights will be culturally diverse in nature. At any given time during the construction and manning of the Space Station any combination crew is possible. Crew make-up will be made various criteria for the mission to be accomplished. As Adler (1986) points out, cultural diversity in an organization is often viewed as either a hindrance or an advantage. An advantage of a culturally diversified space crew is that it engenders a greater degree of creativity to solving problems. Many aspects of space are still not understood, and the effects of space on large structures are still being explored. Problems and life threatening emergency can arise out of nowhere.

Because it is human nature to group with those most similar to oneself, cultural diversity can lead to a lack of cohesion. This can manifest itself in mistrust, miscommunication, and stress. An example of this occurred during a Soviet Soyuz multinational space flight. The international guest was an East German flying with two Russians. The East German spoke little or no Russian. The two Russians ignored the East German because of the difficulty to conversing with one another. During the two-week stay, East German felt isolated, and closed off from what was going on around him.

Studies on diverse teams have shown that these teams come up with the best solutions to resolve problems as long as communication remains good. Diversity forces enhanced concentration on the part of group members to understand one another's ideas and meanings, thus better decisions can be made regarding solutions and problems. A further advantage of a diversified crew is that the variety of perspectives and approaches is more likely to spur technological and scientific advances than culturally homogenous groups faced with the same problems.

Establishing and maintaining cultural synergy will be important to ensuring the success of the Space Station's scientific and technological goals. And as the European Space Agency Astronaut and veteran of the 1985 D-1 Space Lab Space Shuttle flight, Wubbo Oeckels stated: "Learn and understand what is different among the cultures, obtain and show respect for those differences, and build trust and confidence."

Intercultural relations should be based on:

- Awareness of cultural differences, and their advantages and disadvantages in the work environment

- Acceptance of cultural relativity

- Creation of an environment which enables individuals and groups to function in a manner adaptive to cultural differences.

Communications

Communications on the Station after completion and habitation will be much simpler than the space assembly crews experienced. However, when people from different cultures converse, communication becomes a source of difficulty that can not be ignored.

Fons Trompenaars and Charles Hampden-Turner (1998) have documented how tone of voice and the spoken word, and non-verbal communications are realized interculturally.

Tone of Voice

Tone of voice in Anglo-Saxon societies is up and down fluctuation, which communicate intent and seriousness. In Latin societies the up and down fluctuation in the voice indicates that "you have your heart in the matter." Oriental societies, tone is a language element, a necessary parameter to distinguish the pronunciation of different words.

Since tone of voice is used by cultures differently, misinterpreting the intent of what was said might have an unintended effect. For example, if a problem should arise during Station assembly, or a life-threatening emergency should arise, what was said and its importance might not be understood by the person from another culture. This could result in delaying responding to the situation, and possible resulting in loss of life. Misunderstanding could also lead to conflict between the communicators from different cultures.

Spoken Word

Individuals who are similar and from the same culture often have difficulty understanding each other. When members from different countries speak English as a second language, mispronouncing words and use of a heavy accent could lead to further misunderstanding. The wrong choice of words may further create misunderstanding and confusion.

As members from the same culture are assigned to the Space Station it is only natural to converse in one's own language. However, as mentioned before, fellow astronauts who don't know the language may feel left out of the conversation, or during stressful episodes or group conflict may feel that the crew are talking about them. Penwell suggest that it is better to avoid the conflict before it starts (Penwell, 1989). International crewmembers should receive training in cross-cultural communication and conflict avoidance prior to a flight.

Non-verbal Communication

As humans make the transition from the earth's gravitational pull to zero-g, the human physiology changes. A phenomenon called "puffy face" takes place. This condition occurs in "zero gravity when fluids collect in the upper body, leaving the body bloated" (Bluth, 1981). Facial expressions that are interpreted by one's fellow citizen may be unrecognizable. Facial expressions viewed from one of an international crew may incorrectly interpret the meaning behind the expression of another.

In general, in a weightless environment it becomes more difficult to move one's hands and arms; to gesture in a weightless environment takes an even greater amount of effort. Gesturing under these conditions may be mistaken by both a citizen of one's own culture and from the international crewmembers.

Communication may be more critical on long space missions. During stress, voice and facial gestures are generally the first indication that the person is undergoing a mood change. These indicators should be a tip-off to take action and assure that the problem is taken care of. When an international crewmember is involved, the signs may not be recognized by others of the crew.

Space in Space

Harris has defined the concept of "sense of self and space" as "the comfort we have with others, and the sense of space we maintain between ourselves and others." E. Hall (1990) has identified different types of space that we establish between others and ourselves: territoriality, personal space and multisensory space.

Territorial Space

Earlier space stations/spacecraft were very utilitarian and had very limited space. Crew selected turf where they could retreat to. The turf might be their sleeping area or space by a porthole that looked out on Earth. Often, the claimed space would lead to conflict by two or more of the crew who would claim it. Conflicts often lead to bad feelings between those involved. Unlike situations on Earth where those involved can get away from each other, on the space vehicle there is "no where to run" and be out of sight of those with whom they are in confrontation.

Personal Space

Culture socializes its citizens to define personal space and public space. In the United States citizens define personal space as more distance between themselves and other. Others may view close space as being comfortable, such as the Japanese and Latins who may define less than three inches between themselves and the person with whom they are communicating (Harris and Moran 1979). Hall (1987) compares the difference between Northern Europeans and Southern Europeans. Northern European require large amounts of space between them, while with Southern Europeans, such as those from southern France, Italy, Greece, and Spain the spaces between individuals are smaller. And the distance that is perceived as "intimate in North Europe is classified as normal conversation distance in the South."

The Station should pose a less threatening environment than did smaller space vehicles, however, it will still pose challenges for individuals living and working in close proximity. Further, depending on the number assigned to the Station there may be a crowding effect on those who are used to more space.

Multisensory Spatial

Hall explains that space is not perceived by sight alone, but by all the senses. "Auditory senses is perceived by the ears, thermal by the skin, kinesthetic space by the muscles, and olfactory by the nose." Also, Hall indicates that "culture programs our senses."

Different groups may be able to live and work differently based on the sight, sound, smell, and temperature that they experience in the Station environment. Hall gives an example that U.S. American and Germans "rely heavily on auditory screening when they want to concentrate," while people from Southern Europe, Asia, Latin America, or Africa "reject auditory screening and open to interpretation and tune in with what is going on around them."

Establishing a Third Culture

Beyond the Space Station and into the next millennium, when spacefarers go to the moon, Mars and beyond, a *third culture* phenomenon will emerged. A third culture is when several cultures come together, and a blending takes place. Over time no one culture emerges as being dominant; a single culture unfolds with the features of the cultures that existed before.

According to Harris (1992) the new culture will blend the old and new world ways. New values, beliefs, behaviors, and attitudes will form. The emergence of myriad cultures melding into a single culture will be instrumental in reducing intercultural conflict and competition. Future cooperative efforts in space such as the Station will provide opportunities that neither present Earthlings nor Spacefarers have to change our world.

Summary

International Space construction and operation projects are similar in some ways, different in others from earth-based multinational large projects. Culture plays an important part in space as it does on earth.

The ability of international spacefarers best to accomplish the goals of building and manning the Space Station and achieve each international space agency goal depends in part on understanding how a culture is affected by physiological changes due to weightlessness and the environment of living and working conditions in space.

Understanding these changes by the international crewmembers can assist in reducing miscommunication and misunderstanding between the multinational spacefarers and help develop a culture which will further aid future efforts of these types.

References

Nancy Adler, *International Dimensions of Organizational Behavior* (Boston, The Kent Publishing Company, Division of Wadsworth, Inc.)

Roger E. Axtell, *Gestures: The Do's and Taboos of Body Language Around the World* (New York, Chichester: John Wiley and Sons, Inc., 1991)

B. J. Bluth, in *Science,* 81, Vol. 2, No. 7. "Soviet Space Stress." American Association for the Advancement of Science, 1981. Pp. 30–35.

Anne E. Campbell, Multicultural Dynamics in Space Station. Paper presented at the session Role of the Social Science in Space Activities, XXXVIth International Astronautical Congress, October 7–12, 1985, Stockholm, Sweden.

Edward Hall and Mildred Read Hall, *Understanding Cultural Difference: Germans, French, and Americans.* (Garden City, NY, Intercultural Press, Inc., 1977)

A. A. Leonov, B. F. Lomov, and V. I. Lebedev, in International Space Flights "The Problem of Crew Interrelationships." *Voprospy Filosofi* #1., 1976.

Brian O'Leary, *Mars 1999.* (Harrisburg, PA, Stackpole Books, 1987)

NASA Russian Training Brief Document. Johnson Space Flight Center, Mission Operation Directorate, Space Station Training, Houston, TX, 1993.

Jim Oberg, and A. E. Oberg, *Pioneering Space: Living on the Next Frontier.* McGraw-Hill, 1986.

Larry Penwell, "The Problems of Intergroup Behavior in Human Spaceflight Operations," *Journal of Spacecraft,* Vol. 27, No. 5, September/October 1990. Pp. 464–467.

Silvia Novo Peña, "The Next Frontier: Hispanics in the Space Program," *Hispanic* January/February 1989.

Devera Pine, "The Human Factor," *Final Frontier* November/December 1989. Pp. 22–50.

Patricia Santy, "The Journey Out and In: Psychiatry and Space Exploration." *American Journal of Psychiatry,* Vol. 140, No. 5, May 1983. Pp. 519–527.

V. I. Sevast'yanov, "The Appearance of Certain Psychophysiological Characteristics of Man Under Conditions of Space Flight." *Psychological Problems of Space Flights.* Moscow: "Nauka" Press. 1979. Pp. 41–54.

Larry Livingston is the President of International Training Resources. His training career has spanned two continents, and he has worked for a variety of Fortune 500 companies.

He has provided just-in-time international training to corporations and not-for-profit organizations doing business internationally. Training programs that Larry teaches are preparing employees for international assignments, building global work teams, and preparing managers to manage a multinational workforce.

Larry's international training expertise has been valuable to the International Space Station Training Working Group, where he worked with the International Space Station Training cadre to design the training requirements for the International Space Station Partners.

He is a certified Instructional Design trainer that has led results oriented customer specific training workshops. Also, he is certified as a Ropes Course Facilitator. He is known for his professionalism and his flexibility to apply training examples to the student's specific training situation.

He has a Bachelor of Science degree from Illinois State University in Sociology and Anthropology and a Masters of Science degree in Sociology from Illinois State University.

To receive more information on International Training Resources we can be found at www.internationaltraining.com.

Article Review Form at end of book.

What are intercultural communication competencies? Is it possible to learn them in a classroom or training setting? How can we assess intercultural interaction?

Intercultural Communication Competencies

Using behavioral objectives for the introductory course

Dorothy Lawrence Franzone, Ph.D.
Texas Southern University

Many first time instructors of the introductory course in Intercultural Communication are overwhelmed by the mass of data available and compiled into texts for such courses. In addition to the many pedagogical questions confronting teachers are the additional tasks of selecting the text itself, preparing the course syllabus, selecting and scheduling supporting materials and guest speakers, preparing class lectures and finally, choosing assessment techniques and making out the exams. Some new instructors may find themselves midway through the semester before they realize that many of their overall educational objectives, as stated on the syllabus, and some specific instructional objectives for the course cannot be measured by the usual tests for cognitive data. Quantitative measurement techniques is most often used for the assessment of knowledge or cognitive data. Intercultural communication concepts, methodologies and definitions of culture, comparative world views, nomenclature for the course, the citation of personal characteristics and traits of the "effective" intercultural communicator and other cognitive data are effectively tested in this way. But what about the affective and behavioral dimensions of intercultural communication which comprise an essential part of the definition of competency when interacting with other cultures.

Questions of qualitative assessment arise in intercultural communication as it does in interpersonal communication when the instructor attempts to evaluate applied theory or the practical application of an intercultural construct. Although many of the recent theorists in the disciplines of intercultural and interpersonal communication are still debating the question of the exact locus of competence in the interaction process, most agree that "competency" should include a behavioral component. Meaning, that one's competency should demonstrate the ability to apply knowledge in such ways which demonstrate awareness and attitude change as well as communicative behavior changes. Different researchers have identified different behaviors as core components of the construct "competency" which, in some readings, may be called skills, effectiveness, successes, understandings or behavioral adjustments. The questions are "Who should assess intercultural interaction?" Should the interactants themselves give self-reports of the dyad interactions based on their own cultural rules of "effective" or competent behavior or using culture-specific models as a base? Or should significant others (instructor, observers, raters) who observe the interaction between dyads or among group members rate the interaction according to universal culture-general guidelines of competence? There are advantages and disadvantages in the use of both approaches. Some of the problems may be solved for the beginning instructor by deciding in advance which theoretical and pedagogical approaches to use,

---

Intercultural Communication Competencies: Using Behavioral Objectives for the Introductory Course by Dorothy Lawrence Franzone, Ph.D., Texas Southern University. Used by permission.

by the goals he/she selects for the teaching of the course, and by selecting the appropriate, measurable behavioral objectives to achieve these goals.

Historically, three approaches have been used to teach intercultural communication. One perspective measures intercultural communication "effectiveness" and focuses on cognitive components of a culture-general model. The study of personal characteristics of the sojourner and his/her knowledge of self (beliefs, values, behaviors and attitudes) and knowledge of universal cultural differences and world views and a demonstration of the awareness of these differences are used as a measure of competency. Others incorporate competencies of interpersonal communication and seek a more culture-specific application of cultural knowledge and include measures which assess situation-appropriate social interaction between culturally different interactants. In this paradigm, the primary focus of the measure of communication effectiveness shifts from the participant's judgement of his/her success in accomplishing his/her own personal goals, to that of the perceived judgements of others of the appropriateness of the communicative behavior of the participant, i.e., intercultural communication proficiency was thus determined by how successful the sojourner (participant) was judged by the host culture and other observers. Competence thus was defined as the ability "to demonstrate a knowledge of socially appropriate communicative behaviors in a specific situation" (Backlund, 1978 as quoted by Guo-Ming Chen, 1989).

A third perspective combines the original cognition-based culture-general model with that of the behavior-oriented culture-specific model thereby integrating measures of effectiveness (related to reaching one's own goals) and appropriateness (not violating cultural norms) into what some researchers see as a better model for studying intercultural communication (Guo-Ming Chen, 1989; Judith N. Martin, 1993).

Each perspective has its own criteria for measuring intercultural competence. Many of these evolved from interpersonal communication theories and research. Wiemann's (1977) model based upon the attainment of the speaker's own personal goals, defined communication competence as "the ability of an interactant to choose among available communicative behaviors in order that he/she may successfully accomplish his/her own interpersonal goals . . . while maintaining the face and line of his/her fellow interactants within the constraint of the situation" (Martin, 1993). Martin reports that competence for this model is the measure of the degree to which *one's expectations* of what constitutes the ideal behavior is achieved. Assessment sets into motion preconceived cognitive notions of competency, forming impressions of what should or should not be, then judging the interaction of both persons based upon those impressions. Wiemann's model of competence cites the five components of empathy, affiliation/support, social relaxation, behavioral flexibility, and interaction management (Martin, p. 17). Spitzberg and Brunner (1991) suggest that "impressions of competence are based not only on the interactants' motivations (goals), knowledge, and skill but also on the extent to which *contextual expectations* are met" (Martin, p. 18). Expectations within this conceptualization are expanded to include cultural contexts (nationality, ethnicity, race); type of situation (task, social); degrees of intimacy of the relationship, and the function or goals and objectives for the interaction (Martin, p. 18).

Martin further suggests that the strength of the above model and other similar models is the identification of behaviors and skills that lead to impressions of competence. However, she warns of its Eurocentric perspective. The approach and data obtained from such studies can only be applied to middle-class, college-educated Euro-Americans.

In contrast, the perspective to which this writer subscribes is the more culture-specific theories and models which are used by researchers to study variations of speech communication across cultures. Research reveals that the very idea of "competence" is different from one culture to the next. Some researchers employ the ethnographic research methodology and incorporates participant-observation and participation in other cultures. Such a view allows the culture, microculture, co-culture, etc. to speak for itself, to label its own reality and identify its own rules of behavior or "components of communication competency." This view, like the culture-general, universal cultural models has its limitations. It is not generalizable to the main body of intercultural communication research. And because it is situation or culture-specific, it must have sufficient corroborating replications of its findings before the data is considered for inclusion into the overall general communication rules.

This writer has utilized variations of these approaches for more than two decades of teaching the introductory intercultural communication course and discovered that for a culturally diverse student body the combination of the etic and emic approaches work best. The semester is equally divided into (etic) cultural-general universal concepts, theories and comparative world views and religious beliefs; and (emic) culture-specific studies of culture. Qualitative testing of cognitive constructs prevail for the first half and qualitative assessment is used for culture-specific participation. It is however, this final assessment period that can create a problem for beginning teachers if there are no measurable guidelines used to measure student intercultural competency.

Clearly worded behavioral objectives can help a beginning instructor assess student communication competencies. Broad dimensions of intercultural competence call for more subjective judgements when assessing student participation. That is, to measure a student's "attitude change" as a test of achieving competency is much more subjective than measuring components of attitude change which Chen (1989) identifies as the use of "self disclosure," "self-awareness," "self-concept," and "social relaxation." These measurable components should therefore be the focus of behavioral objectives within courses rather than broad abstract educational descriptions of course content. The components which identify the behavioral dimensions of intercultural communication have been clearly identified in the literature. The original seven dimensions of intercultural communication components—display of respect, interaction posture, orientation to knowledge, empathy, self-oriented behavior, interaction management and tolerance for ambiguity were identified by Ruben (1976), Ruben and Lealey (1979). Others have been identified by other researchers. Each has its criteria for assessment. Guo-Ming Chen (1989) used this and research to further divide the construct of communication effectiveness and appro- priateness (competency) into four main dimensions, each of which is divided further into behavioral components. This example and others could, in this writer's opinion, be the basis for wording behavioral objectives for the course.

To illustrate the idea that I have advanced, below are examples of broad based intercultural communication objectives using Chen's four "dimensions," and instructional or student objectives which use Chen's "components."

Educational Objectives: Upon completion of the course the student will:

1. Have a fundamental knowledge of essential personal attributes necessary for an effective communicator interacting across cultures.

2. Have acquired verbal and nonverbal communication skills sufficient to interact effectively with individuals of other cultures.

The suggested behavioral objective replacement requires four distinct statements to fulfill each of the above. Two examples for objective one above are:

1. Demonstrate self-disclosure techniques appropriate to the culture and context.

2. Demonstrate self-awareness by monitoring his own speech in intercultural situations.

The addition of these specifically worded behavioral objectives to the class syllabus helps both teacher and students to work toward the goal of more effective communication across cultures and to more objective assessment of student performance.

Suggested Readings

Chen, Guo-Ming. "Relationships of the Dimensions of Intercultural Communication Competence," *Communication Quarterly*, 1989, 37, No. 2, 118–133.

Hammer, Mitchell R. "The Effects of an Intercultural Workshop on Participants' Intercultural Communication Competence: An Exploratory Study." *Communication Quarterly*, 1984, 32, 252–260.

Kim, Young Yun. "Intercultural Communication Competence: A Systems-Theoretic View." in Stella Ting-Toomey and Felipe Korzenny (Eds.), *Cross-Cultural Communication*. Newbury Park, Ca. Sage Publishers, 1991.

Klopf, Donald. *Intercultural Communication: The Fundamentals of Intercultural Communication*, 3rd. ed. Englewood, Col. 1995, 218–225.

Martin, Judith N. "Intercultural Communication Competence: A Review" in R. L. Wiseman and Jolene Koester (Eds.), *Intercultural Communication Competence*. Newbury Park, Ca. 1993.

Ruben, B. D. "Assessing Communication Competency for Intercultural Adaptation," *Group and Organizational Studies*, 1976, 1, 334–354.

Ruben, B. D., and Kealey, D. J. "Behavioral Assessment of Communication Competency and the Prediction of Cross-Cultural Adaptation." *International Journal of Intercultural Relations*, 1979, 3, 15–47.

Samovar, Larry and Porter, Richard E. "Multicultural Teaching Competency," *Communication Between Cultures*. 2nd ed. Boston, Mass. Wadsworth Publishers, 1995, 241–260.

Wiseman, Richard L. and Koester, Jolene. (Eds.) *Intercultural Communication Competence*, Newbury Park, Ca. 1993.

Zimmermann, Stephanie. "Perceptions of Intercultural Communication Competence and International Student Adaptation to an American Campus." in *Communication Education*, Oct. 1995, 44, 321–335.

Professor Franzone received her undergraduate degree in English and Education, masters degrees from University of Michigan in Speech Correction and in Interpersonal and Intercultural Communication, and Ph.D. in African American Studies from Temple University. Additionally she studied at Stanford University's Summer Institutes and the University of Houston in the area of psychology. She is currently a member of the Communications faculty at Texas Southern University where she has conducted annual Intercultural Communication Conferences for the past two decades. These annual Spring conferences have drawn the attention of national and international conferees and participants. Professional papers have been presented at SCA, ICA, and SIETAR and have earned her friendships and intercultural connections in the Netherlands, Toronto, Mexico City, Hong Kong, Malaysia, Belize, Honduras, and the Virgin Islands. In these sites she either researched aspects of the culture, presented papers, chaired sessions or workshops or critiqued presentations.

Article Review Form at end of book.

Attitudes, values, and beliefs about time can differ among cultures. Are there differences you have observed? Differences may include doing one or multiple things at a time; take the test to discover your pattern. How might differences impact relations? Would this interfere with getting work completed?

How Many Things Do You Like to Do at Once?

An introduction to monochronic and polychronic time

Allen C. Bluedorn
University of Missouri-Columbia

Carol Felker Kaufman
Rutgers University

Paul M. Lane
Western Michigan University

Right now you are reading this article in one of two fundamentally different ways. You may be reading and deliberately doing nothing else, or you may be reading and watching television or eating or conducting a conversation or perhaps doing all of these while you read. The former approach, focusing entirely on one task, is the *monochronic* approach to life: do *one* thing at a time. The latter approaches, simultaneously being actively involved in *two* or more activities, are termed *polychronic* approaches. And as is implied by the word "approaches," there are degrees of polychronicity, ranging from people who tend to be very monochronic to those who are extremely polychronic.[1]

A question that often arises about the idea of polychronicity concerns the meaning of "simultaneously" and "at once." For example, is working on three different projects during a one-hour period an example of polychronic or monochronic behavior? Are they actually carried out at the same time, or are the parts of one activity interspersed or "dovetailed" with the others? Actually, both patterns are considered to be polychronic time use.

If three projects are dealt with completely and in sequence—A is begun and completed before B is started, B is begun and started before C, and C is begun and completed before any other project is started—the behavior is clearly monochronic, extremely monochronic. However, if the following intermittent pattern occurs—resume A from a previous time, stop A and begin B, stop B and return to A, stop A and begin C, stop C and return to B, etc., always making progress on each task, albeit slowly—a much more polychronic behavior pattern is being followed. Even more polychronic would be someone who is writing a letter, talking on the telephone, eating an apple,

---

Reprinted with permission of Academy of Management, PO Box 3020, Briar Cliff Manor, NY 10510-8020. *How Many Things Do You Like to Do at Once? An Introduction to Monochronic and Polychronic Time.* Allen Bluedorn, Carol Kaufman & Paul Lane, The Executive, November 1992. Reproduced by permission of the publisher via Copyright Clearance Center, Inc.

and listening to the *War of 1812 Overture* simultaneously.

In addition to the directly observable patterning of your activities, your subjective reactions to events are also indicators or polychronicity. Compare, for example, two managers who are both planning to write a report in the morning. Both begin writing, and after thirty minutes, both managers receive a phone call. Manager A regards the phone call as an interruption and attempts to reschedule the call for a time later in the day. Manager B answers the phone, has a complete conversation with the caller, and returns to work on the report after the call. Manager A is relatively monochronic because unplanned, unscheduled events are considered interruptions that should be minimized and not allowed to interfere with scheduled activities. Manager B is relatively polychronic because the unscheduled event was handled as a normal part of life, of equal or greater importance than planned activities (i.e., writing the report).

Thus, we need not consider the concept of "simultaneous," of "at the same time" as an absolute. Were we to do so, we would not be able to speak of degrees of polychronicity and would be forced to classify people as being either polychronic or monochronic. Instead, we can identify time use behavior more accurately along the monochronic/polychronic continuum presented in Exhibit 1.

Individuals vary in their orientation along this continuum as do organizations and entire cultures. You will soon be able to identify your own orientation along this continuum as well as recognize how monochronic or polychronic the cultures of your employing organization and department are.[2]

Donna Vinton's preceding article introduced you to time and some of the ways in which time varies between individuals and cultures. As she explained, many of these fundamental variations are so subtle that they often go unrecognized because they exist beneath the level of conscious awareness. Differences in patterns related to time horizon, pace, and punctuality can be found as well as tendencies to use time monochronically or polychronically. However,

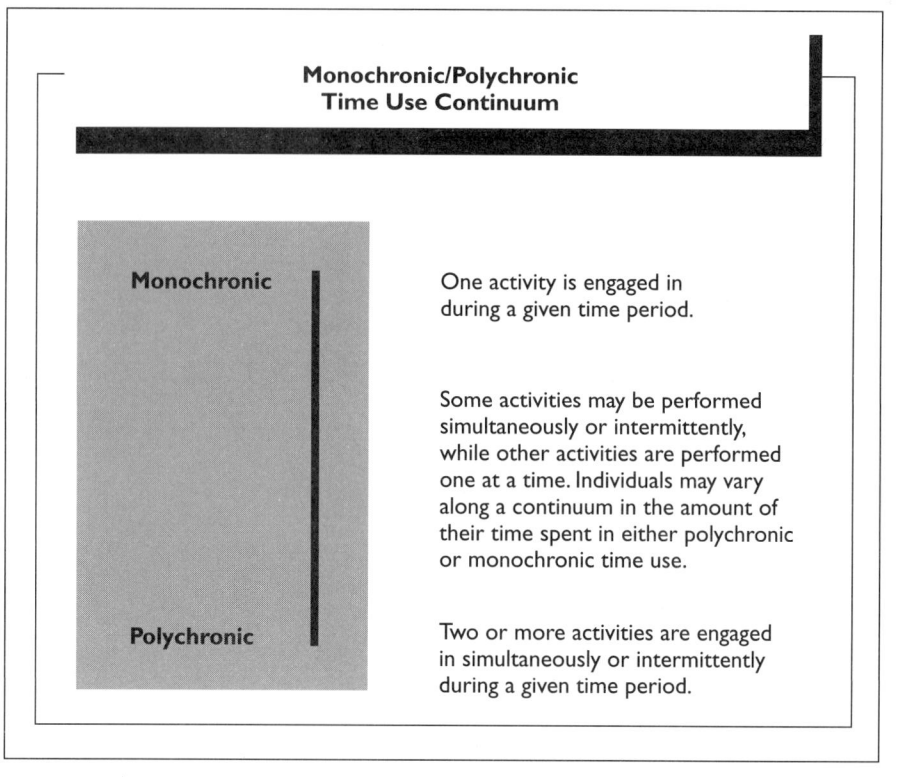

Exhibit 1

```
┌─────────────────────────────────────────────────────────┐
│              Monochronic/Polychronic                    │
│                 Time Use Continuum                      │
│                                                         │
│   ┌──────────────┐                                      │
│   │ Monochronic  │   One activity is engaged in         │
│   │       │      │   during a given time period.        │
│   │       │      │                                      │
│   │       │      │   Some activities may be performed   │
│   │       │      │   simultaneously or intermittently,  │
│   │       │      │   while other activities are performed│
│   │       │      │   one at a time. Individuals may vary│
│   │       │      │   along a continuum in the amount of │
│   │       │      │   their time spent in either polychronic│
│   │       │      │   or monochronic time use.           │
│   │       │      │                                      │
│   │ Polychronic  │   Two or more activities are engaged │
│   │              │   in simultaneously or intermittently│
│   └──────────────┘   during a given time period.        │
└─────────────────────────────────────────────────────────┘
```

individuals are sometimes unaware of the particular aspects of their "time personalities," although they can readily report actual time use preferences and behaviors. Furthermore, polychronicity is important, not only because it is a fundamental distinction in and of itself, but because pioneering research indicates that it is related to many of our other important behaviors and attitudes.

Anthropologist Edward Hall has observed that differences in space utilization and the priorities given to human relationships over task accomplishment vary with monochronic and polychronic cultural orientations.[3] His observations indicate that people with a monochronic orientation are task-oriented, emphasize promptness and a concern for others' privacy, stick to their plans, seldom borrow or lend private property, and are accustomed to short-term relationships with other people. Conversely, people with a polychronic orientation tend to change plans, borrow and lend things frequently, emphasize relationships rather than tasks and privacy, and build long-term relationships with family members, friends, and business partners. Because of these relationships and polychronicity's stature as a core defining characteristic or temporal attitudes and behaviors, an understanding of monochronic and polychronic orientations is vital to understanding our own behaviors, the ability to manage in the international arena, and the ability to manage in an increasingly culturally diverse workplace.

How Polychronic Are You?

Researchers Carol Kaufman, Paul Lane, and Jay Lindquist conducted an extensive survey of polychronic time use in which they examined individuals' tendencies to use time either polychronically or monochronically. They developed a scale, the Polychronic Attitude Index (PAI), which attempted to capture the respondent's general attitude toward performing more than one activity at a time.[4] Respondents were also requested to report the likelihood of their participation in some specific types of activity combinations. As anticipated, several activity combinations were found to be significantly correlated with the PAI. Thus, one's score on the PAI provides a preliminary indication of whether an individual has the potential and desire to combine activities in the same block of time. In contrast, prior research on polychronicity has been primarily qualitative and observational.

Kaufman, Lane, and Lindquist's work produced the four-item scale presented in Exhibit 2. We suggest that you complete the four-item scale right now and then score yourself. By completing this scale you will gain a better understanding of the monochronic/polychronic continuum and learn about an element of your own personality most people do not know about themselves.

Kaufman, et al.'s survey was completed by 310 employed adults in southern New Jersey. Their sample is fairly representative of the general U.S. population and provides the only existing baseline against which your response may be compared. The mean score in their sample was 3.128, which you can use as a point of comparison for your own score. Kaufman, et al. found that polychronic time use was negatively correlated with role overload (the more polychronic the individual, the less role overload the individual tended to experience), and positively correlated with education (the higher the education level, the more polychronic the respondent tended to be), working more than 40 hours per week (the more polychronic tended to work more than 40 hours per week), and social group and club membership (the more polychronic were more likely to belong to social groups and clubs). Polychronic time use was not, however, correlated with gender (contrary to Hall's suggestion), age, income, or marital status.

How Polychronic Are Your Department and Organization?

After Kaufman, et al. had completed the first phases of their work, Bluedorn built upon it to develop a five-item scale for measuring the monochronic/polychronic continuum as a component of organizational culture.[5] Unlike Kaufman, et al.'s original scale, his scale asks

Exhibit 2 Polychronic Attitude Index

Please consider how you feel about the following statements. Circle your choice on the scale provided: strongly agree, agree, neutral, disagree or strongly disagree.

	Strongly Disagree	Disagree	Neutral	Agree	Strongly Agree
I do not like to juggle several activities at the same time.	5 pts	4 pts	3 pts	2 pts	1 pt
People should not try to do many things at once.	5 pts	4 pts	3 pts	2 pts	1 pt
When I sit down at my desk, I work on one project at a time.	5 pts	4 pts	3 pts	2 pts	1 pt
I am comfortable doing several things at the same time.	1 pt	2 pts	3 pts	4 pts	5 pts

Add up your points, and divide the total by 4. Then plot your score on the scale below.

1.0	1.5	2.0	2.5	3.0	3.5	4.0	4.5	5.0
Monochronic								Polychronic

The lower your score (below 3.0), the more monochronic your orientation; and the higher your score (above 3.0), the more polychronic.

respondents to report on the general time use orientations they perceive in their departments and organizations rather than about their own individual orientations. This scale, tested in a sample of 205 employees drawn from a medium-size bank in Missouri, is presented in Exhibit 3. We suggest that you complete the scale in Exhibit 3 for both your department and your entire organization at this time. Then follow the instructions to score your department and organization.

The results in Exhibit 3 reveal your perceptions of your department's and organization's location on the monochronic/polychronic continuum (they will not necessarily be at the same place on the continuum). To determine the "real" locations of your department and organization on the continuum, a survey drawn from a large sample of your department and organization would be necessary. However, your perception by itself is still useful because you can now use it to compare to your own orientation, as measured by the scale in Exhibit 2, your perceptions of your department and organization in Exhibit 3. We suggest that you now plot your results from Exhibits 2 and 3 on the scales in Exhibit 4, which will allow you to compare your personal time use orientation with that which you perceive in your department and organization.[6]

The more polychronic the department, the more externally focused it tended to be. The more polychronic departments also tended to have longer time horizons. These results, which should be considered preliminary findings, may indicate that more polychronic individuals would also have better matches with departments that have longer time horizons and more of an external orientation.

Managerial Implications

Although the monochronic-polychronic distinction creates as many potential implications for behavior and action as there are people, three behavioral domains are particularly prominent: individual

Intercultural Communications **13**

Exhibit 3 Monochronic/Polychronic Orientation Scale

Please use the following scale to indicate the extent to which you agree or disagree that each statement is true about 1) your organization and 2) your department.

		Strongly Disagree	Somewhat Disagree	Slightly Disagree	Neutral	Slightly Agree	Somewhat Agree	Strongly Agree
We like to juggle several activities at the same time.	Organization	1 pt	2 pts	3 pts	4 pts	5 pts	6 pts	7 pts
	Department	1 pt	2 pts	3 pts	4 pts	5 pts	6 pts	7 pts
We would rather complete an entire project everyday than complete parts of several projects.	Organization	7 pts	6 pts	5 pts	4 pts	3 pts	2 pts	1 pt
	Department	7 pts	6 pts	5 pts	4 pts	3 pts	2 pts	1 pt
We believe people should try to do many things at once.	Organization	1 pt	2 pts	3 pts	4 pts	5 pts	6 pts	7 pts
	Department	1 pt	2 pts	3 pts	4 pts	5 pts	6 pts	7 pts
When we work by ourselves, we usually work on one project at a time.	Organization	7 pts	6 pts	5 pts	4 pts	3 pts	2 pts	1 pt
	Department	7 pts	6 pts	5 pts	4 pts	3 pts	2 pts	1 pt
We prefer to do one thing at a time.	Organization	7 pts	6 pts	5 pts	4 pts	3 pts	2 pts	1 pt
	Department	7 pts	6 pts	5 pts	4 pts	3 pts	2 pts	1 pt

Add up the points for your organization, and your department. Divide each total by 5. Then plot both scores on the scale below.

1.0   1.5   2.0   2.5   3.0   3.5   4.0   4.5   5.0   5.5   6.0   6.5   7.0
Monochronic   Polychronic

The lower the score (below 4.0), the more monochronic your organization or department; and the higher the score (above 4.0), the more polychronic.

---

time management, supervision/coordination, and cultural diversity.

Individual Time Management

Much of traditional prescriptive time management emphasizes a monochronic orientation. To wit: In an orderly fashion carefully plan your day by organizing a schedule based on your priorities with a specific allotment of time allocated for each activity. Kaufman, et al. have suggested that more polychronically oriented consumers may be more successfully marketed to by learning which types of activities they would like to have combined with others. For example, many people may like to drive and conduct business at the same time (cars and cellular phones) or watch the news and a ball game at the same time (picture-in-picture televisions). Their idea of identifying activities whose combination is attractive to customers can readily be extended to the personal time management enterprise through a series of questions.

- Which activities require your undivided attention?
- Which activities do you prefer to do in combination with other tasks?
- Which activities do you prefer to have grouped together?
- Which activities would you prefer not to be grouped together?

Candid answers to these questions and their corollaries can lead to a more sophisticated approach to time management by moving beyond the general use of priorities to establish schedules. Using this approach in addition to priorities establishes multiple criteria for deciding what things you plan to do when. By identifying which types of things seem to go together and which do not, a self-managed process of job enrichment can accompany the more traditional time management task.

Your own orientation—relatively monochronic or relatively polychronic—will naturally make some of the preceding questions and issues easier to deal with than others, and it will also lead you to different ways to deal with them.[7]

Earlier in this article we discussed behaviors associated with monochronic and polychronic orientations, one of which was the individual's degree of flexibility in

14   Intercultural Communications

Exhibit 4 Orientation Comparison

To compare your individual Monochronic/Polychronic orientation with your department and organization, copy your scores from the three scales onto this chart.

Individual

1.0	1.5	2.0	2.5	3.0	3.5	4.0	4.5	5.0
Monochronic								Polychronic

Department

1.0	1.5	2.0	2.5	3.0	3.5	4.0	4.5	5.0	5.5	6.0	6.5	7.0
Monochronic												Polychronic

Organization

1.0	1.5	2.0	2.5	3.0	3.5	4.0	4.5	5.0	5.5	6.0	6.5	7.0
Monochronic												Polychronic

To interpret the scores, rather than using exact numerical values, use general comparisons such as "middle of the scale" or "clearly above" or "clearly below" the midpoint.

regard to plans and schedules. The time management fundamental of the daily To-Do list that identifies your activities and assigns priorities to them is a plan and a schedule. Given the association of polychronic orientations with greater flexibility toward plans and schedules, polychronic individuals may be more flexible in their approach to the To-Do list.

First, they are likely to be less precise in scheduling completion times for tasks, if they even use them at all. Second, they should be more likely to modify the items on their lists (add, postpone, delete) as well as alter item priorities as the day proceeds; but this flexibility is neither a universal advantage nor a disadvantage. Flexibility in one situation may lead to the exploitation of an unanticipated opportunity, but in other situations it may lead to unproductive dithering. Third, the practice of using priorities to say no to lower priority requests, especially when the requested activities involve interaction with other people, should be more difficult for more polychronic people too.

Supervision and Coordination

Regardless of whether you are a first-line supervisor managing a single work group or a CEO managing multiple divisions or departments, the polychronicity issues described for individual time management have direct analogues at these higher levels. Which tasks and assignments do your people seem to be able to handle simultaneously (e.g., selling computers and teaching customers how to use them), and which do they have trouble handling if assigned together (e.g., selling computers and repairing them)? Which tasks do they like to handle simultaneously and which ones are better if given one at a time (e.g., taking inventory)? And which tasks might the organization be able to *learn* to handle simultaneously (e.g., designing new computers and repairing current models), giving it competitive advantages in any environment where time-based competition exists?

All of these issues imply the universal management activity of *delegation*, an act that can be influenced by your own monochronic/polychronic orientation as well as that of your subordinate.

Or consider the very monochronic boss. He is so insistent on a tightly planned schedule—everything has its time and only one thing at a time is scheduled—that he delegates almost everything to ensure his ability to be working on only one task at a time. The resulting avalanche of delegated tasks may overwhelm the constantly inundated subordinate, especially if the subordinate has a relatively monochronic orientation too. The subordinate in this case will gain very little in terms of skill enhancement from the delegated tasks and will probably feel continuously overwhelmed and miserable.

Overall, you need to recognize your own orientation and that of your subordinate because you must take *both* into account to successfully delegate over the long term. If you and your subordinates differ in orientation, do not consider such differences impediments. Such differences may actually be complementary and provide opportunities to improve the results of delegation in your department.

Cultural Diversity

". . . when people or groups with different [temporal] perspectives interact, conflicts often arise. Misunderstandings occur when intention and action are judged, by different participants, on different temporal scales. Values are attached to these scales. The *differences in temporal perspective often go unrecognized by the participants.* [Emphasis added] But the differing temporal scales have values associated with them nonetheless, and the temporally divergent actions lead to value inferences by the participants about each other."[8]

Thus has James Jones succinctly described the *raison d'etre* for understanding temporal concepts such as monochronic/polychronic

> The closer your individual preference score is to that of your organization or department, the closer your "fit" or "match" in terms of the monochronic/polychronic orientation, but the closeness of the match may indicate more than just a fit or misfit with the monochronic/polychronic continuum alone. Bluedorn's bank study revealed some very large correlations between a department's polychronicity and the extent to which it emphasizes an external focus (on customers, suppliers, changing technologies, etc.) rather than an internal focus (interpersonal relations and development, rules, procedures, etc.).

orientation when working with culturally diverse groups. To illustrate the problems that may occur if you do not understand these temporal differences, put yourself into the following situation.

You are a sales representative for a U.S.-based company that is attempting to expand into overseas markets. As part of the expansion effort, you are travelling around the world to call on several potential customers. Your itinerary includes appointments in New York, Paris, Berlin, Tunis, and Seoul. You want to make a good impression on your firm's prospective clients in each location, but you are far from an expert on France and Germany, let alone Tunisia and South Korea. Thus, you are quite anxious about how people in these different cultures will react to your behavior, and you are equally concerned about your own abilities to attribute the correct meanings to the treatment you will receive from the French, Germans, Tunisians, and Koreans.

That there will be language differences is obvious, but you were recently briefed that some of the greatest non-language difficulties in cross-cultural interactions are those arising from differences in beliefs, values, and behaviors concerning time. For example, what does it mean when a French manager keeps you waiting for thirty minutes after your scheduled appointment time? Does it mean the same thing that it means when an American or a Korean manager keeps you waiting? Similarly, should you end your appointment at the scheduled time if you have not covered everything you want to discuss, or should you attempt to continue your meeting even if you would be going beyond your scheduled time allotment? And should you try to keep going in Tunis, but not in Berlin?

Although you may not know the exact answers to the questions raised in the scenario, you have a competitive advantage over anyone who does not even know that there are questions, that there may be a difference in these matters between cultures, and that these differences are often crucial differences.

It is hackneyed now to expound on the increasingly diverse nature of the American workforce, let alone the greater diversity of the global economy. But if, as analysts such as Hall and Jones assert, the temporal components of culture are the most fundamental, recognizing and understanding those components, and hence the differences among cultures concerning them, becomes essential for productive cross-cultural management and interaction.

For example, when a relatively monochronic North American interacts with a more polychronic Latin American, misinterpretations and misattributions of behavior, if not friction and conflict, are likely to occur unless some attention has been paid to identifying and learning such differences in temporal behavior and norms. The situation may be even more complex in interactions with the Japanese who tend to be monochronic in their use of technology and in dealing with non-Japanese, but who are very polychronic in respect to most other matters. Similarly, misunderstandings may occur among major subcultures within the United States.[9] And monochronic/polychronic time use, however important, is but one of many ways cultures may differ temporally. If people coming from different cultures and traditions understand these differences, or even that there may be differences, conflicts related to polychronicity and other temporal differences can be managed more effectively.

Conclusion

The more polychronically oriented among you have not only finished this article, but have also finished lunch or are about to change the subject of your conversation; the more monochronically oriented are about to begin lunch or will now make that phone call. Either way, you have learned about one of the subtler yet more profound ways individuals can differ from one another.

As we have seen, an understanding of the monochronic/polychronic continuum can lead to better self-management as well as better management of our organizations and our relationships with people from different cultures and traditions. Given the increasingly international nature of business and management, the strategic competitive advantages will be held by the individuals, companies, and nations who learn how to successfully manage cultural diversity. And temporal differences such as monochronic/polychronic orientations are among the most basic cultural differences to manage.

Endnotes

This article was written with the support of a Summer Research Fellowship from the College of Business and Public Administration at the University of Missouri–Columbia, which was awarded to the first author. We are grateful to

---

If you are relatively polychronic, you may find it more difficult giving an activity your undivided attention than will your monochronic counterpart. Conversely, if you are relatively monochronic, you may have more difficulty than your polychronic colleague grouping certain tasks together to be performed during the same time period; and the more diverse the activities, the more difficulty you are likely to have grouping them together.

Although similarity between delegator's and subordinate's degree of polychronicity would seem to be the obvious route to harmony and successful delegation outcomes, the issue may be more complex than it appears at first glance. For example, an extremely polychronic boss may so enjoy the stimulation of multiple activities carried out simultaneously or in a short period that she fails to delegate enough tasks to subordinates. Not only would polychronic subordinates be potentially experiencing a too-monochronic environment for their own work satisfaction, but they would not be developing skills in a variety of activities, which is a major benefit and purpose of delegation.

Betty Bluedorn, Ronda Callister, Marshall Hamlett, Earl Lundgren, and Donna Vinton for their thoughtful comments on earlier versions of this article.

1. Edward T. Hall developed the concepts of monochronic and polychronic time and presented them most extensively in his book, *The Dance of Life: The Other Dimension of Time,* which was published in 1983 by Anchor Press. Additional material is provided in *Understanding Cultural Differences* by Edward T. Hall and Mildred Reed Hall, published in 1990 by Intercultural Press.
2. Some time writers (not all) such as James W. Gentry, Gary Ko, and Jeffrey J. Stoltman in "Measures of Personal Time Orientation," in Jean-Charles Chebat and Van Venkatesan (eds), *Time and Consumer Behavior,* (Val Motin, Quebec, Canada: Universite du Quebec a Montreal, 1990) reserve the use of the word "orientation" to refer to an individual's relative emphasis on the past, present, or future. Throughout this article we have used "orientation" in its more traditional, more generic sense of establishing a location or position with respect to some phenomenon.
3. See Hall and Hall, Endnote 1.
4. Kaufman, Lane, and Lindquist's research is reported in their article, "Exploring More Than 24 Hours a Day: A Preliminary Investigation of Polychronic Time Use," *Journal of Consumer Research,* 18, 1991, 392–401. The scale presented in Exhibit 2 produced an alpha reliability coefficient of 0.67 in their study.
5. Allen Bluedorn's study is reported in the working paper, "Time and the Competing Values Model of Culture: Adding the Fourth Dimension," which is available from him at the University of Missouri–Columbia. The scale in Exhibit 3 produced an alpha reliability coefficient of 0.74 in the bank sample, and he is currently involved in research on a large insurance company to see if his results will replicate.
6. Carol Kaufman, Paul Lane, and Jay Lindquist provide a much more extensive discussion of matching individual and organizational time styles land orientations in their article, "Time Congruity in the Organization: A Proposed/Quality of Life Framework," which is forthcoming in *The Journal of Business and Psychology.*
7. We would like to thank the following individuals who suggested some of the implications of MP orientation for individual time management: Kevin, Adam, Barbara Braungardt, Greg Boivin, Steven Briggs, James Dawes, Matthew Harper, Mary Hass, Mike Ondracek, and Julie Witte.
8. The quotation is from page 27 of James M. Jones' article, "Cultural Differences in Temporal Perspectives," in J. E. McGrath (ed), *The Social Psychology of Time,* (Newbury Park, CA: Sage Publications, 1988).
9. The relative orientations of North and Latin Americans are taken from Hall, *The Dance of Life.* The description of the Japanese is from Edward T. Hall and Mildred Reed Hall, *Hidden Differences: Doing Business With the Japanese,* which was published in 1987 by Anchor Press/Doubleday.

Article Review Form at end of book.

Culture consists of the values, attitudes, and behaviors of a particular group; might differences in work-related values have communication implications? In working with various cultures, what communication objectives might be reasonable within time constraints? What would be the most effective communication style?

Cross-Cultural Communication for Managers

Mary Munter

Managers must become proficient cross-cultural communicators if they wish to succeed in today's global environment. The purpose of this article is to synthesize multiple insights—from fields as diverse as anthropology, psychology, communication, linguistics, and organizational behavior—and apply them specifically to managerial communication.

Let's start with two definitions. *Culture* consists of the values, attitudes, and behavior in a given group of most of the people most of the time. Though nearly all of the examples in this article are drawn from different countries, managers can apply precisely the same kind of analysis to the culture of any given region, industry, organization, or work group.

Managerial communication is communication in a management context to achieve a desired result (writing a memo, interviewing an applicant, running a meeting, preparing a presentation). To be effective in any given culture, however, managers should consider the following seven issues *before* they begin to communicate:

1. Setting communication objectives
2. Choosing a communication style
3. Assessing and enhancing credibility
4. Selecting and motivating audiences
5. Setting a message strategy
6. Overcoming language difficulties
7. Using appropriate nonverbal behaviors

Setting Communication Objectives

As a general rule, manages should delineate consciously and specifically what it is they want their audience to do as a result of the communication—sign a contract, provide information, approve recommendations, or come up with a solution. If you are working in a different culture, you may have to reconsider your communication objective, asking yourself the following two questions:

Is my objective realistic, given the culture?

A realistic goal in one culture may not be so in another. One way to get at what might be realistic is to analyze what psychologists call the "locus of control." People in some cultures tend to believe in "internal control" over destiny—that is, that people can control events themselves. People in other cultures believe in "external control" over destiny—that is, events are predetermined and uncontrollable.

For example, suppose you are trying to communicate in an Islamic culture—anywhere from North Africa to the Middle East to Indonesia (the largest Islamic nation). What an American might see as a perfectly reasonable goal, such as "construct the new building on schedule," a Muslim might see as irreligious, because Muslims believe that human efforts are determined by the will of Allah, not by a schedule. Non-Muslims may have to adjust their expectations accordingly. Muslims are not the only ones who believe in external control over events: Filipinos, though predominantly Christian, also tend to be fatalistic. A well-known saying in Tagalog is *bahala na*, or "God wills it." Filipinos may view the achievement of your objective as predetermined by fate rather than as controllable by individual effort.

Is my time frame realistic, given the culture?

What constitutes an appropriate time frame in one culture may not be achievable in another. It all depends on the culture's concept of time.

In some cultures, timetables are exact and precise; one can expect peo-

"Cross-Cultural Communication for Managers" by Mary Munter. Reprinted from BUSINESS HORIZONS, May–June 1993. Copyright 1993 by the Foundation for the School of Business at Indiana University. Used with permission.

Figure 1 — Cultural Values Systems

Attitude Toward...		Range		Communication Implications
Nature	Submit to nature — Life determined by God/fate	Harmony with nature — Live in harmony with nature	Mastery over nature — Control and challenge nature	Communication objective
Time	Past tradition — Goals of past are sufficient	Present moment — Goals reflect present demands	Future goals — Goals directed toward future	Communication objective
Social relations	By rank or class — Authoritarian decision making	By entire group — Group decision making	By individual — Individual decision making	Audience selection
Activity	Being, not accomplishing, most important; minimize work	Inner development most important	Accomplishment and future most important; maximize work	Audience motivation
Humanity	Basically evil — Initial lack of trust, people won't change, control necessary	Mixture good and evil — Initial choice, people can change	Basically good — Initial trust, controls unnecessary	Audience motivation

Source: Adapted from Kluckhohn and Strodtbeck (1961)

---

ple to start meetings on time and meet deadlines. Examples of such cultures include Germany and Switzerland. Other cultures have more relative and relaxed attitudes toward time; one may be kept waiting; projects may move more slowly. Examples here are Latin and African countries. An executive in Cameroon tells of a meeting scheduled for 9:00 a.m. in Yaoundé. People began to arrive at 1:00 p.m. Surprisingly, however, when the last person showed up at 2:00 p.m., the other Cameroonians admonished him for being late.

A useful framework for adapting a communication objective in any given culture comes from the field of anthropology. Figure 1 summarizes Kluckhohn and Strodtbeck's "Cultural Values Systems" framework and adds managerial implications. To set an effective communication objective, one should analyze a culture by what the authors call "nature" and "time."

As an example, imagine you are working in Saudi Arabia. American and Saudi Arabian cultures fall on opposite ends of Kluckhohn and Strodtbeck's "nature" and "time" orientations. American beliefs are based on internal control and future orientation toward time, as aptly summarized in the phrase "can do." Saudi beliefs are based on external control and past orientation toward time, and are epitomized by the phrase *Insha'allah*, "If Allah wills."

Choosing a Communication Style

Once you have established a communication objective, consider the most effective communication style to accomplish it. Use different styles in different situations:

- "Tell": to inform or explain, when you need to control the content of what you are communicating and don't need audience involvement;
- "Sell": to persuade people to do something differently—needs some audience involvement;
- "Consult": to interact with the people with whom you are communicating and whose input you need.
- "Join": when you want to collaborate or brainstorm with your audience, whose ideas form the message content.

Some styles, however, will be more effective in some cultures than in others. You may need to be more autocratic or more democratic than usual if you cross cultural barriers.

What is the cultural attitude toward authority?

Tell styles may be more acceptable in autocratic cultures, in which power is unequally concentrated and the leader is seen as automatically right. Consult styles may be more acceptable in democratic cultures, in which power is more dispersed and the leader has to earn respect.

Figure 2, Hofstede's "Differences in Work-Related Values," shows ways of analyzing a culture's attitude toward authority. This figure summarizes the communication implications of the author's research studies on managers in 40 countries. One of his four dimensions is "power distance," the extent to which power is autocratic. Cultures such as those in Sweden, Norway, and Israel rank low in power distance. They are, therefore, more democratic; communication may be participative to the point at which either subordinates or superiors control the communication. The United States has a rather low

Figure 2 Differences in Work-Related Values

Dimensions Differentiated	Communication Implications
1. Power distance Extent to which power is unequally distributed, centralized, and autocratic—and such leadership is accepted by all members • Highest power distance cultures: Philippines, Venezuela, Mexico • Lowest power distance cultures: Israel, Denmark, Austria • United States: Somewhat low (15 out of 40)	*Communication style, audience selection*
2. Individualism/collectivism Extent to which people define themselves as individuals or part of a larger group • Most individual cultures: United States, Australia, Great Britain • Most collective cultures: Saudi Arabia, Venezuela, Colombia, Peru • United States: Highest (40 out of 40)	*Communication style, audience selection*
3. Uncertainty avoidance Extent to which people feel threatened by ambiguous situations • Highest uncertainty avoidance: Japan, Portugal, Greece • Lowest uncertainty avoidance: Singapore, Hong Kong, Denmark • United States: Fairly low (9 out of 40)	*Audience motivation*
4. Masculinity/femininity Extent to which dominant values emphasize assertiveness and materialism ("masculine") versus people, concern for others, and quality of life ("feminine") • Most masculine cultures: Japan, Austria, Switzerland, Italy • Most feminine cultures: Sweden, Norway, Netherlands, Denmark • United States: Somewhat masculine (28 out of 40)	*Audience motivation*

Source: Adapted from Hofstede (1980)

---

power distance (ranked 15 out of 40); communication is somewhat participative, although usually controlled by the manager. French culture exemplifies high-power distance, a country in which Hofstede finds "little concern with participative management American-style, but great concern with who has the power."

How do people define themselves: primarily as individuals or as a group?

Tell/sell styles might be more typical in individualistic cultures, with their emphasis on individual achievement, decision making, and efficiency. Consult/join styles might be more typical in group-oriented collectivist cultures, with their emphasis on group belonging and loyalty.

Referring again to Figure 2, one should analyze a culture in terms of "individualism/collectivism." According to Hofstede, Anglo cultures are the most individualistic, with the United States ranking as the most individualistic of all. On the other hand, various South American cultures are collectivist: identity is based in the social system, not the individual. Hofstede points out that in individualistic cultures, value standards apply to everyone. In collectivist cultures, however, value standards differ for in-groups and out-groups. Similarly, James Fallows (1989) defines group boundaries in terms of the group's "radius of trust"—how many people considered "us," who deserve decent treatment, and how many considered "them," who can be devalued or abused.

Divisions between "them" and "us" are found in a variety of boundaries. For example, in many parts of Africa, the tribe is the most important unit in society—more important than the nuclear family or the nation. The tribe is a source of social and moral sanctions as well as political and physical security. In some South American countries, the family is the most important unit. You may have a hard time doing business unless you are connected to the right families. In Egypt, class standing may be of paramount importance.

As a final note on communication style, Americans will probably feel most comfortable using the range of styles appropriate in the United States when they are in Australia, Great Britain, the Netherlands, Canada, and New Zealand. These cultures combine tell/sell styles when needed for the efficiency of individualism and consult/join styles when needed for the democracy associated with a small power difference. On the other hand, Americans may have to adjust their styles in various South American and Asian countries, which combine tell/sell styles when needed for the autocracy of a large power distance and consult/join when needed to enhance the group loyalty of collectivism.

Assessing and Enhancing Credibility

Regardless of what communication style you use, your credibility will always have a tremendous impact on your communication effectiveness. Five factors, based on a synthesis of the social power theories of French and Raven (1959) and Kotter (1979), affect your credibility: 1) rank or hierarchical power; 2) personal goodwill toward an audience; 3) expertise or knowledge; 4) image or attractiveness; and 5) the values and standards shared with your audience. Different cultures value different aspects of credibility more than others.

What is the relative importance of rank credibility?

Clearly, rank credibility is more important in Hofstede's high-power-distance countries, such as the Philippines, Venezuela, and Mexico, and less important in low-power-distance countries, such as Israel and Denmark. Not only might you "pull rank" differently in different cultures, you may also need to gain rank credibility by association in some cultures. For example, you might need to establish rank through family status in South America, village chiefs in Samoa, and schooling in France.

What is the relative importance of goodwill credibility?

Goodwill credibility is based on your personal relationship and personal "track record" with your audience. In many cultures, business relationships are built entirely on this kind of social and personal trust. You must take the time to build these relationships before you get down to business.

Communication expert Edward Hall's analysis of cultures, summarized in Figure 3, provides yet another useful method for managers to differentiate cultures. He classifies cultures as ranging from "high-context" (establishing a context or relationship first) to "low context" (getting right down to business). Examples of high-context cultures, in which goodwill credibility is particularly valued, include many cultures in Asia and the Middle East. In these cultures, you need to learn about the expectations regarding food and hospitality—when, where, what, and how food is prepared, presented, and eaten—and should expect to socialize and establish a relationship before you start doing business.

What is the relative importance of expertise credibility?

Many other cultures place a higher value on expertise than on personal trust. These cultures Hall classifies in Figure 3 as low-context cultures, which include German, Swiss, and Scandinavian cultures. If you are working in these cultures, you may need to establish you competence or prove your expertise. You may not need the elaborate socialization process or personal rapport needed in high-context cultures.

What image is valued?

Image credibility is based on your audience's desire to look like you (your attractiveness). That image varies tremendously across cultures. For example, being older is an advantage in Korea and many places in Africa, as is being from the upper class in Great Britain and India and being male in Iran. Obviously, you cannot change your age, class, or sex, but you may have to work harder to establish credibility in cultures where your image is not highly regarded.

What values do you share?

Classic American business culture values—such as improving next quarter's bottom line, making more money, or meeting a challenge—are not necessarily universally admired. Search to find values you have in common with a foreign culture, such as the good of the society, organization, or department; increased status or prestige; or appeals to excellence or moral correctness. Establishing an initial common ground is a powerful way to build credibility.

Selecting and Motivating Audience Members

Just as credibility analysis ascertains how your audience perceives you, audience analysis gets at how you perceive them. The culture in which you are communicating often has a huge impact on how you choose and appeal to your audience.

Should you select or include different people?

Many management situations involve multiple audiences. Depending on cultural expectations about rank, authority, and group definition, you may need to include additional or different primary audience members—those who receive your message directly. You may need to add different secondary audiences—those who hear about, need to approve, or are affected by your message. Finally, you may need to reevaluate who represents the key decision maker in your audience. For example, are superiors usually addressed directly, or at least included, in all decisions? Are subordinates? Do you need to add influential officials, leaders, power brokers, contacts, tribe or sect members, or family members?

What will appeal to them?

Once you have decided whom to include in your audience, consider what audience appeals or benefits will work best. Research on influence, persuasion, and motivation offers a wide variety of audience appeals, including material wealth and acquisition, task enhancement, career advancement, achievement and challenge, self-worth, security, satisfaction and fulfillment, personal relationships, group relationships, and altruism.

Referring again to Figure 2, think about where the culture falls in terms of Hofstede's "uncertainty avoidance," or tolerance for ambiguity. Try appeals to security issues in such high uncertainty avoidance cultures as Japan, Portugal, and Greece; consider appealing to risk and challenge in such places as Singapore, Hong Kong, and Denmark.

Figure 3 — High Context and Low Context Cultures

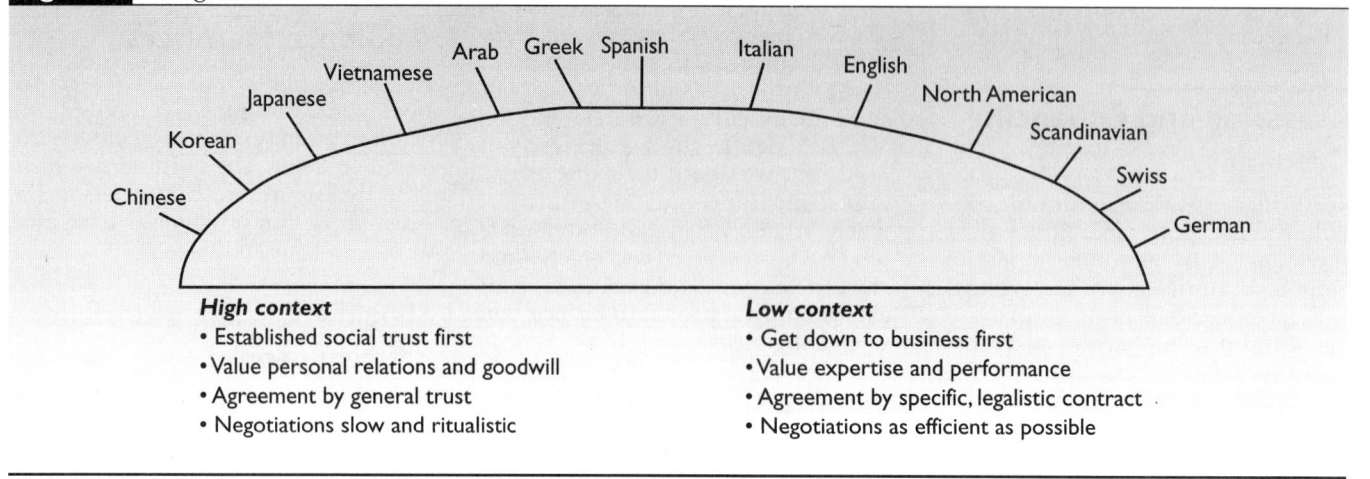

Arranged along an arc from high to low context:
Chinese, Korean, Japanese, Vietnamese, Arab, Greek, Spanish, Italian, English, North American, Scandinavian, Swiss, German

High context
- Established social trust first
- Value personal relations and goodwill
- Agreement by general trust
- Negotiations slow and ritualistic

Low context
- Get down to business first
- Value expertise and performance
- Agreement by specific, legalistic contract
- Negotiations as efficient as possible

Source: Adapted from Hall (1976)

Hofstede's "masculinity/femininity" dimension in Figure 2 measures the importance a culture places on material wealth versus quality of life. You might, for instance, appeal to people in such "masculine" countries as Austria and Switzerland with promises of material rewards. In contrast, those in such "feminine" countries as Sweden and Norway may respond to appeals tied to quality of life issues, such as job satisfaction and flexibility.

Managers should reserve typical American audience appeals—material wealth and achievement—for masculine cultures with low uncertainty avoidance. "This combination," Hofstede notes, "is found exclusively in countries in the Anglo-American group and in some of their former colonies. . . . One striking thing about the concept of achievement is that the word itself is hardly translatable into any language other than English" (1980).

What is their attitude toward work?

You may be able to motivate your audience more effectively by analyzing cultural attitudes toward work itself. How central is work as a life role—as opposed to leisure, community, religious, and family activities? How fully do people identify with their profession, as opposed to some other subgroup, sect, or elite? If they do identify with their work role, is their identity associated with their product or service, their company or organization, or their profession or occupation?

The MOW International Research Team has come up with a "work centrality index," which ranks responses from people in various countries in terms of how committed they are to work, how much they identify with work, and how much importance they attach to work. This study found that work centrality was high in Japan, average in the United States, and low in Great Britain (MOW, 1985). Appeals to corporate affiliation, for instance, might work better with the Japanese than with the British.

Kluckhohn and Strodtbeck's framework in Figure 1 also differentiates cultural attitudes toward work on a scale they label "activity." In such cultures as the United States, the dominant mode of activity is *doing*: to achieve fully, people tend to maximize work. In other cultures, by way of contrast, the dominant mode of activity is *being*: to live fully, people tend to minimize work. For example, offering to raise salaries of Mexican workers might result in decreasing the number of hours the Mexicans want to work. Offering overtime pay to Malaysians might not change the numbers of hours worked, because Malaysian workers might be more interested in spending extra time with family and friends.

Setting a Message Strategy

Based in part on audience analysis, message strategy represents a fifth set of issues to consider for effective communication. Cultural norms will affect decisions about the message structure, channel, and format.

What kind of structure is appropriate?

Some cultures prefer business messages to be structured fairly directly—getting right to the point and stating conclusions or the bottom line first. Such cultures value what they perceive as openness and honesty. In other cultures, however, business messages are typically indirect, building up to the point and stating conclusions or the bottom line last.

To make decisions regarding direct or indirect structure, international managers may find Hall's framework in Figure 3 useful. Low-context cultures (such as German, Swiss, Scandinavian, North American, and British) may favor direct structures. High-context cultures (such as Chinese, Korean, Japanese, Vietnamese, and Arabic) may favor indirect structures.

In high-context cultures, directness may be seen as abrupt, demanding, or intrusive. Worse still, inappropriate directness may cause people in these cultures to "lose face." As international experts Copeland and Griggs point out (1985):

> . . . much has been written about "face-saving" in Japan and China, but face-saving is important absolutely everywhere, the United States included. The difference is only a matter of degree and nuance. Where an American might feel a little guilty or inadequate, an Asian, Arab or South American may feel deep shame and humiliation. What an American might see as a little honest and constructive criticism, the foreigner may take as a devastating blow to pride and dignity.

In authoritarian cultures, managers may need to use more direct structures than they are used to for "downward" communication to subordinates, and more direct structures than they are used to for "upward" communication to superiors.

What message channel is appropriate?

Communication channels change constantly. To communicate across cultures, managers need to stay aware of advances in technology—computers, electronic mail, cellular phones, videoteleconferencing, and facsimile transmissions, just to name a few—and be sensitive to what technology is available, compatible, and acceptable in another culture.

In addition to affecting technological channels, cultural norms affect the most basic kind of channel choice: the decision to write or speak. In Figure 3, the high-context cultures valuing personal trust tend to prefer oral communication and oral agreements. Low-context cultures, which value efficiency, tend to prefer written communication and written agreements. In high-context cultures, confirming an idea in writing may imply that you think their word is no good. For example, Ford Motor Company agreed to acquire the production site of Ferrari and use the Ferrari name in the United States,

> . . . the deal was made on handshakes between gentlemen. Soon, though, Ford's attorneys arrived in Italy with contracts, and a crew arrived to take inventory. This was normal business procedure to the Americans, but Ferrari was disgruntled—to his thinking he had an understanding with a gentleman, not with a group of attorneys and accountants. The deal fell through. (Copeland and Griggs, 1985)

What message formats are appropriate?

You may need to adjust the physical format of your message in different cultures. For example, in many countries, standard paper sizes differ from those in the United States. These size differences can affect duplication, printing, filing, page breaks, and other document design issues. In addition, standard business formats such as memos or reports may be different from those to which Americans are accustomed; in Japan, memos are neither as prevalent nor as lengthy as in the United States. Similarly, presentation formats differ across cultures—including issues of presentation length, timing, number of visual aids, flamboyance, and the nature of interaction with audience members.

Overcoming Language Difficulties

Language difficulties represent one of the biggest barriers to cross-cultural communication. Even if English is spoken by everyone involved, dialects, accents, slang, jargon, and code words vary tremendously among different countries, regions, subcultures, industries, organizations, and professions. For instance, the word "billion" means a thousand million in the United States, and a million million in Britain; the verb "to table" used during a meeting means to postpone discussion in the United States, and to discuss right away in Britain.

Conducting business in a foreign language compounds any problems. If you are going to spend more than a year in a country, do your best to learn the language. At the very least, you can overcome some vulnerability and isolation; at best, you can achieve much better relationships and other business advantages. If you don't know the language well, use your foreign language for socializing but not for business activities. If you don't know the language at all, you have two options:

- Use English, speaking carefully and without unnecessary large words or jargon (remember that non-native English speakers are often embarrassed to admit when they don't understand English); or
- Use an excellent interpreter who is thoroughly briefed in advance, pausing after every short paragraph or thought.

Even with excellent fluency or interpretation, however, language itself poses at least four kinds of problems.

Barriers Caused by Semantics

The first level of potential problems has to do with semantics, or word meanings. Some words are literally untranslatable. For example, to conduct business in Korea, you must understand the concept of *kibun,* which does not translate into English. Its meaning is something similar to "inner feelings" or "mood"; people must communicate in a manner to enhance one another's *kibun* or risk creating an enemy and destroying the relationship. Similarly, understanding the word *sisu* will help you understand the character of your Finnish business associates. This untranslatable word means something akin to "guts," "against-all-odds stamina," or "dogged persistence"; in some ways the word encapsulates two centuries of historical Finnish struggles. As a final example, Russians may find their current economic transition even more difficult because several key English words and phrases—such as "efficiency," "free market," and "regulation"—are not directly translatable into Russian.

Barriers Caused by Word Connotations

The second level of language problems has to do with "connotation," or implications of words. For example, the words *mañana* in Spanish and *bukara* in Arabic translate as "tomorrow." Their connotation, however, may be closer to "some time in the future." In Japanese, the word *hai* translates as "yes," but its connotation may be "yes, I'm listening," rather than "yes, I agree." In Polish, *nie ma* translates as "there is none" or "we don't have any." Its connotation can be "there hasn't been any in a long time and there probably never will be." For a treasury of examples, see D. Ricks' book, *Big Business Blunders* (1983). The author points out, for instance, that "Come Alive with Pepsi" was translated as "Come Out of the Grave with Pepsi" in German and "Bring Your Ancestors Back from the Grave" in Asia.

Barriers Caused by Tone Differences

A third set of potential linguistic barriers has to do with tone—the mood or feeling your words convey. For example, in some cultures tone is usually more formal, whereas in others it is more informal; in some it is more polite, in others more offhand; in some more impersonal, in others more personal; in some more dry, in others more colorful. Decide if and when you want to make marginal adjustments in the tone of your writing or speaking when you are in another culture.

Barriers Caused by Differences Among Perceptions

A final level of potential difficulties emerges when you stop to realize that, according to many linguists, people who speak different languages actually view the world in different ways. Eskimos perceive snow differently because they have many words for it; Hopi Indians perceive time differently because they do not distinguish among past, present, and future verb tenses; Japanese perceive responsibility differently because they have a grammatical form called "adversative passive" used for reporting unpleasant events. Thais perceive "no" differently because there is no such word in their vocabulary.

Using Effective Nonverbal Behaviors

Although managers generally understand that language differences can cause major barriers to communication, they may not recognize that nonverbal barriers can cause even greater problems. Some scholars, such as Knapp (1980), estimate that 65 to 90 percent of what we communicate is, in fact, nonverbal. Keep in mind three sets of challenges in cross-cultural nonverbal communication: body language and vocal qualities, space around you, and greeting behaviors.

Body Language and Vocal Qualities

Notions of appropriate posture, gestures, eye contact, facial expression, touching, pitch, volume, and rate differ across cultures. As a simple but potentially disastrous example, nodding the head up and down in Bulgaria means "no," not "yes."

Successful executives must avoid using any gestures considered rude or insulting. For instance, in Buddhist cultures, the head is considered sacred, so you must never touch anyone's head; in Muslim cultures, the left hand is considered unclean, so never touch, pass, receive, or eat with the left hand. Pointing with the index finger is rude in cultures ranging from the Sudan to Venezuela to Sri Lanka. The American circular "A-OK" gesture carries a vulgar meaning in Brazil, Paraguay, Singapore, and Russia. Crossing your ankle over your knee is rude in such places as Indonesia, Thailand, and Syria. Pointing your index finger toward yourself insults the other person in Germany, the Netherlands, and Switzerland. Avoid placing an open hand over a closed fist in France, saying "tsk tsk" in Kenya, and whistling in India.

On the receiving end of nonverbal communication, prepare yourself to recognize gestures that have meaning only in the other culture. Chinese stick out their tongues to show surprise and scratch their ears and cheeks to show happiness. Japanese suck in air, hissing through their teeth to indicate embarrassment or "no." Greeks puff air after they receive a compliment. Hondurans touch their finger below their eyes to indicate caution or disbelief.

Finally, resist applying your own culture's nonverbal meanings to other cultures. Vietnamese may look at the ground with their heads down to show respect, not to be "shifty." Russians may exhibit less facial expression, and Scandinavians fewer gestures, than Americans are accustomed to, but that does not mean they are not enthusiastic. People in Latin and Mediterranean cultures, on the other hand, may gesticulate and touch more often than Americans, but don't infer that they're "pushy." Southerners in the United States tend to speak slowly, but don't infer that they're dumb; northerners may speak more quickly, but don't infer that they're arrogant. Compared to Americans, Brazilians may interrupt more, Asians may respect silence more, and Arabs may speak more loudly.

Space Around You

A second aspect of nonverbal communication has to do with norms regarding space. In general, Americans feel comfortable in the following zones of space: zero to 18 inches for intimacy only (comforting or greeting); 18 inches to four feet for personal space (conversing with friends); four to 12 feet for social space (conversing with strangers); and more than 12 feet for public space (standing in lobbies or reception areas). Different cultures define the acceptable extents of these zones differently. Venezuelans tend to prefer much closer personal and social space and might consider it rude if you back away. The British, on the other hand, may prefer more distant personal and social space and might consider it rude if you move too close.

Closely related to this is the concept of touch. Anglos usually avoid touching each other very much. In a study of touching behaviors (Knapp, 1980), researchers observed people seated in outdoor cafés in each of four countries, and counted the number of touches during one hour of conversation. The results were: San Juan, 180 touches per hour; Paris, 110 per hour; Gainesville, Florida, 1 per hour; and London, 0 per hour.

Greeting Behaviors

Because first impressions are long-lasting, greeting behavior is particularly important. Hand-shakes can range from the hearty, firm *G'day* shake of an Australian to the gentle, light, single shake of the French. Many Latin and Mediterranean cultures greet with an *abrazo*—some combination of handshake, hugs, and shoulder pats. In Algeria (with its Arabic and French roots), anything less than a handshake plus embrace might be alienating. The Hindu *namaste*, the Thai *wai*, and the Laotian *nop* all involve a palms-together praying motion coupled with a bow. The Japanese bowing conventions, however, are so complex that most non-Japanese are well advised to stick with a handshake.

What name should you use? Americans tend to be too quick to use first names. A general rule is, don't use first names unless invited to do so. In addition, find out about naming conventions. In some cultures, the surname comes first: in Hungary, the composer known in the West as Béla Bartók is actually named Bartók Béla; in China, Zhou Enlai is "Mr. Zhou." In some cultures the surname is second; in Spain, Miguel Ortega Gonzales is "Señor Ortega." Some cultures use a polite familiar with the Mr. or Mrs. equivalent followed by the first name: in Brazil, Enrique Lopez is "Senhor Enrique"; in Poland, Stanislaw Musial is "Pan Stanislaw."

Perhaps the most unusual naming convention comes from Iceland, where people are officially known by their first names; listings are alphabetized by first name. A man's last name is his father's first name plus *son*; a woman's last name is her father's first name plus *dottir*. Because a woman does not change her name with marriage, husband, wife, son, and daughter each has a different last name.

What title should you use? In a country such as Sweden or Israel, titles are relatively unimportant. In other places, such as Germany or Austria, titles are very important; even the wife of a German professor carries her husband's title: "Frau Professor Schmidt" or "Frau Professor." In Korea, titles are often used in place of names because of Confucian attitudes about saying names aloud.

As we have seen, culture permeates every aspect of management communication, from basic decisions about setting a realistic communication objective to specific behaviors when greeting people. At the same time, seemingly superficial behaviors such as greetings can often reflect important and deep-rooted cultural values. The next time you are communicating in a different country, region, industry, or organization, keep in mind the following points:

- Read about and discuss the culture before you go. A single party conversation on the topic will probably not be sufficient; the more you can learn about economics and industry, politics and government, religion and philosophy, history, symbols and traditions, social structures, cultural achievements, language, sports, and food, the more successful you are likely to be.

- Listen, react, and interpret the culture while you are there. All you can learn from studying in advance is never the same as what you can learn when immersed in the culture. Stay alert; be flexible; be willing to modify your ideas. Use your new associates as resources: most people are happy to explain their customs to interested foreigners.

- Imitate group members to learn by example, especially for nonverbal communication. Be particularly aware of how group leaders behave; follow their example when appropriate.

- Perhaps most important, try to maintain an open attitude—of

---

Are Cultures Growing More Similar?

Are cultures becoming more similar worldwide or are they maintaining their differences? Is the world moving toward one way of doing business or does each different culture maintain its own unique approach?

John Child's comparison of myriad cross-cultural studies reveals two groups of equally reputable researchers—one group concluding that the world is growing more similar and the other concluding that cultures are maintaining dissimilarity. In the words of international expert Nancy Adler, "Looking closer, Child discovered that most of the studies concluding convergence focused on macro issues—such as the structure and technology of the organizations themselves—while most of the studies concluding divergence focused on micro level issues—the behavior of people within organizations. Therefore organizations worldwide are growing more similar, while the behavior of people within organizations is maintaining its cultural uniqueness."

Many managers, however, assume that people from different cultures are basically similar to themselves. Researchers Burger and Bass worked with managers from 14 countries, asking each manager to describe the work and life goals of a colleague from another country. In every case, the managers assumed their foreign colleagues were more like themselves than they actually were.

Americans in particular believe that other countries are becoming more like us. "The assumption is erroneous," notes economic analyst James Fallows. "The United States is not an ordinary society. The differences between America and other cultures run deep and matter profoundly. They are differences of kind, not just of degree. Of course, people are essentially the same anywhere on earth, but cultures are not."

Sources: N. Adler, *International Dimensions of Organizational Behavior* (Belmont, Calif.: Wadsworth, 1986), pp. 45 and 66; J. Child, "Culture, Contingency and Capitalism in the Cross-National Study of Organizations," in L. L. Cummings and B. M. Staw, eds., *Research in Organizational Behavior*, Vol. 3 (Greenwich, Conn.: JAI Press, 1981), pp. 303–356; P. Burger and B. Bass, *Assessment of Managers: An International Comparison* (New York: Free Press, 1979); J. Fallows, *More Like Us: Making America Great Again* (Boston: Houghton-Mifflin, 1989), pp. 1–2.

patience, tolerance, objectivity, empathy, and respect—to increase your understanding, cooperation, and effectiveness.

References

N. Adler, *International Dimensions of Organizational Behavior*, 6th ed. (Belmont, Calif.: Wadsworth, 1991).

M. Asante and W. Budykunst, eds., *Handbook of International and Intercultural Communication* (Newbury Park, Calif.: Sage Publications, 1989).

L. Copeland and L. Griggs, *Going International: How to Make Friends and Deal Effectively in the Global Marketplace* (New York: Random House, 1985).

Culture-grams for the Nineties (Provo, Utah: Brigham Young University, David M. Kennedy Center for International Studies, published yearly).

D. Evans, *The Cultural and Political Environment of International Business: A Guide for Business Professionals* (Jefferson, N.C.: McFarland and Company, 1991).

J. Fallows, *More Like Us: Making American Great Again* (Boston: Houghton-Mifflin, 1989).

J. French and B. Raven, "The Bases of Social Power," in D. Cartwright, ed., *Studies in Social Power* (Ann Arbor: The University of Michigan Press, 1959), pp. 150–167.

E. Hall, *Beyond Culture* (Garden City, New York: Doubleday, 1976).

E. Hall, *The Silent Language* (New York: Premier Books, 1971).

E. Hall, *Understanding Cultural Differences* (Yarmouth, Maine: Intercultural Press, 1990).

P. Harris and R. Moran, *Managing Cultural Differences*, 3rd ed. (Texas: Gulf Publishing Company, 1990).

G. Hofstede, "Motivation, Leadership, and Organization: Do American Theories Apply Abroad?" *Organizational Dynamics*, Summer 1980, pp. 42–63.

F. Kluckhohn and F. Strodtbeck, *Variations in Value Orientations* (Evanston, Ill.: Row, Peterson, 1961).

M. Knapp, *Essentials of Nonverbal Communication* (New York: Holt, Rinehart and Winston, 1980).

J. Kotter, *Power and Dependence* (New York: AMACOM, 1979).

J. Mole, *When in Rome . . . A Business Guide to Cultures and Customs in Twelve European Nations* (New York: AMACOM, 1991).

R. Moran and W. Stripp, *Dynamics of Successful International Business Negotiations* (New York: Gulf Publishing Company, 1991).

MOW International Research Team, *The Meaning of Working: An International Perspective* (London: Academic Press, 1985).

Multinational Travel Companion Executive (Stamford, Conn.: Suburban Publishing of Connecticut, Inc., published yearly).

M. Munter, *Guide to Managerial Communication*, 3rd ed. (Englewood Cliffs, New Jersey: Prentice Hall, 1992).

M. Nydell, *Understanding Arabs: A Guide to Westerners* (Yarmouth, Maine: Intercultural Press, 1987).

D. Rearwin, *The Asia Business Book* (Yarmouth, Maine: Intercultural Press, 1991).

Y. Richmond, *From Nyet to Da: Understanding the Russians* (Yarmouth, Maine: Intercultural Press, 1992).

D. Ricks, *Big Business Blunders* (Homewood, Ill.: Dow Jones-Irwin, 1983).

J. Rotter, "Generalized Expectancies for Internal Versus External Control of Reinforcement," *Psychological Monographs*, 80 (1966): 1–28.

L. Samovar and R. Porter, *Intercultural Communication: A Reader*, 4th ed. (Belmont, Calif.: Wadsworth Publishing Company, 1985).

C. Storti, *The Art of Crossing Cultures* (Yarmouth, Maine: Intercultural Press, 1990).

D. Strand, ed., *Multinational Travel Companion* (Stamford, Conn.: Suburban Publishing of Connecticut, revised yearly).

R. Tannenbaum and W. Schmidt, How to Choose a Leadership Pattern," *Harvard Business Review*, March–April 1958, pp. 95–101.

D. Victor, *International Business Communication* (New York: Harper Collins, 1991).

H. Wenzhong and C. Grove, *Encountering the Chinese: A Guide for Americans* (Yarmouth, Maine: Intercultural Press, 1991).

B. Whorf, *Language, Thought, and Reality* (Cambridge, Mass.: MIT Press, 1984).

Article Review Form at end of book.

In the 1950s, Edward Hall was director of the Point IV Training Program at the Foreign Service Institute, where he and others trained diplomats in intercultural communication. He and George Trager wrote the first manual for cross-cultural training. In this article, he offers insights into the Arab cultures. Are his comments accurate today? What changes in the Arab cultures do you believe have occurred, or what has remained the same? Does culture change or remain constant?

Learning the Arabs' Silent Language

In bargaining with the Arabs, we Americans too often speak the language of power and profit. The Arabs reply in kind. But they are also looking for a thousand-and-one body clues to the human relationship. An eminent cultural analyst explains what we ignore in our dealings with the Arabs—and at what cost.

Edward T. Hall interviewed by Kenneth Friedman

When it comes to the Arabs, we Americans may still be suffering from a case of culture shock. Because we depend on them for vital oil supplies, we must pay close attention when they lecture us on conservation. They are not only making us pay almost a dollar a gallon for gasoline, but they are also using those dollars to buy hotels, businesses, even farmland in our own country. Increasingly, Arab students are entering our universities, and Arabs are endowing university professorships and research institutes in the U.S.

Not only is the nose of the camel under the tent, but the whole hump as well. The Arabs are, as the anthropologist Edward T. Hall might put it, invading our cultural space.

What do we make of them now? Have we come any closer, since the energy crunch first began in 1973, to understanding the Arabs and learning how to deal with them? Our government's failure to anticipate the coming to power of a Muslim regime in Iran, suspicious of the U.S., suggests that we haven't. On the other hand, the recent peace accord between Egypt and Israel—put together with the help of tireless face-to-face diplomacy by Jimmy Carter—may provide clues to dealing with the Arabs. For an informed opinion on how to get along with the Arabs, Psychology Today went back to Edward T. Hall, probably the best-known authority in the country on face-to-face contact between peoples of different cultures. Hall, who now lives in Santa Fe, New Mexico, has served as a consultant to government and business for more than 40 years; at one time, he helped train our diplomats in the cultures of their assigned countries. Hall, whose books The Silent Language, Beyond Culture, and The Hidden Dimension stress the importance of nonverbal language in cross-cultural communication—for instance, touching, distance between speakers, concepts of time—was interviewed by Psychology Today in July of 1976 on his general theories. Recently, we asked anthropologist Kenneth Friedman to visit Hall and talk in more detail about our relations with the Arabs. Although "Arab" peoples differ in a number of respects from country to country, region to region, and sect to sect, Hall talked about a few things that are common to the Arab culture and important for Americans to know. Here are excerpts.

Kenneth Friedman: Do we Americans understand the Arabs, or do we tend to caricature or stereotype them?

Edward T. Hall: I don't think we understand them. We tend to think of Arabs as underdeveloped Americans—Americans with sheets on. We look at them as undereducated and rather poor at anything technological. All we have to do is to make believers out of them, get them the proper education, teach them

Reprinted with permission from PSYCHOLOGY TODAY Magazine, Copyright © 1979 (Sussex Publishers, Inc.)

English, and they will turn into Americans.

To Americans, everyone is "like us" underneath. It just isn't true. Anwar Sadat, for instance, wears Western clothes, but he's not a Westerner. When he's sitting and talking with someone, he often has has hand on the other person's knee. This touching is very Egyptian and it's an important part of communication in Arab culture.

The problem is that most Americans don't really believe in the cultural dimension. A friend of mine, a political scientist who is an extraordinarily successful scholar in international relations and has done a lot of work throughout Asia, said to me, "You anthropologists, you just made up all that culture stuff." Whatever it is I am seeing, many other people are just not seeing.

Friedman: How do you explain this denial of cultural factors?

Hall: Well, I've developed a model of what motivates people to do almost anything. There seem to be economic, political, and ideological considerations, all of which exist on the level of awareness. Then, there are habitual, illusional, and cultural factors that exist mostly behind awareness. Economic, political, and ideological aspects get most of the attention because they have a clear impact on people. Communication is the cultural part, and it tends to function automatically. People know as much about it as they do about the inner workings of their automobile, which isn't very much. So we're working at a level, an analytical level, that is not commonly recognized. But once you talk about communication in other cultures with people who have had actual experiences with it, the lights begin to go on. This whole thing is very personal and what you're doing is telling people some of the rules governing behavior that they have already experienced.

One time, a colleague and I were in a nightclub in Beirut—when there were nightclubs in Beirut—watching the show. There was an American black woman in the show, a singer who was quite good, so afterward, we asked her over for a drink. She made a remark that was sort of telling. "You know, I used to be married to a Lebanese in the U.S. and he was strange," she said. "I thought it was just him, but over here, they're all that way!"

This is a person who has experienced cultural difference and understands the depth of it. In contrast, Dean Rusk once told a friend of mine that he had made a big discovery: people have different conversational distances. This was almost 20 years after I wrote a book about it [*The Silent Language*].

Friedman: How are Arabs different from North Americans?

Hall: The basic difference is that Arabs are highly "contexted." They examine the entire circumstance in which events are happening in order to understand them. Everyone is aware there is a relationship between the context of a statement and its meaning. If a man says, "I love you" to a woman on the first date, she knows it doesn't mean the same thing that it might a year later.

The cultures of the world can be placed on a continuum, based on the amount of communication contained in the nonverbal context compared with the amount in the verbal message. A legal contract, for instance, is supposed to be context-free—all the meaning is in the words of the contract. Some cultures, like our own, are low context; they tend to put more emphasis on the verbal message and less on the context. In a low-context culture, you get down to business very quickly. The high-context culture takes considerably longer, and that's simply because the people have developed a need to know more about you before a relationship can develop. You might say that they simply don't know how to handle a low-context relationship with other people.

Friedman: What's the best way to approach an Arab in a business deal?

Hall: In the Middle East, if you aren't willing to take the time to sit down and have coffee with people, you have a problem. You must learn to wait and not be too eager to talk business. You can ask about the family or ask, "How are you feeling?" But avoid too many personal questions about wives, because people are apt to get suspicious. Learn to make what we call chit-chat. If you don't, you can't go to the next step. It's a little bit like a courtship, and without all the preliminaries, sex becomes just like rape.

People will be watching you and getting to know you, developing feelings about you. They're probably even watching the pupils of your eyes to judge your responses to different topics.

Friedman: What can they tell from the pupils? Are the Arabs really more skilled than other peoples at "reading" emotions in the eyes?

Hall: Eckhard Hess, a psychologist at the University of Chicago, discovered that the pupil is a very sensitive indicator of how people respond to a situation. When you are interested in something your pupils dilate; if I say something you don't like, they tend to contract. But the Arabs have known about the pupil response for hundreds if not thousands of years. Since people can't control the response of their eyes, which is a dead giveaway, many Arabs, like Arafat, wear dark glasses, even indoors.

These are people reading the personal interaction on a second-to-second basis. By watching the pupils, they can respond rapidly to mood changes. We're taught in the U.S. not to stare, not to look at the eyes that carefully. If you stare at someone, it is too intense, too sexy, or too hostile. That's one of the reasons why they use a closer conversational distance than we do. At about five feet—the normal distance between two Americans who are talking—we have a hard time following eye movements. but if you use an Arab distance—about two feet—you can watch the pupil of the eye.

Friedman: What kinds of clues to the other person can they pick up at this close range?

Hall: Overall, what they're doing is coding, sort of synthesizing, their reactions. They say to themselves, "How do I feel about this person?" In contemporary American terms: "What kind of vibes am I getting from him?" They are also

> "The eyes are a dead giveaway to people's responses. Many Arabs—like Arafat—wear dark glasses indoors."

responding to smell and to the thermal qualities of the other person. We talk about someone with a very warm personality, This is literally true, and there is a very cold fish. This is the person who draws heat from you. So they're picking up thermal, olfactory, and kinesthetic cues also. A lot of touching goes on during conversations in the Middle East, as with Sadat.

Friedman: You seem to be saying that there is a much stronger emphasis on personal contact and much less on procedures.

Hall: Yes, and we're not willing to accept this about Middle Eastern culture. Once I was interviewing American bankers working in the Middle East who said that they couldn't make loans above a certain amount unless they sent a profit-and-loss statement to New York. Being masters of financial manipulation, Arab businessmen were willing to provide any kind of profit-and-loss statement that they wanted. But by the time they get around to filling out such statements, they may not need the money anymore—and the American bankers will lose the deal. Americans were using criteria for insuring loans that were applicable in the United States, whereas in the Middle East, if you know the man and you know his business and he knows you and you're part of the same social group, he cannot afford not to pay back the loan.

Friedman: How really different is that from the U.S.? In American business, the people at the top do know each other. There is a pressure to socialize and major business deals take shape in face-to-face negotiations, not over the telephone.

Hall: In general, Arabs know more about each other than we do. The group is smaller and more intimate, and there are differences in what people take for granted in negotiating. Having had experience working with American business in negotiations, I find that usually things are not hammered out at the negotiating table. This is because people need to discover what kind of cards the other fellow is holding. It is essential to ascertain the rock-bottom dollar that the other fellow is going to take. Or what the minimal conditions for a deal are—I use the word "dollar" symbolically. Then, you must decide whether there's an overlap between what each side wants. If there isn't, you can't get together. The overlap is where the "give" in the system is. When there's a big overlap, both sides have a greater likelihood of coming out with the feeling that they have made a good deal. The bargaining table for us is a place for ratifying a decision that's been made informally outside the room. And usually it's the lower- or middle-echelon people who do the negotiating. The top people do not participate in the lengthy process of face-to-face haggling.

The whole thing [in the U.S.] is based on how much you can find out about the other fellow's position, to assess his strength. How bad is he hurting? If he's hurting badly enough, you're going to drive a harder bargain.

Essentially, the American strategy is to find out what percentage of the asking price to offer at the start of negotiations. But Arabs have many asking prices. They have what they consider the "insult price," the "go-away price," the "don't-bother-me price," the "I-don't-want-to-sell price." They may also indicate: "I'm willing to sell, but I'm not very enthusiastic." Or: "I would like to sell; I'm very anxious to sell; you're a very close friend of mine." There are all those different asking prices and you must know which one you're working with before you even start bargaining.

Friedman: How does an Arab tell an "insult price" from a genuine one?

Hall: Suppose you have a Rollex watch to sell that costs around $1,000. You're with two Arabs and one of them says, "That's a nice watch. Would you like to sell it?" The seller says, "Well, I don't know," and the Arab replies, "How much would you take for it?" If the Arab knows the market price of a new watch and the seller says $1,500, that's an insult—because that's 50 percent more than he would have to pay in a store. The seller might say, "I've had it for years, and you're a very close friend of mine, I'll sell it to you for $900." That's a decent price, because the Arab buyer will know that he's taking $100 away from you.

Friedman: It's one thing to sell a watch, but it's quite a different matter to sell 10 jet planes.

Hall: I've never sold 10 jet planes to an Arab. That certainly complicates the negotiations. There is a market price for those jet planes, and the Arabs know what it is. But different countries are competing with different kinds of planes, it gets a little more complex, and you get into the whole matter of influence peddling.

Our answer in the U.S. has been simply to pay such tremendous bribes that people cannot afford not to do business with us. If I read Arab people correctly, and if my own experience means anything, in many instances we could have sold the 10 planes for much closer to the market price, without paying exorbitant bribes—if we had taken the time to form proper relationships with the people. We think that price is everything. In this sense, we're kind of naive. Profit isn't as important to these people as a human relationship.

Friedman: Why haven't we developed these personal ties with Middle Easterners?

Hall: Let's go back to the ways of motivating people—the economic, political, and ideological ways. In the past, our attitude has been that if you have the power, why bother with all these things? The trouble with this approach is that by insisting on having things your own way, eventually other people learn your strategies and will use them against you.

This is precisely what the Arabs have done. They didn't invent the cartel. The cartel is a European invention. The question is: have we gone too far? Can we recoup our losses?

The Arabs seem to have learned that power is the only language Americans speak, and it's very difficult to argue with men of power. I've tried. Power is simple-minded; it's easy, but it takes a long time to build relationships in many parts of the world.

Friedman: How should the U.S. go about building those relationships?

> "When Sadat is talking with someone, he often has a hand on the person's knee. This is very Egyptian."

Hall: We could start by being less paranoid. American bureaucrats and businessmen have a feeling that if we leave an American overseas too long, if he learns a foreign culture and he establishes relationships with the people, he's then going to be on their side. He will cease to represent the U.S. We'd much rather rotate people and not allow them to develop relationships. This is kind of nutty when you think about it: we can't trust our own citizens to learn a language, learn a culture, make friends, and still represent our government.

We're getting better, of course, particularly in the State Department, whose personnel are frequently required to learn the language. Unfortunately, they are not evaluated on either their mastery of the culture or the behavioral matrix in which all languages are set.

Friedman: Do the oil companies or other firms doing business in the Middle East follow the same policy as the State Department? Or do they value the personal relationship?

Hall: Companies vary considerably. But look at what happened in Iran as a case history. There was very little general understanding of how the country really works, and how Americans could adapt to it. What you had were enclaves of Americans.

In general, the big companies tend to do better in business operations than do small ones. The big ones are clued in at the higher levels of government. In some cases, they've just fallen into it, simply because the attorneys or bankers they hired have the proper connections in the country. But this doesn't take care of people who can't afford such high-class connections.

Friedman: Have you trained people to work in the Middle East?

Hall: I trained a lot of people who were part of the Point IV [Truman's technical assistance] program. We didn't have time to teach people what to do or even to teach them the language. But we did have enough time to get them started on the right foot and to develop some effective shortcuts. We went to a lot of trouble to get them together with someone from the local culture. Their assignment was to find out how many times they had to meet with a person in the country they were going to before they could really get down to business. We had learned that Americans were getting down to business much too fast in the Middle East. They were skipping important steps in the action chain—we didn't have the action-chain model then because it hadn't been discovered yet, but we knew what an action chain was.

Friedman: Can you explain what you mean by an "action chain"?

Hall: An action chain is a behavioral sequence with two or more participating organisms, in which there are standard steps for reaching a goal. If you leave out one of those steps, the chain gets broken, and you have to start all over again. For example, a greeting has several parts. If you leave out a part, such as the proper body motions, people are confused and have trouble completing the chain. So we thought that maybe it would be possible to have our trainees discover the beginning segments of an action chain for getting down to business.

But this strategy was a mistake. The experience of a Ph.D. in agronomy who was going to Cuba—those were the days before Fidel Castro—illustrates how important it is to stick to basics. He was very ingenious at getting some notion of the soils from the Cuban we had found for him. When he reported on his three-day conference, he said: "You know, I couldn't get the answer to your question, because it wasn't until we had met three times that we got to know each other and could start talking about these things."

That in itself was an important lesson, however. In training people to work in another culture, the real job is to put them in a situation in which they continue to learn on their own.

Friedman: What advice can you give someone who is going to live in another culture? Lacking training in that culture, how can one begin to feel oriented?

Hall: Once you are in a country, and you have personal ties, it's possible to find a sort of cultural advisor, a friend who knows the place. For instance, Americans were paying two to three times as much rent as they should have in Syria. So I asked an Arab-Syrian friend, "If I were a Syrian going to go to Damascus and wanted to rent a house, how would I go about it?" He said: "First, you would *not* let anybody know that you were interested in a house, but you would drive around and decide where you wanted to live, and once you picked a neighborhood, you would get hold of an intermediary you could trust and ask him to find you a place in that neighborhood. Then, the intermediary would find somebody who is anxious to rent a place, but he wouldn't tell them that he has a client. He then returns to the client and says, 'I've got a place. What I want you to do now is to walk down such-and-such street, but don't look at houses. Just walk down the street. Do this a couple of times.' Then, the intermediary goes to the man who has the house to rent and says, 'You know this foreigner who has been through this neighborhood? Maybe we could interest him in your house?'" And it goes on like that, step by step. Eventually, if matters go well, the house is yours for about a third of what the average American is paying. It's a different action chain. The trouble is it's hard to get an American to take each step seriously and to be coached. Most Americans are too eager to buy and reluctant to take coaching. Only actors and athletes are accustomed to being coached. Doctors and industrialists and lawyers are the most difficult to coach. Even when you try to teach them to ski or fly an airplane, a lot of instructors tell me, they don't take directions very well.

Friedman: In the negotiations with Israel and Egypt, did Carter successfully bridge American and Middle Eastern cultures?

Hall: I think his approach was well adapted to the Middle East. The personalized part was important, as it was with Kissinger. We know this because Sadat kept asking about Kissinger. On several occasions, he was reported as saying, "I want to see Henry," because he felt that he had a personal relationship with Kissinger. The more the President can establish a personal relationship with

> "We could have sold planes without paying exorbitant bribes if we had taken time to form proper relationships."

these people in situations of this sort, the better his chances for success. This is an expensive way in terms of time, but it's probably worth it.

Even more so because the Middle East is a top-man culture. Americans have intermediaries between the top and the bottom of an organization, but in Islamic society there are no intermediaries between man and God, and really no intermediaries, in the bureaucratic sense, between the sheik and the peasants. They're used to the fact that the top man makes the decisions. In this instance, Carter's willingness to take the time was probably a very good thing.

> "The Middle East is a top-man culture. Carter's personalized approach was well adapted to peace talks."

Also, Arabs tend to depend upon outsiders to intervene in disputes, and we haven't always understood this. This is one case that Carter, and before him, Kissinger, did understand. The Arabs were depending on the U.S. to play the role of a strong interventionist in a dispute.

Friedman: You mean something closer to a mediator . . . ?

Hall: I mean intervention. For instance, the law in the Middle East is: if there's a fight and somebody is injured, the crowd is guilty because the crowd didn't stop it. This means disinterested third parties who watch disputes going on share the blame for the disputes. When you grow up in an atmosphere of this type, you can tell people all kinds of things in public because you know there are others there who will stop you from hurting someone or getting hurt. It makes for a very different kind of communication—more volatile but less risky.

Friedman: When you are talking about the people of the Middle East, the mass of the population, the cultural differences seem strong. But when you get to the government and business elites, aren't they all educated in France and the U.S.? Isn't there homogenization of the leaders?

Hall: Leaders these days come from the middle levels of society more and more. It is rare for such people to be bicultural. Children growing up in two cultures can be bicultural, but adults seldom are. Learning another culture is a bit like learning another language. People can learn how to deal with Americans, how to live with Americans. But as soon as they get back on their own home turf, they become what they were in the beginning. Learning another culture simply adds another layer onto the person. But that new culture doesn't change them that much. It doesn't eliminate what's underneath.

When Europeans come to this country, the thing that they appreciate most is what they call "freedom." They feel as though a 10-ton weight had been lifted off their backs. But when you look into what "freedom" is all about to them, it turns out to be a freedom from European bureaucracies and from social pressures to conform. In Switzerland, if you don't sweep your sidewalks every day, your neighbors will get on you. And, also in Switzerland, you can only wash your dishes until a certain time at night because the noise might disturb the neighbors. You can't even flush the john after certain times because that will disturb the neighbors. Freedom from the coercive cloak of your neighbors, the police, and the tax collectors is what American freedom means to many Europeans. So they have adapted to American culture, but in terms of the European culture they experienced first.

Friedman: Most people only experience foreign cultures as tourists. Is there anything tourists could do that would give them perspective on the depth of cultural differences?

Hall: Anything that brings them into much closer contact with the local population, like staying with a family, would help; but they move through so quickly that most people remain isolated. What they can do is train themselves to pay attention, rather close attention, to what they are feeling when things are happening—keeping their own emotional pulse. Keep diaries of what it is about different situations that makes people feel happy, sad, hostile, or anxious. Is it because of voice loudness or because those people are too far away and you can't get close to them? Is it the intensity of the transaction or the abruptness of it? What are the details that set transactions apart from what one is used to? It's these little things that make up the entire culture and it's the little things we should pay attention to. When you're walking down the street and some Frenchman talking to a friend steps backward without looking, throws up his arms, and hits you in the face, you get used to watching out for people who are talking and gesticulating. You also give them a lot of room.

Friedman: You seem to have a bias toward cultures with more elaborate systems of nonverbal communication, toward cultures that stress human relationships. Would you prefer to live in a high-context culture?

Hall: Of course, there is no real choice involved. As an American, I know my own culture better than any other in the world and what I know of other cultures, inevitably, is relatively superficial. I can analyze behavior and tell people about things they don't know about themselves. But I also know that the only culture that I'm deeply contexted in is my own, so that regardless of what I know about another culture, I will never really know what is going on.

I want to stress that there is tremendous strength and vitality in this country. We have our problems, as every country has, and we've had more than our share in the last few years. But this is still a very vital, dynamic country. Like all countries, though, we could do some things better and we could be more effective.

In terms of high and low context, the U.S. is toward the middle of the scale. The low-context Swiss around Zurich don't even know their neighbors, and colleagues don't know one another. When I was on a cruise some time ago, attending a conference, I was talking with a famous Swiss geographer friend and said, "I suppose you know our friend and

> "Arabs depend on others to intervene in their disputes. If there's a fight and someone is hurt, the crowd is guilty."

Intercultural Communications **31**

colleague, Professor-Doctor Heine Hediger [who was a professor of animal psychology in the University of Zurich]?" This man laughed and said, "You Americans don't understand us Swiss. One of the functions you perform for us is to get us together. We don't know each other!" So they are much more isolated, much more particular.

Friedman: Are we all trapped in our own culture?

Hall: You can't be a person without having a culture and you can't have a body without genes. Culture is the underlying pattern, but how you develop is up to you. Like a body, culture is the end product of multiple evolutionary changes. Whether people are trapped or not depends on the degree to which they allow themselves to perceive and believe in the reality that we call culture. Awareness is our key to freedom.

Article Review Form at end of book.

IBM USA, Siemens AG of Germany, and Toshiba Corporation of Japan brought a multinational team together to develop a computer chip; what got in the way? What might be done differently if they were to attempt it today?

Computer Chip Project Brings Rivals Together, But the Cultures Clash

Foreign work habits get in way of creative leaps, hobbling joint research.

Softball is not the answer.

E. S. Browning
Staff Reporter of The Wall Street Journal

East Fishkill, N.Y.—Life can be tough out here on the frontier of international business corporation. Just ask Matt Wordeman.

Mr. Wordeman, an International Business Machines Corp. research scientist, works at the heart of one of the most ambitious cross-cultural business projects ever attempted. Three competing companies from three continents—Siemens AG of Germany, Toshiba Corp. of Japan and IBM—are trying to develop a revolutionary computer memory chip together. The Triad, as they call themselves, has been working for a year at the IBM facility in this small Hudson River Valley town on research scheduled to last until at least 1997. The undertaking is cutting-edge, both in technology and in the scope of its cross-cultural cooperation.

Initially, some organizers wondered whether more than 100 scientists from competitive, culturally diverse backgrounds could work together on such a large project. They were right to worry.

Meeting Etiquette

At East Fishkill, Siemens scientists were shocked to find Toshiba colleagues closing their eyes and seeming to sleep during meetings (a common practice for overworked Japanese managers when talk doesn't concern them). The Japanese, who normally work in big groups, found it painful to sit in small, individual offices and speak English; some now withdraw when they can into all-Japanese groups. IBMers complained that the Germans plan too much and that the Japanese—who like to review ideas constantly—won't make clear decisions. Suspicions circulate that some researchers are withholding information from the group.

The human issues raised in this venture offers lessons not just for the three prominent firms involved, but for companies in a wide variety of businesses across the globe.

Cooperative projects of this kind are likely to proliferate, and the reason is money. In business after business, development costs are ballooning, driving more and more cash-strapped companies to look for ways to cooperate with competitors. Participants in the Triad project won't give a precise figure, but its development costs have been estimated in the hundreds of millions of dollars. In the semiconductor business alone, cost pressure has driven Texas

"Computer Chip Project Brings Rivals Together But the Cultures Clash." E. S. Browning, THE WALL STREET JOURNAL, May 3, 1994. Reprinted by permission of THE WALL STREET JOURNAL, © 1994 Dow Jones & Company, Inc. All Rights Reserved Worldwide.

Instruments Inc. and Japan's Hitachi Ltd. to set up their own joint project to develop the same kind of memory chip—although their researchers work apart, in separate labs. Japan's NEC Corp. and South Korea's Samsung Electronics Co. are making similar plans.

The memory chip being developed here in East Fishkill is intended to be the backbone of computers for the early 21st century. Each thumbnail-sized silicon chip is to hold 256 million bits of information, 16 times as much as today's most advanced chip. The chips must hold so much in such a tiny space that their working parts will have to be smaller than the wavelength of light—hard even to detect, much less assemble.

In theory, bringing together scientists with diverse backgrounds to design such an advanced technology is supposed to generate creative leaps, yielding new approaches and dazzling discoveries. "For example," says cultural anthropologist Edward T. Hall, "Americans tend to look at objects. The Japanese look at spaces between objects. If you can relax and let everyone be himself, you can get a lot of strengths from that."

No problem, thought IBM; after all, the company hires people from all over the world. Mr. Wordeman says he figured he had plenty of experience working with foreigners, even those lacking English language skills.

"But most of those people had studied in the U.S.," he says. "They tend to become very Americanized very quickly. What's different this time is that there are entire groups of people who came with their own company ties. People have been able to stay more separate. . . . We don't trust each other entirely."

A disappointed Mr. Wordeman says he hasn't seen the kinds of technical leaps he had hoped for. If it weren't for the financial savings implicit in such a joint research venture, he says, he thinks IBM could do the work more easily on its own.

Mr. Wordeman and other Triad participants emphasize that, despite the huge extra effort required, the project isn't in trouble. Work is on schedule—even a bit ahead in parts—and they are finding ways to overcome communications problems,

they say. Members of all three teams say they have learned huge amounts, both about technology and about cooperating with outsiders. They say it is far too soon to evaluate successes and failures, and that the hoped-for technological leaps still may emerge.

But they agree that cooperation has come much harder than anyone imagined. Part of the problem was a businesslike effort to get a quick start on the daunting microchip technology. International joint ventures need to pay early attention to team-building and understanding various approaches to work, says Nancy Adler, a professor of management at Montreal's McGill University. Otherwise, cultural differences quickly switch from opportunities to obstacles: "They are used to explain problems rather than solve them. People say, 'We missed the deadline because those Japanese are so slow.' "

Needed: Joint Training

That is precisely what happened with the Triad companies.

Toshiba gave employees its normal courses on working and living abroad. But, says Takaaki Tanaka, a Toshiba human-resources expert in New York, "We should have done more cooperative efforts with human-resources people from Siemens and IBM, to develop joint training programs."

Siemens briefed employees on what it calls America's "hamburger style of management." American managers, Siemens says, prefer to criticize subordinates gently. They start with small talk: "How's the family?" That is the top of the hamburger bun. Then Americans slip in the meat—the criticism. And they exit with encouraging words—more bun.

"With Germans," says Alf Keogh, an Irishman who does cross-cultural training for Siemens, "all you get is the meat. And with the Japanese, it's all the soft stuff—you have to *smell* the meat."

The project's planners tried to address cultural differences by stipulating all work would be done in English and by creating mixed research teams of employees from all three companies. That basic plan, which seemed an obvious starting

point for working together, became the first obstacle.

"My biggest problem is the English language," says Motoya Okazaki, a Toshiba researcher, who had been a student of foreign languages and cultures before coming to East Fishkill. "It took me almost one year to learn to communicate slightly well."

The Toshiba researchers also faced the biggest adjustment problem in terms of corporate culture. They are accustomed to working together in big tank-like rooms, which they compare to classrooms. By overhearing conversations, everyone knows what others are doing—from research to family problems. Senior people constantly look over subordinates' shoulders. "They live in a sea of information," says Mr. Hall, the anthropologist.

Toshiba wanted such a system here. But IBM's building already was cut up into a maze of small offices. To save time, the Japanese finally agreed to keep it that way, knocking out a few walls to improve communication.

"For us," explains Toru Watanabe, a senior Toshiba researcher, "very important information exchanges are handled in informal situations—just after finishing lunch, while relaxing and discussing baseball. We say, 'I have a new idea, what do you think?' But here, you have to go to someone's office and say, 'Do you have a minute?' Small talk doesn't come naturally."

The Germans had difficulty adjusting to their American work space, too. In Germany, Siemens people say, no one would be asked to work in a windowless office; in East Fishkill, Siemens engineers learned to their horror, most of the offices are windowless. Office doors have narrow panes of glass so that visitors can see before entering whether occupants are busy; German and Japanese researchers, not accustomed to this, sometimes hand their coats over the glass, annoying IBMers. Equally annoying to some of the foreign visitors is IBM's strict no-smoking policy, requiring them to go outdoors in any weather if they want to light up.

Then comes the delicate question of how to make suggestions. Siemens engineer Klaus Roithner says he spent days analyzing IBM's pilot manufacturing system and then made some gentle proposals for improving it. IBM colleagues first told him to be more specific, he says; then they accused him of simply wanting to do things the Siemens way. Concluding that IBMers don't like outside suggestions, he finally resorted to amateur psychology. Nowadays, he says, "I indirectly suggest an idea to IBM engineers, and let them think they have come up with it themselves."

Also, Mr. Roithner says, deep corporate rivalries may be at work. "I have never been reluctant to share secrets," he says. "But I have had the feeling that this problem exists. Here you are working in a team, but you are still employed by your mother company. Some people still have to think, 'Don't tell too much about your company secrets.'"

For the first few months of the Triad project, the researchers say, everyone was on best behavior—and having fun. People spoke slowly and carefully to one another, making extra efforts to be understood. But with time, people fell into more normal speech and behavior patterns. The honeymoon ended; little slights were felt. The three groups grew more isolated, and some Japanese in particular began speaking less English.

"They do read English all day, but most of their communication now will be done in Japanese," says Mr. Wordeman. "People will talk if you seek them out, but there is very little casual chatting and dropping in the office across company lines—whereas there is a great deal of that kind of contact within each of the three companies."

"I see it most often at 7 or 8 in the evening," says Mr. Roithner, the German engineer. "The American engineers are gone. Most of the German engineers are gone. And half the Japanese engineers are in the aisles, talking. You can see that real work is going on—unplanned and informal."

The separation has prevented the hoped-for big creative leaps that researchers call Aha! effects. "I wish I had a good example of breaking through that and coming up with a great new idea, but unfortunately that hasn't happened very much," says Mr. Wordeman. He adds, however, that the engineers themselves are extremely talented, and this has permitted them to overcome disappointments and wasted time, keeping the project on track.

One program that could have helped smooth over differences was a "buddy system" created by IBM to teach foreign colleagues the internal IBM computer system. Once that technical information was passed on to the first wave of researchers, project leaders ended the buddy system—figuring that later arrivals could learn faster from people of their own nationality. IBM's senior person on the project, John Abernathey, now says that if he had it to do again, he would keep the buddy system in place, to help build friendships outside the office.

After-Hours Socializing

"It takes time to get to know one another," says Mr. Hall, the anthropologist. "One thing that seems to work across all three cultures is to go out and get drunk together."

But project organizers also were reluctant to push after-hours socializing, and now, in their second year of the project, Triad researchers tend to spend free time with colleagues from their own countries.

"For the Germans and the Japanese, this is a big adventure," says Mr. Abernathey. "But for the U.S. people, this is their home. They have school-board meetings, PTA meetings and other activities."

One effort at cross-cultural schmoozing, a softball game, backfired.

"The Americans and Japanese know this game well, but the Germans don't," explains Mr. Roithner of Siemens. Determined to measure up in the new sport— "highly motivated," as he puts it—he hit the ball and raced for first. He beat the throw, but made the mistake of hitting the base stiff-legged, fracturing his hip. A Japanese co-worker took him to the hospital. An American colleague lent him a laptop computer to use at home. The cross-cultural softball project was canceled.

One small consolation: Mr. Roithner found what he calls "the perfect doctor." Why was he perfect? "He spoke German—he had studied in Switzerland. It is hard to explain where something hurts in a foreign language."

Article Review Form at end of book.

Putting different cultures into tight quarters may create difficulties. Stone's article presents some funny and not so funny cross-cultural situations that have occurred in space. How should the international space effort resolve some of the issues of communication style, gender expectations, and privacy issues? Have there been any cross-cultural problems during recent joint space efforts on the Russian Space Station *Mir*? What might be future issues on the International Space Station?

It's a Small World After All

Judith Stone

Japanese astronauts worry that the Americans aboard space station *Freedom* will make ill-considered, split-second decisions. The Americans fear that the Japanese preference for protracted group deliberation could prove fatal in an emergency. The Italians are anxious about whether their privacy will be respected. And I'm terrified the French will make everyone watch Jerry Lewis movies.

Anthropologist Mary Lozano is chronicling the concerns of international partners in the space station, scheduled to be built from modules assembled on the ground, launched on the shuttle, then deployed and linked by space crews on 17 flights beginning in November 1995 (Lord willin' and the deficit don't rise).

Lozano, the first anthropologist to explore cultural differences among space travelers, works for the space station division of McDonnell Douglas in Huntington Beach, California. After polling potential participants from the U.S., Japanese, European, and Canadian space agencies, Lozano wasn't surprised to unearth some troublesome myths and stereotypes. "The non-Americans expect the Americans to be arrogant," she reports. "The Americans expect the *French* to be arrogant. And they consider the Italians emotional, the Germans strict and pompous, and the Japanese clannish."

How will those prejudices play in close quarters? By December 1999 the space station will have what NASA calls PMC—permanently manned capability. Eventually a four-person international PMC crew will remain aloft for 90 days, rotating with other crews and lengthening the stay on later flights if all goes well. *Freedom* duty will ultimately serve as a dress rehearsal for the two-year flight to Mars.

"We know from our astronauts, although they're reticent about public discussion," Lozano says, "that they sometimes get on each other's nerves, especially after several days in what we call a trapped environment. Imagine the problems that could occur if you're living together for years—and if you're from very different cultures."

"What we hope to do is ward off trouble by learning in advance what those differences are likely to be." She's working with human-factors engineer Clifford Wong, who was already researching multicultural hardware designed for the space station when Lozano arrived at McDonnell Douglas a year and a half ago. Before that, she had been investigating stress among non-English-speaking U.S. soldiers for the Department of Defense.

Wong wanted to avoid intercultural confusion over dials, switches, and gauges. "Here in the United States, flipping a switch up means on; in other countries, like England, for example, up can mean off. Some cultures turn a dial clockwise to indicate an increase, others counterclockwise. American warning lights are red, because to us that color means danger. But to the Chinese, it signifies good luck and prosperity."

Dials and switches appear to be the least of potential problems. Lozano and Wong asked nearly 100 astronauts and others involved in the various space programs what cultural issues they considered important. Both Japanese and Americans are interested in understanding each other's decision-making styles, Lozano says. "The Japanese like to make decisions by consensus. If they're asked how they feel about something, they need time to come up with a decision. When the Japanese say yes, it doesn't always mean yes; they try to avoid conflict and maintain group harmony.

"Americans, on the other hand, debate the issues and come up with a decision right at the table. The rapidity appears irrational to the Japanese; the slowness seems dangerous to the Americans."

"The Italians asked Lozano and Wong to look at the way privacy differs from culture to culture. "An American's sense of privacy has to do with personal space: Don't sit too close, don't come in while I'm bathing," Lozano says. "In Italy privacy is a mental thing. You can be in

Judith Stone/© 1992. Reprinted with permission of Discover Magazine.

a crowd and feel private, but that means others have to respect that privacy by not talking to you. One Italian said his idea of privacy is that he should be allowed to have his opinions without anyone trying to change them. The Italians we spoke to think Americans are aggressive and forceful and will want to pry into other people's business. They think Americans are afraid to spend time alone, but for Italians, that's a healthy thing."

The Canadians, Lozano said, are convinced that Americans think the two cultures are identical, when they're not. (Well, of course they're not! Canadians have a small birthmark shaped like Lorne Greene on their right buttock, and their bacon is round. No letters please—I'm just kidding. I could just as easily have said that Americans have small birthmarks shaped like Pernell Roberts, okay? And I happen to adore William Shatner, Joni Mitchell, Guy Lafleur, Mordecai Richler and the Blue Jays.) (You don't know the famous Canadian doo-wop group Mordecai Richler and the Blue Jays?)

"And the rest of the international partners are concerned about language," Lozano says. "English will be the official station language. The Japanese are having the most difficulty with it, not that others are finding it easy. Everyone worries about mastering technical language and whether Americans will be sensitive to their not knowing slang. We know that's a problem in space, because a Czech cosmonaut who spoke perfect Russian still felt he was treated like an outsider because he had trouble with idiomatic slang."

I'd also worry that Americans in general and aerospace types in particular are jargonauts and acronymphomaniacs. An international partner could, for example, easily confuse PMC with PMS. (I used to be condescendingly enchanted by mistakes foreigners made with English. I loved it when a South American colleague said he was so tired he had to take a snap, and when a Finnish friend asked my why the insect that eats cotton is called a Bowl of Evil. But then the foot was in the other mouth. In Ecuador, I proudly ordered fried trout in Spanish—then learned that I had basically asked for a sautéed sexual act.)

Food is also a major topic of concern. The French and Dutch fret that no one else will take dinner seriously. Astronaut wannabes from the Netherlands told Lozano they're afraid that not enough time will be spent indulging in meals, and Europeans in general seem to think Americans eat because it's time, not because it's a pleasure. (Could we please not tell the Europeans about Tang and Space Food Sticks? That could be very embarrassing.) "We need to find out whether people will be repulsed by each other's cuisine," Lozano says. "Will the smell get to them after weeks? How will different nationalities handle KP? What time should meals be served? Will the postprandial siesta favored by some cultures be possible? What about keeping kosher?"

Others Lozano and Wong spoke to thought the anthropologist and the engineer should ask questions like these: Are you disgusted by the idea of somebody who doesn't bathe frequently? Is religious practice an issue? What will happen if we misunderstand each other's jokes? Will you prefer to speak your own language in the recreational area? (Astonishingly, no one is worried about the possibility of having to sing "Kumbaya" in several different tongues on Space Station Hootenanny Night.)

Based on this preliminary survey of cross-cultural issues, Lozano and Wong have designed a questionnaire that's been given a test run and revised with the help of an anthropological consulting group called LTG Associates. They're asking 20 space program participants in each country to fill it out. When that process is complete, which they hope will be late this spring, they'll conduct indepth ethnographic interviews, asking people why they responded the way they did.

"We think that what we're learning will reduce a lot of pressure and tension in the trapped environment," Lozano says. "We hope it will be applied to training and crew operations, and we think it will ultimately save money by minimizing human error caused by misunderstanding."

U.S. and foreign astronauts are now trained in survival, the physical sciences, and flight-specific systems during simulations, but not in interpersonal or intercultural skills, Lozano notes. The theory is that folks who train together for a long period of time automatically form a strong bond.

"But the Russians tell us that this isn't necessarily so," she says. The "cosmonaut Valentin Lebedev, who spend 211 days aboard the space station *Salyut 7* in 1982, says relations grew strained under stress; he thinks all spacefarers should have interpersonal training. And we're thinking, if people who share a culture have these problems, imagine the problems that could arise with an intercultural crew." A survey of the literature, Wong adds, reveals that in simulation studies, when people are confined to a module, group cohesiveness decreases over time, and psychosocial conflicts increase.

Lozano and Wong have found a model for intercultural harmony in space—on television. "Clifford and I watch the new *Star Trek,* and we respect its outlook. Captain Picard is very sensitive to cultural differences. He doesn't immediately dismiss aliens as infantile, hostile, or aggressive; he tries to find out why they behave the way they do. He doesn't force our culture on other cultures they come across; the Prime Directive won't let him." (But you notice that the captain does make beings from other galaxies eat festive plastic cubes. Please don't tell the Europeans.)

"And the crew of the *Enterprise* seems to have taken care of gender issues, which also make the international partners somewhat anxious. It's already happened, for example, that on one European space flight, a Middle Eastern prince refused to take orders from the woman in command. Men in some cultures still aren't completely comfortable working as equals with women."

What do the men think will happen—that the radiation shield will be replaced by a panty shield? If I were aboard the *Freedom,* I'd worry that male crew members might experience a synchronized testosterone surge and spontaneously bond, suddenly holding a Get in Touch with Your Positive Fierceness Weekend. All the drumming in such a small place!

Article Review Form at end of book.

WiseGuide Wrap-Up

- Developing awareness of the variety in both verbal and nonverbal aspects of intercultural communication is a critical first step toward being able to operate in an international environment. Also, becoming aware of one's own culture is critical when working in the global arena.

- Increasing one's knowledge of the cross-cultural communication process can improve relationships. Taking the time to learn more about a particular group or multiple groups is also necessary to be effective. In addition, recognize that developing effective teams with a multinational make-up may take more time and will generally be more challenging. Strong multinational teams, however, are frequently more creative and productive, as a result of the synergy that the blending of different cultures produces.

- The real test of cross-cultural awareness and knowledge is application to specific intercultural relationships or contexts. The ability to understand one's own culture and adapt where appropriate with other societies is an application of intercultural communication skills.

- It is important to also recognize that this is a lifelong learning process, for the only culture we truly understand is our own.

R.E.A.L. Sites

This list provides a print preview of typical **coursewise** R.E.A.L. sites. (There are over 100 such sites at the **courselinks**™ site.) The danger in printing URLs is that web sites can change overnight. As we went to press, these sites were functional using the URLs provided. If you come across one that isn't, please let us know via email to: webmaster@coursewise.com. Use your Passport to access the most current list of R.E.A.L. sites at the **courselinks**™ site.

Site name: Cross-Cultural Resource Library
URL: http://darkwing.uoregon.edu/~oieehome/oiee/resourcelibrary.html
Why is it R.E.A.L.? This site has an extensive intercultural communication bibliography, with topics ranging from blunders to international employment. This is a good preliminary stop for selecting topics for papers, researching a subject, and gathering information for a particular training situation.
Key topic: intercultural communication bibliography
Try this: Select one of the topics under current discussion in class and find three sources listed in the bibliography.

Site name: Idealist
URL: http://www.idealist.org/
Why is it R.E.A.L.? Readers interested in an international internship with a nonprofit organization will find worldwide listings. Nonprofit organizations will be able to list their organizations worldwide. The idealist site also offers listings of nonprofit programs and services worldwide.
Key topics: international internships, nonprofit organizations worldwide
Try this: Select an area of the world and list what type of volunteer internships are available.

Site name: Latin American Network Information Center
URL: http://lanic.utexas.edu/
Why is it R.E.A.L.? This includes information on Latin America by country and/or subject directory. It provides a wide range of information on specific countries as well as regional areas.
Key topics: Latin American countries, regions, subjects, projects
Try this: Select a Latin American country and summarize information regarding historical events which influenced the culture.

section 2

Learning Objectives

- Increase knowledge of how to successfully enter the global marketplace.
- Develop insight into managing a multinational team.
- Recognize the importance of learning about a culture prior to entering it via technology or face-to-face.
- Develop a tolerance for the ambiguity that occurs in learning about and working with another culture.

Global Business

WiseGuide Intro

In this section, we examine the expansion of global business. Large and small firms are rapidly entering the international marketplace. Employees, from the purchasing clerk level to the senior manager, conduct business every day with customers in various regions of the world. The quality of customer service provided for this international clientele has a direct impact on repeat business. In addition, the office around the corner may be filled with multinational teams, as cities become more international in makeup. The success of a transnational firm may hinge on its worldwide teams' abilities to not let cultural patterns interfere with completion of successful projects.

This renewed interest in the global marketplace is reflected in the series of articles gathered for this section. The articles focus on the management skills necessary to supervise diverse teams, as well as organizational issues at hand when people are involved in joint ventures of an international nature. The articles also provide examples of how workers respond to the ambiguity which naturally occurs when working within an unfamiliar environment.

Business professionals also recognize that intercultural communication expertise is of benefit to their careers. Many more advertisements for jobs, ranging from sales to engineering, now include such phrases as "international experience helpful," "second language preferred," "customer service for a diverse market," and "ability to be a multinational team player." Charlene Marmer Solomon, in her article "Women Expats—Shattering the Myths," discusses the increased opportunities of international assignments for women and the importance of this experience for all professionals.

In addition, Richard Reeves-Ellington's case study, "Using Cultural Skills for Cooperative Advantage in Japan," provides insight into how a company can research a particular culture and use that information to its competitive advantage. Geert Hofstede, well known for his seminal intercultural research of IBM International, provides application of research in his article "Cultural Constraints in Management Theories."

The business section of the **courselinks** site for Intercultural Communications allows the reader to research business prospects in a particular country for a global business plan. There are sites for quick, updated international news summaries for a manager, prior to an overseas meeting. It allows a sales representative, being sent to Japan, quick access to country-specific information, in order to avoid cultural mistakes on the first intercultural sales call. These web sites will be continually updated. Neophyte business graduates as well as experienced professionals will find many uses for material readily available via the **coursewise** Passport.

Questions

Reading 8. As business expands globally, managers find themselves with different ways of doing business which have national cultural origins. Hofstede is one of the major theorists regarding cultural dimensions in business. What are these dimensions and how might these differences affect joint ventures or the global expansion of an organization?

Reading 9. Bob Kimmons has been training people to manage multinational teams which are typical of large projects around the world. How might such teams avoid the pitfall of miscommunication? How can a manager motivate such a team?

Reading 10. How did Pharmco transform its managers from people with only home office experience to professionals who successfully work with foreign colleagues? In what way were employees involved in creating this intercultural education process?

Reading 11. What implications does multinational composition have for group functioning? In creating corporate policy in a global business, what cultural sensitivities are necessary for the leadership?

Reading 12. Why is it important for a company to widen its expat candidate pool? What myths have limited women in overseas assignments for global companies?

Reading 13. Why do transnational firms need global human resources management systems? How does a transnational company create a pool of globally competent people?

Reading 14. What are the essential elements for doing business abroad? What mistakes do businesspeople make when expanding their firm globally?

Reading 15. What is meant by the statement "In France, management is not a task. It is a 'state of mind'—one that managers worldwide need to understand"?

As business expands globally, managers find themselves with different ways of doing business which have national cultural origins. Hofstede is one of the major theorists regarding cultural dimensions in business. What are these dimensions and how might these differences affect joint ventures or the global expansion of an organization?

Cultural Constraints in Management Theories

Geert Hofstede

University of Limburg, Maastricht, the Netherlands

In My View

Lewis Carroll's *Alice in Wonderland* contains the famous story of Alice's croquet game with the Queen of Hearts.

Alice thought she had never seen such a curious croquet-ground in all her life; it was all ridges and furrows; the balls were live hedgehogs, the mallets live flamingoes, and the soldiers had to double themselves up and to stand on their hands and feet, to make the arches.

You probably know how the story goes: Alice's flamingo mallet turns its head whenever she wants to strike with it; her hedgehog ball runs away; and the doubled-up soldier arches walk around all the time. The only rule seems to be that the Queen of Hearts always wins.

Alice's croquet playing problems are good analogies to attempts to build culture-free theories of management. Concepts available for this purpose are themselves alive with culture, having been developed within a particular cultural context. They have a tendency to guide our thinking toward our desired conclusion.

As the same reasoning may also be applied to the arguments in this article, I better tell you my conclusion before I continue—so that the rules of my game are understood. In this article we take a trip around the world to demonstrate that there are no such things as universal management theories.

Diversity in management practices as we go around the world has been recognized in U.S. management literature for more than thirty years. The term "comparative management" has been used since the 1960s. However, it has taken much longer for the U.S. academic community to accept that not only practices but also the validity of theories may stop at national borders, and I wonder whether even today everybody would agree with this statement.

An article I published in *Organizational Dynamics* in 1980 entitled "Do American Theories Apply Abroad?" created more controversy than I expected. The article argued, with empirical support, that generally accepted U.S. theories like those of Maslow, Herzberg, McClelland, Vroom, McGregor, Likert, Blake and Mouton may not or only very partly apply outside the borders of their country of origin—assuming they do apply within those borders. Among the requests for reprints, a larger number were from Canada than from the United States.

Management Theorists Are Human

Employees and managers are human. Employees as humans was "discovered" in the 1930s, with the Human Relations school. Managers as humans, was introduced in the late 40s by Herbert Simon's "bounded rationality" and elaborated in Richard Cyert and James March's *Behavioral Theory of the Firm* (1963, and recently re-published in a second edition). My argument is that management scientists, theorists, and writers are human too: they grew up in a particular society in a particular period, and their ideas cannot help but reflect the constraints of their environment.

The idea that the validity of a theory is constrained by national borders is more obvious in Europe, with all its borders, than in a huge borderless country like the U.S. Already in the sixteenth century Michel de Montaigne, a Frenchman, wrote a statement which was made famous by Blaise Pascal about a century later:

Reprinted with permission of Academy of Management, P.O. Box 3020, Briar Cliff Manor, NY 10510–8020. *Cultural Constraints in Management Theories.* Geert Hofstede, The Executive, February 1993. Reproduced by permission of the publisher via Copyright Clearance Center, Inc.

"Vérite en-deca des Pyrenées, erreur au-delà"—There are truths on this side of the Pyrenées which are falsehoods on the other.

From Don Armado's Love to Taylor's Science

According to the comprehensive ten-volume Oxford English Dictionary (1971), the words "manage," "management," and "manager" appeared in the English language in the 16th century. The oldest recorded use of the word "manager" is in Shakespeare's "Love Labour's Lost," dating from 1588, in which Don Adriano de Armado, "a fantastical Spaniard," exclaims (Act I, scene ii, 188):

"Adieu, valour! rust, rapier! be still, drum! for your manager is in love, yea, he loveth."

The linguistic origin of the word is from Latin *manus,* hand, via the Italian *maneggiare,* which is the training of horses in the *manege,* subsequently its meaning was extended to skillful handling in general, like of arms and musical instruments, as Don Armado illustrates. However, the word also became associated with the French *menage,* household, as an equivalent of "husbandry" in its sense of the art of running a household. The theatre of present-day management contains elements of both *manege* and *menage* and different managers and cultures may use different accents.

The founder of the science of economics, the Scot Adam Smith, in his 1776 book *The Wealth of Nations,* used "manage," "management" (even "bad management") and "manager" when dealing with the process and the persons involved in operating joint stock companies (Smith, V.i.e.). British economist John Stuart Mill (1806–1873) followed Smith in this use and clearly expressed his distrust of such hired people who were not driven by ownership. Since the 1880s the word "management" appeared occasionally in writings by American engineers, until it was canonized as a modern science by Frederick W. Taylor in *Shop Management* in 1903 and in *The Principles of Scientific Management* in 1911.

While Smith and Mill used "management" to describe a process and "managers" for the persons involved, "management" in the American sense—which has since been taken back by the British—refers not only to the process but also to the managers as a class of people. This class (1) does not own a business but sells its skills to act on behalf of the owners and (2) does not produce personally but is indispensable for making others produce, through motivation. Members of this class carry a high status and many American boys and girls aspire to the role. In the U.S., the manager is a cultural hero.

Let us now turn to other parts of the world. We will look at management in its context in other successful modern economies: Germany, Japan, France, Holland, and among the Overseas Chinese. Then we will examine management in the much larger part of the world that is still poor, especially South-East Asia and Africa, and in the new political configurations of Eastern Europe, and Russia in particular. We will then return to the U.S. via mainland China.

Germany

The manager is not a cultural hero in Germany. If anybody, it is the engineer who fills the hero role. Frederick Taylor's *Scientific Management* was conceived in a society of immigrants—where large numbers of workers with diverse backgrounds and skills had to work together. In Germany this heterogeneity never existed.

Elements of the mediaeval guild system have survived in historical continuity in Germany until the present day. In particular, a very effective apprenticeship system exists both on the shop floor and in the office, which alternates practical work and classroom courses. At the end of the apprenticeship the worker receives a certificate, the *Facharbeiterbrief,* which is recognized throughout the country. About two thirds of the German worker population holds such a certificate and a corresponding occupational pride. In fact, quite a few German company presidents have worked their way up from the ranks through an apprenticeship. In comparison, two thirds of the worker population in Britain have no occupational qualification at all.

The highly skilled and responsible German workers do not necessarily need a manager, American-style, to "motivate" them. They expect their boss or *Meister* to assign their tasks and to be the expert in resolving technical problems. Comparisons of similar German, British, and French organizations show the Germans as having the highest rate of personnel in productive roles and the lowest both in leadership and staff roles.

Business schools are virtually unknown in Germany. Native German management theories concentrate on formal systems. The inapplicability of American concepts of management was quite apparent in 1973 when the U.S. consulting firm of Booz, Allen and Hamilton, commissioned by the German Ministry of Economic Affairs, wrote a study of German management from an American view point. The report is highly critical and writes among other things that "Germans simply do not have a very strong concept of management." Since 1973, from my personal experience, the situation has not changed much. However, during this period the German economy has performed in a superior fashion to the U.S. in virtually all respects, as a strong concept of management might have been a liability rather than an asset.

Japan

The American type of manager is also missing in Japan. In the United States, the core of the enterprise is the managerial class. The core of the Japanese enterprise is the permanent worker group; workers who for all practical purposes are tenured and who aspire at life-long employment. They are distinct from the non-permanent employees—most women and subcontracted teams led by gang bosses, to be laid off in slack periods. University graduates in Japan first join the permanent worker group and subsequently fill various positions, moving from line to staff as the need occurs while paid according to seniority rather than position. They take part in Japanese-style group consultation sessions for important decisions, which extend the decision-making period but guarantee fast implementation afterwards. Japanese are to a large extent controlled by their peer group rather than by their manager.

Three researchers from the East-West Center of the University of Hawaii, Joseph Tobin, David Wu, and Dana Danielson, did an observation study of typical preschools in three countries: China, Japan, and the United States. Their results have been published both as a book and as a video. In the Japanese preschool, one teacher handled twenty-eight four-year olds. The video shows one particularly obnoxious boy, Hiroki, who fights with other children and throws teaching materials down from the balcony. When a little girl tries to alarm the teacher, the latter answers "what are you calling me for? Do something about it!" In the U.S. preschool, there is one adult for every nine children. This class has its problem child too, Glen, who refuses to clear away his toys. One of the teachers has a long talk with him and isolates him in a corner, until he changes his mind. It doesn't take much imagination to realize that managing Hiroki thirty years later will be a different process from managing Glen.

American theories of leadership are ill-suited for the Japanese group-controlled situation. During the past two decades, the Japanese have developed their own "PM" theory of leadership, in which P stands for performance and M for maintenance. The latter is less a concern for individual employees than for maintaining social stability. In view of the amazing success of the Japanese economy in the past thirty years, many Americans have sought for the secrets of Japanese management hoping to copy them.

> Japanese are to a large extent controlled by their peer group rather than by their manager.

> There are no secrets of Japanese management, however; it is even doubtful whether there is such a thing as management, in the American sense, in Japan at all. The secret is in Japanese society; and if any group in society should be singled out as carriers of the secret, it is the workers, not the managers.

France

The manager, U.S. style, does not exist in France either. In a very enlightening book, unfortunately not yet translated into English, the French researcher Philippe d'Iribarne (1989) describes the results of in-depth observation and interview studies of management methods in three subsidiary plants of the same French multinational: in France, the United States, and Holland. He relates what he finds to information about the three societies in general. Where necessary, he goes back in history to trace the roots of the strikingly different behaviors in the completion of the same tasks. He identifies three kinds of basic principles (*logiques*) of management. In the USA, the principle is the *fair contract* between employer and employee, which gives the manager considerable prerogatives, but within its limits. This is really a labor *market* in which the worker sells his or her labor for a price. In France, the principle is the *honor* of each class in a society which has always been and remains extremely stratified, in which superiors behave as superior beings and subordinates accept and expect this, conscious of their own lower level in the national hierarchy but also of the honor of their own class. The French do not think in terms of managers versus nonmanagers but in terms of *cadres* versus *non*-cadres; one becomes cadre by attending the proper schools and one remains it forever; regardless of their actual task, cadres have the privileges of a higher social class, and it is very rare for a noncadre to cross the ranks. The conflict between French and American theories of management became apparent in the beginning of the twentieth century, in a criticism by the great French management pioneer Henri Fayol (1841–1925) on his U.S. colleague and contemporary Frederick W. Taylor (1856–1915). The difference in career paths of the two men is striking. Fayol was a French engineer whose career as a *cadre supérieur* culminated in the position of Président-Directeur-Général of a mining company. After his retirement he formulated his experiences in a path-breaking text on organization: *Administration industrielle et générale*, in which he focussed on the sources of authority. Taylor was an American engineer who started his career in industry as a worker and attained his academic qualifications through evening studies. From chief engineer in a steel company he became one of the first management consultants. Taylor was not really concerned with the issue of authority at all; his focus was on efficiency. He proposed to split the task of the first-line boss into eight specialisms, each exercised by a different person; an idea which eventually led to the idea of a matrix organization.

Taylor's work appeared in a French translation in 1913, and Fayol read it and showed himself generally impressed but shocked by Taylor's "denial of the principle of the Unity of Command" in the case of the eight-boss-system.

Seventy years later André Laurent, another of Fayol's compatriots, found that French managers in a survey reacted very strongly against a suggestion that one employee could report to two different bosses, while U.S. managers in the same survey showed fewer misgivings. Matrix organization has never become popular in France as it has in the United States.

Holland

In my own country, Holland or as it is officially called, the Netherlands, the study by Philippe d'Iribarne found the management principle to be a need for consensus among all parties, neither predetermined by a contractual relationship nor by class distinctions, but based on an open-ended exchange of views and a balancing of interests. In terms of the different origins of the word "manager," the organization in Holland is more *menage* (household) while in the United States it is more *manege* (horse drill).

At my university, the University of Limburg at Maastricht, every semester we receive a class of American business students who take a program in European Studies. We asked both the Americans and a matched group of Dutch students to describe their ideal job after graduation, using a list of twenty-two job characteristics. The Americans attached significantly more importance than the Dutch to earnings, advancement, benefits, a good working relationship with their boss, and security of employment. The Dutch attached more importance to freedom to adopt their own approach to the job, being consulted by their boss in his or her decisions, training opportunities, contributing to the success of their organization, fully using their skills and abilities, and helping others. This list confirms d'Iribarne's findings of a contractual employment relationship in the United States, based on earnings and career opportunities, against a consensual relationship in Holland. The latter has centuries-old roots; the Netherlands were the first republic in Western Europe (1609–1810), and a model for the American republic. The country has been and still is governed by a careful balancing of interests in a multi-party system.

In terms of management theories, both motivation and leadership in Holland are different from what they are in the United States. Leadership in Holland presupposes modesty, as opposed to assertiveness in the United States. No U.S. leadership theory has room for that. Working in Holland is not a constant feast, however. There is a built-in premium on mediocrity and jealousy, as well as time-consuming ritual consultations to maintain the appearance of consensus and the pretense of modesty. There is unfortunately another side to every coin.

The Overseas Chinese

Among the champions of economic development in the past thirty years we find three countries mainly populated by Chinese living outside the Chinese mainland: Taiwan, Hong Kong and Singapore. Moreover, overseas Chinese play a very important role in the economics of Indonesia, Malaysia, the Philippines and Thailand, where they form an ethnic minority. If anything, the little dragons—Taiwan, Hong Kong and Singapore—have been more economically successful than Japan, moving from rags to riches and now counted among the world's wealthy industrial countries. Yet very little attention has been paid to the way in which their enterprises have been managed. *The Spirit of Chinese Capitalism* by Gordon Redding (1990), the British dean of the Hong Kong Business School, is an excellent book about Chinese business. He bases his insights on personal acquaintance and in-depth discussions with a large number of overseas Chinese businesspeople.

Overseas Chinese American enterprises lack almost all characteristics of modern management. They tend to be small, cooperating for essential functions with other small organizations through networks based on personal relations. They are family-owned, without the separation between ownership and management typical in the West, or even in Japan and Korea. They normally focus on one product or market, with growth by opportunistic diversification; in this, they are extremely flexible. Decision making is centralized in the hands of one dominant family member, but only family members may be given new ventures to try their skills on. They are low-profile and extremely cost-conscious, applying Confucian virtues of thrift and persistence. Their size is kept small by the assumed lack of loyalty of non-family employees, who, if they are any good, will just wait and save until they can start their own family business.

Overseas Chinese prefer economic activities in which great gains can be made with little manpower, like commodity trading and real estate. They employ few professional managers, except their sons and sometimes daughters who have been sent to prestigious business schools abroad, but who upon return continue to run the family business the Chinese way.

The origin of this system, or—in the Western view—this lack of system, is found in the history of Chinese society, in which there were no formal laws, only formal networks of powerful people guided by general principles of Confucian virtue. The favors of the authorities could change daily, so nobody could be trusted except one's kinfolk—of whom, fortunately, there used to be many, in an extended family structure. The overseas Chinese way of doing business is also very well adapted to their position in the countries in which they form ethnic minorities, often envied and threatened by ethnic violence.

Overseas Chinese businesses following this unprofessional approach command a collective gross national product of some 200 to 300 billion US dollars, exceeding the GNP of Australia. There is no denying that it works.

Management Transfer to Poor Countries

Four-fifths of the world population live in countries that are not rich but poor. After World War II and decolonization, the stated purpose of the United Nations and the World Bank has been to promote the development of all the world's countries in a war on poverty. After forty years it looks very much like we are losing this war. If one thing has become clear, it is that the export of Western—mostly American—management practices and theories to poor countries has contributed little to nothing to their development. There has been no lack of effort and money spent for this purpose: students from poor countries have been trained in this country, and teachers and Peace Corps workers have been sent to the poor countries. If nothing else, the general lack of success in economic development of other countries should be sufficient argument to doubt the validity of Western management theories in non-Western environments.

If we examine different parts of the world, the development picture is not equally bleak, and history is often a better predictor than economic factors for what happens today. There is a broad regional pecking order with East Asia leading. The little dragons have passed into the camp of the wealthy; then follow South-East Asia (with its overseas Chinese minorities), Latin America (in spite of the debt crisis), South Asia, and Africa always trails behind. Several African countries have only become poorer since decolonization.

Regions of the world with a history of large-scale political integration and civilization generally have done better than regions in which no large-scale political and cultural infrastructure existed, even if the old civilizations had decayed or been suppressed by colonizers. It has become painfully clear that development cannot be pressure-cooked; it presumes a cultural infrastructure that takes time to grow. Local management is part of this infrastructure; it cannot be imported in package form. Assuming that with so-called modern management techniques and theories outsiders can develop a country has proven a deplorable arrogance. At best, one can hope for a dialogue between equals with the locals, in which the Western partner acts as the expert in Western technology and the local partner as the expert in local culture, habits, and feelings.

Russia and China

The crumbling of the former Eastern bloc has left us with a scattering of states and would-be states of which the political and economic future is extremely uncertain. The best predictions are those based on a knowledge of history, because historical trends have taken revenge on the arrogance of the Soviet rulers who believed they could turn them around by brute power. One obvious fact is that the former bloc is extremely heterogeneous, including countries traditionally closely linked with the West by trade and travel, like Czechia, Hungary, Slovenia, and the Baltic states, as well as others with a Byzantine or Turkish past; some having been prosperous, others always extremely poor.

Let me limit myself to the Russian republic, a huge territory with some 140 million inhabitants, mainly Russians. We know quite a bit about the Russians as their country was a world power for several hundreds of years before communism, and in the nineteenth century it has produced some of the greatest writers in world literature. If I want to understand the Russians—including how they could so long support the Soviet regime—I tend to re-read Lev Nikolayevich Tolstoy. In his most famous novel *Anna Karenina* (1876) one of the main characters is a landowner, Levin, whom Tolstoy uses to express his own views and convictions about his people. Russian peasants used to be serfs; serfdom had been abolished in 1861, but the peasants, now tenants, remained as passive as before. Levin wanted to break this passivity by dividing the land among his peasants in exchange for a share of the crops; but the peasants only let the land deteriorate further. Here follows a quote:

"(Levin) read political economy and socialistic work . . . but, as he had expected, found nothing in them related to his undertaking. In the political economy books—in (John Stuart) Mill, for instance, whom he studied first and with great ardour, hoping every minute to find an answer to the questions that were engrossing him—he found only certain laws deduced from the state of agriculture in Europe; but he could not for the life of him see why these laws, which did not apply to Russia, should be considered universal. . . . Political economy told him that the laws by which Europe had developed and was developing her wealth were universal and absolute. Socialist teaching told him that development along those lines leads to ruin. And neither of them offered the smallest enlightenment as to what he, Levin, and all the Russian peasants and landowners were to do with their millions of hands and millions of acres, to make them as productive as possible for the common good."

In the summer of 1991, the Russian lands yielded a record harvest, but a large share of it rotted in the fields because no people were to be found for harvesting. The passivity is still there, and not only among the peasants. And the heirs of John Stuart Mill (whom we met before as one of the early analysts of "management") again present their universal recipes which simply do not apply.

Citing Tolstoy, I implicitly suggest that management theorists cannot neglect the great literature of the countries they want their ideas to apply to. The greatest novel in the Chinese literature is considered Cao Xueqin's *The Story of the Stone*, also known as *The Dream of the Red Chamber* which appeared around 1760. It describes the rise and fall of two branches of an aristocratic family in Beijing, who live in adjacent plots in the capital. Their plots are joined by a magnificent garden with several pavillions in it, and the young, mostly female members of both families are allowed to live in them. One day the management of the garden is taken over by a young woman, Tan-Chun, who states:

"I think we ought to pick out a few experienced trust-worthy old women from among the ones who work in the Garden—women who know something about gardening already—and put the upkeep of the Garden into their hands. We needn't ask them to pay us rent; all we need ask them for is an annual share of the produce. There would be four advantages in this arrangement. In the first place, if we have people whose sole occupation is to look after trees and flowers and so on, the condition of the Garden will improve gradually year after year and there will be no more of those long periods of neglect followed by bursts of feverish activity when things have been allowed to get out of hand. Secondly there won't be the spoiling and wastage we get at present. Thirdly the women themselves will gain a little extra to add to their incomes which will compensate them for the hard work they put in throughout the year. And fourthly, there's no reason why we shouldn't use the money we should otherwise have spent on nurserymen, rockery specialists, horticultural cleaners and so on for other purposes."

As the story goes on, the capitalist privatization—because that is what it is—of the Garden is carried through, and it works. When in the 1980s Deng Xiaoping allowed privatization in the Chinese villages, it also worked. It worked so well that its effects started to be felt in politics and threatened the existing political order; hence the knockdown at Tienanmen Square of June 1989. But it seems that the forces of privatization are getting the upper hand again in China. If we remember what Chinese entrepreneurs are able to do once they have become Overseas Chinese, we shouldn't be too surprised. But what works in China—and worked two centuries ago—does not have to work in Russia, not in Tolstoy's days and not today. I am not offering a solution; I only protest against a naive universalism that knows only one recipe for development, the one supposed to have worked in the United States.

A Theory of Culture in Management

Our trip around the world is over and we are back in the United States. What have we learned? There is something in all countries called "management," but its meaning differs to a larger or smaller extent from one country to the other, and it takes considerable historical and cultural insight into local conditions to understand its processes, philosophies, and problems; If already the world may mean so many different things, how can we expect one country's theories of management to apply abroad? One should be extremely careful in making this assumption, and test it

Global Business **45**

before considering it proven. Management is not a phenomenon that can be isolated from other processes taking place in a society. During our trip around the world we saw that it interacts with what happens in the family, at school, in politics, and government. It is obviously also related to religion and to beliefs about science. Theories of management always had to be interdisciplinary, but if we cross national borders they should become more interdisciplinary than ever.

Cultural differences between nations can be, to some extent, described using first four, and now five, bipolar *dimensions*. The position of a country on these dimensions allows us to make some predictions on the way their society operates, including their management processes and the kind of theories applicable to their management.

As the word culture plays such an important role in my theory, let me give you my definition, which differs from some other very respectable definitions. Culture to me is *the collective programming of the mind which distinguishes one group or category of people from another.* In the part of my work I am referring to now, the category of people is the nation.

Culture is a construct, that means it is "not directly accessible to observation but inferable from verbal statements and other behaviors and useful in predicting still other observable and measurable verbal and nonverbal behavior." It should not be reified; it is an auxiliary concept that should be used as long as it proves useful but bypassed where we can predict behaviors without it.

The same applies to the *dimensions* I introduced. They are constructs too that should not be reified. They do not "exist"; they are tools for analysis which may or may not clarify a situation. In my statistical analysis of empirical data the first four dimensions together explain forty-nine percent of the variance in the data. The other fifty-one percent remain specific to individual countries.

The first four dimensions were initially detected through a comparison of the values of similar people (employees and managers) in sixty-four national subsidiaries of the IBM Corporation. People working for the same multinational, but in different countries, represent very well-matched samples from the populations of their countries, similar in all respects except nationality.

The first dimension is labelled *Power Distance,* and it can be defined as the degree of inequality among people which the population of a country considers as normal: from relatively equal (that is, small power distance) to extremely unequal (large power distance). All societies are unequal, but some are more unequal than others.

The second dimension is labelled *Individualism*, and it is the degree to which people in a country prefer to act as individuals rather than as members of groups. The opposite of individualism can be called *Collectivism*, so collectivism is low individualism. The way I use the word it has no political connotations. In collectivist societies a child learns to respect the group to which it belongs, usually the family, and to differentiate between in-group members and out-group members (that is, all other people). When children grow up they remain members of their group, and they expect the group to protect them when they are in trouble. In return, they have to remain loyal to their group throughout life. In individualist societies, a child learns very early to think of itself as "I" instead of as part of "we". It expects one day to have to stand on its own feet and not to get protection from its group any more; and therefore it also does not feel a need for strong loyalty.

The third dimension is called *Masculinity* and its opposite pole *Femininity*. It is the degree to which tough values like assertiveness, performance, success and competition, which is nearly all societies are associated with the role of men, prevail over tender values like the quality of life, maintaining warm personal relationships, service, care for the weak, and solidarity, which in nearly all societies are more associated with women's roles. Women's roles differ from men's roles in all countries; but in tough societies, the differences are larger than in tender ones.

The fourth dimension is labelled *Uncertainty Avoidance*, and it can be defined as the degree to which people in a country prefer structured over unstructured situations. Structured situations are those in which there are clear rules as to how one should behave. These rules can be written down, but they can also be unwritten and imposed by tradition. In countries which score high on uncertainty avoidance, people tend to show more nervous energy, while in countries which score low, people are more easy-going. A (national) society with strong uncertainty avoidance can be called rigid; one with weak uncertainty avoidance, flexible. In countries where uncertainty avoidance is strong a feeling prevails of "what is different, is dangerous." In weak uncertainty avoidance societies, the feeling would rather be "what is different, is curious."

The fifth dimension was added on the basis of a study of the values of students in twenty-three countries carried out by Michael Harris Bond, a Canadian working in Hong Kong. He and I had cooperated in another study of students' values which had yielded the same four dimensions as the IBM data. However, we wondered to what extent our common findings in two studies could be the effect of a Western bias introduced by the common Western background of the researchers: remember Alice's croquet game. Michael Bond resolved this dilemma by deliberately introducing an Eastern bias. He used a questionnaire prepared at his request by his Chinese colleagues, the *Chinese Value Survey* (CVS), which was translated from Chinese into different languages and answered by fifty male and fifty female students in each of twenty-three countries in all five continents. Analysis of the CVS data produced three dimensions significantly correlated with the three IBM dimensions of power distance, individualism, and masculinity. There was also a fourth dimension, but it did not resemble uncertainty avoidance. It was composed, both on the positive and on the negative side, from items that had not been included in the IBM studies but were present in the Chinese Value Survey because they were rooted in the teachings of Confucius. I labelled this dimension: *Long-term* versus *Short-term* Orientation. On the long-term side one finds values oriented towards the future, like thrift (saving) and persistence. On the short-term side one finds values rather oriented to-

Table 1 — Culture Dimension Scores for Ten Countries

PD = Power Distance; ID = Individualism; MA = Masculinity; UA = Uncertainty Avoidance; LT = Long Term Orientation
H = top third, M = medium third, L = bottom third
(among 53 countries and regions for the first four dimensions; among 23 countries for the fifth)

	PD	ID	MA	UA	LT
USA	40 L	91 H	62 H	46 L	29 L
Germany	35 L	67 H	66 H	65 M	31 M
Japan	54 M	46 M	95 H	92 H	80 H
France	68 H	71 H	43 M	86 H	30*L
Netherlands	38 L	80 H	14 L	53 M	44 M
Hong Kong	68 H	25 L	57 H	29 L	96 H
Indonesia	78 H	14 L	46 M	48 L	25*L
West Africa	77 H	20 L	46 M	54 M	16 L
Russia	95*H	50*M	40*L	90*H	10*L
China	80*H	20*L	50*M	60*M	118 H

* estimated

wards the past and present, like respect for tradition and fulfilling social obligations.

Table 1 lists the scores on all five dimensions for the United States and for the other countries we just discussed. The table shows that each country has its own configuration on the four dimensions. Some of the values in the table have been estimated based on imperfect replications or personal impressions. The different dimension scores do not "explain" all the differences in management I described earlier. To understand management in a country, one should have both knowledge of and empathy with the entire local scene. However, the scores should make us aware that people in other countries may think, feel, and act very differently from us when confronted with basic problems of society.

Idiosyncracies of American Management Theories

In comparison to other countries, the U.S. culture profile presents itself as below average on power distance and uncertainty avoidance, highly individualistic, fairly masculine, and short-term oriented. The Germans show a stronger uncertainty avoidance and less extreme individualism; the Japanese are different on all dimensions, least on power distance; the French show larger power distance and uncertainty avoidance, but are less individualistic and somewhat feminine; the Dutch resemble the Americans on the first three dimensions, but score extremely feminine and relatively long-term oriented; Hong Kong Chinese combine large power distance with weak uncertainty avoidance, collectivism, and are very long-term oriented; and so on.

The American culture profile is reflected in American management theories. I will just mention three elements not necessarily present in other countries: the stress on market processes, the stress on the individual, and the focus on managers rather than on workers.

The Stress on Market Processes

During the 1970s and 80s it has become fashionable in the United States to look at organizations from a "transaction costs" viewpoint. Economist Oliver Williamson has opposed "hierarchies" to "markets." The reasoning is that human social life consists of economic transactions between individuals. We found the same in d'Iribarne's description of the U.S. principle of the contract between employer and employee, the labor market in which the worker sells his or her labor for a price. These individuals will form hierarchical organizations when the cost of the economic transactions (such as getting information, finding out whom to trust etc.) is lower in a hierarchy than when all transactions would take place on a free market.

From a cultural perspective the important point is that the *"market"* is *the point of departure or base model*, and the organization is explained from market failure. A culture that produces such a theory is likely to prefer organizations that internally resemble markets to organizations that internally resemble more structured models, like those in Germany of France. The ideal principle of control in organizations in the market philosophy is *competition* between individuals. This philosophy fits a society that combines a not-too-large power distance with a not-too-strong uncertainty avoidance and individualism; besides the USA, it will fit all other Anglo countries.

The Stress on the Individual

I find this constantly in the design of research projects and hypotheses; also in the fact that in the U.S. psychology is clearly a more respectable

> The ideal principle of control in organizations in the market philosophy is competition between individuals.

discipline in management circles than sociology. Culture however is a collective phenomenon. Although we may get our information about culture from individuals, we have to interpret it at the level of collectivities. There are snags here known as the "ecological fallacy" and the "reverse ecological fallacy." None of the U.S. college textbooks on methodology I know deals sufficiently with the problem of multilevel analysis.

A striking example is found in the otherwise excellent book *Organizational Culture and Leadership* by Edgar H. Schein (1985). On the basis of his consulting experience he compares two large companies, nicknamed "Action" and "Multi." He explains the differences in culture between these companies by the group dynamics in their respective boardrooms. Nowhere in the book are any conclusions drawn from the fact that the first company is an American-based computer firm, and the second a Swiss-based pharmaceutics firm. This information is not even mentioned. A stress on interactions among individuals obviously fits a culture identified as the most individualistic in the world, but it will not be so well understood by the four-fifths of the world population for whom the group prevails over the individual.

One of the conclusions of my own multilevel research has been that culture at the national level and culture at the organizational level—corporate culture—are two very different phenomena and that the use of a common term for both is confusing. If we do use the common term, we should also pay attention to the occupational and the gender level of culture. National cultures differ primarily in the fundamental, invisible values held by a majority of their members, acquired in early childhood, whereas organizational cultures are a much more superficial phenomenon residing mainly in the visible practices of the organization,

> Managers are much more involved in maintaining networks: if anything, it is the rank-and-file worker who can really make decisions on his or her own, albeit on a relatively simple level.

acquired by socialization of the new members who join as young adults. National cultures change only very slowly if at all; organizational cultures may be consciously changed, although this isn't necessarily easy. This difference between the two types of culture is the secret of the existence of multinational corporations that employ, as I showed in the IBM case, employees with extremely different national cultural values. What keeps them together is a corporate culture based on common practices.

The Stress on Managers Rather than Workers

The core element of a work organization around the world is the people who do the work. All the rest is superstructure, and I hope to have demonstrated to you that it may take many different shapes. In the U.S. literature on work organization, however, the core element, if not explicitly then implicitly, is considered the manager. This may well be the result of the combination of extreme individualism with fairly strong masculinity, which has turned the manager into a culture hero of almost mythical proportions. For example, he—not really she—is supposed to make decisions all the time. Those of you who are or have been managers must know that this is a fable. Very few management decisions are just "made" as the myth suggests it. Managers are much more involved in maintaining networks; if anything, it is the rank-and-file worker who can really make decisions on his or her own, albeit on a relatively simple level.

An amusing effect of the U.S. focus on managers is that in at least ten American books and articles on management I have been misquoted as having studied IBM *managers* in my research, whereas the book clearly describes that the answers were from IBM employees. My observation may be biased, but I get the impression that compared to twenty or thirty years ago less research in this country is done among employees and more on managers. But managers derive their *raison d'être* from the people managed: culturally, they are the followers of the people they lead, and their effectiveness depends on the latter. In other parts of the world, this exclusive focus on the manager is less strong, with Japan as the supreme example.

Conclusion

This article started with *Alice in Wonderland*. In fact, the management theorist who ventures outside his or her own country into other parts of the world is like Alice in Wonderland. He or she will meet strange beings, customs, ways of organizing or disorganizing and theories that are clearly stupid, oldfashioned or even immoral—yet they may work, or at least they may not fail more frequently than corresponding theories do at home. Then, after the first culture shock, the traveller to Wonderland will feel enlightened, and may be able to take his or her experiences home and use them advantageously. All great ideas in science, politics and management have travelled from one country to another, and been enriched by foreign influences. The roots of American management theories are mainly in Europe: with Adam Smith, John Stuart Mill, Lev Tolstoy, Max Weber, Henri Fayol, Sigmund Freud, Kurt Lewin and many others. These theories were replanted here and they developed and bore fruit. The same may happen again. The last thing we need is a Monroe doctrine for management ideas.

The issues explored here were presented by Dr. Hofstede, the Foundation for Administrative Research Distinguished International Scholar, at the 1992 Annual Meeting of the Academy of Management, Las Vegas, Nevada, August 11, 1992.

Article Review Form at end of book.

Bob Kimmons has been training people to manage multinational teams which are typical of large projects around the world. How might such teams avoid the pitfall of miscommunication? How can a manager motivate such a team?

Building Effective Teams in a Multicultural Environment

Robert L. Kimmons
Kimmons-Asaro Group Ltd., Inc.

Businesses throughout the world are encountering serious difficulties in extending their operations globally. There are many problems, but certainly one of the principal ones is getting individuals with differing knowledge, backgrounds, cultures, philosophies, experiences, and skills to work together. Pertinent facts regarding this dilemma can be summarized as follows:

1. Many business efforts today, including introduction of organizational change, are being pursued by setting them up as projects.
2. Most projects require a team of people working closely together to ensure success.
3. Business is becoming more international in nature.
4. Migration of peoples from different areas of the world has created a probability of cultural difference even in basically local endeavors.
5. Team members are recruited to work in multinational teams, with each member working in the areas of his or her particular expertise.
6. Team members, more and more, are bringing the diversity of their own cultural influences and philosophies—this is true whether the project is located in West Texas or in Lagos, Nigeria.

Project management differs from functional management in that the effort has a defined purpose and the work on the project is limited to a finite time period. Projects are also characterized by a shortage of many of the resources needed to do the work, such as skilled personnel, equipment needed for the work, time to accomplish the work, and the funds required to meet the project objectives.

Because of the limited time available, the thinking of the team members must be aligned rapidly. Many successful project managers in the past were characterized by an autocratic approach to dealing with their team members. This meant that the project manager had to have an in-depth knowledge of all aspects of the work. Today, rapidly developing technology and increasingly complex assignments support a team approach to projects.

Studies show that the single cause of an unsuccessful outcome for many projects is the failure to clearly define the desired outcome early. Another factor is the inability to get the project team to become cohesive in the short period of time allowed. Some firms are using a specific approach to maximize the probability of achieving the objectives set forth at the beginning of the project. This approach involves following specific work processes that involve the logical development of project strategies:

- Be sure that all team members *fully understand the scope of work* involved, as well as the part each will play in completing it.

- Inform the team members of the *prioritized project objectives*. These objectives are set by those who are funding the project and who have agreed to the proposed scope of work.

- Communicate any *project constraints*, necessary *assumptions*, and *pending decisions* that may influence how the work will be accomplished.

- Determine what portion of the work will be done with personnel from inside the organization and what part will be contracted out to other firms.

A Project Planning Workshop is an effective way of making sure that these elements are comprehended. All key members of the project team from each organization that might be involved in doing the work are invited to attend the workshop. After the previous three points have been

"Building Effective Teams in a Multicultural Environment," Robert L. Kimmons. Reprinted by permission of the author.

presented and any questions answered, team members are asked to:

- Pinpoint any potential problems that may result in the project objectives not being achieved. These might also be considered risks to the successful project.

This portion of workshop is done using a brainstorming approach to encourage openness. Each team member nominates potential problems from his or her point of view and based on personal experience. All problems/risks are listed at this point in no particular order. The next step is to:

- Evaluate all of the listed potential problems from two aspects:
  1. What will be the impact if the risk occurs?
  2. What is the probability that risk will occur?

Both the impact (usually expressed in monetary terms) and the probability of each risk/problem are evaluated as being "high," "medium," or "low." Note that this evaluation at this point is by no means quantitative.

Those rated as being "high" risk and "high" probability are used in developing the project strategies.

- Develop the project strategies

Up to this point, the question of "what" has been considered. All team members have had an opportunity to question and discuss the completeness of the information. Generally, in a multicultural context, "what" is not a problem if understanding can be reached. The problems come with "how" the work will be done.

A convenient method of coming up with appropriate strategies involves the use of a matrix such as shown in Figure 1. The risks/problems are listed in the left-hand column in descending order of priority based on the evaluation.

The risks are discussed, one at a time, along with the pros and cons of how these risks should be managed.

Risks can be managed by (1) eliminating the risk if possible, (2) minimizing the risk if this can be done, (3) transferring the risk to others if this can be achieved (contracting out or outsourcing), or finally (4) accepting the risk and providing for it with contingency plans.

Figure 1 Matrix Used to Develop Contracting Strategy

Strategies → / Anticipated Risks ↓	Management Strategy #1	Management Strategy #2	Management Strategy #3	Management Strategy #4	Management Strategy #5	Management Strategy #6	Management Strategy #7	Management Strategy #8	Management Strategy #9	Management Strategy #10	Management Strategy #11	Management Strategy #12	Management Strategy #13	Management Strategy #14
Risk #A	✔	✔	✔											
Risk #B		✔	✔							✔				
Risk #C	✔			✔	✔	✔	✔							
Risk #D			✔					✔	✔	✔				
Risk #E								✔				✔	✔	
Risk #F	✔		✔								✔		✔	
Risk #G					✔		✔							✔
Risk #H												✔		
Risk #I	✔			✔										

Individual strategies for managing each of the risks are noted by placing a check mark in the proper square of the matrix. For a given risk, there may be multiple strategies. Everyone is given an opportunity to voice an opinion. During this exercise, all of the team members become aware of not only how each of the risks is to be approached, but more importantly, why it is being done this way. Alignment of the team is underway.

It is during this period that differences in experience, background, culture, and philosophy are all addressed. A consensus is reached as to the most effective manner of handling each of the identified risks.

Multiple check marks in one of the vertical columns of the matrix represent a major strategy. Multiple check marks in one of the horizontal rows of the matrix mean that various strategies will be identified to protect against missing the project objectives because of that one risk.

Based on the information contained in the completed strategy matrix and, after the workshop, the project manager prepares the project strategy in narrative form. The project strategy is a brief but comprehensive document that represents the consensus of how the project is to be done based on the combined input from all of the team members.

The next step is complete documentation of the project execution plan, which sets forth the detail called for by the project strategy. This allows for detailed schedules for the work as well as the ability to firm up the cost estimates.

The workshop is a practical and cost-effective approach to multicultural team building. It is not publicized as a "team-building" exercise, but rather as a planning workshop. The necessary early results are normally obtained because of the opportunity team members have to become acquainted with each other in a nonadversarial environment. *How* the project is to be done comes from joint resolution as to the best methods. Because the team members are all involved and have specific goals for the workshop, they end up understanding *why* things are being done in a specific manner.

The purpose of the Project Planning Workshop is to align the thinking of all of the team members, to consider the input of each member, and to provide a clear road map of how the work will be done. People throughout the world want to do a "good job" but, to achieve the best results, their individual input must be considered wherever there are differences that will impact the way those results are to be obtained.

Article Review Form at end of book.

How did Pharmco transform its managers from people with only home office experience to professionals who successfully work with foreign colleagues? In what way were employees involved in creating this intercultural education process?

Using Cultural Skills for Cooperative Advantage in Japan

Richard H. Reeves-Ellington

Through trial and error, American managers who do business in Japan have learned to gain insight into the Japanese culture. Nonetheless, most American managers remain uneasy dealing with their Japanese counterparts, and "home office" continues to be suspicious of Japanese business practices. This situation produces ineffective business relationships and poor business results. The paradigm of discomfort and suspicion must be replaced by one of confidence and trust if American business is to succeed in Japan.

Pharmco, a pharmaceutical subsidiary of a major US multinational, was saddled with this "home office" attitude of suspicion. Having done business in Japan for more than 20 years, it was dissatisfied with the relationships and financial arrangements with its Japanese licensees. The advent of innovative pharmaceutical technologies provided an opportunity to develop a new strategic alliance with a major Japanese company, Diversity KK. Pharmco anticipated that the alliance would facilitate rapid introduction of its technology in Japan, yield tenfold greater financial returns, and furnish the framework for learning to operate more successfully in Japan. Senior managers in the company understood that they and their staff needed to work effectively at many levels with Japanese managers and scientists in both the Japanese and American cultural environments. They had, however, no plan for learning about Japanese culture; the initial meetings between employees of the two companies resulted in more "damage control" than was desirable. The Pharmco senior manager responsible for Japanese operations, a trained anthropologist, proposed a program offering US-based managers and scientists assistance in learning about Japanese culture. As a result of the program, American-Japanese relations at Pharmco improved considerably and business operations are running smoothly.

This paper provides the practicing anthropologist with a cross-cultural learning process that encompasses business and anthropology concepts, methods, tools, and strategies. It also discusses methods used by a manager-anthropologist to transfer theoretical understanding and practical use skills to people in the organization who needed them. Finally, it demonstrates how individuals used a cultural understanding process, ethnographic data, and participant observation (PO) to get through a business day in Japan, build their own data base, and, eventually, predict Japanese social behavior in different settings. Empirical evidence is provided to demonstrate the value the program had for one company.

Underpinnings of the Program

Employee Needs

The purpose of education in the business setting is to resolve problems. This goal sets the parameters for the types of data transfer, the timing of transfer, and the format of transfer within the corporation. Within the Pharmco context, the people who needed cultural information were based in the US, worked in a variety of functions, and had to operate in several different cultures, not only Japan. Two common learning meth-

"Using Cultural Skills for Cooperative Advantage in Japan." Richard H. Reeves-Ellington. HUMAN ORGANIZATION, Vol. 52, Number 2, 1993. Reprinted by permission.

ods were thereby excluded, i.e., general reading and the use of culture-specific training courses.[1] The manager-anthropologist had to devise another method.

To determine the educational needs, he set up small-group and one-on-one meetings with managers and scientists who would be required to work on the Japanese strategic alliance. He discovered that two questions deterred employees from wanting to work with Japanese in particular and all non-Americans in general: "What do I do during a business day?" and "How can I learn to respond to the various situations I might find myself in while travelling in foreign cultures?"[2] the initial training objective, therefore, was to offer assistance in getting through a Japanese business day while at the same time providing the tools and processes to enable employees to gain cultural understanding and apply their learning to other cultural contexts.

Program Needs

The program required the adoption of total quality tools, a policy deployment model, participant observation methodology, and concepts of culture in ways that employees would understand them intellectually and to be able to use them.[3] The manager-anthropologist relied on previously developed materials as a starting point.[4] These were integrated into a holistic program for the Japan learning program. The resulting cultural learning process was designed to enable its users to generate knowledge that would allow each of them to interact with foreigners in culturally meaningful ways.

Understanding and Predicting Culture

Most anthropological research is geared to understanding societies and their cultures. The needs of business people working in the international environment also need to understand and be able to work successfully in a different culture, i.e., to become at least partially accepted by the natives. To achieve successful behavior, a process is needed for collecting and storing ethnographic values and cultural data. The process discussed below was developed in conjunction with the managers who would use it and had to meet five criteria: (1) be adaptable to a variety of situations and cultures; (2) be easily understood to allow input of data; (3) permit revision as new data became available; (4) allow data to be entered in any data base without being contingent on data in one of the other data bases; and (5) provide a means to develop common vocabulary and understanding amongst those using the process but not force total consensus of data classification in each data base. Each person using the process was responsible for its maintenance and no efforts to audit individual usage were attempted unless requested. Everyone using the process did request such help from the manager-anthropologist on at least two separate occasions.[5]

Developing a Cross-Cultural Understanding Process

Working in a foreign culture with a reasonable comfort level requires a general understanding of the concept of culture and a generalized understanding of the country in which work is to be accomplished. Gaining this cultural understanding demands a grasp of the broad concepts of culture (Redfield 1962) and an understanding that the concept of culture is essentially semiotic (an expression of linguistic logic) (Geertz 1973, White 1949). This level of cultural abstraction is useful to the leader trying to predict cultural events (Reeves-Ellington and Steidlmeier 1991) but Pharmco required an understanding of culture that would raise people's consciousness of implicit assumptions that explain why we do things (Smircich 1985). To make the concept of culture more concrete to Pharmco executives, Schein's concept of culture, *"a set of understandings (habits) shared among persons who are similarly socialized"* (Schein 1985), has been joined to the thought that *"the understandings are the intersection of knowledge, skill, and desire"* (Covey 1989).

A generalized (macro level) cultural understanding is the starting point required to function meaningfully in a culture. The macro level provides the outsider an understanding of the world view of a culture (Geertz 1973). Failure to work within the symbols of a culture dooms one to be an eternal outsider. The cross-cultural understanding process, Understanding and Predicting Culture (Figure 1), was based on the work of Schein (1985) Kluckhohn and Strodbeck (1961), Hofstede (1980), and Finan and van Willigen (1990). It allowed Pharmco managers to examine a culture at both the macro and micro level. The process was also designed as a tool to answer the critical question of how ethnographic knowledge of another culture can be transmitted to others. (Appell and Madan 1988). Total quality techniques, particularly the Plan-Do-Check-Act (PDCA) cycle were incorporated into the process.

ARTIFACTS represent those things that can be seen or heard, e.g., how offices are laid out, how people run meetings, and how honorifics are used in interactional situations, including the "who-what-where-when" part of getting a story. SOCIAL KNOWLEDGE (VALUES) includes the social processes and values that people can explain when questioned, e.g., "why and how" people act as they do. CULTURAL LOGIC provides the facts that will answer the "why" about the most fundamental relationships people have to others, to their environment, to truth and reality, to understanding human nature, to time.

Although the three data bases are important, they are static, inert, and quickly outdated if an improvement step is not incorporated into the process. Improvement, through frequent updating, is demonstrated in the process by encircling the three data bases with a PDCA cycle (Deming 1982, Imai 1986, Ishikawa, 1986, Rohrer 1990). Use of the data bases starts with the PLANNING part of the PDCA cycle and includes issue selection, initial situation, cause analysis, and organizational use plan. An important issue for Pharmco is to understand country cultures in a generalized way and specific company cultures in a detailed way. After selecting a specific issue, one continues the planning process by reviewing the artifact data base, determining what is known, and defining the initial situation. One then moves to step three and looks into the underling values and cultural logic to gain better understanding of what has been seen and heard. One then develops a formal plan to apply the knowledge gained from the data bases. At this point, one enters into the DO part of the PDCA cycle and begins the plan execution by using the learning. Immediately upon completion of the executional phase, one starts the CHECK section of the PDCA cycle by confirming what was learned, adding new information into the appropriate data base, and then adjusting the use of learning by altering the organizational plan. One makes adjustments to the plan and alters the action plan as appropriate in the ACT phase of the PDCA cycle. Then the PLAN cycle begins again. This process keeps the data base current and the action plans based in the latest information available. With this information base and understanding, *from the perspective of a participant of a culture* the user of the model can develop effective means to interact within a foreign culture. The crosscultural understanding process meets Quinn and McGrath's demand: "There is a need for a dynamic theory that can handle both stability and change, that can consider the tensions and conflicts inherent in human systems" (1985:316).

The process has proved valuable because it serves as a process that allows the user to understand what is culturally important in a society and probe more deeply in understanding key elements. It stimulates the user to focus on important aspects of culture that may affect personal and organizational success. This focus is required if coordinated action is to be achieved. It permits the user to handle the data in an organized way and share information learned with others. It also allows the user to review periodically those elements considered important and to analyze further elements not yet clearly understood.

Manager as Ethnologist and Participant Observer

For the "Understanding and Predicting Culture Process" to yield useful information and knowledge, sound ethnographic input is required. As reported by Eliade, "Concreteness (of culture) will be accentuated by the studies of the ethnologist." He further says," . . . the ethnologist will succeed in showing

Figure 1 Understanding and predicting culture.

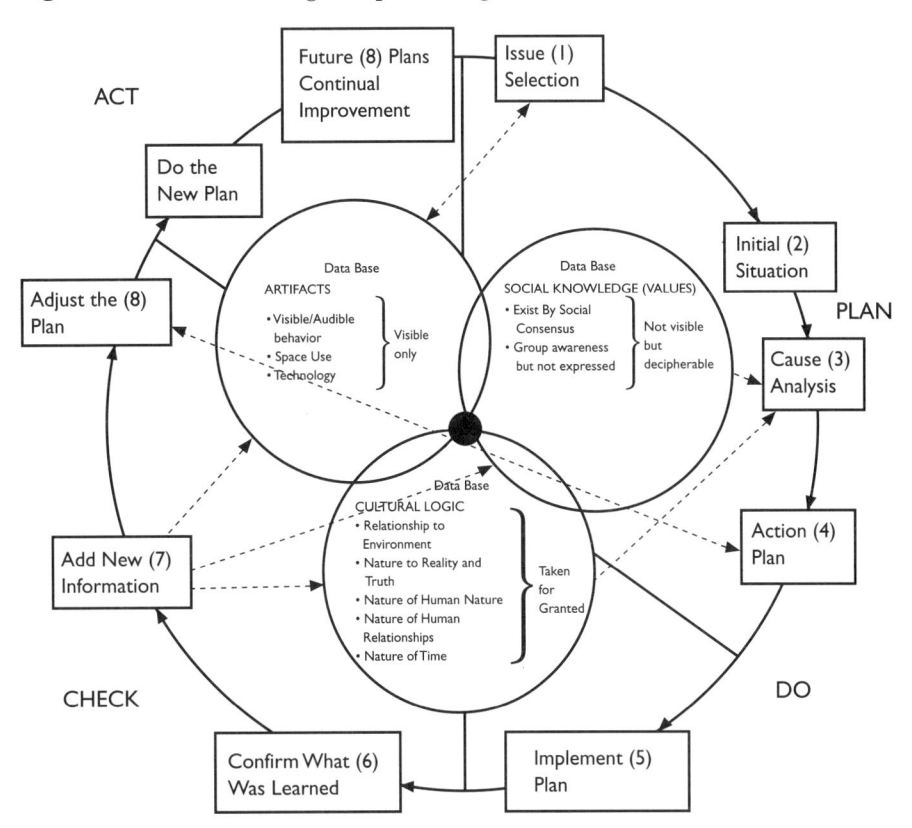

the circulation of the particular motif in time and space . . ." (Eliade 1974:xii–xiii). The anthropological research method of participant observation (PO) provides a preferred technique for collecting ethnographic information that fits the cultural understanding process described and, therefore, warrants detailed discussion of good participant observer methodology.

Managers need a methodological tool to help them comprehend information as others see it. PO skills, traditionally employed by the anthropologist (Chambers 1985, Spradley 1980, Finan and van Willigen 1990), provide a tool that permits the business person to develop and use the needed channels of communication. The task of the participant observer is to find out what is important to others (Jorgensen 1989). It involves making accessible what is normally concealed (that is, backstage and common sense information from another person's point of view) (David 1985). Business people who employ this skill are better able to relate to those around them and to plan meaningful interactions with others.

PO is a style of behavior that creates social relationships between people and a favorable environment for achieving mutually agreed tasks. The key point is that the participant observer spends time with others and does things with them.

Participant Observer Techniques

Participant observation requires a combination of direct observation and questioning techniques. These techniques allow ongoing systematic acquisition of findings about what is important to people.

Gaining needed information about others requires active listening. The two main objectives of active listening are to hear what is meant, if in a language that can be understood, listen for the vocabulary chosen and voice inflections used and to listen (with the eyes) for non-verbal messages (Covey 1989, Hall and Hall 1987).

Participant Observer—Specific Plans

The participant observer requires specific plans for action that will move from what is easily known to what is normally concealed. There are five action strategies that will aid in gaining concealed information (Table 1).

Training Program

The underlying rationale for providing Pharmco managers and researchers with the ability to understand and work in Japanese culture is best expressed by Dorothy Lee (1963:62–63):

> The clarity of the structure within which I find myself—that is, the "social constraint" . . . makes it possible for me to act . . . when I live in dialogue with this structure . . . . It makes it possible for me to proceed in what would otherwise be a confusing jungle: it makes it possible for me to function.

Involvement of an Insider Anthropologist

The manager-anthropologist responsible for Japan operations provided all training that took place over a five year period and involved ten sets of employees. Training content included "horror" stories of what goes wrong in US-Japanese relationships, examples of successful activities and processes for increasing the chances of success,[6] and practice in using all the material discussed and presented. Material selection depended on the previous experience of members of the group in multicultural settings. Initial sessions were timed approximately two weeks before contacts with Japanese counterparts. This timing coincided with the peak interest employees had in learning the information. All training was done at the employees' work site, allowing them a greater comfort level. The manager-anthropologist was present at all initial meetings between US employees and their Japanese contacts, and he continued to be present until the Americans expressed confidence that he was not needed at future meetings. This decision usually occurred after four or five meetings. After each meeting, the US team would meet and undergo a debriefing as to what knowledge had been confirmed and what was new. Differing perceptions were discussed and analyzed. Active participation for the manager-anthropologist with any group was about two years,[7] after which he was present only when business needs dictated, but always on call

Table 1 — Strategies of Action

Appear to know to find out
This is useful in Japan because the Japanese like to gossip and teach. Once Pharmco learned about the transfer of a Diversity colleague before it was common knowledge. When the fact was mentioned to a Diversity employee, he promptly gave the full background of the transfer which provided additional insights into internal power systems and processes of Diversity.

Backstage information gets more backstage information
Building on the above case, another Pharmco manager discussed the matter with yet another Diversity employee, prompting Diversity managers to share information about major reorganization plans currently being considered in Tokyo, including potential winners and losers. This information was extremely helpful in Pharmco's management of relations with Diversity.

Use others as teachers
In order to learn about Diversity corporate culture, Pharmco Staff assumed the role as student to Japanese counterparts. In order to gain information in some degree of order, the old journalism framework of "who-what-where-when-how-why" is suggested for use. Of particular importance is to stress the "why" as most business people fail to grasp the importance of this question.

Rank others as witnesses, informants, backstagers
Pharmco staff, when doing business with Diversity, kept a log of all contacts relating to their value as witnesses, e.g., confirm cultural information learned; informants, e.g., teach about cultural manners; or backstagers, e.g., gossip. A review of classification was required periodically. Often different people classify colleagues differently by different people in the organization.

Claim to really need the information
When supplying information needed by another person, the Japanese responds because he believes that, by doing so, he helps to strengthen social and business bonds; a necessity for doing business in Japan. Pharmco has found that once the strategy is invoked by one of its managers, the manager must be prepared to reciprocate. This is of particular importance as reciprocity is the basis of relationships. Thus much more knowledge transfer is required when doing business in Japan.

---

should his services be required. After withdrawing from direct active participation, the manager continued to provide those working with Japanese information of particular interest to their work.

The goal of training was that, through better understanding of Japan, employees would change their normal behavior patterns when working with Japanese counterparts. All improved their ability to work cross-culturally, but not all applied the material learned equally. Managers, in particular, had less patience to learn "how to do things," but rather just wanted to know "what to do." Scientists, on the other hand, tended to apply the models and processes in a much more diligent manner.

Successful cultural training within Pharmco depended upon an anthropologist being present in Pharmco, working closely with the people who needed the training. Without this inside contact, the program would have been far less successful.

Application of the "Understanding and Predicting Culture Process" in Japan

Pharmco employees started gaining understanding of Japanese culture by gathering and understanding cultural generalities. The process described in Figure 1 was evolved through training as earlier renditions proved inadequate. Employees became more involved in the learning process by working on the tools to be used as well as applying them in a Japanese context.

Employees gathered information through visits, while in Japan, to museums, theaters, shrines, baseball games, and business meetings. They initially use the "Understanding and Predicting Culture" process by entering ethnographic data into three data sets (Table 2). The initial work session was led by the manager-anthropologist but the trainees at the session participated in data entry. While each data base can independently increase understanding, most knowledge is gained when all three sets are understood and related one to the other. After the introduction of the model, the anthropologist made no effort to suggest data classification according to anthropological criteria. Rather, Pharmco employees using the model defined classifications acceptable to and understood by them. For example, in the case of "insider-outsider," discussed under "artifacts" below, the visual artifact was the way people sat at business and dinner tables, with the concept rightly belonging in the cultural logic. Employees, however, skipped the visual and placed the cultural logic in the artifacts section. The point is that they understood what they meant.

The current meta analysis of Japanese culture used by Pharmco as baseline data is as follows:

Artifacts

How are things classified or what are the artifacts of an agreed classification system? In Japan there are two basic classification systems commonly used: (1) insider-outsider and (2) front-rear. The insider is determined in the first instance by what Nakane (1970) refers to as a "frame." By frame, she means criteria that classify and identify individuals as part of a group. In business, the most obvious is the identification by company. When introducing oneself, one says, for example, "I am Pharmco's Reeves-Ellington." Japanese frames can also be determined by locality, such as the city in which one is born or family or household affiliations. In all cases frame indicates a criterion that sets a boundary and gives a common basis to a group of individuals who are located or involved in it. Outsiders are all those who are excluded from the frame. Hence, the use of the word "foreigner" (*gaijin*) is frequent in Japan. If one is not part of the frame, i.e., Japanese (insider), then one is a foreigner (outsider) (Nakane 1970).

Front and rear in the Japanese concept are not linear, as in the western world, but circular. The front, which embodies the concept of *tata-*

Table 2	Cultural Data Bases
Artifacts	Social knowledge	Cultural logic

mae, is what is seen or what is commonly known, or frontstage, whereas the rear is what is hidden or backstage. This rear embodies the concept of *honne* commonly referred to as what is "true." In the western world, these two concepts are the flip side of a coin existing in a dichotomous relationship, but in Japan, the two concepts are a circular continuum. One folds into the next as do the rooms of a house as one walks through it. Outsiders are always kept to the front, whereas insiders are introduced to the rear (Matsumoto 1988).

The artifacts of the classifications are always determined by the situation in which people come together (Hall and Hall 1987). For example, in the inside–outside relationship, obvious manifestations are the family, localities, schools, companies, and association. Tour groups are formed to make a group of people insiders. Outsiders are those not in a particular group, e.g., family members are outsiders to the company inside group. On the other hand, fellow employees are typically outsiders to a colleague's family group. In another context, such as going on a trip together, the family and business colleagues could both be insiders, as members of the XYZ Tour group. The artifacts of the front and rear classifications can be exemplified by business meetings. Humans typically belong to a complex of groups that can be concentrically layered and are variably mutually inclusive and exclusive. The front artifacts are expressed in how people are arranged at a table and the courtesy that is extended to guests. The rear artifacts are expressed in terms of who is attending and the body language that occurs.

Social Knowledge (Values)

What are proper principles for behavior? What are the values that drive the categories and artifacts described above? In Japan, adoption of the classification systems discussed above keeps as many people on the outside as possible. One keeps one's social obliga-tions to a level that encourages self gain but eliminates all that offer less gain than one is required to give. One sees this principle in action in the Tokyo subway system. The proverbial Japanese politeness is totally absent, replaced with a "survival of the fittest" behavior pattern, which is accomplished, in part, by avoiding eye contact, thereby assuring that everyone around stays on the outside.

Keeping people on the outside embodies another principle: minimize obligations to others. The personal value that drives this principle is the desire and need for personal relationships of a meaningful nature. If too many people are insiders, personal relationships would be weakened and a fundamental value diluted.

There is a third human principle at work: everyone needs to be an insider somewhere. All Japanese are striving to be an insider in situations that will provide personal gain. In companies, they have a strong sense of being inside; on tour groups, they all do things together as insiders in a travel experience. The driving value that leads Japanese to strive for insider status is the value of acknowledging and accepting mutual interdependencies with others (*amae*) (Doi 1990).

Cultural Logic

Social knowledge or values are based on underlying cultural logic around relationships to the environment, the nature of reality, truth, human nature, human activities, human relationships, and use of time. Within a culture, these are all taken for granted, rarely understood, and almost never expressible by those living in the culture, but they are of utmost importance to foreigners wishing to live and work in that culture. An explanation of Japanese cultural logic is contained in Table 3.

Learning Ethnology and Participant Observation

Examples of Japanese ethnology and its usefulness was demonstrated by the manager-anthropologist through the use of stories.[8] They were chosen so that the students would be aware that ethnology can show "what" to do by observing what natives do. It also teaches the student to focus and to learn to ask the proper "how" and "why" of what they see. The following story exemplifies the short "ethnography" type used.

An American colleague of mine, well versed in Japanese customs, noticed while at a sushi bar counter that a Japanese gentleman sitting with an empty glass and a half-full bottle of beer next to it was looking around in anticipation. My colleague assumed that the man wanted a drink and wanted someone to fill his glass for him. From the viewpoint of American "common sense," the Japanese gentleman should have picked up the bottle, poured some beer into the glass and taken a drink; but his Japanese "common sense" seemed to preclude this. What was the gentleman's "common sense"? A Japanese gentleman does not normally go to a sushi bar alone, but with colleagues or customers. In this situation, he does not pour his own drinks; someone else in the party does so. In fact, it is rude to pour a drink for oneself. Therefore, the "common sense" thing to do is wait for someone to pour. Understanding this point of view, my American colleague poured the man a glass of beer, which resulted in a pleasant conversation.

Such stories as this demonstrate that ethnography can teach one how things work in a foreign culture (in this case Japan) and that PO skills are indispensable for this learning. The ethnographic data of prime interest to all employees initially concerned the Japanese business day. They wanted to learn about it in order to be able to successfully negotiate a business day when visiting Japan. More specifically, they wanted to know how to get through a business day with Diversity KK.[9] Only by learning what is important to their Diversity colleagues could Pharmco employees begin to appreciate what behaviors the Japanese would expect from them. Even though they collected good ethnographic data, they found the information base meaningless until it was organized into the "Understanding and Predicting Culture Process." Only then could the information be used profitably.

Table 3   Cultural Logic

Environmental relationships
Japanese, as well as other Asians, view the physical environment and human environment as intertwined and not in opposition as do most Christians (Campbell 1960, 1989; Pelzel 1974). As exemplified in Japanese gardens, humans control and shape the environment in ways that suit the artistic feeling of people. The garden denotes the desire for environmental harmony and orderliness.

Nature of truth and reality
Truth and reality are determined by situations and social contexts in which people find themselves (Hall and Hall 1987, Lebra 1976). In a social group, only the insiders determine what is true and real. The accuracy of this determination is based on the degree of harmony and orderliness obtained within the insider group.

Nature of human nature
Humans are driven by emotion and not by logic (Doi 1990b). Mutuality of love and obligation (within the context of the concept of obligation) ties closely with that of hate (Ishida 1974). This mutuality in human relations forces the concept of consensus into human social organization. Since human nature is not believed to be inherently "bad," it is assumed this behavior is caused by ignorance and not evil intent.

Nature of human relationships
Using the concept of relational value orientation (Kluckhohn and Stodbeck 1961), collaterality in human relationships is highly valued. Within this concept is the perception that uncertainty is to be avoided and much effort is put into avoiding it. Within the basic collateral value, there exists a strong power distance within organizations and generational structures (Hofstede 1980)

Nature of human activities
Activity is focused on working toward ideals of harmonious relationships and involves an orientation toward human interdependency (Doi 1990, Lebra, 1976, Hayashi 1988). Activity is necessarily done in groups and by groups.

Use of time
Time is polychronic (Hall and Hall 1988). The time system is characterized by the simultaneous occurrence of many things and by a deep involvement with people. There is more emphasis on completing transactions than holding to a schedule. A person confronted with too many subjects to be covered in too short a time, chooses to expand the time available to complete the tasks rather than reduce the number of tasks.

Theory into Practice

To get theory into practice, Pharmco decided to learn how to do introductions, meetings, leavings, dinner, and drinking in Japan.

This analysis brings to life Pharmco's learning by relating incidents about just how badly things can go wrong when there is no basis for successful behaviors leading to appropriate judgements in the course of cross-cultural activities. In spite of the mistakes made. Diversity employees were gracious and appreciative of the efforts made to behave properly. They understand that Pharmco, being foreign, will never get it exactly right in Japan—just as the Japanese will never get it exactly right in the US. Pharmco employees constantly remind themselves that they are involved in a continuous process they may never get entirely "right." There are always new and more subtle nuances to learn.

The Business Card (meishi)

During the initial meeting with the Japanese, the first item of business is introductions (See Table 4). Proper introductions require proper business cards (*meishi*). The word *meishi* is used by all people in Japan, including foreigners, because the two words, business card and *meishi*, refer to the same card but the meaning behind the card is substantially different. For this reason, *meishi* should be prepared in Japan and be ready upon arrival to do business. At the time of presenting the *meishi*, the Japanese expect the viewer of the *meishi* to examine it carefully and to remember both name and title.

Mistreatment of a Japanese businessman's *meishi* will ruin a relationship, whether new or established. Since the *meishi* is an extension of self, damage to the card is damage to the individual. Explaining this to

Table 4 Introductions at Business Meetings

Artifacts	Social knowledge	Cultural logic
Technology • Business cards • Meishi **Visual behavior** • Presentation of *meishi* by presenting card, facing recipient • Senior people present *meishi* first • Guest presents first, giving name, company affiliation, and bowing. • Hosts presents *meishi* in same sequence. • Upon sitting at conference table, all *meishi* are placed in front of recipient to assure name use.	• Once given, a card is kept—not discarded. • *Meishi* are not exchanged a second time unless there is a position change. • Before the next meeting between parties, the *meishi* is reviewed for familiarization with the people attending the meeting. • The *meishi* provides status for the owner.	**Human relations** • *Meishi* provide understanding of appropriate relations between parties. • *Meishi* takes uncertainty out of relationships. **Environment** • *Meishi* establish insider/outsider environment. • *Meishi* help establish possible obligations to environment. **Human activity** • *Meishi* help to establish human activities.

Pharmco staff was not sufficient. They did not understand the implications of the *meishi* until two stories were told to help their understanding.[10]

The importance of this point is demonstrated in the following story. A major US company was having problems with one of its distributors, and the parties seemed unable to resolve their differences. The president of the US company decided to visit Japan, meet with his counterpart in the wholesaler organization, and attempt to resolve their differences. The two had not met previously and, upon meeting, each followed proper *meishi* ritual. The American, however, did not put the Japanese counterpart's *meishi* on the table; instead he held on to it. As the conversation became heated, the American rolled up the *meishi* in his hand. Horror was recorded on the face of the Japanese businessman. The American then tore the *meishi* into bits. This was more than the Japanese could stand; he excused himself from the meeting. Shortly afterward the two companies stopped doing business with each other.

How Japanese use the *meishi* also helped Pharmco staff understand its importance. Japanese companies value a high degree of consistency in those with whom they work and in the handling of personnel within a company. Failure to demonstrate consistency toward internal employees indicates a probable inconsistency in relationships outside the company. The *meishi* can provide the Japanese executive with some indication of a company's attitude toward its employees. The Pharmco employees learned this lesson with a particularly painful outcome at a meeting with a senior Japanese executive. After the Pharmco team explained the purpose of the visit, this executive took a number of *meishi* from his desk. As he turned each of them up, he asked, "I see that I met with Mr. Hansen of your company ten years ago, where is he now?" Then came the next card, "I see I met with Mr. Harman of your company eight years ago, where is *he* now?" The question went through eight separate *meishi*. The Pharmco team leader responded each time that the particular person was no longer with the company. At the end, the Japanese executive said, "People are not treated well in your company. In our company, people do not leave until retirement." The meeting was not successful.

With this background, Pharmco staff visiting Japan have a good understanding of the *meishi* and treat it and its presentation with the respect Japanese expect.

The Conference Table

As soon as introductions are complete both sides take a seat at the conference table. In Japan, there are no round tables at business meetings. The expression "head of the table" is meaningless in a Japanese context. Understanding conference table arrangements (Table 5) leads to a successful meeting.

Seating is highly ritualistic and stylized. The power position is flanked by advisors; next come suppliers of data and information, should they be requested; and finally interested parties are seated at the extremities of the conference table (Figure 2). The person in the power seat performs all ritualistic duties for

Figure 2 Meeting room.

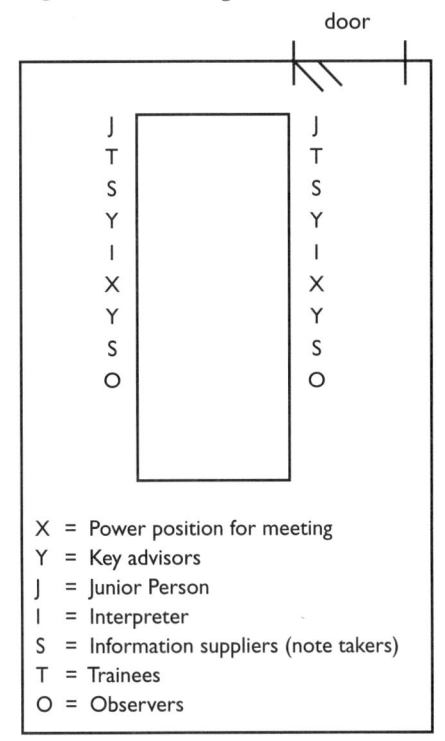

```
                    door
         ┌──────────────┐
    J    │              │    J
    T    │              │    T
    S    │              │    S
    Y    │              │    Y
    I    │              │    I
    X    │              │    X
    Y    │              │    Y
    S    │              │    S
    O    │              │    O
         └──────────────┘
```

X = Power position for meeting
Y = Key advisors
J = Junior Person
I = Interpreter
S = Information suppliers (note takers)
T = Trainees
O = Observers

Table 5 Conference Seating Arrangements

Artifacts	Social knowledge	Cultural logic
Technology • Rectangular table **Visual behavior** • Hosts on one side of the table and guests on the other. • Guests are framed by most attractive background. • The power seat is in the middle of the table. • Junior people are closest to the door.	• Set seating allows all parties social/business understanding. • Person responsible for success has the authority. • Guests are treated as customers.	**Human relations** • Seating arrangements allow established order to be known allowing a proper order and power structure to function between people. **Reality and truth** • Responsibility and authority are combined for success. • The inside and outside are maintained at the conference table. **Environment** • Used to honor customers and guests. • Used to maintain inside–outside definitions.

the side represented. That person directs all comments or questions to particular members of his team who are best qualified to answer them, and also functions as the go-between for his team and the other side.

Contrary to usual western practice, the person in the power seat is not necessarily the most senior person present. Rather, the person designated as the official contact for his company or the person most knowledgeable about the subject matter to be discussed takes the seat. The Japanese want the powerful person to be the one who can accomplish the business at hand.

Not understanding this point led to Pharmco embarrassment. Pharmco managers believed at first that the senior person present always occupied the power seat. This assumption was based on meetings between senior managers of the companies who were addressing subject matter only they could decide. When Pharmco's R&D senior manager led Pharmco's initial discussions with Diversity regarding research philosophy and programs, he correctly took the power seat. At a subsequent meeting, called to address program execution, the senior R&D manager again took the power seat. The Japanese body language indicated he should not be there. A new lesson was learned that day: expertise and subject matter, not status, determine the occupant of the power seat. In the case of program execution, the Pharmco power seat occupant should have been the senior scientist for toxicology, not the head of R&D. By taking the power seat, the R&D manager offended the Japanese scientist because he had less status and therefore felt ineffectual. The meeting was inconclusive.

Knowing who is in the power seat offers insights to the other side's agenda. At a negotiating meeting between Diversity KK and Pharmco, the Pharmco team expected the meeting to be a confirmation of work done. When the meeting started, however, the Diversity power seat was occupied by an attorney, not the familiar businessman known by Pharmco. Pharmco immediately excused themselves for a few minutes. In private caucus, the team discussed the change of people and decided that major changes in the contract under negotiation were about to be introduced. This proved to be a correct interpretation. Even this short notice helped the Pharmco team stay in control of unfolding events.

At the conclusion of the meeting leaving is as ritualistic as arriving. Table 6 provides a grasp of the ritual.

At the conclusion of a business meeting, both sides stand up to leave; the host leads the guests out of the conference room: the host's team escorts the guests to the elevator; the entire team, excluding the host, leaves the guests as the elevator doors close, both sides bowing profusely; the host joins his guests in the elevator. The remaining host and his guests then go to the front door of the office, where, if a car has been arranged, the host will get into the car if there is room and accompany his guests back to their hotel. If no car is arranged, the host will stay with the guests until a taxi is found and the guests are safely in it and driving off. The host will remain at the curb, bowing, until the taxi is well into the traffic. The guests keep eye contact, heads nodding and arms waving until the car leaves the curb.

The respect ritualistically shown is based on the status of the individual's company, not on that of the individual. By showing this level of courtesy, the hosts expect the guests to recognize that they have an obligation to reciprocate in the future, when he is on their turf.

Once Pharmco staff understood the social importance of what the Japanese were doing in seeing them off, they immediately instituted the same policy of courtesy for the Japanese when they visited the Pharmco facilities.

Going Out to Dinner

When foreigners are invited to dinner, they must be prepared to express a preference for the nationality of food to be eaten; in Japan, a preference for Japanese is obligatory because it demonstrates a willingness to engage in things "Japanese." The Japanese

Table 6 Leaving the Conference

Artifacts	Social knowledge	Cultural logic
Visual behavior • Ritualistic thank yous end the meeting while all are seated. • Conclusion of exchange means guests initiate standing. All arise. • Power person stays with guests until they are off company premises. • Bows start upon arising and continue each time one of either side leaves.	• Politeness demands guest be treated as though they were visiting the Japanese at home.	**Environment** • Guests are under control while in the Insider environment. They are left only when they achieve the outside environment. **Truth and reality** • All exchanges are tatamae to assure a smooth transition from one status to another. **Human relations** • All structured interactions require a host and a guest role.

restaurant is likely to be more comfortable and offer more privacy than others, thus creating a better relationship. A Japanese menu includes raw fish. The Japanese host will inevitably ask "Do you like raw fish?" The answer is "yes." Accepting what is offered is a necessity for relationship building in Japan, but it does not include the necessity of eating everything. Being a guest is a simple task as all that is necessary is responding to what the Japanese host suggests or discusses. The intricacies of the organization are the responsibility of the hosts.

Hosting a dinner is much more difficult than being a guest. The host is responsible for assuring a successful relationship-building event. Hosting requires an understanding of Japanese social knowledge if the event is to be successful. Three principles of social knowledge are at work in dinner meetings: (1) have an environment that permits individual members of the companies to start to become acquainted and either start building a relationship or support and maintain one; (2) provide a setting a meal befitting the guests' social position and thereby show that the host respects this position; and (3) send indirect signals of the status of the relationship in terms of the locale and quality of food. The meal can offer a form of celebration, a basis of apology[11] or just a feeling of comfort. The atmosphere created at dinner should be relaxed and enjoyable. The host is responsible for the comfort of the guests and should that comfort be threatened for any reason, the host must make certain that conviviality is restored.

Execution of these social values requires one to know when to host, how to select the right guests, how to select a proper restaurant, how to assure that the meal is a proper one, how to keep the conversation in an acceptable mood, and assure that the events starts and ends within a culturally acceptable time frame.

Determination of who hosts must be settled well in advance of the date of the dinner. The decision should not be left open until the close of a formal business meeting. If one side has an apology to make or if they have a difficult request, then they should certainly offer to host. For dinners following routine meetings, Pharmco works on the basis that if the meetings are in Japan, then the Japanese host, and if they are in the US, Pharmco hosts. This works well. If, however, the Japanese are insistent upon acting as host, it is best to follow their lead.

The attendees of any particular dinner must correlate to reciprocal status of individuals from both companies. Therefore the attendees must be agreed upon well in advance of the dinner. Any changes of attendee by one side must be announced well in advance of the dinner. For one side to change the status level of attendance at the last minute causes problems for the other. If the side making changes lowers the level of attendance, the other side has two problems to sort out. First, is a *honne* message being sent and why? For example, Japanese companies have been known to use this type of last minute change as a way to tell the other company that they want to downgrade the existing relationship between the two companies. Second, how can a Japanese manager explain such changes to his superior? If, on the other hand the level of attendance is increased at the last minute, the other might not be able to reciprocate, leading to embarrassment and a weakening of friendly relations. Attendance, once set, should not change.

The class of the restaurant must be in keeping with the status of the senior member of the party being invited, for Japanese executives have a clear understanding of where their status allows them to dine. Selection of a restaurant considered below a Japanese guest's status results in the guest losing face with his colleagues. Anticipation of this problem makes the Japanese uncomfortable during the meal, precluding the building of good social relationships. An example demonstrates the point.

Pharmco headquarters decided that the cost of entertaining in Tokyo was too high and dictated that cheaper places be found. The dictum was followed and, on the occasion of the next business meeting with a middle manager of Diversity, disaster resulted. When the guest arrived, his first comment was that one of his subordinates often brought suppliers to the restaurant. Pharmco had clearly insulted him in the choice of eating establishment, causing Pharmco managers to spend the rest of the night apologizing. Trying to

Global Business **59**

Table 7 — Going to Dinner

Artifacts	Social knowledge	Cultural logic
Physical • Guests • Restaurant • Meals • Transportation **Visual behavior** • Hosting • Guesting • Timing to eat	• Relationship building is purpose of eating. • Status is honored by correct dinners. • Dinner group has some "insider" attributes.	**Use of time** • Time at dinners is effective use of time for relations. **Relationships** • Identifies how two companies view peoples' position in hierarchy. • Confirms status matching through acceptance or non-acceptance of invitations.

rectify the situation, the next time they hosted the manager, Pharmco managers went to a very exclusive place. The first comment received was, "the president of our company likes this restaurant but I have never been here." This time, Pharmco embarrassed the Diversity manager by taking him to a location beyond his status causing him to explain to his colleagues the next day why he was there.

Avoiding these problems requires only that foreigners ask a Japanese for a restaurant preference. The answer will be "no," followed by a comment indicating a restaurant in which he has never eaten but would like to do so. If this approach fails, a visit to the social director of the hotel in which the foreigner is staying will yield dividends. By showing the director the card of the individual to be entertained, she will make appropriate selections, based on the *meishi* information of the name of the company and the title of the person. She never errs in judgment.

Selection of the restaurant leads to the selection of a suitable menu, which is done by the host in advance and must reflect the status of the guests and the nature of the occasion. For example, if it is a dinner just to end the day, a simple meal is in order. If the relationship is particularly strong, a stop in a noodle shop can be totally appropriate. If the dinner is one of celebration or a form of apology, however, a more elaborate meal is required. As with the choice of a restaurant, use Japanese expertise. A visit to the restaurant with the guest's business card and a discussion of the room and the meal with the major domo of the restaurant (a discussion that should also cover who will attend and the purpose of the meal) assures a proper menu and setting.

When Pharmco management decided to enter a strategic alliance with Diversity KK, they had to inform Nippon Pharmaceutical, a potential partner, that they had decided not to work with them. The business aspects of the decision were discussed with Nippon Pharma at their offices, but then at dinner the relationship aspects of the decision were covered. The choice of location and meal was more elaborate than would normally be the case, given the state of the relationship. At the end of the meal, the Nippon Pharma representatives complimented Pharmco on their ability to be a good Japanese host.

Conversation at dinners does not include heavy business negotiations under any but the most unusual circumstances. Talk focuses on recreational activities, current politics, travel, or other "cocktail party" chat. The point of conversation as well as of the food, is to put everyone at ease. Failure to follow this principle can cause discomfort.

At a dinner hosted by Diversity management, a Pharmco manager discussed matters relating to fundamental changes in the Japanese health care system. He did not notice that the Japanese were becoming upset until one of them exploded that "these matters were not the business of foreigners and they should not express opinions. Rather they should wait to be taught the right way to do business by the Japanese." While the foreigner thought himself at fault by not avoiding the delicate subject matter, he received an extensive apology by a colleague of the Japanese who expressed such a forceful opinion. He said, "As host, I should not permit such things to happen!"

In Japan, dinners are arranged for the end of the business day which is around 6:30 P.M. The foreign host should plan to invite his guests for a 7 P.M. dinner, as doing so will give them a half an hour to get to the restaurant. Always offer an exact time. The American habit of "let's make it around 6:30 to 7" is not acceptable. The host always should arrive a few minutes early and be there to greet his guests. At the close of the meal, the host walks the guests to the front of the restaurant, where he has had the restaurant arrange transportation. The host stands at the curb and stays there, preferably bowing or waving, until the guests have been driven off. Table 7 summarizes the critical cultural factors concerning dinner engagements.

Drinking in Bars

Going out to drink after dinner is the first opportunity for colleagues of different companies to have the chance to behave as a set of "insiders." It also provides a setting in which anyone of the group can express a *honne* sentiment. Drinking provides the foreigner a sense of how relationship-building is progressing between his company, himself and his Japanese counterparts. Therefore, ethnographic understanding of ritual drinking is imperative (Table 8).

"Knowing how to sing," was the key learned by Pharmco management before going out drinking after

Table 8 Going Out Drinking

Artifacts	Social knowledge	Cultural logic
Physical • Karaoke bars • Tabs • Female social managers **Visual behavior** • Singing • Joking • Honest Opinion	• Freedom of speech acceptable. • Drunken behavior acceptable. • Place to get things "off the chest." • Everyone can be an "insider."	**Human relations** • Provides a time for *honne* talk. • Fills the need for business associates to be a set of "insiders." **Environment** • Setting is outside a traditional "insider" setting, allowing a new set of "insiders" to be formed on "neutral" ground. **Reality and truth** • Feelings (reality) must be expressed and understood (truth) by an insider group.

dinner. Drinking in Karaoke bars is the ultimate socializing and relationship building mechanism with and among Japanese. Power and social distance are almost completely broken down at the bars. The president as well as the most junior person present will sing, tell jokes, and generally relax. Although there is still not a round table, all the people together act as though they are at one. The environment has also changed substantially from that of the office. The bar is smaller than the office, and women are an important addition as they are to provide conversation and pour the drinks.[12] The tables are laid out so that there is little structure in physical environment. A basic assumption is that this is the one place in the entire social milieu where uncertainty is acceptable. The assumption is that, with drink, it is totally acceptable to say what is on your mind to whomever you want. A further assumption is that whatever is said cannot be held against a person after leaving the bar.

Being there makes one an insider for the time spent together in the bar. "Insidership" is created only if the proper bar is chosen—one befitting the status of the group. Unlike choosing a restaurant, however, the foreigner must ask his Japanese associates for advice as to where to go, for they know that the foreigner lacks the knowledge to make a proper selection. A Pharmco executive experienced near-disaster the one time he selected a bar without consulting a Japanese businessman. He had found the hotel social relations director helpful with restaurants so thought that person would be a good source of information for bars. It was not. As soon as he walked in the bar recommended by the director, he knew there was a problem: except for one or two Japanese only foreigners were present; the bar was almost empty; and the hostesses ranged in age from 40 to 50—far too old for the tastes of the Japanese guests. Fortunately, relationships between the Pharmco executive and his Japanese guests was strong enough for everyone to get a good laugh from the situation. He is still periodically reminded of the incident.

Business is usually not done at the bar, where drinking offers the Japanese an opportunity to express *honne* opinions about his relationships with colleagues, both foreign and Japanese. These opinions are tolerable as they are expressed when the person expressing them is acceptably drunk. Within the drinking context, everyone is in the same social circle. For this reason, one must constantly be alert for signals that might indicate something is on a colleague's mind. At one drinking session, a Pharmco manager felt that something was bothering his Japanese counterpart but, as the evening wore on, nothing was said. Just before it ended, the Japanese manager put his face down on the table and muttered that he had something important to say. The American leaned forward and asked what it was. All the Japanese said was "Your Johns-san is an asshole." Nothing more was said and the subject was never raised again. The American assumed that just stating the opinion was enough to relieve the tension the Japanese had. The opinion was not reported to Johns. The next business day discussions with the Japanese gentleman were more relaxed than had been previously experienced.

Pharmco Business Improvements

Three critical factors were deemed necessary for the program to be judged a success: (1) effective working relationships with Japanese executives; (2) shortened project times; and (3) improved financial returns. The project is successful based on these factors (Table 9) and is in the process of being applied to other countries.

Before learning the methodologies and skills outlined in this paper, Pharmco executives avoided travel to Japan and working with Japanese whenever possible. Fifty Pharmco executives have been through the training program. Before the program, they were asked to evaluate their comfort level of working with Japanese and their enjoyment of business trips to Japan. The rating scale was 1 to 10 and 1 expressing no comfort and no enjoyment to 10 expressing total comfort and enjoyment. The average score was 3 with a range of 1 to 5. After exposure to the concepts, tools, and material, the average score increased to 6, with a range of 5 to 9. The final measurement was based on 15 executives who used the concepts

Table 9 Critical Factors Outcome

Effective working relationships
1. Pharmco employees are more self-assured when meeting Japanese in Japan.
2. Their Japanese counterparts state they prefer working with Pharmco over other foreign companies.

Shortened project times
1. Prior to introducing the cultural material, projects between Pharmco and Diversity averaged 15 months to completion.
2. Projects run by executives applying cultural methodologies shortened project completion times to an average of 8 months, while all others remain at 15 months.

Improved financial returns
1. Financial returns based on contracts negotiated by personnel not exposed to the cultural material average gross income of 6% of sales.
2. Financial returns of contracts negotiated by personnel applying the anthropological techniques provide gross income equal to 18% of sales.

---

and tools in their next series of meetings. The average score of this group was 8, with a low score of 5 and a high score of 10. Before the program, most employees wanted to be accompanied to Japan by a person experienced in Japan. After the exposure, almost all are comfortable making these trips on their own. This willingness to work in and with Japan has improved personal effectiveness of all these employees working on Japanese projects.

Late delivery of projects was costly to Pharmco and discouraged Diversity managers from working with their Pharmco counterparts. In one case the delays were estimated to cost Pharmco $90 million over a ten year period. The delays were of a nature that a competitor entered the market with a similar product, thereby denying innovator status to Pharmco. The improved delivery times are helping both Diversity and Pharmco in gaining valuable marketing time over their key competitors.

Summary

The ability to work with and within a foreign culture requires an organization to adopt and implement an interpretive strategy that permits its practitioners to set out to work proactively within the perceived meaning of the foreign environment. This strategy requires managers to become transformational in order to operate successfully in other social and institutional environments. Successful implementation of such a strategy demands the use of both business and anthropological tools and skills. By creating a base of these skills and providing a training environment in which employees individually could learn and implement such a strategy, Pharmco achieved dramatic improvements in its Japanese business relationships and business results. This success has led to adapting the training to other countries.

Notes

1. Most consulting companies in this field service the employee transferred to or from the home corporate culture for several years. Few serve employees who travel to different cultures for one or two week assignments. Moreover, many corporations are unwilling to finance such courses for employees on short-term assignments.
2. All the employees lived in a rural environment. None spoke a foreign language, and some had never travelled outside the US.
3. Hamada (1991:6) has confirmed these models, tools, and methods to be useful for foreigners wishing to do business in Japan.
4. The material referenced had been developed specifically for Pharmco and included work on values, based on Kluckhohn (1961) and Kluckhohn and Strodtbeck (1961), participant observer techniques developed by Dr. Kenneth David of Michigan State University, policy deployment concepts and techniques (Rohrer 1990), cultural understanding models originally conceived by Schein (1985) and adapted (Reeves-Ellington 1988).
5. There were requests to provide a computer application for the data bases in the cultural understanding process. This need still exists.
6. The material initially provided came from the manager-anthropologist's personal experience (21 years of doing business with the Japanese). As the employee experience base was accumulated, it was used for explanation and clarification.
7. Over the two years, learning was expanded to the nuances of cross-cultural memo and report writing, understanding how "full information" is defined, agenda setting, and many other activities. The direction of the expanded learning depended on the business problem at hand.
8. This parallels the technique used by Brislin et al. (1986). In the Pharmco case, however, each employee is responsible for writing an individual set of cross-cultural interactions from which proper behavior can be learned and predicted. With Brislin, one is limited to the set of data provided.
9. This was the starting point of learning. As the program progressed, various students applied their learning to far more complex issues, but this discussion is outside the scope of this paper.
10. The most meaningful stories come from incidents that occur inside the company, but when they are not available others will suffice.
11. In Japan, the concept of apology involves a great shame for not having behaved correctly or done something in the right way. To apologize is traumatic for a Japanese.
12. Apologies are necessary for my female colleagues for this chauvinistic viewpoint. It is how things are in Japan, however, I would like to point out that should a female colleague be part of the group visiting the bar, she would be treated as a colleague by her peers and be well received by the employees in the bar.

References Cited

Appell, G. N. and T. N. Madan, eds.
  1988 Choice and Morality in Anthropological Perspective. Albany: SUNY press.
Brislin, Richard W., Kenneth Cushner, Craig Cherrie, and Mehealani Yong
  1986 Intercultural Interactions: A Practical Guide. Beverly Hills, CA: Sage.
Campbell, Joseph
  1960 The Masks of God: Primitive Mythology. New York: Viking Press.
  1989 The Hero with a Thousand Faces. New York: Viking Press.
Caudill, William and Harry A. Scarr
  1974 Japanese Value Orientations and Culture Change. In Japanese Culture and Behavior. Takie Sugiyama Lebra and William P. Lebra, eds. Pp. 37–89. Honolulu: University Press of Hawaii.
Chambers, Erve
  1985 Applied Anthropology: A Practical Guide. Prospect Heights, IL: Waveland Press.
Covey, Stephen R.
  1989 The Seven Habits of Highly Effective People. New York: Simon and Schuster.

David, Kenneth
　1985 Participant Observation in Pharmaceutical Field Selling. Norwich, CT: Norwich Eaton Pharmaceutical Co., Inc.
Deming, Edward W.
　1982 Quality, Productivity, and Competitive Position. Cambridge, MA: Massachusetts Institute of Technology.
Doi, Takeo
　1990a The Anatomy of Dependence. Tokyo: Kodansha International.
　1990b The Anatomy of Self. Tokyo: Kodansha International.
Eliade, Mircea
　1974 Shamanism: Archaic Techniques of Ecstasy. Princeton, NJ: Princeton University Press.
Finan, Timothy J. and John van Willigen
　1990 The Pursuit of Social Knowledge: Methodology and Practice of Anthropology. *In* Soundings: Rapid and Reliable Research Methods for Practicing Anthropologists. John van Willigen and Timothy J. Finan, eds. Pp. 1–9. Washington, DC: American Anthropological Association.
Geertz, Clifford
　1973 The Interpretation of Cultures. New York: Basic Books.
Hall, Edward T. and Mildred R. Hall
　1987 Hidden Differences. New York: Anchor Press.
Hamada, Tomoko
　1991 American Enterprise in Japan. Albany: SUNY Press.
Hayashi, Shuji
　1988 Culture and Management in Japan. Tokyo: University of Tokyo Press.
Hofstede, Geert
　1980 Culture's Consequences: International Differences in Work-Related Values. Beverly Hills, CA: Sage.
Imai, Masaaki
　1986 Kaizen. New York: Random House.
Ishida, Eiichiro
　1974 A Culture of Love and Hate. *In* Japanese Culture and Behavior. Takie Sugiyama Lebra and William P. Lebra, eds. Pp. 27–36. Honolulu: University Press of Hawaii.
Ihsikawa, Kaoru
　1986 Guide to Quality Control. New York: Kraus International Publications.
Jorgensen, Danny L.
　1989 Participant Observation: A Methodology for Human Studies. Newbury Park, CA: Sage.
Kluckhohn, F. R.
　1962 Culture and Behavior. New York: Doubleday.
Kluckhohn, F. R. and F. L. Strodtbeck
　1961 Variations in Value Orientations. Westport, CT: Greenwood Press.
Lebra, Takie Sugiyama
　1976 Japanese Patterns of Behavior. Honolulu: University Press of Hawaii.
Lee, Dorothy
　1963 Freedom and Social Constraint. *In* The Concept of Freedom in Anthropology. David Bidney, ed. Pp. 61–92. The Hague: Mouton.
Matsumoto, Michihiro
　1988 The Unspoken Way. Tokyo: Kodansha International.
Nakane, Chie
　1970 Japanese Society. Tokyo: Charles E. Tuttle Co.
Pelzel, John C.
　1974 Human Nature in the Japanese Myths. *In* Japanese Culture and Behavior. Takie Sugiyama Lebra and William P. Lebra, eds. Pp. 3–26. Honolulu: University Press of Hawaii.
Quinn, Robert E. and Michael R. McGrath
　1985 The Transformation of Organizational Cultures: A Competing Values Perspective. *In* Organizational Culture. Peter J. Frost, Larry F. Moore, Meryl Reis Louis, Craig C. Lundberg, and Joanne Martin, eds. Pp. 315–335. Beverly Hills, CA: Sage.
Redfield, Robert
　1962 A Village That Chose Progress: Chan Kom Revisited. Chicago: University of Chicago Press.
Reeves-Ellington, Richard H.
　1988 Relationships between Multinationals and Peasants. Paper presented at the annual meeting of the American Anthropological Association, Chicago.
Reeves-Ellington, Richard H. and Paul Steidlmeier
　1991 Total Quality, Institutionalism and the Retooling of American Business. Binghamton, NY: SUNY-Binghamton, School of Management.
Rohrer, T. C., ed.
　1990 A Continuing Series for Implementing Total Quality. Cincinnati: Procter and Gamble Co.
Schein, Edgar H.
　1985 Organizational Culture and Leadership. San Francisco: Jossey-Bass.
Smircich, Linda
　1985 Is the Concept of Culture a Paradigm for Understanding Organizations and Ourselves? *In* Organizational Culture. Peter J. Frost, Larry F. Moore, Meryl Reis Louis, Craig C. Lundberg, and Joanne Martin, eds. Pp. 31–35. Beverly Hills, CA: Sage.
Spradley, James P.
　1980 Participant Observation. New York: Holt, Rinehart and Winston.
White, Leslie A.
　1949 The Science of Culture. New York: Grove Press.

Article Review Form at end of book.

What implications does multinational composition have for group functioning? In creating corporate policy in a global business, what cultural sensitivities are necessary for the leadership?

When Groups Consist of Multiple Nationalities

Towards a new understanding of the implications

Donald C. Hambrick, Sue Canney Davison, Scott A. Snell, Charles C. Snow

Introduction

In today's major corporations, task groups consisting of multiple nationalities abound, and the clear trend is towards even more of them in the future. Multinational groups (MNGs) of many types are evident: the management team of an international joint venture, a group developing a product for multiple-country markets, a group responsible for formulating an integrated European strategy, a task force changed with developing recommendations for rationalizing worldwide manufacturing, and, increasingly, even the top management team of the firm itself.

Considerable research has been done on topics peripherally related to multinational groups, resulting in a large body of literature on global organizational design (e.g. Bartlett and Ghoshal 1989), cross-cultural management (e.g. Redding 1992; Roberts and Boyacigiller 1984), cross-cultural interpersonal interaction (e.g. Gudykunst 1991), and heterogeneous task groups (e.g. Hoffman and Maier 1961; Triandis et al. 1965; Jackson 1992; Milliken and Martins 1996). These streams of research have been substantial, both in quantity and in the theoretical advances in their respective domains. Surprisingly, however, very little empirical research or systematic conceptual work has directly addressed the important and timely phenomenon of multinational groups. With some exceptions (noted below), our investigation has uncovered only a few works that deal pointedly or in depth with the specific issues that arise when a task group consists of individuals of diverse national backgrounds.

When we first launched our research programme on MNGs, we discussed it with a group of senior executives from major multinational corporations. The comments of two executives, both from European-based companies, symbolize the complexity and subtlety of the issues involved. One executive said: 'I don't see why this is an important topic to study. Our company puts people of different nationalities together all the time. It's how we do business; there's nothing particularly special about such groups. What's the big issue?'

The second executive responded: 'Wait a minute. In my company, we are having great difficulties with such groups. We've had strategic plans suffer and careers derail because of complications arising from multinational groups. Just last month we killed a global product development project because the team had taken so long that the competition had already sewn up the market.'

"When Groups Consist of Multiple Nationalities: Towards a New Understanding of the Implications." Donald C. Hambrick, Sue Canney Davison, Scott A. Snell, and Charles C. Snow. ORGANIZATION STUDIES, February 19, 1998. Reprinted by permission.

It seems that some MNGs are not particularly noteworthy or problematic and may be barely discernible in their functioning from single-nationality groups. Other MNGs are nettlesome and create organizational challenges that derive specifically from their diversity. In the light of the rapidly increasing use of MNGs, an assessment of the factors that account for such wide variance appears to be very important.

The purpose of this paper is to establish a conceptual understanding of the implications of multinational composition for group functioning. In particular, we build our framework on three key observations about MNGs:

1. Nationality affects a person in numerous interconnected ways, ranging from the deeply underlying to the readily apparent: values, cognitive schema, demeanour, and language. These nationality-derived qualities, in turn, affect a person's behavior, as well as how the person is perceived in an MNG.

2. An MNG's chances of being effective depend on a variety of factors. However, prominent among these is the *combination* of (a) the magnitude and type of nationality-derived diversity among members, and (b) the nature of the group's task. That is, some types of nationality-derived diversity serve as endowments for the group, while other types of diversity create great difficulties. Whether diversity is an asset or a liability, in turn, depends on what the group is trying to accomplish.

3. In contemporary global corporations, multinational groups serve useful purposes in addition to conducting their particular work tasks. Namely, MNGs often exist as a necessary by-product of a concerted global human resource system, in which superior talent from around the world is sought, motivated, and developed.

Our conceptual framework moves across units of analysis, focusing first on the individual group member's characteristics as a reflection of his or her nationality, then on the effects of multinational diversity on the group's functioning and performance, and finally on the association between corporate policies and the use of MNGs.

We do not attempt to set forth prescriptions for the design or management of MNGs. We are engaged in a large, multi-phase field research project which should eventually yield important normative conclusions (some of which we have reported in Snow et al. 1996). Here, our objective is to lay a conceptual foundation for our own and others' research on multinational groups, and we close the paper with a proposed research agenda.

The Group Member's Behaviour as a Reflection of Nationality: A Preliminary Perspective

The nationalities represented in a group are only of consequence to the group's functioning to the extent that they affect members' behaviour. Although there are those who would resist theories of cultural or national relativism, the great weight of evidence, including everyday observation, indicates that national culture has a significant effect on the outlook, perceptions, and behaviour of individuals.

Nationality as an Analytic Construct

Although not the only available construct for considering the orientations of individuals from different cultures, nationality has major advantages: It is analytically tractable, it coincides with the implicit or explicit employee categorizations applied in many global enterprises, and it has been the basis for considerable research on individual differences. A main alternative construct, ethnicity, has the advantage of greater specificity (for characterizing some cultural groups) but potentially yields more atomistic and ambiguous categories, and its relevance depends critically on an individual's personal sense of identity (Fiedler et al. 1961; Phinney 1990; Brass 1991). The arguments we develop in this paper could be directly applied if ethnicity were used instead of nationality. However, empirical tests would be much more difficult, and it is not clear that resultant explanation or understanding would be any greater.

Nationality, while generally a convenient and powerful construct, is itself open to various definitions and operationalizations. It could refer to one's legal status, the identities of one's parents, the place of one's upbringing, and so on (Brass 1991). Conceivably, an index consisting of these components of nationality would be useful in empirical research. Here, though, our conception of nationality is the country in which an individual spent the majority of his or her formative years.

As we will argue, group members drawn from various nationalities tend to differ in ways that have substantial implications for group functioning. However, such differences are not complete and wholesale, as nationality is not completely deterministic. For instance, even though the average American may find a much higher value on individualism than does the average Finn (as observed by Hofstede 1980), some Americans lie far afield from their nation's overall rating of individualism, some even valuing it less than the average Finn.

Several factors may determine whether an individual's dispositional characteristics will be close to, or far away from, their national tendencies: how typical the person's life experiences have been, relative to other members of that nationality (in terms of upbringing, religion, education, etc.); the amount of international life experiences of the person (such as residence or education outside the home country, parents or spouse of different nationalities, or international job assignments) (e.g. Church 1982; Adler 1975); and the degree to which the person has been socialized by an employing organization with a culture similar to (or different from) the person's national culture. Our purpose in noting these factors is not to assess them in depth, but rather to illustrate the forces that can cause a group member to be particularly representative (or unrepresentative) of his or her home country.

Multinational groups essentially never consist of people randomly drawn from their constituent nationalities, and hence such groups may have relatively few of the characteristics—either potentially beneficial or problematic—that might be expected a *priori* from such an admixture of national backgrounds. As illustration, we return to the earlier remarks of the two executives upon hearing about our research. The one who contended that his company had no problems with MNGs was from a major oil company that has long been globally integrated, with a strong worldwide corporate culture, and policies of posting technical and managerial employees to various parts of the world throughout their careers. In short, MNGs in this company tended to consist of experienced 'internationalists' who, additionally, had been significantly influenced by the company's strong culture. In contrast, the executive who said that his company was having considerable difficulties with MNGs was from a large international food corporation that had grown by a series of national acquisitions and whose MNGs, largely consisting of individuals with little international business experience, were working on unprecedented problems of pan-European and global product planning. This contrast illustrates how individuals, through accumulated experience and exposure (such as in the oil company described), can surmount, to some degree, their nationality-based tendencies. When placed together in a group, such people may encounter relatively few nationality-based difficulties in functioning.

However, in noting that individuals may have psychological characteristics that deviate from the central tendencies of their nationalities, we do not mean to imply that nationality imprinting is easily erased. It will be the rare person who does not possess considerable traces of nationality in his or her psychological make-up and behaviour. In this regard, Laurent (1983) found that even seasoned, internationally-experienced executives (who, moreover, were currently enrolled in an internationally-oriented executive programme at INSEAD) exhibited major differences, by nationality, in their beliefs about how to manage effectively. In a later synopsis of his research, Laurent (1991: 201) reported:

When the patterns of differences were analyzed, variations in responses could be partly explained by characteristics such as age, education, job, professional experience, hierarchical level, and company type. Less expected, however—particularly in an institution that places great emphasis on an international ethos—was the fact that the nationality of the respondents emerged as an explanation for far more variations in the data than any of the respondents' other characteristics.'

Implications of Nationality

While not deterministic, nationality is a potent factor in explaining individuals' psychological attributes and behaviour. Nationality can be expected to affect a person in numerous ways. Here we will focus on four important accompaniments of one's nationality: values, cognitive schema, demeanour, and language. These personal characteristics, influenced to some extent by a person's nationality, are conceptually distinct but causally intertwined.

First, nationality affects one's *values*. In fact, probably more has been written about value orientations than about any other psychological correlate of nationality (summarized in Roberts and Boyacigiller 1984). A personal value, as defined by Hofstede (1980: 19), is 'a broad tendency to prefer certain states of affairs over others.' Among the prominent value dimensions identified by theorists are individualism vs. collectivism, universalism vs. particularism, power distance, relationship to time, and uncertainty avoidance (Parsons and Shils 1951; Kluckhohn and Strodtbeck 1961; Hofstede 1980, 1991; England 1975; Triandis 1982; Trompenaars 1993).

The influence of national culture in shaping the values of individuals, including business executives, has been examined by several investigators. For example, studies by Bendix (1956), Sutton et al. (1956), and Chatov (1973) all concluded that the values which business executives bring to their tasks are predominantly due to national systems of beliefs. A study by England (1975), which compared managers from the United States, Japan, Australia, Korea, and India, found that nationality accounted for 30 to 45 percent of the variation in managers' values.

Second, nationality affects one's *cognitive schema*, or what one knows, assumes, or perceives about the world at hand (Lord and Foti 1986). This can include knowledge of facts, events, and trends; knowledge or assumptions about future events; knowledge about alternatives; and knowledge or assumptions about how consequences are attached to alternatives (March and Simon 1958; Maruyama 1980). For example, individuals of two different nationalities tend to know, assume, and perceive different things about their respective countries (Walsh 1995). In fact, individuals are often assigned to MNGs expressly because of their knowledge about conditions, trends, and constituencies in their home countries or regions.

Individuals of different nationalities may also differ widely in their more elemental cognitive orientations, such as the salience of different time horizons (e.g. Hofstede 1991), self-construals (Triandis 1989; Markus and Kitayama 1991), and the way they perceive potentially emotional stimuli (Mesquita and Frijda 1992). That is, nationality affects not only cognitive content, but also the processing and interpretation of new cognitive content, yielding distinct cognitive schemas.

To some degree, nationality-derived differences in cognitive schema are due to differences in values. That is, a person 'sees what he wants to see', 'hears what she wants to hear' (Weick 1969; following from Postman et al. 1948). Values also affect the next category of personal attributes to which we turn—demeanour.

A substantial body of research has dealt with the differences in outward physical behaviour, or *demeanour* of people of different nationalities. For example, differences in eye contact, punctuality, conversational style, interruption patterns, physiological reactions to emotional stimuli, and other types of behaviour have been associated with nationality by various researchers (Gudykunst and Ting-Toomey 1988; Wolfgang 1984; LaFrance and Mayo 1978; Hall 1983; Mesquita and Frijda 1992). Such superficial behaviour may seem incidental to a theory of MNG functioning—not measuring up to the theoretical significance of, say, values. However, it is highly visible factors such as these that primarily give rise to affective conflict within groups (Milliken and Martins 1996; Pelled 1996). Anyone who has observed multicultural groups will attest to the substantial implications of member demeanour on the group's overall functioning. Small, seemingly trivial types of behaviour may matter a great deal, often aggravating stereotypes, causing member disdain and isolation, or resulting in other forms of breakdown in communication and cohesion (Hall 1960).

Finally, nationality obviously has implications for a person's *language*. One's nationality not only determines what will be one's primary language, but it also affects the likelihood of knowing other languages and which specific languages will ever be readily comprehended (Church 1982). For example, it has been widely observed that Americans tend not to know languages other than English, while Europeans often know multiple languages. However, the languages that Europeans are most likely to know are those that use Western-style alphabetic characters, not the characters of Middle Eastern or Asian scripts. Conversely, Japanese individuals are more likely to gain facility with (especially the nuances of) Mandarin Chinese than with Spanish. In short, one's nationality affects one's language repertoire.

The influence of language proficiencies in a multinational group setting has been observed to be profound. For example, an individual's facility with the group's working language greatly affects one's amount and type of participation, as well as one's influence in the group (Gudykunst 1991). Geringer (1988: 214) noted the importance of a mutual language capability in joint venture success: 'The simple ability to communicate with one's counterpart in a partner firm often makes a significant difference in a JV's prospects for success; the absence of this ability has caused more than a few disasters'.

To summarize, a person's nationality (which may be amplified or muted by professional and personal experiences) affects his or her values, cognitive schema, demeanour, and language. These attributes, in turn, shape the person's behaviour in response to task stimuli.

Figure 1 Implications of Nationality for Behaviours in a Group.

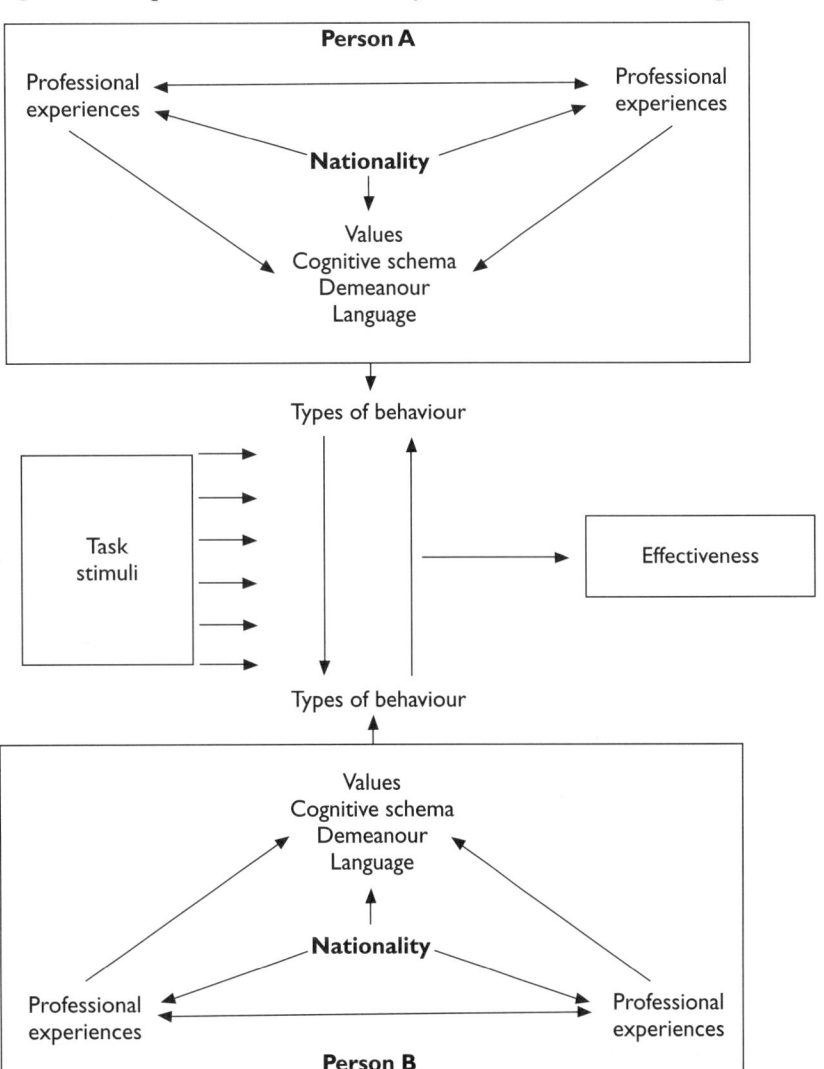

Multinationality as Heterogeneity: Towards a New Understanding

In a group setting, a person's underlying attributes operate interactively and reflexively on the basis of the characteristics and behavioural characteristics of other members of the group. For schematic simplicity, consider a simple 'group' as consisting of two individuals of different nationalities, as shown in Figure 1. The two people can be thought of as complementary, bringing different cognitions and values to the task, and hence broadening the problem-solving capacity beyond what either of them could achieve individually. However, each person's contributions and behavioural patterns are conditioned not only by his or her own characteristics but also by the attributes and behavioural patterns of the other person (Adler and Graham 1989). This reaction can occur through extreme inferential leaps about the other person or through more deliberate empirical observation. For example, in Figure 1, Person A may adjust his or her behaviour merely after observing Person B's nationality (stereotyping) (Devine 1989) and will almost certainly condition his or her behavioural patterns on the basis of those of Person B (Carnevale and Isen 1986).

The members of the group may achieve a constructive 'synergy' (Redding 1992; Adler 1986), or they may experience interpersonal aversion, distrust, and dysfunction. The eventual mutual and collective

Global Business **67**

behaviour of the group may yield a product that is either vastly greater or vastly inferior to 'the sum of the parts'. Herein lie the potential benefits and difficulties of multinational groups. (For major reviews of the literature on group dynamics, the reader is referred to Goodman et al. 1987; and Hackman and Associates 1990.)

Group Heterogeneity: Chief Conclusions from Prior Research

The multinational group presents a special case of heterogeneity, which, as Jackson (1992) states, has achieved the status of a theoretical fulcrum in the study of groups. Contemporary thinking on the implications of group diversity can be traced back thirty years to the research of Hoffman and Maier (1961), who found that heterogeneity (in terms of personality) was positively associated with the quality of problem solutions developed by groups. Since then, a vast number of investigations have been conducted on the implications of group heterogeneity, with widely varying and largely inconclusive results.

Some theorists have hypothesized and observed salutary effects from heterogeneity, as pointed out by Hoffman and Maier (1961). For example, major reviews of basic research on group diversity (largely conducted in laboratory settings) support the conclusion that group heterogeneity aids decision quality (Hoffman 1979; McGrath 1984; Shaw 1981). Using archival and field data, some research has similarly found that top management team diversity is associated with improved decision quality and organizational performance (Eisenhardt and Schoonhoven 1990; Bantel and Jackson 1989; Hambrick et al. 1996). In general, the imputed logic for such a relationship is that diversity enhances the breadth of perspective and overall problem-solving capacity of the group—more vantages are brought to bear on the task at hand.

In contrast, a number of studies have found that group heterogeneity has negative effects on group performance (e.g. O'Reilly and Flatt 1989; Ancona and Caldwell 1992; Tuckman 1965). The general contention of these researchers is that homogeneity promotes integration, trust, and ease of communication, hence conferring implementation advantages that outweigh any disadvantages of narrowness or redundancy within the group.

As a way to resolve these apparent inconsistencies, recent theory has moved beyond the basic question, 'Does heterogeneity help or hurt group performance?' In particular, three theoretical refinements serve to allow much greater subtlety and precision in estimating the effects of group heterogeneity on performance:

1. The benefits and costs of group heterogeneity depend on the nature of the group's task (Filley et al. 1976; Hambrick and Mason 1984; Jackson 1992).

2. The relative benefits and costs of group heterogeneity depend on the specific dimensions on which heterogeneity is being considered (Triandis et al. 1965; Jackson 1992; Pelled 1996).

3. Curvilinear effects must be anticipated. That is, increasing heterogeneity may be helpful to group functioning only up to a point, beyond which the costs outweigh the benefits (O'Bannon and Gupta 1992).

We will draw upon and extend these ideas below, indicating their relevance for a theory of multinational group functioning.

National Heterogeneity as a Continuum

We noted earlier that relatively little theory development or empirical research has been done on multinational groups *per se*. In one of the very few works on the topic, Adler (1986) devotes a chapter of this book to a discussion of 'multicultural teams', drawing from a variety of related literatures. She enumerates both the assets and liabilities of such groups. The negative aspects, or 'process losses', of multicultural groups are similar to those observed by researchers of group heterogeneity in general: dislike, mistrust, stereotyping, communication difficulties, and interpersonal stress. Similarly, the benefits Adler discusses are in line with those envisioned by advocates of group diversity: more and better ideas, and limited 'groupthink' (Janis 1972).

On the basis of these extreme pros and cons, Adler posits that multicultural groups will tend to be either highly effective or highly ineffective, with single-culture groups most likely to be moderately effective. She goes on to discuss several moderating factors, ranging from type of task to the behavioural styles of leaders, that influence the positioning of a given multicultural group in one tail of the effectiveness distribution or the other.

However, what additionally needs to be considered is the concept of 'amount of diversity', or the reality that the differences between nationalities are not binary so much as scalar. That is, a group that consists of Norwegians and Swedes is not as diverse as a group that consists of Norwegians and Saudis, which in turn is not as diverse as a group of Norwegians, Saudis, and Americans. Namely, a potent theory of multinational groups must acknowledge varying 'distances' between nationalities, as well as the fact that the aggregate 'distance' grows as a function of the number of nationalities in the group. Thus, national heterogeneity in an MNG is best viewed as a continuum.

In this respect, the work of the prominent theorists of national values is instructive. Using rigorous analytic methods, both Kluckholn and Strodtbeck (1961) and Hofstede (1980) attempted to calibrate the 'distances' between the nationalities they studied, in terms of overall cultural values. For example, Figure 2 shows the results of the cluster analysis of 40 countries, using their scores on Hofstede's four dimensions of culture: individualism, uncertainty avoidance, masculinity, and power distance (Hofstede 1980: 229). [Hofstede, in subsequent work (1991), added a fifth dimension, 'long-term orientation']. In the dendrogram, cultural similarity is shown both by the proximity of countries in the listing and by how readily they merge to form an analytically compact cluster. Thus, Colombia, Mexico, and Venezuela are very similar and readily form a cluster that is very distant, in terms of value orientation, from the cluster consisting of

Figure 2 Cluster Analysis Results (Dendrogram): 40 Countries Studied by Hofstede (1980), Clustered According to Four Value Orientations (from Hofstede 1980: 229).

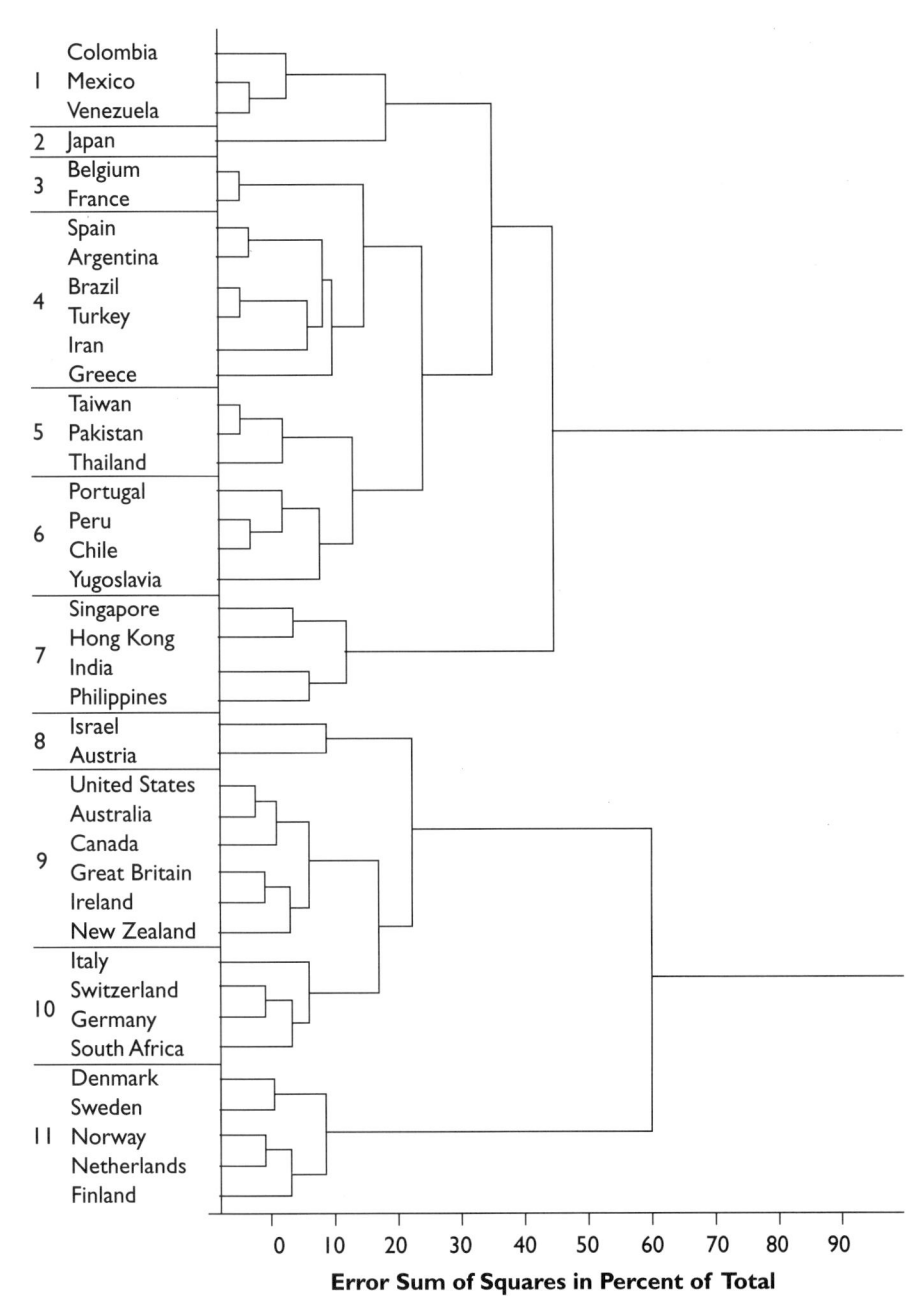

```
 1  Colombia
    Mexico
    Venezuela
 2  Japan
 3  Belgium
    France
    Spain
    Argentina
 4  Brazil
    Turkey
    Iran
    Greece
    Taiwan
 5  Pakistan
    Thailand
    Portugal
    Peru
 6  Chile
    Yugoslavia
    Singapore
    Hong Kong
 7  India
    Philippines
 8  Israel
    Austria
    United States
    Australia
    Canada
 9  Great Britain
    Ireland
    New Zealand
    Italy
    Switzerland
10  Germany
    South Africa
    Denmark
    Sweden
11  Norway
    Netherlands
    Finland
```

Error Sum of Squares in Percent of Total

Denmark, Sweden, Norway, Netherlands, and Finland. Subsequent research, examining dimensions different from Hofstede's, has found different country clusters and sometimes no clear clusters at all (Heller and Wilpert 1979; Trompenaars 1993). Thus, Hofstede's findings should be taken as illustrative of the concept of distances between nationalities, though not as providing definitive gauges.

Indeed, gauging 'differences' between nationalities will ultimately require subtlety and a wide array of considerations. For example, historical animosities between two neighbouring countries may cause great tension between individuals from those countries, even though the countries' values, languages, and so on are very similar. Thus, a group considering of Koreans and Japanese may manifest strained interpersonal dynamics traceable in part to Japan's colonization of Korea earlier this century. Groups consisting of Greeks and Turks, Iranians and Iraqis, or Vietnamese and Cambodians would all experience the possibility of great strains and 'in-group/out-group' tensions (Tajfel 1974) despite their seeming proximity in terms of culture and geography.

Although, as noted earlier, the members of a given nationality vary, for now let us assume that we are studying groups whose members generally tend to adhere to their national tendencies. We can describe some archetypical groups, as a way of illustrating that national differences within a group must be considered in scalar terms . . .*

Obviously, other interesting combinations could be considered as well. For example, when several group members are of highly similar nationalities (say, British, American, and Canadian) but other members are of a wide array of other nationalities, there are the makings of very skewed patterns of influence, control, and participation within the group. In fact, an eventual complete theory of multinational groups must incorporate not only psychological and social phenomena (the conceptual mainstays of the literature on group diversity), but also matters of intragroup power and influence.

The state of theory development on multinational groups is not sufficiently advanced to be able to predict with any precision how the balance of advantages and disadvantages shifts across the cases just discussed. However, what should be clear is that nationalities lie on a series of important continua: some are close together, others far apart; and, generally, the more nationalities represented in a group, the greater the aggregate distance among all members. Just as researchers have come to consider other forms of group heterogeneity (e.g. tenure, functional background, and personality) to have scalar properties (summarized in Jackson et al. in press), so too should theories of multinational groups acknowledge and exploit the concept of 'degrees of diversity' within an

---

*A paragraph that discusses figure 3 has been deleted here; figure 3 does not appear in this publication.

MNG. This is an integral element of the ideas we will develop next.

A New Framework for Predicting MNG Effectiveness

With the rapidly increasing use of multinational groups in companies today, and a severe paucity of integrated theory or research on this important topic, it is appropriate to propose a systematic framework for improving our understanding of MNGs. We must be particularly concerned with the question of why some MNGs are very effective, while others are very ineffective. In the remainder of the paper, we set forth a framework to address this issue.

As will be seen, our framework does not incorporate all factors of potential significance to MNG functioning and effectiveness. At this early stage, no framework could or should attempt to be exhaustive. Rather, our aim is to set forth a general, parsimonious model that will help explain a considerable amount of variance in MNG effectiveness. Other important factors—such as the group's policies and norms, or the leader's behavioural traits—can be captured by using more specific models.

As indicated earlier, our framework for predicting MNG effectiveness is built around three theoretical elements: the nature of the group's task, the specific type of multinational diversity under consideration, and the extent of such diversity. In the preceding section, we developed the concept of 'amount of diversity', arguing that any form of heterogeneity can be considered in scalar terms, ranging from very little to a great deal. In an earlier section, we set forth a scheme for classifying 'types of heterogeneity' within MNGs: cognitive schema, values, demeanour, and language. What remains, then, is to develop our third theoretical element, type of group task.

Types of MNG Tasks

In the literature on small groups, numerous typologies of group tasks have been offered. However, in most analyses of group heterogeneity, the classification scheme that has provided the most theoretical leverage has hinged on the degree of routine in the group's task (Filley et al. 1976; Jackson 1992). A recurring idea is that routine problem solving is best handled by a homogeneous group, while more ill-defined, novel endeavours are best handled by a heterogeneous group, in which diversity of perspective and opinion allows more far-ranging generation and airing of alternatives (Filley et al. 1976; Hambrick and Mason 1984; O'Bannon and Gupta 1992). As intuitively reasonable as is such a contingency approach, it has not been empirically verified, at least not with consistent results.

In a recent in-depth assessment of how group characteristics affect the effectiveness of a group, Jackson (1992) argued that three different types of group tasks, not two, need to be considered in order to make useful predictions about the effects of group heterogeneity. Extending the creative vs. routine dichotomy, Jackson set forth an expanded typology of group tasks: creative, problem solving, and task execution. In our own field research on multinational groups, we have concluded that, with minor modification, Jackson's typology is useful for distinguishing among major types of MNG tasks and, in turn, for considering their implications for heterogeneity. Below, we will discuss what we have come to observe as three major types of tasks engaged in by multinational groups: creative, computational, and coordinative.

The *creative* task is one that can be approached in numerous ways, involving various types of stimuli or information, and for which there is no objectively verifiable 'correct' answer (Jackson 1992). Among the key challenges in facing such a task are to generate a broad array of ideas, use already-generated ideas to develop even more and better-refined ideas, and then eventually to reach consensus on a solution which typically cannot be defended in a rigorous fashion. Multinational groups engaged in creative tasks include those responsible for worldwide or regional product development, market planning, and global strategy.

The *computational* task is one in which a bounded amount of fairly clearcut information needs to be assembled and analyzed, and for which there are relatively objective standards for assessing the correctness or superiority of a particular solution. For such a task, the chief challenges are to make sure that the full range of required information is obtained and processed by the group. [This is essentially the same as Jackson's (1992) 'problem-solving task'—a label we find overly broad] Multinational groups engaged in computational tasks could include those conducting analyses on worldwide manufacturing-site selection, global inventory and logistics planning, and tariff and tax rationalization.

The third type of task is *coordinative*, or one requiring elaborate and well-orchestrated interaction among group members. The successful conduct of this type of task does not require creativity as much as interpersonal reliability, speed and accuracy of interaction, and a great capacity for prompt mutual adjustment among group members. Examples of multinational groups engaged in such tasks are those responsible for executing an already-developed business strategy, environmental crisis-response teams (e.g. oil spill clean-up), and currency arbitrage groups. (This type of group is in the same vein as Jackson's third type—'task execution'—but is broadened to capture any task that requires intensive interpersonal coordination.)

Naturally, some group tasks are hybrids of these three types. Moreover, some groups may go through phases in which they move from one type of task to another, say, from primarily a creative task to a coordinative task. Without ruling out such possibilities, our field research suggests that the three types concisely portray the major differences in most primary MNG tasks. We will now turn to an examination of how multinational diversity affects the likelihood of group effectiveness for each of the three main task archetypes.

MNG Diversity and Effectiveness

As we have emphasized throughout, MNGs vary widely in their effectiveness. Some are very effective, conducting their tasks on a timely basis, with efficient use of resources, and delivering superior output. Other

MNGs are quite ineffective, not delivering the hoped-for results for their organizations.

We conceive of group effectiveness as the economic returns (to the larger organization) that stem from the group's endeavours. This is a composite function of the group's creativity, speed, efficiency, and so on (Hambrick et al. 1996) We exclude from our conception of effectiveness such matters as member satisfaction with the group (Hackman 1990). Over time, member satisfaction and task performance probably greatly co-vary, since chronic dissatisfaction would affect information exchange and collaboration in a way as to impair substantive outputs (Watson et al. 1993).

Our approach will be to address in turn each type of nationality-based diversity discussed earlier: values, cognitions, demeanour, and language. For each of these, we will consider the implications for group effectiveness of varying amounts of diversity under three different task scenarios: creative, computational, and coordinative.

For the sake of analytic framing, we assume that all the tasks we are considering are genuinely 'multinational' in scope, encompassing issues that involve resources, products, markets, or constituencies in multiple geographies. Accordingly, one can conceive, in the abstract, of an amount of national diversity that is expressly required by a task, similar to the systems concept of 'requisite variety' (Ashby 1956). For example, consider a German company with substantial experience in an industry, now attempting to replicate its recent success in Spain with an entry into Portugal. The management team would apparently benefit from consisting of one or more Germans, Spaniards, and Portuguese. Any additional nationalities would be beyond what is expressly needed for the task. Obviously, in cases where the task does not explicitly favour any multinational inputs, the liabilities of diversity will still pertain, but with fewer significant benefits, thus negatively shifting the benefit-cost ratio.

Diversity of Values

The members of a multinational group will tend to possess different values—fundamental preferences for some states of affairs over others—traceable in part to their respective nationalities (Hofstede 1980; Hambrick and Brandon 1988). These values may affect members' preferences for certain task solutions, or for certain group processes, and will affect their cognitions by causing them to interpret stimuli in ways that suit their value structures (Postman et al. 1948).

When the group is engaged in a creative task, diversity of values can be expected to be beneficial for group effectiveness. The varied perspectives and enriched debate that comes from increased diversity will be helpful in generating and refining alternatives (Figure 4a).

When the task is computational, we would expect increases in value diversity to be generally unrelated to group effectiveness. Such tasks typically involve rather clearcut data collection, analysis and solution generation. Operating more in the realm of facts than values (March and Simon 1958), groups engaged in such tasks are not strongly affected by either the homogeneity or heterogeneity of values.

However, when the task is coordinative, involving elaborate interaction among group members, diversity of values will tend to be negatively related to group effectiveness. In such a task situation, fluid and reliable coordination is required; debates or tensions over why or how the group is approaching the task—which will tend to occur when values vary—will be counter-productive. In addition, disparate values create interpersonal strains and mistrust which become damaging when the group is charged with a coordinative task.

Diversity of Cognitions

Group members of different nationalities generally possess different knowledge, assumptions, and schema. They possess different information and process new information through their own base of experience and knowledge (March and Simon 1958; Dearborn and Simon 1958). If the group is engaged in a creative task, each increment in cognitive diversity can be expected to enhance the group's likelihood of effectiveness (as shown in Figure 4b). The differing perspectives that come from different nationalities will serve as resources for solving the unstructured, novel task at hand (Hoffman 1979; Adler 1986; Jackson 1992). Even helpful are increments of cognitive diversity beyond the amount 'explicitly' required by the task. Interestingly, the often-expressed positive views of diverse groups rely on an optimism about precisely these serendipitous benefits of cognitive diversity. For example, Adler (1986: 133) describes such unexpected benefits in a Swedish pharmaceutical firm:

'Once, by accident or design, we brought in an international team to discuss the design of a new allergy product. Due to extreme differences in opinion on what constitutes good medical practice, the team designed the product with maximum flexibility to suit the major demands of each country.'

When the task is computational in nature, increments in cognitive diversity will be helpful to group effectiveness, but *only* up to the point at which all the knowledge explicitly required for the task resides within the group. Cognitive diversity beyond that 'required' amount does not affect group effectiveness either positively or negatively (Figure 4b). For example, a task may require certain facts about conditions in three countries. With the addition of knowledgeable representatives from each of these countries, group effectiveness is likely to improve; but adding a representative from a fourth country brings no further benefit.

Just as with the other types of tasks, when the group is engaged in a coordinative task, there are benefits in increasing the cognitive diversity up to the point explicitly required by the task. Importantly, however, increases in diversity beyond that point become counter-productive (Figure 4b), since the diversity in perspective and assumptions becomes costly to the task of elaborate interpersonal orchestration, without any corresponding benefits.

Diversity of Demeanours

In our estimation, diversity of demeanours—various kinds of surface behaviour involving punctuality, conversational style, body language, and so on—provides no important group benefits yet imposes potentially significant costs in terms of interpersonal strain and mistrust. The

Figure 4 Proposed Relationships between Four Types of Diversity and Multinational Group Effectiveness, for Different Tasks.

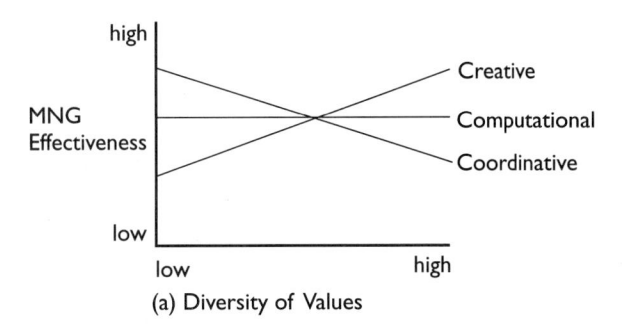

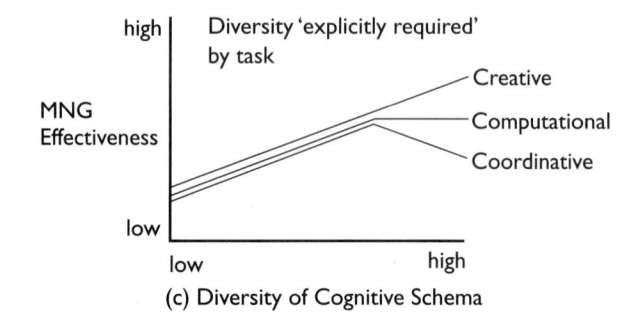

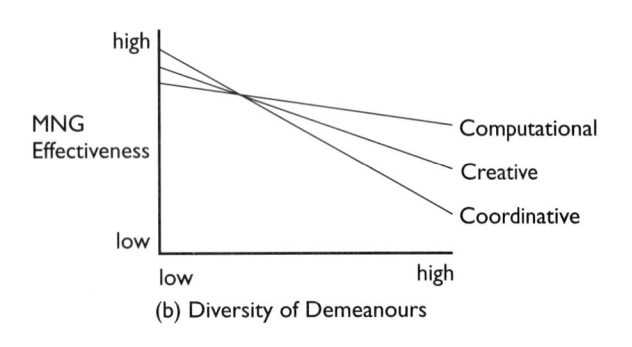

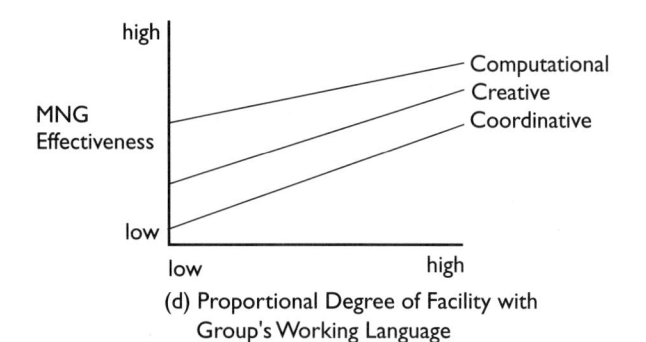

(a) Diversity of Values

(b) Diversity of Demeanours

(c) Diversity of Cognitive Schema

(d) Proportional Degree of Facility with Group's Working Language

greater the diversity of demeanours, the lower the group's effectiveness will be. Such a negative relationship will be strongest for groups engaged in coordinative tasks (Figure 4c), since, as already emphasized, such groups require maximum ease of communication and reliability of interaction in order to perform successfully. Groups engaged in computational tasks are expected to suffer the least from diversity of demeanours among group members, due to the typically objective nature of their problem-solving task. Groups engaged in creative tasks are expected to fall somewhere between the other two types of groups—to be hurt more by increasing diversity of demeanors than groups engaged in straightforward computational tasks, but not to be hurt as much as those engaged in coordinative tasks.

Language Facility

Our conception of language facility is qualitatively different from our treatment of other forms of diversity, because, with language, it is not so much sheer diversity that matters, but rather the group's proportional degree of facility with its working language. For example, a group of Europeans might agree that their working language will be English, even though all the members only have a moderate facility with English (but even less overall facility with any other single language). In such a case, their 'diversity' is low: they *all* have moderate capability with English. More importantly, however, they only have a moderate proportional facility with their working language. Proportional facility is an aggregate concept encompassing both the number of group members who have that facility and the extent to which they possess it.

We expect a low degree of common language facility generally to impair group functioning, hampering the exchange of information and trust. In line with the logic set forth above, the harmful effects of limited shared language facility will be greatest for groups engaged in coordinative tasks, least for computational tasks, and in-between for creative tasks (Figure 4d). Increases in shared language facility result in corresponding increases in group performance for each type of task. However, for the very highest levels of shared language facility, group performance will tend to be equally high for the three types of tasks.

Summary

We have attempted to bring a new precision to predictions about the effects of multinational group diversity on group performance. By refining prior typologies of group tasks, in the light of our own field research on multinational groups, we conclude that the effects of diversity depend on whether the group's task is primarily creative, computational, or coordinative. We also argue that different types of diversity give rise to different performance effects.

It appears that multinational diversity poses the greatest difficulties for groups engaged in coordinative tasks. Except for advantages that come from having the requisite variety of cognitions to handle the task, all other amounts and forms of diversity serve as liabilities for groups such as these, that have to engage in reliable, fluid interaction.

At the other extreme, groups engaged in creative endeavours provide the most promising setting for multinational diversity. Needing diverse, fresh perspectives to deal with their novel and ambiguous tasks, such groups benefit in particular from heterogeneity in values and cognitions. In contrast, those groups engaged in more computational tasks experience the least effects—positive or negative—from multinational diversity.

Diversity of demeanours is almost always costly to MNG effectiveness, and there are no apparent benefits. Differences in outward behaviour such as conversational style, body language, and punctuality bring about interpersonal distrust and disdain. At one level, it could be said that these are simply drawbacks that have to be tolerated in order to reap other benefits from multinational diversity (from varied cognitive schemas, etc.). However, training programmes might help to diminish these potential problems. If group members could be sensitized about how the typical demeanours of their own nationalities are viewed by others, and sensitized to be aware of their own reactions to the incidental demeanours of other nationalities, then group processes and effectiveness might be greatly enhanced.

Time spent together may also play a role in how national differences affect a group's functioning (Watson et al. 1993). Newly-formed MNGs are likely to be the most vulnerable to the drawbacks of diversity, but, over time, if they survive and meet nominal performance thresholds, they develop more trust and rapport. Members come to respect and welcome the group's complementarities, overlooking (perhaps even relishing) differences in demeanour, values, and so on. A corollary idea is that training programmes for enhancing the functioning of MNGs are the most essential at the very formative stage of the group. Similarly, it is at the outset of the group's work together that MNG leaders must be the most vigilant about possible group breakdowns due to diversity.

The Broader Benefits of MNGs

We have argued that groups composed of multiple nationalities do not possess inherent advantages over single-nationality groups. In fact, depending on the nature of the task, some types and amounts of national diversity can be burdensome to the effective functioning of such a team. However, many global corporations still make wide use of MNGs, tolerating the liabilities of diverse group composition, because they are firms that are focused on a bigger, longer-term picture. They are investing in the development of a highly capable, versatile, globally-minded cadre of managers and employees.

The widespread use of multinational groups is a necessary accompaniment to an aggressive global human resource system. If the company wishes to select, retain, and develop exceptional employees in multiple parts of the world—particularly in professional and managerial ranks—then it must establish vehicles by which the employees' current talents are fully tapped, as well as ways to enhance the employees' capacity for making future contributions to the company. Few things are as frustrating to a talented, ambitious, mid-level manager than a company policy or norm, whereby he/she is treated as a 'local' who is expected to make contributions strictly within his or her own country operation, while matters of regional or global significance, or the majority of the most important strategic or innovative endeavours, remain the purview of managers in the headquarters' country or nationality (Bartlett and Ghoshal 1986). If the company wishes to surmount this problem and develop an outstanding global workforce, it will establish worldwide appraisal, training, development and staffing processes.

In addition, multinational task forces, committees, and teams will abound to tap key talent to contribute to the resolution of major company issues. In the process, of course, the company will achieve an additional benefit. By gaining experience with multinational groups, the company greatly enhances its capacity to successfully deploy such groups in the future. Employees with demonstrated aptitudes for working in MNGs can be identified and developed; members of MNGs become more cross-culturally aware; a cadre of adept MNG leaders can be identified and developed; and so on. It takes experience with MNGs—sometimes frustrating experience—to learn about them and about how to improve their chances of success (March 1991). Indeed, it may be that a company's accumulated expertise in successfully using multinational groups will be among the most critical of the capabilities needed for it to prosper during the remainder of the 1990s (Prahalad and Hamel 1990; Snow et al. 1996).

Agenda for Future Research

The importance of multinational groups in today's worldwide enterprises creates the need, as well as the opportunity, for a substantial stream of research. This paper has been inductive in nature, broadly circumscribing some major research questions concerning MNGs: How do individuals' nationalities affect their behaviour patterns in group settings? How does the nature of a group's task interact with the types and amounts of national diversity to affect group functioning and performance? How do company-wide human resource development policies affect the prevalence, form, and functioning of MNGs?

Additional areas of inquiry also need to be pursued in order to develop a fuller theoretical and practical understanding of MNGs. At the firm level, research on the contextual influences on MNGs is needed. For example, what are the strategic configurations (Porter 1980; Bartlett and Ghoshal 1989) and core competencies (Prahalad and Hamel 1990) that give rise, in particular, to the widespread use of MNGs within companies? What are the organizational characteristics—either formal structure (Galbraith 1977; Egelhoff 1982) or company culture (Ouchi 1977; Martin 1992)—that influence the prevalence and form of MNGs? Do companies go through common stages in their use and effectiveness of MNGs? How can companies accelerate their learning about the management of MNGs?

Another level of research needs to focus specifically on the design of MNGs. We anticipate that fruitful investigations will adopt a contingency perspective, in which the type of task or other fundamental factors are examined as moderators of group characteristics and effectiveness. The MNG design features that should be considered include: (a) structure (e.g. role interdependence, role clarify, linking mechanisms); (b) incentives (e.g. group-based vs. individual-based financial incentives, pay dispersion, opportunities and criteria for advancement); (c) processes (e.g. communication and interaction patters, power and influence patterns, meeting norms and policies, and group decision processes); and (d) composition, in terms beyond nationality (e.g. personalities, education, organizational tenure). It is particularly interesting to think about how the effects of nationality-based diversity might be accentuated or ameliorated by other forms of group heterogeneity (e.g. Hurst et al. 1989; Pelled 1996). (See Gist et al. 1987; Goodman et al. 1987; and Hambrick 1992, for extensive reviews of elements of group design.)

Overlaying the design of the group, even presumably orchestrating it, is the group leader. The empirical literature on group or team leadership does not point towards an ideal type of leader for multinational teams. In fact, it is likely that, once multinational teams are better understood, there will be a contingency theory of multinational team leadership. Nevertheless, current knowledge would suggest two main sources of ideas about the role of the multinational team leader:

(a) project or programme managers in matrix organizations and (b) broker roles in network organizations. Matrix and network organizations are similar to multinational teams in the sense that both rely on multifunctional expertise, face complex environments, involve relationships centred on collaboration rather than command and control, and so on.

In addition, team leadership needs to take into account the role of time in influencing group effectiveness. Many MNGs have important contributions to make to the success of business strategies, and are in place for considerable periods of time. Over time, leader behaviour may have to change in order to accomplish team goals or, alternatively, leaders with different skills may have to be put in charge of a particular group.

Finally, the ideal MNG leader will have extraordinary understanding and skills in dealing with interpersonal, social, cultural, and political dynamics within a group. The leader must have enough cultural awareness to anticipate the strains that can accompany multinational group membership; and he or she must have the creativity, temperament, and skills to forestall such problems without suppressing the important advantages of the multinational diversity of the group. In our estimation, the identification and development of MNG leaders will be *the* management staffing challenge of the late 1990s, much as the development of general managers was for the 1970s and 1980s.

Note: Support from the International Consortium of Executive Development Research is gratefully acknowledged. The following individuals have contributed to the development and refinement of ideas in this paper: Gerard Braithwaite-Sturgeon, Ming-Jer Chen, Theresa Cho, Douglas Ready and Albert Vicere.

References

Adler, Nancy 1986 *International dimensions of organizational behavior*. Kent International Business Series. Boston: Kent Publishing.

Adler, Nancy, and John L. Graham 1989 'Cross-cultural interaction: the international comparison fallacy?' *Journal of International Business Studies* (Fall): 515–537.

Adler, Peter 1975 'An alternative view of culture shock.' *Journal of Humanistic Psychology* 15: 13–23.

Ancona, Deborah, and David Caldwell 1992 'Demography and design: predictors of new product team performance'. *Organization Science* 3: 342–355.

Ashby, Ross 1956 *Introduction to cybernetics*. New York: Wiley

Bantel, Karen, and Susan Jackson 1989 'Top management and innovations in banking: does the composition of the top team make a difference?' *Strategic Management Journal* 10: 107–124.

Bartlett, Christopher, and Sumantra Ghoshal 1986 'Tap your subsidiaries for global reach'. *Harvard Business Review* 64/6: 87–94.

Bartlett, Christopher, and Sumantra Ghoshal 1989 *Managing across borders: The transnational solution*. London: Hutchinson Business Books.

Bendix, Reinhard 1956 *Work and authority in industry*. New York: Wiley.

Brass, Paul 1991 *Ethnicity and nationalism*. Newbury Park, CA: Sage.

Carnevale, Peter, and Alice Isen 1986 'The influence of positive affect and visual access on the discovery of integrative solutions in bilateral negotiation'. *Organizational Behavior and Human Decision Processes* 37: 1–13.

Chatov, Robert 1973 'The role of ideology in the American corporation' in *The corporate dilemma*. Dow Votaw and S. Prakesh Sethi (eds.), 50–75. Englewood Cliffs, NJ: Prentice-Hall.

Church, Austin 1982 'Sojourner adjustment'. *Psychological Bulletin* 91: 540–572.

Dearborn, Dewitt, and Herbert Simon 1958 'Selective perceptions: A note on the departmental identification of executives'. *Sociometry* 21: 140–44.

Devine, Patricia 1989 'Stereotypes and prejudice: Their automatic and controlled components'. *Journal of Personality and Social Psychology* 56: 5–18.

Eisenhardt, Kathleen, and Claudia Schoonhoven 1990 'Organizational growth: linking founding team, strategy, environment, and growth among U.S. semi-conductor ventures, 1978–1988'. *Administrative Science Quarterly* 35: 504–529.

Egelhoff, William 1982 'Strategy and structure in multinational corporations: an information-processing approach'. *Administrative Science Quarterly* 27: 435–458.

England, George 1975 *The manager and his values*. Cambridge, MA: Ballinger.

Fiedler, Fred, Willem Meuwese, and Sophie Oonk 1961 'Performance on laboratory tasks requiring group creativity'. *Acta Psychologica* 18: 100–119.

Filley, Alan, Robert House, and Steven Kerr 1976 *Managerial process and organizational behavior*. Glenview, IL: Scott Foresman.

Galbraith, Jay 1977 *Organization design*. Reading, MA: Addison-Wesley.

Geringer, J. Michael 1988 'Partner selection criteria for developed country joint ventures'. *Business Quarterly* 53/2: 79–90.

Gist, Marilyn, Edwin Locke, and M. Susan Taylor 1987 'Organizational behavior: Group structure, process, and effectiveness'. *Journal of Management* 13: 237–257.

Goodman, Paul, Elizabeth Ravlin, and Marshall Schminke 1987 'Understanding groups in organizations' in *Research in organizational behavior*. L.L. Cummings and B.M.Staw (eds.), 1–71. Greenwich, CT: JAI Press.

Gudykunst, William 1991 *Bridging differences: Effective intergroup communication*. Newbury Park, CA: Sage.

Gudykunst, William, and Stella Ting Toomey 1988 *Culture and interpersonal communication*. Newbury Park, CA: Sage.

Hackman, J. Richard and Associates 1990 *Groups that work (and those that don't)*. San Francisco: Jossey-Bass.

Hall, Edward 1960 'The silent language in overseas business'. *Harvard Business Review* 38/3: 118–129.

Hall, Edward 1983 *The dance of life: The other dimension of time*. New York: Anchor/Doubleday.

Hambrick, Donald 1992 'Top management groups: A conceptual integration and reconsideration of the "team" label' in *Research in organizational behavior*. B.M. Staw and L.L. Cummings (eds.), 171–213. Greenwich, CT: JAI Press.

Hambrick, Donald and Gerard Brandon 1988 'Executive values' in *The executive effect: Concepts and methods for studying top managers* D.C. Hambrick (eds.), 3–34. Greenwich, CT: JAI Press.

Hambrick, Donald, Theresa Cho, and Ming-Jer Chen 1996 'The influence of top management team heterogeneity on firms' competitive moves'. *Administrative Science Quarterly* 41: 659–684.

Hambrick, Donald, and Phyllis Mason 1984 'Upper echelons: the organization as a reflection of its top managers'. *Academy of Management Review* 9: 193–206.

Heller, Frank, and Bernhard Wilpert 1979 'Managerial decision making: An international comparison' in *Functioning organizations in cross-cultural perspective*. G.W. England, A.R. Negandhi, and B. Wilpert (eds.), 118–129. Kent, OH: Kent State University Press.

Hoffman, L. Richard 1979 'Applying experimental research on group problem solving to organizations'. *Journal of Applied Behavioral Science* 15: 375–391.

Hoffman, L. Richard, and Norman Maier 1961 'Quality and acceptance of problem solutions by members of homogeneous and heterogeneous groups'. *Journal of Abnormal and Social Psychology* 62: 401–407.

Hofstede, Geert 1980 *Culture's consequences: International differences in work-related values*. Beverly Hills, CA and London: Sage.

Hofstede, Geert 1991 *Cultures and organizations: Software of the mind*. New York: McGraw-Hill.

Hurst, David, James Rush, and Roderick White 1989 'Top management teams and organizational renewal'. *Strategic Management Journal* 10 (Special issue): 87–105.

Jackson, Susan 1992 'Consequences of group composition for the interpersonal dynamics of strategic issue processing' in *Advances in strategic management*, Vol. 8. P. Shrivastava, A. Huff, and J. Dutton (eds.), 345–382. Greenwich, CN: JAI Press.

Jackson, Susan, Karen May, and Kristina Whitney [In Press] 'Understanding the dynamics of diversity in decision making teams' in *Team decision making effectiveness in organizations*. R.A. Guzo and E. Sallas (eds.). San Francisco: Jossey-Bass.

Janis, Irvin 1972 *Groupthink: Psychological studies of policy fiascoes* 2nd Ed. Boston: Houghton-Mifflin.

Kluckholn, Florence, and Fred Strodtbeck 1961 *Variations in value orientations*. San Francisco, CA: Row Peterson.

La France, Marianne, and Clara Mayo 1978 'Cultural aspects of nonverbal communication'. *International Journal of Intercultural Relations* 2:71–89.

Laurent, André 1983 'The cultural diversity of western conceptions of management'. *International Studies of Management and Organization* 13/1–2: 75–96.

Lord, Robert, and Roseanne Foti 1986 'Schema theories, information processing, and organizational behavior' in *The thinking organization* H.P. Sims, Jr. and D.A. Gioia (eds.), 20–48. San Francisco: Jossey-Bass.

March, James 1991 'Exploration and exploitation in organizational learning'. *Organization Science* 2: 71–87.

March, James, and Herbert Simon 1958 *Organizations*. New York: Wiley.

Markus, Hazel, and Shinobu Kitayama 1991 'Culture and the self: Implications for cognition, emotion, and motivation'. *Psychological Review* 98: 224–253.

Martin, Joanne 1992 *Cultures in organizations: Three perspectives*. New York: Oxford.

Maruyama, Magorah 1980 'Mindscapes and science theories'. *Current Anthropology* 21: 589–599.

McGrath, Joseph 1984 *Groups: Interaction and performance* Englewood Cliffs, NJ: Prentice-Hall.

Mesquita, Batja, and Nico Frijda 1992 'Cultural variations in emotions: A review'. *Psychological Bulletin* 112: 179–204.

Milliken, Frances, and Luis Martins 1996 'Searching for common threads: Understanding the multiple effects of diversity in organization groups'. *Academy of Management Journal* 21: 402–433.

O'Bannon, David, and Anil Gupta 1992 'Utility of heterogeneity versus homogeneity within top management teams: towards a resolution of the apparent conundrum'. Paper presented at Academy of Management Annual Meeting.

O'Reilly, Charles, III, and Sylvia Flatt 1989 'Executive team demography, organizational innovation and firm performance'. Working paper, University of California, Berkeley.

Ouchi, William 1977 'The relationship between organizational structure and organizational control'. *Administrative Science Quarterly* 22: 95–113.

Pelled, Lisa H. 1996 'Demographic diversity, conflict, and work group outcomes: An intervening process theory'. *Organization Science* 7: 615–631.

Parsons, Talcott, and Edward Shils, *editors* 1951 *Toward a general theory of action*. Cambridge, MA: Harvard University Press.

Phinney, Jean 1990 'Ethnic identity in adolescents and adults: Review of research'. *Psychological Bulletin* 103: 499–514.

Porter, Michael 1980 *Competitive strategy*. New York: Free Press.

Postman, Leo, Jerome Bruner, and Elliott McGinnies 1948 'Personal values as selective factors in perception'. *Journal of Abnormal and Social Psychology* 43/2: 142–154.

Prahalad, Coimbatore, and Gary Hamel 1990 'The core competence of the corporation'. *Harvard Business Review* 68/3: 79–93.

Redding, S. Gordon 1992 'The comparative management theory 200: getting the elephants and ostriches and even dinosaurs from the jungle into the iron cages'. Paper presented at the Conference on Perspectives on International Business, University of South Carolina, 1992.

Roberts, Karlene, and Nakiye Boyacigiller 1984 'Cross-national organizational research: the grasp of the blind men'. *Research in Organizational Behavior* 6: 423–475.

Shaw, Marvin 1981 *Group dynamics: The Psychology of small group behavior*, 3rd Ed. New York: McGraw-Hill.

Snow, Charles, Scott Snell, Sue C. Davison, and Donald Hambrick 1996 'Use transnational teams to globalize your company'. *Organization Dynamics*. 32 (Spring): 20–32.

Sutton, Francis, Seymour Harris, Carl Kaysen, and James Tobin 1956 'Value orientations and the relationship of managers and scientists'. *Administrative Science Quarterly* 10: 39–51.

Tajfel, Henri 1974 'Social identity and intergroup behavior'. *Social Science Information* 13: 65–93.

Triandis, Harry 1982 'Dimensions of cultural variation as parameters of organizational theories'. *International Studies of Management and Organization* 12: 139–169.

Triandis, Harry 1989 'The self and social behavior in differing cultural contexts'. *Psychological Review* 96: 506–520.

Triandis, Harry, Eleanor Hall, and Robert Ewen 1965 'Member heterogeneity and dyadic creativity'. *Human Relations* 18: 33–55.

Trompenaars, Fons 1993 *Riding the waves of culture: Understanding cultural diversity in business*. London: Economist Books.

Tuckman, Bruce 1965 'Developmental sequence in small groups'. *Psychological Bulletin* 63: 384–399.

Walsh, James 1995 'Managerial and organizational cognition: Notes from a trip down memory lane'. *Organization Science* 6: 280–321.

Watson, Warren, Kamalesh Kumar, and Larry Michaelson 1993 'Cultural diversity's impact on interaction process and performance: comparing homogeneous and diverse task groups'. *Academy of Management Journal* 36: 590–602.

Weick, Karl 1969 *The social psychology of organizing*. Reading, MA: Addison-Wesley.

Wolfgang, Aaron W. 1984 *Nonverbal behavior: Perspectives, applications, intercultural insights*. Lewiston, NY: Hofgrefe.

Article Review Form at end of book.

Why is it important for a company to widen its expat candidate pool? What myths have limited women in overseas assignments for global companies?

Women Expats — Shattering the Myths

Charlene Marmer Solomon

Suzanne Danner doesn't think of herself as a groundbreaker. But the soft-spoken, articulate manager, who is a partner in Price Waterhouse's Audit and Business Services in Warsaw, Poland, blazes new trails and shatters myths wherever she goes.

Not only is Danner a female expatriate in the world of finance, but she's also a human resources partner for the firm's Audit Practice, which gives her a crucial role in establishing new personnel and benefits practices for much of eastern Europe. Indeed, Danner, with her three children and working husband in tow, serves as a role model for other expats as well as for eastern European women she meets. She's such a strong believer in work/family balance and flexibility that she's trying to forge new alternative work policies that are considered radical in eastern Europe.

Ask Danner if she believes the notion that there are so few female expats because of prejudice or a global glass ceiling. Ask her if she has experienced negative consequences overseas as a result of being female. She'll pause, wrack her brain for examples, and then give you an unqualified, "No." In fact, she'll tell you that her gender may actually afford her advantages that allow her to be more effective in her job.

Danner's future is bright. According to New York City-based Catalyst's 1996 study, "Women in Corporate Leadership," almost 50 percent of *Fortune 500/Service 500* CEOs say international experience is crucial to upward movement. But not many women are in a position to take advantage of an overseas assignment to boost their corporate careers.

Women comprise only 14 percent of the expatriate population according to the "1996 Global Relocation Trends Survey Report" conducted by Windham International and the National Foreign Trade Council (both in New York City). Why the disparity"? It's more a reflection of the U.S. domestic glass ceiling than anything to do with women's effectiveness on international assignments or their willingness to go. Expatriates often are selected from upper-middle to senior corporate ranks, where women are still striving to achieve gender parity. (See "Women are Still Undervalued" in the May 1998 issue of *Workforce* for more details.)

Then women face additional hurdles before landing in the expatriate candidate pool. They must challenge two commonly assumed misconceptions. First: Women face overwhelming cultural barriers on international assignments. Second: Women don't want global postings because of career or family concerns.

Guess what? The world is changing, and while some of the same difficulties remain as they have in the past, it's time to re-examine assumptions, question why women's numbers are small and consider ways to make greater use of this valuable labor resource.

The Numbers Show an Upward Trend

The number of female expats is growing. Catalyst's research shows that only 5 percent of expatriates were women prior to 1993. The "Global Relocation Trends Survey Report" also indicates a positive trend, albeit a slow one. These reports for the last several years show the percentage of international assignees who were women to be: 10 percent in 1993, 12 percent in 1994, 13 percent in 1995 and 14 percent in 1996.

"Progress is slow, but there's a steady increase in women who are being considered for—and who are accepting—overseas assignments," says Nina Segal, manager of cross-cultural services at Windham International and previously assistant dean for Career Services at Columbia University's School of International and Public Affairs in New York City. "If you look at organizations that have made special efforts to recruit and promote women, you'll see a larger number of female expatriates."

Indeed, according to Nancy J. Adler, a professor of organizational behavior and cross-cultural management with McGill University in Montreal, the global arena may be more receptive to female managers

---

"Women Expats—Shattering the Myths" by Charlene Marmer Solomon, copyright May 1998. Used with permission of ACC Communications Inc./*Workforce*, Costa Mesa, CA. All rights reserved.

How to Cultivate Female Candidates

Nancy Laben, whose children are now four and six, spent her second maternity leave considering the move to the Hong Kong office of Andersen Worldwide. Her husband took himself off the partnership track at a law firm in Chicago, and they decided to relocate just months after the baby was born because they both wanted international experience. The beginning was horrendous. "Had this not been a lifelong dream for me and had my husband not been so supportive, I wouldn't have made it," says Laben. "Everyone was helpful, but I needed more support." Laben travels between 30 percent and 50 percent of the time, and her husband, who now works as a consultant, provides the child care.

Companies struggle with this adjustment issue in many ways. Currently, competitive HR benefits for families include preassignment visits, predeparture orientation programs, destination and settling-in support (such as local experts helping to arrange appointments for housing and school selection and community orientation) and spouse/partner career counseling. However, there's a dearth of services for accompanying partners and also a lack of support for serious child-care arrangements. These remain big hurdles for dual-career partners. In addition, communicating the benefits and possibilities is something firms aren't doing.

"Any increased support a company provides to the partner or family is really helpful," says Nina Segal of New York City-based Windham International. "It's not just when they get to the destination that it's important, but it's invaluable before they go [because] people have a tendency to self-select out." She suggests information sessions that showcase expatriate women who have had successful assignments.

Eleanor Haller-Jorden of Zurich, Switzerland-based Paradigm Group suggests that companies alter core operational assumptions about what is and isn't appealing about international assignments. They could create a database of their own population and integrate business demographic information with personal demographic information about employees. In other words, companies could track people's careers in the acquisition of technical talent, personal and family status, and interest in overseas opportunities.

There are several steps you can take to improve the odds that high-potential women in your organization find out about and accept international assignments:

1. **Help women break through the glass ceiling.** Clearly, if women aren't making it to managerial positions, they'll never join the expatriate candidate pool. Evaluate gender parity in your organization and, if necessary, implement a diversity program to strengthen women's chances for success.

2. **Create long-term career-development programs.** Encourage male and female top performers alike to include the possibility of an international assignment in their career plans.

3. **Develop an organized approach for identifying potential women expats.** Talk to high-performing women and ask them if they'd consider an international assignment. Save this information in a database of potential expatriate candidates. Also, train your line managers to recognize and dismiss the myths about women on international assignments.

4. **Make sure women assignees receive predeparture cross-cultural training.** It's important that all expatriate families receive predeparture preparation. And women expats should take advantage of this opportunity to learn how to handle some of the unique challenges they may face in other cultures.

5. **Find out what types of support women believe would help them be successful.** Implement policies that support families through the transition, including career services for spouses and partners, destination services and programs addressing child-care needs.

6. **Publicize the successes of women expatriates.** Bring in female repatriates to speak with groups of employees and discuss their experiences.

—CMS

---

than the domestic one. Global corporations are in such a highly competitive business environment that they must select the very best people regardless of gender. Furthermore, she says in her book "Competitive Frontiers: Women Managers in a Global Economy" (co-authored with Dafna Izraeli, Blackwell Business Press 1994) that the less hierarchical, more inclusive structure of global firms is very conducive to women's success.

So, let's examine those outdated beliefs.

Assumption No. 1: Women Are Less Effective Because of Cultural Biases Against Them

Laura Simeone has a broad perspective on the international experience. As senior manager of human resources in Asia for Palo Alto, California-based Cisco Systems, Simeone has supervised dozens of Asians and Europeans during her tenure at headquarters and is currently an expatriate in Singapore.

"There's an interesting dynamic," Simeone says. "Western women are in a unique position and are generally well-received in other countries. They're foreign—and therefore not expected to conform to the same standards that local culture dictates for women. They get the opportunity to function more in their normal roles because they aren't constrained the way local female counterparts would be; they aren't in a subordinate position to men."

Simeone continues, "If people are going to have a difficult time in specific cultures, it's going to be all of

78   Intercultural Communications

the Westerners, not just women Westerners."

According to Simeone, women have the opportunity to succeed in several ways. "It has always been said that women have to be at least as good as men in order to prove themselves. I think there's a natural tendency [among expatriate women] to want to do high-quality work, and it speaks for itself. Furthermore, if a woman has strong support from senior management in her organization, it lends her credibility. Other managers and employees in the country will take their cue from that."

While some cultures are more challenging to women than others, most are manageable with flexibility and planning. For instance, many societies conduct business in environments where there's heavy alcohol consumption. "The tension between a woman wanting to appear to fit in and be on equal footing with local males, yet at the same time not wanting to be viewed in a pejorative way, always brings up tricky dynamics," says Simeone. "Women are going to have to decide how to handle the situation before they get into it." Business networking can become a tough cultural issue. But it's one women can handle with predeparture cross-cultural training.

Nancy Laben is a powerhouse. Based in Hong Kong, she is general counsel for Andersen Worldwide, providing legal support and services to 13 countries in the Asia region. Trotting between Japan, Southeast Asia, Australia and China, she helps negotiate contracts with clients and assists with personnel questions. Laben, who spent part of her childhood in Japan, shows that ingenuity and cultural wisdom can overcome many cultural difficulties.

"In Asia, much of the business-generating activity occurs in surroundings where women are typically not accepted," Laben explains. For example, in Japan it's on the golf course. Although she doesn't see herself teeing off as part of a high-powered foursome, she does construct other opportunities. "What I try to do is to arrange circumstances [requiring us] to work late. Then we go and grab dinner. I try to turn it into a team-building exercise." Others create family barbecues and dinners with couples as a way to network. They take advantage of every occasion that's gender-neutral to build business relationships.

These women acknowledge that cultural sensitivity and awareness are crucial. Women who don't have that cultural experience may not be aware of how to create opportunities and may become severely frustrated.

Assumption No. 2: Women Managers with Families Aren't Eager for Global Assignments

Moving a family internationally isn't an easy task. And, it becomes extraordinarily complicated for expatriate women in dual-career marriages. This is because typically women—even working women—carry the majority of the responsibility for taking care of the family. To emphasize this point, the "1996 Global Relocation Survey Trends Report" shows that of the 71 percent of married expatriates, married men outnumber married women nine to one; but single males outnumber single females only three to one. Clearly, single women have less complicated hurdles to overcome than married women.

But this disparity is a changing reality as well, and it doesn't mean that women who have families don't want international assignments. Just ask Eleanor Haller-Jorden, managing director of the Paradigm Group, a Zurich, Switzerland-based international human resources research and consulting firm. "With the rise of dual-career couples, companies obviously will need to confront this issue more directly," she points out. "I think there have been some dated assumptions in terms of the willingness and ability of male spouses to travel." Line managers and HR professionals need to be more open and direct, speaking to employees about what might be of interest to them and what might get in the way of their taking assignments.

Haller-Jorden, who has two children and a husband who is an international banker, is in the midst of conducting a 10-year longitudinal study on international dual-career families. She's able to reel off examples of couples who have eagerly sought assignments, as she and her husband did.

And why wouldn't they be eager? As stated earlier, CEOs want to see international experience in their executives. In the same Catalyst report, 50 percent of senior women said that high-visibility assignments were important, and 33 percent wanted cross-functional job rotations. Adler's research underscores these findings. As she puts it, there may have been differences in the past, but today, both men and women are equally interested in expat assignments.

Despite this interest, many line managers assume women won't want to move their children overseas. But talk with women who have relocated their children internationally, and they'll wax poetic about the advantages for their children. They're thrilled about providing them with new surroundings, the sense of being an international citizen, and the language and educational opportunities. Although it's not exactly an easy adjustment, most parents claim their children soak up the foreign culture and adapt to it quickly.

By contrast, it's the spouse or partner who has trouble. When Danner landed in Poland she was immediately thrown into a bank privatization. Within three days she was on a plane to Gdansk, working every night until midnight. Her husband and children were living in a hotel. But, she says, even though it was tough for her, it was extraordinarily difficult for her husband. He's a marketing expert who decided to take advantage of this opportunity and agreed to help the children adjust first before looking for work.

"It took him six to nine months to get through the whole shock of language barrier, culture problems and just learning to get around," says Danner. "He'd never been alone with the children in the same way, either," she says. Although the family had some cultural orientation, Danner believes it wasn't enough. "There needs to be more assistance as to what it's going to be like," she says.

An overseas relocation isn't a quick adjustment, and it isn't an opportunity for everyone. But when women with families come forward and express their eagerness for expatriate assignments, they shouldn't be faced with managers who had assumed they wouldn't be interested because of the age of their children or their spouses' careers.

Don't Assume Anything

Just as the global marketplace changes constantly, so do the individuals who work in multinational firms. Greater opportunities and greater knowledge of the expatriate lifestyle will encourage women to step forward.

"I've seen how important international assignments have been in a lot of women's careers in terms of increased mobility and visibility for them in the workplace," says Segal. "There needs to be encouragement and proactive behavior on the part of the organization to empower female executives to feel they have some control over where their careers are going." If career management and effective mentoring of women is successful, if sufficient support and education become commonplace, there will likely be more female expats and more women in the foreign work environments altogether.

But old assumptions won't move the corporate culture or the global business effort forward. HR managers, along with managerial women and their line managers, must shatter stereotypes and create an action plan that works toward making full use of all individuals in the workplace.

Article Review Form at end of book.

Why do transnational firms need global human resources management systems? How does a transnational company create a pool of globally competent people?

Managing Globally Competent People

Nancy J. Adler
McGill University

Susan Bartholomew
McGill University

"Top-level managers in many of today's leading corporations are losing control of their companies. The problem is not that they have misjudged the demands created by an increasingly complex environment and an accelerating rate of environmental change, nor even that they have failed to develop strategies appropriate to the new challenges. The problem is that their companies are incapable of carrying out the sophisticated strategies they have developed. Over the past 20 years, strategic thinking has far outdistanced organizational capabilities."[1]

Today, people create national competitiveness, not, as suggested by classical economic theory, mere access to advantageous factors of production.[2] Yet, human systems are also one of the major constraints in implementing global strategies. Not surprisingly therefore, human resource management has become "an important focus of top management attention, particularly in multinational enterprises."[3]

The clear issue is that strategy (the *what*) is internationalizing faster than implementation (the *how*) and much faster than individual managers and executives themselves (the *who*). "The challenges [therefore] are not the 'whats' of what-to-do, which are typically well-known. They are the 'hows' of managing human resources in a global firm."[4]

How prepared are executives to manage transnational companies? How capable are firms' human resource systems of recruiting, developing, retaining, and using globally competent managers and executives? A recent survey of major U.S. corporations found only six percent reporting foreign assignments to be essential for senior executive careers, with forty-nine percent believing foreign assignments to be completely immaterial.[5]

Which firms are leading in developing globally competent managers and executives, and which remain in the majority and lag behind? That majority, according to a recent survey of 1500 CEOs, will result in a lack of sufficient senior American managers prepared to run transnational businesses, forcing U.S. firms to confront the highest executive turn-over in history.[6]

By contrast, it describes the approaches of some of the world's leading firms that distinguish them from the majority. There is no question that world business is going global; the question raised in this article is how to create human systems capable of implementing transnational business strategies. Based on their research, the authors support the conclusion of the recent *21st Century Report* that "executives who perceive their international operations as shelves for second-rate managers are unsuited for the CEO job in the year 2000, or indeed any managerial job today."[7]

Transnationally Competent Managers

Not all business strategies are equally global, nor need they be. As will be described, a firm's business strategy can be primarily domestic, international, multinational, or transnational. However, to be effective, the firm's human resource strategy should be integrated with its business strategy. Transnational firms need a transnational business strategy. While superficially appearing to be a truism, transnational firms also need a transnational human resource system and transnationally competent managers.

As summarized in Table 1, transnationally competent managers require a broader range of skills than traditional international managers. First, transnational managers must understand the worldwide business environment from a global perspective. Unlike expatriates of the past, transnational managers are not focused on a single country nor limited to managing relationships between headquarters and a single foreign subsidiary. Second, transnational managers must learn about many foreign cultures' perspectives, tastes, trends, technologies, and approaches

---

Reprinted with permission of Academy of Management, PO Box 3020, Briar Cliff Manor, NY 10510–8020. *Managing Globally Competent People*, Nancy Adler and Susan Bartholomew, The Executive, August 1992. Reproduced by permission of the publisher via Copyright Clearance Center, Inc.

Table 1 Transnationally Competent Managers

Transnational Skills	Transnationally Competent Managers	Traditional International Managers
Global Perspective	Understand worldwide business environment from a global perspective	Focus on a single foreign country and on managing relationships between headquarters and that country
Local Responsiveness	Learn about many cultures	Become an expert on one culture
Synergistic Learning	Work with and learn from people from many cultures simultaneously	Work with and coach people in each foreign culture separately or sequentially
	Create a culturally synergistic organizational environment	Integrate foreigners into the headquarters' national organizational culture
Transition and Adaptation	Adapt to living in many foreign cultures	Adapt to living in a foreign culture
Cross-cultural Interaction	Use cross-cultural interaction skills on a daily basis throughout one's career	Use cross-cultural interaction skills primarily on foreign assignments
Collaboration	Interact with foreign colleagues as equals	Interact within clearly defined hierarchies of structural and cultural dominance
Foreign Experience	Transpatriation for career and organization development	Expatriation or inpatriation primarily to get the job done

to conducting business. Unlike their predecessors, they do not focus on becoming an expert on one particular culture. Third, transnational managers must be skillful at working with people from many cultures simultaneously. They no longer have the luxury of dealing with each country's issues on a separate, and therefore sequential, basis. Fourth, similar to prior expatriates, transnational managers must be able to adapt to living in other cultures. Yet, unlike their predecessors, transnational managers need cross-cultural skills on a daily basis, throughout their career, not just during foreign assignments, but also on regular multicountry business trips and in daily interaction with foreign colleagues and clients worldwide. Fifth, transnational managers interact with foreign colleagues as equals, rather than from within clearly defined hierarchies of structural or cultural dominance and subordination. Thus, not only do the variety and frequency of cross-cultural interaction increase with globalization, but also the very nature of cross-cultural interaction changes.

The development of transnationally competent managers depends on firms' organizational capability to design and manage transnational human resource systems. Such systems, in turn, allow firms to implement transnational business strategies. Before investigating firms' capability to implement transnational business strategies, let us briefly review a range of global business strategies along with each strategy's requisite managerial skills.

The Globalization of Business: Strategy, Structure, and Managerial Skills

Since World War II, industry after industry has progressed from dominantly domestic operations toward more global strategies. Historically many firms progressed through four distinct phases: domestic, international, multinational, and transnational.[8] As firms progress towards global strategies, the portfolio of skills required of managers undergoes a parallel shift.

Domestic. Historically, most corporations began as domestic firms. They developed new products or services at home for the domestic market. During this initial domestic phase, foreign markets, and hence international managerial skills, were largely irrelevant.

International. As new firms entered, competition increased and each company was forced to search for new markets or resign itself to losing market share. A common response was to expand internationally, initially by exporting to foreign markets and later by developing foreign assembly and production facilities designed to serve the largest of those markets. To manage those foreign operations, firms often restructured to form a separate international division. Within the new international division, each country was managed separately, thus creating a multidomestic nature. Because the foreign operations were frequently seen as an extension—and therefore a replication—of domestic operations, they generally were not viewed as state of the art.

During this international phase, a hierarchical structure exists between the firm's headquarters and its various foreign subsidiaries. Power and influence are concentrated at corporate headquarters, which is primarily staffed by members of the headquarters' national culture. It is during this phase that firms often send their first home country managers abroad as expatriates. Cross-cultural interaction between expatriate managers and local subsidiary staff thus takes place within a clearly defined hierarchy in which headquarters has both structural and cultural dominance.

During this phase, international management is synonymous with expatriation. To be effective, expatriate managers must be competent at transferring technology to the local culture, managing local staff, and adapting business practices to suit local conditions. Specifically, international expatriate managers require cultural adaptation skills—as does their spouse and family—to adjust to living in a new environment and working with the local people. They must also acquire specific knowledge about the particular culture's perspectives, tastes, trends, technologies, and ways of doing business. Learning is thus single country focused—and culturally specific—during the international phase.

Multinational. As competition continues to heighten, firms increasingly emphasize producing least-cost products and services. To benefit from potential economies of scale and geographic scope, firms produce more standardized products and services. Because the prior phase's multidomestic structure can no longer support success, firms restructure to integrate domestic and foreign operations into worldwide lines of business, with sourcing, producing, assembling, and marketing distributed across many countries, and major decisions—which continue to be made at headquarters—strongly influenced by least-cost outcomes.

During the multinational phase, the hierarchical relationship remains between headquarters and foreign subsidiaries. In addition, with the increased importance of foreign operations to the core business, headquarters more tightly controls major decisions worldwide. However, headquarters' decisions are now made by people from a wider range of cultures than previously many of whom are local managers from foreign subsidiaries posted on temporary "inpatriate" assignments at corporate headquarters. These "inpatriates" are not encouraged to express the diversity of national perspectives and cultural experience they represent. Rather, they are asked to adapt as the firm implicitly and explicitly integrates them into the organizational culture which is still dominated by the values of the headquarters' national culture. While multinational representation increases at headquarters, cultural dominance of the headquarters' national culture continues, remaining loosely coupled with structure.

For the first time, senior managers, those leading the worldwide lines of business, need to understand the world business environment. Similarly for the first time, senior managers must work daily with clients and employees from around the world to be effective. International and cross-cultural skills become needed for managers throughout the firm, not just for those few imminently leaving for foreign postings. Expatriates and "inpatriates" still require cultural adaptation skills and specific local knowledge, but these are not the dominant international skills required by most managers in a multinational firm. For the majority, learning needs grow beyond local context to encompass a need to understand the world business environment. In addition, multinational managers need to be skilled at working with clients and employees from many nations (rather than merely from a single foreign country), as well as at standardizing operations and integrating people from around the world into a common organizational culture.

Transnational. As competition continues to increase and product lifecycles shorten dramatically, firms find it necessary to compete globally, based simultaneously on state-of-the-art, top quality products and services and least-cost production. Unlike the prior phase's emphasis on identical products that can be distributed worldwide, transnational products are increasingly mass-customized—tailored to each individual client's needs. Research and development demands increase as does the firm's need for worldwide marketing scope.

These dynamics lead to transnational networks of firms and divisions within firms, including an increasingly complex web of strategic alliances. Internationally, these firms distribute their multiple headquarters across a number of nations. As a result, transnational firms become less hierarchically structured than firms operating in the previous phases. As such, power is no longer centered in a single headquarters that is coincident with or dominated by any one national culture. As a consequence, both structural and cultural dominance are minimized, with cross-cultural interaction no longer following any pre-defined "passport hierarchy." It is for these firms that transnational human resource strategies are now being developed that emphasize organizational learning along with individual managerial skills.

Moreover, the integration required in transnational firms is based on cultural synergy—on combining the many cultures into a unique organizational culture—rather than on simply integrating foreigners into the dominant culture of the headquarters' nationality (as was the norm in prior phases). Transnational managers require additional new skills to be effective in their less hierarchical, networked firms: first, the ability to work with people of other cultures as equals; second, the ability to learn in order to continually enhance organizational capability. Transnational managers must learn how to collaborate with partners worldwide, gaining as much knowledge as possible from each interaction, and, transmitting that knowledge quickly and effectively throughout the worldwide network of operations. This requires managers who both want to learn and have the skills to quickly and continuously learn from people of other cultures.[9]

Transnational Human Resource Systems

The development of such "transnationally competent managers," as discussed previously, depends upon firms' capability to design and manage transnational human resource systems. The function of human resource systems, in general, is to recruit, develop, and retain competent managers and executives. Beyond these core functions, we add utilization: human resource systems facilitate the effective "utilization" of those managers who have been recruited, developed, and retained. Therefore, a transnational human resource system is one that recruits, develops, retains and utilizes managers and executives who are competent transnationally.[10]

Three Dimensions of a Transnational Human Resource System

For a transnational human resource system to be effective, it must exhibit three characteristics: transnational scope, transnational representation, and transnational process. We will describe each briefly, and then discuss their implications for recruiting, developing, retaining, and using human resources.

Transnational Scope. Transnational scope is the geographical context within which all major decisions are made. As Bartlett and Ghoshal have stated, global management is a "frame of mind," not a particular organizational structure.[11] Thus, to achieve global scope, executives and managers must frame major decisions and evaluate options relative to worldwide business dynamics. Moreover, they must benchmark their own and their firm's performance against worldclass standards. They can neither discuss nor resolve major issues within a narrower national or regional context. An example is Unilever's "Best Proven Practices." This British-Dutch consumer products firm identifies superior practices and innovations in its subsidiaries worldwide and then diffuses the outstanding approaches throughout the worldwide organization.[12]

Transnational Representation. Transnational representation refers to the multinational composition of the firm's managers and executives. To achieve transnational representation, the firm's portfolio of key executives and managers should be as multinational as its worldwide distribution of production, finance, sales, and profits. Symbolically, firms achieve transnational representation through the well balanced portfolio of passports held by senior management. Philips, for example, maintains transnational representation by having "the corporate pool." This pool consists of mobile individuals representing more than fifty nationalities, each having at least five years of experience and ranked in the top twenty percent on performance, and all financed on a corporate budget.[13]

Transnational Process. Transnational process reflects the firm's ability to effectively include representatives and ideas from many cultures in its planning and decision-making processes. Firms create transnational process when they consistently recognize, value, and effectively use cultural diversity within the organization; that is, when there is "no unintended leakage of culture specific systems and approaches."[14] Transnational process, however, is not the mere inclusion of people and ideas of many cultures; rather, it goes beyond inclusion to encompass cultural synergy—the combination of culturally diverse perspectives and approaches into a new transnational organizational culture. Cultural synergy requires "a genuine belief . . . that more creative and effective ways of managing people could be developed as a result of cross-cultural learning."[15] To create transnational process, executives and managers must be as skilled at working with and learning from people from outside their own culture as with same culture nationals.

Today's Firms: How Transnational?

A survey was conducted of fifty firms headquartered in the United States and Canada from a wide variety of industries to determine the extent to which their overall business strategy matched their current human resource system, as well as identifying the extent of globalization of their human resource strategies. The results paint a picture of extensive global business involvement. Unfortunately, however, similar involvement in recruiting, developing, retaining, and using globally competent managers is lacking.

Global Strategic Integration

The fifty firms made almost half of their sales abroad, and earned nearly forty percent of their revenues and profits outside of their headquarters' country (the United States or Canada). Similarly, almost two fifths of the fifty firms' employees worked outside the headquarters' country. Yet, when these firms reviewed their human resource systems as a whole, and their senior leadership in particular, they could not reveal nearly as global a portrait.

For example, in comparing themselves with their competitors, the fifty firms found themselves to be more global on overall business strategy, financial systems, production operations, and marketing. However, they found their human resource systems to be the least global functional area within their own organization. Moreover, unlike their assessment in other functional areas, they did not evaluate their human resource systems as being more global than those of their competitors.

Similarly, the senior leadership of the surveyed firms was less global on all three global indicators—scope, representation, and process—than each firm's overall business performance. For example, an average of only eight countries were represented among the most senior one hundred executives in each firm. Half of the companies reported fewer than four nationalities among the top one hundred executives. Firms therefore have less than a quarter of the international representation in their senior leadership (eight percent) as they have in their global business performance (ie., sales, revenues, and profits: forty percent). Similarly, of the same top one hundred executives in each firm, only fifteen percent were from outside of North America. This represents less than half the internationalization of the senior executive cadre (fifteen percent) as of business performance (forty percent). Moreover, using experience, rather than representation, yields similar results. Of the same one hundred leaders, almost three quarters lacked expatriate experience, with only a third reporting any international experience at all. Not surprisingly, less than one in five spoke a foreign language. On no measure of international experience is the senior leadership of these North American firms as international as the business itself.

Transnational Human Resource Integration

Firms' organizational capability to implement transnational business strategies is supported by transnational human resource management systems. As discussed, such systems should exhibit all three dimensions—transnational scope, transnational representation, and transnational

84   Intercultural Communications

process. These three global dimensions are clearly important for each of the four primary components of human resource systems—recruiting, developing, retaining, and utilizing globally competent people. Each will therefore be discussed separately. Unfortunately, the results of this study indicate that firms' human resource management systems have not become global either as rapidly or as extensively as have their business strategies and structures.

Recruiting. For recruiting decisions, transnational scope requires that firms consider their business needs and the availability of candidates worldwide. Similar to the firm's strategic business decisions, some recruiting decisions must enhance worldwide integration and coordination, others local responsiveness, and others the firm's ability to learn.[16] Local responsiveness requires that firms recruit people with a sophisticated understanding of each of the countries in which they operate; this includes recruiting host nationals. Worldwide integration requires that recruiting be guided by worldclass standards in selecting the most competent people from anywhere in the world for senior management positions. Individual and organizational learning requires that people be selected who are capable of simultaneously working with and learning from colleagues from many nations: people who are capable of creating cultural synergy.

Transnational representation in recruiting requires that firms select managers from throughout the world for potential positions anywhere in the world. In a literal sense, it requires that talent flows to opportunity worldwide, without regard to national passport.

Transnational process in recruiting requires that firms use search and selection procedures that are equally attractive to candidates from each target nationality. Selection criteria, including the methods used to judge competence, must not be biased to favour any one culture.

Similarly, incentives to join the firm must appeal to a broad range of cultures. The antithesis of transnational process was exhibited by one U.S. firm when it offered new college recruits from the Netherlands one of the same incentives it offers its American recruits: free graduate education. The Dutch candidates found this "benefit" amusing given that graduate education in the Netherlands—unlike in the United States—is already paid for by the government and thus free to all students.

Rather than encouraging high potential candidates, this particular incentive made Dutch students hesitate to join a firm that demonstrated such parochialism in its initial contact with them.

The fifty surveyed firms reported that their recruitment and selection activities were less than global in terms of scope, representation, and process. For a summary, see Exhibit 1: Transnational Recruiting.

Development. In managerial development, transnational scope means that managers' experiences both on-the-job and in formal training situations prepare them to work anywhere in the world with people from all parts of the world; that is, it prepares them to conduct the firm's business in a global environment. Transnational firms search worldwide for the best training and development options and select specific approaches and programs based on worldclass standards.

To achieve transnational representation, training and development programs must be planned and delivered by multinational teams as well as offered to multinational participants. To be transnational, programs cannot be planned by one culture (generally representatives of the headquarters' nationality) and simply exported for local delivery abroad. By contrast, using a transnational approach, American Express created a multinational design team at headquarters to develop training approaches and programs which were subsequently localized for delivery around the world. At no time did American cultural values dominate either the process or the programs.

Transnational process in development requires that the approaches taken effectively include all participating cultures. Thus, the process cannot encourage greater participation by one nationality to the exclusion of other nationalities. Ericsson and Olivetti provide examples of a transnational development approach. Each company created a management development center in which both the staff and executive participants come from all regions of the world. To minimize the possibility of headquarters' cultural dominance, neither company located its management development center in the headquarters' country—Sweden or Italy—but rather both chose another more culturally neutral country.[17]

For transnational firms, foreign assignments become a core component of the organizational and career development process. "Transpatriates" from all parts of the world are sent to all other parts of the world to develop their worldwide perspective and cross-cultural skills, as well as developing the organization's cadre of globally sophisticated managers. Foreign assignments in transnational firms are no longer used primarily to get a job done in a foreign country (expatriation) or to

---

Exhibit 1 Transnational Recruiting

The 50 surveyed firms reported that their recruitment and selection activities were less than transnational in terms of scope, representation, and process. In selecting future senior managers, the 50 firms ranked an outstanding overall track record as the most important criterion, with foreign business experience, demonstrated cultural sensitivity and adaptability, and a track record for outstanding performance outside the home country ranked as somewhat, but not highly, important. Moreover, foreign language skills were not considered at all important. Similarly, while considering three out of four transnational scope and process skills to be somewhat important for promotion to senior management (understanding world issues and trends; working effectively with clients and colleagues from other countries; and, demonstrating cultural sensitivity), none was considered highly important. Once again, foreign language skills were not considered important for promotion. Similarly, on transnational representation, only a third of the 50 firms stated that they "recruit managers from all parts of the world in which . . . [they] conduct business."

socialize foreign country nationals into the home country headquarters' culture ("inpatriation"), but rather to enhance individual and organizational learning in all parts of the system ("transpatriation"). Using a "transpatriation" approach, Royal Dutch Shell, for example, uses multifunctional and multinational experience to provide corporate wide, transnational skills. Shell's "aim is that every member of an operating company management team should have had international experience and that each such team should include one expatriate . . . [Similarly, at IBM], international experience is [considered] indispensable to senior positions."[18]

In the survey, the fifty firms reported that their training and development opportunities were less than global on all three dimensions of human resource strategy: transnational scope, transnational representation, and transnational process (for a summary of the research, see Exhibit 2: Transnational Development). Similar to recruitment, training and development approaches currently are not nearly as global as are overall business strategies. To reduce the gap between the relative globalization of firms' strategies and their less-than-global human resource systems, firms must learn how to recognize, value, and uses globally competent managers. As one surveyed executive summarized, closing the gaps begins by having "the key organizational development activity . . . focused on allowing people of different nationalities to meet and to get to know each other, and, through these linkages, to meet the needs of the company."

Retaining. Transnational scope in retaining managers means that decisions about career paths must consider the firm's needs and operations worldwide.

Performance incentives, rewards, and career opportunities must meet worldclass standards such that the firm does not lose its most competent people. Firms must benchmark excellence in their human resource systems against their most significant global competitors in the same ways that they assess the relative competitiveness of their research and development, production, marketing, and financial systems.

Exhibit 2 Transnational Development

In the survey, the 50 firms reported that their training and development opportunities were less than transnational on all three dimensions of human resource strategy: scope, representation, and process. Fewer than one in four of the firms reported that the content of their training programs was global in focus, that they had representatives of many nations attending each program, or that their programs were designed or delivered by multinational training teams. Only four percent reported that cross-cultural training was offered to all managers. However, the firms did report offering a greater number of general development opportunities worldwide than specific international training programs. A third of the firms provide equivalent development opportunities for managers worldwide and 42 percent provide such opportunities for managers of all nationalities.

In reviewing foreign assignments, the 50 firms report using expatriates primarily to "get the job done abroad," not to develop the organization, nor to develop the individual manager's career. Given their emphasis on getting the immediate job done, it is not surprising that they did not report consistently selecting the "stars" (either high potential junior managers or very senior, top-performing executives) for expatriate positions. To increase globalization in their development programs, the surveyed executives strongly recommended "transferring different nationalities to different countries several times in their career" and "making it clear to these employees that international assignments are important to career development." However, to date, the majority of the surveyed films do not have such recommended programs in place.

Transnational representation requires that organizational incentives and career path opportunities be equally accessible and appealing to managers from all nationalities. Firms with transnational human resource systems do not create a glass ceiling beyond which only members of the headquarters' nationality can be promoted.

Transnational process requires that the performance review and promotion systems include approaches which are equally appropriate to a broad range of nationalities. The process by which promotion and career path decisions are made should not be innately biased towards any one culture, nor should it exclude particular cultures. The underlying dynamic in transnational process is not to institute identical systems worldwide, but rather to use approaches which are culturally equivalent. Shell for example, ensures this transnational orientation by having managers' "career home" be in "a business function rather than a geographical place."[19] As one surveyed senior executive summarized, firms considered to be outstanding in transnational human resource management are "flexible enough in systems and practices to attract and retain the best people regardless of nationality."

Utilizing. Transnational scope in utilization means that managers' problem solving skills are focused on the firm's worldwide operations and competitive environment, not just on the regional, national, or local situation. To assess the competitive environment in transnational human resource management, the fifty surveyed firms identified leading North American, European, and Asian companies. The top North American firm was perceived to be IBM, followed by General Electric, and Citicorp. The surveyed firms identified Royal Dutch Shell as the leading European firm, followed by Nestle and Philips, along with British Petroleum and Unilever. Sony was selected as the leading Asian firm, followed by Honda, Toyota, and Mitsubishi. Yet, in reviewing the pattern of responses, a significant proportion of the surveyed firms do not appear to be benchmarking excellence in global human resource management at all, and an even greater number appear to be geographically limiting their perspective to a fairly narrow, parochial scope. For instance, almost a fifth of the surveyed firms (all of which are North American) could not name a single

86 Intercultural Communications

leading North American firm. Even more disconcerting, more than a third could not identify a single excellent European firm, and half could not name a single excellent Asian firm.[20]

Beyond scope, transnational representation in utilization means that managers and executives of many nationalities are included in the firm's critical operating and strategic planning teams. Managers from outside of headquarters are not "out of sight and out of mind;" rather they are integrated into the worldwide network of knowledge exchange, continual learning, and action. For example, as Unilever's director of management development explains:

"In recent years, I have had several product group directors . . . [want] an expatriate on the board of the local company. Not just because they haven't got a national, not just because it would be good for the expatriate, but because it would be good for the company to have a bit of challenge to the one-best-way of doing doings."[21]

Transnational process in human resource utilization means that the organization culture does not inherently bias contributions from or towards any particular cultural group. The human resource system recognizes the firm's cultural diversity and uses it either to build culturally synergistic processes that include all cultures involved or to select the particular process that is the most appropriate for the given situation.

Illusions and Recommendations

From the prior discussion, it is clear that transnational human resource systems are both fundamentally important for future business success and qualitatively different from prior approaches to human resource management. Equally evident is the fact that North American firms' human resource systems are not nearly as global as their business operations on any of the three fundamental human resource dimensions: transnational scope, transnational representation, and transnational process. Competitive demands appear to have "outrun the slow pace of organizational change and adjustment . . . [with] top management beginning to feel that the organization itself is the biggest barrier to competitive and strategic development."[22] It is telling that in most cases the respondents found the survey itself to be important and yet very difficult to complete, primarily because their firms did not systematically collect or keep data on any aspect of global human resource management.

The remaining question is why. There appears to be a series of illusions—of mind traps—that are preventing firms from acting in a global manner, including recognizing the mental gap between their current human resource approaches and those necessary to succeed in a highly competitive transnational business environment. Many of the surveyed executives recognized that their firms simply "lack global thinking" and "lack global business strategies," largely due to the "massive U.S. imprint on human resource practices." According to many of the American executives, firms must "stop thinking that the world begins and ends at U.S. borders," "stop having a U.S. expatriate mentality," and begin to "realize that the world does not revolve around us." This pattern of responses suggests the following seven illusions.

Illusion One: If business has gone well, it will continue to go well
No, today is not like yesterday, nor will tomorrow be a projection of today. Business has fundamentally changed, and human resource systems must undergo similar transformational changes to stay relevant, let alone effective. As Kenichi Ohmae has pointed out, "Today and in the twenty-first century, management's ability to transform the organization and its people into a global company is a prerequisite for survival because both its customers and competitors have become cosmopolitan."[23]

Illusion Two: We have always played on a level playing field and won
No. The North American economies (and therefore North American firms) have had an advantage: they were the only developed economies left intact following World War II and were thus "the only game in town." Today, Asia, Europe, and the Americans each have highly competitive firms and economies, none of which will continue to prosper without being excellent at including people and business worldwide. As Ohmae has observed, "The key to a nation's future is its human resources. It used to be its natural resources, but not any more. The quality and number of its educated people now determines a country's likely prosperity or decline"; so too with global firms.[24]

Illusion Three: If we manage expatriates better, we will have an effective global human resource system
No. Doing better at what was necessary in the past (expatriate management) is not equivalent to creating systems capable of sustaining global competitiveness today. Whereas the temptation is to attempt to do better at that which is known (in this case, the simple expatriation of managers), the real challenge is to excel at that which is new. Transnational firms need transnational human resource systems to succeed. Better managed expatriate transfers will only improve one small aspect of existing human resource management, not create an overall transnational system.

Illusion Four: If we're doing something, we must be doing enough
No. Focusing on only one of the three transnational dimensions—scope, representation, or process—is not enough to transform domestic, international, or multinational human resource approaches into truly transnational systems. Bringing a "foreigner" onto the board of directors, for example, gives the illusion of globalization, but is insufficient to underpin its substance.

Illusion Five: If "foreigners" are fitting in at headquarters, we must be managing our cultural diversity well
No. This is a multinational paradigm trap. In multinationals, foreigners must adapt to the headquarters' culture, including learning its native language. Multinationals typically see cultural differences "as a nuisance, a constraint, an obstacle to be

surmounted."²⁵ In transnational firms, all managers make transitions, all managers adapt, and all managers help to create a synergistic organizational culture which transcends any one national culture.

Illusion Six: As national wealth increases, everyone will become more like us
No. To the extent that the world is converging in its values, attitudes, and styles of doing business, it is not converging on a single country's national pattern, even that of the world's wealthiest nation. "The appealing 'one-best-way' assumption about management, the belief that different cultures are converging at different paces on the same concept of organization, is dying a slow death."²⁶ Moreover, transnational firms need to create transnational cultures that are inclusive of all their members, not wait for the world to converge on a reality that looks like any particular firm's national culture, even one that looks "just like us."

Illusion Seven: If we provide managers with cross-cultural training, we will increase organizational capability
No. Increased cognitive understanding does not guarantee increased behavioral effectiveness, nor is enhanced individual learning sufficient for improved organizational effectiveness. Simply increasing the number of cross-cultural training programs offered to individual managers does not ensure that they will actually use the skills on a regular basis, nor that the firm as a whole will benefit from the potentially improved cross-cultural interaction. To benefit, the individual must want to learn that which is not-invented-here and the organization must want to learn from the individual. To enhance organizational capability, managers must continually work with and learn from people worldwide and disperse that knowledge throughout the firm's worldwide operations.

Despite the seemingly insurmountable challenges, firms are beginning to address and solve the dilemmas posed by going global. To date, no firm believes it has "the answer," the solution to creating a truly transnational human resource system. However, a number of firms are currently inventing pieces of the solution which may cohere into just such a system. For example, as John Reed, CEO of Citicorp, describes:

"There are few companies in the world that are truly global . . . . Our most important advantage is our globality. Our global human capital may be as important a resource, if not more important, than our financial capital. Look at the Policy Committee, the top thirty or so officers in the bank. Almost seventy-five percent have worked outside the United States; more than twenty-five percent have worked in three or more countries. Half speak two or more languages other than English. Seven were born outside the United States."²⁷

Perhaps, then, a primary role of transnational human resource executives today is to remain open to fundamental change and to continue to encourage the openness and experimentation needed to create truly global systems.

Endnotes

The authors would like to thank the Ontario Centre for International Business for generously funding this research. See "Globalization and Human Resource Management," (Nancy J. Adler and Susan Bartholomew) in *Research in Global Strategic Management; Corporate Responses to Global Change*, Alan M. Rugman and Alain Verbeke (eds.), Vol. 3, (Greenwich, Conn.: JAI Press, 1992) for further details of the research design and results of the study.

1. Christopher A Bartlett and Sumantra Ghoshal, "Matrix Management: Not a Structure, a Frame of Mind" *Harvard Business Review*, July–August 1990, 138.
2. See Michael E. Porter, *The Competitive Advantage of Nations* (New York: The Free Press, 1990).
3. Paul A. Evans, Yves Doz, and Andre Laurent, *Human Resource Management in International Firms* (London: Macmillan Press, 1989), xi–1.
4. Ibid.; also see Gunner Hedlund "Who Manages the Global Corporation? Changes in the Nationality of Presidents of Foreign Subsidiaries of Swedish MNCs During the 1980s." Working Paper, (Institute of International Business and the Stockholm School of Economics, May 1990).
5. See Donald C. Hambrick, Lester B. Korn, James W. Frederickson, and Richard M. Ferry, *21st Century Report: Reinventing the CEO* (New York: Korn/Ferry and Columbia University's Graduate School of Business, 1989), 1–94.
6. Ibid.
7. Ibid., 57.
8. See Nancy J. Adler and Fariborz Ghadar "International Strategy from the Perspective of People and Culture: The North American Context," in Alan M. Rugman (ed.), *Research in Global Strategic Management: International Business Research for the Twenty–First Century; Canada's New Research Agenda*, Vol. 1, (Greenwich, Conn.: JAI Press, 1990) 179–205; and "Strategic Human Resource Management: A Global Perspective," in Rudiger Pieper (ed.), *Human Resource Management in International Comparison* (Berlin, de Gruyter, 1990), 235–260.
9. See Gary Hamel, Yves Doz, and C. K. Prahalad "Collaborate With Your Competitors and Win," *Harvard Business Review.*, 89(1), 1989, 133–139.
10. For a review of international human resource management, see Nancy J. Adler, *International Dimensions of Organizational Behavior*, 2nd ed. (Boston: PWS Kent 1991); Peter J. Dowling "Hot Issues Overseas," Personnel Administrator, 34(1), 1989, 66–72; Peter J. Dowling & R. Schuler, *International Dimensions of Human Resource Management* (Boston: PWS Kent, 1990), Peter J. Dowling & Denise E. Welch, "International Human Resource Management: An Australian Perspective," *Asia Pacific Journal of Management*, 6(1), 1988, 39–65; Yves Doz & C. K. Prahalad "Controlled Variety: A Challenge for Human Resource Management in the MNC," *Human Resource Management*, 25(1), 1986, 55–71; A. Edstrom & J.R. Galbraith "Transfer of Managers as a Coordination and Control Strategy in Multinational Firms," *Administrative Science Quarterly*, 22, 1977, 248–263; Evans, Doz, & Laurent, (1989) op. cit.; Andre Laurent "The Cross-Cultural Puzzle of International Human Resource Management," *Human Resource Management*, 25(1), 1986, 91–101; E. L. Miller, S. Beechler, B. Bhatt, & R. Nath, "The Relationship Between the Global Strategic Planning Process and the Human Resource Management Function," *Human Resource Planning*, 9(1), 1986, 9–23; John Milliman, Mary Ann Von Gilinow, & Maria Nathan, "Organizational Life Cycles and Strategic International Human Resource Management in Multinational Companies: Implications for Congruence Theory," *Academy of Management Review*, 16(2), 1991, 318–339; Dan A. Ondrack, "International Human Resources

Management in European and North American Firms," *Human Resource Management*, 25(1), 1985, 121–132; Dan A. Ondrack, "International Transfers of Managers in North American and European MNEs," *Journal of International Business Studies*, 16(3), 1985, 1–19; Vladimir Pucik, "The International Management of Human Resources," in C. J. Fombrun, N. M. Tichy, and M. A. Devanna (eds.), *Strategic Human Resource Management* (New York: Wiley, 1984); Vladimir Pucik & Jan Hack Katz, "Information, Control and Human Resource Management in Multinational Firms," *Human Resource Management*, 25(1), 1986, 121–132; and Rosalie Tung, *The New Expatriates: Managing Human Resources Abroad* (New York: Harper & Row 1988), and "Strategic Management of Human Resources in Multinational Enterprises," *Human Resource Management*, 23(2), 1984, 129–143; among others.
11. Op. cit., 1990.
12. Unilever's "Best Proven Practice" technique was cited by Philip M. Rosenzweig and Jitendra Singh, "Organizational Environments and the Multinational Enterprise," *Academy of Management Review*, 16(2), 1991, 354, based on an interview that Rosenzweig conducted with Unilever.
13. See Paul Evans, Elizabeth Lank, and Alison Farquhar, "Managing Human Resources in the International Firm: Lessons from Practice," in Paul Evans, Yves Doz, and Andre Laurent, 1989, op. cit., 138.
14. Kenichi Ohmae, *The Borderless World: Power and Strategy in the Interlinked Economy* (New York: Harper Business, 1990), 112.
15. Andre Laurent, op. cit., 1986, 100.
16. See C. K. Prahalad and Yves Doz, *The Multinational Mission: Balancing Local Demands and Global Vision*, (New York: Free Press, 1987); also, for a discussion of global integration versus local responsiveness from a business strategy perspective, see Michael E. Porter, "Changing Patterns of International Competition," *California Management Review*, 28(2), 1986, 9–40; and Christopher A. Bartlett, "Building and Managing the Transnational: The New Organizational Challenge," in M. E. Porter (ed.) *Competition in Global Industries* (Boston: Harvard Business School Press, 1986), 367–401, who explicitly developed the concepts, along with initial work and elaboration by: Christopher A. Bartlett & Sumantra Ghoshal, *Managing Across Borders: The Transnational Solution* (Boston: Harvard Business School Press 1989); Yves Doz, "Strategic Management in Multinational Companies," *Sloan Management Review*, 21(2), 1980, 27–46; Yves Doz, Christopher A. Bartlett, & C. K. Prahalad, "Global Competitive Pressures and Host Country Demands: Managing Tensions in MNCs," *California Management Review*, 23(3), 1981, 63–73; and Yves Doz & C. K. Prahalad, "Patterns of Strategic Control Within Multinational Corporations," *Journal of International Business Studies*, 15(2), 1984, 55–72.
17. See Evans, Lank and Farquhar, op. cit., 1989, 119.
18. Ibid., 130–131; 139.
19. Ibid., 141.
20. An even more disconcerting display of ignorance was that four surveyed firms listed 3M, Citicorp, Ford, and General Motors as European firms, and in another four responses, Dupont, Eastman Kodak, Coca-Cola, and Wang were identified as leading Asian firms.
21. Evans, Lank, and Farquhar, op. cit., 122.
22. Paul Evans and Yves Doz, "The Dualistic Organization," in Evans, Doz, & Laurent, op. cit., 1989, 223: based on the earlier work of Doz, "Managing Manufacturing Rationalization Within Multinational Companies," *Columbia Journal of World Business*, 13(3), 1978, 82–94; and Prahalad and Doz, op. cit., 1987.
23. *Beyond National Borders* (Homewood, Illinois: Dow Jones-Irwin, 1987), 93.
24. Ibid., 1.
25. Evans, Lank & Farquhar, op. cit., 115.
26. Ibid., 115.
27. Noel Tichy and Ram Charan, "Citicorp Faces the World: An Interview with John Reed," *Harvard Business Review*, November–December, 1990, 137.

Article Review Form at end of book.

What are the essential elements for doing business abroad? What mistakes do businesspeople make when expanding their firm globally?

Cultural Awareness

An essential element of doing business abroad

Gary Bonvillian and William A. Nowlin

When traveling to other countries to transact business, American usually attempt to make a favorable impression and do their professional best. Unfortunately, behaviors, comments, time orientation, social practices, and etiquette that are considered appropriate professional behavior in corporate America may be perceived as arrogance, insensitivity, overconfidence, or aggressiveness in another culture. This could result in the American business person being perceived as insensitive to other cultures and jeopardize that person's working relationship with international counterparts.

In the domestic market, Americans are comfortable in knowing what to do and how to do it. But to achieve the same objective and success with a minimum of interpersonal and professional errors abroad, advanced preparation is crucial. American corporations have a long way to go in developing executives to function abroad successfully. One retired senior vice president from a major U.S. corporation reports, "We have the technology and we know the business but we are not prepared as a country to deal with cultural differences.... I have seen relatively little progress over the past 30 years."

Recent literature cites an acknowledgment by business executives that understanding cultural differences is absolutely essential for doing business abroad. Unfortunately, this same literature reports that surveys of major corporations indicate that relatively few offer this type of preparation for their people. According to one such survey by the consulting firm of Moran, Stahl and Boyer, only 12 percent of the respondents of 51 multinational U.S. corporations indicated that they offered seminars and workshops on cross-cultural differences and doing business abroad (Callahan 1989).

Similarly, the preparation that is being provided appears to be inadequate, resulting in high costs to companies and frustration for employees. According to one source, in a study of expatriates who were forced to return to the United States before completing their assignment, the failure rate (as measured by coming home before the end of tour in-country) ranged from 20 percent to 50 percent, costing the company between $55,000 and $150,000 per person. This translates into approximately $2 billion per year in costs for U.S. corporations (McEnery and DesHarnais 1990).

Training alone will not solve the problem. Many conditions influence the success of doing business abroad; the individual is merely one variable in the equation. It is perhaps the most critical factor, however, for we know that inadequate attention is being given to this important aspect of executive development.

Other factors that influence success abroad include the nature, scope, and location of the project. Of particular note is the location, as studies have shown that although 18 percent of those sent to London will fail, this increases to 36 percent in Tokyo and 68 percent in Saudi Arabia. Such statistics point to a need for companies to carefully consider the unique nature of differing cultures and direct their executive preparation initiatives accordingly.

This article examines many cross-cultural differences among 25 or more countries in which there is a practice or behavior dissimilar to that in the United States. They rank among the many complex subjects that must be considered by corporations when designing or contracting training for cultural awareness. Among the cultural elements that will be examined are language and communications, aesthetics, time orientation, social institutions, religion, personal achievement, personal space, social behavior, and intercultural socialization.

Cultures include all types of learning and behavior. They are learned, they vary, and they influence the manner in which people behave.

"Cultural Awareness: An Essential Element of Doing Business Abroad" by G. Bonvillian and W. Nowlin. Reprinted from BUSINESS HORIZONS, November–December 1994. Copyright 1994 by the Foundation for the School of Business at Indiana University. Used with permission.

Communications

Of all the cultural elements that an international traveler must study, the language of the host country is among the most difficult to manage. Although it is beneficial for individuals to know the language, one also needs the competency to recognize idiomatic interpretations, which are quite different from those found in the English dictionary. All cultures have verbal and nonverbal communication systems, and each country's vocabulary reflects its primary value and composition. Words spoken by an American may not have the same meaning when translated into another language.

When visiting a country in which English is not spoken, executives often use an interpreter to translate for them. Yet numerous gestures, facial expressions, and motions send different signals, and an interpreter might not be capable of articulating the full intention of the message. For example, Americans are often direct in their conversations, expecting the truth with no hint of deception. At the same time, Americans also tend to be uncomfortable with silent moments. People in some other countries, though, may prefer not to be direct and may shift their eyes away from the American. To them this is a sign of respect. To the American, however, it may be seen as a gesture suggesting withholding of information. And in some cultures silence is appreciated, giving discussants or negotiators time to think and evaluate the situation.

One of the most damaging demands that can be made of an Asian is "Give me a yes or no answer." Although an American would view this as a mild form of confrontation and would expect to get a "yes" or "no" response, Asians rarely say no. This is because of their reluctance to displease another with a negative answer and also to save them the embarrassment of having to admit an inability. There is no word for "no" in Thailand. Similarly, the French often say "no" when they may actually mean "maybe."

In some countries, if a question is asked, the visitor may be told whatever the native thinks the visitor wants to hear. If you ask for directions in Mexico, Lebanon, or Japan, and the natives don't really know the answer, they may still give you one simply to make you happy. In countries such as Paraguay or Pakistan, if directions are requested, regardless of the distance, the answer is likely to be "not far."

In America, a person who is reluctant to maintain eye contact is called shifty-eyed and arouses suspicion. But in some countries an attempt to maintain eye contact may be perceived as a sign of aggression. Accordingly, in Japan, South Korea, Taiwan, and other Asian countries, maintaining eye contact is not an acceptable behavior. On the other hand, in Saudi Arabia, eye contact and gestures of openness are important and could facilitate communications.

Most people who transact business abroad may not be proficient in the spoken language of the host country. However, nonverbal communications, such as signs, gestures, and body cues, can be learned in a short period. The value of knowing what to do and what to avoid should not be underestimated, so that one will not transmit unintended messages. According to several business executives interviewed, these issues are of much greater importance to closing the deal than actually knowing how to speak the native language.

One executive reported that the English language is used in many regions of the world as the accepted form of business communication. In some countries such as the Philippines, you would be expected to use English or risk being considered of a lower class. Even though they risk isolation from the rest of the world, Filipinos no longer require English as a second language for their young, leaving only the upper class the ability to learn it in private schools or from tutors. Power brokers in most of the developing countries recognize the importance of understanding English. In Singapore, for example, it is not unusual to hear the language spoken in the home just for the purpose of further developing the skills of young people.

In the same respect, such regions as the Middle East may prefer that visiting business people not attempt to use the native language, unless they have a high degree of proficiency. According to one source, it is quite common for Arab businessmen to speak English, because their formal education is likely to have come from Western universities. However, it is also recommended that if a company is intending to do a significant degree of business in the Middle East, its employees should be trained in Arabic. Dialects and accents aside, its written form dominates the region.

Aesthetics

Aesthetics refers to attitudes toward beauty and good taste in the art, music, folklore, and drama of a culture. The aesthetics of a particular culture can be important in the interpretation of symbolic meanings of various artistic expressions.

It is important for companies to evaluate in depth such aesthetic factors as product and package design, color, brand name, and symbols. For instance, some conventional brand names that communicate positive messages in America have a totally different meaning in another country, which may substantially stigmatize corporate image and marketing effectiveness.

When General Motors (GM) introduced its Chevy Nova into the Spanish market, it failed to first investigate whether the product name had an adverse meaning. GM subsequently learned that Nova ("no va") in Spanish means "It won't go." Other American product names, shown in Figure 1, impart a negative message when literally translated into another language.

Symbols also are important aesthetic factors that could have an adverse meaning in a different country. For example, the Wise Corporation would have to change or modify its trademark if it decided to test-market potato chips in India. The owl, which is the Wise trademark, is a symbol of bad luck in India even though in America it is associated with intelligence.

This further exemplifies the importance of pre-travel inquiries to avoid making errors that will hamper one's ability to conduct business abroad effectively. They also illustrate the cross-cultural quagmires that can be avoided when a firm leaves little to chance in choosing appropriate and inappropriate behavior or practices.

Figure 1 American Brand Names and Slogans with Offensive Foreign Translations

Company	Product	Brand Name or Slogan	Country	Meaning
ENCO	Petroleum	(Former name of Exxon)	Japan	"Stalled car"
American Motors	Automobile	Matador	Spain	"Killer"
Ford	Truck	Fiera	Spain	"Ugly old woman"
Pepsi	Soft drink	"Come alive with Pepsi"	Germany	"Come out of the grave"

(Griggs and Copeland 1985, p. 62)

Time Orientation

Americans are clock watchers. We live by schedules and deadlines and thrive on being prompt for meetings and "efficient" in conducting business. In many parts of the world people arrive late for appointments, and business is preceded by hours of social rapport. In such places, people in a rush are occasionally thought to be arrogant and untrustworthy.

In the United States, a high value is placed on time. If someone waited outside an office for half an hour or so beyond the appointed time, it would be seen as a signal of his or her lack of importance. In the Middle East, a business person may keep a visitor waiting for a long time. But once the host begins the meeting, it may last as long as required to conduct the business at hand. Of course, others with later appointments on the same day also must wait their turn.

Americans are also deadline-oriented. If a deadline is mentioned to an Arab, however, it is like waving a red flag in front of a bull. Forcing the Arab to make a quick decision may very well cost you the deal. What appears to be inefficiency and muddling on the part of Arab businessmen may be a signal of displeasure with the way things are going. Experienced negotiators recommend slowing down and looking for signals that suggest that negotiations are not going well.

Western cultures view time as a resource that is not to be wasted. The efficient use of time is emphasized in such phrases as "Time is money" and "Time is the enemy." In contrast, Eastern cultures view time as unlimited and unending. In America, meetings sometimes begin with phrases such as "Let's get started" and "Let's dispense with the preliminaries." In Japan, casual conversation precedes business matters, because the Japanese are generally more interested than Americans in getting to know the people involved in the transaction.

Furthermore, it is important to the Japanese that consensus be reached and any misunderstandings be cleared up before proceeding on any problems that may surface in negotiations. The Japanese process of consultation (*ring-seido*) could bring to the surface problems not appreciated or known to Americans. This will require further consultations to remove obstacles.

Many cultures value relationships. Europeans and Asians place a high regard on long-term relationships rather than on short-term gains, which runs counter to what most Americans perceive. Excessive emphasis on speed and time may give the impression that the transaction is more important than the person. This is a fundamental error in professional judgment in many regions of the world.

Social Institutions

Social institutions—business, political, family, or class related—influence the behavior of people. In some countries, for example, the family is the most important social group. So social structures must be examined to understand the culture, because family relationships sometimes influence the work environment and employment practices.

In Latin America and the Arab world, a manager who gives special treatment to a relative is considered to be fulfilling an obligation. From the Latin point of view, it only makes sense to hire someone you can trust. In the United States, however, it is considered favoritism and nepotism. In India there is a fair amount of nepotism. But there too it is consistent with the norms of the culture. By knowing the importance of family relationships in the workplace and in business transactions, embarrassing questions about nepotism can be avoided.

According to the director of sales in the Mideast for a U.S.-based communications company, nepotism is commonplace in this region. He reports that not only are you forced to deal with "large groups of families," but these families often represent the country's aristocracy. Such individuals typically hold high positions in the local government and can rather easily skew a deal in one direction or another. As an outsider, a visiting business executive must learn not only to tolerate but also to appreciate the purpose of these relationships. It is not for us to judge the virtue of these conditions, concludes the sales director, but to adapt and work within the local norms.

Americans should also be cautious of being judgmental or intrusive in the local political structure. Particularly in South America, where each country functions as a distinctive nation-state, it is a mistake to presume that a single political ideology prevails. Rather, these countries have foregone the benefits of functioning as a single market in favor of autonomous units. This results in separate infrastructures of military, customs, currencies, and legal systems.

Religion

Religion is of utmost importance in many countries. In America, substantial effort is made to keep government and church matters separate. Nevertheless, there remains a healthy respect for individual religious differences. In some countries, such as

Lebanon and Iran, religion may be the very foundation of the government and a dominant factor in business, political, and educational decisions.

In the United States, employers are required by federal law to "reasonably accommodate" individual religious beliefs that conflict with job demands. There may be quite a number of them, however, because multiple nationalities, ethnic groups, and religions are represented in the diverse U.S. work force. In other countries, there may be fewer religions, but the dominant religion must be respected in professional, supervisory, managerial, and other business behavior. When abroad, any effort to compare religions should be avoided.

When supervising a work group in some countries, an attempt to modify a policy, behavior, or process that is grounded in religion would not only draw the attention of national corporate officials but that of government officials as well. In Saudi Arabia, for example, during the month of Ramadan, Moslems fast from sunrise to sunset. As a consequence, worker production drops. Many Moslems rise earlier in the morning to eat before sunrise and may eat what they perceive to be enough to last until sunset. This affects their strength and stamina during the work day. An effort by management to maintain normal productivity levels will likely be rejected, so managers must learn to be sensitive to this custom as well as to others like it.

Eating pork is forbidden by law in Islam and Judaism. So if hot dogs are an American's favorite lunch, all-beef hot dogs would have to be substituted for pork. The pork restriction exists in Israel as well as in Islamic countries in the Middle East, such as Saudi Arabia, Iraq, and Iran, and Southeast Asia, such as Indonesia and Malaysia.

Islamic religion also frowns upon excessive profit, which is considered a form of exploitation. This is an important consideration in pricing products and services.

The role of women is also different in Islamic countries. They are, among other things, required to dress in such a way that their arms, legs, torso, and faces are concealed. An American female would be expected to honor this dress code while in the host country.

Islamic worshippers pray facing the holy city of Mecca five times each day. Visiting Westerners must be aware of this religious ritual. In Saudi Arabia and Iran, it is not unusual for managers and workers to place carpets on the floor and kneel to pray several times during the day. Although Sunday is a day of rest for most countries in the world, there are several countries in which the rest day is not Sunday. Figure 2 lists several of these countries.

Figure 2	Countries That Have Official Rest Days Other Than Sunday
Thursday	Iran, Egypt, Saudi Arabia
Friday	Afghanistan, Algeria, Bahrain, Egypt, Iraq, Jordan, Kuwait, Libya, Oman, Pakistan, Qatar, Saudi Arabia, Somalia, Syria, Tunisia, United Arab Emirates, Yemen Arab Republic, Yemen Democratic Republic
Saturday	Israel

Brown and Thomas (1981)

Personal Achievement

For the most part, Americans strive to achieve, be competitive, land the best job, earn the most money, and be promoted. They consider their position in the organization for which they work as an indication of status. We are an individualistic society and have built a nation based on our tenacity to get things done in as little time as possible and with minimal disruption.

By contrast, Hindu teachings suggest that acquisition and achievement are not to be sought, because they are the major courses of suffering in one's daily life. In Japan, positions are not arranged in a status hierarchy, and promotions are determined based on seniority rather than merit, although there is some evidence of movement from seniority-based rewards. Japanese workers are encouraged to work as teams. Cooperation is an art in Asian countries. It is said in Japan that "the nail that sticks out will be pounded down" (Adler 1986). This illustrates that individual competitiveness is less desirable than teamwork and team spirit.

Even the former Soviet Union encouraged teamwork. If a work group failed to meet production goals, no one was rewarded. But if a group exceeded its quota, everyone would benefit. Although cash rewards are often given to high achievers in America, a Japanese, Chinese, or Yugoslav would be humiliated to receive one.

A great deal has been written in U.S. management literature over the past 10 to 15 years on teamwork and a participatory environment of decision making. The currently popular Total Quality Management movement would suggest that more U.S. companies are adopting this ideology. However, some researchers say that the U.S. cultural orientation on this subject is too embedded for us to adapt the normative working relationships of, say, the Japanese. On this comparison, one individual stated, "Harmony has long been important in Japan and is used as a building block to develop consensus in decision-making." In addition, whereas the individual is still the primary unit in American society and the educational system, group welfare prevails in Japan (Fram 1985).

Personal Space

Different cultures have varying rules on personal space and touching. Americans sometimes touch others on the hand or arm or shoulder when talking. In some cultures, such behavior may not be appropriate, especially with the left hand when in the Middle East.

The distance between individuals when talking is another issue that must be known and respected. Although one may not be able to define the exact distance if asked, most individuals have a specific amount of space that they maintain between themselves and others when conversing. Americans are typically made uncomfortable by the close conversation distance of Arabs and Africans. In the same respect, Arabs and Africans may feel rejected by the lengthy personal distance Americans maintain.

Indonesians operate with less empty space than Americans require, and some touching is permissible. However, an Indonesian should not be patted on the head, and a person of the opposite sex should never be touched. It is important to know the rules for personal touching and space of the culture in which a visit is planned. In some cases, personal touching can be viewed as an extreme act; in addition to violating the norms of culture, it may even be viewed as a criminal offense.

Social Behavior

There are a number of social behaviors and comments that have different meanings in other cultures. For example, Americans generally consider it impolite to mound food on a plate, make noises when eating, and belch. However, some Chinese feel it is polite to take a portion of every food served and consider it evidence of satisfaction to belch.

Other social behaviors, if not known, will place the American international traveler at a disadvantage. For example, in Saudi Arabia, it is an insult to question a host about the health of his spouse, show the soles of one's shoes, or touch or deliver objects with the left hand.

In Korea, both hands should be used when passing objects to one another, and it would be considered impolite to discuss politics, communism, or Japan. Also in Korea, formal introductions are very important. Although in America it might be acceptable to initiate a visit to a corporate or government office to meet an official, in Korea it is not considered in good taste. In both Japan and Korea, ranks and titles are expected to be used in addressing hosts. In the United States, there is not a clear rule on this behavior, except in select fields such as the armed forces or medicine. In Indonesia, it is considered rude to point at another person with a finger. However, one may point with the thumb or gesture with the chin.

When greeting someone, it is appropriate in most countries, as in the United States, to shake hands. In some countries the greeting includes a handshake and more. In Japan, a handshake may be followed by a bow, going as low and lasting as long as that of the senior person. In Brazil, Korea, Indonesia, China, and Taiwan, a slight bow is also appropriate.

In some countries, the greeting involves more contact. For instance, in Venezuela, close friends greet each other with a full embrace and a hearty pat on the back; in Indonesia, a social kiss is in vogue, and a touching of first the right then the left cheek as one shakes hands. In Malaysia, close friends grasp with both hands; and in South Africa, blacks shake hands, followed by a clench of each other's thumb's, and another handshake.

In most countries, addressing someone as Mr., Mrs., or Ms is acceptable, but this is certainly not universal. Monsieur, Madame, and Mademoiselle are preferred in France, Belgium, and Luxembourg, while señor, señora, and señorita are the norm in Spain and Mexico.

It is sometimes the case that conversation occurs as greetings are exchanged. In Sweden, the greeting is "goddag"; in the Netherlands, it is "pleased to meet you"; in the United Kingdom it's "how do you do"; and in Israel it is "shalom." Other greetings vary by country.

In many countries, men do not shake hands with a woman unless she extends her hand first. In India, women, or a man and a woman, greet each other by placing the palms of their hands together and bowing slightly; and in Mexico simply by a slight bow. In some countries, such as India, it is not advisable for men to touch or talk alone with a woman.

Although many of the social behaviors mentioned vary slightly from the American norm, negative judgements should not be made about them. When trying to explain what took so long in closing a deal, home office executives need to understand that drinking tea, socializing, and relationship building are important components in accomplishing corporate international goals.

Intercultural Socialization

In addition to knowing specific courtesies, personal space, language and communication, and social behavioral differences, there are numerous intercultural socialization behaviors that an international business traveler should learn. Knowing a culture means knowing the habits, actions, and reasons behind the behaviors.

Americans often make assumptions about what is culturally proper or incorrect based on their own experiences. For example, in the United States the bathtub and toilet are likely to be in the same room. Americans assume this is the world norm. Some cultures, however, such as that of the Japanese, consider it unhygienic. Other cultures think it unhygienic even to sit on a toilet seat.

It is not always necessary for an international business traveler to understand the "whys" of a culture, but it is important to accept them and to abide by them while on foreign soil. However, if the time is available, becoming thoroughly aware of the culture in which you will be visiting or working will pay excellent dividends.

Pre-Travel Planning and Training

Becoming internationally adept and culturally aware should be a goal of any professional who aspires to do business abroad. This generally means a conscious effort in training and professional development by organizations. The Canadian International Development Agency (CIDA) provides an excellent model. CIDA hosts a five day, pre-departure briefing for Canadians that includes travel information, introduction to the geographical area of the host country, and presentations by a host national or a returnee. Cross-cultural communication, information for family members, and information on skills transfer are also included.

There are numerous sources from which to obtain the training necessary for travel abroad. They range from individual consultants and established pre-departure corporations to state and federal offices that center on foreign trade or other foreign relations matters. Universities with international business centers are excellent sources as well.

Many elements of culture that we believe make America such a pleasant place in which to live and work are not the norm in other countries. But when an American travels abroad on behalf of his or her corporation, the more that is known about potential business partners and their culture, the less the risk of engaging in offensive and insulting behavior. This increases the probability of achieving success rather than missing an opportunity simply because of arrogance or ignorance.

References

Nancy J. Adler, *International Dimensions of Organizational Behavior* (Boston: PWS-Kent Publishing Co., 1991).

Harry Brown and Rosemary Thomas, *Brits Abroad* (London: Express Books, 1981).

Madelyn R. Callahan, "Preparing the New Global Manager," *Training and Development Journal*, March 1989, pp. 28–32.

Lennie Copeland, "Making Costs in International Travel," *Personal Administrator*, July 1984, pp. 47–51.

Lennie Copeland and Lewis Griggs, *Going International* (New York: Random House, 1985).

Lennie Copeland and Lewis Griggs, "Getting the Best from Foreign Employees," *Management Review*, June 1986, pp. 19–26.

Eugene Fram, "Consensus on Campus: Lessons for University Decision Making in Japan," *Speaking of Japan*, April 1985, pp. 20–26.

Shari Gaudron, "Surviving Cross-Cultural Shock," *Industry Week* July 6, 1992, pp. 35–37.

Allen Hixon, "Why Corporations Make Haphazard Overseas Staffing Decisions," *Personnel Administrator*, March 1986, pp. 91–93.

John Ivancevich, James Donnelly, Jr., and James Gibson, *Management* (Boston: Irwin, 1989).

Gavin Kennedy, *Doing Business Abroad* (New York: Simon and Schuster, 1985).

Rose Knotts, "Cross-Cultural Management: Transformations and Adaptations," *Business Horizons*, January–February 1989, pp. 29–33.

Jean McEnery and Gaston DesHarnais, "Culture Shock," *Training and Development Journal*, April 1990, pp. 43–47.

Christopher North, *International Business*, 2d ed. (Englewood Cliffs, NJ: Prentice-Hall, 1985).

Arvind V. Phatak, *International Dimensions of Management*. (Boston: Kent Publishing Co., 1983).

Janet Stern Solomon, "Employee Relations Soviet Style," *Personnel Administrator*, October 1985, pp. 79–86.

H.L. Wills, "Selection for Employment in Developing Countries," *Personnel Administrators*, July 1984, pp. 53–58.

Charles F. Valentine, "Blunders Abroad," *Nation's Business*, March 1989, pp. 54–56.

Article Review Form at end of book.

What is meant by the statement "In France, management is not a task. It is a 'state of mind'—one that managers worldwide need to understand"?

The Making of a French Manager

In France, management is not a task. It is a "state of mind"—one that managers worldwide need to understand.

Jean-Louis Barsoux and Peter Lawrence

While the eyes of the world have been focused on Japan's economic success story, France too has been showing a level of progress that makes it essential for the global executive to understand how French managers are molded. Consider this:

- In 1989, France made one-third of all acquisitions in Western Europe, adding more in 1990. And in 1991, France has surpassed Japan and the United Kingdom in acquiring U.S. companies.

- Nuclear power provides just under half of France's power needs, with enough left over to make France the European Economic Community's largest energy exporter. And energy-intensive French industries enjoy a competitive advantage since the country's electricity prices are 48% below U.K. rates and 54% less than Germany's.

- The French TGV, holder of the world speed record for trains, was chosen by British Rail and the Belgian rail board to link London and Brussels via the Channel Tunnel.

- Many French companies are world leaders. Michelin is the largest tire maker, L'Oréal the largest cosmetics company, L'Air Liquide the leader in industrial gases. Alcatel, formed in 1986 when the French Cie. Générale d'Electricité bought ITT's equipment operations, is the world's second largest telecommunications-equipment supplier. Packaging, tires, cement, steel, and hotels are other industries French companies lead. The French retailer, Carrefour, originated the hypermarket—a large department store that includes a supermarket. And analysts consider Peugeot, S.A. (PSA), owner of Peugeot and Citroën, to have one of the strongest positions in Europe in terms of market and costs.

To understand the style of management responsible for these successes, we went to France to study how its managers think about management—how their views of the management task are formed and their skills developed. We interviewed and observed senior executives, company spokespeople, and typical managers at a range of large and midsize companies, including Accor, Carrefour, Saint-Gobain, L'Oréal, Thomson, L'Air Liquide, Renault, Michelin, and PSA. We quickly determined that the development of French managers did not take place in formal company training programs but began long before employment; therefore we also visited the schools that are said to be the real training ground for managers.

Management in France, we learned, is considered a "state of mind" rather than a set of techniques. According to executives like Michel Lafforgue, directeur général technique at L'Oréal, the successful development of executives depends on creating a distinctive shared identity, a sense of belonging to the French managerial class.

France has come closer than any other nation to turning management into a separate profession, with its own entry requirements and regulations. Managerial status in France is not part of a graded continuum, but rather a quantum leap, involving a change of legal status (for example, in terms of pension entitlement) as well as subtle changes in outlook and self-perception.

Cadre, the French word for manager, is borrowed from the armed forces. The term originally was used to designate the ensemble of commissioned and noncommissioned officers—which, incidentally, has given management a distinctly male aura. Cadre status can be attained through educational credentials or through loyalty to a particular company. Those fortunate enough to graduate from one of the leading *grandes écoles* (highly selective universities) can look forward to immediate cadre status on entering

Reprinted by permission of HARVARD BUSINESS REVIEW. From "The Making of a French Manager," Jean-Louis Barsoux and Peter Lawrence, July/August 1991. Copyright © 1991 by the President and Fellows of Harvard College; all rights reserved.

professional life. Someone with, say, only two years of higher education will likely have to wait five to ten years to become a cadre. And for those without qualifications, their only real chance is to prove themselves over several years with a single employer. One Renault cadre who made it "the hard way" bemoaned the quasi-automatic handing out of cadre status to grandes écoles graduates: "Soon they will be naming them cadre upon admission to the grandes écoles."

Even though companies do not all use the same criteria for admitting people to this elite group, membership alone tacitly binds those inside. The title bestows on a French executive the same sort of social prestige as a lawyer, architect, or doctor. After all, it was the cadres who were seen as the prime architects and beneficiaries of France's postwar economic recovery. To French executives, being named cadre is akin to passing an intelligence test. It proves, for all to see, their ability to think logically and analyze systematically. And this is what sets managers apart from the rest of an organization's personnel.

Management as an Intellectual Activity

French managers see their work as an intellectual challenge, requiring the remorseless application of individual brainpower. They do not share the Anglo-Saxon view of management as an interpersonally demanding exercise, where plans have to be constantly "sold" upward and downward using personal skills. The bias is for intellect rather than for action. People who run big enterprises must above all else be clever—that is, they must be able to grasp complex issues, analyze problems, manipulate ideas, and evaluate solutions. A revealing witticism contains this rejoinder, supposedly from one senior French civil servant to another: "That's fine in practice, but it'll never work in theory."

The emphasis on cleverness shows up even in executive recruiting advertisements. They hardly mention the drive or initiative looked for in Anglo-Saxon recruits; rather they call for more cerebral qualities—an analytical mind, independence, intellectual rigor, an ability to synthesize information. Communication or interpersonal skills are tacked on at the end, if they appear at all.

Recent French industrial achievements have occurred largely in fields requiring a coordinated, technologically and scientifically creative, and research-driven approach—rather than, say, marketing dash, financial wizardry, or manufacturing organization. Take for example vitrification, a technique of sealing nuclear waste in glass. The British invented the process, but the French now dominate the field. Other examples are the Ariane satellite launches and the Minitel Viewdata System. Emphasis on research distinguishes L'Oréal, whose former chairman, Charles Zviak, rose through the research ranks as a specialist in dermatology. Research virtuosity is the reason Citroën supplies Rolls-Royce with the components for braking and assisted steering systems. Indeed, PSA's stunning turnaround in the 1980s involved cutting costs through a variety of technology-based achievements. It used information systems and developed common parts, subassemblies, and body components between the Peugeot and Citroën divisions.

French managers excel in their capacity for quantitative thought and expression and in the numerate dimension of strategy formulation. Michel Bonny, head of publicity for Michelin U.K., noted British managers' discomfort at putting figures to proposals, whereas "in France, we won't make a decision unless we have confidence in the numbers." Even in low-tech sectors such as retailing, we found more qualification consciousness, higher numeracy, and a greater familiarity with management best-sellers (including U.S. ones) than in corresponding British companies.

French managers like to communicate in writing, even for informal interactions. In response to our quite undemanding questions, French managers wanted to write things down, to list options. Jean-Louis Reynal, plant manager at Citroën, explained that "it wouldn't be too much of an exaggeration to say that until they are written, until they are entrusted to the blackboard, the notepad, or the flip chart, ideas have no reality for the French manager. You could even say that writing is an indispensable aid to 'being' for us." This propensity reinforces a formality that permeates French relationships.

The French manager's role is to lead the dissection and synthesis of problems, the presentation and appraisal of arguments. Intellectual ability does not preclude practicality, but practicality may be undervalued or at least underdeveloped. To say that French management is dominated by engineers means something qualitatively different from saying that German management is dominated by engineers. A manager with the materials and packaging group Saint-Gobain explained that "to be an engineer in France doesn't mean you can fix a machine. It implies something about social standing, about outlook, about professional self-esteem and national pride."

But intellect can impede communication in French companies. One of the most striking manifestations is the way that obsession with grammatical rectitude is allowed to interrupt interaction. French managers we observed hated to read or hear their language used incorrectly, especially by fellow citizens. On several occasions, we saw highly educated executives attempting to reaffirm their right to lead by pointing out grammatical errors committed by subordinates. An executive at Accor corrected a missed subjunctive; one at Carrefour pointed out a mistaken preposition. We also watched an internal meeting at L'Oréal brought virtually to a standstill by repeated definitional nit-picking about the terms used.

While intellectual ability serves French executives well when it comes to planning, conceptualization, research, and system design, management involves more than these activities. For one thing, sometimes problems are not well defined. One plant manager at L'Oréal worried about this. "It has become something of a cliché that French managers can solve any problem—assuming they can *detect* the problem in the first place." Spotting problems has less to do with IQ than with talking to people, asking the right questions, listening to the answers, and sometimes improvising solutions. But French managers are trained to distrust makeshift or intuitive solutions. An archetypal product of the French system, PSA chief executive, Jacques Calvet, confessed in a recent periodical, "I have a fault from which I suffer greatly. I am too logical, not sufficiently directed by intuition."

Leadership and Organization

The design of French organizations reflects and reinforces the cerebral manager. France has a long tradition of centralization, of hierarchical rigidity, and of individual respect for authority. French company law resembles the country's' constitution in conferring power on a single person. At the helm of French companies is the *président-directeur-général* (PDG), who decides, executes, and controls company policy. The PDG is what British and U.S. companies would regard as chairman of the board and chief executive rolled into one, or the German *vorstandsvorsitzender* (chairman of the executive committee) plus operating executive. The PDG is not answerable to anyone. Votes are rare; if a proposal is put to vote, it is tantamount to a vote of no confidence in the PDG. Indeed, the head of a small, publicly held company boasted to us that "I can do what I please with the exception of selling off the company."

There is a clear connection between the intellectual manager and organizational centralization. Senior executives in France believe they owe their high position to their intelligence and cunning. It therefore follows that they should make all the critical decisions and that they should be told everything so they can check other people's decisions. When Bernard Attali became PDG of Air France, he told his assembled directors, "I want to be at all times informed of every notable event in your different sectors of activity."

Consider the case of PSA. Jacques Calvet was brought into the car group of Peugeot to effect a turnaround in the midst of a major financial crisis. Through a draconian program of restructuring and job cuts, be engineered a spectacular financial and industrial recovery that brought healthy profits and strong sales gains, especially in Germany and the United Kingdom. Today he is moving ever closer to his stated aim of turning PSA into Europe's biggest selling car group. To do this, Calvet is trying to "decentralize"—for example, promoting the company's younger executives and delegating certain decisions to them. Still, he is criticized by some PSA managers for retaining too many decisions, even to the extent of wanting the last say on the color of the new models' door trims.

Large French organizations are not only hierarchical but also compartmentalized. Vertical differentiation is often quite literal; at L'Air Liquide, the chief executive is on the top floor of the building, and the typing pool is in the basement. Educational and intellectual credentials serve as finely tuned hierarchical discriminators. L'Air Liquide's public relations manager does not occupy the office adjoining the PDG's, as might be the case in a British company. That office is reserved for someone farther up the hierarchy with more education-backed luster. As the PR manager himself put it: "Protocol dictates that the general must be surrounded by his general staff—even if his most valuable ally is actually the radio operator."

Les Grandes Ecoles

The heads of the typical French company were molded by a system that confirmed their intellectual superiority early in life. "French organizations are run by the nation's star pupils," Roger Fauroux, former head of the Ecole Nationale d'Administration, the elite civil-service college, told us. And those star pupils come most often from among the graduates of ENA and the other grandes écoles.

French school children who aspire to management careers are encouraged in high school to renounce vocational preferences in favor of disciplines such as mathematics and physical sciences. Bruno de Fongalland, a Carrefour store director, calls this "mathematical Darwinism—the survival of the most numerate." On completing high school, French students can, if they wish, gain immediate access to a university. But the more ambitious will go to special preparatory schools for two years of intense coaching before taking the entrance exam to one of the grandes écoles. As in Japan, mathematics are compulsory in France for entrance to higher education. And the French go through a rigorous preparation for entrance exams that is not unlike the Japanese "examination hell."

About 170 grandes écoles dispense education specifically geared to technical, administrative, and business needs in the civil service, state, and private industry. Engineering schools are especially preponderant, both in number—they account for about two-thirds of the 23,000 graduating annually from the schools—and in terms of historical influence. Their curriculum involves science and engineering of a fairly theoretical kind, along with English, management, and philosophy. These schools tend to foster an esprit de corps and have a disciplinary ethos that contrasts starkly to the laissez-faire character of France's sprawling universities.

Corporate recruiters prefer the products of the grandes écoles to graduates of ordinary universities, for the schools' seal of approval endorses the individual's capacity for rapid learning and intellectual virtuosity. IBM-France, for instance, is not unusual in having a department titled Relations Grandes Ecoles. According to Pierre Stein, personnel manager in one of Mars' French subsidiaries, "In France, few bluechip companies go in for anything as untargeted as 'graduate recruitment.'"

The grandes écoles are generally viewed as institutions characteristic of the Napoleonic regime (though some of them preceded it). Napoleon, concerned about the efficiency of the state machine, found the grandes écoles well suited to endow the country with trained administrators. Students were selected by the most exacting intellectual criteria and subjected to strict discipline that was often based on the military pattern.

The military influence is clear today in the foremost grande école, Ecole Polytechnique. Established in 1794 as a military college to train engineers for the armed forces, it still resembles a residential officer cadet school, with an active general at its head. Its pupils, the "X" (so nicknamed for the school's emblem, crossed cannons), go on parade four times a year in full-dress uniform, complete with *bicorne*—a military curled hat. The school falls under the jurisdiction of the Ministry of Defense, not Education.

Although not all the grandes écoles have kept their military ties, most of the schools still retain a strong male tradition. Some have begun admitting women only in the last 20 years, and even in those schools, access for women remains limited. This could explain the paucity of women in the higher echelons of French business.

The reputation of the grandes écoles rests heavily on their rigorous admission procedures, with mathematics skills as a critical entry determinant. Some recruiters admit that in new hires, they are primarily purchasing the entrance exam. To executives such as Pierre Salbaing, vice president of the supervisory board at L'Air Liquide, the added value in the end product does not come from the teaching imparted in the schools but from the rigor of the schools' selection process. Because competence in mathematics is deemed a faithful indicator of the ability to synthesize ideas and to engage in abstract reasoning, employers are confident that the company can develop specific expertise.

The depth and intensity of grande école training equips future managers with the mettle to cope with pressure and to work long hours. He or she develops a lengthy span of concentration and tested work methods. And, secure from an early age that they are heading into leadership positions, these students assume the values and poise of would be leaders.

They also acquire invaluable old school ties. The grandes écoles provide alumni with a ready-made and influential network of contacts. To a greater extent than many nations, France pools its elites early—immediately after high school— which fosters the solidarity born of a common educational experience. These networks can dominate French companies. At PSA, graduates of one grande école, Arts et Métiers, dominate—with 461 alumni out of 5,000 employees, according to a recent count. Although distinctive competence may play a part, it is certainly not the entire reason; Arts et Métiers reputedly has the most efficient network of all the schools. And solidarity among grandes écoles alumni can even transcend corporate allegiances. One Peugeot production manager confessed to having illicitly allowed into the plant a fellow graduate, who worked at a rival company, to show him how to solve a recurrent production problem.

Having colonized France's corporate boardrooms and ministerial salons from the start, products of the grandes écoles have tended to recruit their own as successors. Graduates from "mere" universities have tremendous difficulty rising to top management positions. A 1990 *l'Expansion* survey of 100 chief executives in France reveals Polytechnique and 8 ENA graduates—just two of the grandes écoles.

Elitism has its limitations, however. Companies like Carrefour, the leading French retailer, has few grandes écoles alumni. Some French say this is because retailing lacks the intellectual challenge found in other industries. And the dearth of alumni, in turn, means the company has trouble recruiting new grandes écoles graduates. One Carrefour senior manager said that grandes écoles graduates do not want to join a company not already abundant with fellow graduates, for fear they might be working for managers with less education.

Other dysfunctional aspects of this intellectual obsession are frequently discussed in France. Criticism of the management-development system is part of a general concern about the selection of an elite and the inevitable wastage that goes with it. But however pertinent such criticisms, no one is willing to grasp the nettle. Those with the power to do so—politicians, civil servants, industrialists—are themselves products of the system. While they concede certain weaknesses in the system, they are attached to the quality it produces and the standing it bestows and are therefore its staunchest defenders. Pascal Eyt-Dessus, a senior executive at L'Air Liquide, declared flatly that "Ninety percent of the population want to abolish the Ecole Polytechnique, but they all also want their sons to go there."

Career Development

After graduation, the development of French managers continues along these inegalitarian lines, a matter of sponsorship rather than ability. Those apprenticed for general management are chosen for their educational attainment, the standing of the grande école they attended and how well they did on final exams. As in Japan, recruits' initial salary differentials reflect this kind of "authenticated" intellectual caliber.

These criteria allow the brightest prospects to be creamed off early. Formal training is largely irrelevant, reserved primarily for the lower echelons. Grandes écoles graduates instead enjoy an informal apprenticeship system that gives fast trackers a secure setting in which to acquire the necessary skills. General educational capital is thereby converted into more orthodox career capital in the form of broad experience. As one student of ENA explained: "The ideal thing for a graduate is to be named head of planning, development, or strategy—or else to be attached directly to the PDG as personal assistant. Such positions guarantee both high visibility and privileged access to the strategic problems of the group."

At L'Air Liquide, for instance, brilliant young managers are given strategic observation missions by the PDG himself. They are sent abroad for six months with their own budget and access to a team to assist them in observing medium-term market developments. Those who distinguish themselves in this will then be assigned operational responsibilities. As in Japanese companies, French companies like L'Air Liquide and L'Oréal often reward rising stars by rotating them through many different jobs.

An alternative route for science and engineering graduates is to start off as specialists, particularly in R&D. Here they might be placed under a mentor who would help them make contacts and oversee their leap from specialist to general manager. While in the United Kingdom and other countries a few ambitious science graduates make a hard-fought transition from R&D to a line-management job, many French science and engineering recruits use R&D as a springboard to an illustrious career.

Managers don't usually move up by going from company to company, except at the very top. For example, Alain Gomez (Thomson electronics group), Francis Mer (Usinor-Sacilor steel group), Jean Gandois (Pechiney aluminum group) Raymond Lévy (Renault automobile group), and Jacques Calvet (PSA) were all brought in from outside in the 1980s to restructure companies. But for the most part, companies grow their own timber. Career development in France means being schooled in the thought, ways, and folklore of the company.

Michelin's approach to corporate acculturation, for example, begins with recruitment policy. Says Jean-Pierre Vuillerme, Michelin's head of corporate communications, "We do not try to fill specific vacancies. We look for people who want a lifelong career with us. So the recruitment policy is biased toward young entrants who are qualified, yet untainted by other corporate practices." Michelin then seeks to fit the job to the person rather than vice versa. Individuals are given a free hand to accumulate what responsibilities they feel capable of taking on. As one manager put it: "We are just like the Michelin Man in the advertisements—we are allowed to inflate our jobs to their natural limits."

Rotation and training through special assignments is also characteristic at Michelin, especially in international markets. A French test driver will be brought to Japan and taught to speak Japanese to work with Honda and other Japanese customers; a Japanese manager will be sent to train in the United States and Europe for a year before returning to Japan to direct regional equipment sales; a Japanese manager will be moved to Detroit to work with Michelin's top Japanese customers on American market needs.

While the strength of Michelin's corporate culture is considered unique even by French standards, its de facto commitment to lifelong employment is shared by other French companies such as L'Oréal. Large French companies resemble their Japanese equivalents in this regard.

Lifelong employment requires corporate commitment to internal promotion. Thus when a post comes up, L'Oréal makes every effort to promote an insider rather than looking outside. Of course, a policy of lifelong employment also means dealing with people whose relative contribution to the company is diminishing. One former leader at L'Oréal remarked: "Being grateful to those who have helped build the company is simply a matter of fairness. But it is also in our interests to stand by them; if we sacrifice the older managers, the younger ones will have no faith in the company." At many companies, ill-defined posts are set aside to accommodate burnt-out managers. One senior manager described them as *voies de garage*—railroad sidings used to store box cars that are out of use. One Thomson executive even spoke of whole departments that had been put out to pasture and whose managers tacitly agreed to help younger managers on the way up.

Executives selected, acculturated, and advanced in this way have presided over France's postwar reconstruction and development. A hallmark of that process has been the close relationship between business and government.

Business and the State: The Japan of Europe?

French business is led by the best of society. What Japan achieves through consensus and groupism, France achieves through elite convergence. And the grandes écoles educational system ensures that a high proportion of the best brains from each generation are pumped into the civil service, business, and government.

Because French establishment is run by a core of like-minded people, it can take concerted action. This action sometimes sets France apart, as in the French withdrawal from NATO. Or consider the impending single European market in 1992. For France, this is act two of an epic production whose act one began in 1957 with the signing of the Rome Treaty and the inception of the Common Market. It is clear from our conversations with French managers, academics, and civil servants, that France sees this as an important challenge, a vital lever for restructuring the country's industry and for internalizing operations. Indeed, John du Monceau, directeur général of Accor, went as far as to call EC '92, a "rendezvous with history."

And for proof of French intentions, we need look no further than the frenetic rate of takeovers initiated by French companies. Virtually every merger or acquisition over the past five years has invoked the need to reach a "critical size" to compete on a European scale; BSN, Michelin, Rhône-Poulenc, and Hachette (a leading French publisher) have been especially voracious. Moreover, the French government is willing to pour money into corporate research to maintain a French position in key industries. Recent subsidies to the state-owned electronics companies Groupe Bull and Thomson dismayed the European Commission.

French management is founded on the qualities its society most reveres: the competitiveness and intellectual brilliance that is bred in the grandes écoles. French management is therefore in tune with society's leading institutions—notably, government and education.

The education system serves as a feeder to both public and private sectors. As we have shown, this system is not so much set up to impart particular skills as to preselect an elite. Diplomas guarantee careers, and the most outstanding guarantee the best careers. Naturally, this common background eases subsequent dialogue between government and industry—a mutual understanding further reinforced by regular midcareer transfers from state service to industry. Polytechnique and ENA were conceived to train engineers and administrators for public service, but in modern times they have supplied leaders for every occasion. Many of the chief executives of France's largest and most admired companies started their careers in public service and moved to positions at or near the top in private industry. The result is that France's largest public and private groups alike tend to be headed by products of the higher echelons of civil service.

The appointment of ex-state officials as company heads is perhaps understandable in the nationalized sector. What is less obvious is why they occupy similar posts in private companies like PSA or even a retail chain like Carrefour. The ubiquitous presence of senior state officials in the private and state sectors makes the conventional distinction between the two groups less relevant.

Consider the career of PSA's Jacques Calvet. After graduating from ENA, he took up various posts in the French administration. The most notable was his position as head of the personal staff of former President Valéry Giscard d'Estaing, while Giscard was finance minister. Calvet moved to the business world when he was appointed deputy managing director of the Banque Nationale de Paris (BNP) in 1974. By the time he joined the Peugeot group in 1982, he had risen to chairman of BNP. In France, Calvet's is considered a model career.

The idea of the state taking responsibility for training individuals to assume leadership positions in businesses highlights the low threshold between state and industry. In France, an accepted career path is to enter public service, then use one's privileged knowledge of its workings to attain a second career in industry. The one-way, midcareer transfer from public service to senior posts in commerce and industry is eased by the social and educational proximity of the two groups, and it helps to cement the government-business relationship. Having themselves been on the receiving end of discreet pressure, former civil servants are able to build and maintain bridges between the company and the state. As François Delachaux, the head of a French midsize engineering company, put it: "This does not mean that the larger companies will necessarily win out, but nor will they lose through not being heard."

Company heads like PSA's Calvet will always be able to call on former public sector colleagues for assistance. And even without personal contact, the likes of Calvet will be fully informed about how political and government networks operate; they know how to lobby and when and where to apply pressure. For example, after major losses at his company in 1983, Calvet asked government approval to eliminate 7,400 jobs at a plant near Paris. The government wanted workweek reductions instead. Calvet refused and eventually prevailed. Today Calvet continues to call on the government for protection from Japanese competition.

This kind of cooperation runs in both directions. Calvet readily links PSA interests with national interests, telling one reporter in 1990, "What was good for General Motors was good for the United States? Well I consider that what is good for France is good for Peugeot. I cannot see how the French car industry can fight for interests contrary to French interests." This reversal of the GM slogan reflects the widespread desire among French industries to do right by the country.

All this makes for a richer relationship between industry and government from what exists in, for example, Britain or Germany. One is reminded again of Japanese economic success, which was founded on a complex interrelationship between a highly trained industry-oriented bureaucracy and big business. Indeed, "nationalized industry" has connotations in France that are different from those in other countries. To be a French public-sector company means to bask in the reflected glory of the French state—it is image enhancing, not image demeaning. So one of the lessons we can draw from France's experience is that the state can be an impelling force in industrial initiative, particularly with regard to nurturing strategic technologies which may turn out to be the mainspring of economic life ten years later (the Minitel Viewdata System already mentioned is a good example of this).

But all is not smooth sailing for French industry. Elite convergence does not preclude elite conflict. Consider the well-publicized struggle for control of Moët-Hennessey Louis-Vuitton or the conflicts between state-owned Unions des Assurance de Paris and private-sector Compagnie de Suez over the running of the insurance company Groupe Victoire.

And because of its distinctiveness, the French managerial model may have problems in the new global environment. For example, L'Air Liquide's Pascal Eyt-Dessus speculated that grandes écoles graduates have resisted moving outside of France because their credentials abroad would not elicit automatic admiration, and they would have to consort with those they considered intellectual inferiors.

The problems at Hachette when it bought Diamandis Communications were a front-page feature of the *Wall Street Journal*. The article singled out the propensity for Hachette executives, as typical French managers, to immerse themselves in tiny details like page designs and photo selection. Other French acquirers have hit some bumps, especially in their U.S. acquisitions. There have been profitability problems at Rhône-Poulenc (acquirer of Rorer pharmaceuticals), Usinor-Sacilor (which acquired J&L Specialty Products), Thomson (buyer of General Electric's consumer electronics business), and Groupe Bull (that bought Honeywell Information Systems and Zenith's computer division).

The French model produces a mixture of strengths and weaknesses. In particular, the emphasis on intellect serves research and strategy formulation well but is perhaps less suited to flexible response in fast-paced industries where planning from the top can be cumbersome. But whatever its perceived merits or shortcomings, the French model is a coherent whole, with its own clear logic and rules providing unambiguous signals that shape managerial action. And such coherence gives French industry a focus and sense of purpose that the rest of the world should not underestimate as a key to strong economic performance.

Article Review Form at end of book.

WiseGuide Wrap-Up

- Business must be oriented to expanding globally but with preparation and intercultural communication expertise.

- In order to remain competitive, transnational firms must create a workforce of globally competent people. Each business must examine how best to meet this challenge.

- Business professionals must expand their intercultural communication skills. They also must learn to tolerate ambiguity in working cross-culturally and with multinational groups.

R.E.A.L. Sites

This list provides a print preview of typical **coursewise** R.E.A.L. sites. There are over 100 such sites at the **courselinks**™ site. The danger in printing URLs is that web sites can change overnight. As we went to press, these sites were functional using the URLs provided. If you come across one that isn't, please let us know via email to: webmaster@coursewise.com. Use your Passport to access the most current list of R.E.A.L. sites at the **courselinks**™ site.

Site name: The ReeseWeb at the University of Pittsburgh
URL: http://www.pitt.edu/~cjp/rees.html
Why is it R.E.A.L.? Sponsored by the Center for Russian and East European Studies, this site offers in-depth material regarding business and cultural issues in this region. It also contains links to other web servers in the former Soviet Union. It is also open to submissions from readers.
Key topics: Baltic states, Caucasus, Central Asia, Central Europe, Eastern Europe, Russian Federation, former Soviet Union
Try this: Explore one national home page and report on the type of information available and its value to firms interested in that market.

Site name: Welcome to Europa
URL: http://europa.eu.int/index-en.htm
Why is it R.E.A.L.? This is the gateway to the European Union site, which also includes a search engine. If a reader is interested in exporting to the EU, this site will answer most questions, as well as provide a mailbox menu for additional inquiries.
Key topics: European, news, institutions, policies, standards
Try this: What are the EU ISO 9000 standards for importing goods and materials to member nations?

Site name: Bureau of Consular Affairs
URL: http://travel.state.gov/
Why is it R.E.A.L.? This is an important site for the U.S. business traveler, as it provides up-to-date travel warnings for countries around the globe. This site is a source of data ranging from passport requirements to judicial assignments. It also has links to U.S. Embassy and Consulate web sites worldwide.
Key topic: international travel
Try this: Select an international "hot spot" and review travelers' advisory information for that region of the world.

section 3

Negotiating Across Cultures

WiseGuide Intro

Negotiating across cultures can take many forms. It may be small—for example, negotiating with an eight-year-old boy for a carved mask in the marketplace of Chichicastananto, Guatemala, as his proud parents watch. It may involve negotiating with trainers from Mexico and Argentina as an intercultural communication workshop is developed. It may be a joint business venture between companies. It may be large—for example, the negotiation of NAFTA between the United States and Mexico.

The negotiation process is complex when similar cultures are representing each side. As different cultures with variations in behavior and expectations negotiate, conflict may arise. The less the cultures have in common in attitudes, beliefs, values, and communication patterns, the more likely that an agreement will be difficult to reach. The more the cultures share on different points, the greater the opportunity for a final agreement. There are, of course, numerous variables which always impact the success or failure of a venture. Cross-cultural communication issues may, however, be a critical factor in reaching a favorable outcome.

Learning Objectives

- Understand the variables that may impact negotiating across cultures.
- Analyze personal negotiating style.
- Enhance ability to adapt to multiple contexts and culturally influenced negotiating patterns.
- Expand use of Internet sources to prepare for international negotiating session.

Questions

Reading 16. What cross-cultural issues impact Ury's attempt to broker a peace agreement between the Russians and Chechens? What strategies does Ury and his negotiating team use to move the talks forward?

Reading 17. What are the seven steps Clarke and Lipp outline to help people from different cultures understand each other's intentions and perceptions as they negotiate agreements?

Reading 18. What impact does the parties' level of familiarity with each other's culture have on the success rate of cross-cultural negotiations?

Reading 19. How does a negotiator select the best strategy for a cross-cultural agreement?

What cross-cultural issues impact Ury's attempt to broker a peace agreement between the Russians and Chechens? What strategies does Ury and his negotiating team use to move the talks forward?

Expand the Pie Before You Divvy It Up

Sound half-baked? Not to Bill Ury, coauthor of the "Negotiator's Bible," as he mediates a peace talk between the Russians and the Chechens.

Doug Stewart

In the marble and varnished-wood lobby of The Hague's grand Hotel Des Indes, William L. Ury is delivering a much-needed pep talk. Seated in armchairs pulled up in a tight circle around him are a dozen jet-lagged international lawyers, ex-diplomats, aid specialists and Kremlinologists. The group has flown in to serve as neutral observers of informal peace talks between Russians and Chechens, the first such international forum since a cease-fire was declared in the breakaway republic of Chechnya a year ago.

The opening reception was to have taken place at the International Peace Palace on Thursday evening, two hours from now, but there's been a snag. According to this morning's newspapers, the airplane bringing the Chechen delegation here was forced down by Russian fighter jets; furious, the Chechen leadership has ordered all Russians out of Chechnya (still recognized internationally as a part of the Russian Federation). As if that weren't bad enough, we now learn that the Chechens, having won belated permission from Moscow to resume their journey, are refusing to use their Russian passports. Extensive negotiations with the Dutch will be necessary for them to enter the country. One of the group wonders idly if the Royal Netherlands Air Force has surface-to-air missiles.

"This doesn't exactly build goodwill," Ury says. "First the Russians force them down. Now the Dutch won't let them in. I imagine they'll be pretty mad once they get here." Worse still, he's just learned that the Chechens on the plane aren't the politically savvy centrists everyone was hoping might attend. Instead, they're part of a militant separatist faction, most of them political hard-liners, Muslims who have never set foot outside the former Soviet Union. Several were field commanders in the recent guerrilla war that humbled the Russian Army.

As the man charged with the nearly impossible task of keeping the forthcoming encounter not only civil but constructive, Ury ought to be having a migraine. But no one's feeling sorry for him. The Harvard-trained negotiation expert runs regular workshops called "Dealing With Difficult People and Difficult Situations," so he asked for it. In fact, as he leans back now amid the whirl of the hotel lobby, he seems almost to be enjoying himself—joking, soothing, offering bits of strategy, cajoling the gloomy faces around him. "One of the things I've learned is, this is like jazz. It's improvised. There's no written score." He shrugs and smiles broadly, his eyes almost crinkling shut. "We'll be in for a wild ride, I suspect."

Bill Ury, 44, was in his late 20s when he and Harvard Law School's Roger Fisher wrote the negotiator's bible, *Getting To Yes: Negotiating Agreement Without Giving In*. Their 1981 book has sold more than two million copies in 21 languages, including Russian, Chinese, Serbo-Croatian and Romanian, and continues to appear on best-seller lists. The book's fans range from Jimmy Carter and Mikhail Gorbachev to Ann Landers. It argues that positional bargaining—staking out a position, usually an extreme one to start with, then reluctantly narrowing the gap between what's asked and what's offered in a series of small, painful steps—makes for bad feelings and worse deals. Instead, Fisher and Ury preach what they call principled negotiation: probe for your adversary's under-lying, often unstated interests, then explore how these may overlap with your own. "Try to expand the pie before you divvy it up," in Ury's words. That win-win solutions are a tiresome mantra of junior sales reps everywhere is a testament to *Getting To Yes's* impact.

"Expand the Pie Before You Divvy it Up." Doug Stewart, SMITHSONIAN, November 1997. Reprinted by permission of the author.

As a mediator, teacher and sometime government adviser, Ury has become a sought-after guru in the booming field of dispute resolution. In the 1980s, he helped the U.S. and Soviet governments replace their obsolete hot line with fully equipped nuclear-crisis centers in each capital. Lately, his focus has shifted to ethnic and secessionist disputes. He's moderated off-the-record talks between Serbs and Croats, Turks and Kurds, and whites and blacks in South Africa—one of many countries where *Getting To Yes* has been a best-seller. Traveling between homes in Colorado and São Paulo, Brazil, Ury maintains ties with Harvard Law School, where he confounded the Program on Negotiation and directs its Project on Preventing War. A social anthropologist by training, he's also advised Pentagon generals, strike-prone coal miners, and IBM, AT&T and American Express executives on the fine art of principled negotiation.

"Bill is very charismatic, but he's not stuffing a message down a channel. He's really teaching people to be curious," says Ed Sketch, a London-based personnel manager at the Ford Motor Company, whose 6,000 top executives worldwide have taken Ury's seminars. "His influence on the company has been incalculable. He inoculated a whole culture with a new way of looking at things."

Few Ford executives are battle-scarred mountain guerrillas, however. In The Hague, where the Chechen delegation finally arrives on Friday morning, a day late, Ury knows his techniques will be hard-tested. The Chechens' arrival at the Peace Palace is delayed several hours more while they protest their accommodations at the deluxe Hotel Des Indes. Only when given a peek at their Russian counterparts' rooms as proof that their own quarters aren't inferior do they acquiesce and head to the Peace Palace, where the other conference-goers have been waiting with more than a little trepidation. "These are the real hard-liners," Ury tells me in the corridor as we wait. "They're looking for insult in everything. There's a drama unfolding here."

The talks are officially the third annual meeting of the Hague Initiative. The high-level but unofficial gatherings are pulled together by a nonprofit consulting group, the Conflict Management Group of Cambridge, Massachusetts—which Roger Fisher cofounded—with the help of Harvard's Program on Negotiation, the Carnegie Corporation of New York, and official bodies in the Netherlands and Russia. The meetings bring together adversaries from ethnic danger zones within the former Soviet Union—Russians, Tatars, Crimeans, Moldovans, Georgians and now Chechens—to talk privately about ways to patch up their differences.

At last, with barely a word or a glance at their lavish surroundings, the half-dozen Chechen delegates and their bodyguards sweep quickly into the Small Hall of Justice and form a tense, inward-facing circle, shoulder to shoulder. None is wearing fatigues or is visibly armed. The presidents of Tatarstan and Ingushetia, semiautonomous republics within the new Russian Federation, join the circle and exchange bear hugs with their fellow Muslims. The four Russian ministers on hand hang back, affecting nonchalance. Ury and Bruce Allyn, a former Harvard colleague and Russia expert, also bide their time on the periphery. Minutes pass with no one speaking. Yes, this is going to be tough: the Chechens are already playing it cagey, refusing to make the first move, refusing even to make eye contact with outsiders.

When everyone is seated, Ury makes the formal introductions. The Chechens sit at tables along one side of the chamber, staring stonily ahead as though the Russians across from them didn't exist. "The purpose of the Hague Initiative is to learn," Ury says soberly as an interpreter in a soundproof booth provides a Russian translation. "I'd like to emphasize that this is going to be very hard work. One hears things from the other side that one does not like to hear."

The sternest of the Chechens, obviously their leader, is stocky, poker-faced Vakha Arsanov, Chechnya's vice president. As a point of pride, he wears a tall Persian lamb's wool hat at all times, even with his earphones. He opens with a prepared speech, a long and withering attack on Russia, which he insists on delivering in Chechen. Through our earphones, we hear a century-by-century recitation of how Russians have massacred, tortured, burned and buried alive generations of Chechens. Arsanov isn't leaving much negotiating room, I notice. To him, Chechnya has never been a part of Russia; it has been an unwillingly subjugated nation since the 16th century. The Russians in the room, to their credit, are keeping their cool. They neither roll their eyes nor shake their heads, though they're rubbing their faces a lot.

In his most recent book, *Getting Past No: Negotiating Your Way From Confrontation To Cooperation*, Ury praised the perspective of Japan's home-run king, Sadahara Oh, who viewed opposing pitchers not as enemies trying to do him in but as partners offering him repeated opportunities to crank another ball out of the park. In a negotiation, Ury advised, don't reject the other side's accusations. Reframe them—treat them as invitations to talk about problems you're both trying to solve. "Reframing works," Ury wrote, "because every message is subject to interpretation."

Now Ury attempts to sum up Arsanov's diatribe as a constructive first step in getting to yes. He thanks him for his "passion" and his "clear articulation" of Chechnya's need for security from attack, acknowledges the importance of preventing another round of war, and agrees that rebuilding is urgently needed. If that's common ground, it's a sliver the width of a rock climber's toehold. Even so, simply allowing someone to vent has its place, Ury had told me earlier. The key is not to react in kind. "You're not trying to control the other person's behavior," Ury had said. "You're trying to control your own."

Two Russian ministers speak. They are, in fact, models of self-control. (Yes, of course, each tells me later, they have studied Bill Ury's books.) In calm tones, they avow their respect for the Chechen people and their horror at the recent bloodshed. One of them, Emil Payin, a short, sleepy-looking adviser to Russian president Boris Yeltsin, suggests the war in Chechnya was never supported by the Russian public. Almost imperceptibly, the mood in the room seems to relax. The Chechens lean back in their chairs and look around the hall a bit. Several take notes. One of the American consultants is writing key points on an easel with a pen. As the sheets of newsprint fill up, he tears them off and tapes them to the walls.

The lull is short-lived. Said-Khasan Abumuslimov, a hawk-faced firebrand and former Chechen vice president, launches into a loud and angry denunciation of Russian treachery. Before he's finished, he's attacked the United States for abetting the Russian war effort and oppressing the people of Puerto Rico. It's quite a performance. The translator labors to keep up, gesturing in the dark booth as he speaks. Payin leans back with the weary smile of someone who's paid to take abuse. Ury listens politely, but his face has grown noticeably paler. He's watching a man pass up an opportunity. Ury's first rule of dealing with angry accusations, he always says, is "go to the balcony"—pretend you're watching him from a distance. I imagine him now willing himself not to react in exasperation.

Ury is a careful orchestrator of the meetings he facilitates, and part of his preparation is gathering the right mix of third parties to call on. Now he decides it's time to cue Hurst Hannum, a professor at Tufts University's Fletcher School of Law and Diplomacy. "Our heavy," Ury jokingly calls him. Professorial but tough, Hannum is an expert on sovereignty. He calmly suggests that the Chechens' obsession with Russian war crimes here has no bearing on self-determination, and that their insistence on independence is naive. Many breakaway regions have declared themselves independent—Biafra, Northern Ireland, the Punjab, Kurdistan—but none exists today as a country. If they're here to be treated like everyone else, Hannum suggests, that's exactly how they're being treated: like Biafra.

The Chechens are paying close attention now, cocking their heads in curiosity and taking notes. Several of the European and American experts weigh in with tactful suggestions that Chechnya do more about its own rampant crime and kidnappings before expecting aid from outside. Sheets of newsprint marked in Russian and English now hang in a double row from the carved wooden mezzanine, giving the judicial chamber the incongruous look of an elementary school classroom. Ury reframes the flow of discussion as optimistically as he dares: "We've made some real progress here in understanding points of view and history and desires." He suggests the fundamental sticking point between Chechens and Russians now is distrust. "The war has left many deep wounds, not all of them physical. How do you begin to heal the wounds that are in people's hearts so that they can treat each other as equal partners?" He calls on a third-party participant, the president of Ingushetia, Ruslan Aushev, who has been nearly silent until now.

Speaking in Russian, Aushev says simply, "The discussion is progressing well. We should continue."

His interjection seems to give everyone a lift—there are nods and smiles all around. By himself, Ury doesn't carry any weight with the Chechens, who may never have heard of Biafra, or Harvard, but Aushev is a wily veteran of secessionist struggles with Moscow and is a Muslim neighbor from the Caucasus to boot. Ury's timing, as he conducts this unwritten score, is perfect.

That evening, the participants gather at a reception and dinner in a private room of the hotel's swank restaurant. The Russians and Chechens are keeping their distance, but the Westerners, at least, make a point of mixing with both, snaring interpreters on the fly. Teetotalers all, the Chechens drink orange juice from their champagne glasses, but they seem to be loosening up all the same. I converse in broken French with a young Chechen officer wounded in the recent war. He gives me a laminated wallet calendar with the Muslim holy days in red and, on the reverse, a photograph of the Chechen guerrilla leader, Shamil Basayev, in beard, headband and grenades. Ury, though fighting a cold and the effects of a flight from Brazil the previous day, is good-humored and unflappable. "The first few hours were very tense. We had to be the container for the Chechens' anger and their hostility. It's like a chemist mixing unpredictable chemicals—is there going to be a nuclear explosion? How far can we let this go?" He laughs.

The level of bombast and vitriol here is nothing new to Ury. His 1982 PhD thesis at Harvard was titled "Talk Out or Walk Out: The Role and Control of Conflict in a Kentucky Coal Mine." The coal mine he studied was so plagued by wildcat strikes that management was threatening to close it down. Ury spent long days and nights underground with miners who viewed their bosses with a distrust that bordered on loathing. Miners wore black hard hats; managers, white ones. Ury took a white hard hat and spray-painted it green. Even so, he had to submit to a hazing his first night underground by a half-dozen miners who gang-tackled him, pulled down his pants and clipped a hair sample with a rusty knife. Having thus been "haired," Ury was accepted by the miners, if not as a full-fledged good old boy, at least as a harmless and amusing alien. With colleagues Jeanne Brett and Stephen Goldberg, he helped devise an orderly system that forced miners and managers to sit down together and listen to each other's complaints (a novelty in many mines), then jointly work out solutions. The frequency of walkouts plunged immediately.

Growing up in a large and sometimes tumultuous extended family, Ury has always been intrigued by dispute resolution. His headstrong parents often quarreled. When he was 6, they failed to resolve a dispute over where they would live. So, for years the family moved back and forth between California, his father's choice, and Switzerland, his mother's. He attended Swiss schools before heading for Yale and then Harvard to study anthropology. Ury himself has had his share of disputes—with roommates, cabdrivers, and his first wife—but he invariably finds an amicable solution. He and his new wife, a Brazilian biochemist, attended his former wife's wedding.

Though Ury personally is a passionate advocate for broad-brush concepts like peace, tolerance and consensus, at the professional level he doesn't take sides. In the coal mines, in the Baltics, in South Africa, in Latin America, Ury always makes a point of teaching the ideas of principled negotiation to both sides in a dispute. Agreements are more likely to stick that way, he says. (One reason *Getting To Yes* has sold so many copies: union leaders will buy stacks of copies for management, and vice versa.) Ed Sketch of Ford describes a workshop Ury ran that brought together 100 of the company's top suppliers with 100 of its own purchasing managers. "The suppliers couldn't believe that we at Ford were teaching them how to be better negotiators," Sketch says. "Bill taught both sides that the essence of a good supplier-purchaser relationship is to get it right, not to screw each other. That's a pretty unusual approach."

Rarely do the two sides in a negotiation have a free hand. Each party is aware of the need to look good when it reports back to its constituency, be it a union's rank and file or a nation's parliament. In his mediation work, Ury likes to ask adversaries to try a deceptively simple exercise: write your opponent's victory speech. "If you can't do that," he tells them, "you know you've got to look again at what you're asking of the other side."

Now, as the second and final day of the truncated Hague conference gets under way, Ury suggests the Chechens imagine that President Yeltsin tells them: fine, you're independent. "Ask yourselves, what is the most persuasive speech Mr. Yeltsin could give that would help his people—including his own opposition—accept your goal? And what could you do that would make his argument more persuasive?"

This the Chechens like. They're leaning forward at their tables, smiling and talking among themselves as they imagine the scenario. Ury asks the Russians to do the same: "Imagine President Maskhadov had to give a speech telling his people they will remain part of the Russian Federation. How would they react?" For Maskhadov, of course, it would be political suicide, as everyone in the room well knows. One of the Russians objects that he would no more presume to give Maskhadov advice than he would the queen of England. Ury explains gently that he meant this as a mental exercise, not a diplomatic strategy. Even Chechnya's impassive foreign minister is smiling now.

Later, as the regular session breaks up, several Russians and Chechens cluster around Arthur Martirosyan, one of several Russian-speaking consultants on hand from Cambridge. A joint statement of the results of the conference must be drafted in time for a press conference at 2 P.M. Martirosyan was up half the night loading a Russian character set into his laptop computer. Now he sits good-naturedly typing and deleting, typing and deleting, as rival delegates dart in and out, leaning over his shoulders like overbearing bosses, dictating their preferred phraseology.

To me, the little group seems to be radiating hostility, but Ury is delighted by the scene. "This is the Chechen hard core," he says quietly. "These are the guys with the guns, the guys you supposedly *cannot* get to yes. And here they are, drafting a joint statement with the Russians." On paper, the result will be a vague call for peace, reconstruction and security, but it's the process that counts, Ury says. However grouchily, the age-old enemies are working together. In the press conference that follows, President Aushev declares, "If we had done this three years ago, there wouldn't have been a war."

Over coffee at the hotel, Ury talks to me about why he believes negotiating has the chance to eclipse force as a tool for settling international disputes. "The traditional way to handle a Chechnya was to beat the guys into the ground. And as in Chechnya, Afghanistan, Vietnam and the West Bank, it doesn't work. Increasingly, it's the Chechens of the world who are defeating, or at least stalemating, the Russians of the world." In modern warfare, there's never a winning side, he says, so countries must devise creative new ways of finding satisfaction together, the way whites and blacks in South Africa have.

The culture of negotiation is spreading far beyond politics and diplomacy, he says. "It's happening in the elementary schools, in the way divorces are handled, in corporations, in the courts. People are realizing that adversarial, win-lose attitudes in an increasingly interdependent world, where I depend on you and you depend on me, don't work anymore. Using those tactics is like asking, 'Who's winning this marriage?'"

Between mediating assignments, Ury has been working on a book about conflict and human evolution. "You hear it said that violence is part of human nature and that warfare is inevitable," he says. "The usual assumption is that we've acquired a thin veneer of civilization. Scratch the veneer, and you get Bosnia." Hobbes and Freud supported this view; crime-happy news reports reinforce it. As an anthropologist, Ury doesn't think the assumption holds up. If violence is as innate as eye color, how can Colombia have a per capita homicide rate 80 times as high as Switzerland's? To Ury, the real question should be: How can a society move from a Colombia to a Switzerland?

To find out, he's spent time studying several remote hunter-gatherer societies—among them the Bushmen of Africa's Kalahari Desert and the Semai of the Malaysian rain forest. These are among the least violent societies in the world, he says. "The Bushmen have no central authority, no policemen, and they have dangerous weapons, like poisoned arrows. You'd think they'd have more violence, not less." Ury recognizes that the Bushman and the Semai aren't necessarily more easygoing than other people. "They have the same quarrels and jealousies that we have, but they've developed a roster of ways to keep it from escalating into violence."

The Bushmen, for example, are almost compulsive about sharing game. As a result, nearly everyone in a community owes everyone else a favor, which makes open hostility more awkward. And when a dispute flares up, friends and family know to hide the parties' poisoned arrows for a few days. Among Malaysia's Semai, says Ury, "if a child hits another child, they have a parliament of children. All the kids in the community get together in a big circle and talk about what happened, how it started, how to prevent it from happening again." The children learn that fights are everybody's affair, not just the fighters'. On a global scale, Ury believes, the same lesson could avert future Bosnias and Rwandas. In both cases, neighboring countries could have quelled the violence early on, had they chosen to get involved.

The conference's final meeting is dinner at an elegant restaurant in the Dutch countryside. At the Peace

Palace earlier in the day, the eldest of the Russians, Ambassador-at-Large Boris Kolokolov, had spoken emotionally of serving alongside loyal Chechen comrades in World War II; he refused to be painted, he said almost angrily, as an enemy of the Chechen people. Now, as we wait to take our seats, the eldest of the Chechens, Daud Akhmadov, gestures to the white-haired Russian to sit with him—the first such fraternization of the gathering.

Ury rises to make a toast. "God gave us two ears and one mouth for a reason," he says to general laughter. More toasts follow, from Russians and Chechens. The atmosphere is still a bit strained—many of the toasts have a chiding undertone of "Why didn't you get to know us sooner?"—but it was only 36 hours earlier that the words "genocide" and "terrorism" were being bandied about. The diminutive Daud Akhmadov, the only Chechen with laugh lines visible on his face, offers a toast to Bill Ury and his dispute-resolving colleagues. "In that you enjoy dealing with conflicts," he says in Russian, raising a juice-filled wineglass, "I am sure you will never be without a job."

Article Review Form at end of book.

What are the seven steps Clarke and Lipp outline to help people from different cultures understand each other's intentions and perceptions as they negotiate agreements?

Conflict Resolution for Contrasting Cultures

Here's a seven-step process that can help people from different cultures understand each other's intentions and perceptions so they can work together harmoniously—based on real-world examples of U.S.-based Japanese subsidiaries.

**Clifford C. Clarke
and G. Douglas Lipp**

An American sales manager of a large Japanese manufacturing firm in the United States sold a multimillion-dollar order to an American customer. The order was to be filled by headquarters in Tokyo. The customer requested some changes to the product's standard specifications and a specified deadline for delivery.

Because the firm had never made a sale to this American customer before, the sales manager was eager to provide good service and on-time delivery. To ensure a coordinated response, she organized a strategic planning session of the key division managers that would be involved in processing the order. She sent a copy of the meeting agenda to each participant. In attendance were the sales manager, four other Americans, three Japanese managers, the Japanese heads of finance and customer support, and the Japanese liaison to Tokyo headquarters. The three Japanese managers had been in the United States for less than two years.

The hour meeting included a brainstorming session to discuss strategies for dealing with the customer's requests, a discussion of possible timelines, and the next steps each manager would take. The American managers dominated, participating actively in the brainstorming session and discussion. They proposed a timeline and an action plan. In contrast, the Japanese managers said little, except to talk among themselves in Japanese. When the sales manager asked for their opinion about the Americans' proposed plan, two of the Japanese managers said they needed more time to think about it. The other one looked down, sucked air through his teeth, and said, "It may be difficult in Japan."

Concerned about the lack of participation from the Japanese but eager to process the customer's order, the sales manager sent all meeting participants an email with the American managers' proposal and a request for feedback. She said frankly that she felt some of the managers hadn't participated much in the meeting, and she was clear about the need for timely action. She said that if she didn't hear from them within a week, she'd assume consensus and follow the recommended actions of the Americans.

A week passed without any input from the Japanese managers. Satisfied that she had consensus, she proceeded. She faxed the specifications and deadline to headquarters in Tokyo and requested that the order be given priority attention. After a week without any response, she sent another fax asking headquarters to confirm that it could fill the order. The reply came the next day: "Thank you for the proposal. We are currently considering your request."

Time passed, while the customer asked repeatedly about the order's status. The only response she could give was that there wasn't any information yet. Concerned, she sent another fax to Tokyo in which she

Copyright February 1998, TRAINING & DEVELOPMENT, American Society for Training and Development. Reprinted with permission. All rights reserved.

outlined the specifications and timeline as requested by the customer. She reminded the headquarters liaison of the order's size and said the deal might fall through if she didn't receive confirmation immediately. In addition, she asked the liaison to see whether he could determine what was causing the delay. Three days later, he told her that there was some resistance to the proposal and that it would be difficult to meet the deadline.

When informed, the customer gave the sales manager a one-week extension but said that another supplier was being considered. Frantic, she again asked the Japanese liaison to intercede. Her bonus and division's profit margin rested on the success of this sale. As before, the reply from Tokyo was that it would be "difficult" to meet the customer's demands so quickly and that the sales manager should please ask the customer to be patient.

They lost the contract. Infuriated, the sales manager went to the subsidiary's Japanese president, explained what happened, and complained about the lack of commitment from headquarters and Japanese colleagues in the United States. The president said he shared her disappointment but that there were things she didn't understand about the subsidiary's relationship with headquarters. The liaison had informed the president that headquarters refused her order because it had committed most of its output for the next few months to a customer in Japan.

Enraged, the sales manager asked the president how she was supposed to attract customers when the Americans in the subsidiary were getting no support from the Japanese and were being treated like second-class citizens by headquarters. Why, she asked, wasn't she told that Tokyo was committed to other customers?

She said: "The Japanese are too slow in making decisions. By the time they get everyone on board in Japan, the U.S. customer has gone elsewhere. This whole mess started because the Japanese don't participate in meetings. We invite them and they just sit and talk to each other in Japanese. Are they hiding something? I never know what they're thinking, and it drives me crazy when they say things like 'It is difficult' or when they suck air through their teeth.

"It doesn't help that they never respond to my written messages. Don't these guys ever read their email? I sent that email out immediately after the meeting so they would have plenty of time to react. I wonder whether they are really committed to our sales mission or putting me off. They seem more concerned about how we interact than about actually solving the problem. There's clearly some sort of Japanese information network that I'm not part of. I feel as if I work in a vacuum, and it makes me look foolish to customers. The Japanese are too confident in the superiority of their product over the competition and too conservative to react swiftly to the needs of the market. I know that headquarters reacts more quickly to similar requests from their big customers in Japan, so it makes me and our customers feel as if we aren't an important market."

Said the U.S.-based Japanese: "The American salespeople are impatient. They treat everything as though it is an emergency and never plan ahead. They call meetings at the last minute and expect people to come ready to solve a problem about which they know nothing in advance. It seems the Americans don't want our feedback; they talk so fast and use too much slang.

"By the time we understood what they were talking about in the meeting, they were off on a different subject. So, we gave up trying to participate. The meeting leader said something about timelines, but we weren't sure what she wanted. So, we just agreed so as not to hold up the meeting. How can they expect us to be serious about participating in their brainstorming session? It is nothing more than guessing in public; it is irresponsible.

"The Americans also rely too much on written communication. They send us too many memos and too much email. They seem content to sit in their offices creating a lot of paperwork without knowing how people will react. They are so cut-and-dried about business and do not care what others think. They talk a lot about making fast decisions, but they do not seem to be concerned if it is the right decision. That is not responsible, nor does it show consideration for the whole group.

"They have the same inconsiderate attitude towards headquarters. They send faxes demanding swift action, without knowing the obstacles headquarters has to overcome, such as requests from many customers around the world that have to be analyzed. The real problem is that there is no loyalty from our U.S. customers. They leave one supplier for another based solely on price and turnaround time. Why should we commit to them if they aren't ready to commit to us? Also, we are concerned that the salesforce has not worked hard enough to make customers understand our commitment to them."

What's the Solution?

Is there an effective way for organizations to deal with conflict between or among the cultural groups represented in their management teams and workforces? We think there is—certainly for Japanese subsidiaries in the United States. The scenario you just read represents only one of many challenges facing multinational companies—how to balance the needs and objectives of the local workforce and customer base with those of the home country and headquarters. To that end, we shall describe a conflict resolution process that has been applied extensively and successfully in a number of Japanese subsidiaries to a variety of seriously disruptive conflict situations. We believe that it constitutes a model for conflict resolution in any multinational organization with offshore subsidiaries.

The core imperative in this process is that managers and other employees from different cultures understand better how culture affects their expectations, reactions, and view of themselves and each other, including possible negative perceptions.

Managers and all employees need to learn how they can keep negative perceptions from escalating into workplace conflict and how to resolve differences when a conflict occurs. Resolution takes time, and the strategies must be thought out carefully. Effective conflict resolution goes beyond mimicking the management style practiced at headquarters in Japan or Europe—and beyond demanding that things be done the "American way."

Instead, resolution is worked out through a process of negotiation between the employees and management of one culture and the employees and management of another. In countless situations, resolving cultural differences has become a valuable way to find creative solutions to other organizational problems.

Resolution involves the concepts of anthropology, uniqueness, and blending.

Anthropology

This discipline teaches that people are affected by the standards and norms of the society in which they grow up, live, and work. The result is *culture*—the values, beliefs, behaviors, thinking patterns, and communication styles that generally characterize the members of a culture and that are neither inherently good nor inherently bad.

Uniqueness

Each of us is a unique individual with our own ways of thinking, behaving, valuing, and communicating—and our own beliefs about what's right and wrong, natural or unnatural, and acceptable or unacceptable. But despite our individual uniqueness, the culture in which we have grown up (and been acculturated) influences us so strongly that we can identify common values and patterns of thinking and behaving. Such values and patterns are shared by a large number of people in any national, linguistic, religious, gender, generational, socioeconomic, ideological or ethnic group.

Blending

The best way to manage is the way that gets the best results. In multinational companies, the best results usually come from a blending of the perspectives and practices of the cultures involved. That approach enables the members of all of the cultures to realize their full potential and to produce positive interpersonal and organizational results.

We developed a seven-step conflict resolution model after examining actual incidents that occurred in U.S.-based Japanese corporations. In each

---

The Seven-Step Conflict Resolution Model

1. **Problem Identification**
   - statement of the problem
   - description of the incident
   - identification of the difficulties
   - development of the explanations

2. **Problem Clarification**
   - comparative intentions
   - comparative perceptions

3. **Cultural Exploration**
   - hidden cultural expectations
   - hidden cultural assumptions and values

4. **Organizational Exploration**
   - global imperatives
   - local conditions

5. **Conflict Resolution**
   - achieving harmony
   - goal setting
   - action planning and implementation

6. **Impact Assessment**
   - monitoring the results
   - modifying the plan
   - assessing the benefits

7. **Organizational Integration**
   - recording the results
   - celebrating the success
   - institutionalizing the benefits

---

case, we were called in as consultants to help resolve a problem. It's our intent to provide a clearly defined framework for analyzing such conflicts so that the recommended strategies can be understood easily and applied effectively in the workplace with any grouping of diverse cultures, including corporate cultures.

Because we emphasize in every step that culture is the root cause of conflicts, it might seem that we're portraying cultural diversity as an obstacle to effective corporate operations. On the contrary, diversity is essential for creating the leading-edge strategies and alternative solutions that enhance a company's competitive capability. Rather than casting culture as the villain, the purpose of this conflict resolution process is to bring culture out into the open so that it can become an organizational strength. Valuing cultural diversity in the workplace leads to greater harmony, more creativity, and a stronger organizational identity or corporate culture. That serves to enhance an organization's teamwork and leadership in the marketplace, both locally and globally. (See the box for the main elements of the model.)

The Model

To enhance the value of the model as a conflict resolution tool, the first five steps include descriptions of several specific facilitation strategies that HRD or organizational development staff can use in implementation. A critical element in applying those strategies and in pursuing the aims of the conflict resolution model as a whole is the creation of an effective bicultural team of facilitators or trainers consisting of Japanese and Americans. In order for such a team, whether internal or external, to be effective, the members need extensive knowledge in the other culture and prolonged contact or experience with it. In resolving the conflict described in the opening scenario, it was especially valuable for the Americans to spend a significant amount of time at the subsidiary's headquarters in Japan. The Japanese members had to understand English, while the Americans, even if they didn't speak Japanese, had to become familiar with Japanese communication styles.

A facilitation team has to be bicultural because no matter how knowledgeable and experienced the parties in a conflict are about each other's culture or how well they speak each other's language, they will still approach their assignments from their own cultural perspectives. And they will act on the basis of culturally conditioned biases of which they may be unaware. Nevertheless, a bicultural facilitation team offers the best way to fuse people's different perspectives to achieve effective conflict management.

Failure to consider those factors caused trouble in one U.S.-based Japanese company. Two well intentioned American HR managers attempting to resolve a conflict only aggravated it by being insensitive to the needs of the Japanese. The HR managers were approached by a group of American operations managers who complained that their Japanese counterparts weren't sharing enough information with them. That, they claimed, limited their ability to make good, timely decisions.

The American HR managers decided to conduct a needs assessment. Recognizing that some of the Japanese were weak in English, they had the questionnaire translated into Japanese. Armed with the questionnaires, the HR staff conducted a series of data-gathering meetings—first with the Americans, which produced a wealth of information, and then with the Japanese, which resulted in far less information and only one suggestion for resolving the problem—that they should improve their English.

After analyzing the information, the HR staff decided to bring together the two groups "to hammer out an agreement." They asked the participants to be open and "put their cards on the table." The American managers shared their feelings and suggested solutions. The Japanese said little, nodded in agreement to the proposed solutions, and promised to practice their English. Predictably, none of the so-called agreements came to fruition—which further frustrated the Americans.

Upon examination of that process, it became obvious why it failed. Although the HR managers were skilled facilitators of conflict resolution meetings, most of their experience was with groups of Americans. Their assumptions about how to motivate people to participate in meetings were based on the American model, which presumes that the Japanese would be also comfortable with public disclosure and asserting themselves in large groups. In fact, they are not, especially in group meetings with nonJapanese. The Americans would have been more successful conducting the meetings with the Japanese one-on-one. An even more effective approach would have been to have a Japanese manager conduct the meetings. That would have helped the Japanese relax and resulted in richer material.

The group meeting in the opening scenario wasn't conducive to the needs of the Japanese to discuss sensitive matters in private and come to a decision before making a public statement. A more effective approach would have been to form small, mono-cultural groups of the Americans and Japanese and ask each group to answer questions provided by the facilitators. Then, the groups could reconvene and report their findings.

That approach can be used effectively in the conflict resolution process even when only Americans are involved, but it's essential when Japanese are on one side of the conflict. It takes effort to help Japanese people open up and disclose sensitive information.

Steps 1 through 5 of the conflict resolution model include specific methodologies (referred to as "facilitation strategies") that can be implemented by trainers, facilitators, and HR staff. The steps are effective regardless of the cultural makeup of the group or groups. Here's the substance of what each step covers.

Step 1: Problem Identification

In this step, an organizational problem arising from a cultural conflict, as perceived by both cultural groups, is identified. A problem represents events that typically occur in U.S.-based Japanese companies and that critically affect operations.

Statement of the Problem

First, you need to state the problem and its background briefly. People can view the same event from different perspectives, but if they agree what the problem is, their shared perception will give them an advantage in trying to solve it.

For example, in the opening scenario, the Americans and Japanese agreed that the problem was multi-faceted and not simply a breakdown in decision making. They realized that, as a bicultural team, they had to improve their effectiveness in the following areas:

- meeting management
- relationship building
- open communication of expectations
- clarification of how to handle customers' requests while balancing the needs of the U.S. and Japanese marketplace.

Description of the Incident

Next, it's useful to have a brief description of a conflict incident or situation that has actually occurred in a U.S.-based Japanese subsidiary—from the Japanese and American viewpoints. That can show why reaching consensus is sometimes a difficult task.

Facilitation Strategies

Within a mono-cultural group, it's important to identify the common or typical approach to dealing with the same type of problem that has been identified. For example, in the opening scenario, the Americans agreed that the typical way to handle that type of problem was to be more upfront with each other, whether communicating face-to-face or via email or other written communication. The Japanese suggested that, from their perspective, the appropriate approach would be to have more one-on-one meetings to discuss delicate issues and not rely so much on large group meetings and email.

Identification of the Difficulties

It's important to describe the difficulties experienced as a result of differences in the way Japanese and Americans approach an issue. In the opening scenario, the Americans agreed that they emphasize "laying one's cards on the table" and find it hard to interpret the indirect answers of the Japanese, such as "It is difficult." The Japanese agreed that they were uncomfortable discussing or brainstorming openly in large meetings. They felt "attacked" and "put on the spot" by their American counterparts.

Development of the Explanations

Have the Americans develop (from their perspective) for the Japanese group a full explanation of how and why difficulties occur. Have the Japanese do the same for the American group. This step is important but often ignored. It's critical for each group, independently, to air their grievances about each other. When that's facilitated properly, the benefits include the following:

- Participants release emotions, which can prepare them for learning.
- They find they aren't alone or abnormal in experiencing the conflict.
- They can explore strategies for cross-cultural interaction that they've found effective in the past.
- They can generate useful, data-based feedback to present to the other culture group.
- They might find that they have different perceptions of the situation and that those might be more personal than cultural.

Step 2: Problem Clarification

In this step, the groups compare their intentions in order to throw light on the nature of the misunderstanding. Because discordance between intentions and perceptions is a frequent cause of conflict, it's necessary to clarify people's intentions and perceptions in order to get at the root of a problem.

Comparative Intentions

It's necessary to understand what the Japanese and Americans intended by their individual actions. People tend to feel that their intentions are positive, but they're often perceived as negative by people in another culture. In the opening scenario, the American sales manager intended to be sensitive to the needs of her Japanese co-workers. "I understand that the Japanese have some difficulty with English," she explained, "so I always send out the agenda in advance." Though the Japanese managers wanted to participate in decision making, they felt uncomfortable. It was hard for them to join in the discussion because it was in English and fast-paced. Said the Japanese, "The Americans need to slow down to allow us to think and respond." The Japanese were hesitant about using memos but eager to participate face-to-face.

Comparative Perceptions

Perceptions of "what really happened" can vary according to culture. So can interpretation and judgment about another person's behavior. In the example, the American sales manager's perspective was that the Japanese in her subsidiary refused to help her make a sale. She said, "The Japanese managers contributed nothing during the brainstorming. At other companies I've worked, it was common sense to send memos to test the water, especially on critical issues. When people responded, you knew who supported you, who didn't, and what the concerns were. Then, we were prepared to work things out in a meeting." She asked, "How can I sell effectively if Tokyo doesn't let me in on what's happening over there?"

Said the Japanese: "The Americans are self-centered and emotionally distant. They send too many memos and email . . . They're quick to commit to a course of action without knowing the big picture." The Japanese thought it was better to discuss matters one-on-one in an informal setting instead of a rushed meeting. From their perspective, the Americans were too concerned about action and not concerned enough about their needs. The U.S.-based Japanese weren't convinced that the American customer was worth the risk of pushing headquarters. "If we put pressure on Tokyo to fill this order and the customer goes elsewhere next year," they said, "we would lose credibility in Japan and have to go back. The Americans should realize that we cannot commit to any action or timeline without discussing them in detail with the appropriate department heads in Japan. In addition, it is hard to know whether the Americans really support each other because they constantly change their minds during brainstorming. They need to put less emphasis on ending a meeting on time and more on meaningful discussion."

Facilitation Strategies

Regarding bicultural groups, it's important to do the following:

- Have the Americans explain to the Japanese the common approaches in the United States for dealing with the same type of problem. It's especially important to clarify the rationale and feelings behind those strategies.
- Have the Japanese adjourn to a separate room to discuss their reaction.
- Reconvene and let the Japanese explain to the Americans the common approaches and strategies used in Japan, clarifying the rationale and feelings behind them.
- Have the Americans adjourn to a separate room to discuss their reaction.
- Reconvene and let them discuss the outcome of their discussion with the Japanese.
- Help the Japanese and Americans reach a mutual understanding (not necessarily acceptance) of each other's approach. That reinforces the idea that within every culture, there are reasonable explanations for a given behavior. That also helps people understand other cultures and to validate differences in their approaches to business and workplace issues.

Step 3: Cultural Exploration

This step examines each culture's values and how they play out in light of people's contrasting expectations and assumptions, which drive their intentions and perceptions, as discussed in step 2.

Hidden Cultural Expectations

"I wish they were more like us" and "Why don't they do it our way?" are common statements. In this step, each group examines how it thinks the other should act, according to what each group considers normal in similar situations. In the case of the lost sale, the Americans said, "We need people to level with us. If you can do something or commit to something, then do it. We can't stand wishy-washy answers. If you don't participate in meetings, don't expect follow-up. Time is money and we can't baby-sit everyone."

The Japanese said, "We want to communicate on a more personal level without the openly aggressive approach often used by Americans." Japanese believe every situation is different and must be treated as such. They don't consider written messages to be adequate communication. They think it's an insult to send an email when you could walk down the hall.

Hidden Cultural Assumptions and Values

Step 3 focuses on how values affect each group's intentions and perceptions of each other. It also helps them look deeper at the origins and assumptions of culturally determined behaviors. They often discover that common sense is different in each culture. Americans tend to think that accomplishing tasks is more important than building relationships. What comes into play is Americans' belief in openness and honesty. The conflict in the opening scenario was caused not because Japanese don't value honesty (they do), but because Americans see openness as an essential element of honesty, even if it hurts someone's feelings.

Typically, if an American asks someone a question and he or she doesn't respond right away or responds vaguely, the American tends to question that person's honesty or reliability. From an American perspective, honesty means expressing exactly what one thinks when the occasion demands it. That belief comes, in part, from a conviction that there's an objective truth in every situation that can be expressed in words. Most Americans believe strongly in the communicative power of words—whether spoken or written, but especially written—which is why they believe that everything they need to know about a situation can be communicated through memos. To Americans, written words are accurate and efficient, and provide a useful record.

The Japanese are more concerned about "losing face." An American might lose face with a customer for a late delivery, but a Japanese would lose face in the eyes of everyone aware of the failure, including friends and co-workers. Americans may feel guilty regarding a person they fail, but the Japanese feel shame in the eyes of society. In Japanese culture, shame damages one's pride and image. Appropriate social behavior is considered to be the ultimate grace. Face is the integrity of behaving appropriately (harmoniously) in a group. Japanese feel that Americans don't have norms of behavior. Face is an issue regarding the unwillingness of Japanese to participate in American-style meetings. If Japanese disagree with another participant, they usually will not say so for fear that person would lose face. They prefer to discuss the matter privately one-on-one. If pushed to answer by aggressive Americans, they may make a hissing sound by sucking air through their teeth and say, "It is difficult."

Facilitation Strategies

Within a bicultural group, it's important to explore and discuss—paying attention to people's different communication styles—the significance of differences in approach. Each group examines how it might feel practicing the other's approach and how easy or difficult that would be. What emotional adjustments would it have to make? What behavioral skills would it have to acquire so that each member could function effectively using the other group's approach.

One way to do that is to use reverse role play. That requires Japanese participants to select role play scenarios using behavior common to Americans. Similarly, it requires Americans to selected role play scenarios using Japanese behavior. For example, regarding communication style, a Japanese participant might be asked in a role play to be aggressive or interactive. Or an American might be asked to be passive and to rely on nonverbal communication. The scenarios can be videotaped and analyzed to reinforce new skills.

Step 4: Organizational Exploration

This step looks at the organizational issues that affect the conflict under discussion. Such issues can impose unexpressed standards, expectations, and values that affect how people work together. Each factor reflects an organization's culture at either the global headquarters level or local subsidiary level. This step is important in that each side of a conflict tends to be unaware of the organizational pressures of the other side. Often, too little time is spent on educating the groups on each other's organizational context.

Global Imperatives

Step 4 focuses on hidden expectations from headquarters, which is what the Japanese managers represent in the scenario that opened this article. Such expectations or imperatives are driven by typical organizational characteristics: corporate values, business strategies, structure, staffing policies, performance standards, operational systems, job skills, and work styles. For a subsidiary to operate effectively, it must take those factors into consideration.

Facilitation Strategies

You should guide conflicting parties in examining the differences between the corporate cultures of headquarters in Japan and the U.S. subsidiary. Ask: What is the corporate culture of the organization in Japan? What is the corporate culture of the U.S. subsidiary? What is the preferred way to manage the issue at hand? Does it support and manifest the organization's core values? Why does headquarters expect a certain approach? Does it meet the needs of the American customers and employees? Are any of the values identified in steps 1 or 2 held by both Japanese and American managers?

In a standard-setting exercise (using the information gathered in steps 1 through 4), challenge participants to analyze their organization's effectiveness from the perspective of employees and customers. Ask the Japanese and American managers to determine how to best use the unique qualities of their cultures. They have to decide where to combine, compromise, or synergize certain elements.

Local Conditions

Step 4 also focuses on the varying factors in the local workplace that affect a company's competitiveness. It's important to examine and understand certain organizational characteristics (such as systems, values, and job skills) with respect to the requirements of the local environment. Often, Japanese managers sent by headquarters are told little about the U.S. structure of their industry or the U.S. workplace—perhaps because the differences are assumed to be insignificant.

Facilitation Strategies

Ask the Japanese these questions: How do state or U.S. government laws affect your approach? Are there industry-specific or labor-directed standards that must be adhered to? What are competitors' standards in the United States? What are American customers' expectations of products and service? What benchmarks suggest alternative approaches to being competitive?

That gives a bicultural facilitation team useful information for making recommendations to management in the United States and Japan. For example, is there strong union representation for hourly wage earners? How sophisticated are the workers? Have they worked for large or small companies?

The local conditions under which the American sales manager was operating were simple. She was under pressure to deliver the product according to the customer's specs and deadline. That was less a function of cultural factors than her role as salesperson. Her desire to fulfill the customer's requirements was also driven by her knowledge that American customers are loyal to price, availability, and quality—not to a particular supplier. Because most U.S. markets have many suppliers, customers tend to believe in shopping for the best deal. The sales manager was also driven by the knowledge that the financial compensation of the entire subsidiary was linked to her ability to perform. She wanted to fill the largest order in the subsidiary's history and help her company achieve profitability.

The global imperatives influencing the actions of the Japanese, on the other hand, were more complicated. Shortly before Tokyo headquarters received the sales manager's faxed order, it had gotten another large order from an established Japanese customer, which it promised to deliver. Headquarters managers were embarrassed that they possibly couldn't fill both orders, so they delayed responding to make sure. The requested changes in specifications was also a problem. The Japanese manufacturer was set up to provide a product for customers who didn't need such changes. Filling the American order would mean delaying delivery of the product to the national account in Japan. From the Japanese perspective, the Americans should have asked (and waited patiently for a response) whether the spec changes could be made, before they promised delivery to the American customer.

Compounding those problems was the fact that the administrators at headquarters weren't convinced of the potential for future business with the new American customer. Because they were aware of U.S. customers' tendency to shop the competition, they weren't willing to sacrifice a proven Japanese customer for an unknown American one. That's not to say that Japanese companies won't take care of American customers. If the relationship is sound and both sides are willing to work together, Americans can expect high-quality products delivered on time.

Step 5: Conflict Resolution

This step emerges from the answers to two questions: What is the goal? How do we attain it? The aim is to develop a team or organization into a unit that can handle inevitable cultural barriers and clarify both the goal and how to attain it. Though steps 5 through 7 are the most difficult, they can ensure the most durable cultural change.

In an effort to support the American sales manager and minimize future problems, the Japanese president suggested examining the system breakdown that had occurred. He said that he wanted to understand how the subsidiary and headquarters could work together more effectively. He also said he was interested in improving relations between the Japanese and American workers in the subsidiary. The sales manager agreed that both goals were important. The president then asked her to analyze the situation objectively, suggesting that she request the HR director to help the subsidiary examine the interface of cultures in its decision making system. The sales manager readily agreed and met with the HR director to develop a plan. They decided that the first step would be for internal HRD staff to interview everyone involved in decision making—the Americans and Japanese at the subsidiary, the relevant people at headquarters, and the American customer. The HR team included a Japanese expatriate who interviewed all of the Japanese employees.

Once it gathered the necessary information the HR staff recommended conducting a team building workshop for the Japanese and American subsidiary employees involved in the conflict. The American sales manager, American vice president, and four other American managers met for two days with the Japanese liaison to headquarters, and Japanese heads of finance and customer support, and three other Japanese managers.

The workshop's structure and facilitation were crucial. For instance, it was important for Japanese managers to make sure the workshop had a balance of cultures. The Americans wanted it held outside of the subsidiary environment, free from interruption. On the first day, the HR staff, as facilitators, began by sharing their understanding of the system breakdown with all 12 participants. The facilitators said the workshop's objective was to analyze how the breakdown occurred and to construct a decision-making system by which the sales division could operate in the future. The facilitators also explained that the solution would involve redesigning systems, clarifying standards, and building communication skills for better teamwork.

Having established goals, the HR team shared the information from the interviews and encouraged participants to tell their sides of the story. The HR staff helped everyone develop a positive explanation of their cultural assumptions and expectations. By explaining their own perspectives and listening to others' explanations, participants were better able to understand the conflict's cultural roots.

By the end of the first day, participants could understand their colleagues' actions and recognize their positive intentions. Both the Japanese and Americans went home with a feeling of accomplishment and optimism.

On day 2, the facilitators drew large diagrams of the various systems involved in the conflict. For each step in a system, there were spaces labeled "Japanese standard" and "American standard." The facilitators asked both groups to explain how they knew when each step in each system was completed. They wrote their answers in the appropriate spaces, creating a map of the decision making system and the different standards the two sides were using to manage it. Once they could see that they were using different standards, they discussed how to resolve the differences.

Next, the group redesigned the entire system, modifying the ordering phase by adding a step for communicating with headquarters before confirming a customer's order, which conformed with the Americans' values on honesty. Participants noted that the added step would take more time, but they saw obvious advantages to customers if salespeople were certain they could deliver an order before accepting it.

The group agreed to other new steps. For instance, the American sales manager agreed to meet with Japanese managers in advance and individually. The sales team said it would have dinner together regularly to provide a less formal atmo-sphere for discussion. Everyone agreed to participate in training on how to communicate more effectively with members of the other group—for instance, the Japanese would learn to read and write memos in English.

Next, participants proposed modifications in how to communicate orders to headquarters. They agreed that it made more sense for the Japanese liaison in the United States to have that responsibility, and they committed to closer teamwork, especially in relaying information to all team members and developing creative alternatives in cases in which information or resources weren't available.

By the end of day 2, the new system's design was complete. The next day, the American sales manager and the Japanese liaison presented it to the president and won his wholehearted support.

Achieving Harmony

By identifying and clarifying the problem (steps 1 and 2), the parties can better understand the conflict and each other's intentions and perceptions. By exploring hidden cultural expectations and assumptions and by becoming aware of the major global imperatives and local conditions (steps 3 and 4), the parties can better comprehend the cultural and organizational framework in which the conflict is occurring. Only when those factors are understood and addressed are the parties ready to achieve the harmony needed to resolve the conflict together.

Because the Japanese regard harmony as the ultimate goal and value in human relationships, they can't work effectively with others until such harmony is desired by all. A frequent cause of continued disharmony is when one member (usually high ranking) assumes the role of bystander or observer. Instead of recognizing his or her part in the problem, that person may accuse others of bad intentions rather than see that he or she manifests the cross-cultural characteristics that are the source of the problem.

A first step to achieving harmony is to determine and clarify the perceived effect of a conflict on employee development, customer service, and business operations. The worksheet, Key Issues, defines conflict issues in a succinct statement. Participants fill in three blanks under the heading, Current Status, on how they think the conflict affects operations, customers, and employees. In discussing such consequences, participants recognize the need to create a framework in which they can work together harmoniously. Their readiness is based on having worked through steps 1 through 4 of the model and having examined the conflict from Japanese and American perspectives, as well as global and local perspectives.

To create the framework, participants have to take responsibility for the problem. They must recognize that their perceptions of people's actions don't necessarily match their intentions. They must understand and accept the other group's cultural assumptions and expectations, and the different local and global conditions central to the conflict. Based on the harmony generated by those actions, participants should be able to commit to working together towards resolution.

Goal Setting

Next, they engage in a process designed to produce a shared goal. Beginning with a discussion of possible goals that are so abstract that they can agree to them readily, participants work together on more concrete definitions of the overall goal. They move from the abstraction of a shared goal—chosen from the universals on which most people in the same organization can agree—to specific indicators of the successful achievement of that goal. That way, they form a shared definition of their goal. If the goal that emerges from that process isn't shared by all parties, there will be no real progress towards conflict resolution. The differences in goals often reflect differences in people's fundamental values—such as the American orientation towards short-term goals versus the Japanese commitment to the long-term.

Given the collaborative effort required to develop a mutually acceptable goal, it's essential to have an effective facilitator with objectivity and a strong bicultural background. A bicultural team of two facilitators can assure cultural equity better than one facilitator if he or she is either Japanese or American. A mutually acceptable goal statement is the foundation for addressing other problem areas.

That approach, a culmination of the previous steps, uses a consensus model. That's a critical point because (1) attaining consensus verifies that harmony has been achieved and (2) the Japanese and American managers must commit to a direction in the form of a company or department goal that has the broadest possible support. However, the goal must be achievable. If it's just an obvious idealistic statement, employees may ignore it. On the other hand, a visionary element in an achievable goal statement can motivate employees. Arriving at agreement on the goal statement is a challenge for managers and facilitators alike. Because consensus and success rely on top management's support, the decision making process in establishing and pursuing a goal must accommodate the cultural needs—such as communication styles, thinking patterns, and behaviors—of both groups. The recommended consensus model emphasizes everyone being heard and attended to instead of unanimous verbal or written agreement. Everyone should feel included so that they buy into the decision to move forward. That's precisely what Japanese mean when they use the word *consensus*.

Facilitation Strategies

Once the parties agree on a goal and specific, measurable indications of its achievement, they must decide on a strategy for taking the organization from its present state to the state embodied in the goal. For instance, the decision whether to "build or buy" often creates conflict because of cultural differences on such issues as time, cost, and work relationships. To facilitate transition planning, it's best to identify any impediments to achieving the goal and to identify the necessary resources from the local organization and global or regional headquarters.

That helps analyze the gaps between the goal statement and the organization's current position on the issue at hand. Refer to the worksheet to see how that is integrated with conflict analysis. That will also contribute to the next step, action planning. Once gaps are articulated, the action planning steps will become clear.

Action Planning and Implementation

At this point, participants translate the strategic plan into specific steps involving who, what, where, when, and how. Next, implementation can begin. It's important to note, however, that making such detailed decisions frequently gives rise to a great deal of culturally based disagreement. Americans and Japanese tend to have different assumptions regarding planning. One major difference that may require facilitation to resolve is the American orientation towards individual assignments versus the Japanese orientation towards teamwork and group assignments.

You can use the worksheet to facilitate the group's planning and implementation tactics and to build on the previous gap analysis. Guide the group in (1) identifying the gaps between the goal statement and organization's current status, (2) finding resources to bridge those gaps, and (3) developing measurable indicators on the achievement of the goal. Typically, participants have many ideas that may be misjudged across cultures, so stay focused on steps 1 through 4 in order to work through such misunderstandings.

Don't hesitate to check people's intentions, perceptions, assumptions, and expectations of both the local subsidiary and global or regional headquarters. Begin by having them complete a worksheet; the Japanese can participate in a small-group worksheet. Then, have participants complete a bicultural group worksheet. When the total-group worksheet is completed with consensus, it's time to implement the actions. Ideally, each participant input his or her strengths and everyone committed to achieving the goal.

A Key Issues analysis, facilitated by the Key Issues Worksheet, can clarify the issues raised in step 5. The worksheet is usually introduced as the core focus of an off-site workshop for Japanese and Americans engaged in a conflict. It involves these actions.

- Identifying the key issue or issues. That will have been done in steps 1 through 4 and just needs to be restated in a way that shows participants' positive intentions.

- Describing the current status. That means, for example, the conflict's effect on these organizational domains: operations, customers, and employees. If the ultimate resolution is going to affect headquarters, then that should be the fourth domain.

- Developing a goal statement. It should be broad enough for both sides to agree on, yet sufficiently specific to be an effective guide and to motivate people to action. This is the most difficult part of using the worksheet.

- Outlining the key benefits. That follows from achieving the stated goal or goals. Benefits also fall into the organizational domains operations, customers, and employees. The benefits will be in areas with the most impact from the conflict. Examining them can help people in the final articulation of the goals.

- Identifying barriers to change. That means describing the obstacles to achieving the goals in specific terms—such as budget limitations and lack of information—rather than blaming individuals or divisions.

- Listing support resources. Such support includes external training, underutilized skills, and funding sources.

- Developing an action plan. The plan for surmounting barriers and achieving the goals should outline and sequence planning from one step to the next—who does what when.

- Noting the success factors. That means drawing up guidelines for monitoring progress in achieving the goals and publicizing the attainment of each milestone.

Step 6: Impact Assessment

This step determines the measures or key indicators that will determine the goal has been achieved and the conflict resolved.

Because the two cultures often have different assumptions about what *success* means, the indicators should be agreed on by consensus in the same way that the goals were. If a solution's effect isn't assessed carefully and systematically, an organization has no way of knowing whether the root problem that caused the conflict has been solved. If no assessment is performed, there can even be uncertainty about whether the strategic plan was ever implemented. We've often seen the hopes of enthusiastic subsidiary employees dashed when their constructive suggestions for resolution receive no response

The Key Issues Worksheet

Key Issue:

Current Status: Impact on (1) operations, (2) customers, (3) employees—and (4) headquarters, if applicable

1	2	3

Goal Statement:

Key Benefits to:

1. Operational excellence	2. Quality of service to customers	3. Development of employees

Barriers to Change:

Source of Support (internal and external):

Action Plan:	Responsibility:	Target Dates:

Success Factors:

---

from headquarters management or U.S. representatives. Mutually agreed upon assessment procedures will assure all parties of the seriousness of their work and reflect a high-quality relationship across cultures.

Monitoring the Results

Step 6 involves using the necessary tools and placing the responsible individuals in a position to assess achievements along established timelines in order to monitor progress. During the action planning stage, it's essential to establish a system for monitoring results to clarify who has responsibility for checking progress, what will be used to monitor progress, and when the monitoring will be done.

Monitoring results at different stages is an important part of motivating workers. If they aren't told until the end whether success was achieved, they won't be motivated to make an effort to ensure it.

Modifying the Plan

If in monitoring the plan, you see that it isn't achieving the desired results along the established timeline, it will be necessary to make modifications.

Assessing the Benefits

After achieving the goal, it's important to determine the ways in which the organization has changed as a result. What were the benefits to headquarters and the subsidiary? The most important ones will be resolution of the conflict and increased morale. That can boost productivity. Another benefit might be less absenteeism or turnover. A significant accomplishment would be if the conflict's negative effects on the critical parties—the operations, customers, and employees identified on the worksheet—had been turned around. Those benefits can be measured as positive consequences of the conflict resolution.

In the example we've been using, a major part of the resolution plan was customized training focused on all of the communication events that occurred—from sales order to delivery. The resulting programs emphasize intercultural communication between Japanese and Americans and their communication with headquarters. Trainees have been strongly motivated to learn new skills because of the clear connection between those skills and a potential rise in team productivity.

The biggest stumbling blocks in the plan were the lack of information from headquarters and a policy that favored Japan-based accounts. It was necessary for the U.S.-based Japanese president to intercede, including traveling to Japan to act as an advocate for the subsidiary. That demonstrated to customers that the whole subsidiary would fight for their interests, and it gained more respect from American employees for the Japanese president.

Japanese presidents of U.S.-based Japanese subsidiaries are often torn between having to explain the actions of headquarters to the subsidiary and having to explain the subsidiary's actions to headquarters. Subsidiary presidents who push too hard for their workers or American customers are often considered to have "gone native" by headquarters.

Nevertheless, the Japanese president had to be the subsidiary's advocate at headquarters. He saw clearly that to be an effective advocate, he'd have to exchange information regularly with his American employees. In Japan, he met with the vice president of international business to explain the subsidiary's needs and argue for a change in the practice that favored Japanese customers. The vice president agreed to become an advocate for the subsidiary. The practice of assigning priority to Japanese customers was redesigned to give the American subsidiary equal access to products. Upon his return to the United States, the Japanese president asked the salesforce to offer the lost customer a new delivery schedule. Though the customer had used another company, he was impressed by the new proposal and said he'd consider the subsidiary for future needs.

The subsidiary experienced several benefits from the steps it had taken. One, its new system and training increased and improved communication between the Japanese and Americans employees. They checked with each other regularly to ensure that communication was adequate and understood. Meetings became more even-paced, and the Japanese were better able to understand and participate in what was going on. The time that the sales team spent at dinner together helped enhance teamwork through improved personal relationships. Despite the fact the system had been modified to include additional steps, the sales cycle time decreased due to less controversy and misunderstanding.

The Japanese liaison to Tokyo headquarters began accompanying the American sales manager on customer calls, which gave the liaison a better sense of U.S. customers' needs. Consequently, he became a more effective advocate for American customers at headquarters. His ability to convey information about the U.S. marketplace more accurately and in a more appropriate style persuaded his colleagues at headquarters to respond to the subsidiary's needs more efficiently.

Last, the Japanese president's trip to headquarters increased the Americans' trust in their subsidiary's leadership, and they passed along that trust to customers, improving the firm's competitiveness in the marketplace.

Step 7: Organizational Integration

In this step, the results of the conflict resolution and assessment processes are distributed throughout the company, integrating individual success stories into corporate learning systems. A conflict (and its resolution) can occur in a department without people in other departments hearing about it. Through integration, the entire company can benefit from the process and results. At the same time, the people involved in the conflict can integrate the key lessons of the conflict resolution into their work styles and, perhaps, be celebrated for their creative contributions.

Recording the Results

The entire process—identifying the root problem, approaching the problem, and resolving the problem—is documented (for example, in the company newsletter or case study report) so that the development path is clear to anyone who wants to follow it. A record of the results prevents the misperception that resolution was haphazard. It also provides information for determining accountability, revamping reward systems, and creating models for future conflict resolution.

Celebrating the Success

You can draw attention to the achievements by pausing, reflecting, and celebrating as a group—for example, a departmental dinner, team excursion, or special staff meeting. Such celebrations are part of an intrinsic reward system: They foster solidarity, teamwork, and excellent role models.

Institutionalizing the Benefits

An organization can apply the benefits from a conflict resolution in other areas or business units to avoid similar conflicts. One conflict resolution can suggest changes for resolving other conflicts involving the same issues. By integrating the key lessons of one department into operating systems, an organization can decrease the effort and energy wasted in culturally based misunderstandings. The competencies and skills learned by experiencing the resolution process can be institutionalized in training, evaluation, and reward systems.

In our example, the results of the conflict resolution were recorded in several interesting ways. First, the American vice president presented the subsidiary's new system to headquarters during a trip to Japan. Understanding how the subsidiary operated got headquarters staff to be more active participants in the "American system." The system's success reflected well on the international vice president, who made sure that the American vice president's presentation was recorded for the benefit of other worldwide subsidiaries.

At the U.S. subsidiary, the HR manager added new courses to the curriculum, in which new American employees and Japanese transferees are required to participate. The result of sales managers having new skills was that the Americans began communicating more directly with headquarters. As they became better at that, it was possible for the Japanese liaison to return to Tokyo headquarters in a position to facilitate communications further because the Americans were dealing with someone they knew and who knew them.

Though there weren't any formal celebrations marking the new system's success, subsidiary employees found ways to honor people who had contributed. The sales team, for instance, had regular meetings and social events that became occasions for them to reaffirm the value of their teamwork and achievements. On a larger scale, employees who completed the intercultural training programs were awarded certificates and encouraged to hang them in their offices. If an employee of one culture entered the office of an employee of another culture and saw the certificate, he or she could feel confident of cross-cultural receptiveness. The result was an environment in which more employees expressed a desire to communicate effectively across cultures.

Our experience in dealing with U.S.-based Japanese subsidiaries has led us to believe that completing all seven steps of the conflict resolution process is crucial to the long-term success of managing cultural conflict. We realized, however, that some of the Japanese and Americans in the companies we've worked with just wanted to know what their cultural counterparts were thinking so they could at least feel less frustrated. They didn't necessarily expect or want others' behavior to change.

For people who just want a better understanding of their cultural counterparts, we recommend that they focus on steps 1 through 4 of the conflict resolution model: problem identification, problem clarification, cultural exploration, and organizational exploration. After completing those steps towards harmony, many Americans are relieved to find that Japanese managers tend to criticize staff to motivate them. We've heard from countless Americans comments like this: "After I realized why my Japanese manager constantly criticized his staff—Japanese and Americans—I was relieved. Until then, I worried that I'd done something wrong. Now that I know it's a common Japanese management style, I don't take it personally. It's simply a Japanese management tool."

Americans who recognize the reason for such criticism realize that their Japanese managers aren't biased against them. They also understand that their managers probably won't change and will continue to dole out mostly critical feedback. That understanding can be extremely helpful in enabling them to adapt to a foreign management style and to enjoy a more harmonious workplace.

The most critical dimension of the conflict resolution model is the centrality of global (headquarters) and local relations. At the heart of almost every cross-cultural conflict in U.S.-based Japanese companies lies a difference in values, perspectives, and priorities between headquarters and local staff. The overriding challenge the Japanese face is one imposed on them—and the rest of the world—by the globalization of business. The kind of self-serving economic aggression that has characterized overseas business operations in many companies in the past is becoming less acceptable in local environments. The countries that recognize that quickly and find ways to accommodate local conditions—especially when conflict arises—will have a marked advantage over their global competitors.

If global-local relations lie at the heart of a problem, cultural mediation lies at the heart of the solution. Broadly viewed, the effective application of the seven-step conflict resolution model ultimately leads to the development of a synergistic corporate culture in which the cultures in conflict are integrated step-by-step at all levels to form a unique third culture. As difficult as that may sound, synergy can be achieved. The key player is the cultural mediator. That's often an experienced trainer who—present from the outset and armed with substantive intercultural skills—guides the resolution process and mediates the differences in people's values and behaviors that fuel the conflict. It's a role that many business executives undervalue but, as with global-local relations, those who do value it will have a marked advantage in the emerging global marketplace.

Article Review Form at end of book.

What impact does parties' level of familiarity with each other's culture have on the success rate of cross-cultural negotiations?

Negotiating with "Romans"—Part 1

Stephen E. Weiss

"Smith," an American, arrived at the French attorney's Paris office for their first meeting. Their phone conversations had been in French, and Smith, whose experience with the language included ten years of education in the United States, a year of residence in France with a French family, and annual trips to Paris for the previous seven years, expected to use French at this meeting. "Dupont," the Frenchman, introduced himself in French. His demeanor was poised and dignified; his language, deliberate and precise. Smith followed Dupont's lead, and they went on to talk about a mutual acquaintance. After ten minutes, Dupont shifted the topic by inquiring about Smith's previous work in international negotiations. One of Dupont's words—"opérations"—surprised Smith, and he hesitated to respond. In a split second, Dupont, in fluent English, asked: "Would you like to speak in English?"[1]

Smith used the approach to cross-cultural interaction most widely advocated in the West, with a history dating back to St. Augustine: "When in Rome, do as the Romans do." It had seemed to be a reasonable way to convey cooperativeness, sensitivity to French culture, and respect for Dupont as an individual. But Smith overlooked important considerations, as have many other people who continue to recommend or follow this approach.[2]

The need for guidance for cross-cultural negotiators is clear. Every negotiator belongs to a group or society with its own system of knowledge about social interaction—its own "script" for behavior.[3] Whether the boundaries of the group are ethnic, organizational, ideological, or national, its culture influences members' negotiations—through their conceptualizations of the process, the ends they target, the means they use, and the expectations they hold of counterparts' behavior. There is ample evidence that such negotiation rules and practices vary across cultures.[4] Thus cross-cultural negotiators bring into contact unfamiliar and potentially conflicting sets of categories, rules, plans, and behaviors.

Doing as "Romans" do has not usually resolved this conflict effectively. (Throughout this article, the terms "Romans" and "non-Romans" are used as shorthand for "other-culture negotiators" and "own-culture negotiators," respectively.) "Fitting in" requires capabilities that relatively few non-Romans possess; most cultures involve much more than greeting protocols.[5] The approach takes for granted that Romans accept a non-Roman's behaving like a Roman when, actually, many Romans believe in at least some limits for outsiders.[6] Also, the approach presumes, misleadingly, that a Roman will always act Roman with a non-Roman in Rome.

Today's challenges should motivate a cross-cultural negotiator to search for additional approaches or strategies. An American negotiator may meet on Tuesday with a group of Japanese who speak through an interpreter and meet on Thursday one-on-one with a Japanese who is fluent in English and a long-time personal friend. In addition, geographical referents are blurring: just off of Paris's Boulevard St. Germain, an American can go to a Japanese restaurant in search of Japanese food and customs, yet find there Chinese waiters who speak Chinese to each other and French to their customers. Indeed, Americans negotiate with Japanese not only in Tokyo and Los Angeles but at third sites such as London. They may forgo face-to-face meetings to communicate by fax, E-mail, telephone, or video conference. Some of these negotiators have one day to finalize a sale; others have fourteen months to formulate a joint venture agreement. This variety of people and circumstances calls for more than one strategic approach.

What are the options for conducting negotiations in culturally sensitive ways? What should non-Roman negotiators do, especially when they lack the time and skills available to long-time expatriates? How should the non-Roman businessperson prepare to use a culturally responsive strategy for negotiation with a particular Roman individual or group in a particular set of circumstances?

This article presents a range of eight culturally responsive strategies

Reprinted from "Negotiating with 'Romans'"—Parts I and II by Stephen E. Weiss. SLOAN MANAGEMENT REVIEW REPRINT SERIES, Winter 1994, by permission of publisher. Copyright 1994 by Sloan Management Review Associates. All rights reserved.

for Americans and other groups involved in cross-cultural negotiations at home and abroad. The corresponding framework takes into account the varying capabilities of different negotiators across different circumstances and thus provides options for *every* cross-cultural negotiator. Among other benefits, it enables a negotiator to move beyond the popular, one-size-fits-all lists of "dos and don'ts" for negotiating in a particular culture to see that what is appropriate really depends on the negotiating strategy. In short, this article offers the manager a broadened, realistic view of strategies for effective cross-cultural negotiation.

Eight Culturally Responsive Strategies

Stories of cross-cultural conflict—faux pas and "blunders"—abound.[8] They highlight feelings of anxiety, disorientation, misunderstanding, and frustration, and they tempt negotiators to try to minimize apparent behavioral differences by "matching" or "imitating" their counterparts' ways. But there are more fundamental goals for a cross-cultural negotiator.

Consider what often happens when Americans negotiate with Japanese. Viewing negotiation as a process of exchange involving several proposal-counterproposal iterations, Americans inflate their demands in initial proposals and expect later to give and receive concessions. Their Japanese counterparts often do not promptly reciprocate with a counterproposal. Thus the Americans offer concessions, hoping that they will kick the exchange model—"the negotiations"—into gear. The Japanese, however, ask many questions. By the end of the talks, the Americans feel frustrated with the extent of their concessions and conclude that Japanese do not negotiate. Although the Americans may believe that the Japanese are shrewdly trying to determine how much their American counterparts will concede, it is quite likely that these Japanese are operating from a different model of negotiation: negotiation as a process of gathering information, which, when consistent and complete, will reveal a "correct, proper, and reasonable" solution.[9]

Research on communication suggests that the minimal, fundamental goal for non-Romans is to ensure that both sides perceive that the pattern of interaction makes sense.[10] For negotiation to occur, non-Romans must at least recognize those ideas and behaviors that Romans intentionally put forward as part of the negotiation process (and Romans must do the same for non-Romans). Parties must also be able to interpret these behaviors well enough to distinguish common from conflicting positions, to detect movement from positions, and to respond in ways that maintain communication. Yet a non-Roman's own script for negotiation rarely entails the knowledge or skills to make such interpretations and responses.

Figure 1 shows the range of negotiation characteristics that may vary across cultures. The basic concept of the process, for instance, may be one of distributive bargaining,

Figure 1 Cultural characteristics of negotiation

General Model

1. Basic Concept of Process
   Distributive bargaining/Joint problem-solving/Debate/Contingency bargaining/Nondirective discussion

2. Most Significant Type of Issue
   Substantive/Relationship-based/Procedural/Personal-internal

Role of the Individual

3. Selection of Negotiators
   Knowledge/Negotiating experience/Personal attributes/Status

4. Individual's Aspirations
   Individual ◄─────────────► Community

5. Decision Making Groups
   Authoritative ◄─────────────► Consensual

Interaction: Dispositions

6. Orientation toward Time
   Monochronic ◄─────────────► Polychronic

7. Risk-Taking Propensity
   High ◄─────────────► Low

8. Bases of Trust
   External sanctions/Other's reputation/Intuition/Shared experiences

Interaction: Process

9. Concern with Protocol
   Informal ◄─────────────► Formal

10. Communication Complexity
    High ◄─────────────► Low

11. Nature of Persuasion
    Direct experience/Logic/Tradition/Dogma/Emotion/Intuition

Outcome

12. Form of Agreement
    Contractual ◄─────────────► Implicit

Source: Adapted from S.E. Weiss with W. Stripp, *Negotiating with Foreign Business Persons* (New York: New York University Graduate School of Business Administration, Working Paper #85-6, 1985), p.10.

joint problem solving, debate, contingency bargaining, or nondirective discussion. Groups and organizations may select their negotiators for their knowledge, experience, personal attributes, or status. Protocol may range from informal to formal; the desired outcome may range from a contract to an implicit understanding.

A culturally responsive strategy, therefore, should be designed to align the parties' negotiating scripts or otherwise bring about a mutually coherent form of negotiator interaction. This definition does *not* assume that the course of action is entirely premeditated; it can emerge over time. But a culturally responsive strategy does involve a clear goal and does consist of means by which to attain it. Effectively implemented, such a strategy enables the negotiators to convey their respective concerns and to respond to each other's concerns as they attempt to reach agreement.

By contrast, strategies that do not consider cultural factors are naive or misconceived. They may sometimes be successful for non-Romans, but they are hardly a reliable course of action. One such strategy is to deliberately ignore ethnic or other group-based differences and operate as if "business is business anywhere in the world." A "business is business" approach does not avoid culture; it actually represents a culture, one usually associated with U.S. businesspeople or a cosmopolitan elite. Negotiators cannot blithely assume the predominance of this particular business culture amid the multiple cultures represented in their negotiations.

The framework shown in Figure 2 organizes eight culturally responsive strategies according to the negotiator's level of familiarity with the counterpart's culture; the counterpart's familiarity with the negotiator's culture; and the possibility for explicit coordination of approaches.[11] For the sake of clarity, it focuses on negotiations between two parties, each belonging to one predominant culture.

"Familiarity" is a gauge of a party's current knowledge of a culture (in particular, its negotiation scripts) *and* ability to use that knowledge competently in social interactions.[12] Operationally, high familiarity denotes fluency in a predominant Roman language, extensive prior exposure to the culture, and a good track record in previous social interactions with Romans (which includes making correct attributions of their behavior).[13] This is no mean accomplishment; it takes some twenty-four to thirty-six months of gradual adaptation and learning for expatriates to "master" how to behave appropriately.[14] Note that negotiators can consider using the strategies feasible at their level of familiarity and *any* strategies corresponding to lower levels of familiarity.

The strategies in brackets in the figure are those that require coordination between parties. Although all negotiators must ultimately coordinate their approaches with counterparts during the talks, if only tacitly, sometimes parties can explicitly address coordination and coherence issues.

Low Familiarity with Counterpart's Culture

The negotiator who has had little experience with a counterpart's culture has a choice of two culturally responsive strategies and, depending on the counterpart's familiarity with the negotiator's culture, a possible third. If the counterpart's familiarity level is low, neither party is well equipped cross-culturally; their interaction can be facilitated by changing the people involved.[15] That is, the negotiator can employ an agent or advisor or involve a mediator. If the counterpart's familiarity level is high, a third strategy becomes feasible: inducing the Roman to follow the negotiating script of one's own cultural group.

- **Employ Agent or Adviser.** To augment his or her own capabilities, a business negotiator can employ cultural experts, translators, outside attorneys, financial advisers, or technical experts who have at least moderate and preferably high familiarity with both the counterpart's and the negotiator's cultures. These experts serve two distinguishable roles, as "agents" who replace the negotiator at the negotiating table or as "advisers" who provide information and recommend courses of action to the negotiator.

In 1986, a U.S. chemical company that had bartered chemicals for tobacco from Zimbabwe hired an American commodities trader in London to negotiate the sale of the tobacco and some chemicals to Egyptian officials and executives. The Egyptians were offering payment in commodities; the U.S. company sought $20 million cash. As an agent, the American trader engaged in lengthy meetings, rounds of thick coffee, and late-night talks with the Egyptians and succeeded in arranging cash sales of the Egyptian commodities to the United Kingdom, Bangladesh, and other countries.[16]

The value of this strategy depends on the agent's attributes. Skilled, reputable agents can interact very effectively with a negotiator's counterpart. However, their employment may give rise to issues of increased structural complexity, trust, and ownership of the process, not to mention possible cultural tensions between principal and agent.[17] Clearly decipherable by a counterpart, this strategy works well when the counterpart accepts it and the particular agent involved.

Employing an adviser involves other actions and effects.

Between 1983 and 1986, IBM prepared proposals for a personal computer plant for approval by Mexico's National Commission on Foreign Investment. The company hired Mexican attorneys, consulted local experts such as the American Chamber of Commerce and U.S. embassy staff, and met with high-level Mexican government officials. These advisers provided information about political and social cultures and the foreign investment review process, access to influential individuals, and assessments of the leanings of key decision makers on the commission.[18]

A negotiator can select this strategy unilaterally and completely control its implementation. Of all eight strategies, this one is the least decipherable, sometimes even undetectable, by the counterpart. It is also uniquely incomplete in that it does not directly provide a script for negotiating. The negotiator must go on to select, with or without the adviser's assistance, a complementary strategy.

- **Involve a Mediator.** The use of go-betweens, middlemen, brokers, and other intermediaries is a common practice within many cultures and represents a potentially effective approach to cross-cultural negotiation as well. It is a joint strategy; both negotiator and counterpart rely on a mutually acceptable third party to facilitate their interaction. In its most obvious form, the strategy involves

Figure 2 Culturally Responsive Strategies and Their Feasibility

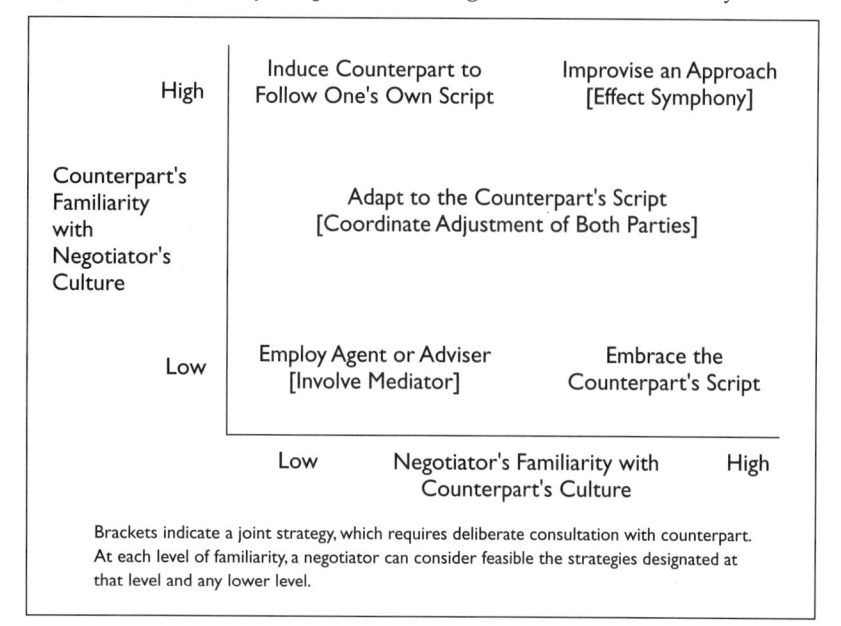

```
              │ Induce Counterpart to        Improvise an Approach
         High │ Follow One's Own Script      [Effect Symphony]
              │
Counterpart's │
Familiarity   │        Adapt to the Counterpart's Script
with          │        [Coordinate Adjustment of Both Parties]
Negotiator's  │
Culture       │
              │ Employ Agent or Adviser      Embrace the
         Low  │ [Involve Mediator]           Counterpart's Script
              │
              └──────────────────────────────────────────────────
                Low      Negotiator's Familiarity with      High
                         Counterpart's Culture
```

Brackets indicate a joint strategy, which requires deliberate consultation with counterpart. At each level of familiarity, a negotiator can consider feasible the strategies designated at that level and any lower level.

contacting a mediator prior to negotiations and deliberately bringing him or her into the talks. A mediator may also emerge, as happens when the "introducer" (*shokaisha* in Japanese[19]) who first brought the negotiator to the counterpart continues to play a role or, in team-on-team negotiations, when an individual involved in the talks who does not initially have authority as a mediator, such as an interpreter, becomes a de facto mediator in the course of the negotiation. Such cross-cultural mediators should be at least moderately and preferably highly familiar with the cultures of both parties.

In the 1950s, an American truck manufacturer negotiated a deal to sell trucks to a Saudi contractor because of the intermediation of Adnan Khashoggi. Khashoggi, the son of the personal physician of the founder of Saudi Arabia, had met the manufacturer while in college in the United States and learned about the contractor's needs upon returning to Saudi Arabia. This was his first "deal," long before his involvement with Lockheed and Northrop. By the 1970s, each of his private jets reportedly contained two wardrobes: "one of three-piece suits, shirts, and ties; . . . the other of white cotton thobes [and] headdresses, . . . the full traditional Arabian regalia."[20]

With this strategy, a negotiator faces some uncertainty about the negotiation process: Will the mediator use one side's negotiation script at the expense of the other's? If the mediator is from a third culture, will he or she use that culture's ways—or introduce something else?[21] In relying on a mediator, the negotiator relinquishes some control of the negotiation. Then again, the mediator can educate the negotiator about the counterpart's culture and bring out ideas and behavior from each side that make the interaction coherent. It is important to find an individual who is not only appropriately skilled but who will also maintain the respect and trust of both parties.[22]

• **Induce the Counterpart to Follow One's Own Script.** Deliberately inducing the counterpart to negotiate according to the model common in one's own culture is feasible when the counterpart is highly familiar with one's culture. Possibilities for inducement range from verbal persuasion to simply acting as if the counterpart will "come along"—as happens when Americans speak English to non-American counterparts known to speak English as a second language.

When U.S.-based ITT and CGE of France conducted merger talks in the mid-1980s, negotiators used "an American business—American M&A [merger and acquisition]" approach, according to French participants. The French went along with it (despite their unfavorable impressions that it consisted of a "vague" general concept of the deal, emphasis on speed, and formulation of long contracts), because only U.S. law and investment firms had the capacity to carry out this highly complex negotiation. Although their motivations are not exactly known, ITT lawyers have stated that their chief negotiator followed their own methodical style, one developed within ITT.[23]

The pros and cons of this strategy hinge on the counterpart's perception of the negotiator's motivations for pursuing it. The counterpart may conclude that the negotiator is naive or deliberately ignorant of cultural differences; arrogant; culturally proud but not antagonistic; or merely using an expedient strategy.[24] It is reported that IBM's Thomas Watson, Sr., once said: "It's easier to teach IBM to a Netherlander than to teach Holland to an American."[25] Using one's own ways could also be the result of mistakenly concluding that the two parties share one culture (e.g., Americans and English-speaking Canadians).

For this strategy to work most effectively, the negotiator should convey that it is not based on a lack of respect for the counterpart or for the counterpart's culture. It is the counterpart, after all, who is being called on to make an extra effort; even with a high level of familiarity with the negotiator's culture, a counterpart usually feels more skilled and at ease with his or her own ways. (Were the counterpart to *offer* to follow the negotiator's script, we would be talking about an embrace strategy by the counterpart, which is described below.)

Moderate Familiarity with Counterpart's Culture

The negotiator who already has had some successful experience with a counterpart's culture gains two more strategic options, provided that the counterpart is at least moderately familiar with the negotiator's culture. The unilateral strategy is to adapt one's usual approach to the counterpart's. The joint version is to coordinate adjustment between the two cultures.

• **Adapt to the Counterpart's Script.** Negotiators often modify their customary behavior by not expressing it to its usual degree, omitting some actions altogether, and following some of the counterpart's ways. The adapt

124   Intercultural Communications

strategy refers to more than this behavior, however; it refers to a broad course of action usually prompted by a deliberate decision to make these modifications.[26]

In the early 1980s, American negotiators in the Toyota-Ford and GM-Toyota talks over car assembly joint ventures prepared by reading books such as James Clavell's Shogun and Edwin Reischauer's The Japanese, watching classic Japanese films (e.g., "Kagemusha"), and frequenting Japanese restaurants. Then they modified their usual negotiating behavior by (1) paying extra attention to comportment and protocol, (2) reducing their expectations about substantive progress in the first few meetings, (3) providing Japanese counterparts with extensive, upfront information about their company and the U.S. business environment, and (4) trying "not to change positions too much once they had been voiced."[27]

A major challenge for the negotiator considering this strategy is to decide which aspects of his or her customary negotiating script to alter or set aside. The aspects most seriously in conflict with the counterpart's may not be easily changed or even readily apparent, and those most obviously in conflict or easily changed may not, once changed, markedly enhance the interaction. Marketing specialists have distinguished between customs to which non-Romans must conform, those to which non-Romans may but need not conform, and those from which non-Romans are excluded.[28] Although a marketing specialist has a fixed, one-sided target in seeking entry into the counterpart's arena, these distinctions may also guide some of the cross-cultural negotiator's deliberations.

A counterpart usually notices at least some evidence of a negotiator's use of the adapt strategy. Deciphering all of the modifications is difficult. It may also be difficult for a counterpart to distinguish an adapt strategy from a badly implemented embrace strategy (described below). Further, if both the negotiator and the counterpart pursue this strategy on their own initiative, their modifications may confuse rather than smooth the interaction. Still, a negotiator can independently make the choice to adapt and usually finds at least some areas within his or her capacity to do so.

- **Coordinate Adjustment of Both Parties.** The parties may develop, subtly or overtly, a joint approach for their discussions; they may negotiate the process of negotiation. The jointly developed script is usually a blend of elements from the two parties' cultures; it is not totally distinct from them yet not wholly of one or the other. It may take various forms.

At the outset of a 1988 meeting to discuss the telecommunications policies of France's Ministry of Industry and Tourism, the minister's chief of staff and his American visitor each voiced concern about speaking in the other's native language. They expressed confidence in their listening capabilities and lacked immediate access to an interpreter, so they agreed to proceed by each speaking in his own language. Their discussion went on for an hour that way, the American speaking in English to the Frenchman, and the Frenchman speaking in French to the American.

In a special case of this strategy, the parties "bypass" their respective home cultures' practices to follow the negotiating script of an already existing, third culture with which both have at least moderate familiarity. The parties know enough about the other's culture to recognize the limits of their capabilities in it and the desirability of additional guidance for their interaction.

Negotiations over MCA's acquisition by Matsushita Electric Industrial Company in 1990 were conducted largely via interpreters. At one dinner, MCA's senior American investment banker and Matsushita's Japanese head of international affairs were stymied in their effort to communicate with each other until they discovered their fluency in the same second language. They conversed in French for the rest of the evening.[29]

Professional societies, trade groups, educational programs and institutions, and various other associations can similarly provide members with third scripts for conduct. This phenomenon is dramatically illustrated, within and between teams, when people who do not share a language play volleyball or soccer socially. The sport provides a script for behavior.

Overall, this strategy has the benefits of the adapt strategy while minimizing the likelihood of incompatible "adjustments." For some Roman counterparts (e.g., Arabs and Chinese), verbally explicit implementation of this strategy for interaction will be awkward—even unacceptable.[30] Other groups' members will appreciate its decipherability and the shared burden of effort that it implies. Since both parties must go along with it, the negotiator's opportunity to "veto" also preserves some control over its implementation.

High Familiarity with Counterpart's Culture

Finally, the negotiator highly familiar with a counterpart's culture can realistically contemplate, not only the five aforementioned strategies, but at least one and possibly two more. If the counterpart is not familiar with the negotiator's culture, the negotiator can unilaterally embrace the other's negotiating script (i.e., "do as the Romans do"). If both parties are highly familiar with each other's cultures, they can jointly or unilaterally search for or formulate a negotiating script that focuses more on the individuals and circumstances involved than on the broader cultures. Such strategies may radically change the process.

- **Embrace the Counterpart's Script.** The embrace strategy calls for the negotiator to use the negotiation approach typical of the counterpart's culture.

In the 1970s, Coca-Cola undertook negotiations with a state-run, foreign trade organization in the People's Republic of China in order to produce and sell cola drinks there. The company sent one of its research chemists, a China-born man with no business background, to Cambridge University to study Chinese language and culture studies for a full year. Later acclaimed to be highly knowledgeable about China, this chemist was the most active negotiator for Coca-Cola in what became a ten-year endeavor.[31]

Relatively few individuals should attempt this strategy. It demands a great deal of the negotiator, especially when the cultures involved differ greatly. In general, it requires bilingual, bicultural individuals—those who have generally enjoyed long-term overseas residence.

When implemented well, especially when very different cultures are involved, this strategy is clearly decipherable by a counterpart. (When it is not, a counterpart may confuse it with an adapt strategy.) Furthermore, the embrace strategy can make the interaction relatively easy and comfortable for the counterpart. The strategy requires considerable effort by the negotiator, and its implementation remains largely—but not completely—within the negotiator's control.

- **Improvise an Approach.** To improvise is to create a negotiation script as one negotiates, focusing foremost on the counterpart's particular attributes and capabilities and on the circumstances. Although all negotiators should pay some attention to the Roman counterpart as an individual, not all can or should improvise. The term is used here as it is used in music, not in the colloquial sense of "winging it" or of anyone being able to do it. Musical improvisation requires some preconception or point of departure and a model (e.g., a melody, basic chord structure) that sets the scope for performance. Similarly, the negotiator who improvises knows the parties' home cultures and is fully prepared for their influence but can put them in the background or highlight them as negotiation proceeds.

In the early 1990s, Northern Telecom, a Canadian-owned telecommunications equipment supplier with many Americans in its executive ranks and headquarters in both Mississauga, Ontario, and McLean, Virginia, maintained a "dual identity." Its personnel dealt with each other on either an American or a Canadian basis. On the outside, the company played up its Canadian identity with some governments (those unenthusiastic about big American firms, or perhaps not highly familiar with American ways), and played up its American identity with others.[32]

This strategy is feasible only when both parties are highly familiar with the other's culture. Without that level of familiarity, the negotiator would not know what the counterpart is accustomed to or how he or she is affected, and would not be able to invoke or create ways to relate to the counterpart effectively; nor would the counterpart recognize or respond to these efforts appropriately. At the same time, since the counterpart is highly skilled in at least two cultures and may introduce practices from both or either one of them, it is extremely important to consider the counterpart as an individual, not just as a member of a culture. High familiarity enables the negotiator to do just that, because he or she does not need to devote as much effort to learning about the counterpart's culture as other negotiators do.

During the Camp David "peace" talks between Egypt, Israel, and the United States in the late 1970s, then President Jimmy Carter set up a one-on-one meeting with Prime Minister Menachem Begin to try to break an impasse. Carter took along photos of Begin's eight grandchildren, on the backs of which he had handwritten their names. Showing these photos to Begin led the two leaders into talking about their families and personal expectations and revitalized the intergovernmental negotiations.[33]

This strategy is often used at high levels, especially at critical junctures, but it need not be limited to that. It can counteract the treatment of a counterpart as an abstraction (e.g., stereotype) and can facilitate the development of empathy. It also seems particularly efficacious with counterparts from cultures that emphasize affective, relationship factors over task accomplishment and creativity or presence over convention.

On the down side, the cultural responsiveness of the improvise strategy is not always decipherable by the counterpart. When a top-level negotiator is involved, the counterpart may assume that the negotiator's strategy is to appeal to status or authority rather than to recognize cultural issues. If the strategy overly "personalizes" negotiation, its implementation can lead to the kinds of problems once pointed out in former U.S. Secretary of State Henry Kissinger's "personal diplomacy": becoming too emotionally involved, failing to delegate, undercutting the status of other possible representatives, and ignoring those one does not meet or know.[34] The strategy may not be appropriate for all cultures and may be difficult to orchestrate by a team of negotiators. It also offers fewer concrete prescriptions for action and greater uncertainty than the four other unilateral strategies. Nevertheless, its malleability should continue to be regarded as a major attribute.

- **Effect Symphony.** This strategy represents an effort by the negotiator to get both parties to transcend exclusive use of either home culture by exploiting their high familiarity capabilities. They may improvise an approach, create and use a new script, or follow some other approach not typical of their home cultures. One form of coordination feasible at this level of familiarity draws on both home cultures.

For their negotiations over construction of the tunnel under the English Channel, British and French representatives agreed to partition talks and alternate the site between Paris and London. At each site, the negotiators were to use established, local ways, including the language. The two approaches were thus clearly punctuated by time and space. Although each side was able to use its customary approach some of the time, it used the script of the other culture the rest of the time.[35]

Effecting symphony differs from coordinating adjustment, which implies some modification of a culture's script, in that both cultures' scripts may be used in their entirety. It is also one resolution of a situation where both parties start out independently pursuing induce or embrace strategies. Perhaps the most common form of effecting symphony is using a third culture, such as a negotiator subculture.

Many United Nations ambassadors, who tend to be multilingual and world-traveled, interact more comfortably with each other than with their compatriots.[36] Similarly, a distinct culture can be observed in the café and recreation area at INSEAD, the European Institute of Business Administration, which attracts students from thirty countries for ten intensive months.

Overall, the effect symphony strategy allows parties to draw on special capabilities that may be accessible only by going outside the full-time use of their home cultures' conventions. Venturing into these uncharted areas introduces some risk. Furthermore, this strategy, like other joint strategies, requires the counterpart's cooperation; it cannot be unilaterally effected. But then, as former U.S. Ambassador to Japan Edwin Reischauer suggested about diplomatic protocol, a jointly established culture—the "score" of a symphony—makes behavior predic- table.[37] It can also make it comprehensible and coherent.

Implications

A cross-cultural negotiator is thus not limited to doing as the Romans do or even doing it "our way" or "their way." There are eight culturally

Table 1. Recommended Behavior for Americans Negotiating with the Japanese* (by type of culturally responsive strategy)

Employ
- Use "introducer" for initial contacts (e.g., general trading company).
- Employ an agent the counterpart knows and respects.
- Ensure that the agent/advisor speaks fluent Japanese.

Induce
- Be open to social interaction and communicate directly.
- Make an extreme initial proposal, expecting to make concessions later.
- Work efficiently to "get the job done."

Adapt
- Follow some Japanese protocol (reserved behavior, name cards, gifts).
- Provide a lot of information (by American standards) up front to influence the counterpart's decision making early.
- Slow down your usual timetable.
- Make informed interpretations (e.g., the meaning of "it is difficult").
- Present positions later in the process, more firmly and more consistently.

Embrace
- Proceed according to an information-gathering, *nemawashi* (not exchange) model.
- "Know your stuff" cold.
- Assemble a team (group) for formal negotiations.
- Speak in Japanese.
- Develop personal relationships; respond to obligations within them.

Improvise
- Do homework on the individual counterpart(s) and circumstances.
- Be attentive and nimble (improvising entails different behaviors for different Japanese).
- Invite the counterpart to participate in mutually enjoyed activities or interests. (e.g., golf).

*These are examples, not a complete listing, of attitudes and behaviors implied by a negotiator's use of each strategy.

---

responsive strategies. They differ in their degree of reliance on existing scripts and conventions, in the amount of extra effort required of each party, and in their decipherability by the counterpart. As a range of options, these strategies offer the negotiator flexibility and a greater opportunity to act effectively.

Because the strategies entail different scripts and approaches, they also allow the negotiator to move beyond the simplistic lists of behavioral tips favored to date in American writings. For example, an American working with Japanese counterparts is usually advised to behave in a reserved manner, learn some Japanese words, and exercise patience.[38] Such behavior applies primarily to an adapt strategy, however, and different strategies call for different concepts and behaviors. Table 1 gives some examples of how an American might behave with Japanese counterparts, depending on the unilateral strategy employed.

Similarly, for his meeting with Dupont in Paris, Smith could have considered strategies other than "embrace" and its associated script. An adapt strategy may not have necessitated speaking exclusively in French. Table 2 suggests some ways he might have behaved, given each unilateral strategy. Smith might also have contemplated using strategies in combination (e.g., "adapt," then "embrace"), especially if meetings had been scheduled to take place over a number of months.

At the same time, only the negotiator highly familiar with the counterpart's culture can realistically consider using all eight strategies. The value of high familiarity, as a current capability or as an aspiration to achieve, should be clear. The value of the cultural focus should also be clear, notwithstanding the importance of also focusing on the individual counterpart (Part 2 of this article will expand on this point). Culture provides a broad context for understanding the ideas and behavior of new counterparts as well as established acquaintances. It also enables the negotiator to notice commonalties in the expectations and behavior of individual members of a team of counterparts, to appreciate how the team works as a whole, and to anticipate what representatives and constituents will do when they meet away from the cross-cultural negotiation. As long as the negotiator intends to go on negotiating with other Romans, it behooves him or her to pay attention to commonalties across negotiation experiences with individual Romans—to focus on cultural aspects—in order to draw lessons that enhance effectiveness in future negotiations.

As presented here, the eight culturally responsive negotiation strategies reflect one perspective: feasibility in light of the negotiator's and counterpart's familiarity with each other's cultures. That is a major basis for selecting a strategy, but it is not sufficient. This framework maps what is doable; it should not be interpreted as recommending that the best strategies for every negotiation are those at the highest levels of familiarity—that improvising is always better than employing advisers. The best strategy depends on additional factors that will be discussed in Part 2. In its own right, the framework represents a marked shift from prevailing wisdom and a good point of departure for today's cross-cultural negotiators.

References

I carried out the early stages of this work during my visits at the Euro-Asia Centre at INSEAD and Dartmouth College's Tuck School of Business. For comments on earlier drafts, I thank Ellen Auster, J. Stewart Black,

Table 2. Recommended Behavior for Americans Negotiating with the French* (by type of culturally responsive strategy)

Employ
- Employ an agent well-connected in business and government circles.
- Ensure that the agent/adviser speaks fluent French.

Induce
- Be open to social interaction and communicate directly.
- Make an extreme initial proposal, expecting to make concessions later.
- Work efficiently to "get the job done."

Adapt
- Follow some French protocol (greetings and leave-takings, formal speech).
- Demonstrate an awareness of French culture and business environment.
- Be consistent between actual and stated goals and between attitudes and behavior.
- Defend views vigorously.

Embrace
- Approach negotiation as a debate involving reasoned argument.
- Know the subject of negotiation and broad environmental issues (economic, political, social).
- Make intellectually elegant, persuasive yet creative presentations (logically sound, verbally precise).
- Speak in French.
- Show interest in the counterpart as an individual but remain aware of the strictures of social and organizational hierarchies.

Improvise
- Do homework on the individual counterpart(s) and circumstances.
- Be attentive and nimble (improvising entails different behaviors for different French individuals).
- Invite counterpart to participate in mutually enjoyed activities or interests (e.g., dining out, tennis).

*These are examples, not a complete listing, of attitudes and behaviors implied by a negotiator's use of each strategy.

Tamara Johnson, Andre Laurent, Tom Murtha, David Saunders, Susan Schneider, Jim Tiessen, William Weiss, Sloan Management Review editors, and anonymous reviewers. Portions of this material were presented at the Academy of International Business annual meeting (1991), the Pacific Rim Forum of the David Lam Centre for International Communication at Simon Fraser University (1992), the Academy of Management annual conference (1992), the Negotiation Workshop at York University (1993), and the Joint Centre for Asia-Pacific Studies at the University of Toronto (1993).

1. All examples that are not referenced come from personal communication or the author's experiences.
2. Contemporary academic advocates of this approach for negotiators include: S.T. Cavusgil and P.N. Ghauri, *Doing Business in Developing Countries* (London: Routledge, 1990), pp. 123–124; J.L. Graham and R.A. Herberger, Jr., "Negotiators Abroad—Don't Shoot from the Hip," *Harvard Business Review*, July–August 1983, p. 166; and F. Posses, *The Art of International Negotiation* (London: Business Books, 1978), p. 27.
3. The concept of a script has been applied by: W.B. Gudykunst and S. Ting-Toomey, *Culture and Interpersonal Communication* (Newbury Park, California: Sage, 1988), p. 30.
4. See, for example, N.C.G. Campbell et al., "Marketing Negotiations in France, Germany, the United Kingdom, and the United States," *Journal of Marketing* 52 (1988): 49–62; and J.L. Graham et al., "Buyer-Seller Negotiations around the Pacific Rim: Differences in Fundamental Exchange Processes," *Journal of Consumer Research* 15 (1988): 48–54. For evidence from diplomacy, see: R. Cohen, *Negotiating across Cultures* (Washington, D.C.: U.S. Institute of Peace Press, 1991); and G. Fisher, *International Negotiation: A Cross-Cultural Perspective* (Yarmouth, Maine: Intercultural Press, 1980).
5. See J.L. Graham and N.J. Adler, "Cross-Cultural Interaction: The International Comparison Fallacy," *Journal of International Business Studies* 20 (1989): 515–537. The authors conclude that their subjects adapted to some extent, but a lack of adaptability could also be convincingly argued from their data.
6. For an experimental study showing that moderate adaptation by Asians in the United States was more effective than substantial adaptation, see: J.N.P. Francis, "When in Rome? The Effects of Cultural Adaptation on Intercultural Business Negotiations," *Journal of International Business Studies* 22 (1991): 403–428.
7. The majority of leaders of North American firms still lack any expatriate experience and foreign language ability, according to: N.J. Adler and S. Bartholomew, "Managing Globally Competent People," *The Executive* 6 (1992): 58.
8. See, for example, D. Ricks and V. Mahajan, "Blunders in International Marketing: Fact or Fiction?" *Long Range Planning* 17 (1984): 79–83. Note that the impact of faux pas may vary in magnitude across cultures. In some cultures, inappropriate behavior constitutes an unforgivable transgression, not a "slip-up."
9. M. Blaker, *Japanese International Negotiating Style* (New York: Columbia University Press, 1977), p. 50.
10. See V.E. Cronen and R. Shuter, "Forming Intercultural Bonds," *Intercultural Communication Theory: Current Perspectives*, ed. W.B. Gudykunst (Beverly Hills, California: Sage, 1983), p. 99. Their concept of "coherence" neither presumes that the interactants make the same sense of the interaction nor depends always on mutual understanding.
11. Although similar in form, this plot differs in theme from the "model of conflict-handling responses" developed by: K.W. Thomas and R.H. Kilmann, *Thomas-Kilmann Conflict Mode Instrument* (Tuxedo, New York: Xicom, Inc., 1974). It also differs in key variables from the "Dual Concerns" model of: D.G. Pruitt and J.Z. Rubin, *Social Conflict: Escalation, Stalemate, and Settlement* (New York: Random House, 1986), p. 35ff. Moreover, neither of these models appears to have yet been applied cross-culturally.

12. This notion of familiarity draws on Dell Hymes's concept of communicative competence. See: R.E. Cooley and D.A. Roach, "A Conceptual Framework," *Competence in Communication* ed. R.N. Bostrom (Beverly Hills, California: Sage, 1984), pp. 11–32.
13. See, for example, R.W. Brislin et al., *Intercultural Interactions* (Beverly Hills, California: Sage, 1986); A.T. Church, "Sojourner Adjustment," *Psychological Bulletin* 91 (1982): 545–549; P.C. Earley, "Intercultural Training for Managers," *Academy of Management Review* 30 (1987): 685–698; and J.S. Black and M. Mendenhall, "Cross-cultural Training Effectiveness: A Review and Theoretical Framework for Future Research," *Academy of Management Review* 15 (1990): 113–136.
14. J.S. Black and M. Mendenhall, "The U-Curve Adjustment Hypothesis Revisited: A Review and Theoretical Framework," *Journal of International Business Studies* 22 (1991): 225–247.
15. Changing the parties involved is commonly mentioned in dispute resolution literature. See, for example: R. Fisher and W. Ury, *Getting to Yes* (Boston: Houghton Mifflin, 1981), pp. 71–72.
16. S. Lohr, "Barter Is His Stock in Trade," *New York Times Business World* 25 September 1988, pp. 32–36.
17. For empirical research on negotiating representatives and their boundary role, constituents, and accountability within a culture, see: D.G. Pruitt, *Negotiation Behavior* (New York: Academic Press, 1981), pp. 41–44, 195–197. With respect to agents, see: J.Z. Rubin and F.E.A. Sander, "When Should We Use Agents? Direct vs. Representative Negotiation," *Negotiation Journal*, October 1988, pp. 395–401.
18. S.E. Weiss, "The Long Path to the IBM-Mexico Agreement: An Analysis of the Microcomputer Investment Negotiations, 1983–1986," *Journal of International Business Studies* 21 (1990): 565–596.
19. J.L. Graham and Y. Sano, *Smart Bargaining: Doing Business with the Japanese* (New York: Ballinger, 1989), p. 30.
20. R. Lacey, *The Kingdom: Arabia and the House of Sa'ud* (New York: Avon Books, 1981), pp. 464–466. See also: P.E. Tyler, "Double Exposure: Saudi Arabia's Middleman in Washington," *The New York Times Magazine*, 7 June 1992, pp. 34ff.
21. For additional ideas about what a mediator may do, see: P.J.D. Carnevale, "Strategic Choice in Mediation," *Negotiation Journal* 2 (1986): 41–56.
22. See J.Z. Rubin, "Introduction," *Dynamics of Third Party Intervention*, ed. J.Z. Rubin (New York: Praeger, 1981), pp. 3–43; and S. Touval and I.W. Zartman, "Mediation in International Conflicts" *Mediation Research*, eds. K. Kressel and D.G. Pruitt (San Francisco: Jossey-Bass, 1989), pp. 115–137.
23. S.E. Weiss, "Negotiating the CGE-ITT Telecommunications Merger, 1985–1986: A Framework-then-Details Process," paper presented at the Academy of International Business annual meeting, November 1991.
24. Such positions have been associated with people in nations with long-established cultures, such as China, France, and India. For instance, some Mexican high officials who speak English fluently have insisted on speaking Spanish in their meetings with Americans. While this position could be influenced by the historical antipathy in the U.S.-Mexico relationship and the officials' concern for the status of their office, it also evinces cultural pride.
25. "IBM World Trade Corporation," Harvard Business School, reprinted in S.M. Davis, *Managing and Organizing Multinational Corporations* (New York: Pergamon Press, 1979), p. 53.
26. Adapting has been widely discussed in the literature. See, for example: S. Bochner, "The Social Psychology of Cross-Cultural Relations," *Cultures in Contact*, ed. S. Bochner (Oxford: Pergamon, 1982), pp. 5–44.
27. S.E. Weiss, "Creating the GM-Toyota Joint Venture: A Case in Complex Negotiation," *Columbia Journal of World Business*, Summer 1987, pp. 23–37; and S.E. Weiss, "One Impasse, One Agreement: Explaining the Outcomes of Toyota's Negotiations with Ford and GM," paper presented at the Academy of International Business annual meeting, 1988.
28. P.R. Cateora and J.M. Hess, *International Marketing* (Homewood, Illinois: Irwin, 1971), p. 407.
29. C. Bruck, "Leap of Faith," *The New Yorker*, 9 September 1991, pp. 38–74.
30. See C. Thubron, *Behind the Wall* (London: Penguin, 1987) pp. 158, 186–187.
31. L. Sloane, "Lee, Coke's Man in China," *The New York Times*, 5 February 1979, p. D2.
32. W.C. Symonds et al., "High-Tech Star," *Business Week*, 27 July 1992, pp. 55–56.
33. Found among the exhibits at the Carter Center Library and Museum, Atlanta, Georgia.
34. R. Fisher, "Playing the Wrong Game?" *Dynamics of Third Party Intervention*, ed. J.Z. Rubin (New York: Praeger, 1981), pp. 98–99, 105–106. On the additional problem of losing touch with constituencies, see the 1989–1991 Bush-Gorbachev talks described in: M.R. Beschloss and S. Talbott, *At the Highest Levels* (Boston: Little, Brown, 1993).
35. See C. Dupont, "The Channel Tunnel Negotiations, 1984–1986: Some Aspects of the Process and Its Outcome," *Negotiation Journal* 6 (1990): 71–80.
36. See, for example, C.F. Alger, "United Nations Participation as a Learning Experience," *Public Opinion Quarterly*, Summer 1983, pp. 411–426.
37. E.O. Reischauer, *My Life between Japan and America* (New York: Harper and Row, 1986), p. 183.
38. N.B. Thayer and S.E. Weiss, "Japan: The Changing Logic of a Former Minor Power," *National Negotiating Styles*, ed. H. Binnendijk (Washington, D.C.: Foreign Service Institute, U.S. Department of State, 1987), pp. 69–72.

Article Review Form at end of book.

How does a negotiator select the best strategy for a cross-cultural agreement?

Negotiating with "Romans"—Part 2

Stephen E. Weiss

Managers are increasingly called on to negotiate with people from other cultures. Cross-cultural negotiation need not be as frustrating nor as costly as it is often made out to be; it can be a productive and satisfying experience. Which of these outcomes a manager achieves depends in part on the negotiation strategies taken in response to—or better, in anticipation of—the counterpart's plans and behavior. There are eight culturally responsive strategies for a manager to consider (see Figure 1*).[1] Clearly, the quality of a negotiation outcome and a manager's satisfaction with it also depend on how well he or she chooses and implements one of these approaches.

This article presents five steps for selecting a culturally responsive strategy and then offers various tips for implementation, such as making the first move, monitoring feedback, and modifying the approach. These guidelines reflect four basic, ongoing considerations for a strategy: its *feasibility* for the manager, its fit with the counterpart's likely approach and therefore its capacity to lead to *coherent interaction*, its *appropriateness* to the relationship and circumstances at hand, and its *acceptability* in light of the manager's values. There are challenges involved in all of these efforts, and they are pointed out below rather than ignored or belittled, as happens in much cross-cultural negotiation literature. Thus, from this article, managers stand to gain both an operational plan and the heightened awareness necessary to use a culturally responsive negotiation strategy effectively.

Selecting a Strategy

Every negotiator is advised to "know yourself, the counterpart, and the situation."[2] This advice is useful but incomplete, for it omits the relationship—the connection—between the negotiator and the counterpart.[3] (For clarity, the negotiator from the "other" culture will be called the "counterpart" in this article.) Different types of relationships with counterparts and even different phases of a relationship with a particular counterpart call for different strategies.

For the cross-cultural negotiator, the very presence of more than one culture complicates the process of understanding the relationship and "knowing" the counterpart. In contrast to the "within-culture" negotiator, the cross-cultural negotiator cannot take common knowledge and practices for granted and thereby simply concentrate on the individual. It becomes important to actively consider the counterpart in two respects: as a member of a group and as an individual.

The right balance in these considerations is not easily struck. An exclusive emphasis on the group's culture will probably lead the negotiator off the mark because individuals often differ from the group average. Members of the same group may even differ very widely on certain dimensions. At the same time, the degree of variation tolerated between group members is itself an aspect of culture. For example, Americans have traditionally upheld the expression, "He's his own man," while Japanese believed that "the protruding nail is hammered down." The cross-cultural negotiator should thus consider both the counterpart's cultural background and individual attributes, perhaps weighting them differently according to the culture involved, but mindful always that every negotiation involves developing a relationship with a particular individual or team.[4]

For years, Japanese managers have come to one of my classes each term to negotiate with graduate students so the students can experience negotiating first-hand and test the often stereotypical descriptions they have read about Japanese negotiating behavior. I deliberately invite many Japanese, not just one or two. The students invariably express surprise when the Japanese teams "deviate" from the Japanese negotiating script, as the students understand it, and when differences appear in the behavior of various Japanese teams.

The five steps for selecting a culturally responsive negotiation

---

*Figure 1 appears in the preceding reading as Figure 2; see page 124.

Reprinted from "Negotiating with 'Romans'"—Parts I and II by Stephen E. Weiss. SLOAN MANAGEMENT REVIEW REPRINT SERIES, Spring 1994, by permission of publisher. Copyright 1994 by Sloan Management Review Associates. All rights reserved.

strategy take into account these complexities:

1. Reflect on your culture's negotiation script.
2. Learn the negotiation script of the counterpart's culture.
3. Consider the relationship and circumstances.
4. Predict or influence the counterpart's approach.
5. Choose your strategy.

These steps take minutes or months, depending on the parties and circumstances involved. Each step will probably not require the same amount of time or effort. Furthermore, the sequencing of the steps is intended to have an intuitive, pragmatic appeal for an American negotiator, but it should not be treated rigidly. Some steps will be more effective if they are coupled or treated interactively. Nor should these efforts start at the negotiation table when time, energy, resources, and introspection tend to be severely limited. Every one of these steps merits *some* attention by every cross-cultural negotiator before the first round of negotiation.

It is important to remember that the procedure represented by these five steps is itself culturally embedded, influenced by the author's cultural background and by that of the intended audience (American negotiators).[5] Not all counterparts will find the pragmatic logic herein equally compelling. As two Chinese professionals have observed, "In the West, you are used to speaking out your problems. . . . But that is not our tradition," and "In our country, there are so many taboos. We're not used to analytic thinking in your Western way. We don't dissect ourselves and our relationships."[6] Even with this procedure, culture continues to influence what we do and how we do it.

One way to deal with this inescapable cultural bias is to acknowledge it and remain aware of the continual challenges of effectively choosing and implementing a strategy. Often these challenges do not stand out—books on international negotiation have not addressed them—yet they can hamper, even ruin, a negotiator's best efforts. Each step below thus includes a list of cautions for cross-cultural negotiating.

1. Reflect on Your Culture's Negotiation Script

Among members of our "home" group, we behave almost automatically.[7] We usually have to impetus to consider the culture of the group because we repeatedly engage in activities with each other without incident or question. It is easy to use these "natural," taken-for-granted ways in a cross-cultural situation—too easy.

A book on international negotiation published by the U.S. State Department displays the flags of six nations on its front cover. On initial copies of the book, the French flag appeared in three bands of red, white, and blue. The actual French flag is blue, white, and red.[8]

A cross-cultural negotiator should construct a thoughtful, systematic profile of his or her culture's negotiation practices, using personal knowledge and other resources. Let's say you want to develop an "American negotiator profile." There is a vast amount of research and popular literature on negotiation in the United States.[9] For insights about American culture more broadly, consider both Americans' self-examinations and outsiders' observations.[10] Then organize this information into the profile represented in Figure 2.*[11] The profile consists of four topic areas: the general model of the negotiation process, the individual's role, aspects of interaction, and the form of a satisfactory agreement. The left side of the ranges in Figure 2 generally fit the American negotiator profile (e.g., the basic concept is distributive bargaining, the most significant issues are substantive ones, negotiators are chosen for their knowledge, individual aspirations predominate over community needs, and so forth).

This profile should also uncover the values that support these tendencies. For instance, distributive bargaining implies certain attitudes toward conflict and its handling (direct), toward business relationships (competitive), and toward the purpose of negotiation (to maximize individual gains). Sine some of your group's tendencies and values may not align with your own, develop a

*See figure 1 on p. 122.

personal profile as well. Doing so does not require probing deeply into your unconscious. Simply ask yourself, "What do I usually do at times like this? Why? What do I gain from doing it this way?" These kinds of questions resemble those used in basic negotiation training to distinguish an underlying interest from a bargaining position, namely, "What does this bargaining position do for me? Why?"

In the mid-1980s, a white American banker planned to include an African-American analyst on his team for a forthcoming visit to white clients in South Africa. When they learned about this, the clients intimated their preference that she not attend. While the banker wanted to serve his clients, he also had strong feelings about including the analyst and about basing qualifications on merit. She was the best analyst on his staff. The banker's values swayed his decision: he told his clients that he would not make the trip without this analyst on his team.[12]

Developing cultural and personal profiles is an ongoing task. Instead of writing them up once and moving on, return to them and refine them as you gain experience and understanding. The value of such a process is considerable. It increases your self-awareness; it helps you explain your expectations and behavior to a counterpart; it prepares you to make decisions under pressure; it allows you to compare your culture to another on a holistic rather than fragmented basis; it helps you determine a counterpart's level of familiarity with your culture; its products—profiles—can be used in future negotiations with other cultural groups; it motivates interest in other cultures; and it enables you to act consistently and conscientiously.

This process demands a good deal of effort, especially at the outset (note the cautions in Table 1). But as a negotiator, you will find such reflection to be a good basis for developing a cross-cultural negotiation strategy.

2. Learn the Negotiation Script of the Counterpart's Culture

This step applies to both the negotiator highly familiar with a counterpart's culture and the one who knows next to nothing about it.[13] The highly familiar negotiator should review what he or she knows and gather additional information to stay

| Table 1 | Cautions: Understanding Your Own Culture's Script |

- Beware of psychological and group biases, such as denial and "groupthink."
- Probe for assumptions and values; they are seldom identified explicitly in day-to-day life.
- Don't become rigidly wedded to your own ways.
- Take time during negotiations to step out of the action and reflect on your behavior.

current. The uninitiated negotiator should begin to construct a negotiator profile from the ground up. Ideally, this process involves learning in the active sense: developing the ability to use the counterpart's cultural and personal negotiation scripts, as well as "knowing" the scripts and related values.

Learning these scripts enhances the negotiator's ability to anticipate and interpret the counterpart's behavior. Even a negotiator with low familiarity who is likely to employ an agent needs some information in order to interact effectively with the agent and to assess the agent's performance. Although few negotiators learn everything about a counterpart before negotiation, advance work allows for assimilation and practice, provides a general degree of confidence that helps the negotiator to cope with the unexpected, and frees up time and attention during the negotiation to learn finer points.

Again, the negotiator profile framework is a good place to start. Try especially to glean and appreciate the basic concept of negotiation because it anchors and connects the other dimensions. Without it, a negotiator, as an outsider, cannot comprehend a counterpart's actions; they appear bizarre or whimsical. Moreover, if you focus merely on tactics or simple "do and don't"-type tips and reach a point in a transaction for which you have no tip, you have no base—no sense of the "spirit of the interaction"—to guide you through this juncture. For instance, the "spirit" of French management has been described like this:

French managers see their work as an intellectual challenge requiring the remorseless application of individual brainpower. They do not share the Anglo-Saxon view of management as an interpersonally demanding exercise, where plans have to be constantly "sold" upward and downward using personal skills. The bias is for intellect rather than for action.[14]

Continuing with this example, let's say you are preparing to negotiate with a French counterpart. You may find information about French negotiation concepts and practices in studies by French and American researchers and in natives' and outsiders' popular writings.[15] In addition to general nonfiction works on French culture, novels and films can convey an extraordinary sense of interactions among individuals and groups.[16] Other sources include intensive culture briefings by experts and interviews with French acquaintances, colleagues, and compatriots familiar with French culture, and, in some cases, even the counterpart.

Here, as in reflections on your own culture, make sure to consider core beliefs and values of the culture. Keep an eye on the degree of adherence to them as well as their substantive content.

A Frenchman involved in the mid-1980s negotiations between AT&T and CGE over a cross-marketing deal revealed his own culture's concern for consistency in thought and behavior as he discussed AT&T's conduct. He described the AT&T representatives' style as "very strange" because they made assurances about "fair" implementation while pushing a very "tough" contract.

Moving from information gathering to assimilation and greater familiarity with a culture usually requires intensive training on site or in seminars.[17] Some Japanese managers, for example, have been sent overseas by their companies for three to five years to absorb a country's culture before initiating any business ventures. When the time comes, familiarity may be assessed through tests of language fluency, responses to "critical incidents" in "cultural assimilator" exercises, and performance in social interactions in the field.[18]

Whether or not you have prior experience working with a particular counterpart or other inside information, try to explore the counterpart's own negotiation concepts, practices, and values. They can be mapped in a negotiator profile just as you mapped your own values.

This entire undertaking poses challenges for every negotiator, regardless of the strategy ultimately chosen. One of the highest hurdles may be the overall nature of the learning itself. Learning about another culture's concepts, ways, and values seems to hinge on the similarity between that culture and one's own. Learning is inhibited when one is isolated from members of that culture (even if one is living in their country) and "may fail to occur when attitudes to be learned contradict deepseated personality orientations (e.g., authoritarianism), when defensive stereotypes exist, or at points where home and host cultures differ widely in values or in conceptual frame of reference."[19] Other significant challenges can be seen in Table 2. Remember that, ultimately, you have access to different strategies for whatever amount of learning and level of familiarity you attain.

3. Consider the Relationship and Circumstances

Negotiators and counterparts tend to behave differently in different relationships and contexts.[20] One does not, for instance, act the same way as a seller as one does as a buyer. So a negotiator should not count on the same strategy to work equally well with every counterpart from a given cultural group (even if the counterparts have the same level of familiarity with the negotiator's culture) or, for that matter, with the same counterpart all the time. The peaks and valleys that most relationships traverse require different strategies and approaches. In the same vein, circumstances suggest varying constraints and opportunities.

To continue your preparations for a negotiation, consider particular facets of your relationship with the counterpart and the circumstances. The most important facets on which to base strategic choices have not yet been identified in research and may actually depend on the cultures involved. Furthermore, laying out a complete list of possibilities goes beyond the scope of this article.[21] But the following considerations (four for relationships, four for circumstances) seem significant.

Table 2 — Cautions: Learning about the Counterpart's Culture

- Don't be too quick to identify the counterpart's home culture. Common cues (name, physical appearance, language, accent, and location) may be unreliable. The counterpart probably belongs to more than one culture.
- Beware of the Western bias toward "doing." In Arab, Asian, and Latin groups, ways of being (e.g., comportment, smell), feeling, thinking, and talking can more powerfully shape relationships than doing.
- Try to counteract the tendency to formulate simple, consistent, stable images. Not many cultures are simple, consistent, or stable.
- Don't assume that all aspects of the culture are equally significant. In Japan, consulting all relevant parties to a decision (*nemawashi*) is more important than presenting a gift (*omiyage*).
- Recognize that norms for interactions involving outsiders may differ from those for interactions between compatriots.
- Don't overestimate your familiarity with your counterpart's culture. An American studying Japanese wrote New Year's wishes to Japanese contacts in basic Japanese characters but omitted one character. As a result, the message became "Dead man, congratulations."

Table 3 — Cautions: Considering the Relationship and Circumstances

- Pay attention to the similarities *and* differences, in kind and in magnitude, between your negotiator profiles and those of the counterpart.
- Be careful about judging certain relationship aspects as major (big picture issues) and minor (fine details). This dichotomy, let alone the particular contents of the two categories, is not used in all cultures.
- Consider the relationship from the counterpart's perspective.
- Identify the relationship factors and circumstances most significant to you *and* the counterpart.
- Beware of the use and abuse of power.
- Discover the "wild cards" either party may have.
- Remember that the relationship will not remain static during negotiation.

• **Life of the Relationship.** The existence and nature of a prior relationship with the counterpart will influence the negotiation and should figure into a negotiator's deliberations. With no prior contact, one faces a not-yet personal situation; general information and expectations based on cultural scripts will have to do until talks are under way. Parties who have had previous contact, however, have experienced some form of interaction. Their expectations concerning the future of the relationship will also tend to influence negotiation behavior.[22] In sum, the negotiator should acknowledge any already established form of interaction, assess its attributes (e.g., coherence) and the parties' expectations of the future, and decide whether to continue, modify, or break from the established form. These decisions will indicate different culturally responsive strategies.

• **Fit of Respective Scripts.** Having completed steps 1 and 2, you can easily compare your negotiator profiles, both cultural and individual, with those of the counterpart. Some culture comparisons based on the negotiator profile in Figure 2 have already been published.[23] Noting similarities as well as differences will enable you to identify those aspects of your usual behavior that do not need to change (similarities) and those aspects that do (major differences) if you choose a strategy that involves elements of both your negotiation script and the counterpart's (e.g., the adapt strategy). The number and kinds of differences will also suggest how difficult it would be to increase your level of familiarity with the counterpart's culture or to use certain combinations of strategies.

Do not allow such a comparison to mislead you. Some people overemphasize differences. Others, focusing on superficial features, overestimate similarities and their understanding of another culture (e.g., when Americans compare American and Canadian cultures). The cautions in Table 3 can help you stay on track.

Of course, a negotiator highly familiar with the counterpart's culture who plans to adopt an embrace strategy, operating wholly within that culture, has less need for these comparisons.

• **Balance of Power.** It may seem that power would have a lot to do with the choice of strategy. A more powerful party could induce the other to follow his or her cultural script. A less powerful party would have to embrace the other's script. A balance of power might suggest an adapt or improvise strategy.

But the issue is not so simple. The tilt of the "balance" is not easily or clearly determined; parties often measure power using different scales.[24] Indeed, forms of power, their significance, and appropriate responses are all culturally embedded phenomena.[25] Furthermore, it makes little sense to rely on power and disregard a counterpart's familiarity with one's culture when one's goal is coherent interaction. This is not to say that one could not benefit from an imbalance of power *after* choosing a culturally responsive strategy or in other areas of negotiation. Still, since power is culturally based and Americans have a general reputation for using it insensitively, American negotiators should be extremely careful about basing the strategy decision on power.

• **Gender.** Consider the possible gender combinations in one-on-one cross-cultural relationships: female negotiator with female counterpart, male negotiator with male counterpart, male negotiator with female counterpart, and female negotiator with male counterpart. Within most cultures, same-gender and mixed relationships entail different negotiating scripts. There are few books on negotiation designated for American women, but communication research has shown that men tend to use talk to negotiate status, women tend to use it to maintain intimacy, and they are often at cross-purposes when they talk to each other.[26] The debates over how American women should act in male-dominated workplaces further substantiate the existence of different scripts. In a sense, gender groups have their own cultures, and mixed interaction within a national culture is already cross-cultural.

Mixed interaction across national and other cultures holds even greater challenges. One of the primary determinations for a woman should be whether a male counterpart sees her first as a foreigner and second as a woman, or vice versa. According to some survey research, Asian counterparts see North American businesswomen as foreigners first.[27] The opposite may be true in parts of France. Edith Cresson, former French prime minister, once said, "Anglo-Saxons are not interested in women as women. For a [French] woman arriving in an Anglo-Saxon country, it is astonishing. She says to herself, 'What is the matter?'"[28] Thus, although current information about negotiating scripts for other countries tends to be based on male-male interactions, complete culturally-based negotiator profiles should include gender-based scripts.

Whether your negotiation involves mixed or same-gender interaction, try to anticipate the counterpart's perception of the gender issue and review your core beliefs. Gender-based roles in France, for instance, may appear so antithetical (or laudable) that you will not entertain (or will favor) the embrace strategy.

With regard to circumstances, the second part of step 3, there are at least four relevant considerations.

• **Opportunity for Advance Coordination.** Do you have—or can you create—an opportunity beforehand to coordinate strategy with your counterpart? If so, consider the joint strategies. If not, concentrate at the outset on feasible, unilateral strategies.

• **Time Schedule.** Time may also shape a negotiator's choice in that different strategies require different levels of effort and time. For the negotiator with moderate familiarity of the counterpart's culture but an inside track on a good agent, employing an agent may take less time than adapting to the counterpart's script. The time required to implement a strategy also depends on the counterpart's culture (e.g., negotiations based on the French script generally take longer than the American script). And time constrains the learning one can do to increase familiarity. Imagine the possibilities that open up for a diligent negotiator when discussions are scheduled as a series of weekly meetings over a twelve-month period instead of as one two-hour session.

• **Audiences.** Consider whether you or the counterpart will be accompanied by other parties, such as interpreters, advisers, constituents, and mass media. Their presence or absence can affect the viability and effectiveness of a strategy. If no one else will attend the meeting, for instance, you have no one to defer to or involve as a mediator at critical junctures.

During the early months of the ITT-CGE telecommunications negotiations in 1985 and 1986, fewer than ten individuals were aware of the talks. That permitted the parties to conduct discussions in ways not possible later, when over a hundred attorneys, not to mention other personnel, became involved. At the same time, that choice may have ruled out the initial use of some culturally responsive strategies.

• **Wild Cards**. Finally, you should assess your own and the counterpart's capacities to alter some relationship factors and circumstances. Parties may have extra-cultural capabilities such as financial resources, professional knowledge, or technical skills that expand their set of feasible options, bases for choice, or means of implementation.

During the GM-Toyota joint venture negotiations in the early 1980s, Toyota could afford to and did hire three U.S. law firms simultaneously for a trial period in order to compare their advice and assess their compatibility with the company. After three months, the company retained one of the firms for the duration of the negotiations.

4. Predict or Influence the Counterpart's Approach. The last step before choosing a strategy is to attempt to determine the counterpart's approach to the negotiation, either by predicting it or by influencing its selection. For the effectiveness of a culturally responsive strategy in bringing about coherent interaction depends not only on the negotiator's ability to implement it but also on its complementarity with the counterpart's strategy. Embracing the counterpart's script makes little sense if the counterpart is embracing your script. Further, reliable prediction and successful influence narrow the scope of a negotiator's deliberations and reduce uncertainty. And the sooner the prediction, the greater the time available for preparation. While these concerns relate to the parties' relationship (step 3), they have a direct impact on interaction that merits a separate step.

Assuming that your counterpart will not ignore cultural backgrounds and that each of you would adopt only a unilateral strategy, you can use Figure 3 to preview all possible intersections of these strategies.[29] They fall into three categories: complementary, potentially but not inherently complementary, and conflicting. Thus the figure shows the coherence of each strategy pair.

Among these pairs, adapt-adapt and improvise-improvise might seem inherently complementary. The catch is that parties can adapt or improvise in conflicting ways. Of all the potentially complementary cells, the improvise-improvise interaction may, however, be the most likely to become coherent, given the nature of the improvise strategy and the capabilities it entails.

Not all of the strategies in Figure 3 will be available to you in every situation. Remember that in addition to potential coherence, your choice will be based on your familiarity with the counterpart's culture, the counterpart's familiarity with yours, appropriateness, and acceptability.

• **Prediction.** Sometimes a counterpart will make this step easy by explicitly notifying you of his or her strategy in advance of your talks. If the counterpart does not do that, there may be telling clues in the counterpart's prenegotiation behavior, or other insiders (associates or subordinates) may disclose information.

Without direct and reliable information, you are left to predict the counterpart's strategy choice on the basis of his or her traits and motivations. Some counterparts will have a rational, task-directed orientation. Strategy research based on this perspective shows that counterparts

Figure 3 The Inherent Coherence of Parties' Culturally Responsive Strategies

	Counterpart's Strategy				
Negotiator's Strategy	Employ agent / Employ adviser	Induce	Adapt	Embrace	Improvise
Employ agent / Employ adviser	▓	□	▓	■	■
Induce	□	■	□	□	■
Adapt	▓	□	□	■	□
Embrace	▓	□	■	□	□
Improvise	▓	■	□	□	□

□ Complementary strategies   ▓ Potentially but not inherently complementary strategies   ■ Conflicting strategies

Table 4 Cautions: Predicting or Influencing the Counterpart's Approach

- Try to discern whether the counterpart's culture categorically favors or disfavors certain strategies.
- Don't fixate on "what's typical" for someone from the counterpart's cultural group.
- Recognize the difficulty in accurately assessing the counterpart's familiarity with your culture's negotiating script.
- Heed the line, however, fuzzy, between influencing and "meddling"—a U.S. diplomat was detained in Singapore in 1988 for interfering in internal affairs.*
- Track changes in the counterpart's strategic choices over time.
- Don't focus so obsessively on parties' strategies that you ignore the richness of the relationship or the context.

*F. Deyo, *Dependent Development and Industrial Order* (New York; Praeger, 1981), p. 89.

seeking to coordinate their actions with a negotiator often select the course of action most prominent or salient to both parties (e.g., choosing a river as a property boundary).[30] Other counterparts will focus on what is socially proper. Indeed, whether a counterpart even responds to the cross-cultural nature of the interaction may vary with his or her cosmopolitanism. A cosmopolitan counterpart may lean toward adapt and improvise strategies, whereas a counterpart having little experience with other cultures may be motivated primarily by internal, cultural norms. In the latter case, the counterpart's negotiator profile may be used to predict some behavior. For example, the internally focused individual from a culture with high communication complexity (reliance on nonverbal and other contextual cues for meaning), which often correlates with low risk-taking propensity, would be more likely to involve a mediator than to coordinate adjustment (which is too explicit) or to embrace or improvise (which are too uncertain).[31]

- **Influence.** Whether or not you can predict a counterpart's strategy choice, why not try to influence it? If you predict a strategy favorable to you, perhaps you can reinforce it; if unfavorable, change it; and if predicted without certainty, ensure it. Even if prediction proves elusive, it behooves you to try to influence the counterpart.

The first task in this process is to determine your own preferred strategy based on the criteria in step 5. This may appear to be jumping ahead, but choosing and influencing go hand in hand. They will go on throughout negotiation, for new information will come to light and necessitate reassessments.

Once you have chosen a strategy, use the matrix in Figure 3 to locate interaction targets. Your prime targets should be the coherent (complementary) combinations, followed by the potentially coherent ones. For example, if you intend to employ an agent, influence the counterpart to use the induce strategy.

Some negotiators may also contemplate targeting conflicting strategies. In this line of thinking, a conflict could bring out the parties' differences so dramatically as to provide valuable lessons and "working" material for both the negotiator and counterpart. Influencing the counterpart to pursue a strategy that conflicts with one's own (or selecting one by oneself if the counterpart has already set a strategy) might establish that one is not a negotiator who can be exploited. However, these effects lie outside of our main purposes of demonstrating responsiveness to cultural factors and establishing a coherent form of interaction. Furthermore, such conflict often confuses, causes delays, and provokes resentment. (Note also the other cautions in Table 4.)

With respect to means of influence, Americans sometimes preemptively take action, such as using English in conversation without inquiring about a non-American counterpart's wishes or capabilities, but there are other, often more mutually satisfactory, ways to influence a counterpart. They range from direct means, such as explicitly requesting a counterpart to choose a particular strategy, to tacit means, such as disclosing one's level of familiarity with the counterpart's culture, revealing one's own strategy choice, or designating a meeting site likely to elicit certain types of conduct. For example, in 1989, then U.S. Secretary of State James Baker hosted his Soviet counterpart Eduard Shevardnadze in Jackson Hole, Wyoming, instead of Washington, D.C. Prenegotiation communications may also be carried out by advance staff or through back channels. As you evaluate these options, bear in mind that their effectiveness will probably differ according to the counterpart's culture and personal attraction to you.[32]

5. Choose Your Strategy

When you have completed the previous steps, it is time to choose a strategy or a combination of strategies. Four selection criteria emerge from these steps. The strategy must be feasible given the counterpart and cultures involved; able to produce a coherent pattern of interaction, given the counterpart's likely approach; appropriate to the relationship and circumstances; and acceptable, ideally but not necessarily, to both parties. These criteria apply to the prenegotiation choice of strategy, but you may also use them to assess your strategy during negotiation.

A possible fifth criterion would be your degree of comfort with a strategy. Even negotiators highly familiar with two cultures' scripts favor one script over another in certain circumstances. So if the four criteria above do not direct you to only one right strategy, consider, at the end, which of the remaining strategies you would be most comfortable implementing.

Apply the four criteria in order, for this sequence is deliberate and designed for negotiators with a pragmatic orientation (e.g., Americans). Feasibility, after all, appears first. Acceptability appears later because the value judgment it involves impedes deliberation in cross-cultural situations when used too early.[33] (Note that counterparts from other cultural groups may prefer to use a list that begins with appropriateness or acceptability.)

Each criterion deserves attention. Feasibility and coherence considerations may narrow your choices down to one unilateral strategy, yet you should still check that choice for its appropriateness, given the relationship and circumstances, and its consonance with core beliefs and values. For a negotiation scheduled to take place over many years, for example, the negotiator might look at a strategy that is potentially but not inherently complementary to the counterpart's (see Figure 3) or at combinations or progressions of strategies. For a negotiation where the negotiator cannot narrow strategy options by reliably predicting the counterpart's strategy, the negotiator may actually have to rely on the last two criteria. And when a negotiator wishes to consider joint strategies, relationship factors and circumstances are essential to consult. In sum, the support of all four criteria for a particular strategy choice should give you confidence in it.

Occasionally, criteria may conflict. Feasibility and coherence point to an embrace strategy for a counterpart's induce strategy, but the negotiator may find aspects of the counterpart culture's script unacceptable (e.g., *fatwa*, Iran's death threat.) Or the embrace-induce strategy pairing may have worked well in a cross-cultural relationship for years, but now you expect your counterpart to be at least moderately familiar with your culture. The resolution of such conflicts begs for further research. In the meantime, you may want to defer to your core beliefs and values. Values define the very existence of your home group and your membership in it; by ignoring or violating them you risk forfeiting your membership.[34]

As an example of strategy selection based on all four criteria, consider an American, Smith, who is preparing for a confidential, one-on-one meeting with a Frenchman he has never met before, Dupont.

Smith once lived in France and, as the meeting is being held in Dupont's Paris office, his gut feeling is to speak in French and behave according to Dupont's culture—that is, to use an embrace strategy. However, he takes the time to evaluate his options. Smith realizes that he is no longer familiar enough with French language and culture to use an embrace strategy, and the short lead time prevents him from increasing his familiarity. With a moderate level of familiarity, he has five feasible strategies: employ an agent or adviser, involve a mediator, induce Dupont to follow his script, adapt to Dupont's script, or coordinate adjustment by both parties. Smith does some research and learns that Dupont has only a moderate level of familiarity with American negotiation practices. That rules out the induce strategy. The relationship and circumstances make an agent or mediator inappropriate. An adapt strategy would be hit-or-miss because Smith has no cues from previous face-to-face interaction and only one meeting is planned. Overall, the best strategy choice is to coordinate adjustment.

A complicated situation will require more complex considerations. (See also the cautions on choosing a strategy in Table 5.) But the five steps above—reflect, learn, consider, predict, and choose—constitute a sound and useful guide for strategy selection.

Implementing Your Strategy

The full value of the most carefully selected strategy rests on effective implementation, a formidable task in the general fluidity of negotiations

Table 5 Cautions: Choosing a Strategy

- Don't assume the counterpart will use the same criteria or order you do (e.g., efficiency is not a universal concern).
- Watch out for parties' miscalculations and conflicting impressions (e.g., the counterpart's assessments of your respective levels of cultural familiarity may differ from yours).
- Proceed carefully when criteria conflict; further research may help.
- Don't treat an embrace strategy, by mere definition, as costly or a concession.

and especially in the multifaceted process of most cross-cultural negotiations. It is here, in a negotiation's twists and turns, that a negotiator deals head on with distinctions between the counterpart's attributes as an individual and as a member of a cultural group. Simply adhering to one's own plan of action is difficult—and may become undesirable. For the negotiator must ensure that the strategy complements the counterpart's approach and enables the two of them to establish and maintain a coherent form of interaction.

Whatever the chosen culturally responsive strategy, a negotiator may enhance the effectiveness of first moves and ongoing efforts by generally respecting the counterpart and his or her group's culture and by demonstrating empathy (both of which may take different forms for different cultures). These qualities, among others, have been recommended in the literature on cross-cultural competence and are consistent with cultural responsiveness.[35] They do not necessitate lowering one's substantive negotiation goals.[36]

First Moves

The strategies of employ agent, embrace, and induce entail complete, existing scripts for negotiation. Pursuing one of these strategies essentially involves following the script associated with it. The adapt strategy involves modifications of your own script, at least some of which should be determined beforehand. With the improvise strategy, you ought to give some advance thought to a basic structure even if much of the path will emerge as you travel on it. Thus you have a starting point for each of the five unilateral strategies.

These strategies assume that when a counterpart recognizes your strategy, he or she will gravitate toward its corresponding script.[37] The counterpart wants to understand you and to be understood; that is what occurs in *coherent* interaction. If you have accurately assessed the counterpart's level of familiarity with your culture and ability to use a particular script, and if the counterpart recognizes the strategy you are using, you stand a better chance of achieving coherence.

Should you make the first strategic move or wait until the counterpart does? This decision affects the transition from preliminary "warm-up" discussions to negotiation of business matters. It depends, in part, on whether you need to gather more information about the counterpart's strategic intentions and abilities. This would matter when both parties have at least moderate familiarity with each other's cultures and have more than one unilateral strategy they can realistically choose, and when you have chosen a strategy (e.g., adapt, improvise) that relies on cues from the counterpart. The decision over timing also depends on whether you need to make the strategy you have chosen distinguishable from another one (e.g., improvise from adapt) and want to clearly establish this strategy at the outset. (Note that if a negotiator has chosen to employ an agent or has successfully influenced the counterpart, then timing should not be an issue.) In sum, to decide on timing, you should weigh the benefits of additional information against the costs of losing an opportunity to take leadership and set the tone of the interaction, a loss that includes being limited in your strategy options by the counterpart's strategy choice.

The three joint strategies are explicit and coordinated by definition. Once parties have decided to use a joint strategy, first moves consist of fleshing out particulars. Which mediator? What kinds of adjustments? What basic structure will underlie improvisation? These discussions may require the intermediate use of one of the five unilateral strategies.

Parties coordinating adjustment might consider trading off their respective priorities among the twelve cultural aspects in the negotiator profiles. If your counterpart values certain interpersonal conduct (protocol) more than the form of the agreement, for example, and you value the latter more than the former, the two of you could agree to adhere to a certain protocol and, on agreement, to draw up a comprehensive legal document. This pragmatic approach will probably appeal more to Western counterparts than to Asian ones, however, particularly if the Asian counterparts have only low or moderate cultural familiarity. So take this approach with caution rather than presuming that it will always work.

Whichever joint strategy you adopt, pursue it visibly in your first moves. Especially in first-time encounters, a counterpart reads these moves as indications of one's integrity ("sincerity," in Japan) and commitment to coordination.

Ongoing Efforts

A cross-cultural negotiator has myriad concerns and tasks, including vigilant attention to the cautions in the tables presented thus far. Still, as negotiation proceeds, one's most important task is concentrating on interaction with the counterpart. Parties' actions and reactions evidence adherence to and departures from a given negotiation script, fill out the incomplete scripts associated with some strategies (i.e., adapt, improvise, effect symphony), and determine the ultimate effectiveness of every one of the eight culturally responsive strategies. These interactions occur so quickly that analyzing them makes them seem fragmented and in "slow motion." Nevertheless, some analysis can have tremendous value.

As you negotiate, shift most of your attention from the counterpart's culture to the counterpart as an individual. Specifically, monitor feedback from him or her, be prepared to modify, shift, or change your strategy, and develop *this* relationship.

• **Monitor Counterpart's Feedback.** A counterpart's reactions to your ideas and conduct provide critical information about the counterpart personally and about the effectiveness of your chosen strategy with this particular individual. As you use that information to make continual adjustments and to evaluate your strategy, you may want to return to the four criteria of feasibility, coherence, appropriateness, and acceptability.

Some verbal and nonverbal cues transcend cultures in signaling positive or negative reception to a negotiator's use of a certain script. They range from a counterpart's statements ("Things are going well," "We don't do things that way") to a tightening of the corner of the mouth and cocked head, which convey contempt.[38]

In one film of the "Going International" series, an American manager urges his Saudi counterpart to expedite delivery of supplies from the docks to the hospital building site. He points out that the supplies have already sat at the dock for a week just because of paperwork, he personally is "in a crisis," "nobody works here" on Thursday and Friday (it is now Tuesday), and during the upcoming Ramadan observance "things really slow down." At various points during these remarks, the Saudi does not respond at all to a direct question, perfunctorily sets aside a written schedule he receives, and looks disparagingly at the American's shoes. In the end, the Saudi states, "Mr. Wilson, my people have been living for many years without a hospital. We can wait two more weeks."[39]

Admittedly, a counterpart's statements can be more or less honest or truthful, and the gradations are often fuzzy to an outsider. A number of cultures distinguish between saying what is socially acceptable (*tatemae* in Japanese) and saying what is truly on one's mind (*honne*). Other standards may also differ across cultures.

Many cues (e.g., silence) do not carry consistent meaning from culture to culture. Generally, individuals learn the culturally specific meanings as they become familiar with a culture. Negotiator profiles include some cues and imply others under dimensions such as "communication complexity" and "nature of persuasion." A negotiator can use these cues when he or she embraces the counterpart's culture.

Then again, some singularly powerful cues are very subtle. (See other cautions for strategy implementation in Table 6.)

In the 1950s, an American couple—the lone foreigners—at a Japanese wedding banquet in Tokyo were socializing and dining like everyone else. All of a sudden, everyone else finished eating and left the reception. Residents of Japan for many years, the Americans concluded later that a signal had been sent at some point, and they had not even detected it.

In cross-cultural interactions that do not involve embracing or inducing, or when a negotiator cannot clearly decipher the counterpart's strategy, nonuniversal cues are disconcertingly difficult to detect and interpret correctly. You can handle ambiguous cues (e.g., the hesitation of a counterpart who has so far been loquacious) by keeping them in mind until additional cues and information convey and reinforce one message. Other ambiguous cues may be de-

Table 6 Cautions: Implementing Your Strategy

- Remember that cross-cultural interaction can be creative and satisfying, not always taxing.
- Stay motivated.
- Separate your observations of the counterpart's behavior from your interpretations and conclusions about his or her intentions.
- Notice the changes as well as the constants in the counterpart's behavior over time.
- Try to pick up even the subtle cues.
- Give some thought to whether the counterpart might be feigning low familiarity with your culture and language.
- Don't get in too deep; don't unwittingly lead the counterpart to think your familiarity with his or her culture is higher than it actually is.
- Accept some of the limitations that the counterpart's culture may impose on outsiders; not all limitations can be surmounted no matter how well or long you try.
- Balance your responsiveness to cultural factors with your other aspirations and needs as a negotiator.

coded only by asking the counterpart; alternatively, they remain unclear. Dealing with these cues is a very real and ongoing challenge.

• **Be Prepared to Modify, Shift, or Change.** Even the well-prepared negotiator faces some surprises and some negative feedback in a negotiation. You want to be nimble enough to respond effectively. "Modifying" refers to refining implementation of a strategy without abandoning it; "shifting" refers to moving from one strategy to another within a previously planned combination of strategies; and "changing" refers to abandoning the strategy for another, unplanned one.

Making alterations is relatively easy with some counterparts.

For the first round of the 1980–1981 Ford-Toyota talks, Ford negotiators employed a bilingual Japanese staffer from their Japan office. The Toyota team, apparently confident in their English language abilities, suggested that Ford not bring the interpreter to subsequent meetings, so that the negotiators could "talk directly." Ford negotiators obliged and changed their approach.

On other occasions, one may have to explain modifications, shifts, and changes before they are made in order to minimize the odds of being perceived as unpredictable or deliberately disruptive. One may also deflect criticism by directly or indirectly associating these actions with changes in circumstances, the subject on the agenda, phase of the discussion, or, when negotiating as part of a team, personnel. For ideas about specific modifications to make, other than those prompted by your counterpart, review the counterpart's negotiator profile. Changes in strategy should be shaped by both a negotiator's culturally relevant capabilities and the strategy being abandoned. You may go relatively smoothly from an adapt to a coordinate adjustment strategy, for example, but not from inducing to embracing or from involving a mediator to employing an agent.

Over time, some movement between strategies may occur naturally (e.g., adapt to coordinate adjustment), but a *shift* as defined here involves a preconceived combination, or sequence, of strategies (e.g., coordinate adjustment, then effect symphony). A negotiator could plot a shift in strategies for certain types of counterpart feedback, variation in circumstances or relationship factors, or, especially during a long negotiation, for a jump in his or her level of cultural familiarity.

• **Develop *This* Relationship.** Pragmatic Americans may view the cultivation of a relationship with the counterpart primarily as an instrument for strategy implementation. Concentrating on coherent interaction and a satisfactory relationship usually does enhance a culturally responsive strategy's effectiveness. But the strategy should also—even primarily—be seen as serving the relationship.

Riding describes the views of Mexican negotiators when they returned home from Washington after the negotiations over Mexico's insolvency in 1982: "'We flew home relieved but strangely ungrateful,' one Mexican official recalled later. 'Washington had saved us from chaos, yet it did so in an uncharitable manner.' Even at such a critical moment, the substance and style of the relationship seemed inseparable."[40]

Many of your non-American counterparts will be accustomed to an emphasis on relationships. Indeed, greater attention to relationship quality may be the most common distinction between negotiators from American and non-American cultures.

Developing a relationship with a particular counterpart requires an attentiveness to its life and rhythms. The form of your interaction can evolve across different scripts and approaches, especially after many encounters. There is also the potential for culturally driven conflict, which you should be willing to try to resolve.

Clearly, such a relationship should be treated dynamically, whether time is measured in minutes or in months. In that light, you can continuously learn about the counterpart and the counterpart's culture *and* educate the counterpart about you and your culture. Over a long period, you may experiment with a counterpart's ways in noncritical areas (at low risk) to develop skills within and across culturally responsive strategies. In this way, you can expand the number of feasible strategies, giving both you and the counterpart more flexibility in the ways you relate to each other.

Toward Cross-Cultural Negotiating Expertise

A friend of mine, a third-generation American in Japan who was bilingual in Japanese and English, used to keep a file of items that one must know . . . to function in Japan . . . . [He] never stopped discovering new things; he added to the file almost every day.[41]

Over the years, many cross-cultural negotiators have essentially asked, "What happens when you're in Rome, but you're not Roman?" The most common advice available today was first offered 1,600 years ago: "Do as the Romans do." Yet these days, a non-Roman in Rome meets non-Romans as well as Romans and encounters Romans outside of Rome. The more we explore the variety of parties' capabilities and circumstances and the more we question the feasibility, coherence, appropriateness, and acceptability of "doing as Romans do," the more apparent the need becomes for additional culturally responsive strategies.

The range of strategies presented here provides every negotiator, including one relatively unfamiliar with a counterpart's culture, with at least two feasible options. Combinations of strategies further broaden the options.

If there is "something for everyone" here, the value of developing and sustaining cross-cultural expertise should still be clear. That includes high familiarity with a "Roman" culture—knowing the cognitive and behavioral elements of a Roman negotiating script and being able to use the script competently. The negotiator at the high familiarity level enjoys the broadest possible strategic flexibility for negotiations with Romans and the highest probability that, for a particular negotiation, one strategy will solidly meet all four selection criteria.

A negotiator can also gain a great deal from learning about more than one other culture. For lack of space I have concentrated on negotiations between two individuals, each belonging to one cultural group, but most cross-cultural negotiations involve more than two cultures: most individuals belong to more than one group; negotiations often occur between teams that have their own team cultures in addition to the members' ethnic, national, and organizational backgrounds; and multiparty, multicultural negotiations occur as well. In short, the non-Roman highly familiar with culture A still encounters cultures B, C, and D. Even though a negotiator may need to focus only on the one culture that a counterpart deems predominant at any one point in time, there are several to explore and manage across time, occasions, and people.[42]

As soon as he was assigned to GM's Zurich headquarters in the mid-1980s, Lou Hughes, one of GM's main representatives in the GM-Toyota negotiations of the early 1980s, began taking German lessons because GM's main European plant was located in Germany. Now president of GM Europe, Hughes' effectiveness as an executive has been attributed in part to his cultural sensitivity and learning.[43]

In the process of exploring other cultures, one may discover an idea or practice useful for all of one's negotiations.

Another American negotiator in the GM-Toyota talks was so impressed with the Toyota negotiators' template for comparing parties' proposals that he adopted it and has relied on it since for his negotiations with others.

It is in this spirit of continuous learning that this article has presented culturally responsive strategies, selection criteria, key steps in the choice process, and implementation ideas. If negotiators with a moderate amount of cross-cultural experience have the most to gain from these tools, first-time negotiators have before them a better sense of what lies ahead, and highly experienced negotiators can find some explanation for the previously unexplained and gain deeper understanding. In addition, the culture-individual considerations and ongoing challenges highlighted throughout the article will serve all cross-cultural negotiators. Perhaps we can all travel these paths more knowingly, exploring and building them as we go.

References

1. S.E. Weiss, "Negotiating with 'Romans'—Part 1," *Sloan Management Review*, Winter 1994, pp. 51–61. All examples that are not referenced come from personal communication or the author's experiences.
2. See J.K. Murnighan, *Bargaining Games: A New Approach to Strategic Thinking in Negotiations* (New York: William Morrow and Co., 1992), p. 22.
3. G.T. Savage, J.D. Blair, and R.L. Sorenson, "Consider Both Relationships and Substance When Negotiating Strategically," *The Executive* 3 (1989): 37–47; and S.E. Weiss, "Analysis of Complex Negotiations in International Business: The RBC Perspective," *Organization Science* 4 (1993): 269–300.
4. Attending to both culture and the individual has also been supported by: S.H. Kale and J.W. Barnes, "Understanding the Domain of Cross-National Buyer-Seller Interactions," *Journal of International Business Studies* 23 (1992): 101–132.

5. To speak of an "American culture" is not to deny the existence of cultures within it that are based on ethnic, geographic, and other boundaries. In fact, the strategies described in Part 1 of this article and the five steps described here can be applied to these cross-cultural negotiations as well. These ideas deserve the attention of those, for example, who are concerned about diversity in the workplace.
6. C. Thubron, *Behind the Wall* (London: Penguin, 1987), pp. 158, 186–187.
7. See R. Keesing as quoted in: W.B. Gudykunst and S. Ting-Toomey, *Culture and Interpersonal Communication* (Newbury Park, California: Sage, 1988), p. 29.
8. H. Binnendijk, ed., *National Negotiating Styles* (Washington, D.C.: Foreign Service Institute, U.S. Department of State, 1987).
9. For a review of popular books, see: S. Weiss-Wik, "Enhancing Negotiator's Successfulness: Self-Help Books and Related Empirical Research," *Journal of Conflict Resolution* 27 (1983): 706–739. For a recent research review, see: P.J.D. Carnevale and D.G. Pruitt, "Negotiation and Mediation," *Annual Review of Psychology* 43 (1992): 531–582.
10. For self-examinations, see: G. Althen, *American Ways: A Guide for Foreigners in the United States* (Yarmouth, Maine: Intercultural Press, 1988); E.T. Hall and M.R. Hall, *Understanding Cultural Differences* (Yarmouth, Maine: Intercultural Press, 1990); and E.C. Stewart and M.J. Bennett, *American Cultural Patterns* (Yarmouth, Maine: Intercultural Press, 1991). The views of outsiders include: A. de Tocqueville, *Democracy in America*, 1805–1859 (New York: Knopf, 1980); L. Barzini, *The Europeans* (Middlesex, England: Penguin, 1983), pp. 219–253; and Y. Losoto, "Observing Capitalists at Close Range," *World Press Review*, April 1990, pp. 38–42.
11. The original framework appeared in: S.E. Weiss with W. Stripp, "Negotiating with Foreign Business Persons: An Introduction for Americans with Propositions on Six Cultures" (New York: New York University Graduate School of Business Administration, Working Paper No. 85–6, 1985).
12. Although I am not certain, my recollection is that the clients relented, and the bank team made the trip to South Africa. The point, however, is that the banker took a stand on an issue that struck values dear to him. Other examples include whether or not to make "questionable payments" and how to handle social settings in France and in Japan when one is allergic to alcohol or cigarette smoke. On payments, see: T.N. Gladwin and I. Walter, *Multinationals under Fire* (New York: John Wiley & Sons, 1980), p. 306. On smoking, see: W.E. Schmidt, "Smoking Permitted: Americans in Europe Have Scant Protection," *New York Times*, 8 September 1991, p. 31. On the other hand, some customs, while different, may not be abhorrent or worth contesting. An American male unaccustomed to greeting other men with "kisses" (the translation itself projects a bias) might simply go along with an Arab counterpart who has initiated such a greeting.
13. Murnighan (1992), p. 28; and Kale and Barnes (1992), p. 122.
14. J.L. Barsoux and P. Lawrence, "The Making of a French Manager," *Harvard Business Review*, July–August 1991, p. 60.
15. For example, for each of the four categories respectively, see: D. Chalvin, *L'entreprise négociatrice* (Paris: Dunod, 1984) and C. Dupont, *La négociation: conduite, théorie, applications*, 3rd ed. (Paris: Dalloz, 1990); N.C.G. Campbell et al., "Marketing Negotiations in France, Germany, the United Kingdom, and the United States," *Journal of Marketing* 52 (1988): 49–62 and G. Fisher, *International Negotiation: A Cross-Cultural Perspective* (Yarmouth, Maine: Intercultural Press, 1980); L. Bellenger, *La négociation* (Paris: Presses Universitaires de France, 1984) and A. Jolibert and M. Tixier, *La négociation commerciale* (Paris: Les éditions ESF, 1988); and Hall and Hall (1990).
16. Nonfiction writings include: J. Ardagh, *France Today* (London: Penguin, 1987); L. Barzini, (1983); S. Miller, *Painted in Blood: Understanding Europeans* (New York: Atheneum, 1987); and T. Zeldin, *The French* (New York: Vintage, 1983). Fictional works include the classics by Jean-Paul Sartre and Andre Malraux and, more recently, A. Jardin, *Le Zèbre* (Paris: Gallimard, 1988).
17. I will leave to others the debate over the effectiveness of training focused on "skills" versus other types of training. Somewhat surprisingly, some research on individuals' perceived need to adjust suggests that "interpersonal" and documentary training have comparable effects. See: P.C. Earley, "Intercultural Training for Managers," *Academy of Management Review* 30 (1987): 685–698. Note also that a number of negotiation seminars offered overseas do not directly increase familiarity with negotiation customs in those countries. These seminars import and rely on essentially American concepts and practices.
18. On cultural assimilator exercises, see: R.W. Brislin et al., *Intercultural Interactions: A Practical Guide* (Beverly Hills, California: Sage, 1986).
19. J. Watson and R. Lippitt, *Learning across Cultures* (Ann Arbor, Michigan: University of Michigan Press, 1955), as quoted in: A.T. Church, "Sojourner Adjustment," *Psychological Bulletin* 91 (1982): 544.
20. See Savage, Blair, and Sorenson (1989), p. 40. The following all include relationship factors (e.g., interest interdependence, relationship quality, concern for relationship) in their grids for strategic selection: R. Blake and J.S. Mouton, *The Managerial Grid* (Houston, Texas: Gulf, 1964): Gladwin and Walter (1980); and K.W. Thomas and R.H. Kilmann, *Thomas-Kilmann Conflict Mode Instrument* (Tuxedo, New York: Xicom, Inc., 1974).
21. For more extensive lists, see: Weiss (1993).
22. D.G. Pruitt and J.Z. Rubin, *Social Conflict: Escalation, Stalemate, and Settlement* (New York: Random House, 1986) pp. 33–34.
23. Weiss with Stripp (1985); F. Gauthey et al., *Leaders sans frontières* (Paris: McGraw-Hill, 1988), p. 149–156, 158; and R. Moran and W. Stripp, *Dynamics of Successful International Business Negotiations* (Houston, Texas: Gulf, 1991).
24. P.H. Gulliver, *Disputes and Negotiations* (New York: Academic, 1979), pp. 186–190, 200–207.
25. G. Hofstede, *Culture's Consequences* (Beverly Hills; Sage, 1984).
26. The literature on women and negotiation includes: M. Gibb-Clark, "A Look at Gender and Negotiations," *The Globe and Mail*, 24 May 1993, p. B7; J. Ilich and B.S. Jones, *Successful Negotiating Skills for Women* (New York: Playboy Paperbacks, 1981); and C. Watson and B. Kasten, "Separate Strengths? How Men and Women Negotiate" (New Brunswick, New Jersey: Rutgers University, Center for Negotiation and Conflict Resolution, Working Paper). On gender-based communication, see: D. Tannen, *You Just Don't Understand* (New York: William Morrow and Co., 1990).
27. N.J. Adler, "Pacific Basin Managers: Gaijin, Not a Woman," *Human Resources Management* 26 (1987): 169–191. This corresponds with the observation that "the different groups a person belongs to are not all equally important at a given moment." See: K. Lewin, *Resolving Social Conflicts* (New York: Harper & Row, 1948), p. 46, according to: Gudykunst and Ting-Toomey (1988), p. 201.
28. A. Riding, "Not Virile? The British Are Stung," *New York Times*, 20 June 1991, p. A3. See the disguises used by a female American reporter in: S. Mackey, *The Saudis: Inside the Desert Kingdom* (New York: Meridian, 1987). On the other hand, the all-woman New York City-based firm of Kamsky and Associates has been widely recognized for their business deals in the People's Republic of China. See also: C. Sims, "Mazda's Hard-driving Saleswoman," *New York Times*, 29 August 1993, Section 3, p. 6; and M.L. Rossman, *The International Business Woman* (New York: Praeger, 1987).
29. This interaction format draws on a game theoretic perspective and borrows more directly from: T.A. Warshaw, *Winning by Negotiation* (New York: McGraw-Hill, 1980), p. 79.

30. T.C. Schelling, *The Strategy of Conflict* (New York: Oxford University Press, 1960), p. 53–58. The prominence of many courses of action would seem, however, to rest on assumptions that are culturally based and thus restricted rather than universal.
31. On risk-taking propensity, see: Gudykunst and Ting-Toomey (1988), pp. 153–160.
32. For discussions of similarity-attraction theory and research, see: K.R. Evans and R.F. Beltramini, "A Theoretical Model of Consumer Negotiated Pricing: An Orientation Perspective," *Journal of Marketing* 51 (1987): 58–73; J.N.P. Francis, "When in Rome? The Effects of Cultural Adaptation on Intercultural Business Negotiations," *Journal of International Business Studies* 22 (1991): 403–428; and J.L. Graham and N.J. Adler, "Cross-Cultural Interaction: The International Comparison Fallacy," *Journal of International Business Studies* 20 (1989): 515–537.
33. N. Dinges, "Intercultural Competence," in *Handbook of Intercultural Training*, vol. 1., D. Landis and R.W. Brislin, eds. (New York: Pergamon, 1983), pp. 176–202.
34. Individual members do instigate change and may, over time, cause a group to change some of its values. Still, at any given point, a group holds to certain values and beliefs.
35. See Dinges (1983), pp. 184–185, 197; and D.J. Kealey, *Cross-Cultural Effectiveness: A Study of Canadian Technical Advisors Overseas* (Hull, Quebec: Canadian International Development Agency, 1990), p. 53–54. At the same time, Church cautiously concluded in his extensive review of empirical research that effects of personality, interest, and value on performance in a foreign culture had not yet demonstrated strong relationships. See: Church (1982), p. 557.
36. This advice parallels the now widely supported solution for the classic negotiator's dilemma of needing to stand firm to achieve one's goals and needing to make concessions to sustain movement toward an agreement: namely, "be firm but conciliatory," firm with respect to goals, but conciliatory with respect to means. See: Pruitt and Rubin (1986), p. 153.
37. Sometimes counterparts do not actually desire an agreement but some side effect. Thus their behavior may differ from that described here. See: F.C. Ikle, *How Nations Negotiate* (Millwood, New York: Kraus Reprint, 1976), pp. 43–58.
38. See "Universal Look of Contempt," *New York Times*, 22 December 1986, p. C3.
39. "Going International" film series, Copeland Griggs Productions, San Francisco.
40. A. Riding, *Distant Neighbors: A Portrait of Mexicans* (New York: Vintage Books, 1984), p. 487.
41. E.T. Hall, *Beyond Culture* (Garden City, New York: Anchor Press, 1977), p. 109.
42. The assertion concerning the predominance of one culture at a time was made by: Lewin (1948).
43. A. Taylor, "Why GM Leads the Pack in Europe," *Fortune*, 17 May 1993, p. 84.

Article Review Form at end of book.

WiseGuide Wrap-Up

- Prenegotiation preparation is particularly critical for cross-cultural negotiations to succeed. It is critical that the negotiator increase his or her level of familiarity with the culture or cultures involved in the discussion process.

- The use of negotiation facilitators should be explored when the negotiations involve multiple cultures or people with animosity toward the other group. These facilitators, however, need to have extensive intercultural communication experience, as well as knowledge of the specific cultures involved in the negotiation.

- Individuals can also apply these negotiating-across-cultures concepts if they live and work in a diverse community. These are skills which improve with practice. The neophyte should not expect errorless negotiations the first time he or she attempts to apply this knowledge.

R.E.A.L. Sites

This list provides a print preview of typical **coursewise** R.E.A.L. sites. There are over 100 such sites at the **courselinks**™ site. The danger in printing URLs is that web sites can change overnight. As we went to press, these sites were functional using the URLs provided. If you come across one that isn't, please let us know via email to: webmaster@coursewise.com. Use your Passport to access the most current list of R.E.A.L. sites at the **courselinks**™ site.

Site name: Adil Najam: MIT Chlorine Negotiation Simulation Global Environment

URL: http://www.mit.edu/people/anajam/cl-game.html

Why is it R.E.A.L.? This Massachusetts Institute of Technology site provides an example of a simulation of a United Nations international negotiation to shape a global organochlorine treaty.

Key topics: simulation, United Nations, global treaty, negotiation

Try this: Analyze the simulation and suggest three areas of conflict which may affect negotiation of the treaty.

Site name: Harvard Law School: The Program on Negotiation at Harvard Law School

URL: http://www.pon.harvard.edu/

Why is it R.E.A.L.? Bill Ury's co-author, Roger Fisher, of the best-selling book *Getting to Yes: Negotiating Agreement Without Giving In*, is a faculty member at the Harvard Law School. The Program on Negotiation site provides a clearinghouse of simulations, publications, journals, and training material on negotiating.

Key topics: negotiating theory, role play simulations, dispute resolution

Try this: Review the role play simulations. Which one would you recommend? Why?

section 4

Global Human Resources and Training

Learning Objectives

- Understand the role human resources and training play in global organizations.
- Evaluate the effectiveness of intercultural communication training programs.
- Increase sensitivity regarding the untapped resources of expatriates and inpatriates.

WiseGuide Intro

Managing the human resources and training functions of a global organization is increasingly complex. Even though the Internet and very sophisticated software designed for international organizations have eased some of the problems of interconnections within the organizational structure, some difficulties still exist. Human resources departments still face problems of different pay structures in different countries, varied benefit packages, and multiple management styles. The challenge remains of how to respect cultural differences while creating the organizational culture necessary to produce a quality product and a profitable company.

International training also benefits from technological advances. Multimedia training materials can be created in which trainees select the language of choice when using the program. Certain types of training can now be offered on the worker's desktop via an Intranet system. However, there still remains the need, as Odenwald states in "A Guide for Global Training," to build employees' skills in working across national and cultural boundaries.

Recently, a trainer with an excellent track record for training U.S. workers was scheduled to conduct a training class in Japan. With less than a week's notice and preparation, he found himself in Tokyo, confronting a group of serious young men waiting for his eight-hour training program to begin. Dressed in dark suits and ties, they silently waited. He began his usual course design, which in the past had been repeatedly judged as interesting as well as very informative. The design called for initial audience interaction with the suggestions and questions laying the foundation on which to build the training session. However, the trainer immediately recognized that he was in deep trouble when his questions and attempts at audience feedback in problem identification were met with a wall of silence. He realized that within hours he would use up all of his prepared material. Moreover, he was uncomfortable with a silent group who carefully wrote down his every word. At the first break, he consulted with his Japanese counterpart regarding the lack of audience response. He then learned that giving one's own opinion in this public group setting was seen as being forward and possibly disrespectful to senior workers. He was also advised that writing down detailed notes was standard practice, enhanced by trainees' concerns about weak English skills. The trainer quickly adapted and rearranged people in groups, with senior members as the designated leaders. He then asked each leader to facilitate discussion of the questions and report the group consensus. This structure met with better success. When coupled with a change in speaking rate and a listing of major concepts on the board, what appeared to be a disastrous training session was salvaged.

It is this adaptability and sensitivity to cultural differences which international human resources and training professionals must possess. In addition, as firms are streamlining to be more profitable in this global market place, managers are increasingly being asked to include human resources and training functions as part of their responsibilities. Adjusting to global issues in these areas will require flexibility and openness to change on the part of all company employees.

Questions

Reading 20. What are some of the obstacles businesses face in operating effectively at the global level? How might the human resources and training professionals partner with other divisions within the firms to maximize success?

Reading 21. What ramifications does the rapid international expansion of a firm have for the human resources and training area?

Reading 22. What components are necessary to put together a complete roster of training classes for building employees' skills in working across national cultural boundaries?

Reading 23. How does a company develop global managers who are able to complete global assignments and use their international expertise within the firm once they are repatriated?

Reading 24. What does a global human resources and training department need to know to avoid sexual discrimination liability and increase the company's chances for harassment-free business relationships?

Global Business Issues

Patty Lynam

What are some of the obstacles businesses face in operating effectively at the global level? How might the human resources and training professionals partner with other divisions within the firms to maximize success?

This article will identify challenging issues that employees at all levels, working for and within global organizations, face daily in their work environment. The purpose will be to create awareness, for students pursing their educational goals, of the business world that lies beyond the classroom. As the world becomes smaller due to globalization, there is an excellent chance that any of today's students will have the opportunity to work for a company that is actively involved in the global economy.

To begin, a short description of a global organization will be useful. A global organization conducts business internationally, has a presence around the world, including offices and employees in more than one country. This may not be agreed to by all, but it will be the description used for the purpose of this article. Global companies communicate to their customers that, as a business entity, they are committed to operating around the world, in the global market. By way of capital investment and human resources, global companies are prepared to provide goods and services to a world market. By electing to operate in multiple countries, organizations position themselves to better service their customers. Global organizations may, although not guaranteed, experience greater credibility with customers because they are generally in a better position to have a broader understanding of local needs, market and labor trends, regulatory requirements, and cultural influences or differences.

Companies having a global presence also have problems to match resulting from market and labor conditions that can change rapidly; country specific regulatory requirements imposed by other governments; and cultural differences that exist between employee populations in each country. External forces beyond the direct control of the company, or the organizational headquarters bring about these problems. Perhaps the most difficult of these conditions is that of cultural differences and the resulting miscommunication that can occur because of lack of understanding between people.

As an employee of a global company, there have been opportunities to observe, experience, and under certain conditions, quantify through the use of surveys how culture or communication can present unique challenges. Having offices throughout the world lends itself to pressures brought about by the mere distance that exists between locations. While it is morning in one part of the world, it may be the evening of the following day somewhere else. Hence, there is difficulty in effectively communicating in real time; there is a time lapse that cannot be overcome since no one can control time.

Not only does time create obstacles in communication, but language as well can stand in the way of effective communication. With a multinational work force, there may well be many languages spoken and that immediately presents difficulty for those not fluent in one or the others native language. Even if there are locations where everyone speaks English, assuming that globally one is operating within an English speaking environment, one must ponder for a moment and ask which English is being spoken.

During World War II Sir Winston Churchill, then Prime Minister has been quoted as saying that the United States and England were ". . . two great nations separated by a common language." He was referring to the difference in language usage and phrasing in each country. The English language had changed and evolved independently between the two countries leaving gaps in clarity and meaning. If one adds in regional accents and slang, other problems develop in the communication of an idea or thought. Australia provides yet another instance whereby the language spoken is English, but due to their geographic location their language has evolved somewhat independently in common usage or phrasing with its own unique slang.

As another example, one could identify a country where the native language is not English, but English is spoken in the course of conducting business. For those who speak English there is still the challenge of taking the words from English, converting them into meaningful thoughts, then responding to or conveying ideas that are interpreted correctly. Again, which

"Global Business Issues" by Patty Lynam. Reprinted by permission of the author.

English might they be operating in, American English or British English, and is the interpretation the same as was originally intended?

As if communication is not enough to deal with, recognizing and respecting cultural differences presents perhaps the most difficult, yet possibly the most rewarding, challenge. Unfortunate as it may be, this is the one area where there is the greatest opportunity for failure, most of which is due to the presence of an ethnocentric attitude held by individuals that can filter through an organization. This in turn can surface as conflict caused by the inability to recognize that each person or individual has value, and something to contribute to the organization, regardless of their ethnicity, belief or value system. Because of cultural differences, others may not have the same work habits as one might have previously encountered, or thought processes may be different: ideas and solutions are based upon a different point of reference.

Culture is by definition the shared attitudes, beliefs, values, norms, and symbols of a social system. Many layers in a complex system to be explored, experienced, and internally processed before there can be some degree of understanding as to what culture truly means within a society. All too often, when given the opportunity to operate or work in another country, little thought or value is given to learning, for the purpose of understanding, anything that will truly prepare one to appreciate the experience and comprehend the full meaning of another culture.

As harmful or embarrassing as cultural ignorance may be, equally as bad is moving forward with an illusion that one has full knowledge of another culture by picking up a handy reference book that offers brief advice on what to do or not to do in another country. While this may be handy to prevent the businessperson from making a foolish remark or gesture, it does nothing to educate the reader in the sense of cultural understanding.

In this brief article only a small glimpse of what one may encounter working globally has been discussed. As a closing thought, if one is truly interested in what exists beyond country borders take the time to research an area. Learn about the culture, historical events, and political systems. The world is getting smaller due to globalization, information is more accessible than ever before, and it is becoming more important as each day passes to acknowledge and appreciate the diverse cultures of the world.

If you are interested in visiting the Web site of a company that operates in the global market place, please refer to the following:

www.kvaemer.com

Article Review Form at end of book.

What ramifications does the rapid international expansion of a firm have for the human resources and training area?

Colgate's Global HR Unites Under One Strategy

Dawn Anfuso

Imagine calling the world your home. Not just your home as in your country, state, city and ultimately your address, but more precisely, where you hand your hat.

For Colgate-Palmolive Co., the world is where the company hangs its hat, its coat and all its belongings. Because although the household and personal-care products conglomerate has an official corporate headquarters in New York City, it has businesses and people all over the world—and has for more than half a century.

Indeed, 70% of the company's more than $8 billion in sales comes from overseas, as Colgate-Palmolive markets such products as Colgate toothpaste, Palmolive soap and Ajax cleanser in 194 countries. The company's product line is immense, so extensive, in fact, that at one point the parent company began to lose track of where all of its "children," or businesses producing its myriad products, were. So, in 1989 Colgate remodeled its home so as to contain its products in five "rooms": oral care, personal care, hard-surface care, fabric care and pet nutrition.

With the remodeling came new business strategies. But as these strategies began to roll out, one fact became painfully clear—there was a gap between the business strategies and the company's current people strategies. For the businesses to succeed, the company would need to better align its human resources with its business objectives.

It has done so by creating a true partnership between senior line management and human resources leaders. The alignment has resulted in a human resources strategy tied to business needs, and a strong link between Colgate's 35,000 people throughout the world.

HR and Business Leaders Strategize Together

The partnership effort began with the creation of a Global Human Resources Strategy Team. "The objective of the team was to work in partnership with management to build organizational excellence," says Brian Smith, director of global HR strategy. "We define organizational excellence as the continuous alignment of Colgate people, business processes and the organization in general with our vision, values and strategies, to become the best."

The team itself constituted a partnership. Approximately half of its 25 members were human resources leaders, the other half senior line managers. Among the members were the president of the Far East division, the president of the pet nutrition business and the global leader of the oral-care business, as well as senior staff people, such as general managers. "We wanted to ensure that our major HR activities were helping the business achieve its primary objectives," says Douglas M. Reid, senior vice president, global HR for Colgate-Palmolive.

One of the first actions the team took was to articulate a global HR vision. It was based on three values which the team determined needed to be shared globally: care, teamwork and continuous improvement. The statement reads: "We care about people. Colgate people, consumers, shareholders and our business partners. We are committed to act with compassion, integrity and honesty in all situations, to listen with respect to others and to value cultural differences. We are also committed to protect our global environment and enhance the local communities where we work.

"We are all part of a global team, committed to working together across functions, across countries and throughout the world. Only by sharing ideas, technologies and talents can we sustain profitable growth.

"We are committed to getting better every day in all we do, as individuals and as teams. By better understanding consumers' and customers' expectations, and by continuously working to innovate and improve our products, services and processes, we will 'become the best.' "

Although the vision statement originated with the Global HR Strategy Team, it was circulated among 75 general managers and the entire senior management team for revisions and approval. Then, based on the principles that the vision espoused, the team worked together for

"Colgate's Global HR Unites Under One Strategy" by Dawn Anfuso, copyright October 1995. Used with permission of ACC Communication, Inc./*Personnel Journal* (now known as *Workforce*), Costa Mesa, CA. All rights reserved.

Colgate Grooms HR Talent

New York City-based Colgate-Palmolive Co. expects a lot from its HR staff. Its management recruitment program ensures it gets just that.

For years Colgate has recruited much of its HR leadership through MBA programs. In 1990, however, it formalized the policy with the HR Professional Development Program. Fashioned after its Global Marketing Program, started in 1987, which brings top-caliber people into the organization via the marketing function—the program targets graduate students at college campuses with top human resources programs, such as the University of Minnesota and Cornell University. "We select the brightest people from the best schools in the country," says Brian Smith, director of global HR strategy at Colgate.

Candidates for the program must be highly regarded by their instructors and peers, must have performed well scholastically and must have had some HR experience, either through employment before grad school or internships, for which they have good recommendations. Senior management takes a keen interest in the review process and the selection process and takes a personal interest in how these people are performing around the world.

Since the program's inception, the company has been bringing two or three people through it each year. "There's no set numbers," says Smith. "It's just the top people." Once brought on board, these candidates spend 15 to 18 months rotating through different parts of the business. They'll work in the sales force for a while, in marketing, in manufacturing and in technology. "Just like the marketing program, the objective is to expose the new hire to Colgate's businesses, because #1 on the list for succeeding at Colgate is understanding Colgate's business," says Smith.

There is a model the company follows to determine how much time the new hire spends in each segment, but, Smith says the company basically tries to schedule their work assignments to coincide with interesting projects happening or to fulfill a particular need. "We don't have a hundred people coming through so we have that flexibility to build a real development program," says Smith. The HR associates in the program also run through various compensation, employee relations and staffing functions.

Although the ideal is to have the new associates complete 15 to 18 months in the program, they're often deployed shortly after completing a year's worth of training. "These people are pretty powerful HR talent, so the various HR communities in Colgate start bidding for them, they start chatting them up about opportunities in their shops," says Smith.

Where the worker ends up going depends both on the person's career aspirations and the company's needs. So, for instance, if someone's particularly interested in compensation as a career, and the company has an opportunity for a compensation specialist in Germany, the company would try to make the connection. "But it isn't 'What do you want to do?'" says Smith. "It's 'Where is the business need and how does that align to the person's personal career aspirations?' We try to balance that and, so far, that has worked successfully."

Wherever in the company the HR associates go, they start out in middle management, with company expectations that they excel toward leadership.
—DA

---

nearly a year crafting an HR strategy that would align with business objectives. To do so, it solicited customer feedback through interviews with Colgate people across the globe. "The line managers [both the ones on the team and those interviewed] provided invaluable perspective and insight as to the needs of the organization and the role of HR in achieving business goals," says Smith.

The team identified several areas for which business managers needed HR's support. One of the most crucial was career planning. "Career planning was an important need from a management perspective," says Reid. "[A big question always is] are we going to have enough managers with the right skills and experiences to fill our forecasted openings?"

Career planning also was a concern of employees, the team learned. Workers wanted a legible road map for charting a meaningful career, a system to help them determine what experiences and skills they would need to achieve their career objectives. "That need existed in virtually every one of the countries in which we operate," says Reid.

The second area the team identified as crucial for HR to align with business needs was education and training. "We discovered that in many of our operating companies—and we now have approximately 75 operating companies around the world—HR was reinventing the wheel," says Reid. "They were all trying to address the education and training needs in their own way." The global team realized that, because there was a need for certain education and training across the globe, it made sense to provide global programs.

HR Strategy Meets Business Leaders' Needs

Based on these two crucial elements, the team created an HR strategy that it broke into three parts: generating, reinforcing and sustaining organizational excellence through a partnership with business leaders.

Generating organizational excellence requires selecting and developing Colgate people. Therefore, selection processes, including recruitment programs and education and training programs, would fall under this category of the human resources strategy.

Reinforcing organizational excellence means helping to focus and align Colgate people. This category encompasses performance management, rewards and recognition.

The final strategy category, sustaining organizational excellence, basically houses continuous improvement initiatives. Constant communication of Colgate's values, visions, strategies and programs to the world of Colgate falls under this section, as does continual data gathering from employee insight surveys.

The centerpiece of this strategy rests on the formation of global

All Colgate Asks for Is a Little Respect

When you operate on a global basis, it's egocentric to define diversity in Western terms. But what if valuing diversity is a priority at your company?

New York City-based Colgate-Palmolive Co. addresses this by focusing its diversity training program, "Valuing Colgate People," on respecting all people, their differences and their similarities.

But, when you're talking close to 200 countries and nearly that many cultures, how do you define respect? That, says Colgate, depends on which country you're in. For example, in the United States, having respect for someone may mean providing him or her open and honest feedback. But in some Asian cultures, this would be an insult. The key is just understanding each culture and respecting people according to those cultural norms.

The Valuing Colgate People program was designed to help business managers understand that "We're only going to achieve our business objectives if we demonstrate respect and concern for all individuals in the company," says Douglas M. Reid, senior vice president, global HR for Colgate-Palmolive. "We value all Colgate people, not just the executive group, not just managers, not just women, not just minorities. We value them all because of the unique talents they bring and the experiences they have that will help solve business problems."

Valuing Colgate People is a two-day program. The first day is common around the Colgate World. On this day, the company vision, its values and its business fundamentals are shared. Also, the company defines respect for the individual in terms of the country in which the training is being done. "It's teaching managers how to manage people to maximize their motivation, making sure they treat all employees with respect and creating an environment in which they feel free to come forward with constructive suggestions," says Reid.

The second day is unique to each particular country and focuses on the issues that prevent people from treating each other with respect there. In the United States, for example, a big piece of that is legal requirements, such as the laws and regulations governing affirmative action. "We want to ensure all managers are aware of these regulations and, more importantly, behave in accord with the spirit of these regulations."

Senior managers were first to receive the training, and because management is responsible for setting the corporate environment, all management levels now are being trained.

"The message from Valuing Colgate People is if you can learn to respect each other for what each has to offer, be it education, friendship, whatever, you too will learn and grow from it," says Ron Martin, director of global employees relations. "There may be differences as far as skin color, language spoken or cultural attitudes, but our commonality is that we respect each other."

—DA

---

competencies for every job function. During the strategy-development phase, the strategy team created competency-development teams. Each team was led by the head of the function for which it was developing competencies. For example, for the finance function, the chief financial officer of Colgate set up a team of finance people from the corporate office, the divisional offices and the operating companies. Together, they identified the skills and experience that are required for each job level, and then they developed career paths that properly reflect these skills and experiences.

So, for example, it's spelled out as to what skills and experiences are required to be an associate accountant, what further skills and experiences would be needed to move into an accountant position and what new skills would be required to become a senior accountant or a supervisor of accounting. "The key in the competency development was that in each case, the work was led by the functional head, whether it was the head of finance, marketing, manufacturing or human resources," says Reid.

The competencies are the centerpiece of the strategy because they're used to select people, for identifying training needs, for promotion decisions and in performance appraisals. In other words, they're the foundation for both career planning, and education and training—the two biggest needs identified as HR's primary role. "Armed with competencies, which are tiered through the organization and are functionally focused, we can target our efforts and be much more effective in bringing the best talent to Colgate," says Smith. (To learn more about the competencies and about Colgate's staffing strategy, see the end of this article.)

Leadership Support Strengthens Strategy Kickoff

After getting buy-in from senior line management on the global HR strategy, the Global HR Strategy Team called together a Global Human Resources Conference in February 1992 to launch the strategy and vision. "We decided that if we were going to have a global HR strategy, we should call all the key HR operating people from around the Colgate World together to discuss the strategy and how to implement it," says Reid.

More than 200 HR leaders from around the world, representing approximately 35 countries, attended the week-long conference. However, also in attendance were the company's chairman, president, COO, every division president and every global category leader. "We took advantage of this global meeting to hear from the president and the chairman about overall objectives for the company—and also to hear firsthand from the various presidents of the operating units what their expectations were from HR people," says Reid.

This was key. According to Smith, having the major players at the conference "emphasized a terrific partnership and commitment from our senior management for the HR program. It was a watershed event for the function, if not the company."

Adds Reid: "The fact that line managers wanted the kind of

assistance HR could provide—and that they were willing to invest their own time in the development of these programs and their subsequent implementation—is key to why it has been successful. We built a strategy to satisfy their needs with their help. So the final plan reflected their needs and their wishes."

The needs of management, as expressed at the conference, were that they wanted pragmatic, succinct programs that easily could be implemented at the operating country level. Design of these programs began at the conference. Prior to the event, Smith sent out questionnaires to HR people across the Colgate World asking them what they'd like to get out of the conference. Smith took these ideas and combined the key issues surrounding them with the issues related to the new Global HR Strategy to create the conference itinerary.

He then asked around and identified the Colgate people best suited to address these issues. "I found our centers of excellence and asked [the people there] to present workshops," says Smith. "All of the myriad activities that go on around the world of Colgate—such as high-commitment work systems, targeted selection, career planning and individual development plans—had workshops presented about them."

HR professionals returned from the conference to their corners of the world with a plan of attack for the future. The Global HR Strategy provided them with a vision of the next half decade or so. The conference workshops gave them the tools to succeed. And annual HR business plans linked to the vision provided them ways to gauge their success.

The business plan basically is an action grid, detailing for each country, each division, each function, the steps to be taken and the timeline for taking them. HR creates the plan—division presidents sign off on it. The business plan enables HR and senior management to evaluate strategy implementation. And it keeps HR around the world of Colgate working off the same page.

Strategy Implementation Moves HR Professionals to Business Partners

According to Reid, the conference served as the rallying cry uniting the HR people of Colgate worldwide around some common initiatives. "Previously, they were focused entirely on their local operating company and not on global issues," says Reid. "We provided them specifics in terms of how to implement the programs and how to monitor their success, and we trained them in how to use these new tools."

Indeed, the structure of global HR, with approximately 500 HR people sprawled across the world, presents a challenge for keeping them linked. There's a global HR crew in New York City, headed by Reid, who reports to the chairman of Colgate-Palmolive. This global HR function is organized around traditional lines—compensation, benefits, labor relations, career planning, education and training, succession planning and so on. Then, each operating company has its own HP organization, with the HR director at the local operating company level reporting to the general manager of that company. These HR people also are pretty much organized around functions. Also, the president of each geographic division—Europe, Far East, Latin America, and so on—has a small HR team. And, as HR becomes more integrated into the business, HR positions are being formed to support particular functions. For example, there's an HR director supporting the CFO and global finance, and another supporting marketing.

Despite their positions, and the distances they may be from other HR people performing the same functions, the HR people today feel they're part of a continuous chain. According to Reid, it's the Global HR Strategy that provides that link across the world of Colgate. "Whether you're in Chile or Greece, Canada or Malaysia, you're working to implement the new career-planning system, the new succession-planning system, the competencies for finance, marketing or sales. In other words, you're working toward common initiatives. That's what ties people together."

This link is vital. But, according to Reid, the strategy team and the conference that followed had an even greater outcome—"The realization by the HR people around the Colgate World that senior line management was counting on human resources to help them achieve their business objectives. HR heard directly from senior line managers that they were a critical component of the business and needed to contribute more than they had been contributing."

The level of contribution by HR today, based on a partnership with line management, is high. But, says Smith, it can still get better. "My expectation is that HR will continue to integrate itself more seamlessly into the business," he says. "I've always taken the view that we should be invisible, that is, fully integrated into the business. HR has much to offer, but can't be on the sidelines. We've made tremendous progress—today HR leaders are business leaders working through strategic issues and people issues in partnership [with line leaders]. That's a model I hope to expand on."

Certainly, with the world as a workshop, there's plenty of room for HR's global role to grow.

Article Review Form at end of book.

A Guide for Global Training

What components are necessary to put together a complete roster of training classes for building employees' skills in working across national cultural boundaries?

Sylvia Odenwald

"Whether corporations like it or not, they are competing globally," says John Garrison, manager of recruitment and development for Colgate-Palmolive in New York. *The global business environment demands employees who can work effectively across national and cultural boundaries—or who can, in author Kenichi Ohmae's words, manage "in a borderless world." Many international corporations are presenting some form of global management training—most often for managers who are sent on international assignments. Cross-cultural training gets high marks for helping people adjust to assignments in other countries and for improving task performance, according to a study by J. Stewart Black (of Dartmouth's Amos Tuck School of Business) and Mark Mendenhall (of the University of Tennessee's School of Business Administration). Black and Mendenhall examined several studies on the effectiveness of cross-cultural training and found that the training is considered an important tool for successful expatriate assignments.*

Here are some of the outcomes training can produce for companies doing business in a global environment:

- Improve a firm's ability to identify viable business opportunities.
- Avoid wasting resources on ill-conceived ventures.
- Give a company a competitive edge over other global players.
- Improve job satisfaction and retention of overseas staff.
- Prevent lost business due to insensitivity to cultural norms.
- Improve effectiveness in changing business environments.

The secret of effective, cost-efficient cross-cultural training lies in targeting training to the person and the job responsibility.

Cross-cultural training is often described in terms of differing interpersonal behaviors. For example, Americans are said to be direct in approach, specifically expressing what they want, while the Japanese are described as being more circumspect. But global success requires more than an understanding of such differences.

Hal Gregersen of Brigham Young University and Stewart Black have identified underlying traits for success in global settings. Some of these traits can be developed through training; others can't always be "trained in" to a person, but should be considered when choosing people for global assignments.

Some traits for global effectiveness:

- a lack of ethnocentrism
- sociability—the desire to meet and be with people
- an interest in communicating
- the ability and desire to substitute host-country food, customs, and so forth, for home-country ones
- nonauthoritarian leadership styles
- negotiating rather than controlling styles of conflict resolution.

Black and his colleagues at the Tuck school have identified five areas of key cross-cultural differences that can lead to difficulties for people trying to conduct business between countries:

- monetary systems in which the relative values of currencies fluctuate (and with them wages, profits, and other financial indicators)
- legal systems that vary not only in particulars but in underlying assumptions
- political structures that differ in operation and in how they influence and are influenced by business
- market structures that require subtle changes in products and marketing techniques from country to country.

Additionally, the balance of control between corporate headquarters and local business units can be a problem in itself.

Cross-cultural training for corporate executives may be of a general nature, making executives aware of the issues present in global dealings, or it can be country-specific. Language is also an important skill.

Cross-cultural skills entail an understanding of differences in communication and style. Some of them

Copyright July 1993, TRAINING & DEVELOPMENT, American Society for Training and Development. Reprinted with permission. All rights reserved.

may be considered "soft" skills, but that doesn't mean they are unimportant. Failure to understand appropriate and courteous behavior in another country has doomed or endangered many international endeavors. American executives will not pick up such skills in the U.S. education system, in their normal life experiences, or in their business careers. So corporations must provide them with relevant training.

Let's look at examples of the types of global training curriculum used in three corporations. These three case studies are from Intel Corporation, Eastman Kodak, and Procter & Gamble.

Intel Corporation

Intel, a high-technology firm, has manufacturing and sales offices around the world. Each major site has a training organization, with a training manager from the local country.

As Intel has engaged in greater multinational partnerships, one of its major thrusts has been to increase the quality of international relationships and the exchange of information and training technology. Once a year, the training organizations take part in a week-long international training summit. The purpose of the meeting is to decide on a corporate-wide training strategy for the year, as well as to promote communication and relationship-building among the training organizations around the world.

Intel is a culturally diverse company, with a lot of diversity among its engineering and manufacturing talent, both worldwide and within the United States. In 1983 Intel launched its intercultural training program, with the development of multicultural-integration classes for foreign-born professionals. Sharon Richards was appointed intercultural training manager, Intel's first position focused solely on intercultural training.

Intel's global training is offered in five areas:
- intercultural awareness
- multicultural integration
- culture-specific training
- training for international assignments
- intact-team training.

Intercultural Awareness

"The main objective of intercultural training is the development of cross-cultural awareness," says Richards. At Intel, intercultural training for first-line supervisors, midlevel managers, and senior managers is integrated with management topics and business objectives.

"Our goal is to incorporate cross-cultural education into all training," she explains. For example, in a course on how to conduct effective meetings, the trainer would address the ways in which culture influences meeting processes and procedures.

It is impossible to work in a global company without working with people of many different cultures. So, teaching Intel's managers—and all employees—to be culturally aware and sensitive is the first step in the company's intercultural training.

Culture-specific information and lists of "dos and don'ts" are important, but around-the-world expertise is unrealistic. Many managers simply cannot be trained in the culture of every employee they manage. Instead, they must learn what it means to manage various cultures. Then they must develop their ability to know when to seek additional culture-specific information or help.

"Even employees' expectations of their manager are different in different cultures," Richards says. "Some countries expect managers to know how to perform every step of the jobs they supervise. Other cultures see managers as those who provide the tools necessary for their groups to be productive and perform well. So, intercultural awareness is the foundation level of all of our training.

"We want to extend and expand our managers' competencies in culture as well as business areas. In today's global competitive environment, a successful manager or executive must have a global mentality and intercultural skills."

Multicultural Integration

This series of classes developed for foreign-born professionals focuses on communication-skill building and career development. Classes include Accent Improvement, Effective Oral Presentations, Speaking Under Pressure, Technical and Business Writing, American Idioms and Vocabulary in the Workplace, and American Business Culture.

In the Multicultural Integration Workshop, managers who were born and raised in different countries and who have been successful within the company are used as role-model presenters. They discuss their own careers and speak of career planning and personal growth and development.

The workshop also offers an informal environment for individual questions and networking.

Culture-Specific Training

This training focuses on working and doing business in or with people from different cultures, including those from Japan, Israel, the Philippines, Malaysia, Ireland, Korea, and Taiwan. Not only do employees learn about the cultures of these countries, but they also analyze their own cultures. Then they learn how to bridge the communication gap and work together.

Training for International Assignments

Competing in a global environment necessitates worldwide cross-training and business communication, especially given the increasing numbers of joint ventures and business partnerships.

Intel managers going on international assignments—and their families—are given language training and country-specific orientations. The training is usually presented by an external consultant with extensive experience living and working in that country and culture.

Intact-Team Training

This level of training is designed to support business initiatives. When Intel forms a joint venture with a non-U.S. company, training for team members is imperative. The role played by corporate and national cultural differences is often underestimated.

Intel is increasingly incorporating intercultural perspectives into team building. For example, when a group of engineers from Japan was brought to the United States for training, an external consultant who is fluent in Japanese was available to work with them and their families during their stay. The consultant served as their translator and helped teach them English.

The consultant acted as a liaison during meetings and clarified information in one-on-one situations. The consultant was also available for family emergencies; for instance, to speak with hospital employees.

The intercultural support enabled the work team to get off to a fast start and facilitated employee and family adjustment to a culturally different lifestyle.

Richards emphasizes the importance of selecting consultants who provide detailed, comprehensive, culture-specific training.

"The criteria should not only be that they are from that country and know the language and culture. They should also be versed in current business practices. They must be able to apply intercultural theory and training to business situations, needs, and applications. Corporate intercultural training must go beyond the 'surface' culture of food, dress, and language to provide the deeper understanding of individual awareness—how we operate and communicate from our own culture—and how all cultures can best work together."

Intel uses mostly external consultants for its intercultural training. It also leverages that expertise by selecting international employees from its own workforce to present "words of wisdom" and serve as role models in the training sessions. Whenever possible, employees from the focus culture are included in classes to share their perspectives. Increasingly, managers from the home culture are co-teaching with consultants from the target culture, as bicultural training teams.

One of the major trends Richards has noticed in the last year is the increased level of intercultural awareness among Intel managers. "Their willingness and commitment to international training is growing," she says. And within the training organization itself, whenever a new training course is discussed, designers seek cultural input up front so the course can be effective for all employees worldwide.

"Managers must develop a repertoire of skills and must become aware that there is not just one way of operating in a multicultural environment. There may be a preferred way of communication, but individuals do not have to give up their primary cultural values to communicate effectively."

Richards believes that it is often easier to recognize the need for cultural training when the culture is very different from your own. When differences are more subtle—as between Ireland and the United States—questions arise about the need for training. Anyone in the intercultural-training arena hears the debate over emphasizing cultural similarities or cultural differences.

Richards points out that the similarities do not get us into trouble in other cultures, but that differences can cause major problems. "Anyone working in a global workforce must also realize that, unfortunately, no matter how much intercultural training and experience you have had, you will at some time make a 'cultural error.' How you handle the situation, and what you do about it to take the sting out of the words or behavior, its extremely important."

Global training for the multinational corporation must be real-time business training. In fact, it is just-in-time training. Richards says it is difficult to plan what international programs Intel will need six months from now. Change happens fast. Decisions are made quickly.

"We in human resources cannot always anticipate what our company's next business venture will be. An executive walks in and says that we have just signed a joint-venture agreement and need to send 20 employees to a specific country within a few weeks. It may be a national culture that is not already included in our training program.

"The training manager must be flexible enough to know that the best ways of developing and presenting that program may not be possible because of the time constraints. You must be flexible and able to implement what you need when you need it. This is a major challenge in supporting the company's intercultural training needs.

But it is both an incredible challenge and an opportunity."

Eastman Kodak Company

Eastman Kodak has been a multinational corporation for more than 90 years, with marketing and manufacturing operations in 140 international locations. The company has a reputation for being committed to the development of employees through many avenues, one of which is a large investment in training.

Currently, regional marketing offices and major manufacturing plants add up to a total employee population of approximately 133,000. Each region and major plant has responsibility for the training and development of its own managers. The locations generally link their employee-development planning to training resources at their own sites. Most of the training organizations are self-sufficient, but they are free to draw on Kodak's Corporate Executive Education function, as well as the Imaging Training Resources unit in Rochester, New York.

Until now, Kodak has not had a "worldwide human resource plan," says Mary Anne Williams, corporate director of executive education. Instead, "a decentralized, customized approach has been our strategy."

The company provides cross-cultural training as needed, in most cases to employees or units that are conducting business in other countries or planning to work abroad. The training ranges from language instruction to cultural and business immersion training for expatriates and their families.

For the past six years, Corporate Education has provided a five-segment program, International Business Operations, which includes a lot of time spent on cross-cultural awareness and skills. The program is targeted at professionals and managers who are in the early stages of interacting with non-U.S. operations and customers.

"With increasing emphasis on globalization in all three Kodak sectors (Imaging, Health, and Chemicals), we are seeing an increase in the number of international and cross-cultural learning initiatives," Williams says.

"For example, the Chemicals Group is currently committing a significant amount of time to cross-cultural training for its entire management team. This team of approximately 50 managers has attended a five-day program focusing on countries in the Asia/Pacific region. Additionally, it will be launching study trips to selected countries in Asia for in-depth learning, focused on strategic issues."

Chairman Kay R. Whitmore has led a group of Kodak's corporate executives—including all three sector presidents, their leadership teams, and staff executive vice-presidents—in two- to three-day management conferences focusing on dimensions of globalization. The faculty for the conferences has come from the United States and abroad. Whitmore is also sponsoring six executive forums in Japan, bringing in world-renowned speakers to further develop global mindsets among the senior leaders. Study trips will probably follow the forums.

"In the case of corporate-sponsored events like management conferences and executive forums, the design originated from within Kodak, and the delivery is made by worldwide faculty. All of the events are work/action oriented, not lecture or strictly case-based learning," Williams explains.

Corporate Executive Education also runs a two-and-a-half week corporate program for high-potential middle managers from all three sectors of the corporation. The focus is on broadening their knowledge and skills as general managers, with a decidedly global tone.

For every Kodak management program held in the United States, two are held in a non-U.S. location, to take advantage of international political and economic developments, faculties, and business speakers.

"A management program was held in Brussels in 1992, and a heavy emphasis was placed on issues and opportunities emerging from the formation of the EEC," says Williams. "For such programs, we bring in senior Kodak executives as speakers, exposing participants to both corporate and regional strategies and cross-cultural issues, and reinforcing a vision of our global firm."

Whether you are providing training to individual expatriates and operating teams, or providing support for a long-haul cultural-change process, Williams' advice is about the same.

"Start where your customers' needs start. Identify what practical issues are on their minds and satisfy those needs with action-oriented learning. It won't be long before longer-range cultural issues present themselves, and the customer will desire to learn more about the culture, customs, language, and even the strategic mind of the country or region.

"Beginning with the seemingly esoteric information can be a big turn-off, unless the customer buys in to and really understands the value of total-immersion techniques. Normally, we find customers turned off by too much too soon. A sensitive needs analysis up front is absolutely essential.

"The second most important factor is to think of this kind of learning as a progressive journey, not one-time training."

Procter & Gamble

Procter & Gamble has subsidiaries in 50 countries around the world. Thirty are manufacturing sites; the other locations are for advertising, financial, and sales functions.

Before 1979, P&G used a common 1970s model for sending U.S. employees to international subsidiaries. The U.S. employees managed a site and trained local employees until the local employees became proficient in their jobs. Then the U.S. employees turned the operation over to them and returned home. American managers were selected for international assignments on the basis of technical competence and availability. Another criterion was the ability to persuade others that the assignment would be best for the company and the manager.

That model is no longer used at Procter & Gamble. The corporation found that it is more efficient to train local employees in the technology as they manage their own site.

In 1979, Procter & Gamble initiated strategic planning for a major technology transfer to Japan. With the help of external consultants, the company developed a three-pronged approach to multicultural training:

- U.S. employees were given the opportunity to learn the Japanese language, and Japanese employees were given the opportunity to learn English.

- Cross-cultural training was presented for employees in both Japan and the United States.

- All employees were given training in P&G's corporate culture, to provide a common base of operations.

This leading-edge approach is time- and labor-intensive. But it has been a major factor in the success of the company's Japanese operations.

In 1992, P&G had a total employee population of 100,000; about 1,000 of these were expatriates around the world.

Most of P&G's standard training curriculum is adopted worldwide. The local training staffs adapt the courses and present them locally.

"So often human resource professionals want a checklist on global training issues; it just doesn't work that way," says Mike Copeland, international training and development manager. "International company needs are in continual flux, and employees in a multicultural environment are also adapting and changing.

"As companies become more global and employees spend more time working in other cultures, the lines between the cultures become less distinct. If you are training someone from Europe on how to do business with Americans, do you present the cultural nuances of New York, California, Minnesota, or Texas? Even American culture differs according to region."

Copeland believes that one of the critical problems with multicultural training is that results data are nonexistent.

"It is so hard to prove that cross-cultural training improves performance and productivity. If increased employee success and productivity from this training could be measured, then training departments would have criteria to sell the importance of multicultural training to top management. A control group should be set up and provided with cross-cultural training and then compared to a group that is not given this training.

"Of course, the study would need to include pretraining testing and posttraining testing and an evaluation at the end of an expat assignment. This type of training evaluation is always difficult, but it would be very valuable."

The faster a company can have indigenous training in the local country organization, the more effective that training will be, says Copeland.

"You cannot run a successful training program from the United States alone," Copeland says. "The best training is localized and run by managers from that country. As multicultural training opportunities increase, I believe there will be more emphasis on multinational effectiveness and big-picture training in specific cultures for more employees.

"Also, we do not do a good job of using our successful expats as a cadre to train others in the skills they have learned. Usually, after their transfer back to home base, they are immediately absorbed into the workforce, and the value of their experience is lost to other corporate employees. Unfortunately, this is true in many other corporations as well.

"Another point that corporations often miss is the preparation the receiving organization should make before an expat is transferred or a manager travels to that location. Just as the individual is prepared for the culture change, so the receiving site should be prepared with specific expectations and outcomes of the transfer.

"It would be interesting if companies would design a 'time off for good behavior' model. The expatriates would have the responsibility to recruit and develop their replacements. Then when the replacements performed at the same level of competence, the expats would return to home base. If a successful transfer was made in record time, then the expats could be rewarded with an early return to the home base."

International Training for Competition

With so much at stake, from the success of business negotiations to the effective operation of global subsidiaries or joint ventures, companies have little rationale for failing to invest time and money in training employees who must work in a global workforce. The training costs are small, compared to the potential costs of early returns from expatriate assignments—and compared to business losses due to the lack of multicultural competency.

As with any large-scale training, top-management support is imperative. Senior executives must start initiating and supporting company-wide global-training programs.

In addition to the gains in productivity and profits, corporations may want to consider the issue from a social perspective as well.

"The military trains its soldiers before sending them into battle," say Black and Mendenhall. "Churches educate and train their missionaries before sending them out to proselytize, and governments train secret agents before they go under 'deep' cover. But U.S. firms send employees overseas cold."

Such a sink-or-swim approach would seem irresponsible and unreasonable to the military, the clergy, and most governments. Why, then, does it seem logical to businesses?

If U.S. firms are to compete successfully in what is becoming a global battleground, they must provide their employees with the ammunition and weapons necessary to fight effective and victorious campaigns.

Article Review Form at end of book.

How does a company develop global managers who are able to complete global assignments and use their international expertise within the firm once they are repatriated?

Developing Global Managers

Stephen Gates

One of the most important HR activities is management development. Today, however, the HR function must incorporate in its general management development activity the special task of developing *global* managers. This consists primarily of three activities: assignment planning for international positions; ensuring that the entire global assignment cycle is a success; and utilizing and retaining managers with international experience upon repatriation.

Yet evidence shows that the gap between rhetoric and reality is very wide:

- According to recent surveys, nearly half of all firms continue to reduce the number of expatriates (U.S. firms more so than European or Japanese).[4]

- A survey of U.S. expatriates found 80 percent felt their international experience was not valued by their company.[5]

- More alarming still, a recent study revealed that 77 percent of U.S., 43 percent of Japanese, and 54 percent of Finnish expatriate managers were actually demoted after returning from a global assignment.[6]

- Twenty percent of U.S. managers sent abroad fail even though they are selected precisely because of their prior business and technical success.[7]

For most firms, global assignments remain a fire-fighting exercise to fix an immediate problem, not an investment of strategic value. Moreover, much of the attention given to global managers focuses on salaries rather than on utilizing valuable international experience. Expatriates generally receive substantial monetary rewards. Estimates of average annual expatriate expense are between $150,000 and $250,000, or up to $1 million over a typical four-year posting. This investment seems especially wasteful when compared with the rate of attrition. Among U.S. firms, 20 percent of repatriated managers leave their company within one year, and rates as high as 40 to 50 percent within three years have been reported.[8] While the short-term cost of the expatriate payroll may be cut back slightly, the true long-term strategic cost of lost global expertise may be very high indeed.

Strategic Role of Global Assignments

If the human resource function is to play a significant role in implementing global strategy, it must accept responsibility for managing global assignments as long-term investments. More often, however, they are treated as a short-term concern (see box, p. 157, comparing the two approaches). In the more common tactical-reactive approach, the most technically suitable manager is chosen under a severe time constraint. Moreover, the company has little concern for training, performance evaluation or repatriation.

HR Guidelines for Developing Global Managers

- Develop a strategic approach to international assignments and avoid succumbing to a reactive, hasty selection decision.

- Increase predeparture and in-country language and cross-cultural training for the expatriate, as well as for the spouse and the entire family.

- Modify the performance evaluation system to incorporate the distinctive conditions of the local country.

- Send strong signals that international experience is critical for promotion to top management.

- Set up a repatriation team for each expatriate consisting of the expatriate's supervisor, an expatriate who has returned from the region, and a corporate HR professional. Plan the specific return position to be consistent with the original strategic purpose of the global assignment.

"Developing Global Managers," in *The Changing Global Role of the Human Resource Function: A Research Report.* Stephen Gates. THE CONFERENCE BOARD, Report Number 1062-94-RR, 1994. Reprinted by permission.

In companies with the long-run approach, global assignments can play three strategic roles: management development, coordination and control, and information sharing and exchange.[9]

Management Development

In many companies, the highest priority goes to management development. To build global strategy formulation capability, future top managers must have worked outside their home country. Middle managers must also work in global markets with customers, suppliers and competitors. Corporate home country managers may transfer to subsidiaries to learn how to operate abroad and to gain specific expertise, while regional or local managers may transfer to corporate headquarters to learn how the company works, as well as to be evaluated.

Coordination and Control

The second strategic role takes on increasing importance as more firms expand their overseas operations. The trend is for global corporations to build more dispersed production and marketing organizations but to integrate them more tightly through better transportation and communication. Such efforts can pit subsidiary managers against headquarters, product or functional managers. As subsidiaries mature and gain significant resources of their own, in terms of capital, technology and market access, headquarter controls take more indirect and informal forms, such as manager transfers, assignments, careers and meetings.[10] Subsidiary managers can then share objectives and execute global strategy with less resistance.

Information Sharing and Exchange

The third strategic role of global assignments has particular importance in technology-driven firms. Since learning a technological process is difficult to encode in blueprints, a global assignment allows the manager sufficient time to assimilate, synthesize and transfer complex information. It also gives the manager time to develop rapport and trust at the host site to facilitate future information exchanges across geographical and organizational boundaries.

How Important Are Global Assignments?

Although managers may agree with the strategic goals of international assignments, are such assignments important to careers? Survey results show that HR managers feel such assignments are most important for top managers. Fewer respondents feel they are significant to subsidiary manager and young manager development.

Top Managers

Forty-three percent of HR professionals believe that international experience is a highly important factor in filling top management posts, and this figure may reflect a positive bias on the part of HR professionals (see Table 1 on p. 158). In a recent survey, 65 percent of HR professionals indicate that they believe international assignments have a positive career feedback,[11] but, in another survey, 77 percent of expatriates on assignment think they have a negative impact.[12] Top management can respond by sending a powerful signal that international experience is an important consideration in filling senior positions.

Strategic-Systematic vs. Tactical-Reactive Approach

Strategic-Systematic Approach: Global Assignment Is a Long-Term Investment	Tactical-Reactive Approach: Global Assignment Is Short-Term Expense
• Develops future executives with essential global perspectives and experiences to formulate and implement competitive strategies. • Increases the effectiveness of critical coordination and control functions between the home country and international operations. • Increases the volume and efficiency of international knowledge, technology and innovation transfers throughout a firm.	• Focuses on quick-fix approach to a short-term problem in a foreign country. • Randomly and haphazardly performs some functions outlined in the strategic-systematic approach to global assignments.

Source: *Global Assignments: Successfully Expatriating and Repatriating International Managers*, J. Stewart Black, Hal B. Gregersen, Mark Mendenhall. (San Francisco: Jossey-Bass Publishers), 1992.

National Subsidiary Managers

Only 20 percent of HR professionals believe that international experience is important. Yet managers with international experience are more likely to support the global strategy and promote it at the local level.

Young Managers

Only 12 percent of HR professionals consider international experience highly important for young managers. However, by programming early transfers, a company creates a flexible group of global managers more willing to accept and successfully execute a global assignment later. Managers also gain important cross-cultural skills early in their careers. Credit Lyonnais is an example of a company committed to promoting international experience among its young managers (see box on p. 158). Early international transfers, however, can pose a tradeoff, especially for U.S. firms. Upon return, often these young, highly marketable managers move to competitor firms.

Selection and Succession Planning

In the tactical-reactive approach, selection for global assignments often occurs under extreme time constraints. When a technically qualified manager is immediately available,

Table 1	Importance of International Experience By Percentage of Respondents Who Rate It Highly
Top management position	43%
National subsidiary manager	20
Young managers	12

Note: Only 20% of respondents to The Conference Board survey consider a young manager with less than three years' experience eligible for an international transfer (N=133).

Promoting International Experience for Young Managers

Credit Lyonnais, the largest bank in Europe with a network of 3,500 branches, has initiated a program to promote international experience among its young managers: the Credit Lyonnais International Program (CLIP). The bank now offers young graduates with less than five years of experience in the company the opportunity to enhance their skills in familiar spheres of activity in another country. Exchanges between European subsidiaries for 40 young people have already been organized by the Group Human Resources Division. The program should be expanded out of Europe in 1994.

CLIP contributes to developing synergies and enriching the culture within the Group Credit Lyonnais. CLIP participants broaden their approach to business, and their skills, built on international experience, facilitate their access to higher levels of responsibility in the future. Furthermore, non-French young managers assigned to the parent company learn about its procedures, techniques or new activities to the benefit of the unit of origin.

For Credit Lyonnais, internationalization of management has become a priority activity. The expatriate French corps now numbers 380, while non-French expatriates should soon double to 200.

---

line managers terminate their search right away. Only when such a candidate is not readily available are they likely to involve the human resource function, to define the required skills and appropriate performance measurements, and to extend the search throughout the company, both internationally and domestically. Indeed, survey results show that HR determines the required qualifications for the international position only 30 percent of the time. Involving HR, however, increases the likelihood of uncovering one or more technically qualified managers who also possess superior cross-cultural adaptation and communication skills.[13]

When the company institutes a strategic-systematic approach, each global assignment is analyzed for its potential to advance global executive development, coordination and control, and information exchange. The skills, knowledge and experience of the manager is matched with the primary purpose of the assignment. Different selection criteria come into play according to the objective of the assignment:

- *Global executive development* calls for advancement potential and experience within the firm.

- *Coordination and control* requires broad experience in the firm, including a wide network of contacts throughout the company.

- *Information exchange* benefits most from relevant headquarters experience and superior cross-cultural communication skills to facilitate information flow from the subsidiary to the headquarters.

To date, most studies of the selection process reveal a lack of identification of strategic goals and the corresponding appropriate skills and inconsistency among the desired criteria.[14] While adaptation traits, such as flexibility, tolerance, and interpersonal skills rank high, business and technical skills rank first among the reasons for selecting a particular manager for a global assignment. To a degree, this reflects the conflict between objectives designed for short-term success and long-term strategic goals. (See box on p. 159 for an outline of the best practices for a global selection process). Within the strategic-systematic approach, the focus widens to include technical and cross-cultural skills as well as family considerations. Multiple selection methods and criteria are also used.

A recurrent theme among corporate HR managers is that subsidiary managers hide their best talent for fear they will be swept up into the company's global system. Meanwhile, corporate HR managers argue that if high potentials are not offered global opportunities they will leave for better advancement opportunities. One solution to this problem is to require subsidiary managers to submit lists of high potentials and to reward them for developing these managers. When global assignments become available, the human resource group has available a list of talent. Another means of uncovering talent is to enable subsidiary managers to reward their best performers with stock options and then track who receives awards.

Preparation/Training

The next step in the global assignment cycle is the preparation and training of managers selected for an expatriate assignment. Many expatriate managers consider predeparture training to be absolutely essential to improve overseas performance. Nevertheless, only 32 percent of U.S. firms conduct international training programs compared with 57 percent of Japanese companies and 69 percent of European countries.[15] This lack of predeparture training may contribute to the higher rate of failure of U.S. expatriates relative to Japanese and European expatriates.

Respondents indicate that language training is the most frequently provided preparation for international managers (60 percent), after visits to host country subsidiary (77 percent) (see Chart 3 on p. 160). Only 45 percent of companies make language instruction available to all family members and only 32 percent provide families with cross-cultural training (see Chart 4 on p. 160).

Global Assignment Selection Process

1. *Create the selection team.*
   Team members should include home and host country managers and a human resource manager. The home country manager should be designated as the expatriate's sponsor.

2. *Define strategic purpose for global assignment.*
   Global executive development, coordination and control, information exchange.

3. *Assess the global assignment content.*
   The more interaction required with local nationals, the more important cross-cultural and language skills will be.

4. *Establish appropriate selection criteria.*
   Technical, advancement potential, cross-cultural skills, ethnocentricity.

5. *Define the candidate pool.*
   Via referrals, internal job postings, global candidate database.

6. *Utilize multiple selection methods.*
   Assessment center, standardization tests, preselection interviews.

7. *Interview expatriate and spouse.*
   Outline strategic purpose of assignment and career path of potential expatriate. Determine unique dual-career and family needs. Provide realistic preview of job and living overseas.

8. *Make global assignment offer.*
   Base it on relevant, factual and comprehensive information.

9. *Transition into training program.*
   The selection should be well enough in advance to initiate appropriate training and preparation.

Adapted from *Global Assignments: Successfully Expatriating and Repatriating Managers*, J. Stewart Black, Hal B. Gregersen, Mark Mendenhall. (San Francisco: Jossey-Bass Publishers), 1992.

Cross-Cultural Training

Research has shown that cross-cultural training programs improve expatriates' job performance, adjustment to the new culture, and development of cross-cultural skills.[16] However, cross-cultural training (offered by 43 percent of companies) often consists of watching films, reading books, and talking with people who have visited the country. Rarely do companies employ substantial, skills-oriented, cross-cultural training.

Only 18 percent of firms provide cross-cultural training once a manager arrives in the host country. In-country training can be beneficial since the manager's motivation at that point is often higher, and he or she has immediate opportunities to apply training and has some familiarity with his or her new environment. A best practice recommendation is to provide survival-level instruction prior to departure, with more cultural training once the expatriate is in the country.[17]

Managers should also vary the amount of cross-cultural training according to the assignment. Three important factors should determine the degree of training: the difficulty of dealing with the culture, the job itself, and the required communication level. Clearly, more cross-cultural training is necessary when there is a greater difference in culture, more job difficulty in terms of demands and constraints, and a high degree of interaction with local employees.

The Importance of the Family

Ignoring the family when sending out a manager is risky. One of the most common reasons cited for expatriate failure is the spouse's inability to adjust to a foreign environment.[18] To minimize this possibility, the human resource function can initiate several actions:

- Multiple interviews to determine whether the spouse is dissatisfied about accompanying an international transfer. Only 8 percent of respondents indicate this practice in their companies.

- Psychological testing to assess spousal cross-cultural adaptability. Only 3 percent of responding companies conduct such testing.

- Assist spouse in finding employment abroad. Only 20 percent of respondents currently offer such assistance. Companies could also reimburse spouses for education or business activities.

- Finally, if spouses do not wish to alter their present career path, the global assignment might be shortened or include frequent visits back to the home country.

Performance Evaluation

Expatriate performance evaluation has receive little research attention, though some guidelines for improving the process do exist.[19] While the performance appraisal system should be linked to global strategy implementation, it should also reflect the most significant local country differences. In effect, an expatriate should not be punished by a performance evaluation system that fails to incorporate distinctive conditions of the local country. In addition, poor evaluations are often due to a lack of communication between expatriates and their managers in the home office as well as to a lack of international experience among home country managers. To mitigate these factors, HR managers can:

- Recommend how to adjust evaluations to reflect the level of difficulty of an assignment. Difficulty can be assessed in terms of the firm's operational language, the "cultural" distance of the region, and the stability of factors affecting the expatriate's performance (e.g., exchange rate). A simple rule-of-thumb difficulty factor can be multiplied by the performance evaluation rating.

- Delay first performance evaluation since adaptation to the local country takes at least three to six months.

- Encourage more objectivity in the evaluation. Typically, the home-site manager continues to write the actual performance evaluation. It is more effective for the on-site manager to write the evaluation in consultation with the home-site manager. Another strategy is to incorporate on-site managers' viewpoints into evaluation.

Chart 3*
Preparation of Expatriate Managers
By Percentage of Respondents Who Undertake This Activity

- Organize visits to host country subsidiary: 77%
- Provide language training: 60%
- Provide cross-cultural training: 43%

N=158

Chart 4
Preparation of Expatriate Managers
By Percentage of Respondents Who Undertake This Activity

- Provide language training for family: 45%
- Provide cross-cultural training for family: 32%
- Assist spouse to find employment abroad: 20%
- Spouses undergo psychological testing: 3%

N=158

*Note: Charts 1 and 2 do not appear in this publication.

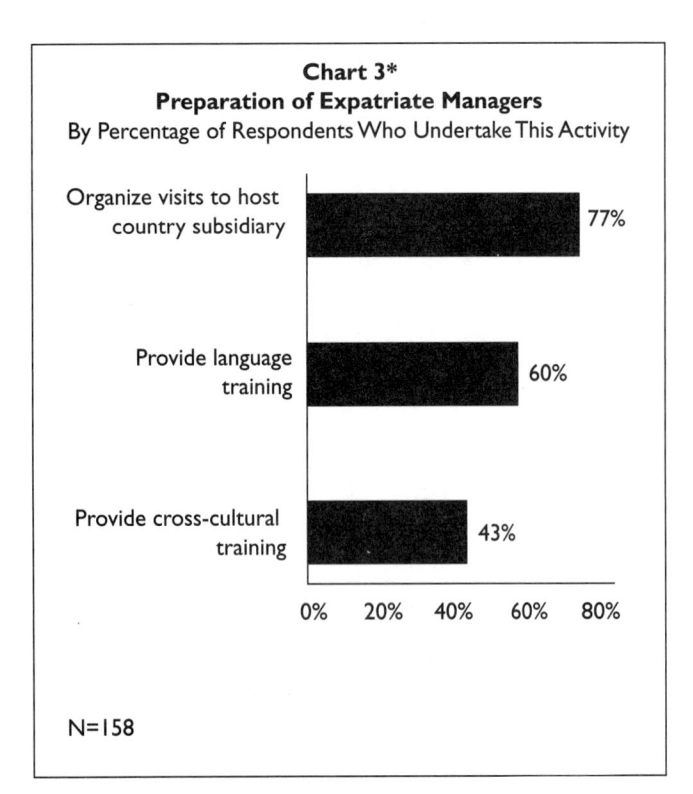

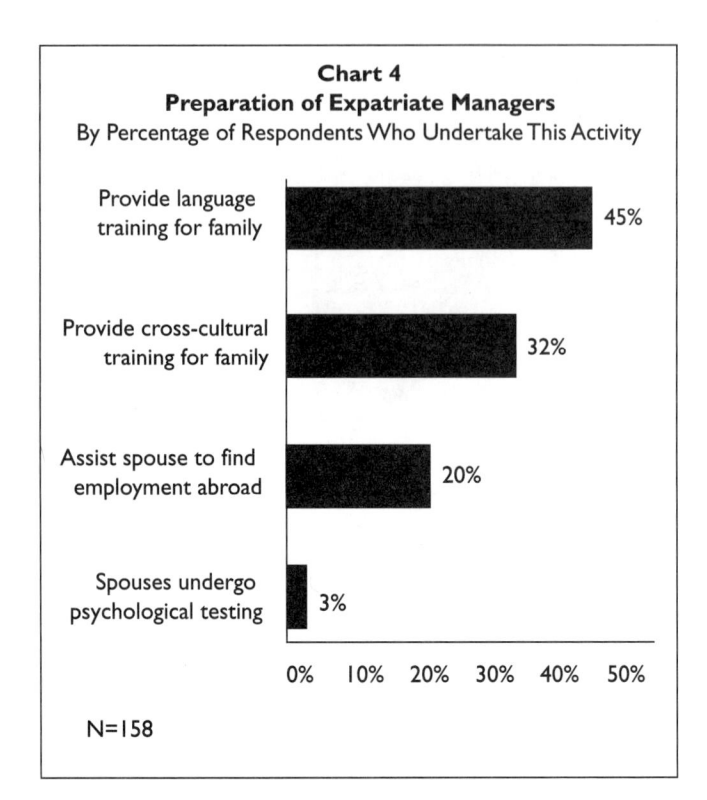

- Performance criteria should be modified according to the local country environment. For example, in a country where strikes are common, success in labor negotiations should be measured.

- Lastly, an expatriate's insights and observations should be solicited periodically and taken into account in the final evaluation.

Repatriation

In terms of global assignments, selection and deployment of the manager have been viewed as the most important considerations. Return planning, however, is just as key. Lack of planning can affect international assignments in many ways. For example, "war stories" of disgruntled repatriates can cause other managers to turn down offers. Moreover, managers think twice about accepting such assignments especially when there is no guarantee of a return job. In a recent survey, 68 percent of expatriates report high uncertainty concerning what their return position would be.[20] Even more common, expatriates are overlooked for promotions in the home country.

Table 2 HR Preparation for Repatriation
By Percentage of Respondents Who Undertake This Activity

Systematically considers expatriates' eligibility for home office positions	43%
Actively plans expatriates' return to specific, identified home positions	20
Guarantee expatriates a return job by contract	12
Pairs expatriates with mentors	11

N=158

The human resource function can ease the return of expatriate managers in several ways (see Table 2). The most common practice, found in 43 percent of responding firms, is to consider systematically the expatriate's eligibility for home office positions. Less frequently do companies identify a specific position at home office and actively plan for the expatriate's re-entry into it (20 percent of firms). Even less common is guaranteeing the expatriate a return job by contract (12 percent of companies). The most infrequent activity is to pair expatriates with mentors at the home office. In these cases, the mentor helps plan for the expatriate's re-entry by trying to locate suitable positions along with the HR group.

A manager of a U.S. subsidiary of a European company observes that headquarters often selects return assignments with only executive development in mind. However, identifying a specific position should be accomplished with a clear sense of the global assignment's strategic purpose:

- For executive development, the return assignment logically should be a critical next step in developing skills and knowledge.

- To increase coordination and control, the return assignment should use the expatriates' foreign contacts for headquarters-subsidiary coordination and control.

- To transfer information and technology, the next home assignment should be in the home-country unit, which would benefit most from receiving the information and technology.

In all cases, global expertise should be utilized whenever possible. A repatriation team can include the expatriate, an HR representative and the expatriate's supervisor in the home country. This is even more beneficial when the HR representative has experienced expatriation and repatriation personally.

Greater attention should be focused on returning expatriates at higher risk for poor readjustment. These include ex-patriates and spouses who return from extended international experience, or those who return from a region very different from the home country. Special efforts, such as home-country visits, pre-return training and orientation, home-country information sources, and sponsors ease such returns. Finally, if expatriates cannot find suitable positions on return, it can be extremely destabilizing to the entire global management effort. When requesting that senior management review the severance package of the returning expatriates, the human resource manager can take the opportunity to explain the consequences of such an important decision.

Retaining the Returning Expatriate

An important advantage for the company as a whole is to retain the knowledge gained by returning expatriates. A debriefing session with senior managers is one method. A second is more permanent written or recorded documentation. In both cases, the returning expatriate should be asked to serve as a mentor for future managers.

One way to retain expatriate knowledge is to provide incentives for such managers to stay with the company; for example, make international experience, perspectives and skills major criteria for advancement. The company's culture should also reflect the shared value of global assignments.

The ultimate purpose of global assignment management is to provide a pool of international managers as a company expands worldwide. One of the primary activities of the global HR role, international executive development, has become both more challenging and more important to successful strategy implementation. The global HR function should advocate more international experience among management and assume the role of planning and executing each step of the global assignment cycle.

Notes

Note: footnotes 1–3 do not appear in this publication.

4. Berenbeim, R. E., *Managing the International Company: Building a Global Perspective,* The Conference Board, 1982, p. v. Kobrin, S. J., *International Expertise in American Business,* New York: Institute of International Education, 1984, p. 43. *Global Assignments: Successfully Expatriating and Repatriating International Managers,* p. 237.
5. "When Yankee Comes Home: Repatriation and Adjustment of U.S. Managers."
6. *Global Assignments: Successfully Expatriating and Repatriating International Managers,* p. 23.
7. *Global Assignments: Successfully Expatriating and Repatriating International Managers,* p. 11.
8. *Global Assignments: Successfully Expatriating and Repatriating International Managers,* p. 14.
9. *Global Assignments: Successfully Expatriating and Repatriating International Managers,* pp. 3–32.
10. C. Prahalad, and Y. Doz, "An Approach to Strategic Control in Multinational Companies," Sloan Management Review, Vol. 22, No. 4, Summer 1981.
11. H. Gregersen, J. Black, and J. Hite, "Performance Appraisal Practices for Expatriates in U.S. and Canadian Firms." Paper presented at the Academy of International Business meeting. Maui, Hawaii, 1993.
12. "When Yankee Comes Home: Repatriation and Adjustment of U.S. Managers."
13. E. Miller, "The International Selection Decision: A Study of Managerial Behavior in the Selection Decision Process," *Academy of Management Journal,* Vol. 16, No. 2, 1973, pp. 239–252.
14. The Economist Intelligence Unit, *The Quest for the International Manager,* Special Report No. 2098, London, 1991.
15. R. Tung, "Selecting and Training of Personnel for Overseas Assignments," *Columbia Journal of World Business,* Vol. 16, No. 1, 1991, pp. 68–78.
16. J. Black and M. Mendenhall, "Cross-Cultural Training Effectiveness: A Review and Theoretical Framework for Future Research," *Academy of Management Review,* 1990, pp. 15, 113–136.
17. *Global Assignments: Successfully Expatriating and Repatriating International Managers,* pp. 90–114.
18. R. Tung, *The New Expatriates: Managing Human Resources Abroad.* (New York: Ballinger), 1988.
19. G. Oddou, and M. Mendenhall, eds., "Expatriate Performance Appraisal: Problems and Solutions," Readings and Cases in International Human Resource Management (Boston: PWS-Kent), 1991.
20. "When Yankee Comes Home: Repatriation Adjustment of U.S. Managers."

Article Review Form at end of book.

What does a global human resources and training department need to know to avoid sexual discrimination liability and increase the company's chances for harassment-free business relationships?

When Sexual Harassment Is a Foreign Affair

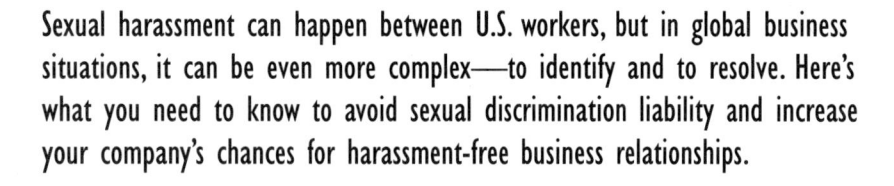

Sexual harassment can happen between U.S. workers, but in global business situations, it can be even more complex—to identify and to resolve. Here's what you need to know to avoid sexual discrimination liability and increase your company's chances for harassment-free business relationships.

Wendy Hardman and Jacqueline Heidelberg

Scenario #1: Sandra Whitney is on a three-year, career-enhancing assignment in Mexico for her company and finds herself the target of unwanted sexual attention from her new male manager—a citizen of the host country. Whitney complains to a female co-worker (who's also a citizen), but is told this behavior is "normal." When the behavior persists after Whitney has made it clear she isn't interested, she consults with the human resources manager in her host country. She finds there are not laws protecting women from sexual harassment on the job, although she's assured that her company's policy and the U.S. laws will be maintained.

Scenario #2: Connie Bosworth in working on a team with several men from Europe who have been sent to the United States for six months. Bosworth finds these mens' flirtatious language and gestures charming and endearing, but she feels ambivalent because she realizes that if an American man said the same things to her, it wouldn't be acceptable. Are Europeans bound by the same rules?

Sexual Discrimination Is a Little-Discussed Problem in Cross-Cultural Relationships

Both of the scenarios above, and other tales of sexual discrimination, are realistic for today's multinational companies and the emerging global workplace. In the past five years alone, the number of female expatriates of U.S. companies has more than doubled according to a recent news item in *The Wall Street Journal* on September 5, 1995. New York City-based Windham International, which conducted the survey, predicts the number of expatriate women will reach 20% (of all U.S. expatriates) by the year 2000. In addition, the U.S. workforce is ethnically and culturally more diverse than ever and this trend is expected to continue. As we struggle to understand and negotiate both the subtle and more complicated issues related to sexual harassment in our domestic marketplace, we also must be aware of the added concerns of working overseas with co-workers, customers and vendors of many different nationalities.

To find out what individuals and organizations experience in the international marketplace, we asked several companies to share their stories. As consultants with extensive backgrounds in human resources management and cross-cultural business settings, we also reviewed what has been written on the subject. A key question we posed: "What have you encountered as far as sexual harassment incidents that occurred between people of two different cultures, whether they were employees, customers, vendors or clients?"

While exploring this relatively uncharted territory, several corporate human resources executives from multinational organizations told us we'd have trouble getting any information. Because of the potentially liability, and the potential threat to an organization's image, they suggested that candid responses would be scarce. Indeed, the most frequent response we got was

---

"When Sexual Harassment Is a Foreign Affair" by Wendy Hardman and Jacqueline Heidelberg, copyright April 1996. Used with permission of ACC Communications, Inc./*Personnel Journal* (now known as *Workforce*), Costa Mesa, CA. All rights reserved.

that companies had limited experience with the issue, and therefore, they had little to report. The topic of sexual harassment is one that many organizations find difficult to address. And when it's complicated by cross-cultural issues, it becomes even more foreboding.

In fact, several organizations refused to return our calls or stated that they didn't want to participate. Some respondents, including human resources managers at Akron, Ohio-based The Goodyear Tire & Rubber Co. and Chicago-based Amoco Corp., stated they either have had "no incidents" or none that couldn't be handled at the local level.

Is this possible for firms having thousands of employees working both domestically and internationally? Yes, but it's highly unlikely. At Wilmington, Delaware-based E. I. du Pont de Nemours (DuPont), a company noted for its work in sexual harassment training, there were no reported cases of sexual harassment internationally that have reached HR representatives at the corporate level. Bob Hamilton, a diversity consultant with DuPont, conceded that there may have been some situations, but they would have been handled as close to the front lines as possible. He added that third party cases of sexual harassment aren't rare, but DuPont doesn't keep records of these events.

George Krock, manager of EEO and selection at Pittsburgh-based PPG Industries Inc., told us: "In the last couple of years, there have been four incidents involving employees of PPG: two in North America, one in Asia and one in Europe." Similar numbers were quoted by a senior human resources manager in a large pharmaceuticals company: Approximately one to four sexual harassment complaints are filed each year internationally.

Both of these corporations (typical of an increasing number of multinational organizations) employ tens of thousands of employees outside the United States—although many are citizens of the host country. Philadelphia-based SmithKline Beecham, for example, operates in nearly 80 countries and currently has approximately 250 expatriates. When you consider that there are many more expatriate women these days, the actual number of cases of sexual harassment globally seems surprisingly small. Have we triumphed over sexual harassment in cross-cultural settings? Have employers managed to eliminate "unwelcome conduct of a sexual nature," not to mention ridding their workplaces of "hostile or intimidating environments?" Are individuals in cross-cultural work environments more careful, better informed and generally more respectful of each other?

That's certainly one possibility. More believable, however, is the interpretation by one head of international HR for several financial-service organizations over the last several years. He suggests that companies might not have accurate information to report because employees are cautious about disclosing sexual harassment incidents—particularly when they occur cross-culturally. There are many reasons for this. One is the problem that sexual harassment is often under-reported, understated or trivialized—regardless of where it occurs or who's involved. Jim Yates, manager of human resources for international operations with Amoco, says another problem may be the desirability of the overseas assignment. "People may not want to jeopardize their jobs," he says. These positions are highly valued, sometimes taking years to attain.

Training Employees about Cultural Differences Before International Assignments May Help Avert Problems

Craig Pratt, of Craig Pratt and Associates based in Alameda, California, is an investigator of sexual harassment complaints for San Francisco Bay Area companies. Having been an expert witness in 40 sexual harassment court battles over the past four years, he finds that a disproportionate number of cross-cultural sexual harassment complaints involve perpetrators and victims from differing ethnic, racial or national-origin groups. He often has thought about the complexity presented by sexual harassment situations in cross-cultural contexts. His experiences strongly support the idea that when individuals from two different cultures interact, the potential for problems with sexual harassment is greater, not smaller.

Cultural relativism—the notion that ethics, values and behavior are a function of culture—is one way to understand, and perhaps to dismiss, the issue. In fact, all of the HR and international managers we spoke to raised the notion of a cultural context as central to the discussion. Pratt frequently encounters situations which might be better understood (although not necessarily forgiven) when cultural frameworks are considered. What's acceptable in one culture may be disrespectful and confusing in another. What U.S. citizens may construe as sexually provocative or offensive, for example, isn't shared by most—or even many—cultures.

Bill Ferra, director of U.S. management and development services for Heinz USA in Pittsburgh, reports that Europeans think Americans are "crazy" with all of our laws about sexual harassment. Some behaviors that deeply violate norms of U.S. culture may not be perceived as a problem in another cultural context. In many Mediterranean and Latin countries, physical contact and sensuality are a common part of socializing. For example, one Brazilian senior HR executive was surprised when he was admonished for calling the women at work "girls." While this label was appropriate and acceptable in his native culture, he wasn't aware it was insulting to North American women and could contribute to a "hostile or intimidating work environment" by U.S. standards.

Rudiger Daunke, VP of international HR for Bausch & Lomb Inc. based in Rochester, New York, notes that U.S. citizens proceed carefully in their cross-cultural relationships abroad because of cultural differences. The organizations we surveyed unanimously agreed that the incidence of sexual harassment across cultures can be diminished with adequate cultural preparation of employees. Interestingly, many international companies have such programs in place.

Bill Mossett, vice president and director of employee relations and diversity for SmithKline Beecham, says its program *Managing Transculturally*, is currently being rolled out for managers with assignments in the United

States and the United Kingdom. This newly instituted program has both a general component as well as culture-specific information. Theoretically, managers might go through it three or four times during their careers—each time they go on assignment to a different country.

Similarly, Amoco offers its expatriates and spouses a two- to three-day, cross-cultural program. The topics covered include such issues as social behaviors, relationships, titles, dining practices and American perceptions. In addition, once a U.S. expatriate is in the host country, he or she receives another cultural orientation.

While this cross-cultural training is a proactive measure that helps diminish the potential for cultural misunderstandings between men and women, it may be inadequate and limited. None of the programs surveyed includes specific information about sexual harassment or sexual discrimination. Moreover, many U.S. companies don't offer standalone sexual harassment training (although it's sometimes included as part of diversity awareness training) for their domestic employees. Such training is rarer still for host-country nationals. One exception, DuPont, reports that as many as 90% of its domestic employees have attended sexual-harassment training. In addition, the company says most of its offshore leaders have participated, as well as its international employees on assignment in the United States. But this is rarely the case.

When sexual harassment training is provided, the content is specific to the laws and customs of the United States, *not* to the international destinations of increasing numbers of employees in multinational companies. The sexual-harassment programs in multinational companies—if they're even offered or required—are for domestic, not international employees. And their focus is local, not global.

Another inadequacy to the cross-cultural preparation for most expatriates is that the courses are usually offered for employees on long-term assignment, not for the occasional visitor or business traveler. One international HR executive says that because of the lack of preparation, the occasional visitor becomes the company's greatest liability. He says: "When [U.S. citizens abroad] aren't culturally sensitive, they may use inappropriate gestures or names that can be perceived as harassment, even when it's not intentional."

One example of a cross-cultural preparation course we encountered is the *Passport/Visa Program* used at Amoco for its international business travelers and U.S. employees who host foreign visitors. The passport section is a fairly generic cross-cultural review, while the visa component is country-specific. The organization has visa programs for countries such as China, Russia, Azerbaijan, Egypt, Trinidad and the United States. HR currently is developing programs for Europe and Latin America. Benefits to the learners include being able to "identify, anticipate, avoid, minimize and resolve areas of potential conflict resulting from cultural differences." The only drawback is brevity—the program is only a half-day course.

Finally, cross-cultural training is designed for employees destined for overseas assignments. But it's rarely an option for domestic employees who'll be interacting with foreigners on a regular basis in their jobs.

Should You Define Sexual Harassment by Home- or Host-Country Standards?

Even when cultural preparation is adequate, it begs the question of cultural relativism. Should an organization operating in a host country with different customs and moral traditions insist that all behavior be measured according to home-country standards? If men and women have interacted in a certain way for hundreds of years in a culture, who shall judge that certain language or behavior is wrong or *bad*? Sexual harassment is one manifestation, of sexual discrimination. Values and behaviors about women's rights aren't as deeply entrenched in many societies as in our own.

Mahbub ul Haq, a United Nations development program team leader and the author of a recent U.N. report cited by *USA Today* on August 29, 1995, states: "There isn't a single society in the world that treats its men and women equally, not even by accident." Undoubtedly, expatriate women face unique problems.

Jim Yates of Amoco echoes a common sentiment about the difficulties women encounter cross-culturally: "In some countries, there are barriers that have affected the ability of females to be fully integrated into a project or team." Another senior HR executive notes: "Particularly in 'macho' cultures, it's strange to interact with women in a professional capacity." In these environments, men may take advantage of women because they're accustomed to relating in traditional ways. Even on the egalitarian ground of the United States, the same problems may arise.

Jane Henderson-Loney, of the Timner Consultant Group in the San Francisco suburb of Clayton, California, describes a Middle Eastern-born man working in the United States who was accused of sexually harassing an American-born woman. She remembers him saying: "In my country, women can't behave like this to men!"

Literature on the subject goes beyond mere sexual discrimination. It supports the view that sexual harassment is common in many countries. The *Harvard International Law Journal* reported in 1992: "Sexual harassment is a pervasive problem in the Japanese workplace." In 1991, *IABC Communication World* reported that in Mexico, "sexual harassment has been recognized as a problem, but is accepted in our culture where many men consider themselves superior over women . . ." The same source reported that a national survey in Australia revealed one in four Australian women suffered from sexual harassment at work. Sexual harassment also is happening in Africa. Pratt says when he read the 1992 deposition testimony by a Nigerian woman in preparation for a sexual harassment case, he concluded that it's common in Nigeria—in fact expected—that male supervisors can have sexual access to female subordinates.

If sexual discrimination, including sexual harassment, is the norm in some cultures, should it be ignored when it occurs? In the book *Essentials of Business Ethics*, edited by Peter

Madsen and Jay Shafritz, one respected contributor, Norman Bowie, states that he believes universal ethics do exist that should guide business conduct. However, they often aren't obvious, and may be difficult to decipher. Probably every culture would say it believes in, and upholds, the respect and dignity of every human being. It's hard to imagine a society that would openly condone sexual harassment. The *Essentials of Business Ethics* states: "Such moral rules are not relative; they simply are not practiced universally. . . . However, multinational corporations are obligated to follow these moral rules."

In fact, the few incidents of sexual misconduct in international situations that we heard about were frequently resolved once the employees were informed that the women in question were offended by the behavior. Senior HR executives from several companies concluded that these incidents often are caused by lack of awareness of cultural differences—they aren't malevolent in nature. Once an explanation is offered and the woman's perspective is explained, the male (the usual perpetrator) is frequently surprised: He's not aware that his behavior could cause such a degree of anxiety or uneasiness. The universal ethic—not to offend—seems to transcend the customary behavior and interaction of a particular culture.

On the other hand, perhaps it isn't so innocent or simplistic. In at least two incidents we heard about, the offender was clearly told that his behavior was unacceptable. The Middle Eastern employee accused of sexual harassment was told—in no uncertain terms—that to continue working for his employer he would have to conform to treating women as total equals, or be terminated. Perhaps the explicit or implied threat of losing a job or a contract results in a change in behavior more often than the desire not to offend. The excuse that it was a cultural misunderstanding and totally unintended, may be just that—an excuse.

Regardless of personal values and beliefs, the employees in question were motivated to change their behavior to conform to the standards that were expected by the company. Most of the organizations we interviewed have explicitly stated values and policies regarding sexual harassment that are maintained worldwide. Several senior HR executives emphasized workplaces should be free of harassment for all their employees. PPG Industries' Krock shares a viewpoint that's typical of his HR peers: "[Sexual harassment] isn't only contrary to our U.S. law, it's contrary to the policies established by PPG Industries. . . . We don't believe that employees can operate effectively if they don't feel safe."

Consider the Legal and Business Implications of International Sexual Harassment

Do the laws worldwide, and in the United States, support companies' internal policies against sexual harassment? The U.S. laws that govern sexual harassment are covered under Section 109 for both Title VII of the Civil Rights Act and the Americans with Disabilities Act (ADA). Section 109 addresses two distinct issues: 1) circumstances in which Americans and American-controlled employers can be held liable for discrimination that occurs abroad; and 2) circumstances in which foreign employers can be held liable within the United States.

If sexual harassment occurs abroad, American and American-controlled corporations will be covered under Title VII. However, significant interpretation of the law occurs when determining if the company is, American-controlled. Section 109 establishes four factors to consider in interpreting whether a company is, or isn't American-controlled. Not all four factors need to be present in all cases:

- Interrelation of operations
- Common management
- Centralized control of labor relations
- Common ownership or financial control of employer and the foreign corporation.

If a workplace is located in the United States, Title VII and ADA apply to a foreign employer when it discriminates within the United States, except when that individual(s) is protected by a *Friendship, Commerce and Navigation* (FCN) treaty. (The FCN treaty grants jurisdiction to one country over another country's corporation, and vice versa.)

In either case, abroad or within the United States, Section 109 doesn't explicitly discuss sexual harassment, although sexual harassment is a part of Title VII. The sexual harassment guidelines that have been issued in this country, increasingly familiar to U.S. employees, have no counterpart in Section 109.

Furthermore, as we mentioned earlier, in most countries there are no laws protecting against sexual harassment in the workplace. A 1992 article published in the *International Labour Review* revealed that in a study of 23 industrialized countries, only nine had statutes that specifically define or mention the term sexual harassment—Australia, Belgium, Canada, France, Germany (Berlin), New Zealand, Spain, Sweden and the United States. The author, Robert Husbands—of the International Labour Organization, based in Geneva, Switzerland—says that the law is in a state of evolution in most of the 23 countries he studied, and that different legal approaches reflect different cultural attitudes and legal systems. In 1994, the European Parliament adopted a resolution to enact legislation obliging employers to "appoint an in-house counselor to deal with cases of sexual harassment." (Belgium is the only European Community country currently with specific legislation on confidential counselors.) This builds on the European Commission's 1991 Code of Practice to define and combat sexual harassment.

In addition, a November 1992 article in *The New York Times* said: "Legislators in some countries are also reluctant to go too far forward what they see as the desexualization of the United States." When cultures accept and value gender familiarity and unequal roles, it may be difficult to prohibit sexual harassment at work.

The ramifications of sexual harassment when it occurs cross-culturally are more confusing and difficult from both an emotional and legal standpoint. From a business perspective, it's an extremely important area to explore and one that has significant cost implications. With many HR concerns, the human costs of sexual harassment can be high because they directly translate into losses from absenteeism, dissatisfaction and low productivity.

The global nature of the problem adds another cost—expatriate employees are expensive employees. They tend to be high-level and require a great deal of money to support in relocation, schooling their children, tax differences and training, to name just a few. The average expatriate may take approximately $300,000 to replace. When we lose one to a sexual-harassment incident, it's a loss that's costly.

One question mysteriously looms on the horizon of global business: When the practices and laws of two cultures clash, which will apply? This is a question which, apparently, hasn't been widely tested. Perhaps it hasn't even been raised—as some of the organizations we interviewed implied.

It's difficult to believe that a problem that has been so widespread within the United States isn't a problem elsewhere, but the complexities of intercultural socialization blur the lines of what is proper and what is improper. It's HR's job to understand the associated risks when business personnel travel out of—or into—the United States. We also must make training a priority. If our expatriates don't even know which side of the road they'll be driving on when they go abroad on business (or which side of the road their foreign visitors are used to traveling on when they come to the United States), how can we possibly expect them to know what the requirements are regarding intercultural business relationships and the potential for sexually harassing behavior? It's our job to inform our people. Only then can we be sure that the road to international business is a safe one.

Article Review Form at end of book.

WiseGuide Wrap-Up

- Human resources and training departments must be flexible and open to change as organizations expand internationally. The use of Intranets and new software can allow employees worldwide to pose questions to human resources and training personnel and can increase their access to information about programs and services.

- The development of strategies to address this organizational culture shift can be facilitated by human resources and training, if these professionals take the initiative. Human resource and training professionals must be proactive leaders of change in this effort to build employees' skills in working across national and cultural boundaries.

- The ability to prepare employees and their families effectively for company assignments in a culture other than their own will result in fewer resignations, increased job productivity, and easier transition to the new position. By offering assistance with the transition back home and the use of international expertise, the firm gains an additional return on the investment.

R.E.A.L. Sites

This list provides a print preview of typical **coursewise** R.E.A.L. sites. (There are over 100 such sites at the **courselinks**™ site.) The danger in printing URLs is that web sites can change overnight. As we went to press, these sites were functional using the URLs provided. If you come across one that isn't, please let us know via email to: webmaster@coursewise.com. Use your Passport to access the most current list of R.E.A.L. sites at the **courselinks**™ site.

Site name: American Society for Training and Development (ASTD)
URL: http://www.astd.org/
Why is it R.E.A.L.? This site provides information on the organization, its membership, international interest groups, and conferences. ASTD also has a discount for student membership. It also includes an inventory of more than 200 books on different aspects of training.
Key topics: training, development, membership
Try this: Select an area of interest in training and find three books on that topic.

Site name: Society for Human Resource Management (SHRM)
URL: http://www.shrm.org/
Why is it R.E.A.L.? This site provides extensive information on SHRM. It has an enormous number of links to other human resources sites. It also links to the Institute for International Human Resources and the World Federation of Personnel Management Associations.
Key topics: training, research, education, intercultural
Try this: Explore three linked organizations. Are they relevant for a person in the human resources field. Why or why not?

Site name: International Society for Performance Improvement
URL: http://www.ispi.org/home.htm
Why is it R.E.A.L.? This site provides information regarding both performance improvement and training. Publications information as well as conference sites and dates and membership are included in this site.
Key topics: performance improvement, training
Try this: What is performance improvement as ISPI defines it?

section 5

Intercultural Communication Research

WiseGuide Intro

As a relatively new field, intercultural communication research traces its beginnings to the 1950s, starting with Edward Hall and his work with the Foreign Service Institute. It is noteworthy that his initial objective was to apply some of his theoretical concepts to an intercultural communication training program. As Moon reports in her article "Concepts of "Culture": Implications for Intercultural Communication Discourse," his efforts were met with mixed success.

Historically, the field has drawn from many disciplines, such as anthropology, psychology, sociology, history, political science, business, and communications. A great deal of the research has focused on a particular culture or on cross-cultural dyads. Increasingly, many people find themselves working in groups which are multinational; however, limited research is available regarding the dynamics of this type of team. In addition, variables such as gender, class, education level, historical conflict, and context have not been explored completely. There is, however, a cadre of researchers and practitioners that continues to work for a better understanding of this process.

Many of the following readings have been repeatedly referenced by students in intercultural communication and international training courses, for the answers they provide as well as for the questions they raise. These students have also found the bibliographies to be of great help in gathering material regarding their particular interest in the field of intercultural communication. Many of the R.E.A.L. sites at the **courselinks** site for Intercultural Communications have also been recommended by students as a way to move out of one's geographical or cultural perspective and ask new questions. Perhaps today's readers, as researchers and practitioners, may advance the intercultural communication research field that much closer to answers to those very difficult questions.

Learning Objectives

- Expand knowledge of the historical development of the intercultural communication field.
- Recognize the advances that have been made in intercultural communication theory development.
- Increase awareness of what constitutes intercultural communication competency.
- Understand the role of the researcher and practitioner in applying intercultural communication theory to training situations.
- Identify aspects of intercultural communication that require further research.

Questions

Reading 25. What are the alternate ways in which "culture" can be conceptualized, according to Moon?

Reading 26. What are some of the alternative concepts of cross-cultural competency?

Reading 27. What are some of the flaws in previous intercultural communication research that Hannigan identifies?

Reading 28. Paige advocates that trainer intercultural communication competency rests on knowledge, performance, and personal attributes. How does he characterize each of these?

What are the alternate ways in which "culture" can be conceptualized, according to Moon?

Concepts of "Culture"

Implications for intercultural communication research

Dreama G. Moon

A discursive formation can be seen as a system of statements that "set the context in which constitutive statements are held to . . . be 'true' " (Rice, 1992, p. 339). For Foucault, "truth" is an "ensemble of rules . . . [and] a system of ordered procedures for the production, regulation, distribution, and operation of statements" (1980, pp. 132–133). In essence, a Foucaultian genealogical inquiry seeks to trace the "descent" and "emergence" of new discursive formations and to chart a discourse's lineage across the path of contradictions and logical discontinuities, particularly the "accidents, chance, passion, petty malice, surprises . . . and power" (Davidson, 1986, p. 224) that foster discursive formations (Rice, 1992).

In this Foucaultian sense, I interrogate the historical emergence of intercultural communication as a field of inquiry and the subsequent impact this has had on intercultural communication scholarship. In addition, I examine how the configuration of the field affects the ability of scholars to engage in current theoretical debates. If it is true that disciplines as a group "constitute systems of control in the production of discourse" (Foucault, 1972, p. 222), inquiry into the formation of intercultural communication discourse should serve to create a vision of not only where we have been, but where we are and where next we might want to go as intercultural communication scholars.

The task is to highlight a historical moment in the formation of intercultural communication discourse in which particular statements came to be taken as "truth" within the field. In course, I briefly revisit the era encompassing the work of Edward T. Hall at the Foreign Service Institute (FSI), review a sample of intercultural communication scholarship published in communication journals during the 1970s, and then discuss current theoretical debates and their impact—or lack of—on intercultural communication scholarship. From a Foucaultian frame of power and knowledge, I then examine the construction of the discipline of intercultural communication and how certain statements became hegemonic and defining while others did not.

In the course of developing the above argument, I pay particular attention to the text of Leeds-Hurwitz (1990) as it attempts to provide the definitive history of the field. I deconstruct that text to show the absence of alternative readings of culture. Next, I examine published work in the 1970s and 1980s, when the discipline of intercultural communication becomes crystallized. Finally, I end by examining contemporary work in the field and indicating some contributions that critical feminist theory can make to a broader intercultural communication inquiry.

A Genealogy of Intercultural Communication

Employing a dialectic of continuity and discontinuity, Foucault (1980) argues that "historical breaks always include some overlapping, interaction, and echoes between the old and

---

"Concepts of 'Culture': Implications for Intercultural Communication Research." Dreama G. Moon. COMMUNICATION QUARTERLY, Winter 1996. Reprinted by permission of Eastern Communication Association, Department of Communication Arts, Salisbury State University, Salisbury, MD 21801.

the new" (p. 361). Through examining such ruptures, one can begin to "grasp historical events in their real complexity" (Best & Kellner, 1991, p. 46). One such "break" with respect to intercultural communication encompasses the creation of the Foreign Service Institute (FSI) and the role played there by anthropologist Edward T. Hall. Indeed, this era is often marked as the "beginning" of the field of intercultural communication (Leeds-Hurwitz, 1990); its importance to the development and formation of intercultural communication as a field has been documented (e.g., Harman & Briggs, 1991; Leeds-Hurwitz, 1990). However, according to Leeds-Hurwitz (1990), Hall's work "was shaped by the specific context of the FSI" (p. 260). More to the point, his vision of and approach to the study of "culture" was substantially altered by his experiences at the FSI. Though acknowledged by Leeds-Hurwitz (1990), the implications of Hall's transformative experience at the FSI remain unexamined. In light of this, I revisit the development of the FSI and Hall's experience there, paying particular attention to the connection between power and knowledge.

Disabling Legacy? Edward T. Hall and the FSI

The Foreign Service Institute was formally established in 1947 to provide career-long inservice training to Foreign Service officials. In 1951, Edward T. Hall joined the staff (Leeds-Hurwitz, 1990). It should be noted that the duties of Service officers were not limited to diplomatic ones in the strictest sense of the word. Much of their role included feeding important information regarding their countries of assignment back to the U.S. government. If Foreign Service personnel were to be the "eyes and ears" of the government, however, they would require a variety of specialized cultural training.

The training that Hall and his associates offered to foreign service personnel consisted of "beginning instruction in the language of the country of assignment, orientation to the mission and its philosophy, limited study of the country and area," as well as limited anthropological and linguistic conceptualizations of "culture" (Leeds-Hurwitz, 1990, p. 267). However, many of the FSI students found the anthropological concept of culture as a shared historically transmitted system of codes—or in Hall and Hall's (1989) words, "shared information along with shared methods of coding, storing, and retrieving that information" (pp. xiii–xiv)—difficult to understand and irrelevant, preferring more specific and concrete information. The trainees' limited perceptions and emphasis on goal achievement complicated the training task for Hall and his associates. Hall (1965) writes:

The younger officers . . . because of the emphasis on "political" reporting, often were left with the idea that there was nothing of importance to be learned from the foreigner as a member of his culture, and that if they could just get to the "right person," in the political sense, the cold dope on any given situation could be obtained. (p. 7)

This attitude reflected what Hall (1956) called the "self-evident truths" of the trainees—unquestioned, unexamined, taken for granted beliefs assumed to be "true" and "common sensical"—against and with which Hall struggled. Two of these taken-for-granted beliefs were particularly problematic: the first being the old saw that "people are the same wherever you go" and the other being "the best way to learn is through personal experience" (Hall, 1956). The training situation was further complicated by other problems including bureaucratic red tape, disrespect for academics in general and anthropologists in particular, and the view that training was unneeded and unimportant (Hall, 1956).

Unable to overcome these obstacles, Hall and his colleagues were forced to abandon an anthropological view of "culture" and to treat "culture" in a pragmatic, goal-oriented manner. According to Leeds-Hurwitz (1990), this decision set the agenda for intercultural communication as a field of inquiry. She summarizes the connections between Hall's work and current intercultural communication research in the following ways: (1) comparison of (national) cultures rather than focus on a single culture, (2) a move from macroanalysis (i.e., culture in general) to microanalysis (i.e., smaller cultural units such as tone of voice, gestures, time and spatial relations), (3) a focus on interaction between members of different cultures (i.e., dyadic emphasis), (4) communication as patterned, learned, and analyzable, (5) use of "real life" intercultural experiences as teaching tools, (6) use of descriptive linguistics, and (7) an expanded audience for intercultural training (i.e., international business) (pp. 263–264). In short, when taken together, these statements comprise the current discursive rules of inquiry within the field of intercultural communication. As such, they set the conditions of possibility for producing, regulating, and distributing knowledge about intercultural communication discourse.

While it is clear that political interests of the time dictated how the notion of "culture" was configured at the FSI, it is not clear why or under what circumstances this notion of "culture" was later adopted by intercultural communication scholars. In fact, there is evidence that at least during the decade of the seventies, what was defined as "culture" and as "intercultural communication" was less constrained.

The 'Habeas Corpus' of the 1970s

In this section I focus on intercultural communication articles found in journals published within the discipline of communication and identified as such in the Index to Journals in Communication Studies Through 1990 (Matlon, 1992)—the so-called Matlon Index.[1] As Matlon's Index is published by the field's national professional association (Speech Commu- nication Association), it serves as an indicator of what is formally understood as "intercultural communication" research within the field. Publication in journals such as those listed in Matlon's Index have an impact on tenure and other career achievements made by communication scholars. With only three articles published during the 1950s and six in the 1960s, Matlon (1992) cites 52 additional intercultural communication articles published in the following communication scholarly journals during the 1970s:[2] *Journal of Communication* (28), *Communication*

Quarterly (5), *Southern States Communication Journal* (2), *Communication Monographs* (3), *Communication Research* (5), *The Quarterly Journal of Speech* (3), *Journalism Quarterly* (2), *Western Journal of Communication* (1), *Central States Speech Journal* (2), and *Communication Education* (1). Several trends are noted in this literature. These trends are discussed in turn. Most significant in this body of work is the diverse ways in which "culture" is defined.

Although a series of articles dealing with the global impact of media define "culture" in terms of nation-state (e.g., Pipe, 1979; Porat, 1978; Righter, 1979), most others conceptualize "culture" in terms of race, social class, and gender identity. For instance, Daniel (1970a, 1970b) argues that communication between the poor and the affluent should be viewed as a case of cross-cultural communication. Whiting (1971) and Whiting and Hitt (1972) examine code-restrictedness and problem-solving communication among lower and middle class black and white teenagers. Philipsen (1975, 1976) examines how talk is used by working class white men. Rich (1971) investigates interracial communication in the classroom between Black, Chicano, Anglo, Native, and Japanese American students. Cheseboro (1973) juxtaposes the goals and beliefs of "establishment" and "counter" cultures that result in rhetorical conflicts.

While many of the studies cited above compare two or more cultures, a number of other studies are concerned with the explication of one culture. For instance, Dubner (1972) examines nonverbal aspects of Black English. Daniel and Smitherman (1976) explicate the Traditional African Worldview and argue for its significance in understanding African American communication. Shuter (1979) investigates the use of the "dap" in the military—a handshake used by African American soldiers to express solidarity.

Also of note are the variety of methods employed in studying intercultural communication. Philipsen (1975, 1976) utilizes ethnographic methods, Rich (1971) employs case studies, Whiting and Hitt (1972) use a quasi-experimental design, and Dubner (1972) conducts a textual analysis of film, previous research, and popular literature.

Evident too in this body of research is a concern for and an involvement with social debates of the 1970s. Gregg, McCormack, and Pedersen (1970), Daniel (1970a, 1970b), Rich (1971), Dubner (1972), Lumsden, Brown, Lumsden, and Hill (1974), Daniel and Smitherman (1976), Colquit (1977), Sayer (1979), and Shuter (1979) in various ways attempt to come to terms with or offer insight into the ways in which communicative differences play into the social problems between Anglo and African Americans. In a similar vein, Daniel (1970a, 1970b), Whiting and Hitt (1972), and Philipsen (1975, 1976) attempt to highlight how social class differences negatively affect communication. Indeed, a 1977 special issue of *Journal of Communication* entitled "When Cultures Clash" is devoted to the examination of the effects of new technologies, products, and systems of communication on "authentic" or traditional cultures (e.g., Katz, 1977; Lomax, 1977). In addition, a number of articles address the effects of the "New World Information Order" on developing countries (e.g., Grossberg, 1979; Nordenstrong, 1979; Righter, 1979).

Lastly, a number of articles call into question some of the underlying assumptions of communication inquiry. For instance, in a study of communication competence across social class, Whiting (1971) suggests that as most researchers are middle class and insensitive to working class communication strategies, scholarly investigations of "competence" may be class-biased. In a similar vein, Colquit (1977) argues that definitions of "competence" are race-biased and privilege the communicative style of middle class white Americans. Dubner (1972) argues that many of the communication problems between African Americans and Anglo Americans are largely due to (faulty) interpretations of the behaviors of "Others" by dominant group members. Shuter (1977) finds that Edward Hall's assumptions about nonverbal forms of communication (i.e., proxemics and haptics) do not bear out when the gender of the participants is taken into account. Noting the ethnocentrism of American communication scholarship and its isolation from European thought (e.g., Marxism, structuralism), Carey (1975) asks:

Where, if anywhere, does ideology leave off and science begin?

In examining the articles published in the 1970s, some patterns emerge. Up until about 1977, "culture" is conceptualized in a variety of ways (i.e., race, social class, gender, and nation), diverse analytical methods are utilized, and there is deep interest in how intersections between various nodes of cultural identity both play out in, and are constructed by, communication. Starting about 1978, "culture" comes to be conceived almost entirely in terms of "nation-state" and by 1980, "culture" is predominantly configured as a variable in positivist research projects (see Appendix [p. 176] for a chronological listing of published articles throughout the eighties). As shown below, this view of "culture" becomes further entrenched throughout the decade of the eighties.

Into the Eighties

The first article published in the decade of the eighties (Jin, 1980) is an empirical test of acculturation. By 1983, the intercultural communication literature begins to be dominated by Gudykunst and associates and cross cultural tests of uncertainty reduction theory (e.g., Gudykunst, 1985; Gudykunst & Hammer, 1988; Gudykunst, Seung-Mock, & Nishida, 1985; Gudykunst, Sodetani, & Sonoda, 1987). Working out of a positivist tradition, the studies of Gudykunst and associates account for almost one-half of the articles published during the 1980s—12 out of the 29 published works. The conceptualization of "culture" as nation-state, comparison of cultures, a focus on dyadic interaction between members of different cultures, and microanalysis characterize much of the work published during this decade. Furthermore, Gudykunst and Nishida (1989) outline their "objectivist" approach to the study of intercultural communication which strikingly corresponds to the discursive rules for intercultural communication scholarship as laid out by Leeds-Hurwitz (1990) and attributed to Hall.

Clearly, the year of 1980 represents a "disjuncture" in the study of intercultural communication. It is during this time that a heterogeneous notion of "culture" gets displaced. Foucault (1972) observes that such "breaks" or "ruptures" are so radical that an entire way of knowing a phenomenon is altered irrevocably. This certainly appears to be the case in regards to what was published from the 1970s to the 1980s in the field of intercultural communication. It is of more than passing interest that this disjuncture occurs in conjunction with other ruptures, in particular the rise of Reaganomics in the United States and Thatcherism in great Britain.

How is this "disjuncture" to be accounted for, and what are the ramifications for the study of intercultural communication? Casmir and Asuncion-Lande (1990) offer some insight into these issues. Toward the end of the 1970s, many studies were published that addressed the diffusion of innovations from one culture to another, particularly so in the *Journal of Communication*. Indeed, a special issue of the *Journal of Communication* was devoted to this topic in 1977 and diffusion studies dominated in both the 1978 and 1979 issues of the journal as well (see Appendix for a chronological listing). Casmir and Asuncion-Lande (1990) suggest that the impact of these studies on the field of intercultural communication was in "moving the locus of communication research from the United States to various cultures in which communication concepts, structures, styles, and functions were not similar to our own" (p. 288). In other words, the emphasis on defining "culture" as nation-state is attributed to the international interest created by these diffusion studies.

In addition, the late 1970s witnessed dissent within the field regarding the status of the discipline of intercultural communication itself. Following the social sciences and eschewing the "faddism" of the seventies, intercultural communication scholars extolled "methodological rigor" as a means of transforming the discipline into one that would be taken seriously both within and outside the academy (Casmir & Asuncion-Lande, 1990, p. 282). Not surprisingly, "methodological rigor" involved the "careful application of statistical and mathematical models" (Gudykunst, 1983a) and placed a priority on theory development and testing (Gudykunst, 1983b). Shuter (1990) observes that:

Intercultural studies in national and regional speech communication journals are neither of an etic or emic nature; they are products of a nomothetic model developed in psychology that drives communication research and aims at identifying laws of human interaction rather than describing cultural patterns. (p. 239)

Shuter goes on to argue that much intercultural communication research is concerned with refining existent communication theories (i.e., uncertainty reduction) wherein "culture" serves principally as a "research laboratory for testing the validity of communication paradigms" (p. 238). Although Shuter argues for the importance of "culture" in intercultural communication inquiry, he does not question the conceptualization of "culture" in terms of national boundaries. In fact, his above remarks are located in an introductory essay of a 1990 special issue of the *Southern Communication Journal* dealing with intracultural communication within and across national boundaries.

In summary, it appears that the "disjuncture" that occurred around 1980 within the field of intercultural communication had its roots in a variety of influences, including the political and capitalist interests of the United States, the impact of diffusion studies, and the felt need to establish disciplinary status through the adoption of social scientific approaches. What so often gets lost in the traditional rhetoric of historical accounts is the interplay of power relations. This is the single issue that intercultural communication research published in the 1970s speaks to most clearly and one that the majority of the work in the 1980s obscures. By conceptualizing "culture" in a variety of ways and challenging dominant definitions of taken-for-granted communication concepts such as that of "competence," these scholars brought into question hegemonic assumptions about the nature of "culture" and often "centered" the voices of the less powerful (e.g., Daniel's 1970 discussion of communication from the perspective of the poor). Diverse readings of "culture" encourage the inclusion of a power analytic in the study of intercultural communication and contest the notion of "culture" as unproblematically shared.

A plurality of perspectives also encourages debate. For example, Colquit (1977) challenges definitions of "competence" that privilege the communicative style of middle class white Americans, while, in vehement disagreement, Sayer (1979) claims that mastery of a "socially superior" (dominant) language is not racist. These and similar debates in much of the work published in the 1970s show evidence for the inherently contested nature of "culture." As Dirks, Eley, and Ortner (1994) remind us, "culture may be seen as multiple discourses, occasionally coming together in large systemic configurations, but more often coexisting within dynamic fields of interaction and conflict" (p. 4). This contested nature of "culture" often gets lost in homogenizing views of "culture as nationality" where dominant cultural voices are often the only ones heard, where the "preferred" reading of "culture" is the only reading. This certainly seems the case in most of the intercultural communication work published in the eighties. As we have seen, in many of these studies the experiences and self-reports of privileged members of the United States and Japan represent "culture" for all cultural members.

Discussion

From my reading of the intercultural communication scholarship published in the 1970s, it is clear that this body of literature deviates—often dramatically so—from the discursive rules that, according to Leeds-Hurwitz (1990) now define intercultural communication scholarship. Indeed, according to Leeds-Hurwitz, this body of work is clearly not intercultural communication and is therefore absent in her account of intercultural scholarship. How might intercultural communication scholars recover the seventies in order to create a broader intercultural communication in the 1990s? Rumblings of this move to recover are already being heard within the field.

This essay calls for the insertion of more complex notions of "culture" into intercultural communication scholarship. Such reconceptualizations would entail substantive rethinking of the field and attendant goals, desires, needs, and visions of our work. We must again, as in the 1970s, seriously consider whose interests are served by continuing to construct "culture" primarily in terms of national boundaries and by maintaining the current focus on the development of "intercultural cookbooks" for interaction. This revisioning needs to be a collective effort by a community of scholars. I would like to offer some possible directions as suggested by critical feminist theoretical perspectives.

Most immediately, insights derived by critical/feminist scholars have the potential to expand the predominant conceptualizations of "culture" currently accepted in intercultural communication inquiry. As a rule, intercultural communication scholars are not interested in the idea of "culture" per se, but use operationalized notions of cultural variation (e.g., individualism/collectivism) as one among many independent variables that affect the dependent variable (i.e., communicative phenomena such as uncertainty reduction, Gudykunst & Nishida, 1989). "Culture," at this level, is most often defined as nationality, and the constructedness of this position and its intersection with other positions such as gender and social class is not considered. The outcome is that diverse groups are treated as homogeneous, differences within national boundaries, ethnic groups, genders, and races are obscured, and hegemonic notions of "culture" are presented as "shared" by all cultural members. Moreover, intercultural communication of this sort is most often studied within dyads wherein two disembodied, ahistorical beings communicate across cultures.

The utilization of critical/feminist perspectives would allow intercultural communication scholars to employ more sophisticated and politicized analyses of cultural identity in general and to examine how these identities are constructed in communication, as well as how they affect communication. For instance, feminist scholars such as Marsha Houston (1992), Patricia Hill Collins (1993), and bell hooks (1989) argue that inquiry must address interlocking and overlapping nodes of identity (i.e., race, class, and gender) rather than focus on any one node alone. Wood (1994) reminds us that notions of femininity and masculinity, constructed differently across lines of race, class, nation, inform the communication process. Cultural feminists such as Johnson (1989) argue that women are culturally different from men and that "woman's culture" should be treated as analytically distinct from that of men.

Regarding the notion of "culture" as shared, Dirks et al. (1994) asks "By whom? In what ways? and Under what conditions?" (p. 3). Such insights have major implications for intercultural communication scholarship. For instance, in light of the fact that Shuter (1977) discovered that commonly accepted ideas about nonverbal communication across and within cultures derived from the work of Edward T. Hall do not pertain when gender is taken into account, the exclusion of this aspect of cultural identity in intercultural communication inquiry is difficult to understand or justify.

Another critical feminist notion that intercultural communication scholars could find useful is Alcoff's (1988) idea of "positionality," as it directs attention to the context in which subjects are situated rather than focusing on the individual characteristics of the person. In this way, subjects become embodied, contextualized, historicized—a site of contradiction rather than one that is static, unitary, stable, fixed, and thereby indifferent to context and history. Assuming a different positional perspective has interesting implications for intercultural communication research. For instance, research employing a construction of "culture-as-nationality" could include an examination of interactants' positions within their own social structures in relation to gender, social class, status group, ethnicity, religion, and so forth, and could explore how this positionality affects and/or is constructed in intercultural interactions. In short, if "culture" signifies the intersection of various subject positions within any given society, then ways of studying intercultural communication that acknowledge this multifacetedness are needed.

These approaches would require a vastly deeper understanding of intracultural communication than is currently available. Without a sense of how communication is patterned within groups, we can have little understanding of how that communication differs from or resembles communication between groups (Shuter, 1990). All too often intercultural communication scholars focus their research efforts on privileged Anglo American and Japanese college students. The result has been the formation of what vanDijk (1987) calls "elite" discourse and what I call "colonizer" discourse. In short, we know quite a bit about the communication patterns of social elites in this and other countries, but little or nothing about those of "Others." In part, our lack of knowledge stems from the imposition of dominant definitions and constructs onto the communication of "Others," with the resulting comparison of their communication to that of the dominant group(s) in the language of dominance.

Nakayama's (1994) "Other/wise" reading of texts offers an alternative approach to colonizer/ing discourse. In Nakayama's (1994) terms, an "Other" is called up—essentialized and centered—in order to view social relations and communication from an "Other" place. This strategy enables insights and perspectives usually ignored or marginalized. What would intercultural communication look like when viewed from these "Other" places? Would uncertainty reduction theory "hold water" when viewed through the lens of Collins's (1993) Acrocentric feminist epistemology which assumes that making connections is a primary motive in human interaction rather than the reduction of uncertainty? How would understandings of intercultural communication be enriched if the reduction of uncertainty/anxiety was assumed to be a Western rather than a global concern? What could be learned if notions such as intercultural communication competence were studied "Other/wise?" How would theories of intercultural communication be enriched or expanded by taking such positions?

In this decade, we are seeing more scholarly work that takes communication within cultural groups as a primary focus which, in turn, allows us to gain insight into intracultural communication patterns (e.g., Collier, M. J., Ribeau, S., & Hecht, M. L., 1986; Collier, M. J., 1988; Hecht, M. L., Ribeau, S., & Alberts, J. K., 1989; Hecht, M. L., Larkey, L., Johnson, J., & Reinard, J. C., 1992). This work allows us to understand communication patterns within groups in their own terms without the distraction of comparisons with dominant group patterns. However, much of this research remains limited to cultural groups within the United States.

In writing about ethnography, Kauffman (1992) makes several points from which intercultural communication researchers can benefit. Kauffman argues that the positionality of the researcher is implicit in every research effort, thus rendering research an explicitly political act. This brings to mind Houston's (1992) metaphor of "multiple jeopardy" in that not only are our subjects infused with multiple, interlocking identities, but so are researchers. When researchers perceive themselves as positioned and embodied beings—gendered, racial, sexual, and social class—we can begin to acknowledge how these particularities shape our research. We can affect what gets constituted as a "problem" worthy of study, whose reality/knowledge will be constructed as "answers," and what findings will be selected or reported as "facts" (Kauffman, 1992, p. 192).

Cultural studies, with its focus on popular culture, provides another alternative frame. Hall (1981) argues that the media produce "representations of the social world, images, descriptions, explanations, and frames for understanding how the world is and why it works as it is said and shown to work" (p. 35). In a similar vein, vanDijk (1987) claims that most of what white Americans know about "Others" is gleaned from mass media. If we are to agree with Hall (1981), then much of how we understand ourselves as cultural members and our interactions with "Others" is too impacted by media representations. By examining these discourses, we can better understand these processes and how they affect and are played out in intercultural interactions.

With its emphasis on popular culture, feminist cultural studies suggests an alternative to the study of intercultural communication that moves away from focusing on dyadic intercultural encounters to popular representations of intercultural communication. In an age when media images abound in "first, second, and third worlds" and keeping in mind vanDijk's (1987) claim that much of what we know about "others" we learn from media, what we can learn from analyses of popular cultural forms of intercultural communication and their audiences seem especially promising. For example, one could argue that intercultural communication scholarship should rightly include studies of the impact of foreign media communication on cultural members. If one envisions the interaction between text and audience as another case of communication, then one's watching of an Italian film as a white American woman is a form of intercultural communication. Indeed, cultural norms, values, and beliefs are communicated in media which are actively constructed and deconstructed by audience members. This is worthy of intense study.

Into the Nineties: A Note in Closure

Matlon's Index (1992) indicates twelve articles classified as intercultural communication published in communication journals in the first year of the decade of the nineties. The first such work is a historical piece by Leeds-Hurwitz (1990) which lays out the discursive rules of the field attributed to Hall. In a 1990 special issue of the *Southern Speech Communication Journal* devoted to intracultural communication, Shuter (1990) calls for the reinsertion of "culture" into intercultural communication scholarship. He argues that the development of intracultural communication theory is critical for three reasons: First, it provides a conceptual framework for analyzing interaction within a society and world region. Second, intracultural theories demonstrate the inextricable linkage between communication patterns and sociocultural forces. And, lastly, it provides a conceptual basis for making intercultural communication comparisons between dissimilar societies. (p. 243)

The articles in this special issue describe patterns of intercultural communication in groups as diverse as the Yoruba of Nigeria (Asante, 1990), Greeks (Broome, 1990), Mexicans and Mexican Americans (Gonzalez, 1990), the North Yemini (Frye, 1990), Chinese and Americans (Ma, 1990), and Japanese (DiMare, 1990). Interestingly, these research efforts do not "qualify" as intercultural communication scholarship under the discursive rules laid out in Leeds-Hurwitz (1990). As discussed earlier, the late 1980s and early 1990s also exhibit a turn to the intracultural in terms of domestic cultures within the United States (e.g., Hecht, Ribeau, & Alberts, 1989). These are hopeful signs. These efforts alone, however, are insufficient to move the field of intercultural communication to include an analytic that recognizes the contested and power-infused nature of "culture" within intercultural communication.

In this essay, I have examined how the field of intercultural communication has been constructed and how certain definitions have become hegemonic, thereby reading others out. I have paid attention to Leeds-Hurwitz's historical account of the field and have shown how this account leaves out the prolific intercultural communication scholarship published in communication journals during the 1970s. Moreover, I have traced the emergence of the discipline identifying the disjuncture at which current conceptualizations of intercultural communication inquiry became hegemonic. Lastly, I suggest how critical/feminist insights might contribute to a broader intercultural communication inquiry.

Notes

1. Matlon's Index is utilized as an external indicator of what is considered as "intercultural communication" research within the field of communication. It is published by the Speech Communication Association, the discipline's national professional and academic association. Since Matlon's as yet has not published an index covering the years 1992–1995, the intercultural communication articles published in the field's journals during these years could not be considered here.

2. The Appendix (p. 176) provides a chronological listing of these research articles so that the reader may see the foci of these inquiries as they evolved during the decade of the seventies. In addition, all of the published works termed as "intercultural communication" by Matlon are contained in the Appendix in chronological order by decade as well.

References

Alcoff, L. (1988). Cultural feminism versus post-structuralism: The identity crisis in feminist theory. *Signs: Journal of Women in Culture and Society, 13,* 405–436.

Asante, M. K. (1990). The tradition of advocacy in the Yoruba courts. *Southern Speech Communication Journal, 55,* 250–259.

Best, S., & Kellner, D. (1991). *Postmodern Theory: Critical interrogations.* NY: The Guilford Press.

Broome, B. J. (1990). "Palevone": Foundations of struggle and conflict in Greek interpersonal communication. *Southern Speech Communication Journal, 55,* 260–275.

Carey, J. W. (1975). Communication and culture. *Communication Research, 2,* 173–191.

Casmir, F. I., & Asuncion-Lande, N. C. (1990). Intercultural communication revisited: Conceptualization, paradigm building, and methodological approaches. In James A. Anderson (Ed.), *Communication Yearbook* 12 (pp. 278–309). Newbury Park, CA: Sage.

Cheseboro, J. W. (1973). Cultures in conflict—a generic and axiological view. *Communication Quarterly, 21,* 11–20.

Collier, M. J. (1988). A comparison of conversations among and between domestic groups: How intra- and intercultural competencies vary. *Communication Quarterly, 36,* 122–144.

Collier, M. J., Ribeau, S., & Hecht, M. L. (1986). Intracultural communication rules and outcomes with three domestic cultures. *International Journal of Intercultural Relations, 10,* 434–457.

Collins, P. H. (1993). *Black feminist thought: Knowledge, consciousness, and the politics of empowerment.* New York: Routledge.

Colquit, J. L. (1977). The student's right to his own language: A viable model or empty rhetoric? *Communication Quarterly, 25,* 17–20.

Daniel, J. (1970a). The facilitation of white-black communication. *Journal of Communication, 20,* 134–141.

Daniel, J. (1970b). The poor: Aliens in an affluent society: Cross-cultural communication. *Communication Quarterly, 18,* 15–21.

Daniel, J. L., & Smitherman, G. (1976). How I got over: Communication dynamics in the Black community. *Quarterly Journal of Speech, 62,* 26–39.

Davidson, A. (1986). Archaeology, genealogy, ethics. In D. C. Hoy (Ed.), *Foucault: A critical reader* (pp. 221–233). NY: Basil Blackwell.

DiMare, L. (1990). Ma and Japan. *Southern Speech Communication Journal, 55,* 319–328.

Dirks, N. B., Eley, G., & Ortner, S. B. (1994). Introduction. In N. B. Dirks, G. Eley & S. B. Ortner (Eds.), *Culture/power/history: A reader in contemporary social theory* (pp. 3–45) Princeton, NJ: Princeton University Press.

Dubner, F. S. (1972). Nonverbal aspects of Black english. *Southern Speech Communication Journal, 37,* 361–374.

Foucault, M. (1972). *The archaeology knowledge.* New York: Pantheon Books.

Foucault, M. (1990). *The history of sexuality.* NY: Vintage Books.

Frye, P. A. (1990). Form and function of North Yemeni Qat sessions. *Southern Speech Communication Journal, 55,* 292–304.

Gonzalez, A. (1990). Mexican "otherness" in the rhetoric of Mexican Americans. *Southern Speech Communication Journal, 55,* 276–291.

Gregg, R., McCormack, A. J., & Pedersen, D. (1970). A description of the interaction between black youth and white teachers in a ghetto speech class. *Communication Education, 19,* 1–8.

Grossberg, L. (1979). Interpreting the "crisis" of culture in communication theory. *Journal of Communication, 29,* 56–68.

Gudykunst, W. B. (1983a). Intercultural communication theory, current perspectives. In W. B. Gudykunst (Ed.), *International and Intercultural Communication Annual 7* (pp. 13–20) Beverly Hills: Sage.

Gudykunst, W. B. (1983b). Toward a typology of stranger-host relationships. *International Journal of Intercultural Relations, 7,* 401–413.

Gudykunst, W. B. (1985). The influence of cultural similarity, type of relationship, and self-monitoring on uncertainty reduction processes. *Communication Monographs, 51,* 203–217.

Gudykunst, W. B., & Hammer, M. R. (1989). The influence of social identity and intimacy of interethnic relationships on uncertainty reduction processes. *Human Communication Research, 14,* 569–601.

Gudykunst W. B., & Nishida, T. (1989). Theoretical perspectives for studying intercultural communication. In M. F. Asante & W. B. Gudykunst (Eds.), *Handbook of international and intercultural communication* (pp. 17–46). Newbury Park, CA: Sage.

Gudykunst, W. B., Seung-Mock, Y., & Nishida, T. (1985). A cross-cultural test of uncertainty reduction theory: Comparisons of acquaintances, friends, and dating relationships in Japan, Korea, and the U.S. *Human Communication Research, 11,* 407–455.

Gudykunst, W. B., Sodetani, L. L., & Sonoda, K. T. (1987). Uncertainty reduction in Japanese-American/Caucasian relationships in Hawaii. *Western Journal of Communication, 51,* 256–278.

Hall, E. T. (1956). Orientation and training in government for work overseas. *Human Organization, 15,* 410.

Hall, E. T., & Hall, M. R. (1989). *Understanding cultural differences.* Yarmouth: ME: Intercultural Press.

Hall, S. (1981). The whites of their eyes. In G. Bridges & Rosalind Brunt (Eds.), *Silver linings: Some strategies for the eighties* (pp. 28–52). London: Lawrence and Wishart.

Harman, R. C., & Briggs, N. E. (1991). SIETAR survey: Perceived contributions of the social sciences to intercultural communication. *International Journal of Intercultural Relations, 15,* 19–28.

Hecht, M. L., Larkey, L., Johnson, J., & Reinard, J. C. (1992). African American and European American perceptions of problematic issues in interethnic communication effectiveness. *Human Communication Research, 19,* 209–236.

Hecht, M. L., Ribeau S., & Alberts, J. K. (1989). An Afro-American perspective on interethnic communication. *Communication Monographs, 56,* 385–410.

hooks, b. (1989). *Talking back: Thinking feminist, thinking black.* Boston: South End Press.

Houston, M. (1992). The politics of difference: Race, class and women's communication. In L. F. Rakow (Ed.), *Women making meaning* (pp. 45–59). NY: Routledge.

Jin, K. (1980). Explaining acculturation in a communication framework: An empirical test. *Communication Monographs, 47,* 155–179.

Johnson, F. L. (1989). Women's culture and communication: An analytical perspective. In C. M. Lont & S. A. Friedley (Eds.), *Beyond boundaries: Sex and gender diversity in communication* (pp. 301–316). Fairfax, VA: George Mason University Press.

Katz, E. (1977). Can authentic cultures survive new media? *Journal of Communication, Z 7,* 113–121.

Kauffman, B. J. (1992). Feminist facts: Interview strategies and political subjects in ethnography. *Communication Theory, 2,* 187–206.

Leeds-Hurwitz, W. (1990). Notes on the history of intercultural communication: The Foreign Service Institute and the mandate for intercultural training. *Quarterly Journal of Speech, 76,* 262–281.

Lomax, A. (1977). Appeal for cultural equity. *Journal of Communication, 27,* 125–138.

Lumsden, G., Brown, D. R., Lumsden, D., & Hill, T. A. (1974). An investigation of differences in verbal behavior between Black and white informal peer group. *Communication Quarterly, 22,* 31–36.

Ma, R. (1990). An exploratory study of discontented responses in American and Chinese relationships. *Southern Speech Communication Journal, 55,* 305–318.

Matlon, R. J. (Ed.). (1992). *Index to journals in communication studies through 1990.* Annandale, VA: Speech Communication Association.

Nakayama, T. K. (1994). Show/down time: "Race," gender, sexuality, and popular culture. *Critical Studies in Mass Communication*, II, 162–179.

Nordenstrong, K. (1979). Behind the semantics—a strategic design. *Journal of Communication*, 29, 195–199.

Philipsen, G. (1975). Speaking like a "man" in Teamsterville: Cultural patterns of role enactment in an urban neighborhood. *Quarterly Journal of Speech*, 61, 13–22.

Philipsen, G. (1976). Places for speaking in Teamsterville. *Quarterly Journal of Speech*, 62, 15–25.

Pipe, R. (1979). National policies, international debates. *Quarterly Journal of Speech*, 29, 114–123.

Porat, M. U. (1978). Global implications of the information society. *Journal of Communication*, 28, 70–80.

Rice, J. S. (1992). Discursive formation, life stories, and the emergence of co-dependency: "Power/knowledge" and the search for identity. *The Sociological Quarterly*, 33, 337–364.

Rich, A. L. (1971). Some problems in interracial communication. *Central States Speech Journal*, 22, 228–235.

Righter, R. (1979). Who won? *Journal of Communication*, 29, 192–194.

Sayer, J. E. (1979). The student's right to his own language: A response to Colquit. *Communication Quarterly*, 27, 44–46.

Shuter, R. (1979). A field study of nonverbal communication in Germany, Italy, and the United States. *Communication Monographs*, 44, 298–305.

Shuter, R. (1979). The dap in the military: Hand-to-hand communication. *Journal of Communication*, 29, 136–142.

Shuter, R. (1990). The centrality of culture. *The Southern Communication Journal*, 55, 237–249.

vanDijk, T. A. (1987). *Communicating racism: Ethnic prejudice in thought and talk.* Newbury Park, CA: Sage.

Whiting, G. C. (1971). Code restrictedness and opportunities for change in developing countries. *Journal of Communication*, 21, 36–57.

Whiting, G. C. & Hitt, W. C. (1972). Code-restrictedness and communication dependent problem solving: An exploratory study, *Communication Monographs*, j8, 68–73.

Wood, J. T. (1994). *Gendered lives: Communication, gender, and culture.* Belmont, CA: Wadsworth.

Appendix

Decade of the 1950s

1951 November Campa, A. L. Language barriers in intercultural relations. *Journal of Communication*, 1, 41–46.

1952 May Knode, D. P. The Iron Curtain refugee in a new world. *Journal of Communication*, 2, 1–5.

1958 Spring Bakonyi, S. Divergence and convergence in culture and communication. *Journal of Communication*, 3, 24–30.

Decade of the 1960s

1963 June Keller, P. W. The study of face-to-face international decision-making. *Journal of Communication*, 8, 67–76.

1964 Autumn Chu, G. C. Problems of cross-cultural communication research. *Journalism Quarterly*, 61, 557–562.

1966 December Wedge, B. Nationality and social perception. *Journal of Communication*, 16, 278–282.

1966 December Flack, M. J. Communicable and uncommunicable aspects in personal international relationships. *Journal of Communication*, 16, 283–290.

1966 December Stewart, E. C. The simulation of cultural differences. *Journal of Communication*, 16, 291–304.

1968 December Lorimar, E. S., & Dunn, S. W. Reference groups, congruity theory, and cross-cultural persuasion. *Journal of Communication*, 18, 354–368.

Decade of the 1970s

1970 January Gregg, R., McCormack, A. J., & Pedersen, D. A description of the interaction between black youth and white teachers in a ghetto speech class. *Communication Education*, 19, 1–8.

1970 Spring Bostian, L. R. The two-step flow theory: Cross-cultural implications. *Journalism Quarterly*. 67, 109–117.

1970 June Daniel, J. The facilitation of white-black communication. *Journal of Communication*, 10, 134–141.

1970 Winter Daniel, J. The poor: Aliens in an affluent society: Cross-cultural communication. *Communication Quarterly*, 18, 15–21.

1971 March Whiting, G. C. Code restrictedness and opportunities for change in developing countries. *Journal of Communication*, 51, 36–57.

1971 Winter Rich, A. L. Some problems in interracial communication. *Central States Speech Journal* 22, 228–235.

1972 March Whiting, G. C. & Hitt, W. C. Code-restrictedness and communication dependent problem solving: An exploratory study, *Communication Monographs*, 39, 68–73.

1972 Summer Dubner, F. S. Nonverbal aspects of Black english. *Southern Speech Communication Journal*, 37, 361–374.

1973 Spring Cheseboro, J. W. Cultures in conflict—a generic and axiological view. *Communication Quarterly*, 21, 11–20.

1974 Fall Lumsden, G., Brown, D. R., Lumsden, D., & Hill, T. A. An investigation of differences in verbal behavior between black and white informal peer group. *Communication Quarterly*, 12, 31–36.

1975 February Philipsen, G. Speaking like a "man" in Teamsterville: Cultural patterns of role enactment in an urban neighborhood. *Quarterly Journal of Speech*, 41, 13–22.

1975 March Miller, D. T. The effect of dialect and ethnicity on communication effectiveness. *Communication Monographs*, 6t, 69–74.

1975 April Carey, J. W. Communication and culture. *Communication Research*, 2, 173–191.

1975 Winter Woodward, G. C. Mystification in the rhetoric of cultural dominance and colonial control. *Central States Speech Journal*, 26, 298–303.

1976 February Philipsen, G. Places for speaking in Teamsterville. *Quarterly Journal of Speech*, 62, 15–25.

1976 February Daniel, J. L., & Smitherman, G. How I got over: Communication dynamics in the Black community. *Quarterly Journal of Speech*, 61, 26–39.

1976 Summer Fine, G. A. Obscene joking across cultures. *Journal of Communication*, 16, 134–140.

1977 January Stevenson, R. L. Studying communications across cultures. *Communication Research*, 4, 113–128.

1977 Spring Katz, E. Can authentic cultures survive new media? *Journal of Communication*, 27, 113–121.

1977 Spring Dissanalyaki, W. New wine in old bottles: Can folk media convey modern messages? *Journal of Communication*, 17, 122–124.

1977 Spring Lomax. A. Appeal for cultural equity. *Journal of Communication*, 27, 125–138.

1977 Spring Pool, I. del Sola. The changing flow of television. *Journal of Communication*, 17, 139–149.

1977 Spring O'Brien, R. C. Professionalism in broadcasting in developing countries. *Journal of Communication*, 17, 150–153.

1977 Spring Cassirer, H. R. Radio as the people's medium. *Journal of Communication*, 27, 154–157.

1977 Spring Martin, T. H., Byrne, R. B., & Wedemeyer, D. J. Balance: An aspect to the right to communicate. *Journal of Communication*. S7, 158–162.

1977 Autumn Kent, K. E. M., & Rush, R. R. International communication as a field: A study of Journalism Quarterly citations. *Journalism Quarterly*, 54, 580–583.

1977 Fall Colquit, J. L. The student's right to his own language: A viable model or empty rhetoric? *Communication Quarterly*, 15, 17–20.

1977 November Shuter, R. A field study of nonverbal communication in Germany, Italy, and the United States. *Communication Monographs*, 44, 298–305.

1977 Winter Goodyear, F. H., & West, A. An organizational framework for cross-cultural communication. *Southern Speech Communication Journal*, 42, 178–190.

1978 July Kreiling, A. Toward a cultural studies approach for the sociology of popular culture. *Communication Research*, 5, 240–263.

1978 July Leed, E. J. Communications revolutions and the enactment of culture. *Communication Research*, 5, 305–319.

1978 July Golding, P., & Murdock, G. Theories of communication and theories of society. *Communication Research*, 5, 339–356.

1978 Winter Rogers, E. M. The rise and fall of the dominant paradigm. *Journal of Communication*, 28, 64–69.

1978 Winter Porat, M. U. Global implications of the information society. *Journal of Communication*, 18, 70–80.

1978 Winter Parker, E. B. An information-based hypothesis. *Journal of Communication*, 28, 81–83.

1978 Winter McAnany, E. G. (1978, Winter). Does information really work? *Journal of Communication*, 28, 84–90.

1979 Spring Masmoudi, M. The new world information order. *Journal of Communication*, 29, 172–185.

1979 Spring Androunas, E., & Zassoursky, Y. Protecting the sovereignty of information. *Journal of Communication*, 19, 186–191.

1979 Spring Righter, R. Who won? *Journal of Communication*, 19, 192–194.

1979 Spring Nordenstrong, K. Behind the semantics—a strategic design. *Journal of Communication*, 29, 195–198.

1979 Summer Pipe, R. National policies, international debates. *Journal of Communication*, 29, 114–123.

1979 Summer Eger, J. M. U.S. proposal for progress through negotiations. *Journal of Communication*, 29, 124–128.

1979 Summer Heintz, A. The dangers of regulation. *Journal of Communication*, 19, 129–134.

1979 Summer Freese, I. The dangers of non-regulation. *Journal of Communication*, 19, 135–137.

1979 Summer Saur, R. A. C. Protection without protectionism. *Journal of Communication*, 19, 138–140.

1979 Summer Mendelsohn, H. Delusions of technology. *Journal of Communication*, 29, 142–143.

1979 Summer Hamelink, C. J. Informatics: Third world call for new order. *Journal of Communication*, 19, 144–148.

1979 Summer Jacobson, R. E. The hidden issues: What kind of order? *Journal of Communication*, 29, 149–155.

1979 Fall Starosta, W. Roots for an older rhetoric: On rhetorical effectiveness in the Third World. *Western Journal of Speech Communication*, 43, 278–287.

1979 Winter Grossberg, L. Interpreting the "crisis" of culture in communication theory. *Journal of Communication*, 29, 56–68.

1979 Winter Sayer, J. E. The student's right to his own language: A response to Colquit. *Communication Quarterly*, 27, 44–46.

1979 Winter Shuter, R. The dap in the military: Hand-to-hand communication. *Journal of Communication*, 14, 136–142.

Decade of the 1980s

1980 August Jin, K. Explaining acculturation in a Communication framework: An empirical test. *Communication Monographs*, 47, 155–179.

1980 Winter Jain, H. C., Kanungo, R. N., & Goldhaber, G. M. Attitudes toward a communication system: A comparison of Anglophone and Francophone hospital employees. *Human Communication Research*, 6, 178–184.

1981 February Stanback, M. H., & Pearce, W. B. Talking to "the man": Some communication strategies used by members of "subordinate" social groups. *Quarterly Journal of Speech*, 68, 21–30.

1981 April Mansell, M. Transcultural experience and expressive response. *Communication Education*, 30, 93–108.

1982 Fall Cheseboro, J. W. Illness as a rhetorical act: A cross-cultural perspective. *Communication Quarterly*.

1982 Winter Yurn, J. O. Communication diversity and information acquisition among Korean immigrants in Hawaii. *Human Communication Research*, 8, 154–169.

1983 Summer Wolfson, K., & Pearce, W. B. A cross-cultural comparison of the implications of self-disclosures in conversational logics. *Communication Quarterly*, 31, 249–256.

1983 Fall Gudykunst, W. B. Similarities and differences in perceptions of initial intracultural and intercultural encounters: An exploratory investigation. *Southern Speech Communication Journal*, 49, 49–65.

1983 Winter Kolzenny, F., Neuendorf, K., Burgoon, M., Burgoon, J. K., & Greenberg, B. S. Cultural identification as predictor of content preferences of Hispanics. *Journalism Quarterly*, 60, 677–685.

1984 March Gudykunst, W. B., & Nishida, T. Individual and cultural influences on uncertainty reduction. *Communication Monographs*, 51, 23–36.

1985 Spring Gudykunst, W. B., Seung-Mock, Y., & Nishida, T. A cross-cultural test of uncertainty reduction theory: Comparisons of acquaintances, friends, and dating relationships in Japan, Korea, and the U.S. *Human Communication Research*, 11, 407–455.

1985 September Gudykunst, W. B. The influence of cultural similarity, type of relationship, and self-monitoring on uncertainty reduction processes. *Communication Monographs*, 52, 203–217.

1985 Fall Gudykunst, W. B. An exploratory comparison of close intracultural and intercultural friendships. *Communication Quarterly*, 33, 270–283.

1985 Winter Johnson, J. D., & Tums, A. R. Communication factors related to closer international ties. *Human Communication Research*, 12, 259–273.

1986 March Wheeless, L. R., Erickson, K. V., & Behrens, J. S. Cultural differences in disclosiveness as a function of locus of control. *Communication Monographs*, 53, 36–46.

1986 Spring Choe, J. H., Wilcox, G. B., & Hardy, A. P. Facial expressions in magazine ads: A cross-cultural comparison. *Journalism Quarterly*, (volume # omitted), 122–126.

1986 September Stewart, L. P., Gudykunst, W. B., Ting-Toomey, S., & Nishida, T. The effects of decision-making style on openness and satisfaction within Japanese organizations. *Communication Monographs*, 53, 236–251.

1986 Winter Gudykunst, W. B., & Nishida, T. The influence of cultural variability on perceptions of communication behavior associated with relationship terms. *Human Communication Research*, 13, 147–166.

1987 February Gudykunst, W. B., Yang, S. M., & Nishida, T. Cultural differences in self-consciousness and self-monitoring. *Communication Research*, 14, 7–34.

1987 Summer Gudykunst, W. B., Sodetani, L. L., & Sonoda, K. T. Uncertainty reduction in Japanese-American/Caucasian relationships in Hawaii. *Western Journal of Communication*, 51, 256–278.

1987 Fall Foeman, A., & Pressley, G. Ethnic culture and corporate culture: Using Black styles in organizations. *Communication Quarterly*, 35, 293–307.

1988 Spring Collier, M. J. A comparison of conversations among and between domestic culture groups: How inter and intracultural competencies vary. *Communication Quarterly*, 36, 122–144.

1988 Spring Ting-Toomey, S. Rhetorical sensitivity style in three cultures: France, Japan, and the United States. *Central States Speech Journal*, 39, 28–36.

1988 Summer Gudykunst, W. B., & Hammer, M. R. The influence of social identity and intimacy of interethnic relationships on uncertainty reduction processes. *Human Communication Research*, 4, 569–601.

1988 December Yum, J. O. The impact of Confucianism on interpersonal relationships and communication. *Communication Monographs*, 55, 374–388.

1989 Spring Chen, G. M. Relationships of the dimensions of intercultural communication competence. *Communication Quarterly*, 37, 118–133.

1989 Fall Gonzalez, A. "Participation" at WMEX-FM. *Western Journal of Communication*, 53, 398–410.

1989 December Kecht, M. L., Ribeau, S., & Alberts, J. K. An Afro-American perspective on interethnic communication. *Communication Monographs*, 55, 385–410.

1989 Winter Gudykunst, W. B., Nishida, T., & Schmidt, K. L. The influence of cultural, relational, and personality factors in uncertainty reduction processes. *Western Journal of Communication*, 53, 13–29.

The Year of 1990

1990 February Leeds-Hurwitz, W. Notes on the history of intercultural communication: The Foreign Service Institute and the mandate for intercultural training. *Quarterly Journal of Speech*, 76, 262–281.

1990 Spring McCroskey, 3. C., Burroughs, N. F., Daun, A., & Richmond, V. P. Correlates of quietness: Swedish and American perspectives. *Communication Quarterly*, 38, 127–137.

1990 Spring Shuter, R. The centrality of culture. *Southern Speech Communication Journal*, j5, 237–249.

1990 Spring Asante, M. K. The tradition of advocacy in the Yoruba courts. *Southern Speech Communication Journal*, 55, 250–259.

1990 Spring Broome, B. J. "Palevone": Foundations of struggle and conflict in Greek interpersonal communication. *Southern Speech Communication Journal* 55, 260–275.

1990 Spring Gonzalez, A. Mexican "otherness" in the rhetoric of Mexican Americans. *Southern Speech Communication Journal*, j5, 276–291.

1990 Spring Frye, P. A. Form and function of North Yemeni Qat sessions. *Southern Speech Communication Journal*, 55, 292–304.

1990 Spring Ma, R. An exploratory study of discontented responses in American and Chinese relationships. *Southern Speech Communication Journal*, 55, 305–318.

1990 Spring DiMare, L. Ma and Japan. *Southern Speech Communication Journal*, 55, 319–328.

1990 Fall Andersen, P. A., Lustig, M. W., & Andersen, J. F. Changes in latitude, changes in attitude: The relationship between climate and interpersonal communication predispositions. *Communication Quarterly*, 38, 291–311.

1990 Fall Collier, M. J., & Powell, R. Ethnicity, instructional communication, and classroom systems. *Communication Quarterly*, 38, 334–349.

1990 Fall McCroskey, J. C., & Richmond, V. P. Willingness to communicate differing cultural perspectives. *Southern Speech Communication Journal*, 56, 72–77.

Article Review Form at end of book.

What are some of the alternative concepts of cross-cultural competency?

The Study of Cross-Cultural Competence

Traditions and contemporary issues

Brent D. Ruben
Rutgers University

A Pragmatic Tradition

Much of the impetus for the study of cross-cultural communication competence arose out of efforts to cope with practical problems encountered by individuals living and working overseas, and by their institutional sponsors (Aitken, 1973; Byrnes, 1966; Cleveland & Mangone, 1957; Cleveland, Mangone, & Adams, 1960; Davis, 1969; Gullahorn & Gullahorn, 1966; Hall & Whyte, 1963; Hawes & Kealey, 1980, 1981; Lysgaard, 1955; Maretzki, 1969; Miller, 1972; Morris, 1960; Oberg, 1960; Russell, 1978; Sewell & Davidsen, 1961; Smith, 1965; Spector, Parris, Humphrey, Aronson, & Williams, 1969; Stein, 1963; Torbiorn, 1982; Tucker, Raik, Rossikr, & Uhes, 1973; Unseem, Unseem, & Donoghue, 1963). There were difficulties of culture shock, personal adjustment, cultural adaptation and cross-cultural effectiveness. The definitions of each were then, as many would argue they remain today, relatively ambiguous and un-

Requests for reprints should be addressed to: Dr. Brent Ruben, Rutgers University, SCILS, 4 Huntington St., New Brunswick, NJ 08903.

differentiated. But regardless of whatever terminological confusion existed, there could be little doubt that these were obstacles of significance. The problems were apparent in the business community, where measurement came in the form of "project failures," "botched negotiations," "early return of workers" and "lost time and money" (Aitken, 1973; Cleveland et al., 1960; Davis, 1969; Russell, 1978). Peace Corp volunteers encountered a similar set of impediments, though these were more typically described not only in terms of "project failure," but with reference to volunteers' personal adjustment difficulties or lack of cultural participation (Harris, 1970, 1973, 1975; Jones & Burns, 1970; Jones & Popper, 1972; Maretzki, 1969; Smith, 1965; Stein, 1963).

In large measure it was these problems, and the efforts to solve them which provided motivation for the kind of academic study that led to interest in the concept of intercultural competence. Perspectives were needed that would help to meet four essential needs:

1. to explain overseas failures;
2. to predict overseas successes;
3. to develop personnel selection strategies; and
4. to design, implement and test sojourner training and preparation methodologies.

Each of these four needs has played an important role in directing theory and research activities in the field since the earliest days, and each has contributed to the development of our thinking relative to cross-cultural competence.

Explaining Failure

Most early efforts to delineate reasons for failure relied heavily on anecdotal methods, where individuals with first-hand experience, recounted and reported on incidents of those who had failed, offering conjectures as to factors presumed to underlie the downfall. Dimensions mentioned included sojourner personality, inadequate language facility, lack of appropriate technical or job skills, poor preparation, lack of adequate family/support system, job or project difficulties, and other culture-specific problems.

Over time, a number of productive and rigorous descriptive efforts have been undertaken in pursuit of the goal of identifying factors and patterns associated with overseas failure and its outcomes. Such efforts

"The Study of Cross-Cultural Competence: Traditions and Contemporary Issues." Brent D. Ruben. INTERNATIONAL JOURNAL OF INTERCULTURAL RELATIONS, Volume 13, 1989. Reprinted by permission of the author.

have served us well in their own right, and also served to lay the groundwork for efforts to predict and control outcomes on an a priori basis.

Predicting Successes

Attempts at predicting cross-cultural success were initially psychological, focusing on characteristics of the prospective sojourner which were thought might predispose the individual to success or failure. Important work in this area was done for the Peace Corp with the goal of identifying individuals who would be well-suited for overseas assignment (Guthrie & Zektick, 1967; Harris, 1970, 1973, 1975; Jones & Burns, 1970; Jones & Popper, 1972; Maretzki, 1969; Mischel, 1965; Smith, 1965; Stein, 1963). Sojourners were assessed based on technical and personal qualities. Thought to be important were an individual's attitudes toward individuals of different cultures, motivation, values, tolerance for ambiguity, adaptability, and personal adjustment in one's own culture.

Most predictive studies employed measurements that were in one way or another *self-report*. Sometimes individuals were asked directly about their attitudes, motives, and values in open-ended interviews. In other instances, measures were more unobtrusive, using scales and Rorschach testing. While these studies provided an important foundation for subsequent study, they generally fell short of their goal of providing clear-cut predictions of individuals who would succeed and those who would fail.

It has been argued that one explanation for the disappointing results using psychological measures, was the measurement system typically employed. As mentioned previously, many of the diagnostic tools relied on self-reports by prospective sojourner of their attitudes, values, motives, goals and the like. The validity of data of this type, rested fundamentally on the presumption that respondents have the *desire* and *ability* to engage in valid self-assessment. Indeed there were circumstances where the desire for candid self-assessment was present. But in many circumstances, these assessments were called for at a time when prospective sojourners may have perceived (often correctly) that their responses would influence the likelihood of their selection for foreign postings—not exactly an ideal circumstance for encouraging candor and full-disclosure.

Perhaps a more significant, if also a more subtle, difficulty was an assumption that potential sojourners were sufficiently self-aware to provide accurate verbal assessments that would usefully predict subsequent behavior patterns. One is reminded here of the imprecision and bias associated with self-perception, and of the many assertions and resolutions that are verbalized with all good intentions, but which, for one reason or another, are never translated in behavior.

Behavioral observation methods were suggested as an alternative to verbal, self-report measures, and were implemented on a limited basis with some promise (Ruben, 1976; Ruben & Kealey, 1979). The objective of the approach was to examine not so much one's desires, motives, personality, or attitudes, but rather the observable communication behaviors. Emphasis was, then, on *the communicated rather than as conceptualized, hoped for, or intended.* Implicit in this approach was the need to identify particular communication competencies that might be important to cross cultural success, an effort which continues systematically in work underway in the field (Hammer, 1984, 1987; Hawes & Kealey, 1980, 1981; Kealey, 1988, 1989a, 1989b; Koester & Olebe, 1986; Martin & Hammer, 1989; Nishida, 1985; Olebe & Koester, 1989).

Efforts to predict cross-cultural outcomes have been frustrated by problems of conceptualization and definition. What exactly do we mean by cross-cultural success, culture shock, adaptation, overseas effectiveness, and how are these related to one another theoretically and operationally? There is little doubt that these nagging and complex issues are still at the heart of research and conceptual difficulties today (Abe & Wiseman, 1983; Adelman, 1988; Adler, 1975, 1982; Bennett, 1977; Benson, 1978; Brein & David, 1971; Brislin, 1981; Church, 1982; Collier, 1989; David 1972; Furnham, 1984; Furnham & Bochner, 1982, 1986; Gullahorn & Gullahorn, 1963; Hall, 1966, 1976; Hammer, Gudykunst, & Wiseman, 1978; Hwang, Chase, & Kelly, 1980; Imahori & Lanigan, 1989; Kim, 1988; Kim and Ruben, 1988; Oberg, 1960; Ruben, 1985; Ruben, Askling, & Kealey, 1977; Sargent, 1970; Spitzberg, 1989; Wiseman, Hammer, & Nishida, 1989).

Selecting Prospects

For those whose work has involved the selection of candidates for overseas placement, the challenge of identifying reasons for failure and methods for predicting success has been of extraordinary significance (Baum, 1976; Kealey & Ruben, 1983; Miller, 1972; Schwartz, 1973; Tucker, 1974; Tucker & Schiller, 1975). Particularly for professionals without behavioral science training, the approach has generally been to recruit and select individuals for overseas assignment based primarily on technical/job qualifications. Such a decision-making framework implicitly utilizes a behavioral observation approach, in that candidates who surface are those with demonstrated records of accomplishment. Many decision makers in corporate and governmental organizations have become painfully aware, however, that there are major limitations of this approach to selection: Often the very persons who are successful in the Western world, are often wholly inappropriate for cross-cultural postings precisely because of the orientations that ensured their success here. An individual who is extremely ambitious and task-oriented, an aggressive problem-solver, who lives out a "time-is-money" philosophy—not infrequently the profile of success in North America—is arguably a person with a profile for failure in many cultures, particularly in the Third-World, where relationships and tradition are priorities (Ruben & Kealey, 1979).

As a consequence of this kind of awareness, increasing attention has been devoted to factoring in assessments of "people skills," and cross-cultural (and communication) competencies alongside more purely technical and occupational competencies.

Training Sojourners

If we knew the reasons for overseas failure and could predict success, we might be able to provide training problems to enhance these skills, and thereby increase the probability of positive outcomes. Indeed it is with this outlook that many educators and trainers looked with interest to research examining overseas failure and successes. Even in the absence of precise knowledge in this area, intercultural training programs of various kinds have been an important activity within the intercultural field for years. These programs and workshops have hopefully been a valuable forum for their many participants. At the same time, these programs have also been a most fertile environment for theory building and testing, and the development of improved concepts of the kinds of communication skills and capabilities which seem critical to meaningful interactions with individuals from other cultures (Ackermann, 1976; Brislin & Pedersen, 1976; Casse, 1981; Hammer, 1984; LaFromboise & Rowe, 1983; Maretzki, 1965; Martin, 1986).

Issues for Today and Tomorrow

The traditions of study of cross-cultural competence have provided a promising foundation built in practical need on the one hand, and theoretical and research advances on the other. Those who have been interested in the area for some time must be very pleased by what seems to be the growing interest in the topic today. Alongside individuals from the cross-cultural communication subdiscipline, are scholars from interpersonal communication who share a baseline interest in issues of human communication competence and its measurement. There are a number of issues worthy of being addressed to further advance our thinking about cross-cultural communication competence, and a broader base of interest and expertise will certainly be welcomed in meeting this challenge. In the sections that follow, six such issues will be listed and briefly discussed.

1. What Are the Facets of Cross-Cultural Competence?

A great deal has been written on the nature and dimensions of competence. Among some scholars of communication competence, much of the writing seems to suggest that *competence* is primarily concerned with relationship-building and maintenance (Bostrom, 1984; Ruben, 1976; Ruben & Kealey, 1979; Spitzberg, 1988; Wiemann, 1977; Wiemann & Backlund, 1980). Unfortunately, for many non-academics and even some traditional cross-cultural scholars, this is not the most obvious, nor necessarily the most important, sense in which the word *competence* is used. Other meanings focus on "an ability to get things done"—suggesting criteria of *task*, as well as *relational orientation*.

At some point it seems important to examine, and if necessary to reconcile, alternative conceptualizations. One alternative may be to conclude that competence has various facets:

1. **Relational-Building and Maintenance Competence**—Competence associated with the establishment and maintenance of positive relationships.

2. **Information-Transfer Competence**—Competence associated with the transmission of information with minimum loss and distortion.

3. **Compliance-Gaining Competence**—Competence associated with persuasion and securing an appropriate level of compliance and/or cooperation.

While facets such as these may be conceptually and empirically related, they are operationally distinguishable—and distinguished—in many cross-cultural theory, research, selection, and training contexts. As such, there could be value in such a differentiation.

2. How Is Cross-Cultural Competence to Be Defined and Differentiated from Related Concepts?

What is the relationship of *cross-cultural competence* to concepts such as *style, adjustment,* and *adaptation*. The need for conceptual clarity of this kind has already been referenced previously. Attention to definition and operationalization in our investigations seems essential if the promise of research and theory that builds on and advances previous work is to be realized.

3. Is Cross-Cultural Competence a Matter of Attitude, Knowledge or Behavior?

Posing the question in this oversimplified manner hopefully will not obscure what continues to be an important issue: Is cross-cultural competence a matter of an attitude, a question of knowledge, and an issue of behavior? Or, is it a combination of two or more of these? Previous research efforts seem to suggest that attitudes alone, are not sufficient to predict patterns of overseas success or failure, but do they contribute to or predispose such patterns?

Certainly some knowledges are important to competence—at least some facets of competence as previously mentioned. Knowledge of language, for instance, is obviously important to cross-cultural *information-transfer competence*. Is such knowledge—and perhaps knowledge of cultural and communication rules—not equally important to compliance gaining and relationship-building? Perhaps the most observable and significant manifestation of attitudes and knowledges is behavior. But, exactly what behaviors?

4. Where Does Cross-Cultural Competence Reside?

Is cross-cultural competence a *sender-based* variable, a characteristic or set of characteristics an individual possesses and/or displays. The implication here is that it is possible to conceive of *an individual who is competent*. Or is competence, like credibility, solely in the eye-of-the-beholder, and thus, a *receiver-based* attribute? Here, the implication is that there would be no competent individuals unless they were so regarded by some receiver.

A third alternative is a *dyadic, systemic,* or *culture-based* conceptualization, where competence is defined based on a set of relational, social or cultural rules. Would this then mean that an individual who is competent (or judged to be competent) in one relationship or culture, would be classed as incompetent in another? Important, and not simple issues.

5. How Should Cross-Cultural Competence Be Measured?

Certainly one of the most difficult issues for those interested in studying cross-cultural competence has to do with its measurement. First, issues of conceptual and operational definition referred to previously are vital.

Assuming clarity of this type, how does one overcome the numerous methodological problems inherent in cross-cultural research of this type? The challenges of research designs utilizing self-report methods which assume candor and self-awareness have already been alluded to previously. Less direct methods, such as content analysis and conversational analysis are subject to the usual problems of interpretation, in addition to the layer of problems that may be introduced by cultural differences.

Behavioral observation methods and other third-party observational approaches have potential problems of interrater reliability and cultural bias to overcome. And perhaps even more than with other approaches, there are inherent obstacles in generalizing findings across cultures. In essence, all of the knotty problems of research design and measurement, interpretation and generalization that present themselves within one's own culture, present particular obstacles in intercultural research settings.

6. Is Interpersonal Communication Competence a Special Case of Cross-Cultural Communication Competence, or the Other Way Around?

If all communication occurs in a cultural context, then all interpersonal communication is intercultural communication, as well. This being the case, is intercultural communication competence the broader category of which interpersonal communication competence is but a special case?

Alternatively, if one conceives of interpersonal communication as the essential form of human interaction, then the study of cross-cultural communication competence becomes the study of a special instance of interpersonal communication.

There is more than simply a semantic or political argument here (Ellingsworth, 1977; Spitzberg, 1988; Spitzberg, 1989). At the least, there are a number of important conceptual and methodological implications of how we resolve this emerging debate. To the extent the dialogue holds promise for stimulating a reexamination of what may be a very arbitrary (and perhaps dysfunctional) delineation between interpersonal and intercultural communication, there is reason to be enthusiastic about the discourse, if only for this reason.

Conclusion

A number of non-trivial issues face theorists and researchers who are interested in cross-cultural communication competence, and there is reason to believe that the energy and resources being directed toward them holds great promise for significant advances in the period ahead. The challenge which presents itself today is, on the one hand to further advance theory regarding one of the most fundamental elements in human interaction.

At another level, the challenge is also to contribute meaningfully to the pragmatic tradition which served to stimulate interest in cross-cultural competence. As the world of commerce and government moves daily closer to the vision of the global village that not long ago seemed merely to be rhetoric, the need for a comprehensive understanding of cross-cultural competence has never been greater.

References

Abe, H., & Wiseman, R. (1983). A cross-cultural confirmation of the dimensions of intercultural effectiveness. *International Journal of Intercultural Relations, 7,* 53–67.

Ackerman, J. M. (1976). Skill training for foreign assignment: The reluctant U.S. case. In L. A. Samovar & R. E. Porter (Eds.), *Intercultural communication: A reader,* Belmont, CA: Wadsworth.

Adelman, M. B. (1988). Cross-cultural adjustment: A theoretical perspective on social support. *International Journal of Intercultural Relations, 12,* 183–204.

Adler, P. S. (1975). The transition experience: An alternative view of culture shock. *Journal of Humanistic Psychology, 15*(4), 13–23.

Adler, P. S. (1982). Beyond cultural identity: Reflections on cultural and multicultural man. In L. A. Samovar & R. E. Porter (Eds.), *Intercultural communication: A reader* (pp. 389–408). Belmont, CA: Wadsworth.

Aitken, T. (1973). *The multinational man: The role of the manager abroad.* New York: Wiley.

Baum, C. (1976). *Selecting personnel for foreign assignments.* Unpublished master's thesis, School of Business and Management, Pepperdine University, CA.

Bennett, J. (1977). Transition shock: Putting culture shock in perspective. *International and Intercultural Communication Annual, 4,* 45–52.

Benson, P. G. (1978). Measuring cross-cultural adjustment: The problem of criteria. *International Journal of Intercultural Relations, 2*(1), 21–37.

Bostrom, R. N. (1984). *Competence in communication: A multidisciplinary approach.* Beverly Hills, CA: Sage.

Brein, M., & David, K. (1971). Intercultural communication and the adjustment of the sojourner. *Psychological Bulletin, 76,* 215–230.

Brislin, R. W. (1981). *Cross-cultural encounters: Face-to-face encounters.* New York: Pergamon.

Brislin, R. W., & Pedersen, P. (1976). *Cross-cultural orientation programs.* New York: Gardner Press.

Byrnes, F. C. (1966). Role shock: An occupational hazard of American technical assistants abroad. *Annals of the American Academy of Political and Social Science, 368,* 95–108.

Casse, P. (1981). *Training for the cross-cultural mind* (2nd ed.). Washington, DC: Society for Intercultural Training and Development.

Church, A. T. (1982). Sojourner adjustment. *Psychology Bulletin, 91*(3), 540–572.

Cleveland, H., & Mangone, G. J. (1957). *The art of overseamanship.* New York: Syracuse University Press.

Cleveland, H., Mangone, G. J., & ADAMS, J. C. (1960). *The overseas Americans.* New York: McGraw-Hill.

Collier, M. J. (1989). Cultural and intercultural communication competence: Current approaches and directions for future research. *International Journal of Intercultural Relations, 13,* 287–302.

David, K. (1972). Intercultural adjustment and applications for reinforcement theory to problems of culture shock. *Trends, 4*(3), 1–64.

Davis, D. (1969). Cultural frictions of American technicians abroad. *Texas Business Review, 43*(11).

Ellingsworth, H. W. (1977). Conceptualizing intercultural communication. *Communication Yearbook*, **1,** 89–98.

Furnham, A. (1984). Tourism and culture shock. *Annals of Tourism Research*, **11,** 41–57.

Furnham, A., & Bochner, S. (1982). Social difficulty in a foreign culture. In S. Bochner (Ed.), *Cultures in contact.* Elmsford, NY: Pergamon.

Furnham, A., & Bochner, S. (1986). *Culture shock: Psychological reactions to unfamiliar environments.* London: Metheun.

Gullahorn, J., & Gullahorn, J. (1963). An extension of the U-curve hypothesis. *Journal of Social Issues*, **19,** 33–47.

Gullahorn, J. E., & Gullahorn, J. T. (1966). American students abroad: Professional versus personal development. *The Annals*, **368,** 43–59.

Guthrie, G. M., & Zektick, I. N. (1967). Predicting performance in the Peace Corps. *Journal of Social Psychology*, **71,** 11–21.

Hall, E. T. (1966). *The hidden dimension.* Garden City, NY: Doubleday.

Hall, E. T. (1976). *Beyond culture.* New York: Doubleday.

Hall, E. T., & Whyte, W. F. (1963). Intercultural communication: A guide to men of action. *Practical Anthropology*, **10,** 216–299.

Hammer, M. R. (1984). The effects of an intercultural communication workshop on participants' intercultural communication competence: An exploratory study. *Communication Quarterly*, **32**(4), 252–262.

Hammer, M. R. (1987). Behavioral dimensions of intercultural effectiveness: A replication and extension. *International Journal of Intercultural Relations*, **11,** 65–88.

Hammer, M., Gudykunst, W., & Wiseman, R. (1978). Dimensions of intercultural effectiveness: An exploratory study. *International Journal of Intercultural Relations*, **2,** 382–393.

Harris, J. G. (1970). Prediction of success on a lonely Pacific island: Peace Corps style. *Trends*, **3,** 1–69.

Harris, J. G. (1973). A science of the South Pacific: An analysis of the character structure of the Peace Corp volunteer. *American Psychologist*, **28,** 232–247.

Harris, J. G. (1975). Identification of cross-cultural talent: The empirical approach of the Peace Corps. *Topics in Culture Learning*, **3,** 66–78.

Hawes, F., & Kealey, D. (1980). *Canadians in development.* Ottawa: Canadian International Development Agency.

Hawes, F., & Kealey, D. J. (1981). An empirical study of Canadian technical assistance. *International Journal of Intercultural Relations*, **5,** 239–258.

Hwang, J., Chase, L., & Kelly, C. (1980). An intercultural examination of communication competence. *Communication*, **10,** 70–79.

Imahori, T. T., & Lanigan, M. L. (1989). Relational model of intercultural communication competence. *International Journal of Intercultural Relations*, **13,** 269–286.

Jones, R. R., & Burns, W. J. (1970). Volunteer satisfaction with in-country training for the Peace Corps. *Journal of Applied Psychology*, **54**(6), 533–537.

Jones, R. R., & Popper, R. (1972). Characteristics of Peace Corps host countries and the behavior of volunteers. *Journal of Cross Cultural Psychology*, **3,** 233–245.

Kealey, D. J. (1988). *Explaining and predicting cross-cultural adjustment and effectiveness: A study of Canadian technical advisors overseas.* Hull, Quebec: Canadian International Development Agency.

Kealey, D. J. (1989a). *Cross-cultural effectiveness: A study of Canadian technical advisors overseas.* Hull, Quebec: Canadian International Development Agency.

Kealey, D. J. (1989b). A study of cross-cultural effectiveness: Theoretical issues, practical applications. *International Journal of Intercultural Relations*, **13,** 387–428.

Kealey, D. J., & Ruben, B. D. (1983). Cross-cultural personnel selection: Criteria, issues and methods. In D. Landis & R. Brislin (Eds.), *Handbook for intercultural training, Volume 1: Issues in theory and design* (pp. 155–175). New York: Pergamon.

Kim, Y. Y. (1988). *Communication and cross-cultural adaptation.* Philadelphia: Multilingual Matters.

Kim, Y., & Ruben, B. D. (1988). Intercultural transformation: A systems theory. *Theories in intercultural communication* (pp. 299–321). Beverly Hills, CA: Sage.

Koester, J., & Olebe, M. (1986, November). *The measurement of intercultural communication effectiveness: An extension of Ruben's behavioral assessment scales.* Paper presented at the Annual Conference of the Speech Communication Association, Chicago, IL.

Lafromboise, T. D., & Rowe, W. (1983). Skills training for bicultural competence: Rationale and Application. *Journal of Counseling Psychology*, **30**(4), 589–595.

Lysgaard, S. (1955). Adjustment in a foreign society: Norwegian Fulbright grantees visiting the United States. *International Social Science Bulletin*, **7,** 45–51.

Maretzki, T. W. (1965). Transition training: A theoretical approach. *Human Organization*, **24**(2), 128–134.

Maretzki, T. W. (1969). Transcultural adjustment of Peace Corps volunteers. In J. C. Finney (Ed.), *Culture change, mental health, and poverty.* Lexington: University of Kentucky Press.

Martin, J. N. (1986). Training issues in cross-cultural orientation. *International Journal of Intercultural Relations*, **10,** 103–116.

Martin, J. N., & Hammer, M. R. (1989). Behavioral categories of intercultural communication competence: Everyday communicators' perceptions. *International Journal of Intercultural Relations*, **13,** 303–332.

Miller E. L. (1972). The overseas assignment: How managers determine who is to be selected. *Michigan Business Review*, **24**(3), 12–19.

Mischel, W. (1965). Predicting the success of Peace Corps volunteers in Nigeria. *Journal of Personality and Social Psychology*, **1**(5), 510–517.

Morris, R. T. (1960). *The two-way mirror: National status in foreign students' adjustment.* Minneapolis: University of Minnesota Press.

Nishida, H. (1985). Japanese intercultural communication competence and cross-cultural adjustment. *International Journal of Intercultural Relations*, **9,** 247–269.

Oberg, K. (1960). Culture shock: Adjustment to new cultural environments. *Practical Anthropology*, **7,** 177–182.

Olebe, M., & Koester, J. (1989). Exploring the cross-cultural equivalence of the behavioral assessment scale for intercultural communication. *International Journal of Intercultural Relations*, **13,** 333–347.

Ruben, B. D. (1976). Assessing communication competency for intercultural adaptation. *Group and Organization Studies*, **1**(3), 334–354.

Ruben, B. D. (1985). Human communication and cross-cultural effectiveness. In L. A. Samovar & R. E. Porter (Ed.), *Intercultural communication: A reader* (pp. 338–346). Belmont, CA: Wadsworth.

Ruben, B. D., Askling, L. R., & Kealey, D. J. (1977). Cross-cultural effectiveness. In D. Hoopes, P. Pedersen, & G. Renwick (Eds.), *Overview of intercultural training, education and research, Vol. 1: Theory* (pp. 92–105). Washington, DC: Society for Intercultural Education, Training, and Research.

Ruben, B. D., & Kealey, D. J. (1979). Behavioral assessment of communication competency and the prediction of cross-cultural adaptation. *International Journal of Intercultural Relations*, **3,** 15–47.

Russell, P. W. (1978). *Dimensions of overseas success in industry.* Unpublished doctoral thesis. Ft. Collins, CO: Colorado State University.

Sargent, C. (1970). *Psychological aspects of environment adjustment.* Unpublished paper.

Schwartz, P. A. (1973). Selecting effective team leaders. *Focus*, **2,** 2–8.

Sewell, W. H., & Davidsen, O. M. (1961). *Scandinavian students on an American campus.* Minneapolis: University of Minnesota Press.

Smith, M. B. (1965). An analysis of two measures of "authoritarianism" among Peace Corps teachers. *Journal of Personality*, **33,** 513–535.

Spector, P., Parris, T., Humphrey, R., Aronson, J., & Williams, C. (1969). *Troop-community relations research in Korea. Technical report.* Washington, DC: American Institutes for Research.

Spitzberg, B. H. (1988). Communication competence: Measures of perceived effectiveness. In C. H. Tardy (Ed.), *A handbook for the study of human communication* (pp. 67–105). Hillsdale, NJ: Ablex.

Spitzberg, B. H. (1989). Issues in the development of a theory of interpersonal competence in the intercultural context. *International Journal of Intercultural Relations*, **13,** 241–268.

Stein, M. (1963). *The criterion, prediction, and changes in the Columbia I PCVs upon completion of their 2 year assignment. Final report.* Peace Corps.

Torbiorn, I. (1982). *Living abroad: personal adjustment and personnel policy in the overseas setting.* Chichester: Wiley.

Tucker, M. (1974). *Screening and selection for overseas assignment: Assessments and recommendations to U.S. Navy.* Denver, CO: Center for Research and Education.

Tucker, M., Raik, H., Rossikr, D., & Uhes, M. (1973). *Improving cross-cultural training and measurement for cross-cultural learning.* Denver, CO: Centre for Research and Education.

Tucker, M. F., & Schiller, J. E. (1975). *Overview summary for an assessment of the screening problems for overseas assignment.* Denver, CO: Centre for Research and Education.

Unseem, J., Unseem, R., & Donoghue, J. (1963). Men in the middle of the third culture: The roles of American and non-Western people in cross-cultural administration. *Human Organization*, **22,** 169–179.

Wiemann, J. A. (1977). Explication and test of a model of communicative competence. *Human Communication Research*, **3**(3), 195–213.

Wiemann,, J. M., & Backlund, P. (1980). Current theory and research in communicative competence. *Review of Educational Research*, **50,** 185–199.

Wieman, R. L., Hammer, M. R., & Nishida, H. (1989). Predictors of intercultural communication competence. *International Journal of Intercultural Relations*, **13,** 349–370.

Article Review Form at end of book.

What are some of the flaws in previous intercultural communication research that Hannigan identifies?

Traits, Attitudes, and Skills That Are Related to Intercultural Effectiveness and Their Implications for Cross-Cultural Training

A review of the literature

Terence P. Hannigan

Rockland Community College and Teachers College/Columbia University

The difficulty of adjusting to life in a foreign culture is an issue that has been with humankind throughout the ages. Today, with improved means of communication and transportation, the amount of cross-cultural contact has increased dramatically; however, our knowledge in this area is still limited. In order to select and train individuals who will function competently in different cultures we must have an understanding of what factors are important as criteria for successful cross-cultural functioning.

Overall, there are three categories into which these factors can be classified: skills, attitudinal factors, and personality traits. The first two categories are directly related to the training process, the implication being that persons can develop the necessary skills in order to function in a different culture and that attitudes can change. Personality traits are generally perceived as previously established in the individual's life or inherent. Therefore, this last factor relates to the selection process.

This review will examine these three factors as related to an individual's cross-cultural effectiveness with special emphasis on two populations which have been the target of numerous studies: Peace Corps Volunteers (PCVs) and International Students. However, before looking at the research on these populations, a brief review of terms is important, particularly *Adjustment, Adaptation, Acculturation, Assimilation,* and *Effectiveness.*

Adjustment

English (1958) defines Adjustment as "a condition of harmonious relation to the environment wherein one is able to obtain satisfaction for most of one's needs and to meet fairly well the demands, physical and social, put upon one." The author continues with a definition of *Relative Adjustment,* ". . . (the only actual

Requests for reprints should be addressed to: Terence P. Hannigan, International Student Services, Rockland Community College, 145 College Road, Suffern, NY 10901.

Reprinted from INTERNATIONAL JOURNAL OF INTERCULTURAL RELATIONS, Volume 14, Terence P. Hannigan, "Traits, Attitudes, and Skills That Are Related to Intercultural Effectiveness and Their Implications for Cross-Cultural Training: A Review of the Literature," 1990, with permission from Elsevier Science.

kind). 3. the process of making the changes needed in oneself or in one's environment to attain relative adjustment."

David (cited in Ruben & Kealey, 1979) conceptualized *Social Adjustment* as the sojourner's effectiveness as measured by interaction with nationals. This definition suggests that mere quantity of contact with nationals is the only criteria for defining the term.

Adler (1975) views *Cultural Adjustment* as "a field problem in adaptation (i.e., learning a language; being able to recognize the names of cities, foods and historical persons; and having a working knowledge of the essential customs and habits of the people)." These examples all deal with the acquisition of knowledge and imply a cognitive view of adjustment without consideration of emotional or behavioral factors.

Several researchers conceptualize adjustment as the sojourner's degree of satisfaction. Ruben and Kealey (1979) define *Psychological Adjustment* as "the general psychological well-being, self-satisfaction, contentment, comfort with, and accommodation to a new environment after the initial perturbations which characterized culture shock have passed." Torbiorn (1982) follows a similar approach with his definition of *Subjective Adjustment* which is an "individual's general satisfaction with his personal situation in the host country." He considers well-being or happiness as more or less analogous with Subjective Adjustment. The novelty in these definitions is the use of the sojourner's emotional state as a measure of the degree of adjustment. The former definition has the added feature of conceptualizing Adjustment as a process rather than a state. However one could argue that the exclusive use of the sojourner's input makes for a highly subjective definition. Church (1982) overcomes this problem by using the basic premise of satisfaction but also includes performance in his definition of *Sojourner Adjustment*, "academic/professional performance and satisfaction." This added element of performance broadens the evaluation of adjustment to parties other than just the sojourner.

Two sources (Church, 1982; American Psychological Association, 1985) view the term Adjustment as too general.

Grove and Torbiorn (1985) developed a more complex view of the term. Adjustment is characterized by a social applicability of behavior and an ability to successfully reach outcomes desired in one's dealings and interactions with others. Adjustment has a second dimension described as confidence that one's view of his/her environment is "accurate, complete and clearly perceived." Adjustment then has two dimensions—one social, the other cognitive which deals with perception. This definition is in line with Ruben and Kealey's (1979), and takes several steps beyond Torbiorn's (1982) definition.

In summary, based on the definitions that have been cited, Adjustment can be conceptualized as a psychosocial concept which has to do with the process of achieving harmony between the individual and the environment. Usually this harmony is achieved through changes in the individual's knowledge, attitudes, and emotions about his or her environment. This culminates with satisfaction, feeling more at home in one's new environment, improved performance, and increased interaction with host country persons.

Adaptation

Nash (1967) defines Adaptation as "changing and reorganizing the sojourner's subjective world, the process being complete when a satisfactory internal balance is restored as characterized by "feeling at home in the new environment."

Pruitt (1978b) views Adaptation as having two components—Adjustment and Assimilation. "Adjustment means coping with one's environment sufficiently well to be happy, comfortable and free of problems. Assimilation means interacting freely with people from the host country and accepting their culture."

Klein (1979) defined Adaptation as "a process of attitudinal or behavioral change in response to new stimuli."

Ruben and Kealey (1979) defined adaptation as having three dimensions: (a) Psychological Adjustment (see the previous section for the definition), (b) culture shock, and (c) intercultural effectiveness.

Grove and Torbiorn (1985) defined Adaptation as a process of reconstructing one's mental frame of reference in the wake of a period during which one has lost confidence in its previous structure and quality. As with Nash's (1967) definition, Grove and Torbiorn (1985) stress cognitive/perceptual change in their definition.

Both Ruben and Kealey's and Pruitt's definitions of Adaptation cite Adjustment and participation with host nationals as components of Adaptation.

All of the above definitions of Adaptation deal with the same factors that were discussed under the definition of Adjustment, or they include Adjustment as a component of Adaptation. Therefore, for some theorists Adjustment and Adaptation overlap to a certain degree or are synonymous.

Tucker (1974) sums up the state of the terminology in this area by commenting that, "The primary weakness in all these studies was the lack of a common definition of adjustment or adaptation to a foreign culture . . ."

Drawing from the definitions cited, Adaptation encompasses cognitive, attitudinal, behavioral, and psychological changes in an individual who lives in a new or foreign culture. These changes result in the individual's movement from uncomfortableness to feeling at home in the new environment. It is a broad term which includes Adjustment and Assimilation.

Acculturation and Assimilation

Acculturation and Assimilation are also used to describe changes that occur as the result of living in a new cultural environment. Herskovits (1965), Teske and Nelson (1974), and Berry (1980) tend to use the terms in reference to groups rather than individuals. Simpson (1968) states that "Assimilation and Acculturation are sometimes considered synonymous, but more often the view is that of Assimilation encompassing Acculturation."

Acculturation is defined in the *International Encyclopedia of the Social Sciences* (Sills, 1968) as "those changes set in motion by the coming together of societies with different cultural traditions."

In short the terms Adjustment, Adaptation, Acculturation, and Assimilation describe change that occurs when individuals or groups have contact with a different culture. These terms are not clearly differentiated. In some cases they are used interchangeably; however some theorists differentiate among them. This lack of consensus on terminology is a stumbling block to research in this area.

Effectiveness

Although many theorists (Taft, 1977; Hammer, Gudykunst, & Wiseman, 1978; Hawes & Kealey, 1981; Abe & Wiseman, 1983; Gudykunst & Hammer, 1984; Szapocznik, Santisteban, Kurtines, Perez-Vidal, & Hervis, 1984) use the term Effectiveness in describing the target behavior of persons working in other cultures, *Competence* or competent behavior is also commonly used (White, 1959; Ezekiel, 1968; Ruben, 1976; Ruben & Kealey, 1979; LaFromboise & Rowe, 1983).

Ruben (1976) comments on this recurring problem of the definition of terms and the important skill of communication:

Systematic attempts to define 'effective', 'successful' or 'competent' communication behavior are relatively scarce . . . For a particular interaction to be termed effective or a person to be termed competent, the performance must meet the needs and the goals of both the message initiator and the recipient.

Success is also used by researchers (Mischel, 1965; Gordon, 1967; Dicken, 1969, Uhes & Shybut, 1971; Harris, 1972) to describe the desired behavior of the sojourner. Tucker (1974) observes that "a so-called 'criterion problem' existed, namely that success overseas had never been adequately described or measured."

Dinges (1984) raises this issue in terms of the lack of focus on person/environment fit. Researchers look at the sojourner to the exclusion of the job requirements and environment in which the task(s) must be performed.

White (1959) offers a concise definition of, *Competence,* calling it "the capacity to make events occur." Although this may be a starting point, there remains to be developed a clear definition of what is meant by the above terms.

One final definition is that of *trait,* which is defined by Hilgard, Atkinson, and Atkinson (1971) as "a persisting characteristic or dimension of personality according to which individuals can be rated or measured . . ." It should be noted that ability is considered a trait by these authors.

Attitudes, Skills, and Traits That Relate to Intercultural Effectiveness

In the literature on intercultural effectiveness, communication skills are frequently mentioned along with certain attitudes of the sojourner as two important factors in the success of the individual who studies or works in a culture different from his/her own.

Hammer, Gudykunst, and Wiseman (1978) cite ability to communicate as one of three dimensions of intercultural effectiveness. This construct is composed of four skills which correlate strongly with effective communication: ability to enter into a meaningful dialogue with other people (+.69), ability to initiate interaction with a stranger (+.68), ability to deal with communication misunderstandings between self and others (+.62), and ability to effectively deal with different communication styles (+.49). However, Brein and David (1971) view intercultural communication as necessary for effective interaction, but it does not guarantee adjustment to the host culture. They speak of the importance of reconciling the differences between the two cultures.

In addition, the literature suggests that ability to deal with different communication styles is an important factor in cross-cultural effectiveness; however, it is of a more general nature and is usually referred to as flexibility (Smith, 1966; Hawes & Kealey, 1981; Torbiorn, 1982; Abe & Wiseman, 1983).

Two studies (Abe & Wiseman, 1983; Hammer et al., 1978) note the ability to establish and maintain relationships as an important factor in intercultural effectiveness.

Uhes and Shybut (1971) state that there is a correlation which reached the .01 level of significance between the scale entitled Capacity for Intimate Contact on the Personal Orientation Inventory and the Final Selection Board ratings of Peace Corps Volunteers. Although this research finding is in agreement with the findings in the literature, it should be noted that much of the research on Peace Corps Volunteers defines effectiveness as the successful completion of training. A more rigorous criteria would be successful completion of overseas service or performance evaluation of service by self, peers, and host national counterparts at the end of service—a standard which is less frequently used in research on Peace Corps Volunteers.

Another aspect of communication, *Interaction Management,* is cited in the work of Ruben (1976). Interaction Management is the skill of being aware of and in control of the amount of input a person has during conversation:

so that needs and desires of others play a critical role in defining how the exchange will proceed. Effective management of interaction is displayed through taking turns in discussion and initiating and terminating interaction based on a reasonably accurate assessment of the needs and desires of others.

In summary, research shows that a high level of social skill plays an important part in success in a different culture. It seems to hold true that what leads to success in one's own culture is also important in other cultures. Perhaps the degree of importance for specific skills varies from culture to culture rather than being a matter of altogether different skills being needed to function successfully in a different culture.

The general rubric of attitudes of the sojourner is also consistently mentioned as an important factor in successful cross-cultural functioning. Ruben (1976) cites *Orientation to Knowledge* as a major factor to be considered. This term refers to how an individual views beliefs, values, and knowledge—as being applicable to everyone, or as being applicable only to the holder of the beliefs, values, and knowledge. In this sense, Orientation to Knowledge is an attitudinal factor. Torbiorn (1982) also addresses this issue and stresses the importance of giving advice, rather than orders. According to Ruben (1976), "The effective cross-cultural sojourner should be ready and able to offer input of his own experience, but does not establish himself as an all-knowing expert."

Ruben and Kealey (1979) cite Orientation to Knowledge as the best of seven communication behaviors in predicting culture shock, with an r of $+0.705$, $p = 0.005$.

An individual who has a relativistic view of knowledge can be said to be low on egocentricity. This argument could be extended to ethnocentrism, if we view certain aspects of knowledge as being culture specific. A relativistic view of one's culture has been cited in the literature as an important attitude for success in cross-cultural interactions. Hanvey (1976) cites examples of PCVs who achieved an understanding of Filipino culture and were quite effective. These were the volunteers who were not tenaciously wedded to American values of efficiency, task orientation, and promptness. Volunteers who were able to accept people for what they were seemed to have more success than those who judged Filipinos by American standards and values. One PCV said:

I consistently believed and followed a life based on getting away from all identity or entanglement with the Peace Corps. My reasons were . . . to figure out a little bit about what was going on in the Philippines, to see what was really significant in my own place, to try to understand life here, and to learn to function in a way that could be meaningful to me and the community.

This quote demonstrates an attitude of surrender to the new culture—of disengaging from the major symbol of the home culture, the sojourner's organization. Particularly when the PCV comments on the distancing from the Peace Corps identity, this suggests that this individual may have avoided such behaviors as speaking English, eating American foods and socializing with other Americans. This is an interesting strategy especially in a time when biculturalism is so popular. A possible explanation for these competing strategies of adjustment is that an individual may have to go through an initial period of rejection of his/her own culture in order to delve into the new environment. Once a basic understanding of the second culture has been grasped, there may be an advantage to striking a balance between the two cultures, that is, becoming bicultural.

Oberg (1960) is not so optimistic about achieving biculturalism. He advises that the sojourner should always be aware that he or she is an outsider and will be treated as such. Rather than speaking of biculturalism, Oberg talks of developing two patterns of behavior, which implies skill building rather than a change in identity.

Dixit (1983) in a study on Asian Indian children living in the United States states that the major concern of the parents of these children was the children's rejection of Indian culture, and the rapid assimilation into the new culture. This study suggests that a bicultural strategy to living in a new culture is difficult to achieve, particularly in the case of children and adolescents.

Taft (1977) by contrast, suggests that there can be equal proficiency in two cultures and that such a person experiences loss when he moves into a monocultural setting. He also enumerates the assets and liabilities of multiculturalism.

A nonjudgmental attitude is also mentioned frequently in the literature as an important attitudinal factor in intercultural effectiveness. Hammer et al. (1978) use the term *Third Culture Perspective* to describe the world view used by the effective sojourner to understand a new environment. It is neither the perspective of the home nor the host culture; however, it is characterized by the sensitivity to pick up on the important cues in the new environment and to respond to them in a socially acceptable manner. The Third Culture Perspective consists of being nonjudgmental and being an astute observer of one's own culture and the host culture. These researchers also cite the ability to establish meaningful relationships as a component of the third culture perspective.

One can conceptualize the nonjudgmental perspective at the zero point of a continuum which runs from the extreme of highly critical to its opposite extreme, highly respectful of a culture. Although some researchers cite a nonjudgmental attitude as important for cross-cultural effectiveness, the research is richer in support of an attitude of respect for the host culture as an important attitude for cross-cultural effectiveness (Hawes & Kealey, 1981; Hanvey, 1976). Harris (1973) demonstrates that six variables are most effective in differentiating successful Peace Corps Volunteers from early terminees. Three of these items are directly related to respect: (a) the traits of Patience, Tolerance, (b) the trait of Courtesy, and (c) Interest in nationals. These three factors had strong correlations with the overall evaluations of the Volunteers ($r = +.81, +.77, +.83$, respectively).

Mischel (1965) uses six dimensions as criterion ratings of Peace Corps Volunteers. Appreciation of Nigerian culture is an attitude that is cited and appears to be another term for respect. Person-to-person contacts (interpersonal behavior with Nigerians) is also cited. This study adds further support to the research cited in the previous paragraph.

Cultural Empathy is also frequently mentioned. Ruben (1976) states that the ability to put oneself in another's shoes is important in human relationships, both within and between cultures. Ruben describes empathy as the capacity to clearly project an interest in others, as well as to obtain and to reflect a reasonably complete and accurate sense of another's thoughts, feelings, and/or experiences. Some people lack interest or fail to display it. In his study, Ruben uses empathy, display of respect, interaction posture, orientation to knowledge, interaction management, self-oriented role behavior, and tolerance for ambiguity as components to evaluate Communication Competency for Intercultural Adaptation.

Cleveland, Mangone, and Adams (1960), who studied Americans living, working, and studying abroad, also cite Cultural Empathy as one of five major components for Intercultural Effectiveness. These researchers define Cultural Empathy as "not merely a matter of 'liking people' or 'getting along with the locals . . .' it has to do with perceptiveness and receptiveness." Cleveland et al. (1960) make the point that this is a skill that can be learned. One aspect of Cultural Empathy involves making use of local resources to solve problems. One Brazilian commented, "You teach baseball by learning soccer."

Hawes and Kealey (1981) do not use the term empathy but they do mention sensitivity to host culture issues. The broad term of Interpersonal Skills was found to be the best predictor of overseas effectiveness in their research. Interpersonal Skills is composed of six factors, one of which was sensitivity to host country issues. This term is not defined, but it may very well be synonymous with Cultural Empathy.

To summarize, the research supports the idea that a relatively relaxed approach to dealing with different cultures and people as characterized by openmindedness, a nonjudgmental, noncritical perspective, and a limited degree of ethnocentrism may be quite important to Intercultural Effectiveness.

Brein and David (1971) stress the importance of the development of understanding between host and sojourner. These researchers state that this development of understanding is the result of the amount and quality of information exchange between the two parties.

Hammer et al. (1978) cited communication ability and ability to establish interpersonal relationships as two major dimensions of intercultural effectiveness. The third dimensions cited in their research is the ability to deal with psychological stress. Hammer et al. (1978) came to this conclusion by having 53 so-called cross-culturally effective university students rate the importance of 24 personal abilities which were collected from a review of the literature on intercultural effectiveness. Principal Factor Analysis was used to identify the above three skills and the abilities that clustered together to compose the dimensions. In the dimension referred to as ability to deal with psychological stress, eight abilities loaded heavily. These include the abilities to deal with (a) frustration (+.72), (b) stress (+.60), (c) anxiety (+.60), (d) different political systems (+.56), (e) pressure to conform (+.49), (f) social alienation (+.48), (g) financial difficulties (+.45), and (h) interpersonal conflict (+.40).

One weakness of this study is that the raters had to have lived *only* three months in another culture in order to participate. This is a relatively short time in which the adjustment process is only beginning. The other criteria for inclusion as a rater in this study was that the individual be recommended as one ". . . who would have functioned effectively in another culture." We have no way of knowing whether the subject would or did actually function effectively in another culture. At best there is only face validity to support this means of selection.

This study was replicated by Abe and Wiseman (1983) using Japanese tourists as subjects, and the data also supported the importance of the ability to deal with stress in intercultural settings. Church (1982) also contends that this is an important factor based on his review of the literature. All the research Church reviewed supports the contention that skill in handling stress is highly correlated with intercultural effectiveness.

Cleveland et al. (1960) describe the preferred overseas candidate as ". . . resourceful and buoyant, whose emotional gyroscope enables him to snap back rapidly from discouragement and frustration." The individual who is able to deal with stress may be the person who can be flexible enough to adjust to his or her new environment. This is characterized by the ability to change goals and methods of reaching goals as needed, given situational variables.

Smith (1966) cited *Persistence with flexibility* as personality traits of PCVs who are considered to be generally competent. Guthrie (1975) echoes this idea when he cites the difficulties a sojourner has when "it is hard to acknowledge the inevitability of mistakes. What appears to be needed is some humility about one's own social competence and enough self-confidence to keep on trying."

Torbiorn (1982) also speaks about the value of being flexible:

The ideal candidate as he emerges from the pages of the literature could be summed up as kind of flexible superman. Most accounts emphasize the importance of adaptability, but what is meant by this is rarely explained. It probably refers to a general ability to cope and function in unfamiliar surroundings, but how far this ability is actually linked to personality is not discussed. An apparently related attribute often mentioned in descriptions of the suitable candidate is flexibility, an equally vague concept. It is probably meant to refer to lack of prejudice, respect for other people's opinions and for ideas and behavior patterns that do not meet expectations, an awareness of the relative and culture-bound nature of personally held views, and an ability to question and if necessary abandon earlier convictions.

Hanvey (1976) also stresses the importance of flexibility if one is to become culturally aware and maintain the sustained participation in the host culture that is needed in order to develop an understanding of that culture.

Gullahorn and Gullahorn (1963) cite sojourner flexibility of role behavior and sensitivity to subtle sanctions and the discrimination of cues for appropriate behavior in the host culture as crucial determinants of the severity of culture shock among International Students. Ruben and Kealey (1979) also cite flexibility of role behavior as important for the effectiveness of technical advisors and their spouses serving in Kenya. Task-oriented role behavior had the highest correlation of six behavioral patterns observed during training, when correlated with Effectiveness ($r = -0.544, p = .05$). One explanation is that North Americans are highly task-oriented in their work. Normally an individual exhibiting this behavior is viewed as competent in the U.S./Canada. However, this trait interferes with several of the previously cited person-oriented skills which play an important part in effective functioning in cultures outside the U.S./Canada. Three factors come into play here: (a) sensitivity to discriminate which strategy will be most appropriate in a new environment, (b) flexibility to use different strategies as needed, and (c) persistence, the ability to maintain a high degree of motivation when results are not always successful. Flexibility can serve the sojourner very well in a host culture situation where the sojourner's initial expectations and the reality of the new environment are widely disparate. The sojourner who can easily adjust expectations so that they are in tune with the reality of his/her experiences will suffer less culture shock. Less dependence on flexibility will be needed if sojourners receive accurate predeparture information about the environments they are about to enter.

There is controversy with a number of the factors that have been mentioned which correlate with Intercultural Effectiveness as to whether these skills can be learned. Certainly there is room for debate about whether Cultural Empathy or the capacity for intimate behavior can be learned. However, in the case of realistic expectations of the overseas experience, a great deal can be accomplished in training to insure that the sojourner has accurate information about the culture he/she will be entering.

Hawes and Kealey (1981) cite realistic predeparture expectations and Identity as "The second most important predictor of overseas success." Unfortunately, the authors do not explain what is meant by Identity.

Torbiorn (1982) focuses a great deal of attention on flexibility, but in terms of realistic expectations. He does warn about the dangers of perfectionism and rigidity or dogmatism, including such consequences as a longer and more difficult culture shock phase for persons possessing these traits.

Gardner (1962) makes an excellent argument about realistic expectations in the cross-cultural context. He suggests that so-called helpers from countries such as the United States may be the least capable of helping those in the third world. His argument is that this is the broadest of attitudinal leaps that a sojourner could make, that is, the mentality shift from one of the most technologically-advanced countries to that of an underdeveloped country. He suggests that intercultural effectiveness in the third world might be more easily attained by individuals from developing countries. This idea makes sense in terms of the increased degree of difficulty in adjusting to the host culture that is substantially different from one's home culture (Gullahorn & Gullahorn, 1963; Torbiorn, 1982). For example, it is generally accepted that an American would have an easier time adjusting and functioning effectively in New Zealand or Germany than in Pakistan or Nigeria, because the cultural change is less extreme in the former than in the latter. Dinges (1984) spoke of person/environment fit and the importance of this relationship in intercultural competence. This idea of effectiveness in 'less foreign' environments also follows the person/environment-fit perspective.

All the research reviewed supports the importance of realistic expectations of the host country. When the sojourner does not have such expectations, Flexibility was cited as an important attitude for the sojourner's successful functioning in the host country. Triandis, Vassiliou, and Nassiakou (1968) and Triandis (1972) presented a series of studies which look at how persons from different cultures perceive different roles and behaviors. This research gives us insight into different attitudes and role expectations in different cultures. This cognitive understanding of difference may be important knowledge for the sojourner faced with the need to be flexible in his or her new environment.

Detweiler's (1978) work on category width is also related to flexibility. He defines category width as "a term used to describe the amount of discrepancy tolerable among category members—how similar do things have to be to be called by the same name? A narrow categorizer might put only highly similar things in the same category, whereas a broad categorizer might put more discrepant things in the same category." Detweiler goes on to comment that, "A narrow categorizer might be less able than the broad categorizer to classify the different behavior of a person from another culture into the normal acceptable category." This researcher demonstrates that there is a linear relationship among three factors. His research shows that culture influences category width, which in turn influences attribution. This model supports the idea that those persons who are less exacting in setting criteria for classifying behavior, do better when they are in environments where behaviors have different meaning. The narrow categorizer finds his or her less flexible classification criteria to be a liability in cross-cultural situations.

Dinges' (1984) review discussed the person/environment fit. He is critical of the lack of research on the environment or task. He rightfully observes that research has focussed on the individual to the exclusion of the environment to which he or she is sent. Although this is a valid observation, it is not surprising that this has occurred. Intercultural trainers train persons, not environments; therefore the research has gravitated toward the individual rather than the environment. Also there is an issue of ethics which enters the picture. Attempts to alter the environment of another culture might be viewed as imperialistic. However, training of persons who will go overseas is generally less controversial, particularly when the trainees seek out such training.

Dinges also speaks of the exposure/experience/expertise fallacy. In short, this refers to the belief that persons who go overseas are viewed as cross-culturally competent by reason of having first-hand experience in a different culture. Dinges is critical of this reasoning but fails to state that research has to be done to prove or disprove this hypothesis. Indeed an argument could be made that exposure and experience in a different culture is necessary but not sufficient to achieve Intercultural Effectiveness.

Another criticism which Dinges raises is the overemphasis on stage theories to describe cross-cultural adjustment. According to Hilgard et al. (1971), stage theories cite critical events or focal points in development. Some go so far as to present specific periods or stages at which certain events should occur in the development of an individual. Dinges feels that the wide range of individual differences in the amount of time needed to adjust to a new culture reduces these theories to a collection of generalizations. However, another approach would be theory-driven research which looks at clearly defined populations and their coping patterns in specific cultures. This thrust in research would be a "fine tuning" of the stage theories that have been developed to date.

A number of other factors were also found in the research literature that are related to Intercultural Effectiveness; however, these were not mentioned as frequently. Cleveland et al. (1960) present five key elements for effective performance overseas: (a) Technical Skill, (b) Belief in Mission, (c) Cultural Empathy, (d) A Sense of Politics, and (e) Organization Skills. These researchers view these five elements as skills that can be acquired. Cultural Empathy was discussed earlier, and much of what is said in this Carnegie Report on a Sense of Politics was discussed under the topic of Interpersonal Relations.

Technical Skill plays a major part in effectiveness, according to Cleveland et al. (1960), as well as being consistently mentioned in the PCV literature labeled as "General competence as a teacher" (Mischel, 1965; Smith, 1966; Harris, 1973). Harris (1973) cites *Knowledge of Subject* as among the most effective factors in distinguishing successful volunteers from early terminees. Smith (1966) uses an ipsative Q-sort technique to evaluate personality and performance based on interviews of PCVs. Competent teaching scored second highest of the items that characterize successful volunteers. Commitment to carrying out the job of Peace Corps Teacher, an echo of Cleveland and colleagues' (1960) Belief in Mission, received the highest rating.

However, Benson (1978) mentions several times the danger in confounding "job performance with adaptation, and exceptional job performance should not be taken as an indication of adjustment." Harris (1973) concluded that measures of job performance, which must be closely related to Technical Skill and Knowledge of Subject as a fundamental aspect of cross-cultural effectiveness, are certainly only a small part of a complex multi-factor concept. In many cross-cultural organizations there is a tendency for members to be either language 'experts' or technicians. Unless training develops the weaker area, persons are placed overseas either knowing a great deal but not being able to communicate the information, or having facility with the language of delivery but with little to communicate to the hosts.

Smith (1966) also coins the phrase *Self-Confident Maturity* to describe personality factors which are typical of successful Volunteers. This concept includes traits such as self-confidence, high self-esteem, energy, principled responsibility, optimistic realism, and persistence with flexibility.

Earlier, reference was made to Interpersonal Skills being an important factor in predicting Intercultural Effectiveness. *Intercultural Interaction* is also cited by researchers as important to cross-cultural success. Hawes and Kealey (1981) define Intercultural Interaction as, "interacting with local people and making local friends; learning the local language and nonverbal communication (gestures, interpersonal space, postures, appropriate eye contact, etc.); demonstrated factual knowledge about local culture, politics, history, current events, economy, etc." These abilities and this knowledge are developed through involvement with the host country community. The literature offers many citations supporting participation in the local culture as a key to cross-cultural adjustment (Gullahorn & Gullahorn, 1963; Sewell & Davidsen, 1956; Morris, 1960). These studies deal with International Students and how their participation in the host cultures relates to adjustment and satisfaction. It follows that the individual who is well-adjusted feels more satisfaction and functions more effectively. Research on PCVs (Harris, 1973) and on Scandinavians working overseas (Torbiorn, 1982) also shows the importance of participation in the host culture and its relationship to effective functioning.

Taft (1977), however, states that "difficulty in coping is a function of the degree to which the new culture is all-encompassing." He goes on to speak of the sojourner's willingness to adapt and how this is reflected in the avoidance of contact with host nationals. His example is the foreign student who fulfills the role of student but finds social and recreational satisfaction among his or her own expatriates. The idea of breathing room for the sojourner is quite relevant, and having some opportunities to interact with others from the home country can be an important means of alleviating culture shock at least temporarily.

Al Ibrahim (1983), in a dissertation on Syrian students who relocate to study in the United States, cited wives of students as the real losers because of their isolation from the host culture. Students' wives suffered from loneliness, boredom, and homesickness more than their student husbands who were deeply involved in the host culture via their studies. Five researchers (Hammer et al., 1978; Pruitt, 1978a; Harris, 1973; Sewell & Davidsen, 1956; Deutsch & Won, 1963) discuss the importance of host culture language proficiency and its relation to cross-cultural effectiveness.

Benson (1978) commented that Peace Corps Volunteers who were identified as well-adapted had more ability in the use of nonverbal communication than their colleagues who were classified as nonadapted. It should be noted that Guthrie (1975) states that although signals are sent through facial expressions, touching, dressing, posture, proximity, as well as volume, speed, and tone of speech, there is a paucity of instructional materials in this area. This lack of instruction in nonverbal communication in our educational and training programs adversely affects the trainee who must work overseas.

Hammer et al. (1978) cite "ability to effectively communicate in the language of the host culture" as 1 of 24 personal abilities that were mentioned in a review of the literature on intercultural effectiveness. These researchers distinguish between linguistic proficiency and effective communication. The former has to do with ability to speak and understand a language, and the latter refers to listening skills, and expressing and understanding needs, values, and ideas. As an aside, the 24 personal abilities mentioned in Hammer et al. (1978) were divided into three general categories which included the abilities (a) to handle psychological stress, (b) to effectively function in interpersonal relationships, and (c) to communicate effectively.

Pruitt (1978a) finds that students who attended an English Language Institute had more adjustment problems than those who did not attend. However, Pruitt suggests that maladjustment is not related to language class attendance. It is a matter of persons with language difficulties generally having more problems of adjustment to the host culture.

Harris' (1973) discriminant analysis of successful Peace Corps Volunteers demonstrates that with four variables, one of which was facility with language, accuracy of classification (high success versus low success) could be achieved in 97.5% of all cases that were evaluated.

Sewell and Davidsen (1956) report that host language proficiency is important, particularly having an understanding of subtleties of vocabulary and use of correct forms of address.

Deutsch and Won (1963) demonstrate that language facility is related to the degree of satisfaction and the amount of social contact that Agency for International Development (A.I.D.) trainees had with host country nationals during their residence in the United States.

It is clear that linguistic proficiency and social interaction are important prerequisites for intercultural effectiveness; however the relationship between linguistic proficiency and social interaction is unclear. Does linguistic proficiency lead to more social interaction, or is the more extroverted sojourner more likely to interact with host culture persons, thus developing new language skills? Oberg (1960) perceives mastery of the host culture language as the means to getting to know the host country nationals. He states that a first hand knowledge of the people of another culture is not possible without host country language proficiency. Further research on this question is needed in order to better understand how the independent variables of intercultural effectiveness are related.

To summarize this section on attitudes, skills, and traits, the following can be noted:

1. Ease of interacting with a variety of persons with different communication styles and personality factors is very important for the sojourner. Closely related to these interpersonal skills are the issues of host culture language proficiency and an understanding and an ability in using the nonverbal communication of the host culture.

2. Attitudes are an important factor in intercultural effectiveness especially patience, courtesy, and a willingness to immerse oneself in the new environment rather than rigidly maintaining the values of the home culture.

3. The research literature cites a positive attitude for the host culture, that is, respect and interest for the customs, traditions, and people of the new environment. This attitude is cited more frequently than nonjudgmental attitude toward the new environment.

4. Another attitude is flexibility. However, it is mentioned in tandem with persistence, which suggests that the sojourner must be able to accurately size up his or her environment so that he or she knows when it is time to follow through on a task and when it is time to be sensitive to host culture priorities. Clearly this shows that a sense of politics is needed to decide whether a flexible or a persistent mode is best in each situation.

5. Ability to deal with psychological stress suggests that the sojourner should have the ability to deal with frustration and change. Another way of dealing with this is to insure that the information about his or her new environment is accurate.

6. Competence in one's content area is cited by several researchers as another fundamental skill if one is to succeed in a culturally different environment.

Factors That Have Inverse Relationships to Cross-Cultural Effectiveness

This section tells us primarily about personality traits that have negative correlations with cross-cultural effectiveness. As mentioned earlier, Torbiorn (1982) cites perfectionism, rigidity, and dogmatism as traits that do not lend themselves to improving one's performance in intercultural functioning. Rigid ethnocentrism is cited by two researchers (Lunstedt, 1963; Rokeach, 1960) as a limiting factor in coping effectively with a new language and new social norms.

Dependent Anxiety tends to be incompatible with good performance of PCVs (Smith, 1966).

Task-related behavior was mentioned earlier as having correlated negatively with effectiveness in the Ruben and Kealey study (1979). This research study shows that self-centered role behaviors ($r = -.502$, $p = .05$) also are inversely related to effectiveness in an overseas setting.

Narrowmindedness is cited by Torbiorn (1982) as inappropriate for a candidate who is planning to live overseas.

Dicken (1969) states that measures of intelligence have no predictive validity for Peace Corps Community Development Workers' success.

Authoritarianism gets mixed reports in the literature as to its relationship in Intercultural Effectiveness. Smith (1966) states that Authoritarianism shows essentially null correlations with loadings on general competence patterns of PCVs. Mischel (1965) presents evidence for measures of authoritarianism on a self-report inventory as being quite effective in the prediction of PCV success.

Training Implications

Based on the above data, it follows that cross-cultural training programs should challenge trainees to become aware of their own dogmatism. Trainees should give some thought to their own criteria for deciding whether an idea is right. Do the criteria change depending on the decision to be made? Are there different ways of knowing?

The area of values clarification should be examined as a source of information and exercises for preparing for the sojourn.

Another area that should be examined is the individual's need for control. How willing is the trainee to be flexible, accept other values, etc.? Under what conditions can/will the trainee surrender to a culturally different way of doing things?

The research (Fiedler, Mitchell, & Triandis, 1971) states that it is important to be able to pick up on cues in a new environment. The culture assimilator is a valuable tool in helping trainees learn which are the significant factors in understanding the new environment.

Trainees should also learn something about assessing their new environment and finding low risk means of testing out their hypotheses about the new environment.

Sojourners learn that different behaviors are valued in the host culture, but even with this information it may be difficult to adjust one's behavior to match the norms of the new environment. Perhaps the sojourner will have to be less assertive or more sociable in order to function effectively. The literature raises the issue of the importance of communication styles, and a fundamental goal of intercultural training should be to make trainees aware of the different styles. A more ambitious goal would be opportunities for trainees to practice different communication styles in order to make decisions about their own capabilities in being flexible in communicating.

Discussion groups can also be used to increase awareness of the importance of being able to deal with frustration, stress, and different political systems as well as the other abilities that were cited in the research of Hammer et al. (1978).

Trainers should also assist trainees in developing realistic goals about the level of language proficiency and biculturalism that can be reached given the amount of time that the sojourner will be in the host culture. The veteran sojourner can be an important resource in helping neophytes develop adjustment goals that are realistic.

Dealing with psychological stress has been cited as important and training should include an assessment of current means of dealing with stress. Trainees should consider whether they are effectively dealing with stress and, if not, programs such as meditation, yoga, and exercise need to be considered. Important questions include: Is it possible to engage in these activities while overseas, individually or in groups? What local means of stress reduction are available in the host country? Will these means be adequate substitutes? How can in-country training programs encourage follow through in using stress reduction techniques?

Because Intercultural Interaction plays an important role in intercultural effectiveness, trainees will need instruction in the areas of local history, politics, economy and culture. This knowledge will give them a foundation in understanding the host culture and will enhance their ability to converse intelligently with host nationals about their new environment.

Foreign language training is also a necessary part of the training process and the depth will be decided based upon the duration of training. Serious consideration should be given to how the sojourner will be able to perfect language skills while overseas. What resources will be available beyond the daily opportunities to converse with host nationals?

Oberg (1960) states that language ability is the key to interaction with host nationals and, if nothing else, trainees should have exposure to polite means of making requests, and to words in the native language that are not easily translated into English yet capture important values unique to the host culture. This approach blends the psychological and the linguistic aspects of a culture and is a more integrated way to learn about the host culture.

It becomes obvious that a training process based on changing so many attitudes and developing so many skills can be an overpowering task. Grove and Torbiorn (1985) stated that cross-cultural training should be an ongoing process which begins in the predeparture stage and continues through Stages 1 and 2 of cross-cultural adjustment. These researchers believe that the sojourner is more receptive to specific information at different stages of their adjustment. Because of the large number of factors influencing cross-cultural effectiveness, it seems logical that ongoing training before and during the sojourn would make the most sense.

Summary

Factors that relate to Intercultural Effectiveness can be broadly classified as either abilities, attitudes, or traits. Under the abilities subheading, the following have been found to relate to successful cross-cultural functioning: Interpersonal and Communication skills including listening skills, the ability to enter into a meaningful dialogue with others, to initiate interaction with others, to deal with communication misunderstandings and different communication styles as well as linguistic ability in cultures that have a different language from that spoken by the sojourner, and interaction management. Organizational ability, competence in one's area of expertise, the ability to effectively communicate one's knowledge to others, and the ability to deal with psychological stress are all components of successful cross-cultural functioning.

Attitudes that are important for the sojourner to possess include Cultural Empathy, a relativistic orientation to knowledge, acceptance of others as people, a nonjudgmental attitude, respect for the host culture, interest in nationals and appreciation of their culture, and a sense of politics.

A number of traits play an important role in Intercultural Effectiveness. These include Patience, Tolerance, Courtesy, Persistence with flexibility, energy, self-confident maturity, and self-esteem.

Traits that correlate negatively with Intercultural Effectiveness include perfectionism, rigidity, dogmatism, ethnocentrism, dependent anxiety, task-oriented behavior, narrowmindedness, and self-centered role behaviors.

Conclusions

The research area of Intercultural Effectiveness is relatively new, having developed since the Second World War. A great deal of the research has been done on International Students and Peace Corps Volunteers.

One of the principal obstacles in this research is the lack of clearly defined terms. Frequently, researchers use terms interchangeably, and there is a paucity of discussion as to the meanings of these terms.

Generally, researchers have made a good start in identifying factors that are related to Intercultural Effectiveness. However, the findings are usually assumed to be culture general. Replication studies in different cultures would go a long way toward adding to our knowledge about whether findings apply to one culture or many and under what circumstances.

Further study is needed to ascertain which methods are most effective and least expensive in training personnel for positions requiring Intercultural Effectiveness.

Some researchers argue that situational factors play a more important role in Intercultural Effectiveness than skills and personality traits. This question also needs further investigation if we are to develop a full understanding of the correlates of Intercultural Effectiveness.

References

Abe, H., & Wiseman, R. L. (1983). A cross-cultural confirmation of the dimensions of intercultural effectiveness. *International Journal of Intercultural Relations, 7,* 53–67.

Adler, P. S. (1975). The transitional experience: An alternative view of culture shock. *Journal of Humanistic Psychology, 15*(4), 13–23.

Al Ibrahim, F. Y. (1983). Adjustment problems facing Syrian students and their families in New York. (Doctoral dissertation, Teachers College/Columbia University, 1983). *Dissertation Abstracts International, 44,* 82. (Teachers College microfilm #06-7700).

American Psychological Association (1985). *Thesaurus of psychological index terms* (4th ed.). Washington, DC: Author.

Benson, P. G. (1978). Measuring cross-cultural adjustment: The problem of criteria. *International Journal of Intercultural Relations, 2,* 21–37.

Berry, J. W. (1980). Acculturation as varieties to adaptation. In A. M. Padilla (Ed.), *Acculturation: Theory, models and some new findings.* Boulder, CO: Westview Press.

Brein, M., & David, K. H. (1971). Intercultural communication and the adjustment of the sojourner. *Psychological Bulletin, 76,* 215–230.

Church, A. T. (1982). Sojourner adjustment. *Psychological Bulletin, 91,* 540–572.

Cleveland, H., Mangone, G. J. & Adams, J. C. (1960). *The overseas Americans.* New York: McGraw-Hill.

Detweiler, R. A. (1978). Culture, category width and attributions: A model-building approach to the reasons for cultural effects. *Journal of Cross-Cultural Psychology, 9,* 259–284.

Deutsch, S. E., & Won, G. Y. M. (1963). Some factors in the adjustment of foreign nationals in the United States. *Journal of Social Issues, 19,*(3), 115–122.

Dicken, C. (1969). Predicting the success of Peace Corps community development workers. *Journal of Consulting and Clinical Psychology, 33,* 597–606.

Dinges, N. (1984). Intercultural competence. In D. Landis & R. W. Brislin (Eds.), *Handbook of intercultural training* (Vol. 1). New York: Pergamon Press.

Dixit, J. L. (1983). An investigation into the social adaptation of Asian-Indian immigrants in the U.S. and their children's academic performance (Doctoral dissertation, Teachers College/Columbia University, 1983). *Dissertation Abstracts International, 44,* 1983. (Teachers College microfilm #06-7776).

English, H. B. (1958). *A comprehensive dictionary of psychological and psychoanalytical terms.* New York: David McKay.

Ezekiel, R. S. (1968). The personal future and Peace Corps competence. *Journal of Personality and Social Psychology, 8*(2), (Monograph Supplement), 1–26.

Fiedler, F. E., Mitchell, T., and Triandis, H. C. (1971). The culture assimilator: An approach to cross-cultural training. *Journal of Applied Psychology, 55,* 95–102.

Gardner, G. H. (1962). Cross-cultural communication. *Journal of Social Psychology, 58,* 241–256.

Gordon, L. V. (1967). Clinical, psychometric, and work-sample approaches to the prediction of success in Peace Corps training. *Journal of Applied Psychology, 51,* 111–119.

Grove, C. L., & Torbiorn, I. (1985). A new conceptualization of intercultural adjustment and the goals of training. *International Journal of Intercultural Relations, 9,* 205–233.

Gudykunst, W. B., & Hammer, M. R. (1984). Dimensions of intercultural effectiveness: Culture specific or culture general? *International Journal of Intercultural Relations, 8,* 1–10.

Gullahorn, J., & Gullahorn, J. (1963). An extension of the U-curve hypothesis. *Journal of Social Issues, 19,* 33–47.

Guthrie, G. M. (1975). A behavioral analysis of culture learning. In R. W. Brislin, S. Bochner, & W. J. Lonner (Eds.), *Cross-cultural perspectives on learning.* New York: Halstead Press Division, Wiley.

Hammer, M. R., Gudykunst, W. B., & Wiseman, R. L. (1978). Dimensions of intercultural effectiveness: An exploratory study. *International Journal of Intercultural Relations, 2,* 382–393.

Hanvey, R. G. (1976). Cross-cultural awareness. In E. C. Smith & L. F. Luce (Eds.), *Toward internationalism: Readings in cross-cultural communication* (pp. 44–56). Rowley, MA: Newbury House Publishers.

Harris, J. G., Jr. (1972). Prediction of success on a distant Pacific island: Peace Corps style. *Journal of Consulting and Clinical Psychology, 38,* 181–190.

Harris, J. G., Jr. (1973). A science of the South Pacific: Analysis of the character structure of the Peace Corps volunteer. *American Psychologist, 28,* 232–247.

Hawes, F., & Kealey, D. (1981). An empirical study of Canadian technical assistance: Adaptation and effectiveness on overseas assignment. *International Journal of Intercultural Relations, 4,* 239–258.

Herskovits, M. J. (1965). African gods and Catholic saints in new world negro belief. In W. A. Lessa & E. J. Vogt (Eds.), *Reader in comparative religion: An anthropological approach* (2nd ed.). New York: Harper.

Hilgard, E. R., Atkinson, R. C., & Atkinson, R. L. (1971). *Introduction to psychology.* New York: Harcourt, Brace & Jovanovich.

Klein, M. H. (1979). Adaptation to new cultural environments. In D. S. Hoopes, P. B. Pedersen, & G. W. Renwick (Eds.) *Overview of intercultural education, training and research: Vol. 1. Theory.* LaGrange Park, IL: Intercultural Network, Inc.

LaFromboise, T. D., & Rowe, W. (1983). Skills training for bilingual competence: Rationale and application. *Journal of Counseling Psychology, 30,* 589–595.

Lunstedt, S. (1963). An introduction to some evolving problems in cross-cultural research. *Journal of Social Issues, 19,* 1–10.

Mischel, W. (1965). Predicting the success of Peace Corps volunteers in Nigeria. *Journal of Personality and Social Psychology, 1,* 510–517.

Morris, R. T. (1960). *The two way mirror: National status in foreign students' adjustment.* Minneapolis: University of Minnesota Press.

Nash, D. (1967). The fate of Americans in a Spanish setting: A study in adaptation. *Human Organization, 26*(3), 157–163.

Oberg, K. (1960). Culture shock: Adjustment to new cultural environments. *Practical Anthropology, 7,* 177–182.

Pruitt, F. J. (1978a). The adaptation of African students to American society. *International Journal of Intercultural Relations, 2,* 90–117.

Pruitt, F. J. (1978b). The adaptation of foreign students on American campuses. *Journal of the National Association for Women Deans, Administrators, and Counselors, 41*(4), 144–147.

Rokeach, M. (1960). *The open and closed mind.* New York: Basic Books.

Ruben, B. (1976). Assessing communication competence for intercultural adaptation. *Group and Organization Studies, 1,* 334–354.

Ruben, B. D., & Kealey, D. J. (1979). Behavioral assessment of communication competency and the prediction of cross-cultural adaptation. *International Journal of Intercultural Relations, 3,* 15–47.

Sewell, W. H., & Davidsen, O. M. (1956). The adjustment of Scandinavian students. *Journal of Social Issues, 12,* 9–19.

Sills, D. L. (Ed.). (1968). *International encyclopedia of social sciences.* New York: Cromwell Collier and Macmillan, Inc.

Simpson, G. E. (1968). Assimilation. In D. L. Sims. (Ed.), *International encyclopedia of the social sciences.* New York: Macmillan.

Smith, M. B. (1966). Explorations in competence: A study of Peace Corps teachers in Ghana. *American Psychologist, 21,* 555–566.

Szapocznik, J., Santisteban, D., Kurtines, W., Perez-Idal, A., & Hervis, O. (1984). Bicultural effectiveness training: A treatment intervention for enhancing intercultural adjustment in Cuban American families. *Hispanic Journal of Behavioral Sciences, 6,* 317–344.

Taft, R. (1977). Coping with unfamiliar cultures. In Neil Warren (Ed.), *Studies in cross-cultural psychology (Vol. 1.).* New York: Academic Press.

Teske, R., & Nelson, B. (1974). Acculturation and assimilation: A clarification. *American Ethnologist, 1,* 351–367.

Torbiorn, I. (1982). *Living abroad: Personal adjustment and personnel policy in the overseas setting.* New York: Wiley.

Triandis, H. (1972). *The analysis of subjective culture.* New York: Wiley-Interscience.

Triandis, H., Vassiliou, V., & Nassiakou, M. (1968). Three cross-cultural studies of subjective culture. *Journal of Personality and Social Psychology, 8*(4, Monograph Supplement), 1–42.

Tucker, M. F. (1974). *Screening and selection for overseas assignment: Assessment and recommendations to the U.S. Navy.* Denver, CO: Center for Research and Education.

Uhes, M. J., & Shybut, J. (1971). Personal Orientation Inventory as a predictor of success in Peace Corps training. *Journal of Applied Psychology, 55,* 498–499.

White, R. W. (1959). Motivation reconsidered: The concept of competence. *Psychological Review, 66,* 297–333.

Article Review Form at end of book.

Paige advocates that trainer intercultural communication competency rests on knowledge, performance, and personal attributes. How does he characterize each of these?

Trainer Competencies

The missing conceptual link in orientation

R. Michael Paige
University of Minnesota

Introduction

The complexities and demands of culture learning require exceptional competencies of the trainer. These include a high degree of self-awareness and a recognition of one's skills limitations, sensitivity to the needs of the learners, the ability to respond to the problems that culture learners encounter, an awareness of the ethical issues involved in cross-cultural training, conceptual/theoretical understanding, program-design skills, and research/evaluation skills (Paige & Martin, 1983, p. 57).

During the past twenty years, there has been enormous growth in the field of international educational exchange and a concomitant increase in the number of cross-cultural orientation programs being conducted. Pusch et al. (1981) estimate that over 20,000 cross-cultural training programs were offered between 1951 and 1981 to cross-cultural sojourners such as foreign students, business personnel, and government officials. Associated with this growth of the field has been the emergence of a relatively sizeable literature regarding cross-cultural training (Batchelder & Warner, 1977; Casse, 1979; Hoopes, 1977; Hoopes & Ventura, 1979; Pusch, 1979; Weeks, Pedersen, & Brislin, 1977), the most recent and significant work being the three-volume *Handbook of Intercultural Training* edited by Dan Landis and Richard Brislin (1983). Cross-cultural specialists now have their own professional journal, the *International Journal of Intercultural Relations,* and their own professional association, the Society for Intercultural Education, Training and Research (SIETAR). In many respects, the field of cross-cultural training is in the very healthy process of coming of age.

It is somewhat surprising, in light of these other advances, that little has been written about cross-cultural trainers and the competencies they must have to be effective in their work. In my view, the literature should more systematically examine (1) the skills the trainer must have, (2) the appropriate settings—time, place and audience—for specific learning activities, (3) the potential difficulties the learners will have with these activities and appropriate trainer responses, and (4) the ethical issues associated with training programs and trainer behavior. The deficiency in the literature on these topics represents a missing conceptual link in orientation.

The purpose of this paper is to address this shortcoming by conceptualizing specific cognitive understandings, behavioral skills and personal qualities that would characterize the competent cross-cultural trainer. First, the author will briefly review two relevant literatures (cross-cultural effectiveness and cross-cultural training) and extract from them the major implications for trainers. A discussion of the central ethical issues will also be presented so that the challenges facing trainers will be seen in their moral as well as pragmatic contexts. The paper will then conclude with an elaboration of the trainer competencies.

Cross-Cultural Effectiveness

Virtually millions of persons . . . have by now successfully interacted with persons from other cultures in obtaining academic degrees, concluding business deals,

Requests for reprints may be sent to R. Michael Paige, International Student Advisor's Office, University of Minnesota, 717 E. River Road, Minneapolis, MN 55455.

Reprinted from INTERNATIONAL JOURNAL OF INTERCULTURAL RELATIONS, Volume 10, R. Michael Paige, "Trainer Competencies: The Missing Conceptual Link in Orientation, 1986, with permission from Elsevier Science.

negotiating treaties, and collaborating to bring about advances in the sciences and arts. Yet it is only within the last two decades that there has been any systematic attempt to understand either the persons or the situations in which these successes occurred (Dinges, 1983, p. 177).

For training programs to have meaningful goals and objectives, it is necessary for trainers to understand what constitutes effectiveness in the target culture and what the factors are that influence success. While the study of cross-cultural effectiveness is still relatively new, there have been noteworthy advances in both the theoretical and research literatures (Hawes & Kealey, 1979; Hawes & Kealey, 1981; Ruben & Kealey, 1979; Kealey & Ruben, 1983; Hammer, Gudykunst & Wiseman, 1978; Hull, 1978; Klineberg & Hull, 1979; Hopkins, 1982). These have been thoughtfully reviewed by David (1972), Benson (1978), Brislin (1981), and Dinges (1983).

The conceptual model that emerges from these studies is a complex one. Cross-cultural effectiveness is positively influenced by (1) *knowledge* about the target culture, (2) *personal qualities* such as openness, flexibility, tolerance of ambiguity, and sense of humor, (3) *behavioral skills* such as communicative competency, culturally appropriate role behavior, ability to relate well to others, (4) *self-awareness,* especially with respect to one's own values and beliefs, (5) *technical skills,* including the ability to accomplish the task within the new cultural setting, and (6) *situational factors* such as relative similarity of the target culture to one's home culture, culture, receptivity to foreigners, political/economic/social conditions in the second culture, or clarity of expectations regarding the role and position of the foreigner.

The complexity of the cross-cultural experience has important implications for trainers. They must know which factors can or cannot be influenced by the program, which types of learning activities can affect different types of learning outcomes, and how to prepare the learner to continue the process of learning abroad. The more clearly trainers can accurately conceptualize cross-cultural effectiveness, the more likely they are to design and implement a sound orientation program. Ignorance of these concepts can result in poorly designed and delivered programs, unrealistic expectations among the learners, and harmful misperceptions regarding the sojourn experience.

Cross-Cultural Training and Orientation

. . . the purpose of a cross-cultural training program is to provide a *functional awareness* of the cultural dynamic present in intercultural relations and assist trainees in becoming more *effective* in cross-cultural situations (Pusch et al., 1981, p. 73).

Trainers now have an extensive literature to draw upon regarding such key topics as: training activities (Batchelder & Warner, 1977; Casse, 1979; Hoopes & Ventura, 1979; Weeks, Pedersen, & Brislin, 1977); training design issues (Gudykunst & Hammer, 1983; Hoopes, Pedersen, & Renwick, 1978; Brislin & Pedersen, 1976; Hoopes, 1977); and evaluation of cross-cultural training (Renwick, 1979; Blake & Heslin, 1983). In this section we will examine some of the major issues associated with training that emerge from the literature.

Content and Pedagogy

In their recent work on cross-cultural training, Gudykunst and Hammer (1983) introduce two issues they consider central to training: didactic versus experiential approaches to instruction, and culture-general versus culture-specific content. The first issue concerns the method of instruction to be employed. Many of the early training programs relied on the didactic approach (alternately referred to as the "intellectual," "cognitive," or "university" models), which emphasized the lecture-discussion format to transmit information about the target culture. The many deficiencies of the university model were articulated in a seminal article by Harrison and Hopkins (1967) and experiential learning activities started to be utilized with increasing frequency. However, many experiential approaches were seriously flawed because the trainers lacked the conceptual framework to assist the learner in reflecting upon and making some sense out of the experience. In their extreme forms, neither the didactic nor the experiential approach alone proved suitable for cross-cultural training (see J. Bennett, this issue).

The intriguing culture-general versus culture-specific issue concerns the content of training. Early programs relied almost entirely on culture-specific content, i.e., information about the target culture, society, political system, economic structure, history, etc. Although at the time this seemed like a logical approach, it eventually became clear that: (1) individual cultures are diverse, fluid, and difficult to comprehend and, (2) self-awareness and an understanding of the dynamics and influence of culture, in general terms, are equally if not more important than information about cultural specifics. An overemphasis on culture-specific training can deceive the learners into thinking that they are much better prepared for the experience than they actually are. Paradoxically, the learners themselves are generally more positive toward culture-specific than culture-general learning because the former is more concrete and less threatening. Trainers thus face the dilemma of having to include learning activities that may be resisted (but according to training design theory will be more relevant to overseas effectiveness) or eliminate those culture-general activities (and risk failing to adequately prepare the learner). An integrated training design is the solution suggested by Gudykunst and Hammer (1983) (refer also to J. Bennett, this issue; Gudykunst, Wiseman, & Hammer, 1977; Gudykunst, Hammer, & Wiseman, 1977; and Hammer, Gudykunst, & Wiseman, 1978).

Three Challenges of Orientation Programs

Orientation programs have some unique features that pose challenges for trainers. *The first is the challenge of helping learners wrestle with the issue of assimilation and acculturation.* The pressures of assimilation are particularly strong upon long term sojourners (e.g., foreign students) who will be completely immersed in a new culture. As the learners begin to recognize that pressure will be placed on them to adapt to new ways of thinking and behaving, they will begin to pose difficult questions about cultural identity, personal integrity with respect to belief and behavior systems, etc. While there are no correct answers to these questions that will apply equally to all learners, trainers must avoid giving simplistic or misleading responses. Rather, they should emphasize that the cross-cultural experience will require learners to make some difficult behavioral and attitudinal choices. Trainers can point out that attaining mastery of another language and culture will be a source of great personal accomplishment. But during the adjustment phase, the sojourner will be facing the dilemma of wanting to become a fully functioning member of the new culture, on the one hand, without having to sacrifice one's own identity, on the other. It takes a skilled trainer to assist learners in working through these questions and maintain their enthusiasm for the forthcoming cross-cultural experience.

The second challenge for trainers is that of helping learners conceptualize and deal with the experience of becoming "multicultural," i.e., the capacity to function effectively in two or more cultures. As Mestenhauser (1981, 1983) points out, acquiring that capacity requires a "paradigm shift," which can be defined as a cognitive, behavioral, and affective shift from one's monocultural frame of reference. Such a shift is often accompanied by a sense of loss and confusion as the learner begins to systematically confront deeply held value orientations, assumptions about human behavior, and perspectives about the world. Unquestionably, the process of culture learning (or becoming multicultural) subjects the learner to certain psychological stresses and tensions (Adler, 1974).

The trainer must be able to assist the learner in sorting out these feelings and in developing new strategies for coping with these stresses (refer to Barna, 1983 for useful suggestions). Some trainers may be sufficiently uncomfortable themselves with the learning issues surrounding the paradigm shift that they do not incorporate any activities into their programs that would induce these more substantive, and difficult, dimensions of culture learning. Avoidance of these issues, however, is not the answer. It is this author's opinion that the effective cross-cultural trainer will be able to provide learners with both opportunities to experience the paradigm shift and conceptual frameworks to help them understand this profoundly important aspect of culture learning. The experienced trainer, above all else, will have the ability to provide personal support to the learner by means of effective listening, advising, and counseling.

The third challenge is for trainers to be able to handle learner resistance, defensiveness, and frustration. These are the normal responses of individuals undergoing a challenging, self-confrontative learning experience. Learners will take their frustrations out on the trainers. They will rationalize inadequate performances. They will resist certain learning activities. They may reject the program in its entirety. Experienced trainers will be familiar with these negative reactions and will know how important it is to be patient, sensitive, open, and nondefensive with the learners. Such trainers will recognize that as the program progresses toward its more provocative segments, the trainer may become *less* rather than more popular with the learners, and they will accept that being liked is not always synonymous with being effective as a trainer.

In summary, cross-cultural trainers must understand and be able to act upon a great deal of information, from the basic assumptions underlying their programs, to content and process issues, to the interpersonal dynamics of the learner-trainer relationship. They must also be aware of the central ethical issues, which are presented in the following section.

The Ethics of Cross-Cultural Training and Orientation

The neglect of ethical concerns and ethical implications of cross-cultural training programs stands in sharp contrast to the extensive discussions on research ethics and professional conduct in the traditional social science disciplines (Brislin, Landis, & Brandt, 1983, p. 27).

There are many ethical questions that confront individual trainers and the profession as a whole, but only recently have these issues become the focus of any systematic attention. This relatively new concern with ethics is the result of several factors: the sizeable increase in the number of cross-cultural practitioners, the absence of certification and licensure mechanisms to govern trainer activities, various instances of abuse (e.g., exaggerated claims made for training programs and trainers, poorly implemented programs), and the desire of many to strengthen the profession. Significant contributions in conceptualizing ethical issues and developing ethical standards have been made by Barnlund (1982), Howards et al. (1982), Howell (1982), and Paige and Martin (1983). The purpose of this section is to further elaborate the emerging definition of the "ethical trainer."

Key Ethical Questions in Cross-Cultural Training and Orientation

The central ethical questions that have been presented in the literature and discussed among the trainers can be categorized into concerns about:

1. *What goals and objectives are appropriate for cross-cultural training and orientation.* For example, is it ethical to attempt to change the individual's behavior, attitudes, or values? Or promote multiculturalism?

2. *What constitutes an ethical training environment.* For example, should cross-cultural training be conducted in an extremely competitive social psychological context? What kind of fit should be established between the learning environment and the personal characteristics of the learners?

3. *What characterizes an ethical training pedagogy.* For example, are there certain types of learning activities (e.g., experiential simulations) that would be inappropriate under certain circumstances?

4. *What characterizes an "ethical client" and under what circumstances might a training program contract be rejected.* Are there ethical standards that can and should be applied to the long term purposes of clients for acquiring cross-cultural skills?

5. *What constitutes ethical marketing of trainers and their programs.* Under what circumstances should we be making claims regarding our own skills and the outcomes attributed to our programs?

6. *What characterizes an ethical trainer-learner relationship.* For example, is the "expert" posture an appropriate one for the trainer to take?

7. *What risks are associated with training for the learners and how would the ethical trainer respond to them.* What skills should the trainer have in order to utilize learning activities that present the risks of failure and self-disclosure, and/or might threaten the learner's self-esteem and personal identity?

8. *What qualities characterize ethical trainers as opposed to unethical practitioners.* Are there behavioral patterns, values, and levels of understanding that distinguish ethical trainers?

9. *What steps can our profession take to promote an ethics of cross-cultural training and orientation.* Are there practical steps our professional associations can take to encourage further development of ethical guidelines and standards?

These are extremely difficult questions to answer, but they are central to the development of our profession, and how it will be perceived in the public mind in the years ahead, and to how we as individual trainers will be received and judged. If we ignore these questions and fail to provide ethical guidelines for our applied work, our profession will be harmed, unethical and ill-informed practices will likely increase, and our collective professional reputation will be compromised.

The Emerging Ethics of Cross-Cultural Training and Orientation

Although an absolute consensus does not yet exist with respect to all of the questions posed above, healthy discussion and debate is occurring. Paige and Martin (1983), for example, have offered useful responses to a number of these issues. Regarding the goals and objectives of training, they suggest that cross-cultural training is inherently "transformative," i.e., is intended to change learner cognition, behavior, and affect. But they add that the ethical trainer is both fully aware of this "person-transformation imperative" and has the capacity to help move learners through the challenges and difficulties of culture learning. The unethical trainer may induce change without being aware of it or lack the skills to assist learners who are going through a period of significant change. Regarding the training environment, the authors suggest that an ethical trainer will seek to establish a climate of trust and will strive to fit the learning environment to the learning styles of the clients. On the matter of training pedagogy, Paige and Martin (1983, pp. 54–56) discuss the sequencing of learning activities and the importance of debriefing skills for trainers. They also address the question of ethical clients, urging trainers to inquire into the long range purposes of the client and to reject contracts if they determine that the acquired cross-cultural skills would be used for unethical purposes (e.g., exploitation of others). An ethical marketing approach would base claims about trainers and programs on solid evaluation research. The trainer's prior experience and skills would be accurately represented, not exaggerated. I discuss the trainer-learner relationship elsewhere in this chapter, emphasizing the need to avoid creating dependency relationships and the importance of helping the learners to become independently resourceful in learning about the target culture. Paige and Martin also identify certain risks (of self-disclosure and failure) related to training and suggest that ethical trainers—through awareness of these risks, proper sequencing of activities, and debriefing skills—can reduce the element of risk for learners.

We can anticipate that these answers will be considerably refined in the future as more is written about ethics, as more conference programs on ethics are presented, and as our reflections on ethics become more sophisticated. Fortunately, a solid start has been made.

The Ethical Trainer

In light of the above considerations, the author will conclude this section by suggesting certain behavioral qualities that would characterize the ethical trainer. Specifically, ethical trainers will:

1. Strive to acquire relevant conceptual/theoretical foundations for cross-cultural training from fields of study such as intercultural communication, cross-cultural psychology, social psychology, anthropology, etc.

2. Keep abreast of ethical issues via the literature, conference programs, and dialogues with professional colleagues.

3. Keep informed about training issues through the literature, professional association meetings, workshops, etc.

4. Seek to constantly develop their professional skills.

5. Use only those training methods and learning activities that are congruent with their own skills as trainers.

6. Be openly self-reflective and critical regarding their own skills, level of self-awareness, training biases, etc.

7. Seek to establish ethical training environments, training pedagogies, and trainer-learner relationships.

8. Market themselves and their programs honestly and accurately.

9. Recognize the change imperative of training and the risks associated with certain learning activities, and acquire the skills to conduct training, in general, and these activities, in particular, with sensitivity to the needs and concerns of the learners.

10. Strive to help the profession identify ethical issues and forge a consensus regarding ethical behavior.

Trainer Competencies

Training design, duration, intensity, and size vary. Participants vary. Countries of destination vary . . . And from that builds my conviction that this most challenging of challenges—helping man related to unknown man—deserves extraordinary, inventive modes of teaching (Ackermann, 1976, p. 304).

In this section, trainer competencies will be categorized in terms of cognitive knowledge, behavioral skills, and personal attributes. Some of these cognitive and behavioral competencies, and many of the personal attributes have been mentioned in the general training and cross-cultural effectiveness literatures. Thus, the author is indebted to his colleagues for their prior work in this field. The intended contribution of this paper is to pull these ideas together and present a detailed description of trainer competencies.

No given trainer, of course, will possess all of these skills and attributes, but the best and most ethical trainers will be constantly striving to improve their knowledge base, behavioral performance and personal qualities. They will recognize their own strengths and weaknesses as trainers, and will seek to function in those areas where they can be most effective.

Trainer Competencies in the Cognitive Domain

Competent trainers must have a sound conceptual foundation for their work. Knowledge serves as the basis for action and must be regularly expanded in the light of new research findings, conceptual models, and theories.

Figure 1 classifies cognitive competency into seven knowledge areas and 29 knowledge specifics, "understandings," that are subsumed under each of these broader areas. Together, these knowledge areas and specifics represent the cognitive competencies of the exemplary trainer.

Cross-Cultural Phenomena

This knowledge area is at the core of the trainer's knowledge foundation. It includes understanding what it means to make the transition to another culture, and to live and work

Figure 1 Trainer Competencies: Cognitive Domain

Knowledge Area	Knowledge Specifics
I. Cross-Cultural Phenomena	I. 1. Understanding cross-cultural effectiveness
	I. 2. Understanding cross-cultural adjustment, culture shock
	I. 3. Understanding re-entry adjustment
	I. 4. Understanding culture learning, paradigm shift
	I. 5. Understanding the cross-cultural experience
II. Cross-Cultural Training	II. 1. Understanding critical training variables
	II. 2. Understanding what training can and cannot accomplish
	II. 3. Understanding the relationship of training to performance in the target culture
	II. 4. Understanding basic training program assumptions
	II. 5. Understanding training design issues including: a) experiential and didactic methods, b) culture-general and culture-specific content, c) integrated training design, d) goals and objectives, e) content versus process factors
	II. 6. Understanding training pedagogy including: a) sequencing of activities, b) selection of activities, c) alternative techniques, d) purposes of different activities
	II. 7. Understanding program planning principles
	II. 8. Understanding program evaluation principles
III. Trainer/Learner Issues	III. 1. Understanding that training prepares "culture learners"
	III. 2. Understanding social-psychological dynamics of trainer/learner relationship: power, role modeling, source of expertise
	III. 3. Understanding demands of training and learner reactions such as stress, anxiety, frustration, anger
	III. 4. Understanding major learner concerns: assimilation/own cultural identity issue, multiculturalism
	III. 5. Understanding nature of learner resistance and principles of debriefing
IV. Ethical Issues	IV. 1. Understanding ethical issues in training: person-transformation imperative; person-environment fit; risk of self disclosure, failure; purposes of the client
	IV. 2. Understanding the emerging code of ethics for trainers
V. Culture-Specific Content	V. 1. Understanding the target culture: political, economic, social, cultural, religious, historical, and other factors
	V. 2. Understanding situational factors of the target culture: host counterpart expectations of the sojourner; job clarity; openness to foreigners; host country relationship to sojourner's nation; host country aspirations, development goals
	V. 3. Understanding the personal characteristics of host country counterparts, if possible
	V. 4. Understanding the nature of the occupational position the sojourner will be entering into, if applicable

(Continued on page 201)

Figure 1 Continued

Knowledge Area	Knowledge Specifics
VI. Trainer Issues	VI. 1. Understanding the role of the trainer in the learning process
	VI. 2. Understanding the pressures that face trainers and the methods for coping with them
	VI. 3. Understanding one's own strengths and limitations as a trainer
VII. International Issues	VII. 1. Understanding theories of social change and development, including "dependencia" theory
	VII. 2. Understanding North–South dialogue issues

effectively in it. The dynamics of cultural adjustment and the challenges of culture learning are well understood, as is the process of re-entry adjustment, which is emerging in the literature as a major cross-cultural issue (Martin, 1984). The trainer who understands the excitement as well as the frustration of the cross-cultural experience will be better able to empathize with and assist the learner on the verge of this experience.

Cross-Cultural Training

There is a great deal to understand in this second knowledge area, as the eight knowledge specifics suggest. From basic programmatic assumptions to follow-up evaluation, the competent trainer must have a command of all aspects of training. A sophisticated program design requires an in-depth awareness of key design issues. The development of a pedagogy relevant to learner needs and program goals requires a detailed understanding of content and process alternatives. The skilled trainer will know what factors influence the process of training as well as how cross-cultural orientation impacts on the sojourner's subsequent effectiveness.

Trainer-Learner Issues

It is critical for the trainer to understand the dynamics of the trainer-learner relationship. Above all else, the competent trainer will understand the principles of "debriefing," that is, the process of providing conceptual and personal assistance to the learner, especially during times of great stress, confusion, anxiety, or frustration. The trainer should have a conceptual grasp of alternative learner reactions to program activities.

Ethical Issues

The competent trainer must be aware of the major ethical issues in the field of cross-cultural training and orientation, such as those mentioned earlier in this paper. There will be an understanding of the code of ethics that is emerging and that this code will be refined in the years ahead.

Culture-Specific Content

This knowledge area compliments the trainer's general understanding of cross-cultural phenomena by including specific items of information about the sojourner's target culture and assignment. Obviously, trainers cannot be experts regarding the many target cultures they are preparing sojourners to enter, but they can and should, (1) learn as much as possible about the host culture and assignment prior to the orientation, and (2) know how to bring together the appropriate human and material resources to convey this information.

Trainer Issues

Competent trainers will have a clear understanding of their role in the learning process. Rather than serve as experts and risk creating dependency relationships with learners, they will understand the principles of culture learning and thus encourage learners to discover for themselves the realities of the target culture. Trainers will also understand the pressures on learners and will know the methods for coping with them. Fundamentally, they will know their own strengths and weaknesses.

International Issues

Many orientation programs today are preparing sojourners to live, work, and study in the so-called developing nations. Trainers preparing persons for these assignments have a special obligation to understand and convey to the learners information about: (1) alternative theories and perspectives of social change, or development, (2) the concerns and aspirations of "Third World" peoples, and (3) the issues associated with the "North-South" debate.

Trainer Competencies in the Behavioral Domain

Figure 2 presents the behavioral competencies. These are organized into the same seven areas as listed in the cognitive domain and are further described in terms of 29 behavioral specifics. In many instances, the behavioral specific is the performance equivalent of the cognitive competency.

Cross-Cultural Phenomena

These behavioral specifics are related to the trainer's ability to prepare learners for their encounters with cross-cultural phenomena such as cultural adjustment (including culture shock), culture learning, intercultural communication and relations, and re-entry adjustment. The competent trainer must be able to construct learning activities that will enable learners to think about, emotionally feel, and behaviorally react to these phenomena prior to their departure. The acquisition of new ways of thinking, behaving, and feeling (i.e., the paradigm shift) must begin during training, irrespective of the target culture, because it can be anticipated that all sojourners will experience these cross-cultural phenomena to some degree.

Cross-Cultural Training

Many behavioral skills are required of the trainer in this area. The capacity to assess the needs of prospective learners is basic. The planning process includes making logistical arrangements, securing funding, conducting staff training, designing the program and its evaluation procedures. The specifics of program design include: identifying goals and objectives, relating training activities to them, integrating a variety of content areas and instructional methods into the program, and doing all of this by systematically considering the critical variables associated with training as they apply to this program. In the specific realm of pedagogy, the trainer must be able to design appropriate learning activities and properly sequence them, making certain that they are reasonably congruent with the learning styles of the trainers and/or that alternative activities are available.

Trainer/Learner Issues

Competent trainers will not only have a keen awareness of learner concerns and dynamics, they will also be able to respond effectively to them. By providing conceptual frameworks and establishing an atmosphere of trust, trainers will be able to promote culture learning and the skills of cross-cultural effectiveness. They will be able to debrief learners and discuss difficult learning issues with them, especially when certain activities have produced strong reactions. They will resist being placed in the "expert" role and will thus avoid forming dependency relationships with learners. At all times, they will demonstrate behavioral sensitivity to what the learner is experiencing.

Ethical Issues

Ethical trainers will conduct themselves in ways that will advance the profession. They will promise only what they can deliver. They will be prepared to design and implement a sophisticated program. They will refuse contracts if the clients' purposes are themselves unethical. They will promote public trust and confidence in cross-cultural training by adhering to the emerging code of ethics.

Figure 2 Trainer Competencies: Behavioral Domain

Behavioral Area	Behavioral Specifics
I. Cross-Cultural Phenomena	I. 1. Capacity to induce a cultural adjustment experience, a paradigm shift during orientation
	I. 2. Capacity to present a culture-general conceptual framework to assist learners in dealing with adjustment, paradigm shift
	I. 3. Capacity to promote learner acquisition of skills, knowledge and personal qualities relevant to cross-cultural effectiveness
	I. 4. Capacity to present theories and concepts regarding cross-cultural phenomena such as culture shock, re-entry, culture learning, intercultural communication/relations, effectiveness
II. Cross-Cultural Training	II. 1. Capacity to assess learner needs
	II. 2. Capacity to design a cross-cultural program that would: a) consider the "critical" variables, b) be appropriate to learner needs, c) be integrated in terms of method and content, d) have clear goals and objectives
	II. 3. Capacity to develop a pedagogical approach that would: a) properly sequence activities, b) utilize activities appropriate to the goals of the program, c) use activities relevant to the learning style of the trainee(s)
	II. 4. Capacity to plan a cross-cultural program that would: a) consider all aspects of the program, b) include staff training and program evaluation
	II. 5. Capacity to implement a cross-cultural program including: a) managing and administering the program, b) conducting the learning activities, c) making adjustments in the program in response to changing trainee needs and training dynamics
	II. 6. Capacity to evaluate a cross-cultural program
III. Trainer/Learner Issues	III. 1. Capacity to assist trainees in becoming culture learners
	III. 2. Capacity to help trainees deal with stress, anxiety, frustration, etc.
	III. 3. Capacity to present conceptual frameworks for the learners to better understand acculturation, cultural identity, multiculturalism
	III. 4. Capacity to "debrief" learners individually or in groups
	III. 5. Capacity to respond effectively and sensitively to learner resistance
	III. 6. Capacity to use own knowledge carefully and avoid becoming the "expert"
IV. Ethical Issues	IV. 1. Capacity to make ethical decisions about who to train as a function of the purposes to which training will be put
	IV. 2. Capacity to conduct training and orientation in an ethical manner, i.e., in accordance with the ethical guidelines of the profession
	IV. 3. Capacity and willingness to improve own professional skills

(Continued on page 203)

Figure 2 Continued

Behavioral Area	Behavioral Specifics
V. Culture-Specific Content	V. 1. Capacity to assess situational factors in the field that will affect the work of the sojourner
	V. 2. Capacity to interview host country counterparts to acquire information for the sojourner
	V. 3. Capacity to instruct about culture-specific content
VI. Trainer Issues	VI. 1. Capacity to serve as a learning resource and to orient trainees toward that trainer role
	VI. 2. Capacity to handle stress and pressure of training
	VI. 3. Capacity to function as a member of a training team
	VI. 4. Capacity to resist engaging in a "popularity contest" with learners, to deal with the tough learning issues that will emerge in training
VII. International Issues	VII. 1. Capacity to instruct about social change and development theories, North-South dialogue issues

Culture-Specific Content

This behavioral area is comprised of two distinct competencies: the ability to secure information about the setting within which the sojourner will be working (using interviews and other assessment strategies) and the ability to provide instruction about the specific features of the target culture. The competent trainer also takes care that learners do not overemphasize culture-specific information and use it as a crutch.

Trainer Issues

The behaviorally competent trainer must possess some unusual abilities: the capacity to serve as a resource, but not an expert; the capacity to create learning activities that are stressful combined with the ability to help learners deal with the stresses of culture learning; the capacity to be a strong individual, but also serve as a part of a team. Competent trainers derive their professional identity from functioning effectively in the many roles of the trainer: programmer, educator, advisor, etc. Unlike many inexperienced trainers, their professional self-concept is not dependent on having lived and worked in a specific culture, nor on praise from the learners. They have moved beyond these initial, but ultimately limiting sources of identity.

International Issues

Cross-cultural trainers, most certainly those preparing sojourners for "Third World" assignments, should have the capacity to build theoretical content into the program related to social change and development. They must be able to instruct learners about the pressing concerns of peoples in developing nations, some perspectives of which may be significantly different from the learner's own perception of the global reality.

Personal Attributes of the Cross-Cultural Trainer

Figure 3 lists twelve personal characteristics the author suggests are positive attributes of the effective and competent cross-cultural trainer. Many of these have been identified in the literature on cross-cultural effectiveness; if we can assume that an orientation program is itself of cross-cultural experience for the participants, then it is reasonable to hypothesize that the attributes associated with effectiveness in a new cultural setting will apply in the training environment.

Tolerance of Ambiguity

Virtually every orientation program is unique and to some degree predictable. The configuration of elements—staff composition, learner characteristics, design features, learning dynamics—changes from program to program. Thus, there is some inherent ambiguity built into orientation programs that trainers must be able to tolerate.

Cognitive and Behavioral Flexibility

Given the complex and somewhat unpredictable nature of training as a learning enterprise, orientation programs demand cognitive and behavioral flexibility on the part of the trainer. Trainers must be able to adjust their expectations and learning activities as the diverse needs, learning styles, and responses to training activities become manifest. The pace of learning may differ from the trainer's assumptions. Certain activities may be effective, while others are not. As a function of the learner's experiences, new conceptual explanations may be required. The competent trainer will be flexible enough to respond effectively to these dynamics of training.

Personal Self-Awareness, Strong Personal Identity

In light of the fact that trainers are often going to be challenged by learners, it is important for them to be confident in their own identity and to possess a high level of self-awareness. Then, they can serve as models for learners, be more open and honest in their relationships with them, and more effectively help them deal with the issues of culture learning.

Cultural Self-Awareness

Cultural self-awareness means understanding the role of culture in the formation of one's own values, beliefs, patterns of behavior, problem-solving orientation, and the like. It also means awareness of one's own uniqueness as well as one's similarity to the prevailing cultural norms. The competent trainer will be aware in this cultural sense and will be able to teach this concept to others.

Patience

This attribute is frequently mentioned in the literature and is definitely a virtue for cross-cultural trainers. In every program, there will be delays, logistical problems and other issues to test the mettle of the trainer. Most importantly, trainers must be patient with learners, whose style and pace in acquiring key concepts and skills may not be congruent with the trainer's expectations. They should also encourage learners to be patient with respect to becoming proficient in a second language and culture, so that learners aren't discouraged when their progress seems slow.

Enthusiasm and Commitment

Many of the most competent trainers inspire learners by communicating a sense of enthusiasm for their subject matter and a spirit of commitment to the pursuit of cross-cultural knowledge and skills. Such trainers never lose sight of the exciting aspects of cross-cultural learning in spite of the many challenges. Their great gift is the ability to motivate learners by means of their own demonstrable enthusiasm and commitment to the culture learning experience.

Interpersonal Sensitivity, Relations

Cross-cultural trainers must be very adept at interpersonal relations and especially sensitive to the needs and concerns of learners. They must be able to relate well to the wide variety of individuals who comprise the learner community. They must also be skilled at working with other trainers, resource people, community volunteers, and administrators who are involved with the program.

Tolerance of Differences

The ability to tolerate differences (e.g., in values, beliefs, behavior) is one of the hallmarks of the effective sojourner. Likewise, this quality characterizes the competent trainer, who is often working in extremely heterogeneous learning communities. This trait will frequently be tested by learners who do not fit the norm, by colleagues with different perspectives on training, or by the inevitable "petty bureaucrats" with whom trainers must interact.

Figure 3 Trainer Competencies: Personal Attributes

1. Tolerance of ambiguity
2. Cognitive and behavioral flexibility
3. Personal self-awareness, strong personal identity
4. Cultural self-awareness
5. Patience
6. Enthusiasm and commitment
7. Interpersonal sensitivity, relations
8. Tolerance of differences
9. Openness to new experiences, peoples
10. Empathy
11. Sense of humility
12. Sense of humor

Openness to New Experiences, Peoples

An authentic openness to new experiences and peoples is a quality which leads many into the cross-cultural field in the first place and it is a most important attribute for culture learning. The competent trainer will be motivated in this way and will communicate that openness to learners in patterns of thought, feeling, and action.

Empathy

Empathy here means the ability to project oneself into the mind, feelings and role of another. The empathic trainer will have the capacity to sense how the learner is doing and to respond appropriately. Such a trainer will appreciate the learner's anxieties and difficulties as well as sense of accomplishment.

Sense of Humility

This does not mean a false sense of modesty, but a real respect for the complexities, challenges, and uncertainties of cross-cultural learning. The competent trainer will first acknowledge that there is much to learn about cross-cultural phenomena. This trainer will also appreciate that training is not a perfect science, that creativity in orientation design and technique is still possible and desirable, and that future research and evaluation will have much to reveal about the cross-cultural experience. Fundamentally, this sense of humility stems from competent trainers' deep respect for the intricate and varied nature of cultures. They approach the learning process with this sense of humility.

Sense of Humor

This particular attribute can help trainers and learners more effectively cope with the pressures of training, and for learners, with the subsequent stresses of adjustment to a new culture. By being able to laugh at themselves and at the peculiarities of cross-cultural relationships, competent trainers can help break the tension and maintain the learner's enthusiasm.

This section has dealt in detail with trainer competencies. In its totality, an ideal type is being presented by means of these cognitive, behavioral competencies, and personal attributes. Unquestionably, other qualities could be mentioned and some exceptions could be taken with those listed here. No ideal type can do complete justice to the variation in style and approach that exists among competent trainers. Nonetheless, the question remains as to how prospective trainers can acquire certain competencies. In the next section, the author will discuss the training of trainers.

The Training of Trainers

If preparing sojourners in a cross-cultural orientation program is a complex educational enterprise requiring many trainer competencies, the training of trainers is even more complex and challenging. Such training requires learners to make a quantum leap from a foundation of cross-cultural experience and skills to a point where they can bring that foundation to bear as cross-cultural educators. That basic foundation, however necessary, does not automatically make persons with cross-cultural skills trainers, although it is sometimes assumed that such is the case. This author has worked with many newly returned sojourners serving as trainers in Peace Corps and other cross-cultural training programs. It generally takes several programs' worth of experience for them to begin to understand the learning dynamics, design questions and pedagogical issues of training. With experience, time, and support of experienced trainers, they can become increasingly more competent trainers themselves.

The point to be made is that one does not quickly or easily become a competent, professional trainer. The problem for the aspiring trainer is that there are few established experiential or academic pathways into the profession. Thus, it is incumbent on the profession and its experienced practitioners to:

1. Identify relevant academic programs at the undergraduate and graduate levels.

2. Continue to articulate and refine the body of knowledge trainers must acquire.

3. Provide more opportunities for prospective trainers to gain needed experience under the guidance of seasoned professionals.

4. Refine and offer more programs for the training of trainers.

Programs intended to train trainers will have to be very sophisticated in combining experiential opportunities to acquire training skills with sound conceptual content regarding the critical training variables, dynamics, and trainer competencies. These programs should include learning exercises regarding overall program design and the construction of specific learning activities. Logistical planning and program evaluation should be reviewed. Program objectives and assessment measures should be examined. The challenging dynamics of the trainer-learner relationship should be thoroughly explored. These are just a few of the elements that would comprise a training-the-trainer program.

Fortunately, there are several cross-cultural training workshops offered annually under the sponsorship of professional associations such as SIETAR (Society for Intercultural Education, Training, and Research) and NAFSA (National Association for Foreign Student Affairs); these include workshops offered at Georgetown University, Stanford University, and the University of Minnesota. They are intensive in nature, but also limited in time (to one or two weeks). Thus, they cannot substitute for the long term effort the prospective trainer must make to acquire experience and knowledge. Indeed, trainers should seek professional development opportunities throughout their careers.

Summary

Cross-cultural observation and orientation probably began the first time a scout from one tribe peeked over the ridge to see what the neighboring tribe was having for lunch . . . According to informed sources, the excited scout returned to his own tribe with a full report of the scenes he had witnessed. This process back in his own camp is the first recorded intercultural orientation (Batchelder, 1978, p. 45).

Today's scouts are cross-cultural trainers and they have moved considerably beyond peeking over the ridge. In the manner of the early scouts, they have the responsibility to help interpret new cultures to those who have not yet experienced them. But they also have the responsibility to help prepare others to experience those cultures, function effectively within them. Now, many thousands of programs have been conducted since that first, mythical orientation and the field has become increasingly sophisticated. Cross-cultural training demands of its practitioners a command of a large body of knowledge, a wide range of behavioral competencies, and a number of personal qualities. This author would submit that it takes years of relevant academic training, experience, and exposure to skilled professionals to become an authentically competent trainer. For those willing to make the commitment to this field, there are many rewards. Hopefully, for a world desperately in need of peace and understanding, but often dangerously close to conflict and war, there will be those special persons who will wish to serve as scouts.

References

Ackermann, J. M. (1976). Skill training for foreign assignment: The reluctant U.S. case. In L. A. Samovar & R. E. Porter (Eds.), *Intercultural communication: A reader* (pp. 298–306). Belmont, CA: Wadsworth.

Adler, P. S. (1974). Beyond cultural identity: Reflections upon cultural and multicultural man. *Topics in Culture Learning*, **2**, 23–41.

Barna, L. M. (1983). The stress factor in intercultural relations. In D. Landis & R. W. Brislin (Eds.), *Handbook of intercultural training: Vol. 2* (pp. 19–49). New York: Pergamon.

Barnlund, D. C. (1982). The cross-cultural arena: An ethical void. In L. A. Samovar & R. E. Porter (Eds.), *Intercultural communication: A reader* (pp. 378–383). Belmont, CA: Wadsworth.

Batchelder, D. (1978). Training U.S. students going abroad. In D. S. Hoopes, P. B. Pedersen & G. W. Renwick (Eds.), *Overview of intercultural education, training and research: Vol. 2—Education and training* (pp. 45–63). Washington, D.C.: SIETAR.

Batchelder, D., & Warner, E. C. (Eds.) (1977). *Beyond experience*. Brattleboro, VT: Experiment in International Living.

Benson, P. (1978). Measuring cross-cultural adjustment: The problem of criteria. *International Journal of Intercultural Relations*, **2**, 21–37.

Blake, B. F., & Heslin, R. (1983). Evaluating cross-cultural training. In D. Landis & R. W. Brislin (Eds.), *Handbook of intercultural training: Vol. 1* (pp. 203–223). New York: Pergamon.

Brislin, R. W. (1981). *Cross-cultural encounters*. New York: Pergamon.

Casse, P. (1979). *Training for the cross-cultural mind*. Washington, D.C.: SIETAR.

David, K. (1972). Intercultural adjustment and applications of reinforcement theory to problems of "culture shock." *Trends*, 4, 1–64.

Dinges, N. (1983). Intercultural competence. In D. Landis & R. W. Brislin (Eds.), *Handbook of intercultural training: Vol. 1* (pp. 176–203). New York: Pergamon.

Gudykunst, W. B., & Hammer, M. R. (1983). Basic training design: Approaches to intercultural training. In D. Landis & R. W. Brislin (Eds.), *Handbook of intercultural training: Vol. 2* (pp. 118–154). New York: Pergamon.

Gudykunst, W. B., Hammer, M. R., & Wiseman, R. (1977). An analysis of an integrated approach to cross-cultural training. *Intercultural Journal of Intercultural Relations*, **1**, 99–109.

Gudykunst, W. B., Wiseman, R., & Hammer, M. R. (1977). Determinants of a sojourner's attitudinal satisfaction. In B. Ruben (Ed.), *Communication yearbook: Vol. 1*. New Brunswick, NJ: Transaction.

Hammer, M. R., Gudykunst, W. B., & Wiseman, R. (1978). Dimensions of intercultural effectiveness. *International Journal of Intercultural Relations*, **2**, 99–110.

Harrison, R., & Hopkins, R. (1967). The design of cross-cultural training: An alternative to the university model. *Journal of Applied Behavioral Science*, **3**, 341–360.

Hawes, F., & Kealey, D. J. (1979). *Canadians in development*. Ottawa: Communications Branch Briefing Centre.

Hawes, F., & Kealey, D. J. (1981). An empirical study of Canadian technical assistance: Adaptation and effectiveness on overseas assignment. *International Journal of Intercultural Relations*, **5**, 239–258.

Hoopes, D. S. (Ed.). (1977). *Readings in intercultural communication: Vol. 2—teaching intercultural communication, concepts and courses*. Pittsburgh, PA: SIETAR.

Hoopes, D. S., & Ventura, P. (Eds.). (1979). *Intercultural sourcebook*. Washington, D.C.: SIETAR.

Hoopes, D. S., Pedersen, P. B., & Renwick, G. W. (1978). *Overview of intercultural education, training and research: Vol 2.—education and training*. Washington, D.C.: SIETAR.

Hopkins, A. R. (1982). *Defining and predicting overseas effectiveness for adolescent exchange students*. Unpublished doctoral dissertation, University of Massachusetts.

Howards, S., Frank, T., Pusch, P., & Renwick, G. (1982). Guest editorial. *International Journal of Intercultural Relations*, **6**, 225–226.

Howell, W. S. (1982). *The empathic communicator*. Belmont, CA: Wadsworth.

Hull, F. W., IV. (1978). *Foreign students in the United States: Coping behavior within the educational environment*. New York: Praeger.

Kealey, K. J., & Ruben, B. D. (1983). Cross-cultural personnel selection criteria, issues, and methods. In D. Landis & R. W. Brislin (Eds.), *Handbook of intercultural training: Vol. 1* (pp. 155–175). New York: Pergamon.

Klineberg, O., & Hull, F. W., IV. (1979). *At a foreign university: An international study of adaptation and coping*. New York: Praeger.

Landis, D., & Brislin, R. W. (Eds.). (1983). *Handbook of intercultural training: Vol. 1–3*. New York: Pergamon.

Martin, J. N. (1984). The intercultural reentry: Conceptualization and directions for future research. *International Journal of Intercultural Relations*, **8**, 115–134.

Mestenhauser, J. A. (1981). Selected learning theories and concepts. In G. Althen (Ed.), *Learning across cultures* (pp. 116–127). Washington, D.C.: NAFSA.

Mestenhauser, J. A. (1983). Learning from sojourners. In D. Landis & R. W. Brislin (Eds.), *Handbook of intercultural training: Vol. 2* (pp. 153–185). New York: Pergamon.

Paige, R. M., & Martin, J. N. (1983). Ethical issues and ethics in cross-cultural training. In D. Landis & R. W. Brislin (Eds.), *Handbook of intercultural training: Vol. 1* (pp. 36–60). New York: Pergamon.

Pusch, M. D. (Ed.). (1979). *Multicultural education: A cross-cultural training approach*. LaGrange Park, IL: Intercultural Network, Inc.

Pusch, M. D., Patico, A., Renwick, G. W., & Saltzman, C. (1981). Cross-cultural training. In G. Althen (Ed.), *Learning across cultures* (pp. 72–102). Washington, D.C.: NAFSA.

Renwick, G. W. (1979). *Evaluation handbook*. LaGrange Park, IL: Intercultural Network, Inc.

Ruben, B., & Kealey, D. (1979). Behavioral assessment of communication competency and the prediction of cross-cultural adaptation. *International Journal of Intercultural Relations*, **3**, 15–47.

Weeks, W., Pedersen, P. B., & Brislin, R. W. (1977). *A manual of structured experiences for cross-cultural learning*. Washington, D.C.: SIETAR.

Article Review Form at end of book.

WiseGuide Wrap-Up

- The intercultural communication process is much more complex than suggested in early theoretical models. As with many evolving fields, once intercultural communication is past the initial phase, conflicting theoretical constructs evolve and there is a lack of agreement regarding both the concepts and application thereof. This is a normal part of theory construction and will continue as more questions are answered and more are raised.

- As McLuhan's "global village" evolves, there is increased awareness of the need for people to develop a basic degree of intercultural communication competency. Research, however, now recognizes that there is not a "quick fix" training formula to increase employees' abilities to work across national cultural boundaries. How best to meet this need for "high touch" to go with "high tech" has not been established.

- Moon and others offer insightful suggestions for new directions in research. As Tulsi Saral did in the 1970s and 1980s, they suggest that some intercultural research is biased or limited by lack of awareness of cultural influence on the part of the researcher. It is often difficult to expand our frame of reference or recognize how it limits our canvas of reality.

R.E.A.L. Sites

This list provides a print preview of typical **coursewise** R.E.A.L. sites. (There are over 100 such sites at the **courselinks**™ site.) The danger in printing URLs is that web sites can change overnight. As we went to press, these sites were functional using the URLs provided. If you come across one that isn't, please let us know via email to: webmaster@coursewise.com. Use your Passport to access the most current list of R.E.A.L. sites at the **courselinks**™ site.

Site name: Society for Intercultural Education Training and Research (SIETAR)
URL: http://www.jyu.fi/~sietareu/
Why is it R.E.A.L.? This site provides extensive information on SIETAR. It has links to a variety of sites. Information on conferences and workshops is available. It also provides updates regarding the *International Journal of Intercultural Relations*.
Key topics: training, research, education, intercultural
Try this: Compare and contrast the home page of SIETAR with the SIETAR Europa home page.

Site name: National Communication Association (NCA)
URL: http://www.natcom.org/
Why is it R.E.A.L.? NCA, formerly known as the Speech Communication Association, has an International and Intercultural Division which is very active. This site provides information regarding the various journals and publications such as the *International and Intercultural Communication Annual* supported by NCA. There is also information about a lower student membership fee and graduate and undergraduate workshops, special institutes, and other activities.
Key topics: communication, intercultural, international, publications, journals
Try this: Find the International and Intercultural Division and summarize the types of activities this division sponsors. Which do you find of greatest interest?

Site name: International Communication Association (ICA)
URL: http://www.icahdq.org/
Why is it R.E.A.L.? This site provides extensive information regarding the ICA, which has worldwide membership. It provides links to the divisions and interest groups within the organization. There is an Intercultural Division; many other groups, such as the Health Communication Division, also have a cross-cultural focus. There is a reduced student fee and special graduate and undergraduate activities. Information regarding the International Communication Yearbook and the journals is also available at this site.
Key topics: international, communication, training
Try this: The yearly ICA Conference is held outside the United States every four years. Where and when will ICA meet again internationally?

section 6

Intercultural Ethics and Discussion Issues

Learning Objectives

- Recognize that intercultural ethical issues do not always offer easy solutions.
- Understand the impact that different contextual environments have on intercultural communication.
- Appreciate the complexity of the cultural norms and value systems that guide human behavior.
- Develop a sensitivity to the unique characteristics of individuals as communicators.
- Transcend invisible cultural boundaries while experiencing the world.
- Expand awareness of the dilemma of preserving the uniqueness of each culture and creating the "global village."

WiseGuide Intro

There is a myth that, if we can just talk together, we can resolve all problems. If only it were that easy. As research expands regarding the intercultural communication processes in different contextual environments, such as ethical dilemmas, negotiations, cultural identity, border disputes, contrasting values, and multinational teams, it is clear that cross-cultural relationships are complex. However, the following readings may provide a beginning point for discussions regarding the multiple levels of issues involved in addressing these concerns. They may also suggest some strategies that individuals and groups have adopted, as beginning steps, toward better understanding of some of the intercultural concerns they represent.

Tulsi Saral sets the tone for this final section of the intercultural reader with his article on "Intercultural Ethics." He addresses the continuing dilemma: how to preserve and enhance the richness and variety of each interacting culture while effectively communicating across cultures.

This concern is echoed in the thirty-year dialogue of the Arizona-Sonora Commission regarding ongoing concerns along the shared United States and Republic of Mexico border, discussed in "Crossing the Line."

In 1995, during a border dialogue involving the states of Texas, New Mexico, Coahuila, Nuevo Leon, Tamaulipas, and Chihuahua, a participant from El Paso offered the following reason people attended the meetings, "One river, one people, a new way of thinking." "Imagining La Frontera: SEDL's Border Colloquy" summarizes this series of seven meetings. A La Frontera participant from the Cuidad Juarez saw the border region in the Year 2010 thus: "We believe that we will have a cultural mixture which will affect our language, art, customs, and other facets of both cultures. This 'hybrid' culture will be neither a cultural integration nor the submission of one culture under another."

Another aspect of the mixing of cultures is addressed in Wheeler's interview with University of California professor Terry P. Wilson, who is the son of a Potawatomi Indian father and a white mother. A comment by Mr. Wilson illuminates the issues people of mixed race contend with: "Most mixed-race people, myself included, have been besieged by others to choose one identification or the other." Most recently, Tiger Woods, the newest golfing star, has also been pressured by the media to make a choice regarding his heritage. Wilson draws from his experiences in offering insight into this issue.

Sometimes when attempting to make decisions which may impact on cultural identity there are no easy answers. Slakey's article, "Cattle, Education, and the Masai Identity," offers insight into this type of intercultural dilemma. Rothenberg's article, "The Sounds of Global Change: Different Beats, New Ideas," appears initially to be a light piece on global music; however, a closer reading reveals the same issues of maintaining cultural identity while musically crossing borders.

Our final reading, Beverly Geber's "Virtual Teams," describes how technology and the invention of groupware allow workers to be widely separated geographically but be global members of a team. For many people, this is not a "new frontier" but a normal method of doing business, nationally and internationally, with people from multiple cultures. In addition, for a large number of workers, this may soon be a standard practice. The issue remains, however: how can different communication patterns be respected without limiting the success of the group? Also, as we use these alternate channels, do we miss nuances of individual communication patterns which might cause us to decode a message inaccurately?

Our goal as effective intercultural communicators is to not miss the message. In order to do that, we must continue to learn more about ourselves as communicators, and not let our invisible cultural boundaries limit our ability to move effectively within and across national and cultural borders.

These are not easy issues to address, but those of us interested in expanding our intercultural communication abilities will continue the quest to create not just a "high-tech" world but one which displays "high touch."

? Questions ?

Reading 29. What are some of the intercultural ethical issues that employees moving across national and cultural boundaries might face? Why are boundaries important to people either at a personal level or at a national level?

Reading 30. Why are boundaries important to people either at a personal or national level?

Reading 31. What are the major components of the "vision of the future" for La Frontera?

Reading 32. How do people of mixed race define themselves culturally? Why are they pushed to make a choice between races, as opposed to being both?

Reading 33. What choice would you make if faced with a set of cultural circumstances that was similar to Francis Slakey's? What is the Masai leader attempting to preserve?

Reading 34. How do musicians and singers create music to contain cultural messages which are in a form that moves across the globe in popularity?

Reading 35. How do you get a team to work like a well-oiled machine when its gears and cogs are scattered across the globe?

What are some of the intercultural ethical issues that employees moving across national and cultural boundaries might face?

Intercultural Ethics

Tulsi B. Saral
University of Houston–Clear Lake

Abstract

Different cultures develop different moral sensitivities, which are the product of their history, traditions and worldviews. The goal of intercultural communication is not to eliminate cultural differences but to preserve and enhance the variety and richness of interacting cultures. Ethical intercultural communicator respects the member of a different culture to think, believe and act differently than his/her own actions, thoughts and beliefs in similar or parallel situations.

Ever since the inception of the human race, men have struggled to define and evaluate their own conduct and character and that of other men. Ethics, as an area of study, has concerned itself with the characterization and evaluation of human conduct. Normative ethics concerns itself with "discovering, justifying, elucidating and applying criteria according to which specific human actions are considered to be morally good or bad." Comparative ethics, on the other hand, studies "the moral beliefs and practices of different people and cultures in various places and times. It aims not only to elaborate such beliefs and practices but also to understand them in so far as they are casually conditioned by social, economic and geographic circumstances." (Encyclopedia Britannica, 1980, p. 977).

Ethicists have been long divided over the questions of the universality and diversity of moral rules and practices. Some believe that morality is rooted in human nature and, if human nature is fundamentally everywhere the same, it will also manifest this similarity in significant ways, including morality. Others maintain that although all societies tend to develop well defined norms for personal, interpersonal and inter-group behavior, not all societies evolve the same norms for the various aspects of human conduct. Whatever the merits and demerits of the two positions, one thing is certain—People tend to identify with their moral beliefs and judge themselves and others often without becoming aware of the basis of their judgments. The difficulty arises when the person judged belongs to a different culture and does not subscribe to the same, moral beliefs as the one who is doing the judging.

The rules of behavior vary greatly from culture to culture, and it is easy to misinterpret and misjudge other people's behavior if we do not have the appropriate awareness of the mores, mythology, rituals and belief systems prevalent in their culture. Just as it is natural for us to read the behavior of others in terms of our own standards, so it is natural to view actions in other cultures from the codes of our own culture. What seems fair to us we assume is fair to them; and when we see an action we regard as unfair from the perspectives of our own culture, we tend to assume that they have violated their code. The only way to penetrate the deception of appearance is to study the cultural context in which the action occurs, determining the circumstances of time, place, and conditions surrounding the action and, most important, learning the reasoning that underlies it and the moral value(s) it reflects.

Each culture evolves its own moral sensitivity, which reflects its unique history, tradition and worldview. It would be inappropriate for one culture to employ its own standards in judging moral beliefs and behavior of a member of another culture in the same way as it would not want its members to be judged by; another culture with ethical norms and standards different from its own. What this implies, of course, is that given the cultural diversity prevalent in the world today, we cannot possibly justify a universal ethical code that would govern the behavior of all human beings. Even Aristotle, in his time-honored treatise on ethics, recognized this fact. Commenting upon his work, Barnes (1979) remarks:

"Morals, he implies, cannot by any means be reduced to a set of universal principles; any principle that may be formulated 'is liable to exception, any universal moral judgment (strictly construed) is false . . . we must not indulge in the vain fancy that a set of true and universal principles is somewhere waiting to be found: ethical absolutism, in that sense, is an illusion. (p. 21–22)"

It is in this light that we must address the question of ethical considerations in intercultural communications. A number of scholars in the recent past have drawn attention to the ethical dilemmas experienced in intercultural encounters and at-

Reprinted by permission of Tulsi B. Saral, University of Houston–Clear Lake.

tempted to resolve the problem by proposing adaptation of certain 'codes of ethics' to be followed by intercultural educators, researchers, scholars and trainers. Sitaram and Cogdell (1976), for example, propose a list of 'do's' and 'don'ts' in intercultural interactions. Asuncion-Lande (1980) attempts to develop a list of similarities and differences in diverse cultural ethical codes in order to come up with a body of rules for ethical conduct in intercultural interactions. Pointing out the limitations of such approaches, Gudykunst (1980) argues that:

"It is impossible to develop a list of 'do's' and 'don'ts' with respect to intercultural ethics given our current state of knowledge with respect to comparative ethical codes. . . . It would be difficult, if not an impossible task to develop a list which recognizes the diversity of ethical codes, allows for making ethical judgments, and is consistent with normative ethical relativism. (p. 18)"

Gudykunst believes, and rightfully so, that developing a code of ethics would be a "fool's errand" and that we would never be able to develop a code which meets the criteria specified above.

"Such a code would have to recognize the situational nature of ethical choice. And within the code, appropriate behavior would have to be specified for every situation (and potentially designating which cultures the communicators come from). Much research is necessary to gather the knowledge needed to write such a code. (p. 29)"

Reality Is Relative

Reality is not fixed and absolute but conditional and relative. What one perceives as real is very much determined by one's cultural conditioning and symbolic and linguistics categories. Saral (1980) points out some of the ways in which different cultures map their 'reality' differently:

"Metaphysical beliefs about the nature of reality differ widely from culture to culture. Concepts of space, for example, may not fully follow the dictums of Euclidean Geometry in all cultures. Time, likewise, may not necessarily be perceived as following a continuous and unidirectional flow. Man may be differentiated from non-man in different ways in different cultures. Even the so called 'ordinary' stimuli may be processed and integrated differently and assigned entirely different sets of meanings. (p. 17)"

The language of culture defines the limitations and possibilities of thinking within the culture. In fact, a distinctive worldview becomes associated with each language. An individual's thinking and consequent behavior are strongly determined by his/her particular and partial way of construing things. There is, therefore, no absolute reality but only subjective and often contradictory conceptions of reality. Watzlawick (1977) explores the confusion between two different aspects of reality:

". . . there is confusion between two very different aspects of what we call reality. The first has to do with the purely physical, objectively discernible properties of things and is intimately linked with correct sensory perceptions, with questions of so-called common sense or with objective, repeatable, scientific verification. The second aspect is the attribution of meaning and value to these things . . . (pp. 140–141)"

Intercultural differences and conflicts arise when we lose sight of this distinction between the first order, 'objective' reality and the 'subjective' reality with its culture-specific roles, norms and value structures. One would like to believe for example, that one's practice of "moral conduct" would not be governed by who the potential beneficiary of such behavior would be. However, as Baelz (1977) points out, it is not always so across all cultures.

"A moral point of view is not always a universal point of view, from which all human beings, whatever their race color or intelligence, can be seen to merit equal consideration. It may be a more limited point of view in the sense that it takes into account only members of the family, or members of the tribe, or members of the nation. One of the substantial moral questions which individuals have to answer is 'who is my neighbor?' How far do the boundaries of the moral community extend? (p. 28)"

Interaction with Context

Human beings exist in a cultural or environmental context. Environment determines the context of space in which they dwell and also to some extent the kinds of interactions they can have with it. Humans are also dynamic beings who are continually in process. An individual is never complete at any one moment and is always in movement and change within time. What choices will be made by an individual in what context will very much depend upon the time-orientation that is preeminent in his/her assumptions. The past is generally based upon the customs, habits, and time-honored traditions, whereas future usually points out toward the possibilities, goals, and intentions.

The critical role of contextual environment in intercultural interactions has been spelled out in greater detail by Saral (1977). The context also determines the moral and ethical imperatives followed by a given culture at a given crossroad. What may be judged right in one context may not necessarily be perceived to be right in another. Baelz (1977) notes:

"Thirdly, situations themselves change. Moral rules which may at one time have had a valid point and purpose become outdated and no longer serve the needs of people. Changed situations demand changed responses. (pp. 101–102)"

The uniqueness of intercultural transactions does not rest merely with their environmental context. It is also the interactional process that distinguishes intercultural communications from any other communication events or experiences. As Saral (1979b) explains:

"Interactions in an intercultural communication transaction do not assume fixed cultural identities and are subject to the usual process of growth, evolution and change at different times in different contexts at their own unique pace. (p. 7)"

The ethical demands in an intercultural setting are thus continually subject to the contextual, environmental and interactional forces. Human values, for example, are the product of an ongoing interaction among a person's psychological ecology, his cultural upbringing, and the situational factors present at a given time.

The Personal Nature of Ethics

One's personal values and conduct are not simple introjections from one's society. They also reflect one's personality and unique response dispositions. Moral development like cognitive and linguistic development is a function of maturation within the age-related experience. Each individual has within him/her an innate structure capable of deciphering the complex rules of moral behavior in his/her Culture and selects for himself/herself the moral code that is most conducive for the growth and nurturance of his/her personal worldview. Ethical norms and principles are thus structures that evolve as a result of one's interaction with environment. They do not represent passive internalization of external rules and codes.

The Overlooked Ingredient

Reviewing the literature on intercultural communication research, Nicassio and Saral (1978) proposed that intercultural communication scholars adopt a new perspective which views the communication process as resulting from the dynamic interplay between the cultures of the communicators, their unique response dispositions, and the situational context in which the communication takes places.

> "In analyzing communication from an intercultural perspective, then, we must acknowledge and study the interaction of three major forces: the cultures under consideration with their attendant norms and value systems which guide human behavior, the situational context or specific environment in which the interaction takes place, and the unique characteristics of the individuals themselves as participants in the communication process. (p. 346)"

These are critical variables and deserve detailed attention by students and scholars of intercultural interaction. However, they also very much reflect certain cultural biases. They follow the mechanical model of looking at the world which fragments the whole into several atomized parts, assigns them individualized substance and meaning, and tries to discover some logical and necessary connection between them. This sharply contrasts with the Eastern way of involving the total experience as an organic whole and intuitively apprehending the meaning.

The major ethical dilemma for the intercultural communicators, educators, researchers and trainers is not that they can not enumerate the cognitive, affective and behavioral differences among different cultures. Numerous scholars in the past several years have come up with valuable descriptions of how different cultures differ from each other in their basic value structures and behavior hierarchies. We know, for example, that "Western thinkers trust reason as providing the way to whatever truth and insight man can gain, whereas Eastern thinkers are deeply convinced that ultimate truth can be achieved only by passing beyond reason and the limitations essential to it. (Burtt, 1968, p. 675)"

What we often overlook is our inability to recognize and transcend the invisible cultural boundaries that limit our modes of perceiving, cognizing, and communicating the experience of encountering our world. Burtt (1968) sums up this frustration in the following way:

> "What is that obstructs us in seeking this kind of intercultural understanding? . . . It is our underlying philosophical presuppositions not the ones that we easily become conscious of, but the ones providing the implicit framework of our whole way of thinking. It is vital to remind ourselves that there are presuppositions that we think with so naturally and constantly that it requires a severe wrench for us to free ourselves from their crutches sufficiently to think about them . . . The inevitable tendency for a philosopher is to assume that every experience he meets, every philosophical assertion he reads, can be assimilated into the framework of presuppositions with which he now thinks. It is the only framework he has available. (p. 674)"

Human behavior, verbal as well as non-verbal, is by necessity selective. What is selected and what is omitted by an individual is reflective not only of his/her personal desires, goals, hopes and fears, but also of a broader cultural context which defines his/her reality. In order to understand the complexity, the richness, and the full content of its meaning a behavior must be returned to the context of its origin so that the needs, the priorities, the values and the assumptions that shaped that behavior could be fully acknowledged and understood. The goal of communicating across cultures is not to integrate various cultures into one uniform system, it is to preserve the uniqueness of the cultures across which communication takes place. This can be accomplished by respecting the members of other cultures, as they actually are, not as how we would like them to be, and respecting their right to act differently from how we would like to see them act.

References

Asuncion-Lande, N. C. (1980). *Ethical Perspectives and Critical Issues in Intercultural Communication.* Falls Church, VA: Speech Communication Association.

Baelz, Peter (1977). *Ethics and Belief.* New York: The Seabury Press.

Barnes, Jonathan (1979). Introduction. In Aristotle. *Ethics.* New York: Penguin Books.

Benedict, R. (1934). *Patterns of Culture.* New York: Houghton Mifflin Co.

Burtt, E. A. (1968). A Basic Problem in the Quest for Understanding Between East and West. In Moore, Charles A. (Ed.). *Philosophy and Culture: East and West.* Honolulu: University of Hawaii Press.

The New Encyclopedia Britannica, Vol. III (1980). Chicago: University of Chicago.

Gudykunst, W. B. (1980). *Communication Ethics and Relativism:* The Implications of Ethical Relativity Theory for Intercultural Communication. Unpublished manuscript.

Nicassio, Perry M. and Saral, Tulsi B. (1978). The Role of Personality in Intercultural Communication. In Ruben, Brent (Ed.). *Communication Yearbook 2.* New Brunswick, N.J.: Transaction Books.

Saral, Tulsi B. (1997). The Role of Families in the Changing Global Scenario. A paper presented at the East–West Center International Conference, New Delhi, India.

Saral, Tulsi B. (1983). Ethical issues in intercultural communication. *Journal of Communication Therapy*, Vol. 1, No. 2, 179–188.

Saral, Tulsi B. (1980). Intercultural Incomprehensibility. *International Popular Culture*, Vol. 1, No. 2., 15–20.

Saral, Tulsi B. (1979a). The consciousness theory of intercultural communication. In Asante M. K., Newmark E. and Blake, C. A. (Eds.) *Handbook of intercultural communication.* Beverly Hills, CA: Sage Publications.

Saral, Tulsi B. (1979b). Metaphysics of Mental Health, Mental Illness and Psychotherapy. A paper presented at the fifth annual conference of Society for Intercultural Education, Training and Research, Mexico City.

Saral, Tulsi B. (1977). Intercultural Communication Theory and Research: An Overview. In Ruben, Brent D. (Ed.) *Communication yearbook I.* New Brunswick, NJ: Transaction Books.

Watzlawick, Paul. (1977). *How real is real? Confusion, disinformation, communication.* New York: Random House.

Biographic Sketch: Dr. Tulsi Saral is a Professor of Clinical Psychology at the University of Houston-Clear Lake and teaches courses in Culture and Psychotherapy, Group Psychotherapy, Transpersonal Therapy and Sex Therapy. At UH–Clear Lake, he served as a Program Director of Human Sciences and founded a Masters degree program in Multicultural Studies which was later renamed as M.A. in Cross-Cultural Studies. Before that, he served as Research Assistant Professor at the University of Illinois Institute of Communication Research and as University Professor at Governors State University. At Governors State University, he also served as Program Coordinator of Communication Science, Assistant Dean, and later as Acting Dean, of the College of Human Learning and Development.

Dr. Saral is the past Chair of the Intercultural Communication Division of International Communication Association and Past Secretary of the Society of Intercultural Education, Training and Research. He is also the past president of the American Association for the Study of Mental Imagery. Dr. Saral is the Founding Editor of the *Journal of Communication Therapy* and founding associate editor of the *International Journal of Intercultural Relations.* He has published numerous articles and book chapters on the various aspects of intercultural communication, transpersonal communication, mental imagery and psychotherapy.

Article Review Form at end of book.

Why are boundaries important to people either at a personal or national level?

Crossing the Line

There is growing worldwide interest in developing closer socioeconomic and political relationships among bordering nations.

J. Stark

The United States and Mexico have had 135 years to develop a relationship across their shared border. According to Ed Williams, professor of political science, the North American Free Trade Agreement (NAFTA) has added both a new quality to that relationship and new importance to the study of borderlands throughout the world. Because those of us in Southern Arizona and the state of Sonora—along with the border generally—are in the physical vanguard, he explains, we have attained a new socioeconomic and political importance. "For the first time since the Treaty of Guadalupe Hidalgo, folks in Washington and Mexico City and elsewhere are beginning to pay attention to us."

"Between Arizona and Sonora, we have achieved some fame in the world," says Dr. Williams. "We get along more easily than many folks do. The Arizona-Sonora Commission, which has been running out of the two governors' offices for more than 30 years, has had some successes. We have established channels of communication, so between the two states there is a highly-developed, long, and moderately successful interaction."

It is this interaction, Williams says, that triggered last fall's visit to Arizona and Sonora by a group of European government officials, academics and businessmen. With the fall of the Iron Curtain in 1989, the Czech-Polish-German borderlands have become increasingly important and are facing issues common to the relationship between the U.S. and Mexico. Interactions between east and west—Poland and the Czech Republic on one hand and Germany on the other—that had been blocked are now possible and in need of structure. People interested in developing closer socioeconomic and political relationships and in solving environmental problems are looking to the experiences and lessons of the U.S.-Mexico bond.

A significant issue in the relationship between the United States and Mexico is the maquiladora industry. As Williams describes it, maquiladora is "production-sharing in an assembly plant context that takes advantage of cheap Mexican labor to make U.S. companies more competitive, leading to significant controversies concerning the environment and working conditions." And, he points out, the problems of this kind of relationship are not confined to Mexico; Polish labor is less expensive than German, for instance. Wherever high prosperity meets poverty, he contends, there will be problems of pollution and production-sharing relationships.

The maquiladora industry, spurred by the threat of economic collapse in Mexico in 1982 and another crisis in 1994, now counts 3,000 plants along the U.S.-Mexico border. Largely because of this industry, NAFTA was negotiated with two side accords. One addressed environmental issues—the sheer proliferation of plants coupled with a lack of enforcement of regulations has led to considerable environmental degradation—the other labor. Stemming in part from his longstanding interest and work in the maquiladora industry, Williams was named to the national advisory committee for the labor side agreement. "With nearly a million workers on the Mexican side, and 80 percent of those in the borderlands, the maquiladora industry is extraordinarily important," he says.

> "Boundaries are important to people. It's that basic animal instinct that separates 'mine' from 'thine.'"

Referring to the "boomlet" in the study of borderlands throughout the world, Williams notes the State Department now has established the position of "border person" in the Office of Mexican Affairs, and the U.S. Information Agency (USIA) has established a program for cross border academic exchanges in areas where there are cities to accommodate it, such as San Diego, Tijuana, and Los Dos Laredos (the two Laredos). He adds that what we learn here, along the U.S.-Mexico border, may help to resolve issues in other places, but, "like Alice in Wonderland, we have to run very rapidly just to stay in place because the problems multiply about as fast as we find solutions."

Article Review Form at end of book.

J. Stark, PEOPLE, PLACES & SOCIETY, College of Social & Behavioral Sciences, The University of Arizona.

What are the major components of the "vision of the future" for La Frontera?

Imagining La Frontera

SEDL's border colloquy

Southwest Educational Development Laboratory

About the Border Colloquy Project

A frontier is not where a world ends, it's where a world begins.

—comment from the El Paso Border Colloquy

We need to stop thinking that what we're doing now is all we need forever. The P-51 Mustang fighter plane was fine for its time. We may be flying a P-51 educational system, but that shouldn't impede our drive to create an F-16 fighter for the year 2010.

—comment from the McAllen Border Colloquy

Purpose and Background

This report describes the results of a series of seven meetings in which residents of *La Frontera*—the region along the boundary between the United States and The Republic of Mexico*—envisioned the future of education for children in an extended "community" that spans that boundary. The Southwest Educational Development Laboratory (SEDL) has sponsored these meetings as part of its Border Colloquy Project, which focuses on the shared border regions of the states of Texas, New Mexico, Coahuila, Nuevo Leon, Tamaulipas, and Chihuahua. The Border Colloquy Project is designed to:

- Develop common understandings about the educational issues and needs facing La Frontera as it experiences massive cultural and economic change.

- Foster a bi-nationally shared vision for the education and well-being of the region's children and youth.

- Encourage the development and use of comprehensive, bi-national plans to fulfill that vision.

The Border Colloquy Project was initiated in March 1994, after SEDL's Board of Directors targeted the educational needs of La Frontera as an area of special concern. Phase 1 of the project consists primarily of the seven planning and information-sharing meetings whose results will be described in this document; Phase 2, from December 1, 1994 through November 30, 1995, will focus on the development of action plans and the cooperative relationships that will be essential to their effective implementation. During Phase 2, SEDL will provide information support and will facilitate interaction among educational communities on both sides of the border through brokering and networking activities.

Overview of the Phase 1 Border Colloquy Meetings

The meetings conducted during Phase 1 were designed to culminate in the creation of a vision statement that reflects a shared, binational perspective on the educational future of La Frontera and its inhabitants; meeting participants also began to consider elements of the action plans that will be fleshed out during Phase 2. To complete these tasks, SEDL first sponsored a series of five regional meetings, followed by a meeting in Monterrey, Mexico, with representatives of the departments of education in each of the Mexican states of Chihuahua, Coahuila, Nuevo Leon, and Tamaulipas. Finally, SEDL sponsored a culminating meeting in Austin, Texas, whose participants were drawn from each of the six preceding meetings.

Regional Meetings

The five regional meetings brought together educators and community representatives from specific areas

*The official designation is the "United Mexican States," while "The Republic of Mexico" is frequently used as well. Because of possible confusion between various shorthand expressions of the "United Mexican States" and the "United States of America," SEDL has elected to use in this paper "The Republic of Mexico" or "Mexico" when referring to the United Mexican States and "United States" or "U.S." when referring to the United States of America.

Note: Southwest Educational Development Laboratory has produced a detailed report exploring educational issues within La Frontera. To receive a copy of *Border Issues in Education,* write or call SEDL, 211 East 7th Street, Austin, Texas, 78701, (512) 476-6861, extension 202.

This excerpt is from a report published originally by the Southwest Educational Development Laboratory, Austin, Texas, 1995, and sponsored wholly or in part, by the Office of Educational Research and Improvement, U.S. Department of Education under contract number RP91002003.

within La Frontera; they were held as follows:

- McAllen, Texas, April 18–19, co-hosted by the Region I Education Service Center, with 16 participants plus SEDL staff and consultants;
- El Paso, Texas, May 9–10, co-hosted by the Region XIX Education Service Center, with 28 participants;
- Las Cruces, New Mexico, May 10–11, co-hosted by the Las Cruces School District #2, with 27 participants;
- Ciudad Juárez, June 9–10, co-hosted by the Universidad Pedagógica Nacional, Cd. Juárez, with 80 participants; and
- Reynosa, June 15–16, co-hosted by El Centro de Actualización de Magisterio de Nuevo Laredo, with 33 participants.

Participants included students, teachers, principals, bilingual supervisors, and superintendents; staff from state and regional education agencies; legislators and legislative staff members; business, church, and community leaders; university faculty; health and human services providers; and immigration officials.

Participants in the regional meetings were asked to imagine what education should be like by the year 2010, when the provisions from the North American Free Trade Agreement (NAFTA) are to be fully implemented. They first described their image of the ideal community of La Frontera in general, then focused specifically on schooling, developing a vision statement to picture what education should accomplish within that community. Finally, participants outlined the work that must be undertaken—changes in attitudes, values, systems, and services—in order to achieve their vision.

Background: Issues Facing La Frontera

It is necessary to acknowledge that current socioeconomic and pedagogic contexts do not particularly favor teamwork.

—comment from the Ciudad Juárez Border Colloquy

If this side of the border is always perceived as better, if this side is always ideal, if this side is always the dreamed place, el norte famoso mágico, then I don't think we're ever going to get the change we're looking for.

—comment from the McAllen Border Colloquy

La Frontera—the region spanning the boundary between the United States and Mexico—is centered on the most populated international border in the world. More than 16.5 million people live along it. Increasingly, the interactions among these people are leading to overlapping and highly interdependent regional economies, societies, and cultures.

The North American Free Trade Agreement (NAFTA) has redefined the economic significance of a 2000-mile political line on the map, while migration and cultural influences are helping to smear that line into a regional blur. Tens of thousands of people cross the border each day; many move back and forth between homes in Mexico and jobs, even schools, in the United States. Among those moving north are many who eventually work or settle permanently in communities as far afield as the states of Washington, Illinois, Michigan, and New York.

With immigration a central fact of life along La Frontera, consideration of border issues carries a huge weight of emotional and political baggage, not only for the region's residents but for U.S. and Mexican citizens throughout the two countries. Many U.S. citizens consider *the border* to be a fence, a barrier designed to maintain stability in the country's population, economy, and services (although the gates through this fence tend to open or close depending on U.S. demand for cheap labor). For its part, Mexico considers emigration a drain on the country's resources; and the government has enacted measures designed to protect its language and cultures from its larger, sometimes overbearing northern neighbor.

However, many border experts believe that NAFTA will serve as a catalyst for the creation of a region that spans current boundaries, a region neither *here* nor *there*, in which neighboring nations remove rather than construct barriers, in which people move freely and the infrastructures that support them—economic, governmental, cultural, and educational systems and services—are compatible and cooperative. The border, then, is conceived not as a line with *us* on one side and *them* on the other but as the central feature in a zone of cooperation, and La Frontera becomes not a sharp edge between peoples but a community with its own energy, direction, and future.

Although this image of community may seem like idealism or fantasy, the present reality is that territories along the border, such as the "twin cities" of El Paso-Juárez or Laredo-Nuevo Laredo, are already as closely bound as Siamese twins joined at the hip. This interdependency is destined to increase as NAFTA's provisions are phased in over the next 16 years.

With migration and interdependence as givens, the questions that arise are not *shoulds* or *ifs* but *hows*. Some of the biggest *hows* relate to education, which must address issues such as the following:

- Poverty and unemployment are serious problems on both sides of the border. Thousands of people live in *colonias*, without basic services such as running water. Many families perform migrant labor, moving with the seasons and earning subsistence wages. How can schools offer poor and transient students the highest quality education? How can schools interact with social service providers to assure all students access to the basic necessities that they must have—food, shelter, health, safety—in order to focus on learning? How can poor communities provide adequate resources for education?

- Mexico and the United States have different educational requirements, systems, and structures. (Contrary to popular perceptions in the U.S., Mexico's requirements are sometimes more stringent than those in the U.S. To graduate from *secundaria*, for example, a student must pass Algebra II, which is not required for a high school diploma in Texas.) Students who try to move from one system to the other face major obstacles; Mexican students entering U.S. schools, for example, are sometimes forced to re-take subjects they have already covered in Mexico. How can educational requirements, curricula, teacher training, and other aspects of schooling be made compatible, so that students and teachers who move from one system to another are not penalized?

- Language is a major educational barrier—and opportunity. Many believe that the full potential of this region cannot be realized until all its citizens are bilingual. Bilingual education is still debated in the United States, yet even certified bilingual teachers may not have mastered the levels of Spanish they need to be able to teach in Mexico or to work most effectively with Mexican students in U.S. schools. Spanish-speaking students in the U.S. are often precluded from learning other subject matter before they learn English. How can schools effectively provide developmental bilingual education for all students in the region, so that they can become fluent in both Spanish and English without any slowdown in content-area learning? And how can teachers receive the language training they may need?

- Government sovereignty, and variations in federal, state, and local government structures and policies, present barriers to cooperation on both sides of the border. How can governments retain the autonomy they need, yet provide policies, structures, and resources to support multi-national initiatives?

Participants in SEDL's Border Colloquy meetings considered these issues and more as they plotted a path from current problems to an imagined future. Although participants agreed that the challenges to La Frontera are immense, they also felt strongly that the region is a resource, not a liability, and that with cooperation and good will, these challenges can be met.

Voices from La Frontera: Conditions and Concerns

If present tendencies continue, we will have a conflictive and asymmetrical border. However, if tendencies change—and here education plays an important role—the border of the year 2010 could be an integrated, dynamic region with a high standard of living.

—comment from the Ciudad Juárez Border Colloquy

Participants in the five regional meetings were asked to imagine what conditions in La Frontera might be like by the year 2010, when NAFTA's provisions are scheduled for full implementation. Participants projected massive changes, and for the most part equated such change with opportunity, imagining that a changing economic climate will help to produce the resources needed to transform the region. They cautioned, however, that it will be essential to maintain a focus on equality and the well-being of people and the environment. UDEM faculty members summarized this concern by calling for a "balance," or "equilibrium": "We want to be competitive and productive, but at the same time we look for social equity, respect for human beings, and opportunities for people to be successful."

The Border Region in the Year 2010

We will see the attitude that the river is to be used, not just to be crossed.

This region will be virtually self-sufficient and consequently able to satisfy the diverse demands of different sectors of its economy.

We believe that we will have a cultural mixture which will affect our language, art, customs, and other facets of both cultures. This "hybrid" culture will be neither a cultural integration nor the submission of one culture under another.

In considering what La Frontera might be like by the year 2010, participants in all five of the regional meetings echoed common themes: economic development that brings with it massive changes in people, cultures, language, resources, and community infrastructures; and the need to assure a continuing focus on human and moral values, with an emphasis on respect for cultural traditions and beliefs. The primary difference among these regional voices was that participants in the two Mexico meetings—in Ciudad Juárez and Reynosa—expressed a more cautious optimism about the anticipated changes, speaking more in terms of what "should" happen rather than what is likely to happen, and emphasizing that current problems will not disappear quickly.

Participants at all the meetings described La Frontera in the next century as an economically and culturally diverse, dynamic and cosmopolitan region. They expect the divisions between the United States and Mexico to blur somewhat; participants in the U.S. meetings described a greater blurring of national boundaries than did participants from Mexico. All generally described the relatively free movement across the border not only of goods but of people, ideas, resources, and services; some anticipate the creation of a regional government or oversight agency that spans national boundaries. Participants see tremendous population growth, leading to the need for improved infrastructures and human services—improved, high-tech transportation, communication, basic facilities such as water, electricity, and sewage, and services such as health and education. All groups perceive technology as increasingly important both to the economy and to education. Participants also were united in a focus on the environment; while some see increased opportunities for "clean" industry, others expressed concern that current environmental problems will increase.

Participants described an open, multicultural society in which bilingualism is an essential skill. However, every group expressed, in some form, the conviction—and the concern—that, no matter how global the economy or cosmopolitan the population, the inhabitants of La Frontera must not lose their individual cultural heritage and values; the region should be characterized by "integration without erasing cultural differences, but rather supporting them." There will be a continuing concern for equality and individual well-being.

Education in La Frontera

The quality of the school systems on both sides of the border would be equal.

Open the school from its isolated condition and engage it with the life of the community on both sides of the border.

We conceive education as an effective means for equalization, mobilization, and transformation.

Participants in the regional meetings were also generally in agreement about the kind of education that will be needed in La Frontera. They described an educational system that is an integral part of community life; two different groups used the phrase "full-service schools" to describe the concept of schools working with other community agencies to provide a full spectrum of services for students and their families—child care, parent education, health services, adult training, and the like.

Education will need to prepare students for both work and citizenship; schooling will include a strong vocational focus, but also will impart values, teaching about students' own cultural traditions and encouraging respect for others. All students will need to become bilingual; technology will be integrated into instruction at all levels. Progress through school will be based on concept mastery rather than on grade levels; students will be able to move freely from school to school as their needs dictate.

To support this kind of education in La Frontera, rules, policies, and resources will need to change. All participants anticipate greater cooperation and exchange between the educational systems in the U.S. and Mexico; some expect the creation of a bi-national, regional governing board. Educational standards will need to be uniformly high; accreditation, teacher certification, and student entry and exit requirements will need to be coordinated. At the same time, almost every group noted the need to maintain local flexibility, so that local school districts can tailor their offerings to meet specific community needs.

Faculty from the Universidad de Monterrey, after analyzing the reports of each of the five regional meetings, identified elements of curricular change that would support economic growth and bi-cultural understandings while helping to maintain each country's identity and cultural and moral values. In their presentation at the Monterrey meeting, they identified six major elements:

- "human development," which includes a focus on respect for oneself, family, and society as well as on an integrated, humanist education;

- "the development of teaching-learning models for a bi-cultural environment," which involves "a personalized education that would use different educational models according to each student's learning pace";

- instruction in both Spanish and English, so that all students on both sides of the border will become fluent in both languages; the presenters noted, "Two neighbors that want to work together have to understand each other";

- the development of multimedia instructional materials, using technology to promote cultural exchanges and interactions;

- teacher training, in language particularly but also in other curricular areas; better training, the presenters noted, should help teachers become more valued and respected in their communities; and

- administrator training, with a focus on new approaches to managing the educational system; new concepts that focus on "bottom-up" decisionmaking hold promise for building new understandings.

Concerns and Priorities

The perception that needs to change is that Mexico has nothing to offer. That Mexico is a negative force, that the U.S. is a positive force and that there's not an equal to that on both sides. That it's an "us" and "them" situation. That the border is responsible for our economic ills. That people who come across are not productive. That education in Mexico has nothing to offer us.

Race and ethnicity are issues in both countries. We need to work together and learn from each other to eliminate prejudice.

Participants in the regional meetings described the kinds of changes they feel must occur in order to assure a productive future for La Frontera and all of its inhabitants. They characterized their concerns in terms of changes in perceptions and attitudes, knowledge, resources, and bi-national cooperation.

Changing Perceptions and Attitudes

Participants in all five regional meetings focused intensively on misperceptions about the border region and on racial and ethnic stereotypes, describing these as major barriers to be overcome. Participants described public perceptions in the U.S. regarding Mexico and the border region as highly negative and seriously inaccurate; Mexico and its people are too often considered only as a drain on the U.S., overlooking the richness of its languages and culture, the resources it has to offer, and the quality of many of its educational policies.

Participants focused strongly on perceptions about language and language differences. One misperception among many Americans, they noted, is "about the superiority of English to Spanish." "We must accept differences in languages," one U.S. group stated; similarly, a participant in one of the Mexico meetings said, "It is time for some organizations and people from the U.S. to stop being intolerant and accept the use of our language in their communities."

Participants also pointed out that the U.S. and Mexico are economically interdependent, but there is a general perception, as a participant in a U.S. meeting stated, "that Mexico needs us and we don't need them." Related to this is the misperception of the border area as "economically deprived" rather than "economically viable."

Finally, participants in three of the five groups noted that people must alter their attitudes about change itself: "We have to get beyond seeing change as a problem all the time; we need to move people to where they embrace change."

Filling Gaps in Knowledge

Participants feel that residents in both Mexico and the United States need to learn more about each other's history, cultures, and educational and social systems:

We must get to know the border and become familiar with the cultural patterns of both countries.

We need knowledge regarding the way in which both sides of the border maintain social, cultural, and economic relationships.

They generally feel that such learning can best occur through working together. Some groups also called for comparative studies focused on public schools and curriculum; one group spoke of the need for greater knowledge about "how to work with diversity."

Filling Resource Gaps

Participants see vast needs for increased resources; the greatest problem, one group noted, lies with "seemingly insurmountable gaps related to federal funding" and the differences in the two countries' relative economic power. Alleviation of poverty is a major priority for most; so is funding to make a quality education accessible to all. One group detailed the need for increased teacher salaries, opportunities for teachers' professional advancement, funds for teacher preparation, and provisions for better educational facilities, technology, and materials.

Extending Bi-National Cooperation

Participants feel that strong leadership is needed at federal, regional, and state levels to accomplish change in La Frontera. The governments of both Mexico and the U.S. need to develop cooperative arrangements that provide for common resources and regulations, while at the same time allowing for greater local autonomy and flexibility for the border region. Most critically, governments need to facilitate the sharing and equalization of financial resources; one group suggested moving toward common financial and currency systems, following the model of the European community.

One group focused in some detail on the need for cooperative efforts to address the environmental problems that have been raised by the development of heavy industry along the border. The border region needs to be able to attract "clean" industry; participants noted, "We need a notion of economic development which could include the promotion of frontera art, culture, music, agriculture—not just heavy industry."

Discussions of bi-national cooperation focused primarily on education. Cooperation in education should focus on development of systems for international accreditation; exchanges of teachers, students, and materials; on bilingual, multicultural education, including teacher training in these areas; and on shared research. Some suggested creating "a similar educational infrastructure on both sides of the border through a common fund" and/or a regional board of education.

Voices from La Frontera: Visions for the Future

One river, one people, a new way of thinking.

—comment from the El Paso Border Colloquy

A major goal of the Border Colloquy Project's Phase 1 activities has been the creation of a common vision regarding the future of education in the border region, a vision that can guide planners, policymakers, and practitioners from both countries as they consider the purposes and practice of schooling in La Frontera. To accomplish this task, SEDL first asked participants in the five regional colloquies to draft vision statements based on their discussions about the future of the border region. These five statements then provided a base from which participants in the regionwide Austin meeting—who included representatives from each of the regional colloquies and the Monterrey meeting—worked to develop a final, bi-national vision statement reflecting the group's shared goals.

Though they were phrased differently, and though some were composed in Spanish and some in English, the vision statements developed in the five regional meetings all reflect remarkably similar goals and concerns. All focus on the "holistic well-being" of students, on assuring that all children have the opportunity to grow up as productive, fulfilled members of society. That society, according to all five vision statements, will be "bicultural" or "multicultural," changing and dynamic. Most of the vision statements picture a close relationship between school and community; according to one statement, "the educational process will integrate school and community"; another states that "schools are the central focus of the community."

The vision statements also focus on character, dignity, moral and democratic values. The goal of education, it is clear, is to prepare students not only vocationally and intellectually but morally and culturally as well; education will offer "academic excellence, moral values, bi-cultural understanding and respect, and preparation for participation in work and society," enabling students to be "dynamic members of a multicultural society." Two of the vision statements address the concept of lifelong learning; one refers to "comprehensive educational, health, and human services."

Participants in the Austin meeting carried each of these concepts into the development of a unified vision statement. This vision statement, drafted, revised, and approved by educational and community leaders representing six of the border states in the U.S. and Mexico, is, to SEDL's knowledge, the first of its kind, a symbol of the movement toward cooperation and mutuality among the inhabitants of La Frontera.

Article Review Form at end of book.

How do people of mixed race define themselves culturally? Why are they pushed to make a choice between races, as opposed to being both?

Helping Mixed-Race People Declare Their Heritage

David L. Wheeler
Berkeley, Cal.

Terry P. Wilson once arrived at his class on "People of Mixed Race Descent" to find a crowd so dense that he couldn't get into the room.

Anxious students tired of being on a waiting list for the course at the University of California campus here showed up to see if they could talk their way in. The students mistook Mr. Wilson for a line-jumper and barred his way until he announced that he was the teacher.

The swelling crowds of mixed-race students and students involved in interracial romances who have arrived at Mr. Wilson's classroom door in recent years have surprised him. "I never anticipated what would happen when I started this class 13 years ago," says Mr. Wilson, who has just retired from his post as professor of ethnic studies at Berkeley. "This has become a social movement and more recently a political movement."

An Intellectual Revolution?

Mr. Wilson believes the rising popularity of the course, whose enrollment grew from 23 students in the first year to 226 last year, mirrors an intellectual revolution among mixed-race people, who see their background as a source of pride instead of something to hide.

"Most mixed-race people, myself included, have been constantly besieged by others to choose one identification or the other," says Mr. Wilson, the son of a Potawatomi Indian father and a white mother. "But those very people who want you to choose are never happy about whatever choice you make because you are mixed and they know it."

Mr. Wilson's course is widely viewed as the first one in the country to address interracial issues exclusively. Cynthia L. Nakashima, a former student of Mr. Wilson's, is teaching the course this fall.

While Mr. Wilson taught the class, he watched the formation of two student groups at Berkeley for mixed-race people, including one called Miscellaneous. Similar groups have been started at more than 13 other colleges and universities around the country.

'Ridiculous Notions'

Some mixed-race students participating in such organizations choose to identify themselves as "multiracial," while others seek full membership in existing ethnic groups.

"I am 100-per-cent black and 100-per-cent Japanese," says Eric Tate, a Berkeley graduate who took Mr. Wilson's course.

One of Mr. Wilson's student had grandparents who were white, Japanese, American Indian, and black. She was in danger of not graduating because she did not want to pick a conventional racial designation on university forms.

"She went through a lot," says Mr. Wilson, "because she said, 'I'm not going to deny three-quarters of my heritage to satisfy somebody else's ridiculous notions about race.'"

Mr. Wilson, who is 52, grew up on a reservation in Oklahoma at a time when mixed-race people rarely talked about their background and were greeted with chilly silence or outright slurs, like "halfbreed," from others. The central lesson he has imparted to mixed-race students who are trying to figure out where they belong is that they need to look for acceptance within.

Mr. Wilson says the existence and the experience of mixed-race people in America has largely been ignored by historians, and he tried to use his class to change that. He told the students that racial categories are shaped by society, rather than defined by science. Students often lined up outside Mr. Wilson's office door, eager to talk to someone about their own racial experiences. "He's really well known for being approachable,"

Copyright 1994, The Chronicle of Higher Education. Reprinted with permission.

Ms. Nakashima says. "He has no airs of superiority or authority."

Mr. Wilson's retirement will actually serve more as a sabbatical. He is working on a book about an episode in the history of the Osage Indians and is planning two books on mixed-race themes. He hopes to teach again next year at a small college.

'Culture Brokers'

Mr. Wilson could easily be mistaken for a white man. He remembers a time in his life when he regularly wore a pow-wow jacket and lots of Indian jewelry such as choker-style necklaces to declare his Indian heritage publicly and to avoid having to listen to racist comments.

Sometimes ugly remarks slipped past his shield. When his picture appeared in *The Billings Gazette* in Montana because he was the first Indian in the state to get a Ph.D., his wife's supervisor at work commented that his achievements weren't that amazing since, after all, he was half white.

In his historical research, Mr. Wilson says he found that many mixed-blood Indians acted as "cultural brokers," representing the interests of their tribe with the outside world. "They weren't caught between two cultures," he says. "They were *in* both cultures."

In and out of the classroom, Mr. Wilson insists that publicly acknowledging a racially mixed background does not indicate a lack of commitment to fighting racial discrimination. He also refuses to be considered less of an Indian because he is mixed blood.

Once, when he was in Riverside, Cal., to give a speech, he went out to lunch with a group of Indian students, many of whom were dark-skinned. A Navajo woman approached the group after lunch and said, "Where's our speaker?"

The students introduced Mr. Wilson. "Oh," she said, "I thought we were going to have an Indian."

Mr. Wilson took that as a not-so-subtle dig. "You seem to have a little problem with me being mixed-blood," he said. "You're Indian because you have no choice about it and you can't get out of it. I'm an Indian partly by choice. I could 'pass' if I want to, but I don't want to. That should tell you something about me."

Article Review Form at end of book.

What choice would you make if faced with a set of cultural circumstances that was similar to Francis Slakey's? What is the Masai leader attempting to preserve?

Cattle, Education, and the Masai Identity

Francis Slakey

Francis Slakey is an adjunct professor of physics at Georgetown University.

I crouch down to fit inside the tiny hut made of mud and sticks. Once inside, Kilembu offers me a hollowed-out calabash that contains the morning meal—a mixture of cow's blood and milk. Somewhere outside, nearby, are the remains of a village elder who was found dead, dragged out of town, and left for hyenas to devour.

In a few days, I'll be deciding whether I think children in this village need rescuing. If this were the United States instead of Tanzania, it would be a nobrainer.

Kilembu picks up his spear, and we crawl back outside. He wears only a red blanket and a pair of sandals that he's fashioned out of a piece of car tire. He introduces me to the key elements of his world, in descending order of importance: two dozen cattle, a few goats, four children, three tiny huts, two wives, a mother. After all the introductions, he takes me back to his cattle for one last look. The cattle are the center of his life, his core. Kilembu lives the typical life of a Masai warrior.

We walk up the hill that rises above the village of Longido. From the top we can see dozens of miles across the African savanna. Kilembu extends his spear out flat to his side, then slowly swings it in front of him. "All Masai," he says proudly, as his spear traverses the entire length of the horizon. Yes, as far as the eye can see, this is Masai country. In fact, all Kilembu has ever seen is Masai country—he has never stepped a foot beyond it. So far, neither have his children.

Kilembu ends our walk at the home of Estomii Molell, a Masai elder. I duck out of the midday sun and into his dimly lit hut. On the floor, with his arms twisted like corkscrews, lies the paralyzed frame of this village elder. A Masai warrior stands at his side, brushing away flies.

"I want you to know, we are not dirty here," Estomii says. He speaks emphatically, anticipating criticism. "There is no extra water for washing. When a woman travels 15 kilometers to get water, and you ask her for some water to wash, what do you think she'll say?" The point made, his face relaxes. He wants me to understand his people. So he starts by talking about mine.

He says he knows the United States. He knows of its phones and its computers and its big roads. "Why would we want that?" he asks. He dismisses all of our modern technological infrastructure with a laugh. "Here we walk and we see people. In the West, you call and you never see." He explains that our sophisticated telecommunications have left us isolated: "In your country, people have everything but company."

"I went to Germany and stayed with a family," Estomii continues, "and you know the conversation over breakfast? 'Pass the sugar.' And over dinner? 'Pass the salt.'" He chuckles, remembering. "I asked this man, 'What is your neighbor doing?' and he said, 'I don't know.'"

Estomii shakes his head in wonder. "In Masai country, you cannot say, 'That is not my business.'" He illustrates his point: "If a boy cringes when he is circumcised, everyone will know the next day. He will never be respected."

Estomii pauses, a chance for a question. I ask about crime. "Yes, we do have killing here," he says gravely. "A Masai killed a Masai here in 1961. It has happened again this month." He falls quiet; he is embarrassed by the number of murders. So am I. "The family of the dead man dragged the body outside the village and left it for the hyenas. Then they demanded the other man pay 49 cows. He paid; he is now accepted back." I'm shocked. "Isn't anyone worried that he might kill again?" I ask. "No," Estomii says, surprised by my question. "That would cost him 189 cows, and he can't afford that."

I'm so stunned by this notion of justice that all I can think to ask is how they determine the number of cows. Estomii says the number varies, but there must always be a nine—49, 189, 199. This doesn't clarify anything. I ask, "Why nine?" He explains: "The nine orifices. A murdered man has been stripped of life from his nine orifices, and that must be repaid." I stop our conversation to count. When I look back up, Estomii has fallen asleep. His warrior motions for me to leave. As I walk out

"Cattle, Education, and the Masai Identity," Francis Slakey. THE CHRONICLE OF HIGHER EDUCATION, December 5, 1997. Reprinted by permission of the author.

the door, I notice the warrior's spear leaning against the wall.

Once a week, Masai come from as far as 20 miles away to trade at the makeshift market. Seventy or 80 warriors gather around a pen to trade cattle. No one is buying, few are talking, all look proud. I've seen this act before in the States. I leave the posing to find some shade and in the process find Mwarimbo. He's built like a Masai—tall, lean, and fit, with an expressive face—but that's where the similarity ends. He is not Masai. He wears pants, a short-sleeved, cotton shirt, and sneakers; he asks me to call him "Johnson." He teaches science in the Longido Secondary School. We start strolling in the direction of his school.

In Tanzania, primary school is free. Unfortunately, you get what you pay for. The primary schools in this part of the country crowd 60 children into a classroom; not much learning goes on during the seven years of primary school. The next four years of education make up secondary school—roughly equivalent to our high school—and it must be paid for by the family. The quality of education is much higher, the benefits seem clear, and yet very few Masai children attend secondary school. It's the father's decision and, for many, education comes at too high a cost. "At $120 a year, it would mean selling a cow to get a child through secondary school," Johnson explains. But the Masai seem to have plenty of cows to spare, I observe. Johnson shakes his head, "You don't understand the problem."

The vast majority of Masai men consider education "trouble," he says. "When a girl completes secondary school, she realizes she is more valuable than a cow." That's trouble. Warriors start to define their place in society when they marry and receive a dowry of cattle. They take three wives, get three dowries, start amassing a herd. So educating girls threatens the cattle business; it threatens the Masai way of life. To Masai warriors, education is a raw deal.

A cinder-block compound interrupts the savanna; we've arrived at the school. "All they think about is cattle," Johnson continues, barely controlling his anger. He is determined to do whatever it takes to break the Masai of their bond to cattle and to give the children an education. He recites his first law: "Masai are not allowed to wear their traditional clothes in this school." Also, they are addressed only by Western names that they are given, not their Masai names. In addition to that initial cultural stripping, Johnson takes a far more extreme measure: All Masai students board at his school. They are not allowed to return home until the school year has finished. I ask if the children miss their homes, their families. He answers quickly, as if to cut off criticism: "The mothers are happy they come."

The first thing students learn is that raising cattle, which graze on whatever grows on the savanna, is not a sustainable livelihood. "Agriculture is inevitable," Johnson declares. Through science courses, students learn basic principles of farming, irrigation, and how to combat drought. They learn about basic medical care and vaccinations—the country is still fighting polio. But not everything they are taught is so practical. Johnson speaks with zeal about the simple excitement of learning. He wants children to identify with a larger world. His world. My world.

Before I leave the school, Johnson introduces me to Anna and Susanna. They are Masai, but I never learn their Masai names. They wear skirts and blouses, socks and dress shoes. They speak only a few words of English, but they seem eager to try. We chat for a few minutes. When I say goodbye, they say it was a pleasure to meet me—a verbal curtsy. As they walk away, Johnson explains that they will be leaving the school after only one year here, because their father will not pay. According to Johnson, the children want to stay.

The next morning I return to Estomii's hut. I tell him about Johnson, about the school. I ask his opinion of modern education. "Let me tell you about one of the best brains in Tanzania. Very brilliant with mathematics. He went to Britain to study aircraft design. He came back, and you know what? We don't design airplanes here." Estomii chuckles. "He is still looking for a job."

His warmth has drawn me into the story; we're both laughing as he delivers the clincher: "He is useless."

Estomii adds: "This Johnson is a fool. He is not Masai; he does not understand. Without cattle, Masai have no identity." Estomii points out that a truly competent teacher would be able to educate children no matter what clothes they wear. "Besides, their clothes are practical. It's hot here, why wear pants?" As he launches into a bitter criticism of Johnson, I tune out and watch the warrior looking after Estomii brush away flies. Estomii has already made his point. He is engaged in a battle, the only battle that a paralyzed old man with twisted arms and a fading voice can still fight. He fights for his identity, his tribe's identity. With a quick mind and a passionate heart, he fights for what it means to be Masai.

I am back in the States now, staring at my checkbook. With some additional money, Johnson can keep Anna and Susanna at school. Without the money, their education ends and they go back to a life in the bush. No one asked me for the money; no one told me not to give it, either. I've been drawn into the battle, and I can choose to arm one side. Estomii or Johnson? Masai or modern world? It is a matter of how they define who they are. But it is also a matter of who I am. I pick up a pen and make a check out to the Longido Secondary School. That is my identity.

Article Review Form at end of book.

How do musicians and singers create music to contain cultural messages which are in a form that moves across the globe in popularity?

The Sounds of Global Change

Different beats, new ideas

David Rothenberg

David Rothenberg, an associate professor of philosophy at the New Jersey Institute of Technology, is currently a Fulbright lecturer at the University of Art and Design, in Helsinki, Finland.

As the United States becomes more ethnically diverse and our economy increasingly international, American universities face pressure to make their curricula more global. For example, the department of humanities and social sciences, in which I teach, in a public, technical-research university, now offers "The World and the West" instead of "Western Civilization," and an upper-division course called "Technology and Global Development."

The latter class is usually taught by an economist, but it can also be taught by a professor who is, like me, a philosopher and musician, and I have taught it twice. That's because the idea of development includes conceptual and cultural issues as well as economic ones: What are the people and nations of the world supposed to be developing into? Is there any clear cultural goal implied in the notion of global development? And, most important, does development mean that the people of the world are moving toward one culture, or, somehow, toward a diversity of compatible cultures?

The last time I taught the global-development class, among my 40 students at the New Jersey Institute of Technology were native speakers of 18 languages. What unites those students, beyond a desire to fit into American society and get a good job after they graduate, is music. Wherever they're from, music is one thing about which students are always passionate. Many of them grew up on the pop-music image of America, with Michael Jackson, Madonna, and other world-renowned pop stars symbolizing a universal fantasy future—of freedom, glamour, and easy wealth—of which anyone who moved to the U.S.A. could partake.

But now that the students are here, the myths have dissolved into complicated realities. Their home cultures often come into conflict with what's expected of them in America, and they long for some way that their own traditions can find a way into the modern world. One way is through music. Though most foreign students grew up on American sounds, many gain a renewed interest in their own culture's music as they enter college. It helps them know who they are and where they come from.

Around the world, musicians are blending different musical styles with their own traditions in a complicated surge that sways back and forth between homogenization and variation.

In Estonia, all you hear is the relentless beat of techno-disco music, which sounds as if it's being piped in from some Big Brother in the sky, announcing that all the world can dance to the same drum machine. But the words to the music are in Estonian, and the tunes are emerging from local bands influenced by Western pop. Although we enlightened Westerners might lament that this influence is just more evidence of our pervasive cultural imperialism, it's important to put it in historical context: Traditional music from Estonia and other parts of Eastern Europe (such as that sung by the fabulous women of *Les Mystères des Voix Bulgares*) thrived under Communist regimes, which promoted a "pure" folk culture. Under democracy, in which the state doesn't enforce musical traditions, old music mixes more promiscuously with the new.

Popular music evolves through contact with the global marketplace, as its rhythms and sounds are altered to appeal to a mass audience. It's up to my students to decide if the modern music from around the world maintains cultural differences, or if the technology of music (such as the worldwide use of the same synthesizers to replace acoustic instruments) blurs different traditions into a kind of bland, multicultural Muzak. I try

© David Rothenberg. First appeared in THE CHRONICLE OF HIGHER EDUCATION.

to convince my students that cultural differences do survive modern musicians' playful, innovative mixing of cultures and their blending of traditional music with new sounds and ideas. Sure, everyone is using synthesizers, I tell them, but did you know that most synthesizers can be programmed with the flick of a button to play an Indonesian or Arabic scale?

What's more, the lyrics, as well as the music, may contain a message of cultural difference. What do pop singers sing about? I ask my students. They say: the struggles and successes of love, most of the time. That's not all, I respond. The popular singers of the developing world, especially, are often concerned with the successes and failures of progress, and distinguish themselves from American and Western European pop singers by their willingness to tackle serious subjects. Consider these words from the Senegalese singer Youssou N'Dour, who usually speaks French but sings this song in English and in his native language, Wolof:

"Rich countries make toxic waste; why should they send it to me? Poor countries know toxic waste; why should we accept it? When I'm in bed I can't stop thinking about it. When I'm awake, I have to warn you. Many of the underdeveloped countries are beginning to say 'No!'"

That 1993 song, "Toxiques," combines lyrics with a fast-moving electronic mix and a danceable beat. The sound is globally listenable but decidedly African, and the sentiment is something we don't immediately expect in a song. I watch my students wake up as they hear it. The message is not new to them, but now they want to get up and dance to it. It will be much harder for them to forget. I like to think that the song has helped to make a difference: With its world-beat style, its international availability, and its mixture of old and new languages, it brings a new voice of protest into the global conversation. Five years after its release, the practice of international trading of toxic waste is under more careful scrutiny.

Or consider the soothing voice and grounded rhythms of the Malian singer Oumou Sangaré, whose first name means "songbird" in Wassoulou, her native language. Being a singer is a traditional role acceptable for women in the culture of Mali, but Sangaré uses her role to sing of the changes that are needed in her country, rather than to uphold imperfect traditions. Here are lyrics, translated into English, from her 1996 record, *Worotan:*

"In the forest the anguished bird sings a song. More and more we live in a world ruled by individualism, a selfish world. I worry about the future of our world."

It sounds like the beginning of a student paper, but the words are embedded in a gentle, lilting melody. Sangaré also protests polygamy, advocating the breaking of her country's entrenched taboos:

"Let us fight for women's literacy. Women, let us fight together for our freedom, so we can put an end to this social injustice."

Her songs are surprising in other ways, too: They combine the traditional sounds of Mali with a blues music stripped of its European-influenced chords and taken down to its true groove, one chord over unstoppable rhythms that seem as if they could go on forever.

Students are drawn in by these enveloping rhythms and melodies. They want to know what she is singing about, and they are surprised by the audacity of the words. Through the beauty of her music, a woman from a culture that traditionally represses women is allowed to speak out in a way that makes her whole country proud. Sangaré's music is now one of Mali's claims to fame; the country is no longer known just as a place of political strife and of resources to exploit, but as a place with music that the world wants to hear.

Popular music gives melody and refrain to people's dreams and hopes. But it also can help people recognize the existing value of a culture under tremendous pressures to change. Consider the anthropologist Steven Feld's 1991 recording, *Voices of the Rainforest,* which presented the music and sonic environment of the people of the Bosavi rain forest, in Papua, New Guinea, singing in haunting harmony with the birds of their home.

These are a people under constant economic and political pressure to give up their subsistence way of life and work in the giant mines that are destroying their homeland—high-paying work that will last only a short time. Their music does not seek to fit global pop conventions, but it touches people all over the world with its captivating blend of human and environmental sounds. Money from the sale of the recordings has been given back to the tribe, and, according to Feld, has helped convince the Bosavi that their traditional culture is worth something in the looming world of international commerce.

Transnational banks think of developing countries as emerging markets, new places in which to sell Western stuff or manufacture Western ideas cheaply. But at the same time, such markets are also rich cultures that are able to offer up their music as part of the global exchange. The global music industry is beginning to realize as much, and the governments of developing countries are beginning to see that they have not only raw materials and cheap labor to offer, but also good, diverse music that can be performed and sold all over the world, while still being played—and produced—locally.

The more that Westerners learn to appreciate new and foreign sounds, the more we become truly part of a global culture. World music helps us appreciate that cultures evolve, and that none is more primitive than any other. We may live according to different precepts, but music is one way we can explore life together.

My students discover that the culture of Brazil, say, is not so foreign, when they hear Gilberto Gil's 1997 album, *Quanta,* which is full of references to science, spirituality, and the modern technological world. In one song, "Pela Internet," over a slightly machine-enhanced samba beat, Gil sings timely sentiments in Portuguese: "I want to enter the Net, have a chat, join via Internet, a group of fans from Connecticut, I want to enter the Net to contact the homes in Nepal, the bars in Gabon. . . . With how many gigabytes does one make a raft, a boat that sails in this info-sea?"

The subject of that song surprises my computer-and-engineering students, and confounds their preconceptions about the place of nations on the march toward progress. Suddenly, the music of what they think is a third-world country seems more up-to-the-minute than what's blaring from their speakers at home: Why don't *we* have pop songs about such things? When we consider ourselves part of a global community, the world's music belongs to all of us.

When the complex subject of global development becomes something to sing about and dance to rather than something simply to calculate and forecast, the personal side of world transformation comes to the fore. Throughout the world, we're singing of our individual troubles and collective responsibilities, and the world is evolving not according to some grand corporate plan, but in the fits and starts of people's own creativity.

Indian, African, Greek, Lebanese, Korean, Japanese—I've got my whole class hearing and singing songs from cultures that somehow fit together. Sure, the world's developing, and no tradition will stay the same. But diverse musical strains need not fade away into one global monotone. If there is such a thing as development, it will include a joyful and chaotic mix of many sounds, a music that plays on while no one knows how it's going to end.

Article Review Form at end of book.

Virtual Teams

How do you get a team to work like a well-oiled machine when its gears and cogs are scattered across the globe?

It's not easy getting a team to work like a well-oiled machine when its gears and cogs are scattered across the globe.

Beverly Geber

Most of the time, Barbara Recchia likes being a "remote" member of her work team. Although she is a communications program manager in the corporate human resources department of Hewlett Packard Co. in Palo Alto, CA, Recchia lives and works in Santa Rosa, CA, a large town woven into the wine country north of San Francisco.

Each day, Recchia fiendishly works the phones and the company's e-mail system to cement herself with her team members. Yet sometimes, in staff meetings she attends in person, it's clear how isolated she is. Someone makes a sly comment and everybody but Recchia giggles, wise to the joke that only insiders would appreciate.

"Sometimes you just feel really lonely and disconnected," Recchia says.

Not that she would consider abandoning the river across the street from her house to move to the "urbanized" environs of Silicon Valley, where the rest of her teammates live and work. Santa Rosa suits her lifestyle and satisfies her yearnings for a quieter, more outdoorsy existence. So she tries hard to make things work even though she faces obstacles that might not exist if she were in the same building as the rest of her teammates.

Recchia may be lonely but she is not alone. She has plenty of kindred colleagues across the country as companies try to get work done through distributed work groups, a more formal title for what many call virtual teams. Virtual teams are groups of people working closely together even though they may be separated by many miles, even continents. Sometimes, as in Recchia's case, the teams are intact work groups whose members stick together indefinitely. Other times the teams are cross-functional groups brought together for a finite time to tackle a project.

They are connected by all the modern appurtenances we take for granted in the 1990s' workplace and some we're still getting used to: telephones, fax machines, e-mail and videoconferencing. Often, they are linked as well by groupware, a powerful new class of project-management software that electronically links workers and allows them instantly to trade and manipulate project information.

The rise of virtual teams is a relatively recent phenomenon, brought about in part by the invention of groupware and the reluctance of many workers like Recchia to relocate for a new job. But virtual teams are a benefit and a necessity for companies too, and are bound to become more prevalent, says Lee Sproull, a professor of management at Boston University.

The reason, Sproull says, has to do with the global nature of marketplaces, the need to get projects done as quickly as possible in order to get new products to those global markets, and the necessity of tapping the best brains for those projects no matter where those brains may be.

A company may prefer to devise a new product by pulling together a group of people in one spot for the duration of the project, but that's impractical if the project will last less than a year or if the product needs to be simultaneously recast for markets around the world. In the latter case, it's a certainty that the workers needed for the project are scattered across a wide geographic expanse.

"Even though the barriers are enormous, companies have no choice," Sproull says. "If you say to a bunch of executives, 'Would you prefer to have this project done face-to-face or by computer?' nine out of 10 would say, 'Face-to-face.' But if you were to ask them if they wanted to do the project by computer or not at all, there wouldn't really be a choice."

To illustrate, she cites a U.S. aircraft manufacturer that recently designed a new-generation jet plane, its most technologically advanced product ever. The project bound together myriad subcontractor teams from around the world, each lending its obscure expertise to the design of a complex new machine. Since it was impractical to assemble all those people in one place, much of the work took place through electronic links, particularly computer networks, Sproull says.

Reprinted with permission from the April 1995 issue of TRAINING Magazine. Copyright 1995. Lakewood Publications, Minneapolis, MN. All rights reserved. Not for resale.

Although the technical challenges of such a project were enormous, one of the thorniest problems this company faced was how to get all those individuals working together compatibly and productively, even though face-to-face contact was limited and communication was confined almost exclusively to phone, fax and computer. Companies that use virtual teams are finding that tending to the human factors of the arrangement is one of the savviest things they can do to ensure the success of the teams' projects.

In the case of the aircraft manufacturer, Sproull says company officials brought many of the "remote" team members to its headquarters for at least six months and up to 18 months so they could get to know other team members face-to-face while learning how to work within the company's project-management system.

Some people maintain that it's not necessary to sponsor bonding fests before asking people to work in virtual teams. Sheldon Laube, national director of information and technology for Price Waterhouse in Menlo Park, CA, says his company seldom does so. That's despite the fact that the accounting and consulting firm is a heavy user of groupware and frequently uses virtual teams.

Some virtual teams at Price Waterhouse work together for just a week or two preparing work for a particular client, Laube says. It would be unrealistic to put everyone on a plane for a get-together when all the necessary information can be coalesced quickly on networked computers. Considering that Price Waterhouse has 45,000 employees in 120 countries, people often work on projects without benefit of having met in person. But Laube maintains that the company's set methodology and common language for conducting audits eases collaboration. Also, he adds, there is a strong unspoken expectation within the company that colleagues share information freely with one another.

But in some companies, in which projects may be of long duration and even include members from other firms, such as suppliers or subcontractors, forming a team without face-to-face meetings may be courting disaster.

At the very least, it's necessary to have a one-day videoconference so the team members can see one another, says Chris Newell, executive director of the Lotus Institute, the research and education arm of Lotus Development Corp., in Cambridge, MA. The company makes Lotus Notes, the most widely used groupware product. Newell says the introductions are crucial because "it's important to develop some level of trust and relationship before you can move into electronic communication."

Others maintain that a brief videoconference is too minimal to be of any help in warding off the interpersonal problems that might arise among people who work closely together without ever being together—especially if the team is going to be together for many months, even years, and particularly if the team members face language and cultural differences.

John Spencer, worldwide manager for the design and development of single-use cameras for Eastman Kodak Co. in Rochester, NY, recently pulled together a product-development team to design a new product that hasn't been announced yet. Although the interior workings of the product will be the same worldwide, Kodak wants to adapt the exterior and the features for the European market.

Since the company didn't want to do a mere cosmetic makeover of the product, it was necessary to involve German design engineers from the start. So Spencer brought two German engineers to the United States for the initial six months of the project.

Why such a long engagement? "The most important part of the project is the up-front time," says Spencer, who doesn't believe that a long-term virtual team can be successful without that personal contact. During the six months, personalities gelled, friendships formed, and the members got used to one another's work styles and temperaments. That's the time for finding out, for instance, that when Kurt says no, he's adamant about it and doesn't tolerate jawboning. Trying to fathom personality quirks like that via computer is much more difficult and time-consuming, and can damage the rapport of the team if tensions develop into flame wars via e-mail.

Often, says Spencer, extracurricular activities do more to cement a team than a passel of team meetings or team-building sessions. The two German engineers who stayed for six months ended up socializing on weekends with their U.S. counterparts, a factor that helped secure their bond. To keep the team members connected, Spencer is also sending U.S. engineers to work in Germany for brief periods of time.

The importance of personal contact and socializing can't be overestimated, says HP's Recchia. In the early months of her remote work arrangement, she visited the HP headquarters just once a month and felt hopelessly out of touch with her colleagues.

"It was a very odd feeling walking in and knowing you weren't exactly connected," she says. She found that she had to curb her hard-driving, let's-get-on-with-it style to sit down and "neighbor" with teammates each time she visited Palo Alto. Eventually, she decided that she needed to drop in once a week instead of once a month in order to maintain her connection to the team.

A lot can be missed when communication is carried on long-distance, Recchia says. Subtle tones and meanings slip away. Recently Recchia's group had been asked to give a presentation on its work to another section of HP. It wasn't really necessary for Recchia to make an extra trip to be there; someone else could describe what she did. But while her boss told her this in a face-to-face meeting, Recchia sensed that the boss really wanted her to come. When she asked, her boss said yes, it would be nice if the entire group could be there.

Would Recchia have picked up the clue during a phone call? She thinks not. "She's kind of hard to read sometimes," she says of her boss. So Recchia attended the presentation, which was followed by an informal luncheon that Recchia says was one of the most enjoyable times she's spent with her team.

Often, the most valuable "team-building" sessions are the informal ones, arranged outside business hours and without the company's imprimatur. Lotus' Newell works in a virtual team whose members are spread across much of New England.

Two months ago, they all went off on a ski weekend "because we decided it was important to do some social things together a couple of times a year," Newell says.

Vince Anderson, director of environmental programs for Whirlpool Corp.'s North American Appliance Group in Evansville, IN, oversaw a two-year project using a virtual team that developed a chlorofluorocarbon-free refrigerator. The expertise came from sites in the United States, Brazil and Italy.

The team met every four months or so to discuss the project, but Anderson found that some of the most valuable events during those visits were the informal get-togethers, including a backyard cookout and volleyball game Anderson hosted at his house.

Informal meetings help team members size up others, a task that would be protracted, if not impossible, on-line. How to tell, for instance, which team member is easily crushed by criticism, especially if criticism makes her clam up? Are any of the teammates devious, likely to manipulate others in order to advance a hidden agenda? Who's power hungry? Who likes handholding? Is anybody downright malicious?

Not all the answers to these questions become apparent during a backyard barbecue, of course, but the informal gatherings go a long way toward developing the understanding and personal trust that individual team members must develop in each other to weather the conflicts that inevitably arise during the course of work.

There is another kind of trust that must be present for teams to work smoothly, says Sproull. It's trust that springs from competence. "Trust comes from performance," she says. "If I see this person is going to do a first-rate job with the information I provide, that he won't undercut it, won't embarrass me, then I'm more likely to trust him."

Building this kind of trust is more difficult to accomplish among cross-functional teams that spring up for a spurt of time to complete a project. "If you take people from finance and marketing and manufacturing and give them the same paragraph to read, you'll get three different interpretations," Sproull says. That may not be as much of a problem if team members are all on-site and meeting frequently to hash out differences. But completing a project by using groupware means that the members are more isolated from one another and the chances for misinterpretation are greater.

Groupware allows information about a project to be fed into a huge, structured database that can be accessed by all team members. You can always tell when a virtual team isn't working well together, Sproull says, because the database doesn't hold all the latest information. People hoard what they know and share it only with teammates they trust. You might get design engineers sharing information only with design engineers and not with their teammates from finance or manufacturing.

Lotus' Newell says trust is a crucial factor in a well-oiled team, but the degree of trust that's needed may depend on the type of project. If a Price Waterhouse accountant needs some information from several colleagues scattered around the world for a client presentation due next month, the task can probably be completed without undue angst or bickering. The need for trust is more pressing in a cross-functional team tackling a difficult long-term project that will require negotiation and compromise.

Newell believes that organizations in general have created cultures in which information-hoarding is rewarded. The task for companies using virtual teams is to get team members to break that habit. Newell knows of one large consulting group that has changed its performance-appraisal system to reward individuals who share information. If a piece of information a consultant puts into the shared database gets accessed a certain number of times by others, the end-of-year bonus for that consultant grows.

Amid all the carping about the difficulties of using distributed work teams, it's easy to lose sight of the fact that there are a few special advantages that electronic distance affords. For one thing, it's a particular boon to shy people, says Newell. Extroverts may resist the isolation of electronic communication, but shy people often thrive on it. For many people, writing is easier than speaking.

"Some people like the barrier. Their interpersonal style lends itself to it," says Recchia. She recalls having many delightful telephone conversations and computer communications with a woman she eagerly anticipated meeting in person. When it finally happened, Recchia was disappointed. She realized the individual dealt with others much better if she was doing it from behind a screen.

There may be formidable interpersonal barriers to overcome in making virtual teams click, but that doesn't mean it can't be done, according to those who have managed them. A few sensible rules apply.

For one thing, says Sproull, a manager needs to fight for the budget to get team members together periodically. It may be hard to justify that need to executives who have invested considerable money in new-fangled electronic communications. Therefore, it's best to use the synergy ploy. Remind executives that often a company's best ideas are born out of chance encounters in a hallway or around a watercooler. Letting virtual team members get together sometimes for extended watercooler discussions improves the chances for serendipity.

Paradoxically, virtual work teams require *more* formal communications, not fewer, says Susan Sowers, manager of the Hewlett Packard corporate client computing group in Palo Alto. Sowers manages a distributed work team of 21 people spread over three U.S. sites.

Precisely because there is less informal chatter among team members, the kind that takes place during birthday gatherings or coffee-machine chats, Sowers finds that she must change her previously informal approach to managing. "I have to do things differently. I can't just walk around to supervise people and call a meeting whenever I think one is needed," she says. To do so would favor the team members who work in her own office and would eventually alienate those at other sites. Sowers tries to make sure the team members in Atlanta and Fort Collins, CO, feel as though they have the same information as someone who works in the office next to Sowers.

The cohesion of the group can be broken when someone new joins, Sowers says. That's why it's particularly important to make sure that nearly all communications are kept in the shared database, so that a historical document of the group's work is available for the new person to peruse.

Whirlpool's Anderson says it's essential to use rigorous project-management principles. Make sure to be as specific and direct as possible in determining who will do what by when. This is especially important if the team is a global one, wrestling with language and cultural differences.

Lotus' Newell recommends that each team establish a mission for what it intends to accomplish. Along with this, team members need to come up with a list of norms and agreements about how the team will operate and how it will handle the technological aspects of its interactions. All this gets written down and stored in the same database that contains the project information, Newell says.

Team norms can be anything that team members feel is important for everyone to commit to doing. For instance, says Newell, a team norm might be that everyone check into the database once a day to monitor the progress of the project, even if he has no new information to add. Other norms might deal with the way information is handled. Which kinds of issues are discussed by the team as a whole, and how often do they get discussed? Does everyone have access to all information, or is some of it restricted?

Other agreed-upon practices might cover ways to deal with conflict. Teams sometimes enforce a rule that if one team member has a conflict with another, it can't be dealt with electronically; one person has to telephone the other, or the two must meet in person.

Newell also recommends that virtual teams have both a team leader (formerly called a manager) and a team facilitator. The facilitator is a member of the team who is assigned to monitor the way in which the team works. For instance, if two team members are having frequent conflicts, the facilitator is the first to intervene to try to smooth things out. In a way, she's like a team conscience.

Eastman Kodak's Spencer believes you can improve the chances of fielding a successful team if you choose members carefully. Select people who are comfortable sharing information and working with computers, he says, but also make sure they're people with strong personalities who can assert themselves in an electronic medium.

Sproull says team members should be chosen in part for their empathic abilities. "You can be the world's best hydraulic engineer, but if you can't put yourself in the shoes of an electrical engineer, it would be problematic," she says. "You can't all sit around a table for the life of a project to hash things out."

And of course, that, in a nutshell, is why virtual teams may become less an oddity than a common—if challenging—way to work.

Article Review Form at end of book.

WiseGuide Wrap-Up

- Intercultural ethics issues are varied and complex. As our "global village" continues to connect and overlap culturally, the ability to facilitate the process of cultural accommodation will be important for the intercultural communication professional.

- These cultural issues, for discussion, are just a tiny sample of the multiple concerns arising from expanded global interaction. The efforts of the communities along La Frontera to envision a new future, and their efforts to make the vision a reality, bear watching as a possible model for creating a new community.

- Expanding one's view of the world, whether via music or cyberspace connections, will assist in widening the frame of reference with which people see reality, to include more than their cultural front yard.

R.E.A.L. Sites

This list provides a print preview of typical **coursewise** R.E.A.L. sites. (There are over 100 such sites at the **courselinks**™ site.) The danger in printing URLs is that web sites can change overnight. As we went to press, these sites were functional using the URLs provided. If you come across one that isn't, please let us know via email to: webmaster@coursewise.com. Use your Passport to access the most current list of R.E.A.L. sites at the **courselinks**™ site.

Site name: Institute for Global Ethics
URL: http://www.globalethics.org/about/default.html
Why is it R.E.A.L.? The Institute for Global Ethics analyzes ethical trends and shifts in values as they occur worldwide. It also provides examples of international dilemmas and the choices people made in different situations.
Key topics: global, ethics, education, dilemmas, publications
Try this: Select the Dilemma: Right vs. Right menu. Review the descriptions and select a cross-cultural scenario. Review the decision that was made and indicate if you would have made the same choice, given those circumstances. Why or why not?

Site name: Student and Educational Development
URL: http://www.dist.maricopa.edu/eddev/
Why is it R.E.A.L.? This site takes a bit of navigating to arrive at the Intercultural & Multicultural Education Resources menu button, but it is well worth the extra steps. It contains an extensive URL list of a multitude of international and intercultural information sources. In addition, there are links to sites with multiple connections to intercultural/multicultural sites on the Internet.
Key topics: intercultural, multicultural, international, education
Try this: Visit a URL site which has a focus on Mexico, Central America, or North America. Review the site to see if it contains any information on border conflicts or other border issues.

Index

Note: Authors of articles are shown in **bold face**.

A

Abe, H., 187, 189
Achievement, cultural differences, 93
Ackerman, J.M., 181
Action chain, 30
Adler, Nancy J., 5, 25, 65, 68, 71, 77, **81**, 82, 121, 134
Adler, P.S., 186, 198
Aesthetics, cultural differences, 91
Aitken, T., 179
Alcoff, L., 173
Althen, G., 131
Ancona, Deborah, 68
Anderson, Vince, 229, 230
Anfuso, Dawn, 147
Appell, G.N., 52
Arabs
    American perception of, 27-28
    business communication with, 28, 29-31
    high-context culture of, 28
    nepotism, 92
    personal space, 28-29, 94
    proximity in communication, 28-29
    pupils of eyes, reading of, 28-29
    relationship building strategies, 29-31
    religious practices, 93
Artifacts of culture, 52, 53, 57
    Japanese, 55, 57, 60
Asante, M.K., 174
Ashby, Ross, 71
Asuncione-Lande, N.C., 211
Attali, Bernard, 98
Audience analysis, for motivational factors, 21-22
Authority, cultural attitudes toward, 19-20

B

Baelz, Peter, 211
Bantel, Karen, 68
Barlund, D.C., 198
Barna, L.M., 198
Barnes, Jonathan, 210
Barsoux, Jean-Louis, 96, 132
Bartholomew, Susan, 81, 122
Bartlett, Christopher, 64, 81
Behavioral competencies, of cross-cultural trainer, 201-203
Behavioral objectives, intercultural communication course, 9-10
Bendix, Reinhard, 74
Benson, P.G., 191
Berenbeim, R.E., 156
Berry, J.W., 186
Best, S., 170

Binnendijk, H., 131
Black, J.S., 129, 159
Blaker, M., 128
Blending of cultures. *See* Third culture concept
Bluedorn, Allen C., **11,** 13
Bluth, B.J., 5, 6
Bond, Michael Harris, 46
Bonvillan, Gary, 90
Bostrom, R.N., 181
Brass, Paul, 65
Brein, M., 189
Brislin, R.W., 123, 132, 181
Broome, B.J., 174
Browning, E.S., 33
Buddy system, 35
Burtt, E.A., 212
Business card, Japanese business custom, 56-57

C

Callahan, Madelyn R., 90
Calvet, Jacques, 98, 101
Campbell, Anne E., 4
Campbell, Joseph, 56
Canadian International Development Agency, 94
Career development
    France, 99-100
    transnational, 85-86
    See also Management development
Carey, J.W., 171
Carter, Jimmy, 30-31
Casmir, F.I., 172
Casse, P., 181
Chalvin, D., 132
Chambers, Erve, 62
Channels of communication, 23
Chatov, Robert, 66
Chen, Guo-Ming, 9, 10
Cheseboro, J.W., 171
Chinese, management theories applied to, 44, 45
Church, A.T., 186, 189
Church, Austin, 65
Clarke, Clifford C., 109
Cleveland, H., 179, 188, 189
Cognitive competencies, of cross-cultural trainer, 200-201
Cognitive schema, and nationality, 66, 71
Cohen, R., 128
Colgate-Palmolive Co., Global Human Resources Strategy Team, 147-150
Collectivist culture, 20, 46
Collins, P.H., 173
Colquit, J.L., 171, 172

Communication objectives, 18-19
Communication styles, types of, 19
Comparative management, 41
Competency. *See* Cross-cultural competency
Conflict resolution, 109-120
    bicultural facilitation team, 111-112
    conflict resolution phase, 115-117
    cultural exploration, 113-114
    impact assessment, 117-119
    organizational exploration, 114-115
    organizational integration, 119-120
    problem clarification, 113
    problem identification, 112
    problems, example of, 109-110
    See also Negotiation
Copeland, L., 23
Copeland, Mike, 154-155
Covey, Stephen R., 52, 53
Credibility
    expertise credibility, 21
    factors related to, 21
    goodwill credibility, 21
    image credibility, 21
Cronen, V.E., 122
Cross-cultural competency, 179-182
    and acculturation/assimilation, 186-187
    and adaptation, 186
    and adjustment, 185-186
    aspects of, 181-182
    best candidates, 180
    communication skills, 187, 189, 192, 197
    competence, aspects of, 187
    cultural empathy, 188-189
    failure, reasons for, 179-180, 192
    flexibility, 189-190
    intercultural communication course assessment, 8-9
    knowledge factors, 187-188, 191
    nonjudgmental perspective, 188
    prediction of success, 180
    social skills, 187, 191
    technical skills, 191
    training implications, 192-193
Cross-cultural trainer
    behavioral competencies of, 201-203
    cognitive competencies of, 200-201
    ethical trainer, 199-200
    personal attributes of, 203-204
    training of, 204-205
Cross-cultural training
    areas for personal development, 192-193
    aspects of culture, 52-53, 54-55
    for competition, 155
    Eastman Kodak Company, 153-154
    ethical questions, 198-199
    ethnography, 55-56
    factors in success of, 61-62, 151

foreign assignments in, 85-86
goals of, 152
Intel Corporation, 152-153
Japanese business practices, 56-61
literature related to, 196
management training, 159
outcomes of, 151
participant observation, 53
Procter & Gamble, 154-155
program needs, 52-53
retraining, 86
in sexual harassment, 163-164
site for training, 54
team training, 152-153
unique challenges of, 197-198
university model for, 197
Cultural differences
aesthetics, 91
bipolar dimensions of, 46-47
eye contact, 1, 28-29, 91
hidden cultural aspects, 113-114
high context/low context cultures, 21, 22
individualism versus collectivism, 20-21
intercultural socialization, 94
locus of control, 18
masculinity/femininity aspects, 22
monochronicity/polychronicity, 15-16
nonverbal communication, 1, 4, 24-25
personal achievement, 93
pre-travel preparation for, 94-95
religion, 92-93
social behavior, 94
social institutions, 92
space (proximity), 6-7, 24-25, 36-37, 93-94
time frame, 15-16, 18-19, 92
values systems, 19
verbal communication, 91
work values, 20, 21
Cultural logic, 52, 53, 57
Japanese, 55, 56, 60
Cultural relativism, meaning of, 163
Culture
artifacts of, 52, 53
cultural logic, 52, 53
four dimensions concept, 21-22, 46-47
meaning of, 18, 46, 52
social knowledge of, 52, 53
Cyert, Richard, 41

D

Daniel, J., 171
Danielson, Dana, 43
Danner, Suzanne, 77, 79
Daunke, Rudiger, 163
Davidson, A., 169
Davis, D., 179
Davison, Sue Canney, 64
Dearborn, Dewitt, 71
Decision making, cultural differences, 36
Demeanour, and nationality, 66-67, 71-72
Deming, Edward, 52
Deutsch, S.E., 192

Development
France, 99-100
transnational, 85-86
See also Management development
Devine, Patricia, 67
Dicken, C., 192
DiMare, L., 174
Dinges, N., 136, 187, 197
Dirks, N.B., 172, 173
Diversity, effects on group dynamics, 71-72
Dixit, J.L., 188
Dubner, F.S., 171
Du Nemours, E.I., 163

E

Earley, P.C., 132
Eastman Kodak Company, global training, 153-154
Egelhoff, William, 73
Eiichiro, Ishida, 63
Eisenhardt, Kathleen, 68
Ellingsworth, H.W., 182
Emic approach, intercultural communication course, 9-10
England, George, 66
English, H.B., 185
Ethical issues, 210-213
basic ethical dilemma, 212
contextual aspects, 211
cross-cultural training, 198-199
and objective/subjective reality, 211
personal values, 211-212
Ethnography, in cross-cultural training, 55-56
Etic approach, intercultural communication course, 9-10
Evans, K.R., 136
Evans, Lank, 87
Evans, Paul A., 81, 84
Expatriates
repatriation training, 160-161
skill requirements, 83
women, 77-80
Expertise credibility, 21
Eye contact
and Arabs, 28-29
cultural differences, 1, 91

F

Failure of project, reasons for, 179-180
Fallows, J., 20
Familiarity with culture, 123-127
high familiarity, 125-127
low familiarity, 123-124
moderate familiarity, 124-125
Family
assessment for overseas assignment, 159
international dual-career families, 79-80
Fauroux, Roger, 98
Fayol, Henri, 43
Feminine cultures, 22, 46, 47
Ferra, Bill, 163
Fiedler, Fred, 65

Filley, Alan, 68
Finan, Timothy J., 63
Fisher, R., 129
Fongalland, Bruno de, 98
Foreign Service Institute, 170
Foucault, M., 169, 172
Fram, Eugene, 93
France, 96-101
Americans/French, negotiation behaviors, 128
career development, 99-100
educational background, 98-99
intellectual aspects of management, 97-98
leadership, 98
management theories applied to, 43, 96-98
organizational structure, 98
state/business connection, 100-101
women in business, 99
Franzone, Dorothy Lawrence, 8
Freedom
cross-cultural crew, 36-37
official language, 37
training areas, 37
French, J., 21
Friedman, Kenneth, 27
Frye, P.A., 174

G

Galbraith, Jay, 73
Garrison, John, 151
Geber, Beverly, 227
Geertz, Clifford, 63
Geringer, J. Michael, 67
Germany, management theories applied to, 42
Gestures, cultural differences, 24
Gist, Marilyn, 74
Globalization process
international companies, 82-83
multinational companies, 83
transnational companies, 83
Global organization
business issues, 145-146
characteristics of, 145
Global village, 1
Gonzalez, A., 174
Goodman, Paul, 68
Goodwill credibility, 21
Graham, J.L., 121, 123
Greetings
cultural differences, 25, 94
first/last names and culture, 25
Gregerson, J., 157
Grossberg, L., 171, 172
Group behavior, multinational groups, 64-74
Grove, C.L., 186, 193
Gudykunst, William, 66, 121, 171, 172, 173, 197, 211
Gullahorn, J., 189, 191
Gulliver, P.H., 133
Guthrie, G.M., 180, 189, 191

H

Hackman, J. Richard and Associates, 68
Hall, Edward T., 1, 6, 11, 12, 21, 34, 53, 66, 67, 139, 169, 170, 174
    interview on Arab culture, 27-32
Hall, Mildred Read, 6, 53
Haller-Jorden, Eleanor, 79
Hamada, Tomoko, 56
Hambrick, Donald C., 64, 68, 81
Hamel, Gary, 83
Hamilton, Bob, 163
Hammer, M.R., 180, 181, 188, 189, 191, 193
Hannigan, Terence P., 185
Hanvey, R.G., 188, 189
Haq, Mahbub ul, 164
Hardman, Wendy, 162
Harman, R.C., 170
Harris, J.G., 179, 180, 191
Harrison, R., 197
Hawes, F., 180, 191
Hecht, M.L., 174
Heidelberg, Jacqueline, 162
Heller, Fred, 69
Henderson-Loney, Jane, 164
Herskovits, M.J., 186
Heterogeneity
    effects on group dynamics, 67-69
    group type of, 68
    national type of, 68-69
High-context cultures, 21, 22
    Arabs, 28
    values of, 22, 23, 28, 31-32
Hoffman, L. Richard, 64, 68, 71
Hofstede, Geert, 21, **41**, 52, 65, 66, 68, 133
Holland, management theories applied to, 43-44
Houston, M., 173, 174
Human relations theories, of management, 41
Human resource systems
    Global Human Resources Strategy Team, 147-150
    transnational, 83-88

I

Image credibility, 21
Incentives, transnational companies, 86
Individualistic culture, 20, 46
Inpatriates, 83, 86
Intel Corporation, global training, 152-153
Intercultural communication
    feminist concepts of, 173
    historical view, 169-175
Intercultural communication course, 8-10
    assessment of competencies, 8-9
    behavioral objectives, 9-10
    teaching approaches, 9-10
International companies, features of, 82-83
International Space Station, 3-7
    construction of station, 3-4
    group interaction, 5
    intercultural relations, basis of, 5
    isolation effects, 5
    official language, 4
    participants in, 3
    sense of space within station, 6-7
    third culture concept, 7
    verbal/nonverbal communication, 4
    zero-gravity effects, 3, 6
Interpreter, use of, 23, 91

J

Jackson, Susan, 68, 70, 71
Janis, Irvin, 68
Japan
    business card (meishi), 56-57
    conflict resolution with, 109-120
    dinner customs, 58-60
    drinking after work, 35, 56, 60-61
    front/rear, meaning of, 55
    management theories applied to, 43
    meeting seating arrangement, 57-58
    time orientation, 92
    -U.S., cross cultural training program, 51-62
Jin, K., 171
Johnson, F.L., 173
Joint projects, 33-35
    after-work socializing, 35
    buddy system, 35
    culture-related adjustment problems, 33-35
    joint training needs, 34-35
Jones, R.R., 179, 180

K

Kaoru, Ihsikawa, 52
Katz, E., 171
Kauffman, B.J., 174
Kaufman, Carol Felker, 11
Kealey, D.J., 10, 180
Keesing, R., 131
Kenneth, David, 53
Kimmons, Robert L., 49
Kissinger, Henry, 30-31
Klein, M.H., 194
Kluckhohn, Florence, 19, 56, 75
Knapp, M., 24
Koester, J., 180
Kotter, J., 21
Krock, George, 163

L

Laben, Nancy, 79
Lacey, R., 124
La France, Marianne, 66
LaFromboise, T.D., 181
La Frontera, 215-219
    Border Colloquy meetings, 215-216
    educational issues, 216-217
    future view, 217-219
    location of, 216
    NAFTA, effects of, 216
Lane, Paul M., 11
Language barriers
    and group functioning, 72
    interpreters, 91
    and nationality, 67
    nonverbal communication, 24-25
    perceptual differences, 24
    semantics, 23
    tone, 24
    word connotations, 23-24
Laube, Sheldon, 228
Laurent, André, 43, 66, 84
Lawrence, Peter, 96
Lebedev, V.I., 5
Lee, Dorothy, 54
Leeds-Hurwitz, W., 169, 170, 171, 172, 174
Leonov, A.A., 5
Lipp, G. Douglas, 109
Livingston, Larry, 3
Locus of control, internal and external, 18
Lohr, S., 123
Lomax, A., 171
Lomov, B.F., 5
Long-term orientation, of culture, 46-47
Lord, Robert, 66
Losing face, 114
Low-context cultures, 21, 22
    values of, 22, 23, 28, 31
Lozano, Mary, 36-37
Lynam, Patty, 145

M

Management
    global assignments, importance of, 157
    global assignment selection process, 159
    linguistic origins of term, 42
    and polychronicity/monochronicity, 13-15
    roles of, 157
    succession planning, 157-158
    transnational skill requirements, 81-82
Management development
    cross-cultural training, 159
    family-related issues, 159
    language training, 158
    performance evaluation, 159-160
    repatriation, 160-161
    strategic systematic approach, 156-157
    tactile reactive approach, 156-157
Management theories
    China, 44, 45
    cultural dimensions applied to, 46-47
    France, 43, 96-98
    in Germany, 42
    Holland, 43-44
    human relations theories, 41
    in Japan, 42-43
    Russia, 45
    and third world countries, 44-45
    United States, 47-48
Managerial communication
    audience perception of, 21-22
    communication styles, 19
    credibility, assessment of, 21
    and cultural values, 19-20
    definition of, 18
    language barriers, 23-24
    message strategy, 22-23
    nonverbal communication, 24-25
    objectives of, 18-19

Maquiladora industry, 214
March, James, 41, 66, 71, 73
Maretzki, T.W., 179, 180, 181
Markus, Hazel, 66
Martin, Joanne, 73
Martin, Judith N., 9, 180, 181, 201
Masaaki, Imai, 52
Masculine cultures, 22, 46, 47
Masia, identity of, 222-223
Matlon Index, 170
Matlon, R.J., 170
Matsumoto, Michihiro, 55
McEnery, Jean, 90
McGrath, Joseph, 68
McGrath, Michael R., 53
McLuhan, Marshal, 1
Mediator, in cross-cultural negotiation, 123-124
Medsen, Peter, 165
Meishi, Japanese business card, 56-57
Mesquita, Batja, 66
Message strategy
  communication channels, 23
  formats of message, 23
  structure of, 22-23
Mestenhauser, J.A., 198
Mexico
  maquiladora industry, 214
  See also La Frontera
Miller, E., 158
Milliken, Frances, 64
Mill, John Stuart, 42, 45
Mircea, Eliade, 53
Mischel, W., 180, 187, 188, 191
Mixed-race persons, 220-221
Monochronicity, 11-16
  assessment of, 14
  cultural differences, 15-16
  meaning of, 11
  and organizations, 13-16
  person characteristics related to, 12
  and supervision/coordination, 15
  time management, 14-15
Montaigne, Michel de, 41
Mossett, Bill, 163
Multinational companies, features of, 83
Multinational groups, 64-74
  benefits of, 73
  diversity effects, 68, 71-72
  effectiveness, factors in, 70-72
  future research directions, 73-74
  heterogeneity effects, 67-69
  nationality effects, 65-67
  tasks of, 70
Multinational teams, 49-50
Munter, Mary, 18
Murnighan, J.K., 130, 140
Music, popular, cultural elements in, 224-226

N

Nakane, Chie, 55
Nakayama, T.K., 173
Names, first/last and culture, 25
Nash, D., 186
Nationality
  as analytic construct, 65-66

effects on group dynamics, 65-67
effects on person/personality, 66-67
Negotiation, 121-140
  Americans/French, recommended behaviors, 128
  balance of power, 133
  conflict resolution, 109-120
  and counterpart's strategy, 134
  cultural characteristics of, 122
  and familiarity with culture, 123-127
  feedback monitoring, 137–138
  with French, 128
  implementation of strategy, 136-139
  influence, effects of, 135-136
  learning skill of, 139
  negotiation script of culture, 124-127, 131-132
  strategy selection, 130, 136
  time schedule, 134
  and women, 133–134
Nepotism, cultural differences, 92
Newell, Chris, 228, 230
Nicassio, Perry, M., 212
Nishida, H., 180
Nonverbal communication, 24-25
  eye contact, 1, 91
  gestures, 24
  greeting behaviors, 25
  International Space Station construction, 4
  pupils of eyes, reading of, 28-29
  space (proximity), 24-25
  touch, 24-25
Nordenstrong, K., 171
North American Free Trade Agreement (NAFTA), 214
  See also La Frontera
Nowlin, William A., 90

O

O'Bannon, David, 68, 70
Oberg, A.E., 5
Oberg, Jim, 5
Oberg, K., 188, 192
Oddou, G., 159
Odenwald, Sylvia, 151
Ohmae, Kenichi, 84
O'Leary, Brian, 5
Olebe, M., 180
O'Reilly, Charles, III, 75
Organizations
  global, aspects of, 145-146
  globalization process, 82-83
Ouchi, William, 73

P

Paige, R. Michael, 196, 198, 199
Parsons, Talcott, 66
Participant observation
  by manager, 53
  methods, 53
Pascal, Blaise, 42
Pelled, Lisa, 67, 68, 74
Pelzel, John C., 63
Peña, Silvia Novo, 5

Penwell, Larry, 6
Perceptual differences, as language barrier, 24
Personal space, and culture, 6
Pharmco, cross-cultural training, 51-62
Philipsen, G., 171
Phinney, Jean, 65
Pipe, R., 171
PM leadership theory, 43
Polychronicity, 11-16
  assessment of, 12-13, 14
  cultural differences, 15-16
  meaning of, 11
  and organizations, 13-16
  person characteristics related to, 12
  and supervision/coordination, 15
  time management, 14-15
Porat, M.U., 171
Porter, Michael, 73, 81
Postman, Leo, 73
Power distance, 46
Prahalad, Coimbatore, 73, 157
Pratt, Craig, 163
Privacy, cultural differences, 36
Procter & Gamble, global training, 154-155
Product names, negative translations, 91, 92
Pruitt, D.G., 123, 133
Pruitt, F.J., 191

Q

Quinn, Robert, 53

R

R.E.A.L. sites
  Adil Najam: MIT Clorine Negotiation Simulation Global Environment, 142
  American Society for Training and Development, 167
  Harvard Law School: The Program on Negotiation, 142
  idealist, 38
  Institute for Global Ethics, 231
  Intercultural & Multicultural Education Resources, 231
  Latin American Network Information Center University of Texas at Austin, 38
  National Communication Association, 207
  SCOS Conference Euro Disney: A Cross-Cultural Communications Failure?, 142
  Society for Human Resource Management, 167
  Society for Intercultural Education Training and Research, 167, 207
  University of Oregon International Communication Cross-Cultural Resource Library, 38
  U.S. State Department-Service-Consular Affairs Bureau of Consular Affairs, 102
  Welcome to Europa, 102
Recruiting, transnational, 85

Redding, S. Gordon, 64, 67
Redfield, Robert, 52
Reeves-Ellington, Richard H., 51, 52
Reischauer, E.O., 126
Religion, cultural differences, 92-93
Repatriation, training for, 160-161
Rice, J.S., 169
Rich, A.L., 171
Richards, Sharon, 152-153
Ricks, D., 24, 122
Riding, A., 134, 138
Righter, R., 171
Roberts, Karlene, 64
Rohrer, T.C., 52
Rothenberg, David, 224
Ruben, Brent D., 10, **179**, 181, 186, 187, 188
Rubin, J.Z., 129
Russell, P.W., 179
Russia
    management theories applied to, 45
    Russia/Chechnya peace talks, 104-108

S

Sadat, Anwar, 28
Santy, Patricia, 5
Saral, Tulsi B., 210, 211
Savage, G.T., 140
Sayer, J.E., 172
Schein, Edgar H., 52
Schelling, T.C., 141
Scientific management, 42, 43
Scripts, negotiation script of culture, 124-125, 131-132
Seating arrangement, Japanese meetings, 57-58
Segal, Nina, 77
Semantics, as language barrier, 23
Sexual harassment, 162-166
    cost implications, 166
    and cross-cultural context, 163-164
    cross-cultural training in, 163-164
    of foreign employee in U.S., 165
    research on, 164
    standards for definition of, 164-165
    Title VII coverage for Americans, 165
Shafritz, Jay, 165
Shaw, Marvin, 68
Short-term orientation, of culture, 46-47
Shuji, Hayashi, 56
Shuter, R., 122, 172, 173, 174
Sills, D.L., 186
Simeone, Laura, 78-79
Simon, Herbert, 41, 71, 73, 75
Simpson, G.E., 186
Slakey, Francis, 222
Smircich, Linda, 52
Smith, Adam, 42
Smith, M.B., 179, 180, 189, 191, 192
Snell, Scott A., 64
Snow, Charles, 64, 65, 73
Social behavior, cultural differences, 94
Socializing
    with Arabs, 28, 35
    with Germans, 35
    with Japanese, 56, 60-61

Social knowledge, 52, 53
    Japanese, 55, 57, 60
Solomon, Charlene Marmer, 77
Sowers, Susan, 229
Space (proximity)
    and Arabs, 28-29, 94
    cultural differences, 24-25, 93-94
    personal space, 6
    and sense of privacy, 36-37
    sensory aspects, 6-7
    territorial space, 6
Space stations
    Freedom, 36-37
    International Space Station, 3-7
Spencer, John, 228
Spitzberg, B.H., 181, 182
Spradley, James P., 53
Stein, M., 179
Stein, Pierre, 98
Stewart, Doug, 104
Stone, Judith, 36
Strategic systematic approach, management development, 156-157
Sutton, Francis, 66
Swell, W.H., 191, 192

T

Tactile reactive approach, 156-157
Taft, R., 186
Tajfel, Henri, 69
Takeo, Doi, 55
Takie Sugiyama, Lebra, 56
Taylor, A., 141
Taylor, Frederick W., 42, 43
Teams
    cultural differences, 93
    multinational teams, 49-50
    virtual teams, 227-230
Territorial space, of space vehicle, 6
Thayer, N.B., 129
Third culture concept
    International Space Station, 7
    meaning of, 7
    musical influences, 224-226
    studies related to, 25
Third world countries, management theories applied to, 44-45
Thubron, C., 140
Tichy, Noel, 88
Time frame
    and communication objectives, 18-19
    cultural differences, 18-19, 92
    monochronicity/polychronicity, 11-16
Time management, monochronicity/polychronicity, 14-15
Ting-Toomey, Ting, 128
Tobin, Joseph, 43
Tone, as language barrier, 24
Torbiorn, I., 186, 187, 189, 191, 192
Touch, cultural differences, 24-25, 94
Training. *See* Cross-cultural training
Transnational companies, features of, 83
Transnational human resource systems, 83-88
    dimensions of, 84
    incentives, 86

    misconceptions about, 87-88
    recruiting, 85
    training/development programs, 85-86
Triad project, as joint project, 33-35
Triandis, Harry, 64, 66, 68
Trompenaars, Fons, 66, 69
Tucker, M.F., 186, 187
Tuckman, Bruce, 68
Tung, R., 158, 159

U

Uhes, M.J., 187
Uncertainty avoidance, 21-22, 46
United States, management theories applied to, 47-48
Ury, William L., 104-108

V

Values
    communication implications, 19, 20
    cultural differences, 19
    Japanese, 55
    and nationality, 66
    work-related values, 20, 21
Virtual teams, 227-230

W

Walsh, James, 66
Watson, Warren, 19, 71, 73, 140
Wealth of Nations, The (Smith), 42
Web sites. *See* R.E.A.L. sites
Weick, Karl, 66
Weiss, Stephen E., 121, 123, 129, 130, 131
Wheeler, David L., 220
White, Leslie A., 52
White, R.W., 187
Whiting, G.C., 171
Whitmore, Kay R., 154
Wiemann, J.M., 181
Williamson, Oliver, 47
Wilson, Terry P., 220-221
Wolfgang, Aaron W., 66
Women
    and cross-cultural negotiation, 133–134
    expatriates, 77-80
    feminists on intercultural communication, 173
    French, 99
    international dual-career families, 79-80
    in Islamic countries, 93
    learning about international assignments, 78
    sexual harassment, 162-166
Wong, Clifford, 36-37
Word connotations, as language barrier, 23-24
Work centrality index, 22
Wu, David, 43

Y

Yates, Jim, 164

Putting it in *Perspectives*
-Review Form-

Your name: _____   Date: _____

Reading title: _____

Summarize: Provide a one-sentence summary of this reading: _____
_____
_____
_____

Follow the Thinking: How does the author back the main premise of the reading? Are the facts/opinions appropriately supported by research or available data? Is the author's thinking logical?
_____
_____
_____
_____
_____
_____

Develop a Context (answer one or both questions): How does this reading contrast or compliment your professor's lecture treatment of the subject matter? How does this reading compare to your textbook's coverage?
_____
_____
_____
_____
_____
_____
_____

Question Authority: Explain why you agree/disagree with the author's main premise.
_____
_____
_____
_____
_____
_____
_____

COPY ME! Copy this form as needed. This form is also available at http://www.coursewise.com
Click on: *Perspectives*.